# BATMAN

# KNIGHTFALL

## PART TWO: WHO RULES THE NIGHT

**Doug Moench   Chuck Dixon   Alan Grant**

writers

**Jim Aparo   Graham Nolan**
**Bret Blevins   Klaus Janson   Mike Manley**

pencillers

**Scott Hanna   Mike Manley   Klaus Janson**
**Bret Blevins   Steve George   Terry Austin**
**Rick Burchett   Dick Giordano**

inkers

**John Costanza   Ken Bruzenak**
**Todd Klein   Richard Starkings   Bob Pinaha**

letterers

**Adrienne Roy   Klaus Janson**

colorists

**Kelley Jones   Glenn Fabry   Brian Stelfreeze**

covers

W9-DDF-014

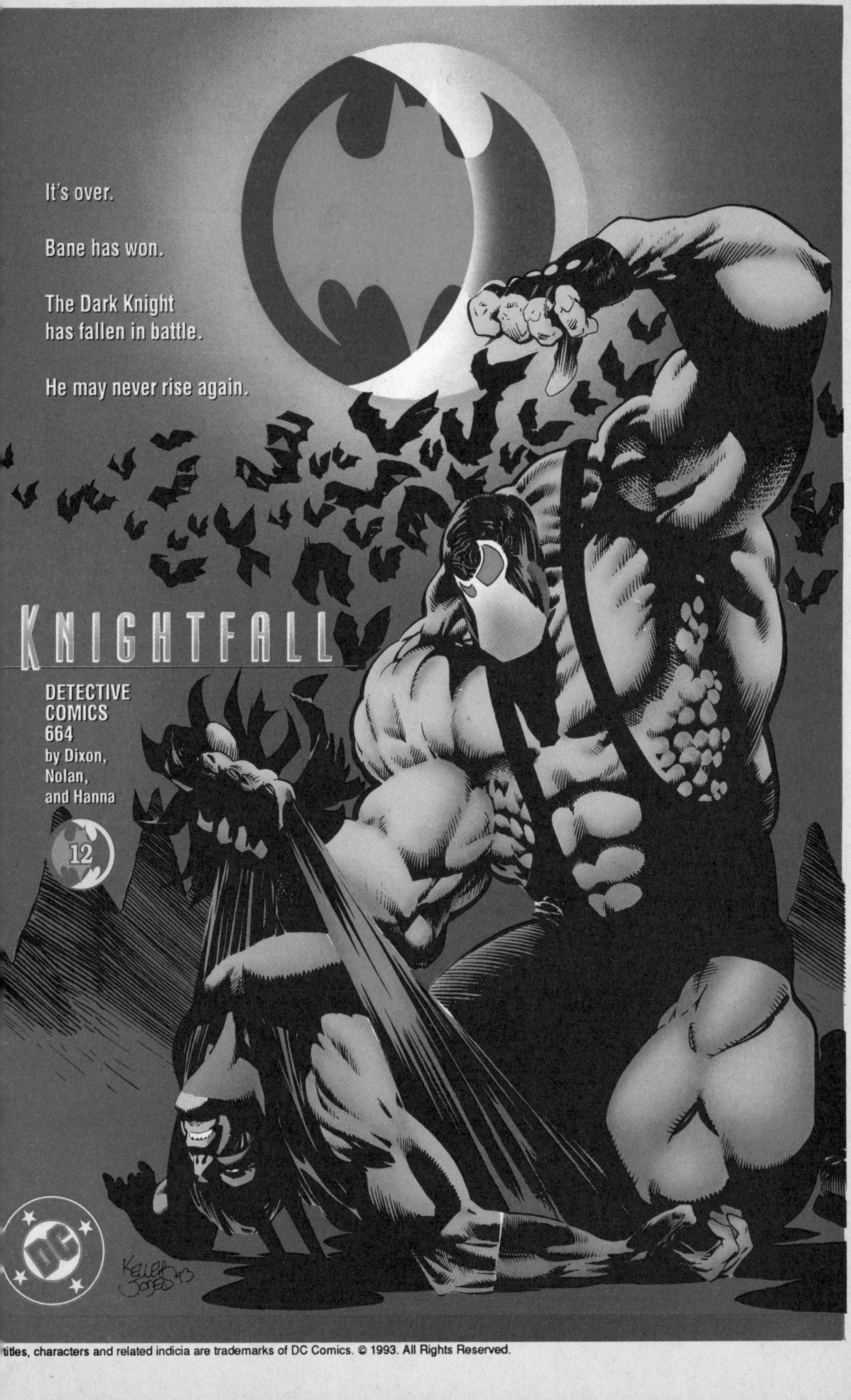
It's over.
Bane has won.
The Dark Knight
has fallen in battle.
He may never rise again.
KNIGHTFALL
DETECTIVE
COMICS
664
by Dixon,
Nolan,
and Hanna
12
DC

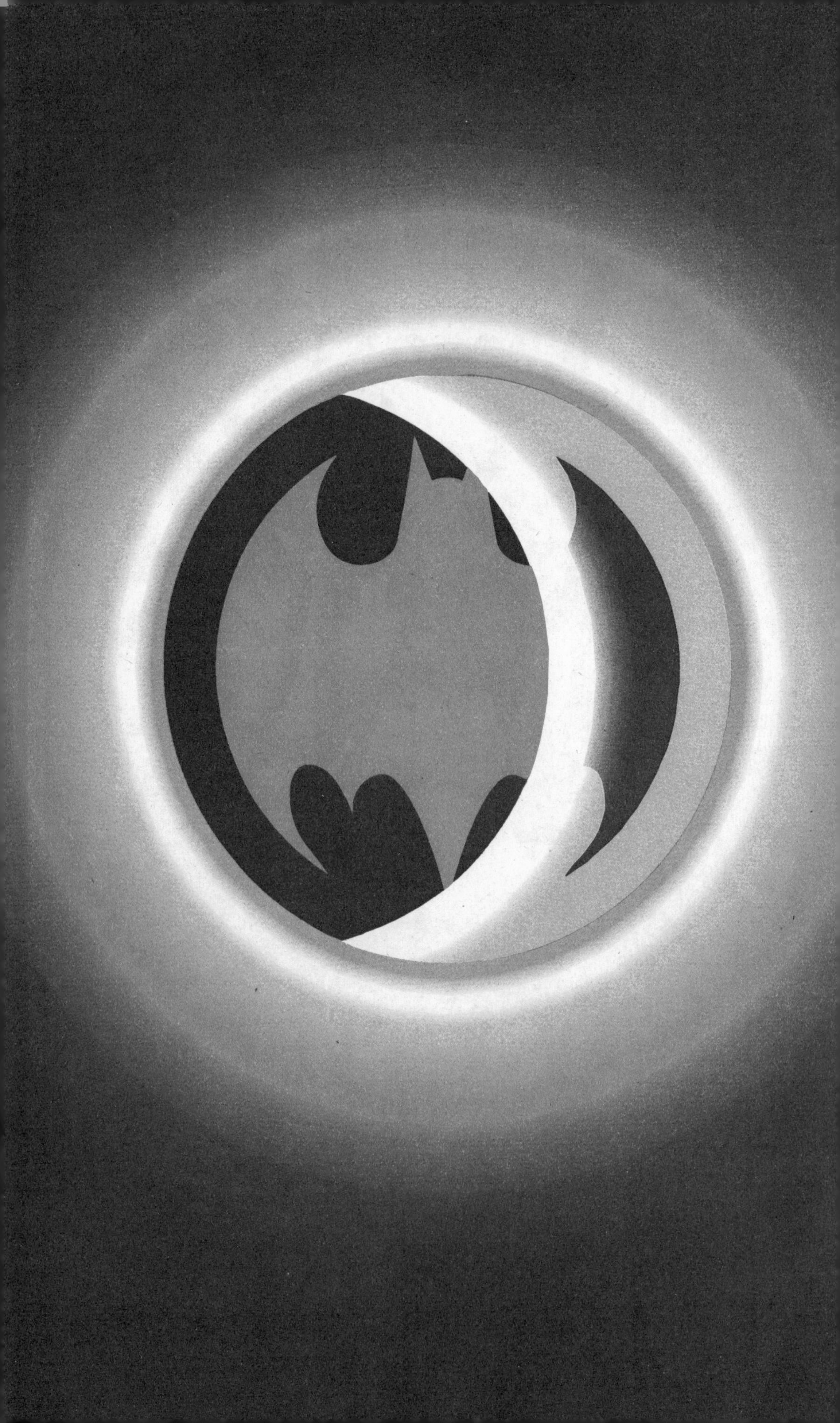

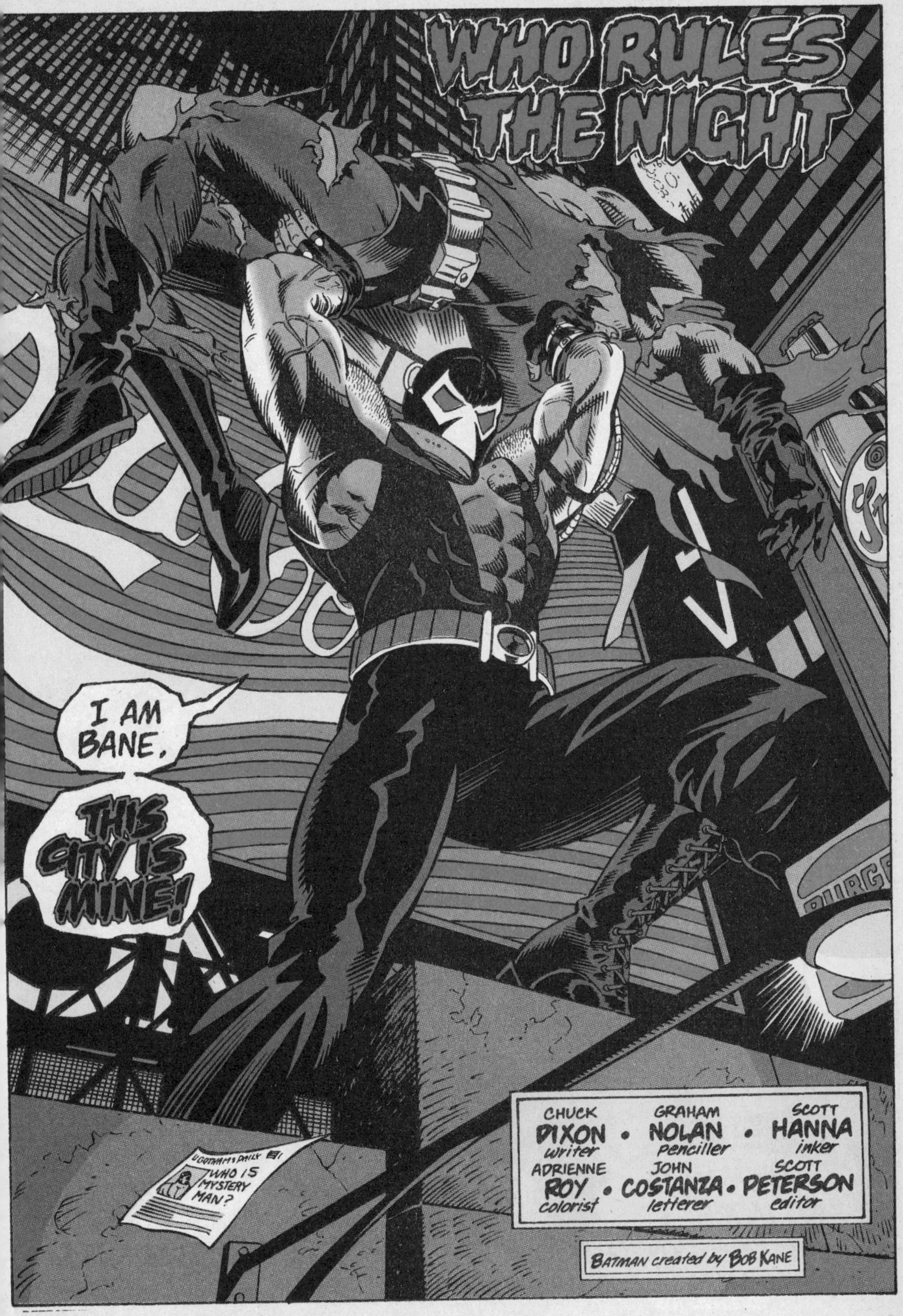
WHO RULES THE NIGHT
I AM BANE.
THIS CITY IS MINE!
GOTHAM DAILY
WHO IS MYSTERY MAN?
CHUCK DIXON writer • GRAHAM NOLAN penciller • SCOTT HANNA inker
ADRIENNE ROY colorist • JOHN COSTANZA letterer • SCOTT PETERSON editor
BATMAN created by BOB KANE

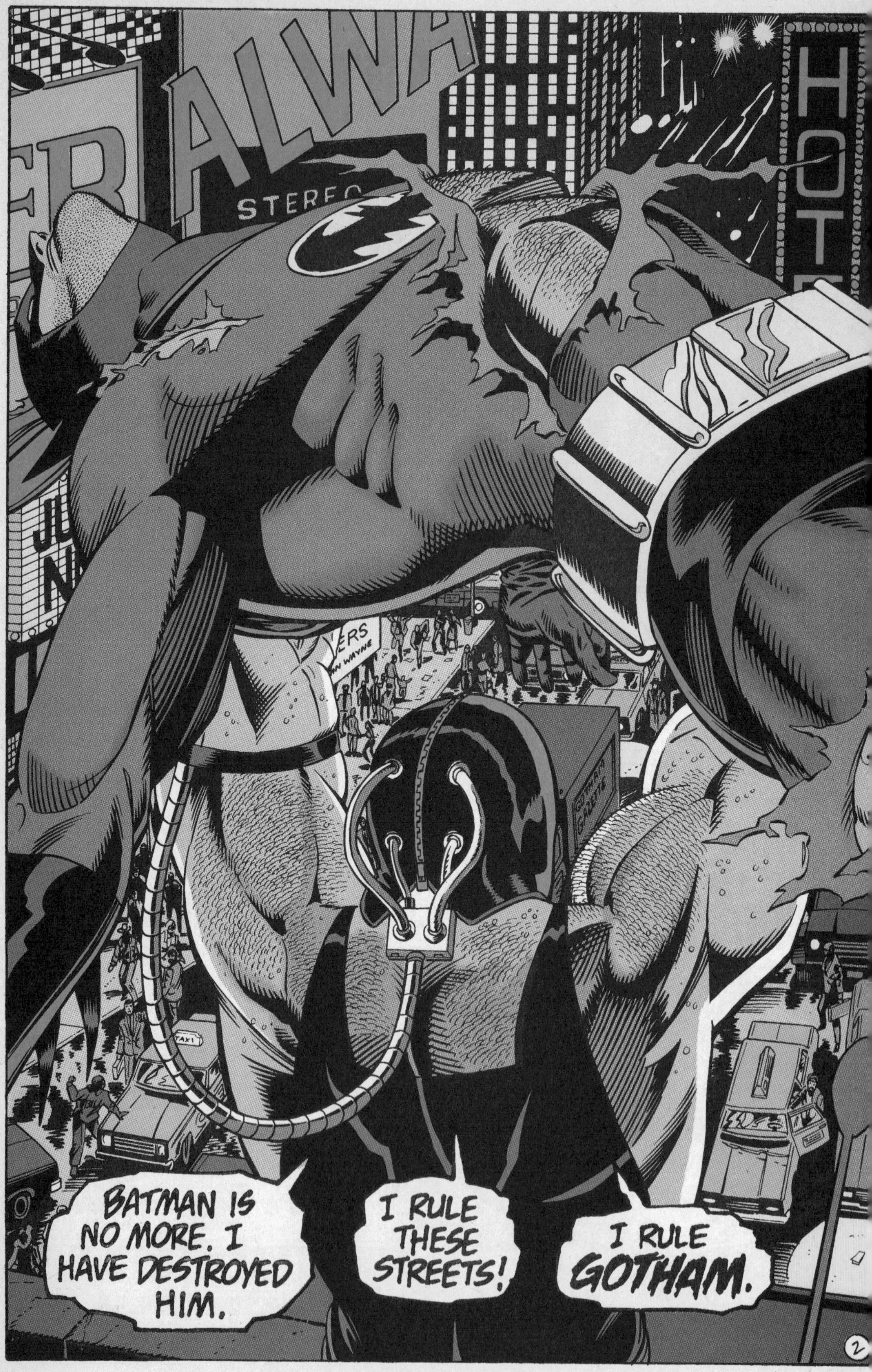
ALWA
STEREO
HOT
BATMAN IS NO MORE. I HAVE DESTROYED HIM.
I RULE THESE STREETS!
I RULE GOTHAM.
2

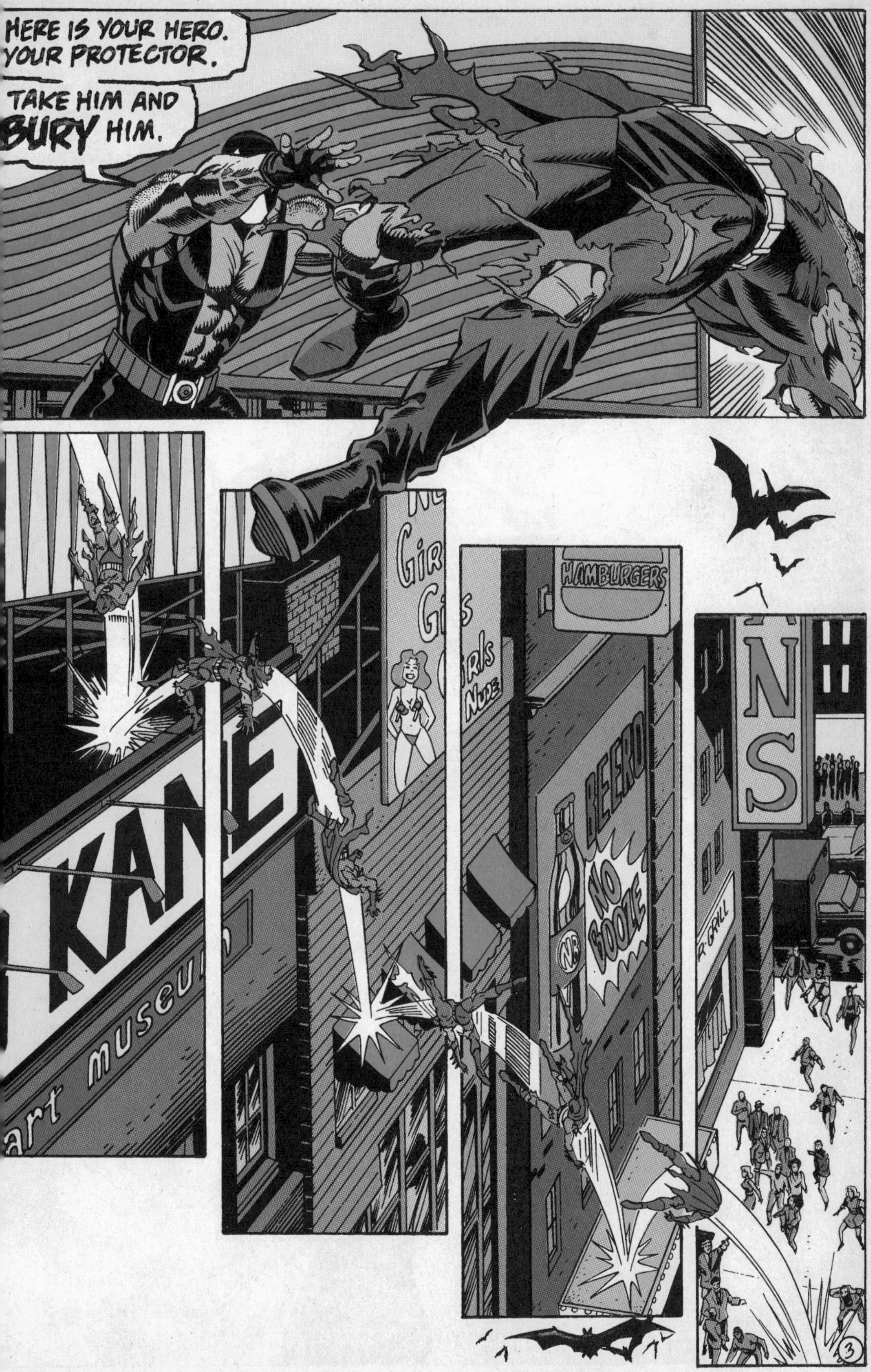
HERE IS YOUR HERO. YOUR PROTECTOR.
TAKE HIM AND BURY HIM.
HAMBURGERS
Girls
Nude
BEER
NO BOOZE
NB
KANE
art museum
GRILL
NS
3

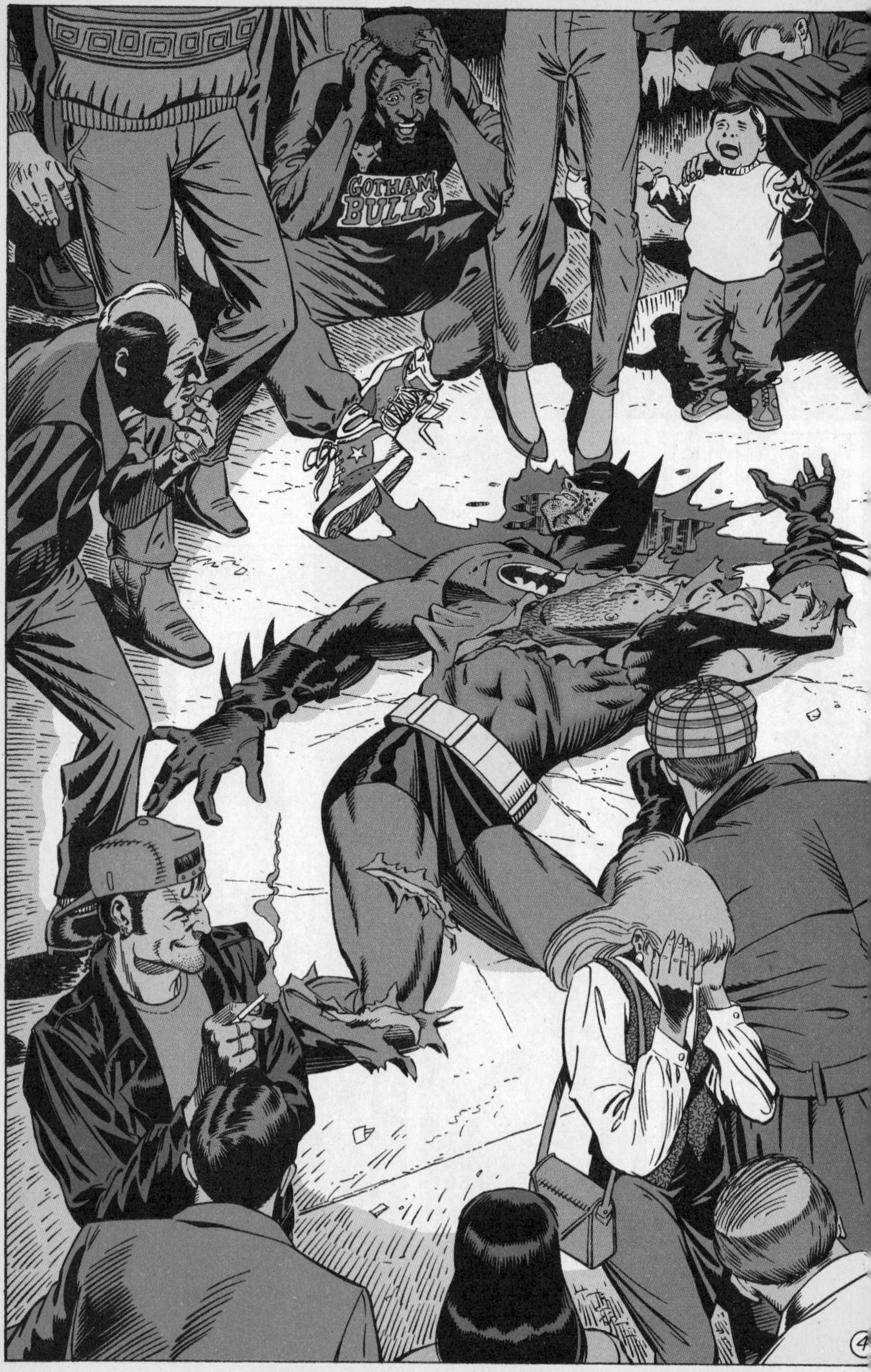
GOTHAM BULLS

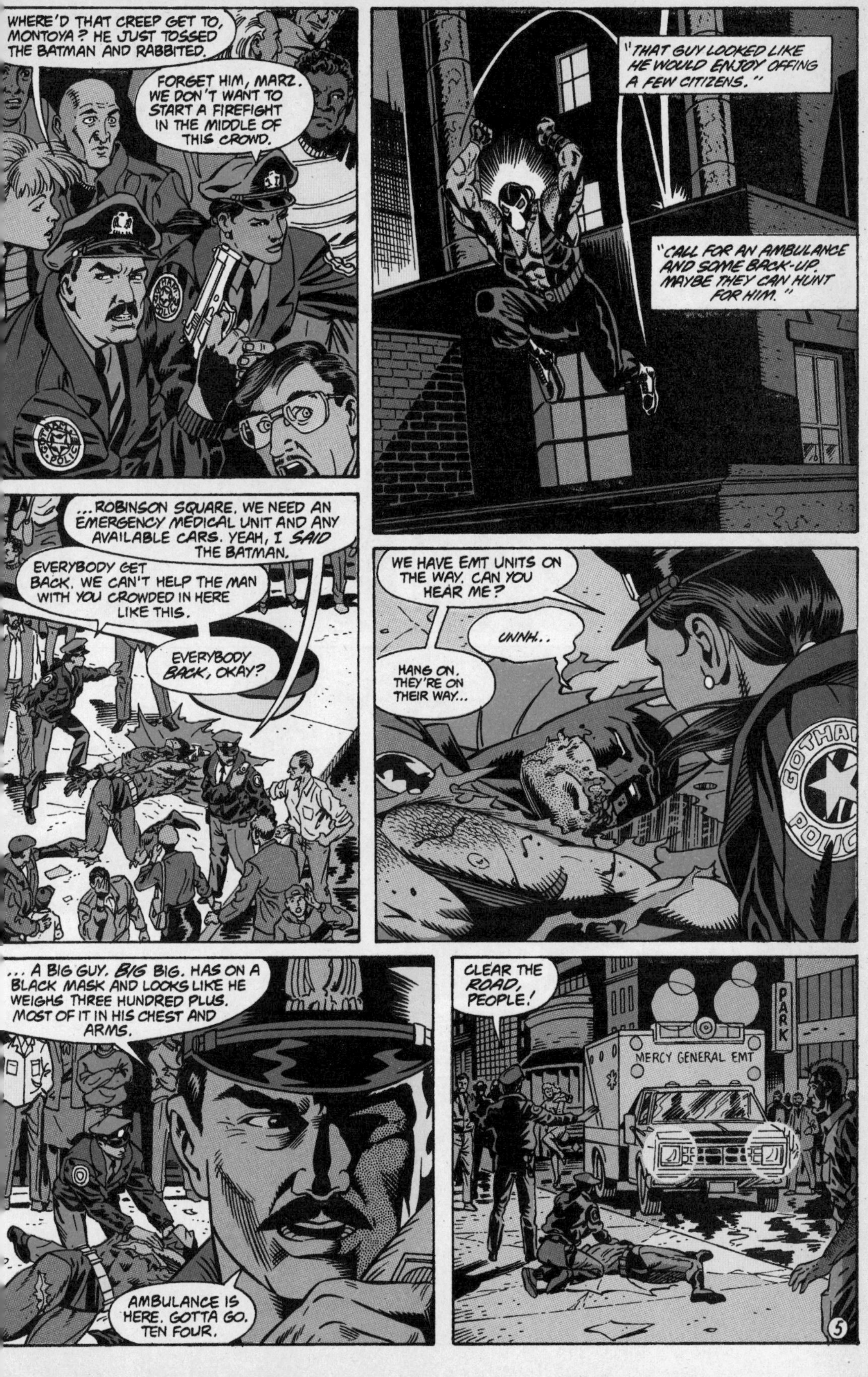
WHERE'D THAT CREEP GET TO, MONTOYA? HE JUST TOSSED THE BATMAN AND RABBITED.
FORGET HIM, MARZ. WE DON'T WANT TO START A FIREFIGHT IN THE MIDDLE OF THIS CROWD.
"THAT GUY LOOKED LIKE HE WOULD ENJOY OFFING A FEW CITIZENS."
"CALL FOR AN AMBULANCE AND SOME BACK-UP. MAYBE THEY CAN HUNT FOR HIM."
...ROBINSON SQUARE. WE NEED AN EMERGENCY MEDICAL UNIT AND ANY AVAILABLE CARS. YEAH, I SAID THE BATMAN.
EVERYBODY GET BACK. WE CAN'T HELP THE MAN WITH YOU CROWDED IN HERE LIKE THIS.
EVERYBODY BACK, OKAY?
WE HAVE EMT UNITS ON THE WAY. CAN YOU HEAR ME?
UNNH..
HANG ON. THEY'RE ON THEIR WAY...
... A BIG GUY. BIG BIG. HAS ON A BLACK MASK AND LOOKS LIKE HE WEIGHS THREE HUNDRED PLUS. MOST OF IT IN HIS CHEST AND ARMS.
AMBULANCE IS HERE. GOTTA GO. TEN FOUR.
CLEAR THE ROAD, PEOPLE!
PARK
MERCY GENERAL EMT
5

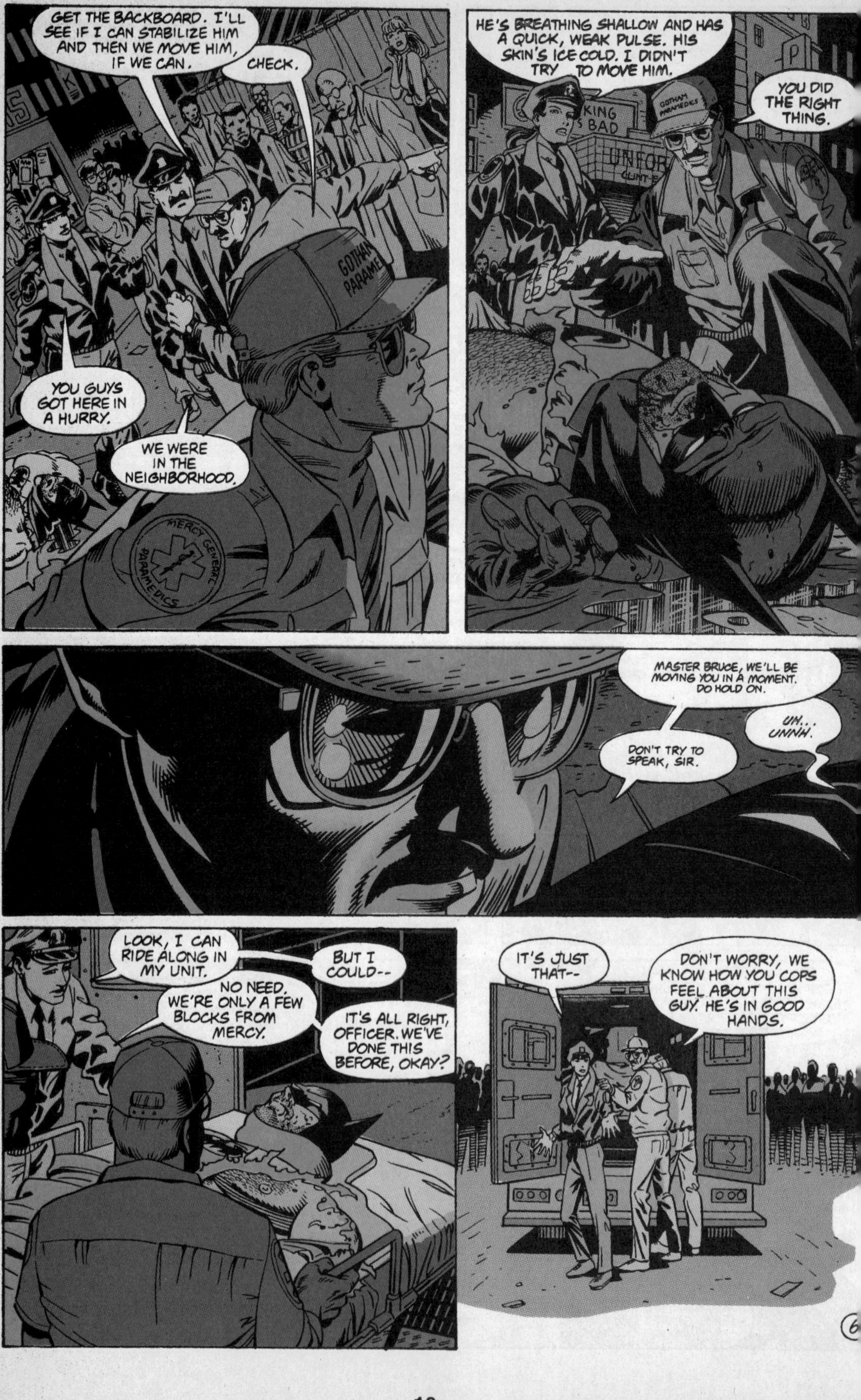
GET THE BACKBOARD. I'LL SEE IF I CAN STABILIZE HIM AND THEN WE MOVE HIM, IF WE CAN.
CHECK.
YOU GUYS GOT HERE IN A HURRY.
WE WERE IN THE NEIGHBORHOOD.
GOTHAM PARAMEDICS
MERCY GENERAL PARAMEDICS
HE'S BREATHING SHALLOW AND HAS A QUICK, WEAK PULSE. HIS SKIN'S ICE COLD. I DIDN'T TRY TO MOVE HIM.
YOU DID THE RIGHT THING.
MASTER BRUCE, WE'LL BE MOVING YOU IN A MOMENT. DO HOLD ON.
UH... UNNH.
DON'T TRY TO SPEAK, SIR.
LOOK, I CAN RIDE ALONG IN MY UNIT.
NO NEED. WE'RE ONLY A FEW BLOCKS FROM MERCY.
BUT I COULD--
IT'S ALL RIGHT, OFFICER. WE'VE DONE THIS BEFORE, OKAY?
IT'S JUST THAT--
DON'T WORRY, WE KNOW HOW YOU COPS FEEL ABOUT THIS GUY. HE'S IN GOOD HANDS.

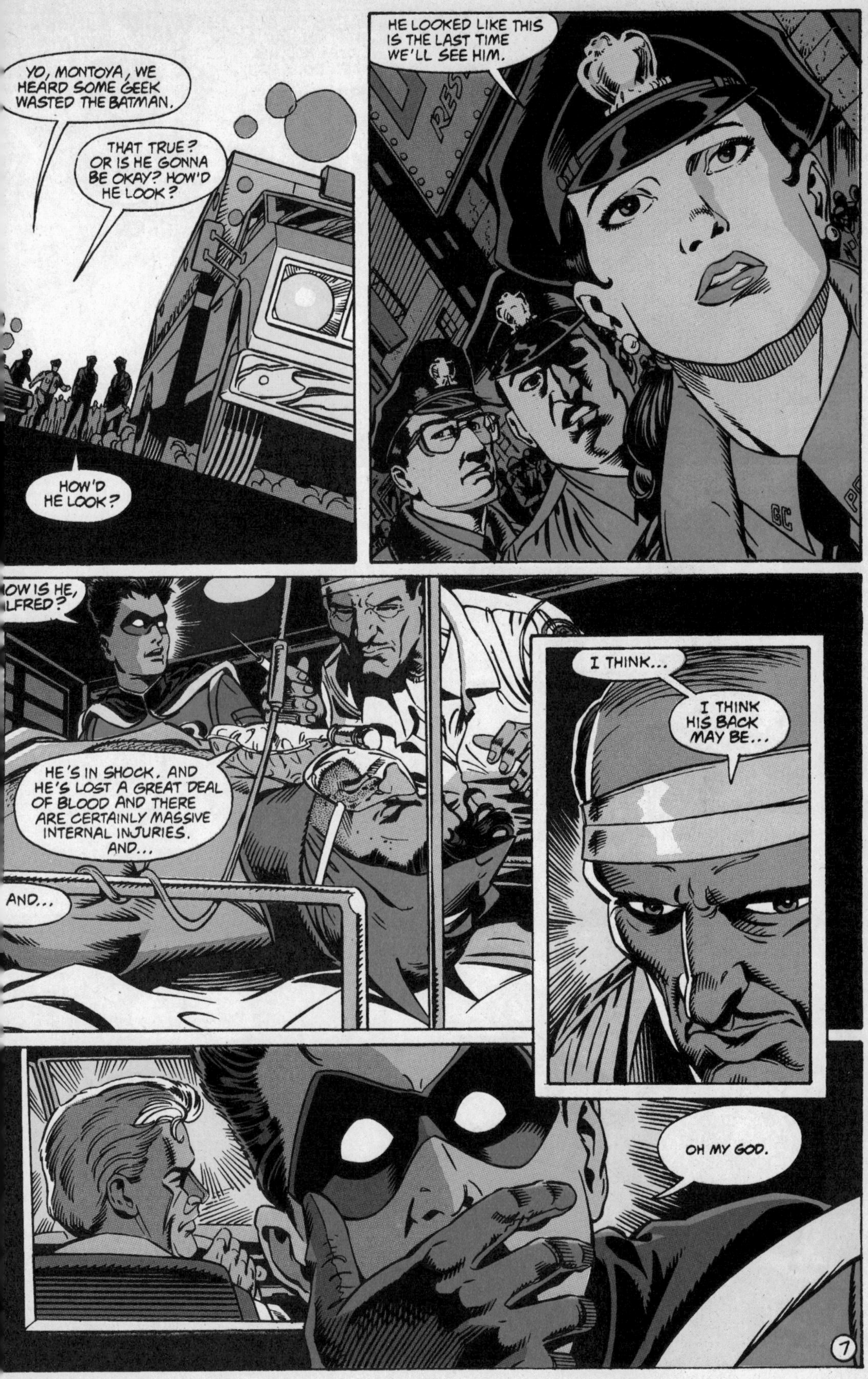
YO, MONTOYA, WE HEARD SOME GEEK WASTED THE BATMAN.
THAT TRUE? OR IS HE GONNA BE OKAY? HOW'D HE LOOK?
HOW'D HE LOOK?
HE LOOKED LIKE THIS IS THE LAST TIME WE'LL SEE HIM.
OW IS HE, LFRED?
HE'S IN SHOCK. AND HE'S LOST A GREAT DEAL OF BLOOD AND THERE ARE CERTAINLY MASSIVE INTERNAL INJURIES. AND...
AND...
I THINK...
I THINK HIS BACK MAY BE...
OH MY GOD.
7

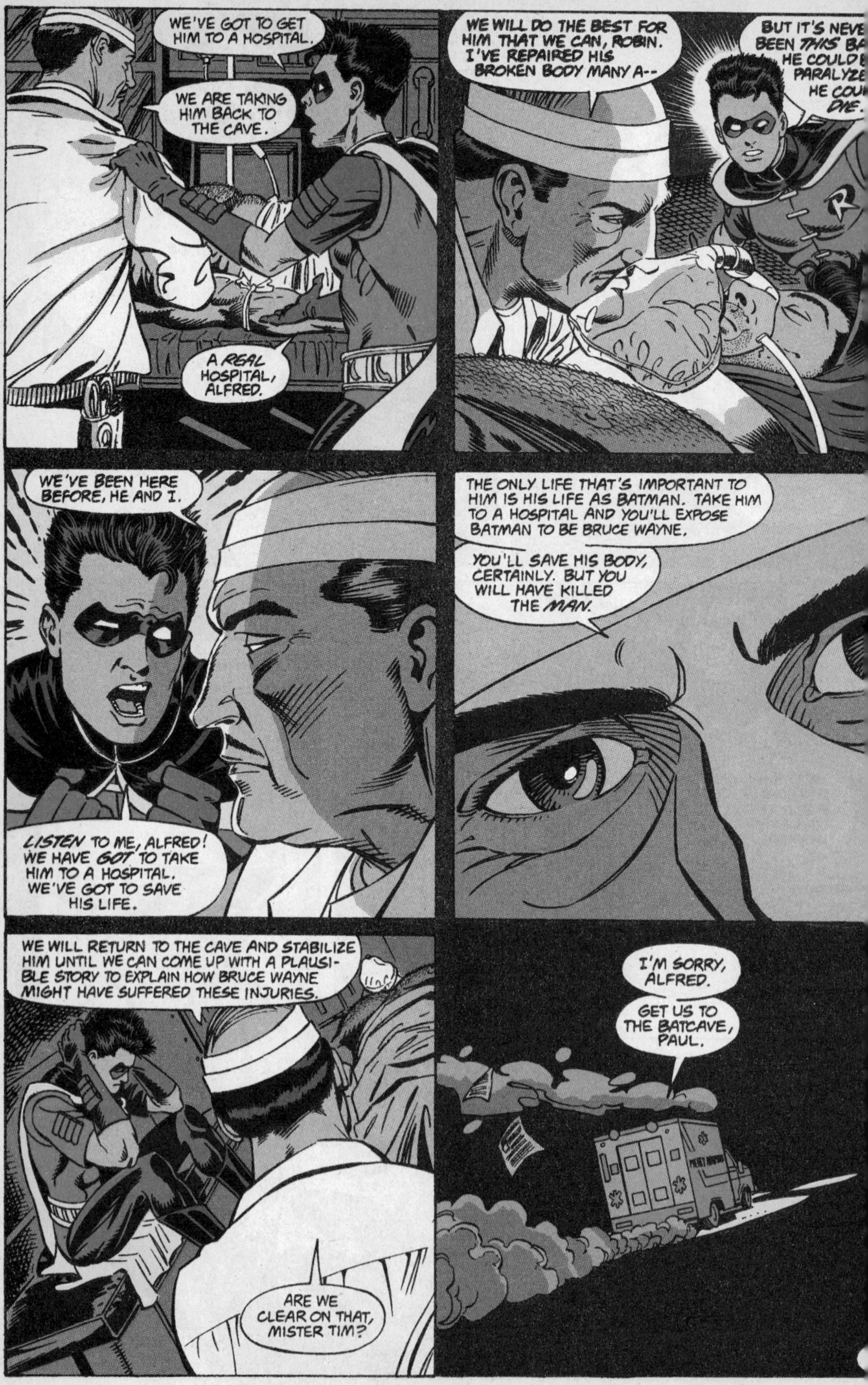

WE'VE GOT TO GET HIM TO A HOSPITAL.
WE ARE TAKING HIM BACK TO THE CAVE.
A REAL HOSPITAL, ALFRED.
WE WILL DO THE BEST FOR HIM THAT WE CAN, ROBIN. I'VE REPAIRED HIS BROKEN BODY MANY A--
BUT IT'S NEVE
BEEN THIS BA
HE COULD
PARALYZE
HE COU
DIE.
WE'VE BEEN HERE BEFORE, HE AND I.
LISTEN TO ME, ALFRED! WE HAVE GOT TO TAKE HIM TO A HOSPITAL. WE'VE GOT TO SAVE HIS LIFE.
THE ONLY LIFE THAT'S IMPORTANT TO HIM IS HIS LIFE AS BATMAN. TAKE HIM TO A HOSPITAL AND YOU'LL EXPOSE BATMAN TO BE BRUCE WAYNE.
YOU'LL SAVE HIS BODY, CERTAINLY. BUT YOU WILL HAVE KILLED THE MAN.
WE WILL RETURN TO THE CAVE AND STABILIZE HIM UNTIL WE CAN COME UP WITH A PLAUSI-BLE STORY TO EXPLAIN HOW BRUCE WAYNE MIGHT HAVE SUFFERED THESE INJURIES.
ARE WE CLEAR ON THAT, MISTER TIM?
I'M SORRY, ALFRED.
GET US TO THE BATCAVE, PAUL.

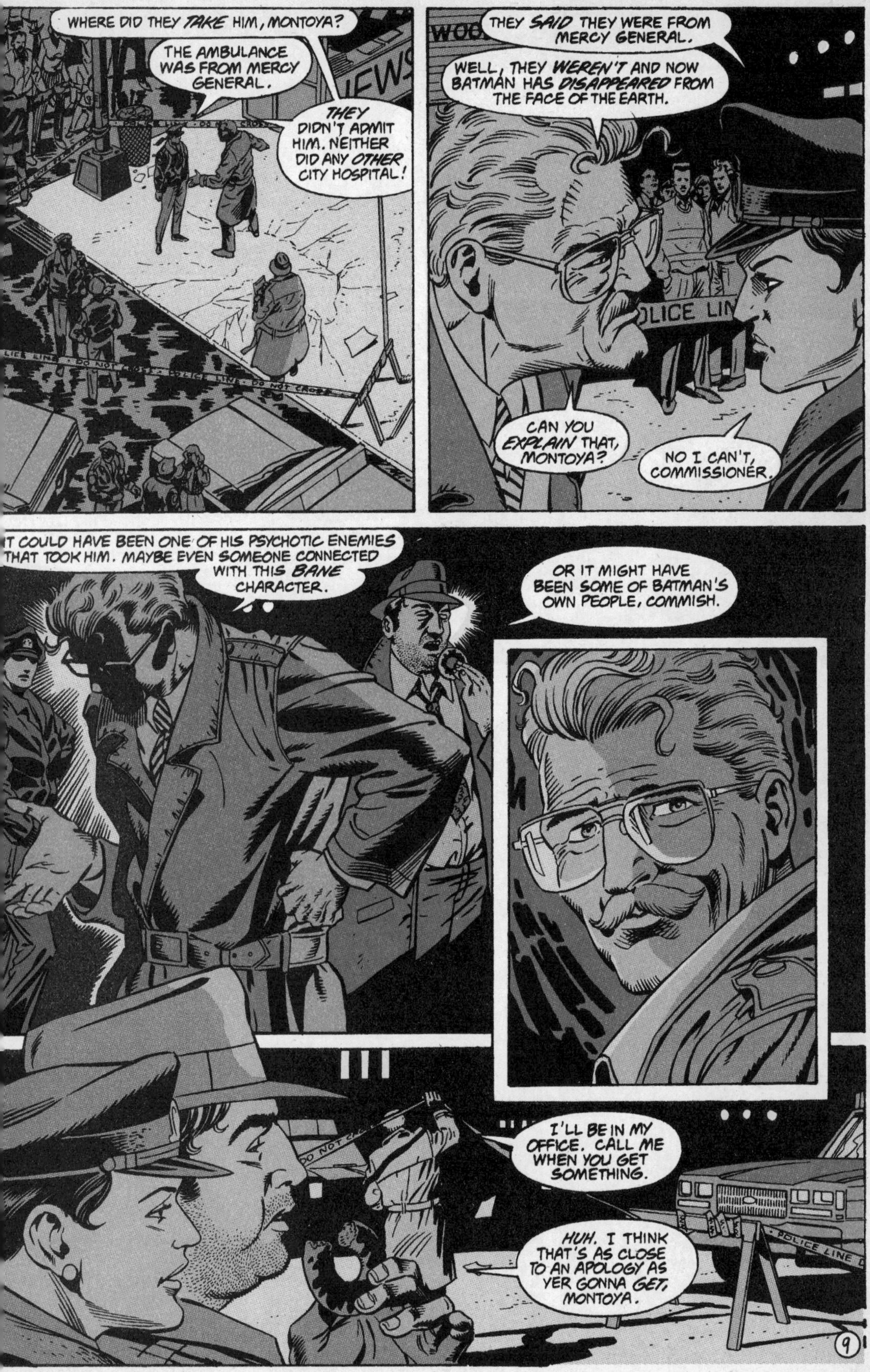

WHERE DID THEY *TAKE* HIM, MONTOYA?
THE AMBULANCE WAS FROM MERCY GENERAL.
*THEY* DIDN'T ADMIT HIM. NEITHER DID ANY *OTHER* CITY HOSPITAL!
THEY *SAID* THEY WERE FROM MERCY GENERAL.
WELL, THEY *WEREN'T* AND NOW BATMAN HAS *DISAPPEARED* FROM THE FACE OF THE EARTH.
CAN YOU *EXPLAIN* THAT, MONTOYA?
NO I CAN'T, COMMISSIONER.
IT COULD HAVE BEEN ONE OF HIS PSYCHOTIC ENEMIES THAT TOOK HIM. MAYBE EVEN SOMEONE CONNECTED WITH THIS *BANE* CHARACTER.
OR IT MIGHT HAVE BEEN SOME OF BATMAN'S OWN PEOPLE, COMMISH.
I'LL BE IN MY OFFICE. CALL ME WHEN YOU GET SOMETHING.
*HUH.* I THINK THAT'S AS CLOSE TO AN APOLOGY AS YER GONNA *GET*, MONTOYA.
9

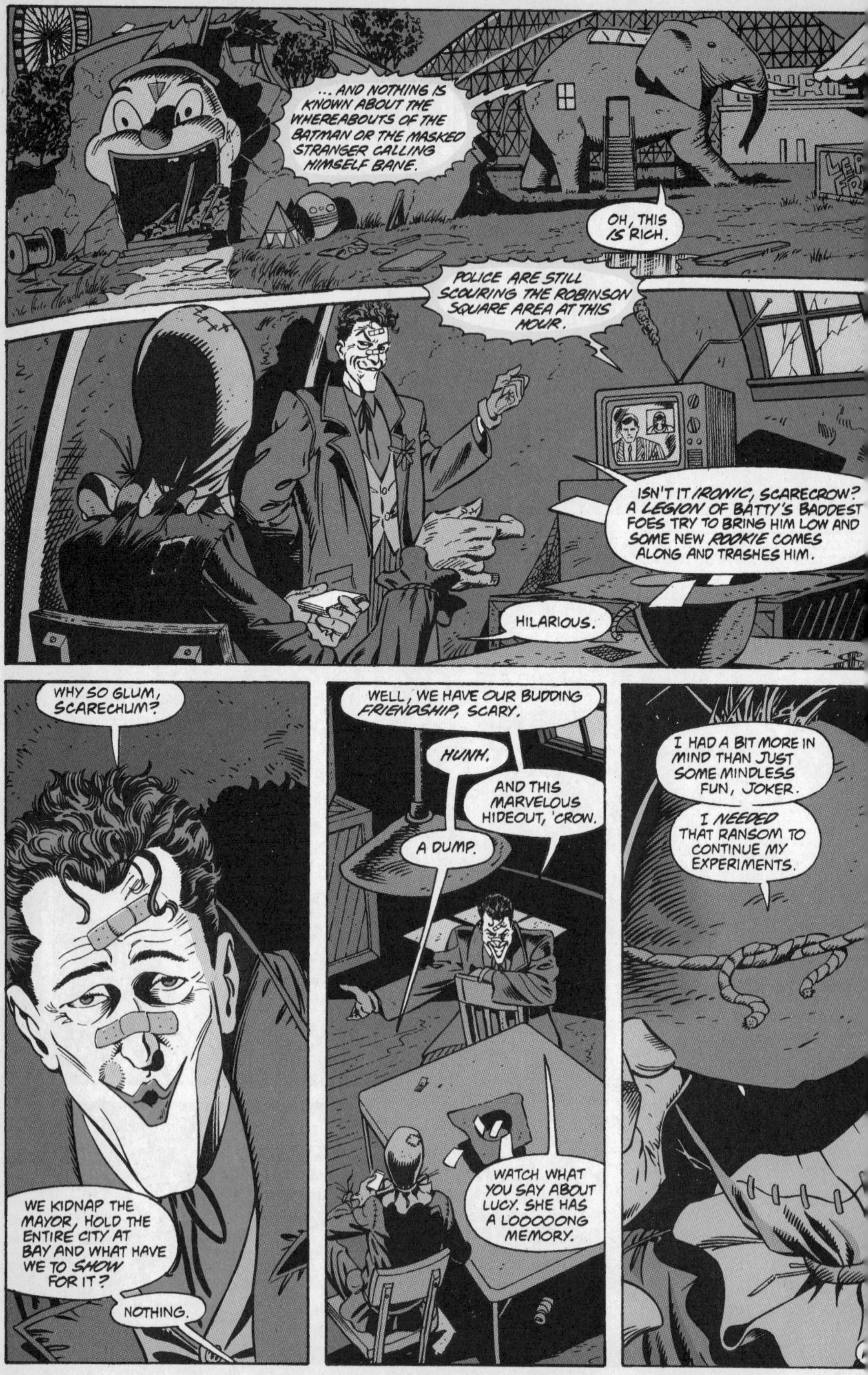

...AND NOTHING IS KNOWN ABOUT THE WHEREABOUTS OF THE BATMAN OR THE MASKED STRANGER CALLING HIMSELF BANE.
OH, THIS IS RICH.
POLICE ARE STILL SCOURING THE ROBINSON SQUARE AREA AT THIS HOUR.
ISN'T IT IRONIC, SCARECROW? A LEGION OF BATTY'S BADDEST FOES TRY TO BRING HIM LOW AND SOME NEW ROOKIE COMES ALONG AND TRASHES HIM.
HILARIOUS.
WHY SO GLUM, SCARECHUM?
WE KIDNAP THE MAYOR, HOLD THE ENTIRE CITY AT BAY AND WHAT HAVE WE TO SHOW FOR IT?
NOTHING.
WELL, WE HAVE OUR BUDDING FRIENDSHIP, SCARY.
HUNH.
AND THIS MARVELOUS HIDEOUT, 'CROW.
A DUMP.
WATCH WHAT YOU SAY ABOUT LUCY. SHE HAS A LOOOOONG MEMORY.
I HAD A BIT MORE IN MIND THAN JUST SOME MINDLESS FUN, JOKER.
I NEEDED THAT RANSOM TO CONTINUE MY EXPERIMENTS.

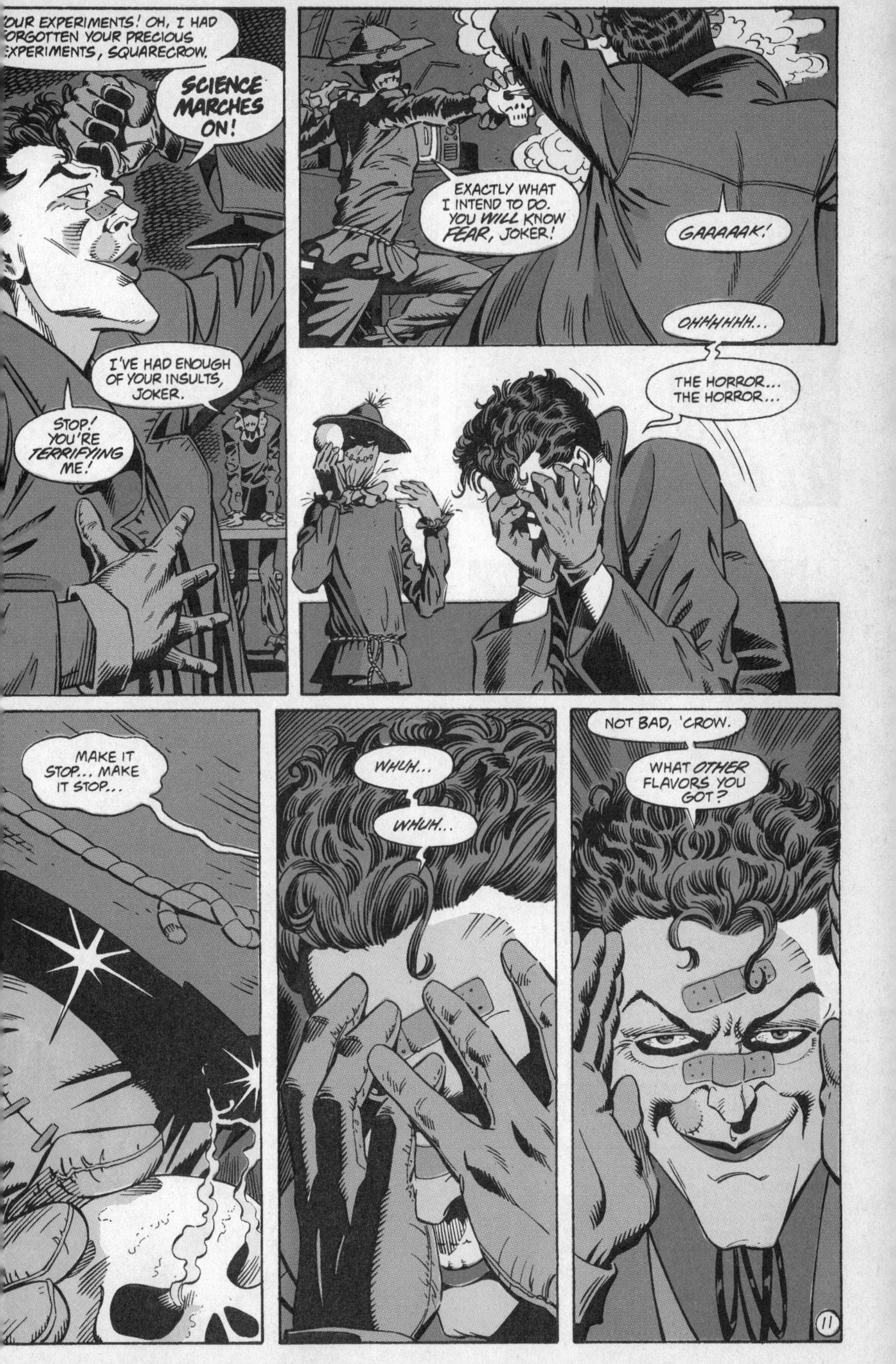
YOUR EXPERIMENTS! OH, I HAD FORGOTTEN YOUR PRECIOUS EXPERIMENTS, SQUARECROW.
SCIENCE MARCHES ON!
I'VE HAD ENOUGH OF YOUR INSULTS, JOKER.
STOP! YOU'RE TERRIFYING ME!
EXACTLY WHAT I INTEND TO DO. YOU WILL KNOW FEAR, JOKER!
GAAAAAK!
OHHHHHH...
THE HORROR... THE HORROR...
MAKE IT STOP... MAKE IT STOP...
WHUH...
WHUH...
NOT BAD, 'CROW.
WHAT OTHER FLAVORS YOU GOT?
11

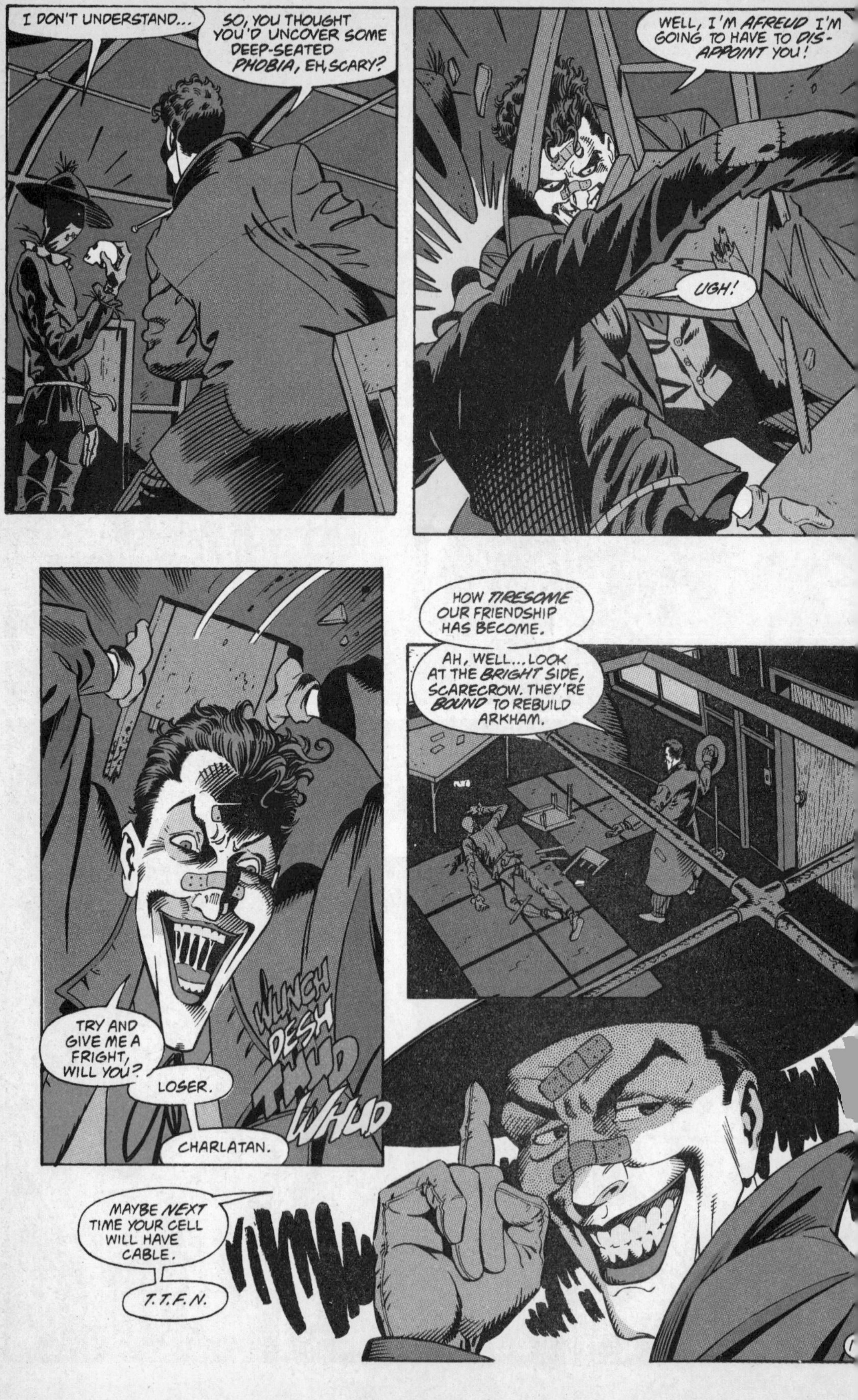
I DON'T UNDERSTAND...
SO, YOU THOUGHT YOU'D UNCOVER SOME DEEP-SEATED PHOBIA, EH, SCARY?
WELL, I'M AFREUD I'M GOING TO HAVE TO DIS-APPOINT YOU!
UGH!
WUNCH
DESH
THUD
WHUD
TRY AND GIVE ME A FRIGHT, WILL YOU?
LOSER.
CHARLATAN.
HOW TIRESOME OUR FRIENDSHIP HAS BECOME.
AH, WELL... LOOK AT THE BRIGHT SIDE, SCARECROW. THEY'RE BOUND TO REBUILD ARKHAM.
MAYBE NEXT TIME YOUR CELL WILL HAVE CABLE.
T.T.F.N.

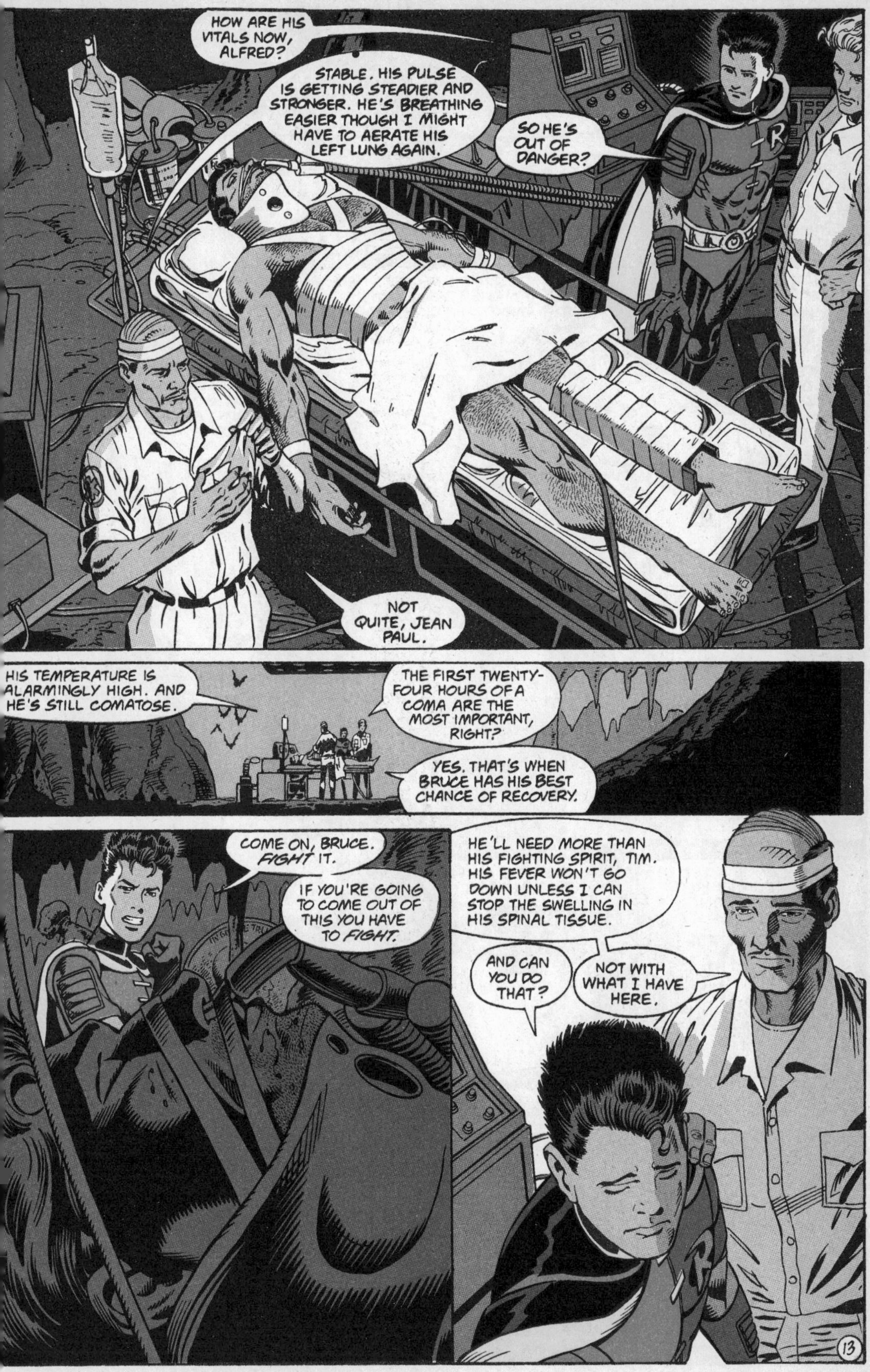
HOW ARE HIS VITALS NOW, ALFRED?
STABLE. HIS PULSE IS GETTING STEADIER AND STRONGER. HE'S BREATHING EASIER THOUGH I MIGHT HAVE TO AERATE HIS LEFT LUNG AGAIN.
SO HE'S OUT OF DANGER?
NOT QUITE, JEAN PAUL.
HIS TEMPERATURE IS ALARMINGLY HIGH. AND HE'S STILL COMATOSE.
THE FIRST TWENTY-FOUR HOURS OF A COMA ARE THE MOST IMPORTANT, RIGHT?
YES. THAT'S WHEN BRUCE HAS HIS BEST CHANCE OF RECOVERY.
COME ON, BRUCE. FIGHT IT.
IF YOU'RE GOING TO COME OUT OF THIS YOU HAVE TO FIGHT.
HE'LL NEED MORE THAN HIS FIGHTING SPIRIT, TIM. HIS FEVER WON'T GO DOWN UNLESS I CAN STOP THE SWELLING IN HIS SPINAL TISSUE.
AND CAN YOU DO THAT?
NOT WITH WHAT I HAVE HERE.
13

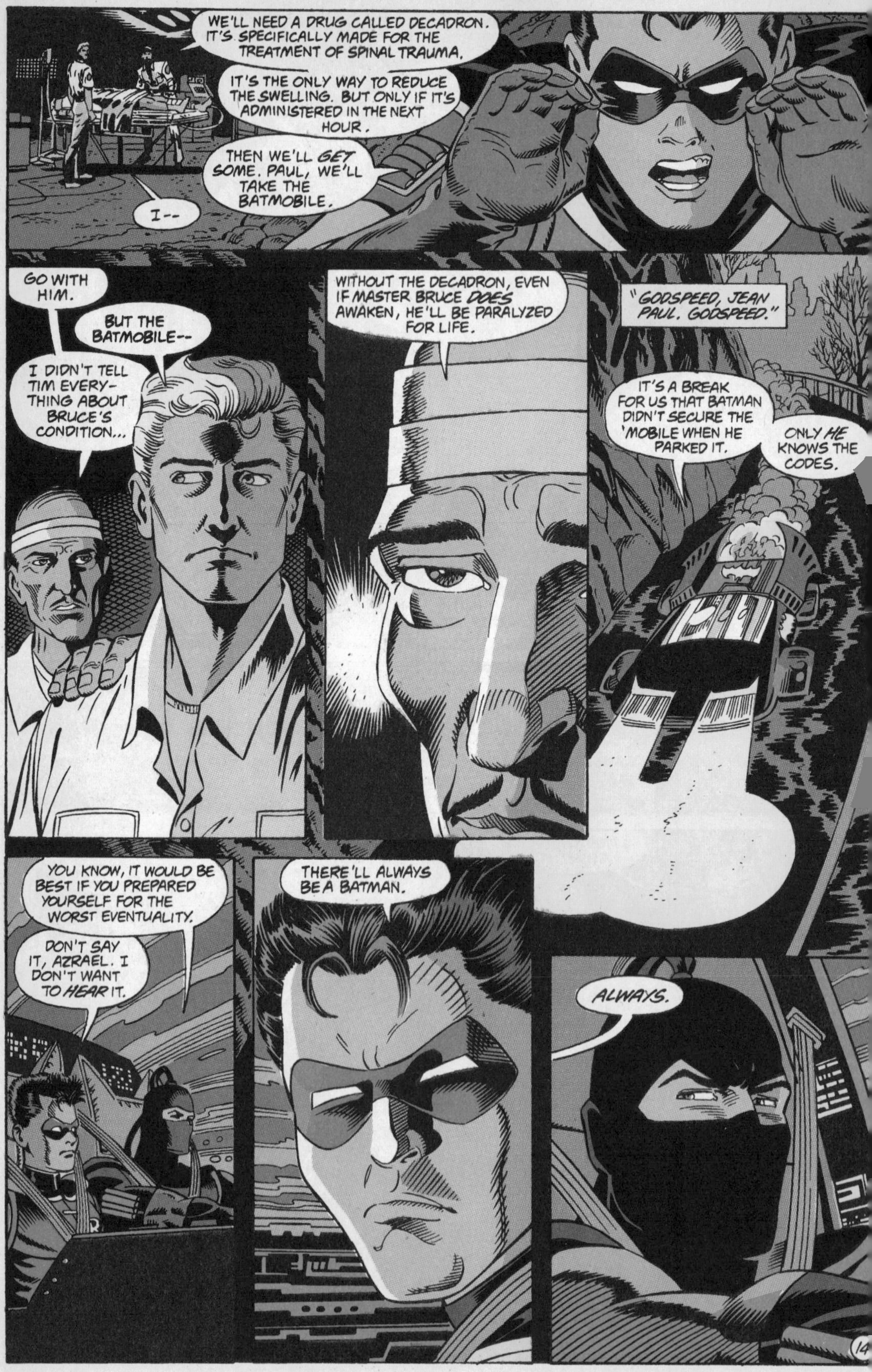
WE'LL NEED A DRUG CALLED DECADRON. IT'S SPECIFICALLY MADE FOR THE TREATMENT OF SPINAL TRAUMA.
IT'S THE ONLY WAY TO REDUCE THE SWELLING. BUT ONLY IF IT'S ADMINISTERED IN THE NEXT HOUR.
THEN WE'LL GET SOME. PAUL, WE'LL TAKE THE BATMOBILE.
I--
GO WITH HIM.
BUT THE BATMOBILE--
I DIDN'T TELL TIM EVERYTHING ABOUT BRUCE'S CONDITION...
WITHOUT THE DECADRON, EVEN IF MASTER BRUCE DOES AWAKEN, HE'LL BE PARALYZED FOR LIFE.
"GODSPEED, JEAN PAUL. GODSPEED."
IT'S A BREAK FOR US THAT BATMAN DIDN'T SECURE THE 'MOBILE WHEN HE PARKED IT.
ONLY HE KNOWS THE CODES.
YOU KNOW, IT WOULD BE BEST IF YOU PREPARED YOURSELF FOR THE WORST EVENTUALITY.
DON'T SAY IT, AZRAEL. I DON'T WANT TO HEAR IT.
THERE'LL ALWAYS BE A BATMAN.
ALWAYS.
14

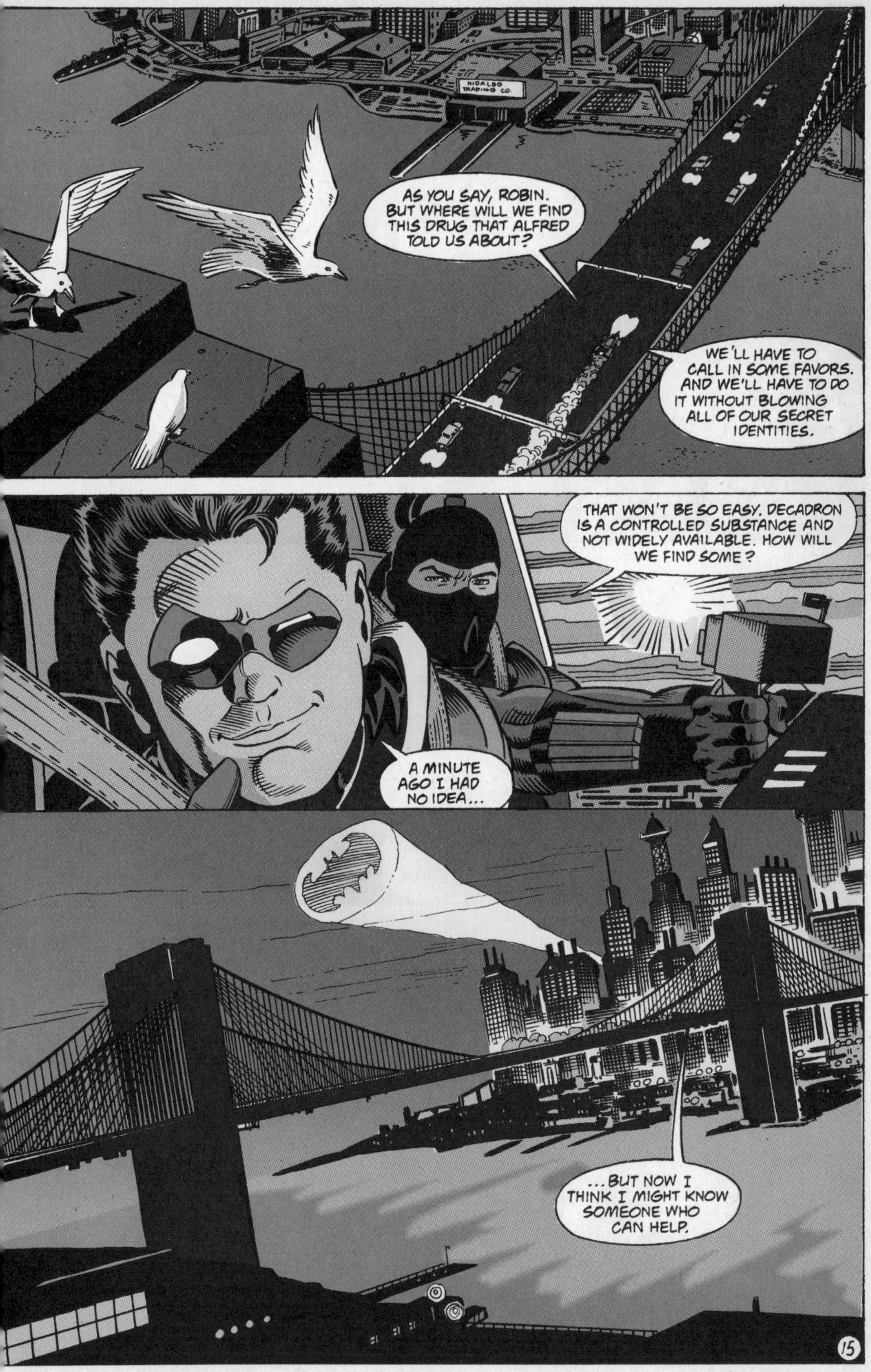
HIDALGO TRADING CO.
AS YOU SAY, ROBIN. BUT WHERE WILL WE FIND THIS DRUG THAT ALFRED TOLD US ABOUT?
WE'LL HAVE TO CALL IN SOME FAVORS. AND WE'LL HAVE TO DO IT WITHOUT BLOWING ALL OF OUR SECRET IDENTITIES.
THAT WON'T BE SO EASY. DECADRON IS A CONTROLLED SUBSTANCE AND NOT WIDELY AVAILABLE. HOW WILL WE FIND SOME?
A MINUTE AGO I HAD NO IDEA...
...BUT NOW I THINK I MIGHT KNOW SOMEONE WHO CAN HELP.
15

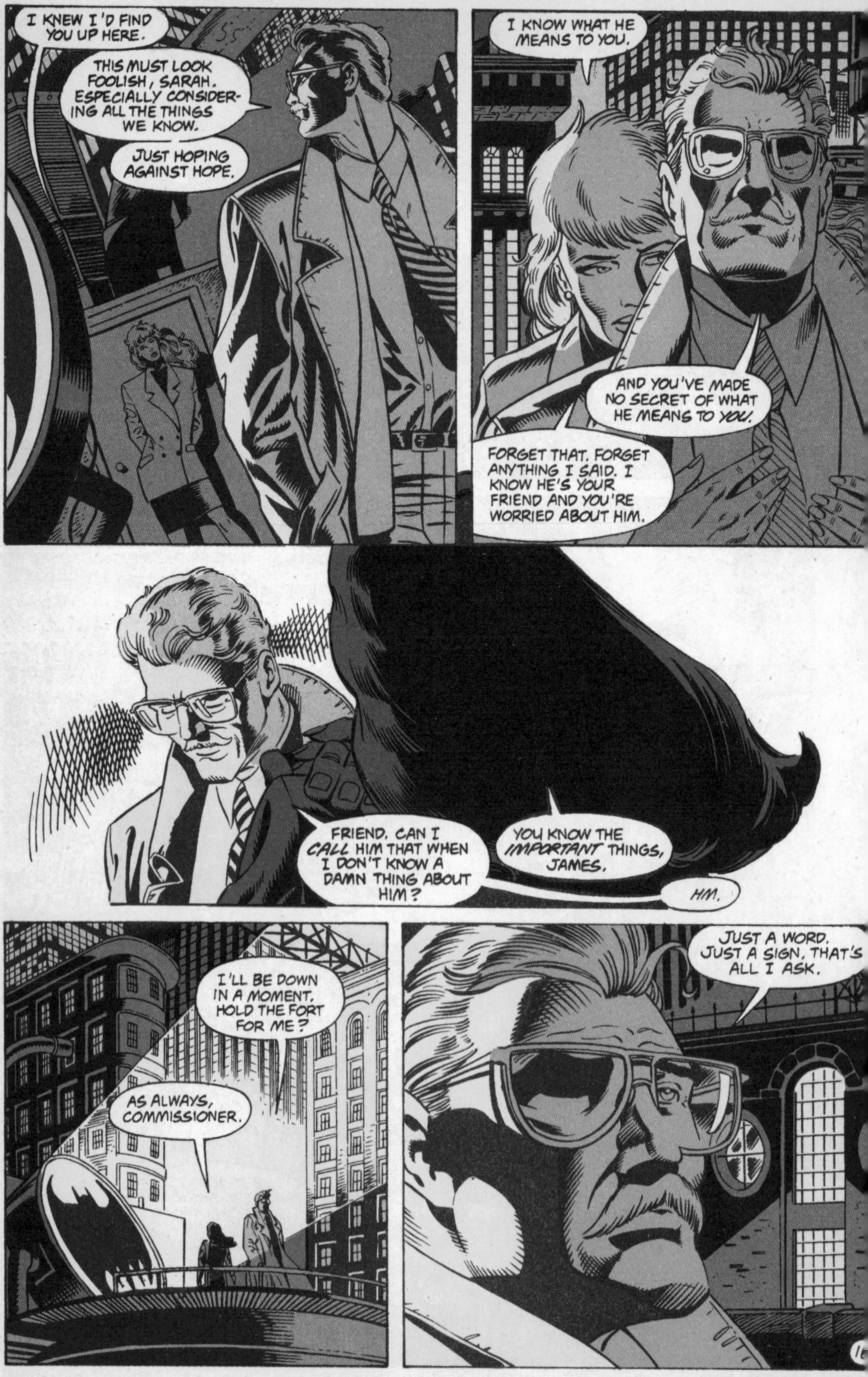
I KNEW I'D FIND YOU UP HERE.
THIS MUST LOOK FOOLISH, SARAH. ESPECIALLY CONSIDERING ALL THE THINGS WE KNOW.
JUST HOPING AGAINST HOPE.
I KNOW WHAT HE MEANS TO YOU.
AND YOU'VE MADE NO SECRET OF WHAT HE MEANS TO *YOU*.
FORGET THAT. FORGET ANYTHING I SAID. I KNOW HE'S YOUR FRIEND AND YOU'RE WORRIED ABOUT HIM.
FRIEND. CAN I *CALL* HIM THAT WHEN I DON'T KNOW A DAMN THING ABOUT HIM?
YOU KNOW THE *IMPORTANT* THINGS, JAMES.
HM.
I'LL BE DOWN IN A MOMENT. HOLD THE FORT FOR ME?
AS ALWAYS, COMMISSIONER.
JUST A WORD. JUST A SIGN. THAT'S ALL I ASK.

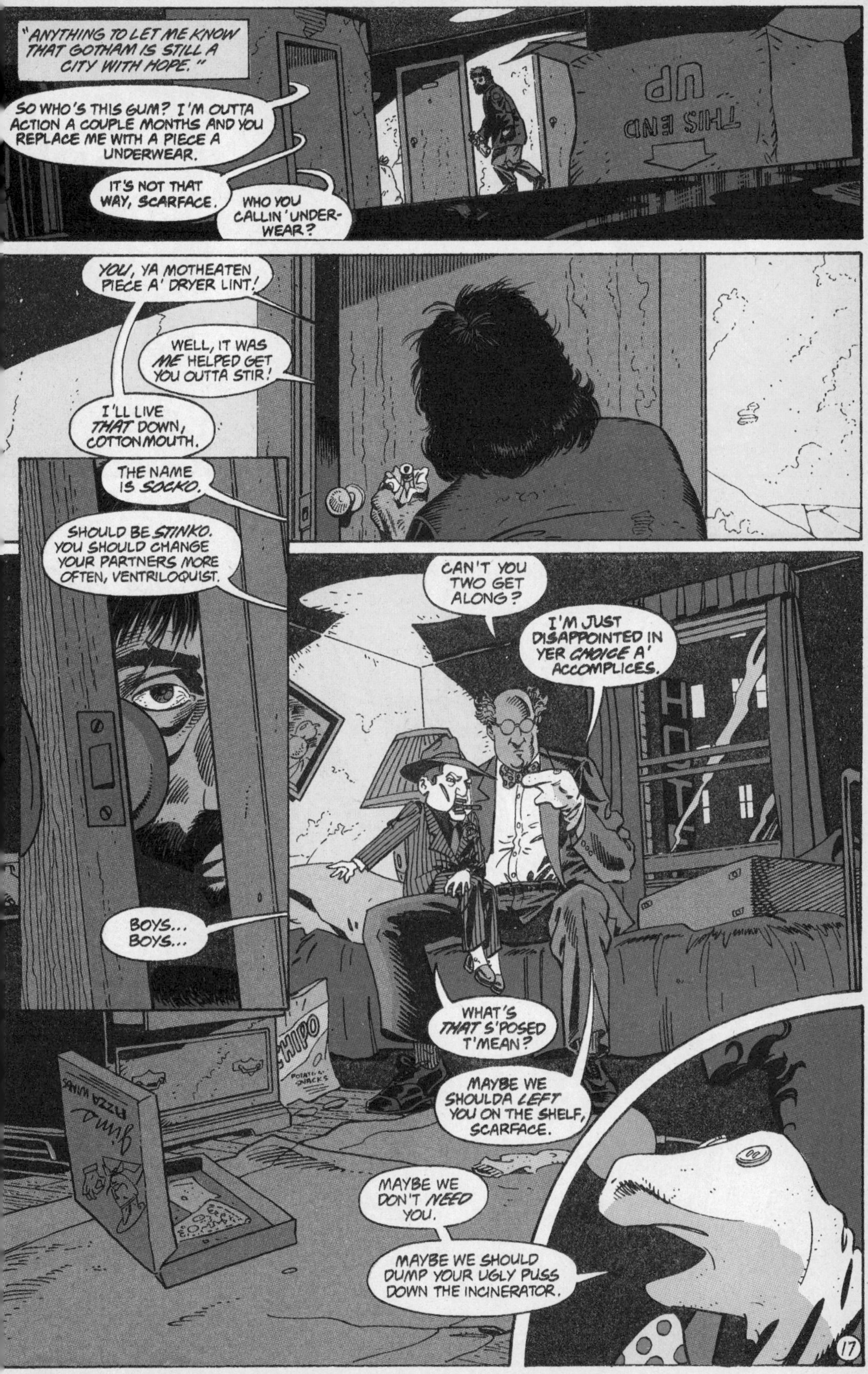
"ANYTHING TO LET ME KNOW THAT GOTHAM IS STILL A CITY WITH HOPE."
SO WHO'S THIS GUM? I'M OUTTA ACTION A COUPLE MONTHS AND YOU REPLACE ME WITH A PIECE A UNDERWEAR.
IT'S NOT THAT WAY, SCARFACE.
WHO YOU CALLIN' UNDER-WEAR?
THIS END UP
YOU, YA MOTHEATEN PIECE A' DRYER LINT!
WELL, IT WAS ME HELPED GET YOU OUTTA STIR!
I'LL LIVE THAT DOWN, COTTONMOUTH.
THE NAME IS SOCKO.
SHOULD BE STINKO. YOU SHOULD CHANGE YOUR PARTNERS MORE OFTEN, VENTRILOQUIST.
CAN'T YOU TWO GET ALONG?
I'M JUST DISAPPOINTED IN YER CHOICE A' ACCOMPLICES.
BOYS... BOYS...
WHAT'S THAT S'POSED T'MEAN?
MAYBE WE SHOULDA LEFT YOU ON THE SHELF, SCARFACE.
MAYBE WE DON'T NEED YOU.
MAYBE WE SHOULD DUMP YOUR UGLY PUSS DOWN THE INCINERATOR.
17

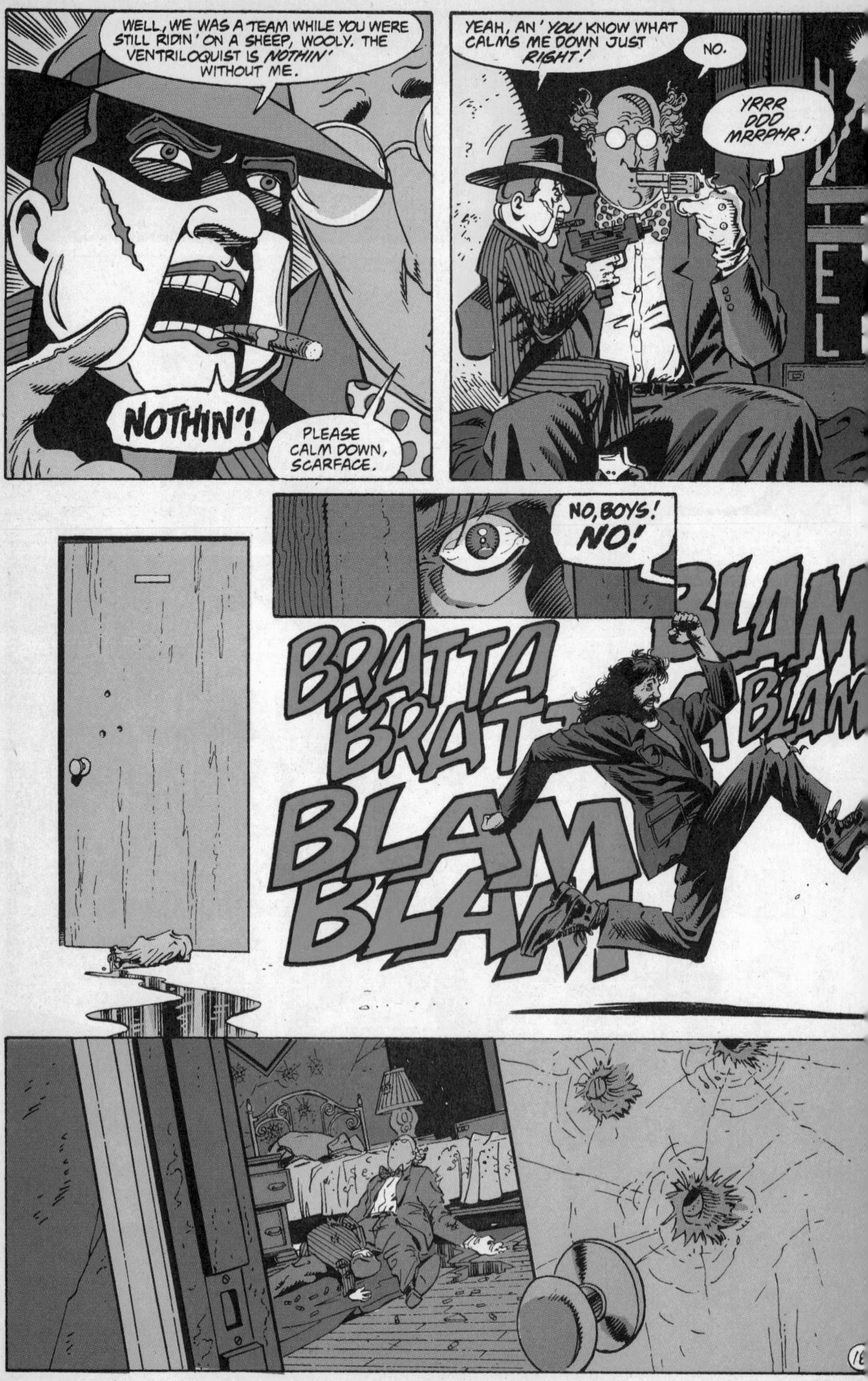

WELL, WE WAS A TEAM WHILE YOU WERE STILL RIDIN' ON A SHEEP, WOOLY. THE VENTRILOQUIST IS NOTHIN' WITHOUT ME.
NOTHIN'!
PLEASE CALM DOWN, SCARFACE.
YEAH, AN' YOU KNOW WHAT CALMS ME DOWN JUST RIGHT!
NO.
YRRR DDO MRRPHR!
NO, BOYS! NO!
BRATTA
BRAT
BLAM
BLAM
BLAM
BLAM
18

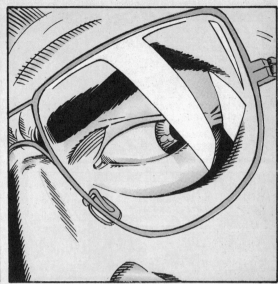

THANKS FOR LEAVING THE WINDOW OPEN.

YOU'RE ALONE.

I NEED YOUR HELP. *HE* NEEDS YOUR HELP.

ANYTHING.

A DRUG CALLED DECADRON. HE MIGHT DIE WITHOUT IT. WE NEED IT FAST.

WAIT HERE.

PATCH ME THROUGH TO BULLOCK'S UNIT.

BULLOCK, THIS IS THE COMMISSIONER, COME IN.

NO SIGN OF THIS BRAIN GUY, COMMISH. BUT HE CAN'T HIDE FOREVER.

IT'S *BANE*, HARV.

FORGET ABOUT THAT AND LISTEN UP...

⑲

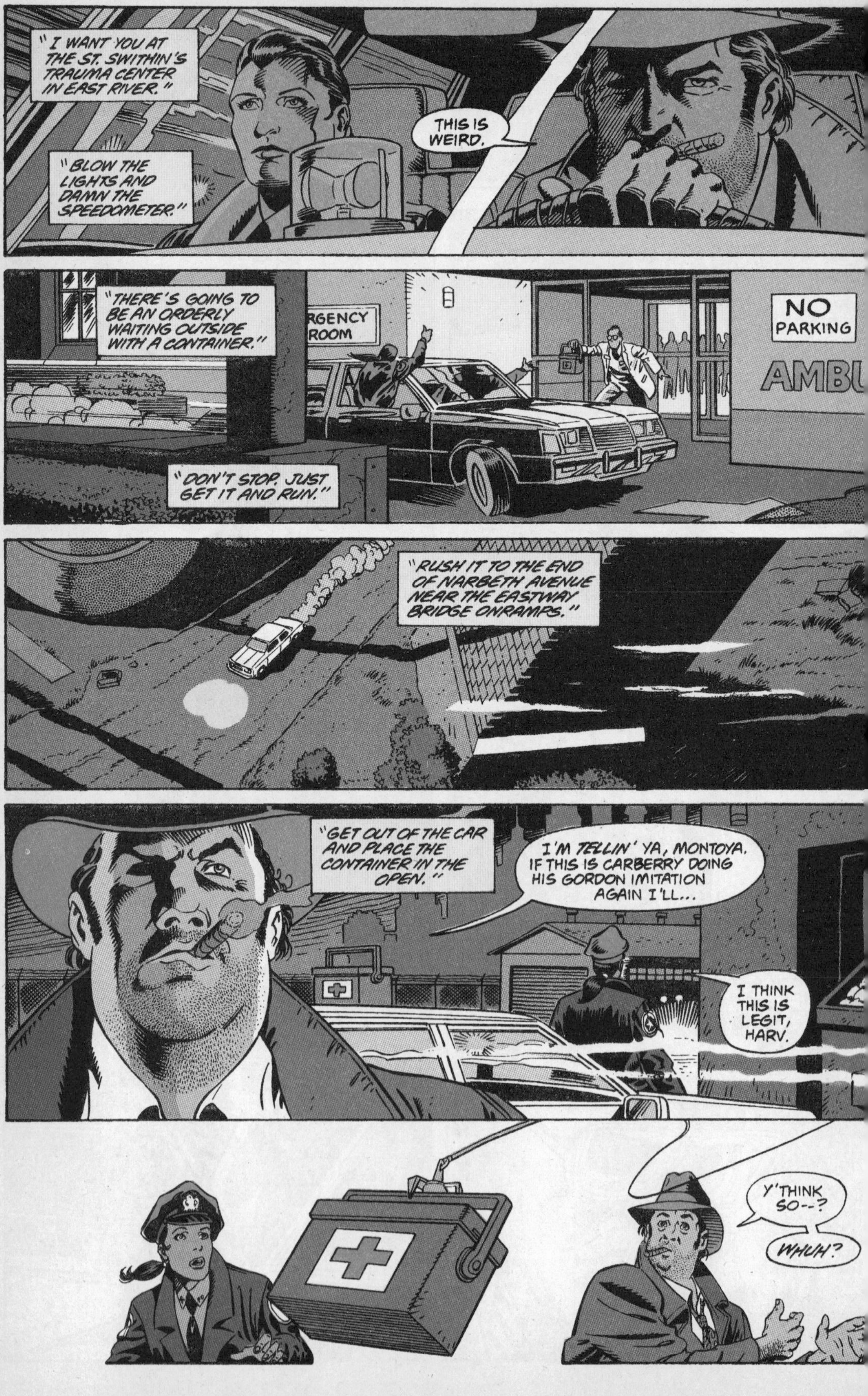
"I WANT YOU AT THE ST. SWITHIN'S TRAUMA CENTER IN EAST RIVER."
"BLOW THE LIGHTS AND DAMN THE SPEEDOMETER."
THIS IS WEIRD.
"THERE'S GOING TO BE AN ORDERLY WAITING OUTSIDE WITH A CONTAINER."
RGENCY ROOM
NO PARKING
AMBU
"DON'T STOP. JUST GET IT AND RUN."
"RUSH IT TO THE END OF NARBETH AVENUE NEAR THE EASTWAY BRIDGE ONRAMPS."
"GET OUT OF THE CAR AND PLACE THE CONTAINER IN THE OPEN."
I'M TELLIN' YA, MONTOYA. IF THIS IS CARBERRY DOING HIS GORDON IMITATION AGAIN I'LL...
I THINK THIS IS LEGIT, HARV.
Y'THINK SO--?
WHUH?

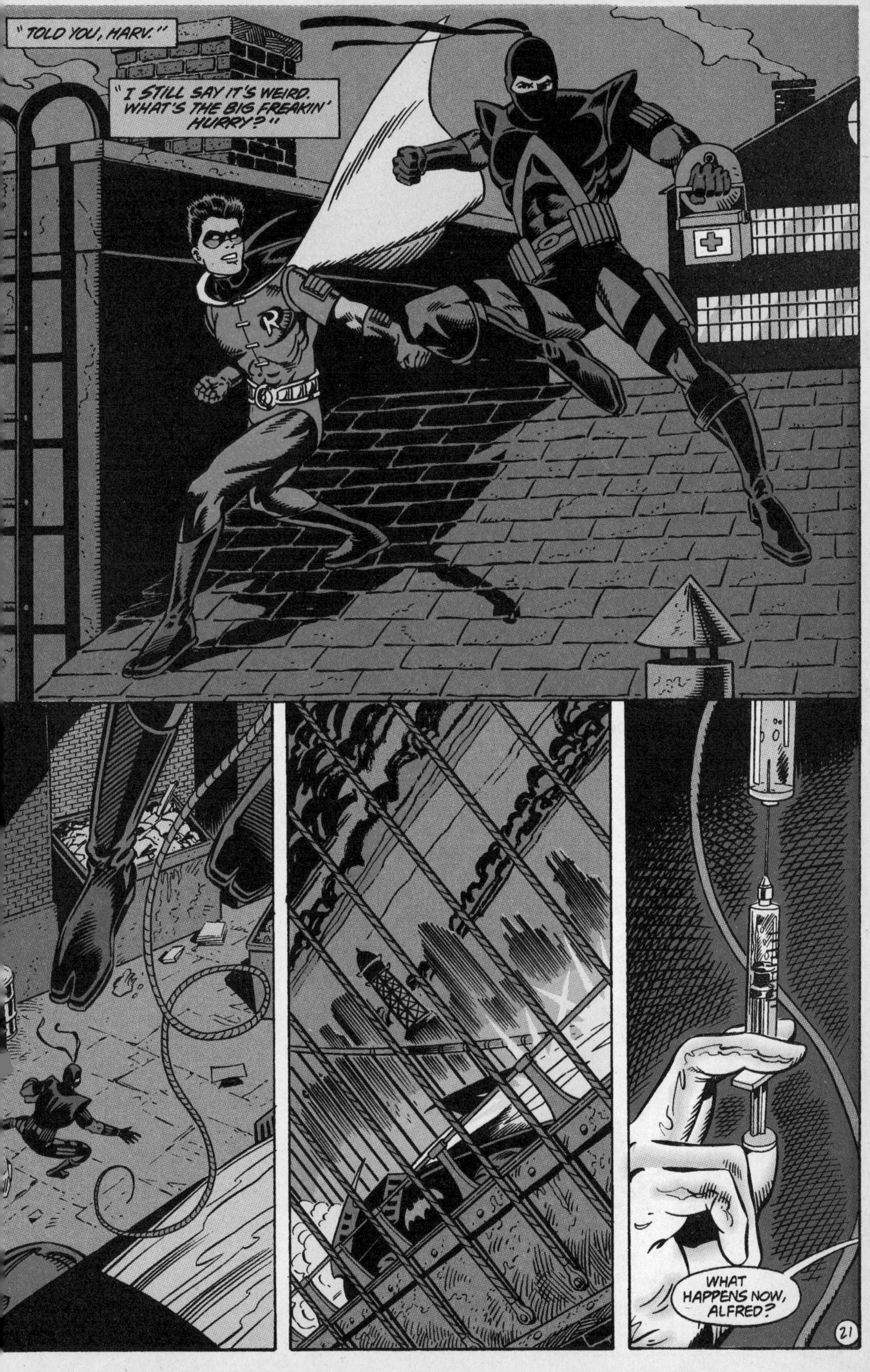
"TOLD YOU, HARV."
"I STILL SAY IT'S WEIRD. WHAT'S THE BIG FREAKIN' HURRY?"
WHAT HAPPENS NOW, ALFRED?
21

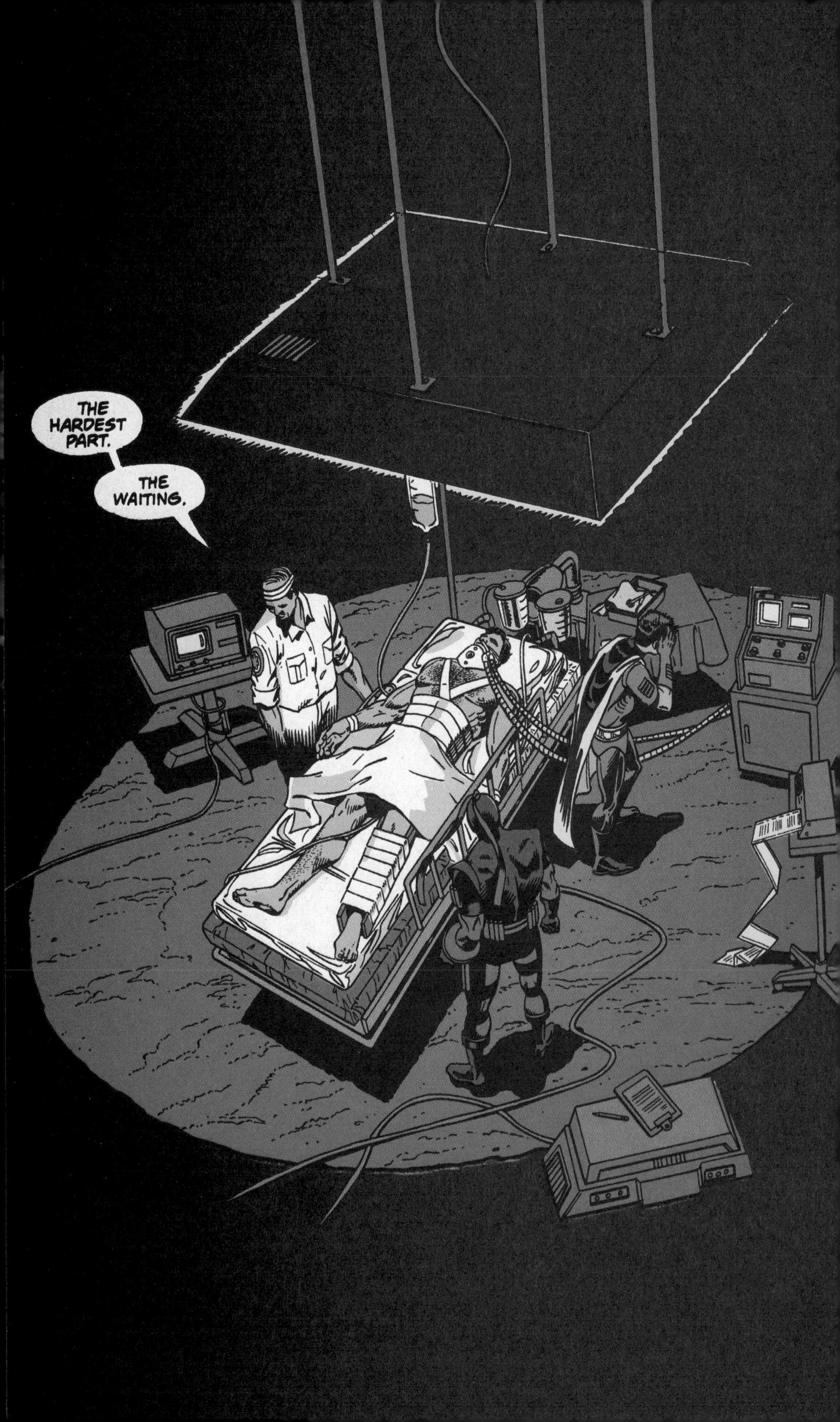
THE HARDEST PART.
THE WAITING.

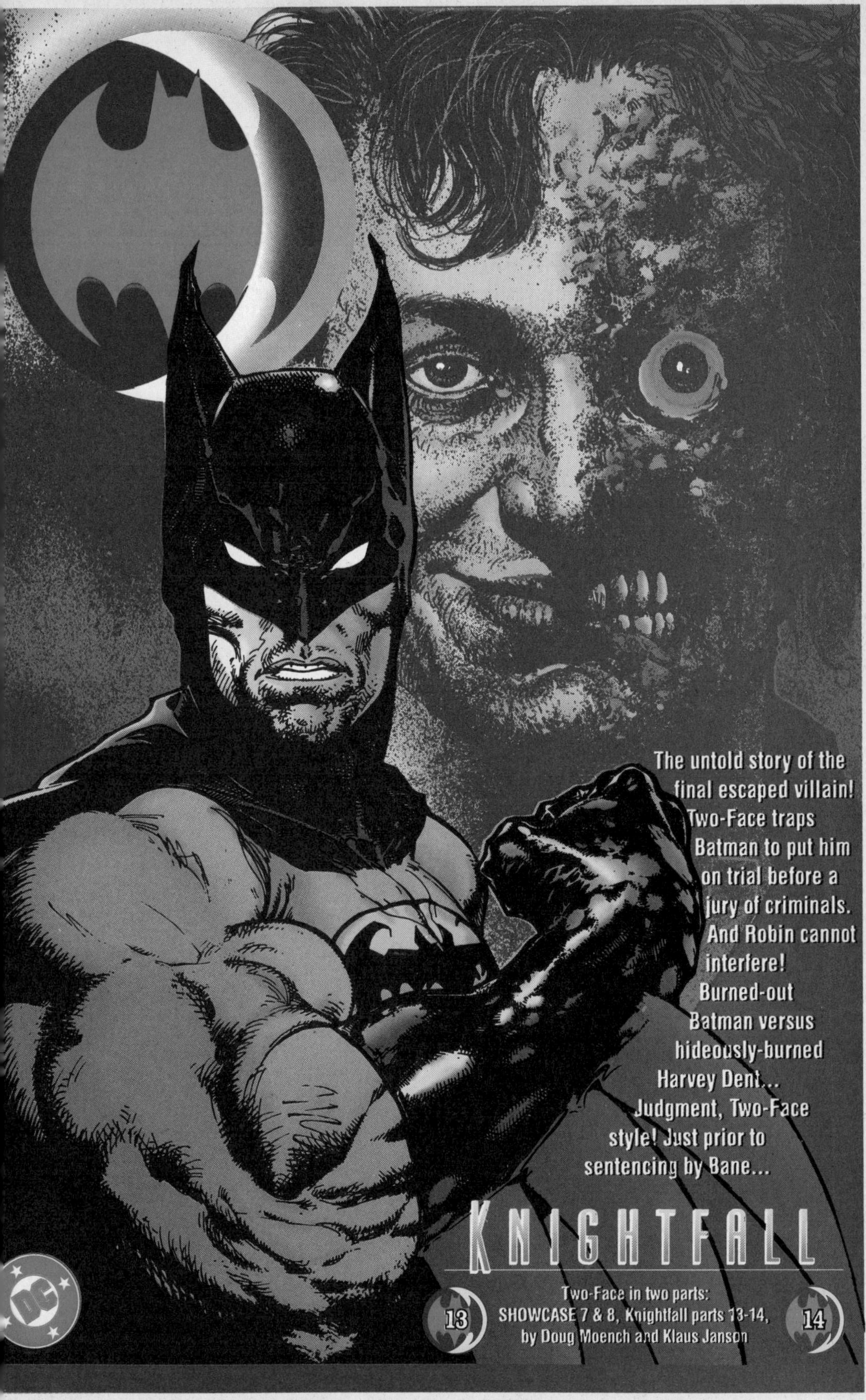
The untold story of the final escaped villain! Two-Face traps Batman to put him on trial before a jury of criminals. And Robin cannot interfere! Burned-out Batman versus hideously-burned Harvey Dent... Judgment, Two-Face style! Just prior to sentencing by Bane...
KNIGHTFALL
13
Two-Face in two parts:
SHOWCASE 7 & 8, Knightfall parts 13-14,
by Doug Moench and Klaus Janson
14

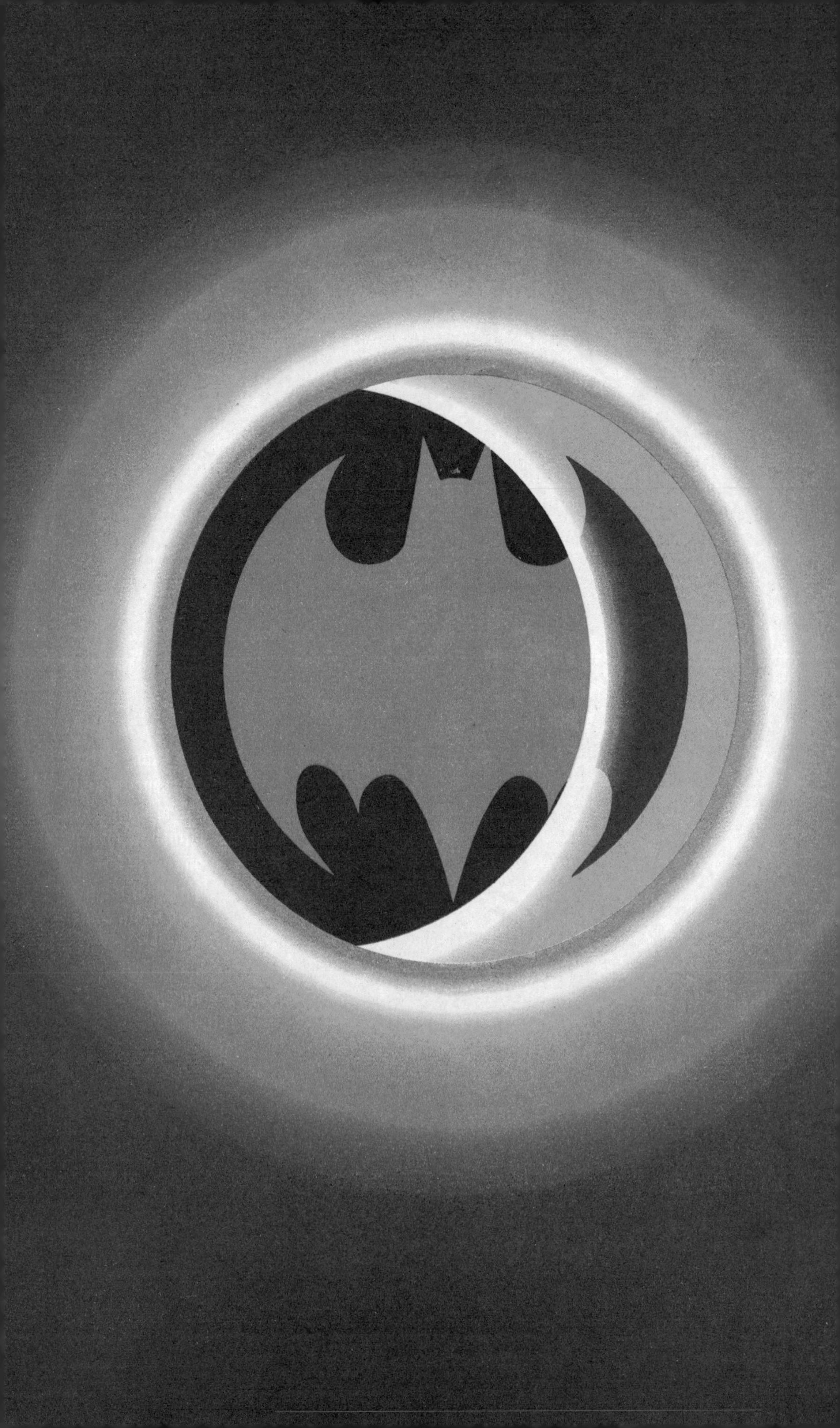

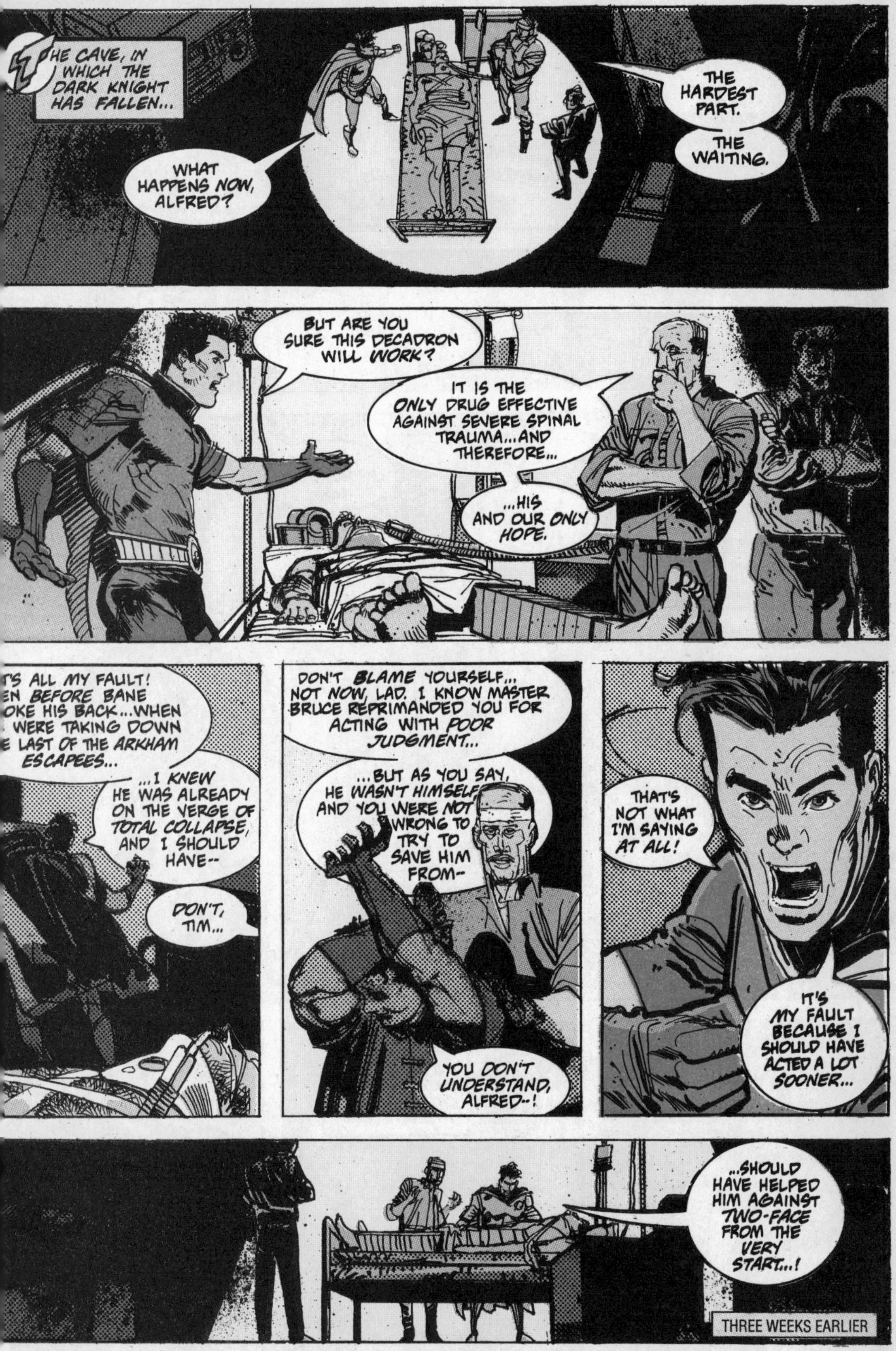
THE CAVE, IN WHICH THE DARK KNIGHT HAS FALLEN...
WHAT HAPPENS NOW, ALFRED?
THE HARDEST PART.
THE WAITING.
BUT ARE YOU SURE THIS DECADRON WILL WORK?
IT IS THE ONLY DRUG EFFECTIVE AGAINST SEVERE SPINAL TRAUMA...AND THEREFORE...
...HIS AND OUR ONLY HOPE.
IT'S ALL MY FAULT! EVEN BEFORE BANE BROKE HIS BACK...WHEN WE WERE TAKING DOWN THE LAST OF THE ARKHAM ESCAPEES...
...I KNEW HE WAS ALREADY ON THE VERGE OF TOTAL COLLAPSE, AND I SHOULD HAVE--
DON'T, TIM...
DON'T BLAME YOURSELF... NOT NOW, LAD. I KNOW MASTER BRUCE REPRIMANDED YOU FOR ACTING WITH POOR JUDGMENT...
...BUT AS YOU SAY, HE WASN'T HIMSELF AND YOU WERE NOT WRONG TO TRY TO SAVE HIM FROM--
YOU DON'T UNDERSTAND, ALFRED--!
THAT'S NOT WHAT I'M SAYING AT ALL!
IT'S MY FAULT BECAUSE I SHOULD HAVE ACTED A LOT SOONER...
...SHOULD HAVE HELPED HIM AGAINST TWO-FACE FROM THE VERY START...!
THREE WEEKS EARLIER

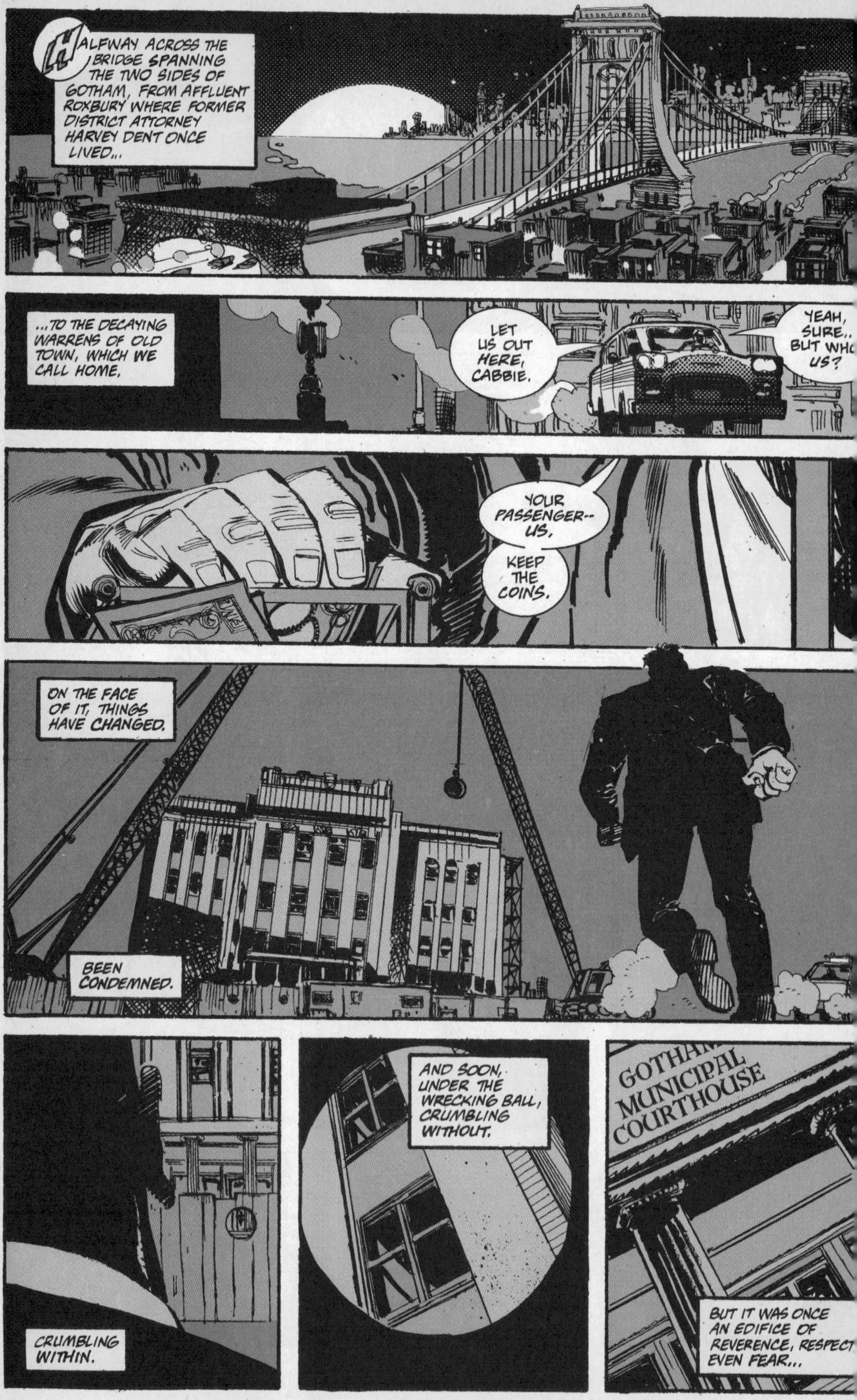
HALFWAY ACROSS THE BRIDGE SPANNING THE TWO SIDES OF GOTHAM, FROM AFFLUENT ROXBURY WHERE FORMER DISTRICT ATTORNEY HARVEY DENT ONCE LIVED...
...TO THE DECAYING WARRENS OF OLD TOWN, WHICH WE CALL HOME.
LET US OUT HERE, CABBIE.
YEAH, SURE.. BUT WHO US?
YOUR PASSENGER-- US.
KEEP THE COINS.
ON THE FACE OF IT, THINGS HAVE CHANGED.
BEEN CONDEMNED.
CRUMBLING WITHIN.
AND SOON, UNDER THE WRECKING BALL, CRUMBLING WITHOUT.
GOTHAM MUNICIPAL COURTHOUSE
BUT IT WAS ONCE AN EDIFICE OF REVERENCE, RESPECT EVEN FEAR...

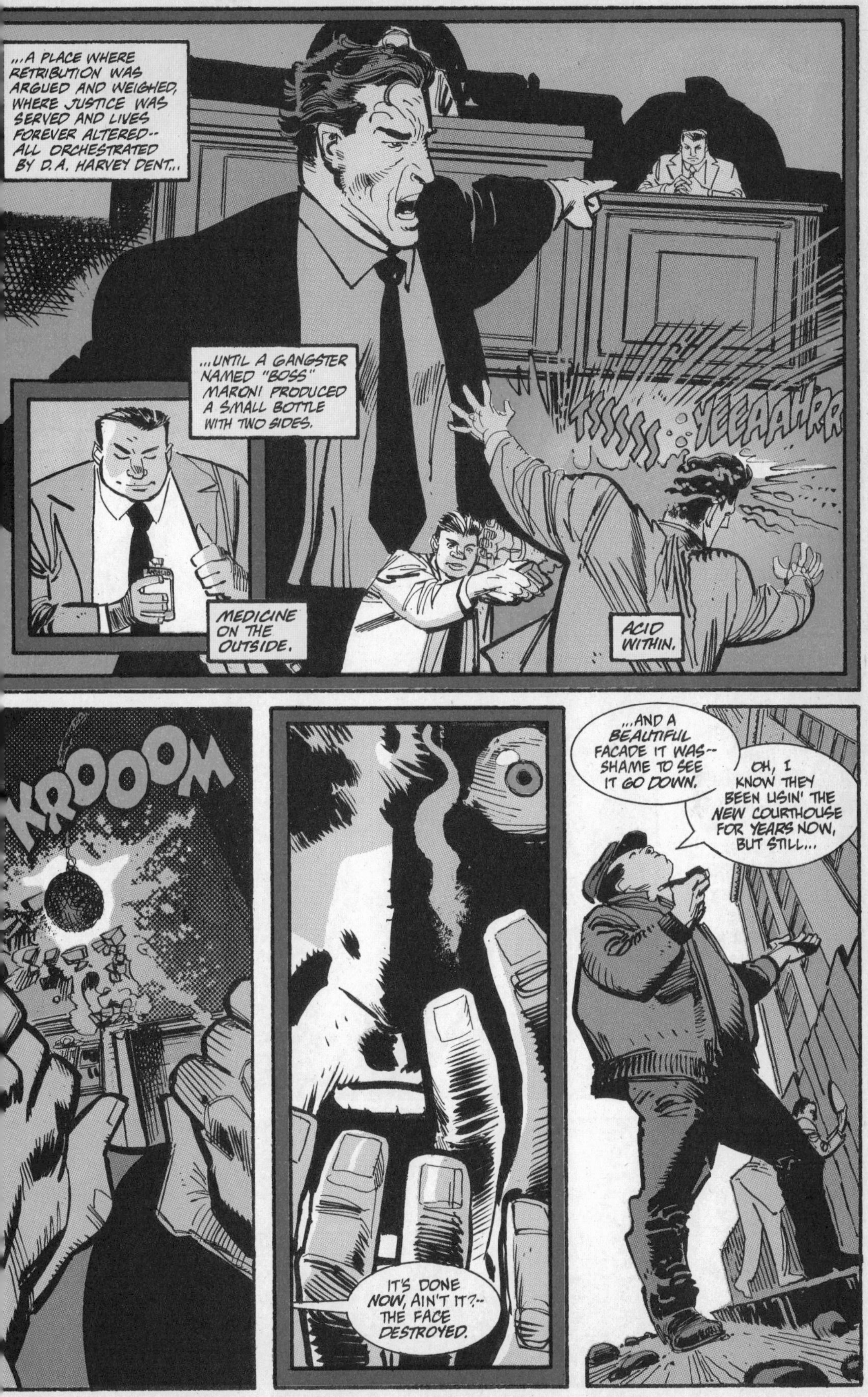

...A PLACE WHERE RETRIBUTION WAS ARGUED AND WEIGHED, WHERE JUSTICE WAS SERVED AND LIVES FOREVER ALTERED-- ALL ORCHESTRATED BY D.A. HARVEY DENT...
...UNTIL A GANGSTER NAMED "BOSS" MARONI PRODUCED A SMALL BOTTLE WITH TWO SIDES.
MEDICINE ON THE OUTSIDE.
ACID WITHIN.
TSSSSS
YEEAAHRR
KROOOM
IT'S DONE NOW, AIN'T IT?-- THE FACE DESTROYED.
...AND A BEAUTIFUL FACADE IT WAS-- SHAME TO SEE IT GO DOWN.
OH, I KNOW THEY BEEN USIN' THE NEW COURTHOUSE FOR YEARS NOW, BUT STILL...

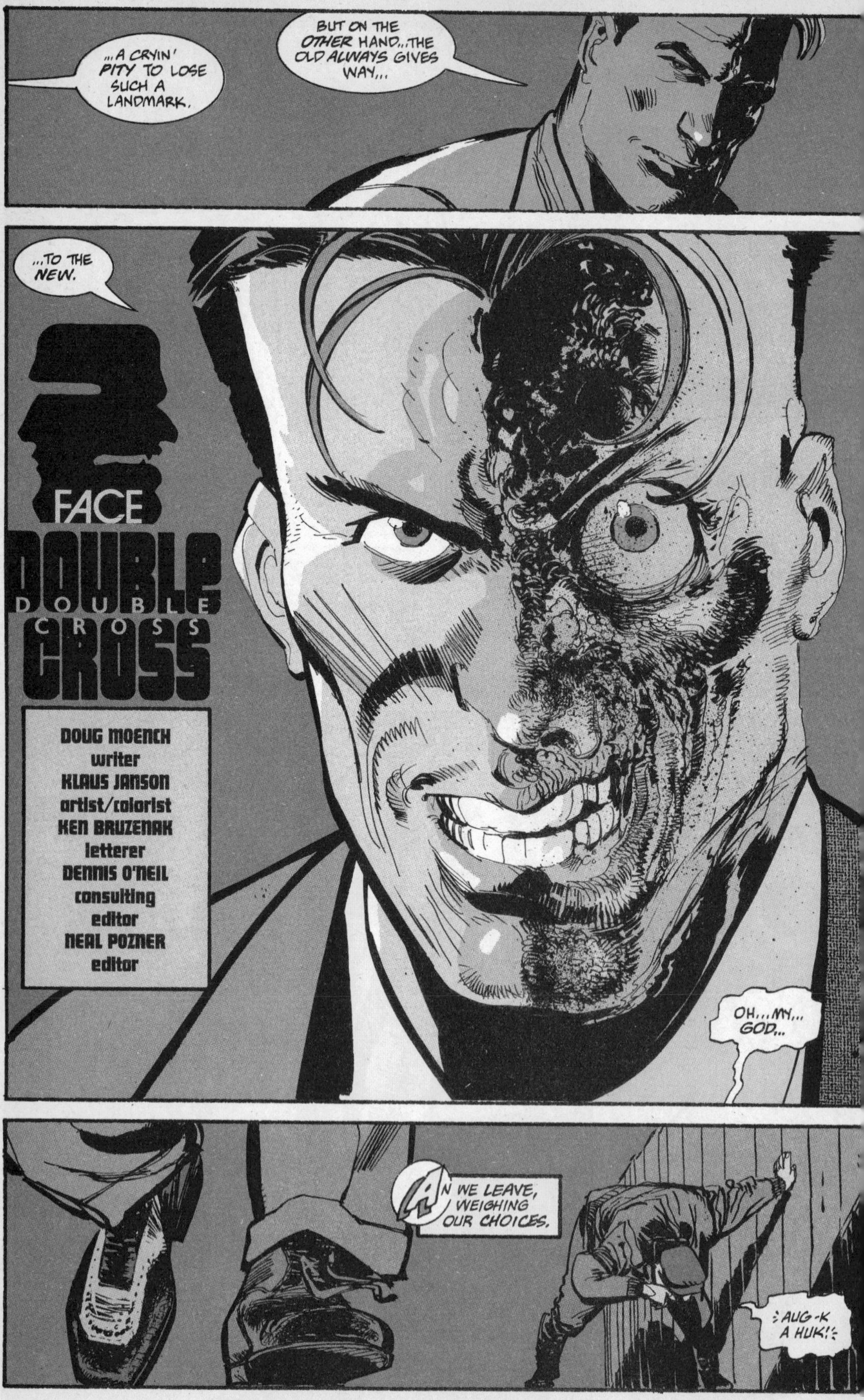

...A CRYIN' PITY TO LOSE SUCH A LANDMARK.
BUT ON THE OTHER HAND... THE OLD ALWAYS GIVES WAY...
...TO THE NEW.
2 FACE
DOUBLE DOUBLE CROSS CROSS
DOUG MOENCH writer
KLAUS JANSON artist/colorist
KEN BRUZENAK letterer
DENNIS O'NEIL consulting editor
NEAL POZNER editor
OH... MY... GOD...
AN WE LEAVE, WEIGHING OUR CHOICES.
AUG-K A HUK!

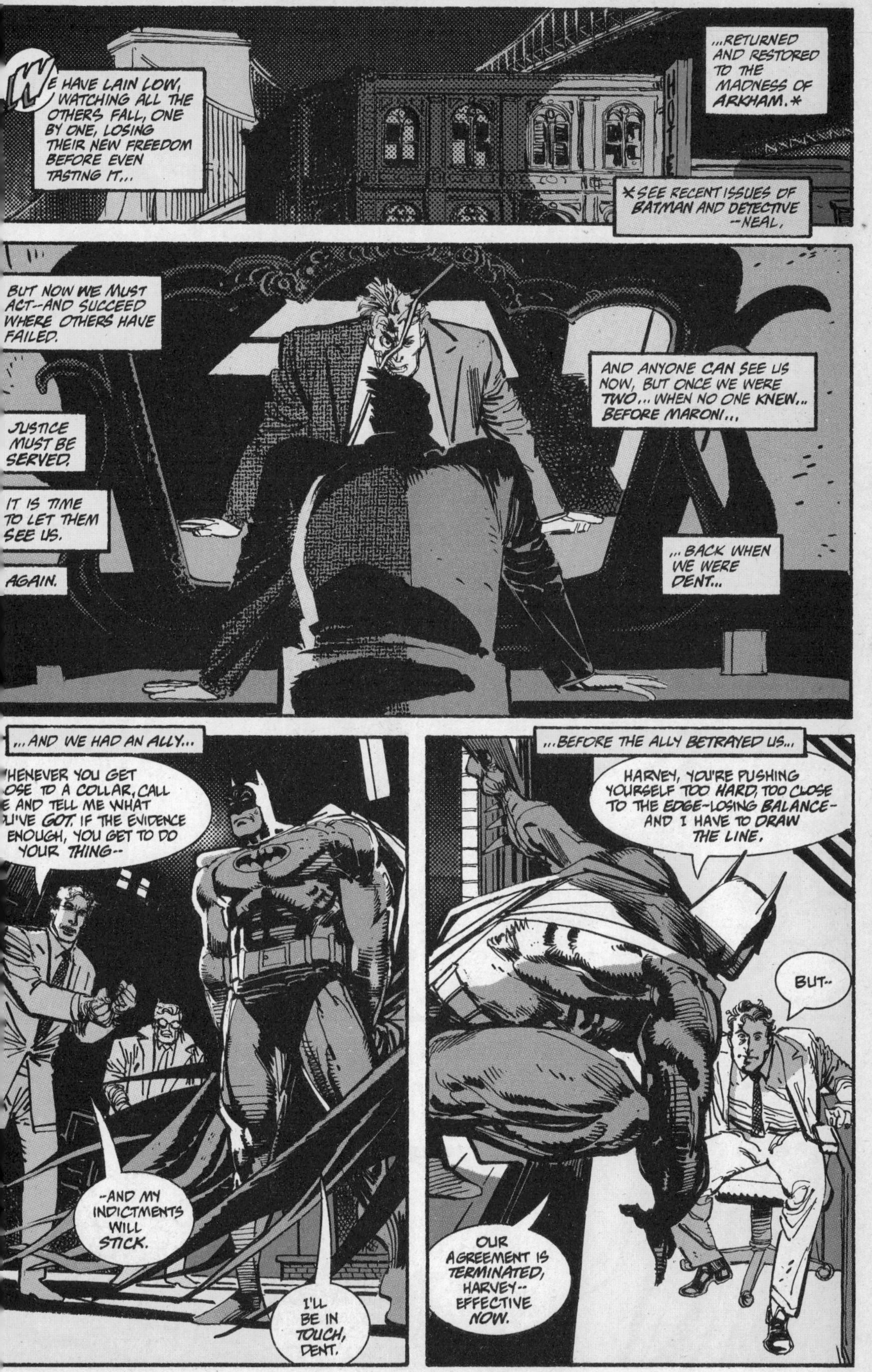
WE HAVE LAIN LOW, WATCHING ALL THE OTHERS FALL, ONE BY ONE, LOSING THEIR NEW FREEDOM BEFORE EVEN TASTING IT...
...RETURNED AND RESTORED TO THE MADNESS OF ARKHAM.*
*SEE RECENT ISSUES OF BATMAN AND DETECTIVE --NEAL.
BUT NOW WE MUST ACT--AND SUCCEED WHERE OTHERS HAVE FAILED.
JUSTICE MUST BE SERVED.
IT IS TIME TO LET THEM SEE US.
AGAIN.
AND ANYONE CAN SEE US NOW, BUT ONCE WE WERE TWO... WHEN NO ONE KNEW... BEFORE MARONI...
...BACK WHEN WE WERE DENT...
...AND WE HAD AN ALLY...
HENEVER YOU GET OSE TO A COLLAR, CALL E AND TELL ME WHAT U'VE GOT. IF THE EVIDENCE ENOUGH, YOU GET TO DO YOUR THING--
--AND MY INDICTMENTS WILL STICK.
I'LL BE IN TOUCH, DENT.
...BEFORE THE ALLY BETRAYED US...
HARVEY, YOU'RE PUSHING YOURSELF TOO HARD, TOO CLOSE TO THE EDGE--LOSING BALANCE-- AND I HAVE TO DRAW THE LINE.
BUT--
OUR AGREEMENT IS TERMINATED, HARVEY-- EFFECTIVE NOW.

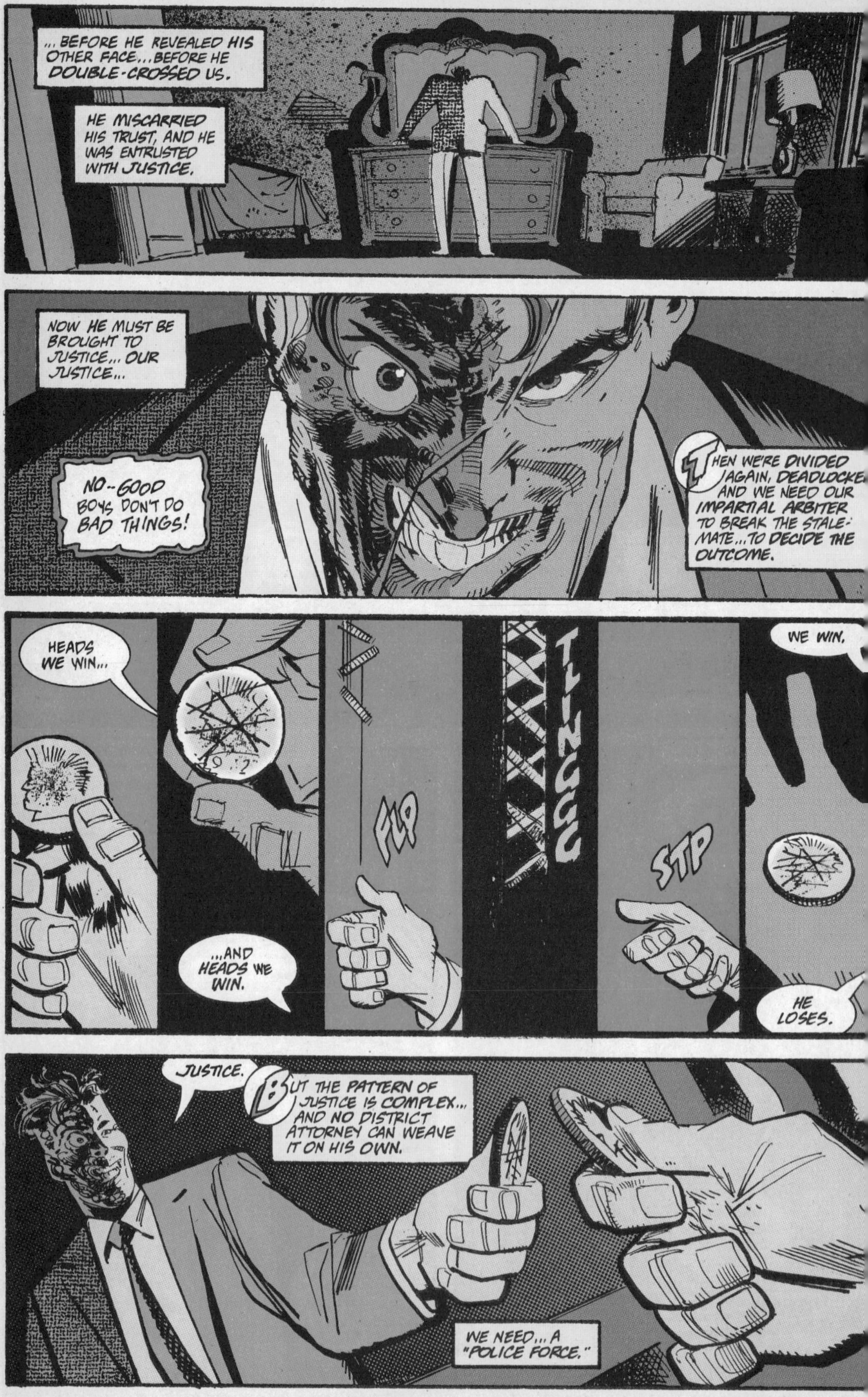
...BEFORE HE REVEALED HIS OTHER FACE...BEFORE HE DOUBLE-CROSSED US.
HE MISCARRIED HIS TRUST, AND HE WAS ENTRUSTED WITH JUSTICE.
NOW HE MUST BE BROUGHT TO JUSTICE... OUR JUSTICE...
NO--GOOD BOYS DON'T DO BAD THINGS!
THEN WE'RE DIVIDED AGAIN, DEADLOCKE AND WE NEED OUR IMPARTIAL ARBITER TO BREAK THE STALE-MATE...TO DECIDE THE OUTCOME.
HEADS WE WIN...
...AND HEADS WE WIN.
FLP
TLINGGG
STP
WE WIN.
HE LOSES.
JUSTICE.
BUT THE PATTERN OF JUSTICE IS COMPLEX... AND NO DISTRICT ATTORNEY CAN WEAVE IT ON HIS OWN.
WE NEED... A "POLICE FORCE."

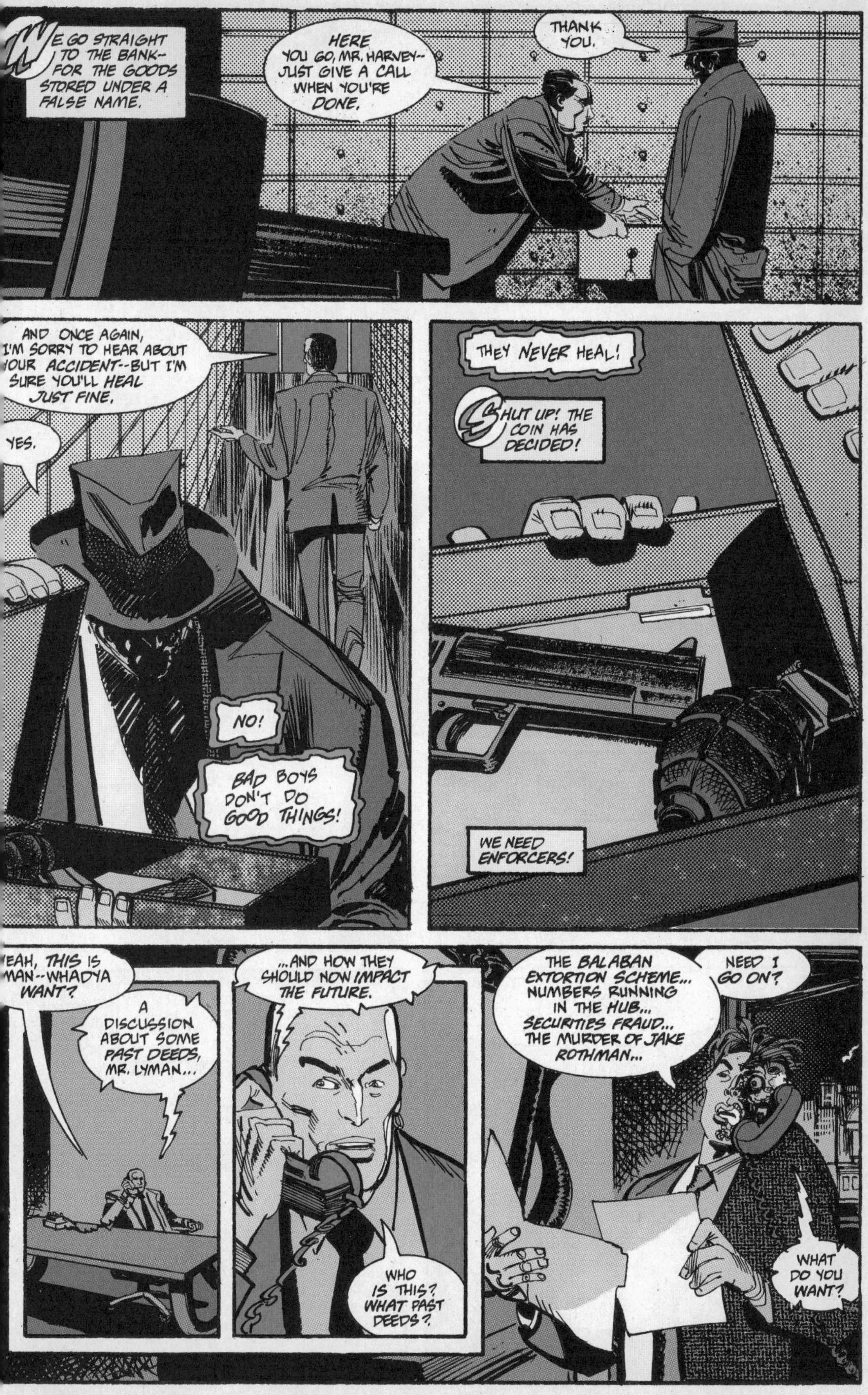
WE GO STRAIGHT TO THE BANK-- FOR THE GOODS STORED UNDER A FALSE NAME.
HERE YOU GO, MR. HARVEY-- JUST GIVE A CALL WHEN YOU'RE DONE.
THANK YOU.
AND ONCE AGAIN, I'M SORRY TO HEAR ABOUT YOUR ACCIDENT--BUT I'M SURE YOU'LL HEAL JUST FINE.
YES.
NO!
BAD BOYS DON'T DO GOOD THINGS!
THEY NEVER HEAL!
SHUT UP! THE COIN HAS DECIDED!
WE NEED ENFORCERS!
YEAH, THIS IS LYMAN--WHADYA WANT?
A DISCUSSION ABOUT SOME PAST DEEDS, MR. LYMAN...
...AND HOW THEY SHOULD NOW IMPACT THE FUTURE.
WHO IS THIS? WHAT PAST DEEDS?
THE BALABAN EXTORTION SCHEME... NUMBERS RUNNING IN THE HUB... SECURITIES FRAUD... THE MURDER OF JAKE ROTHMAN...
NEED I GO ON?
WHAT DO YOU WANT?

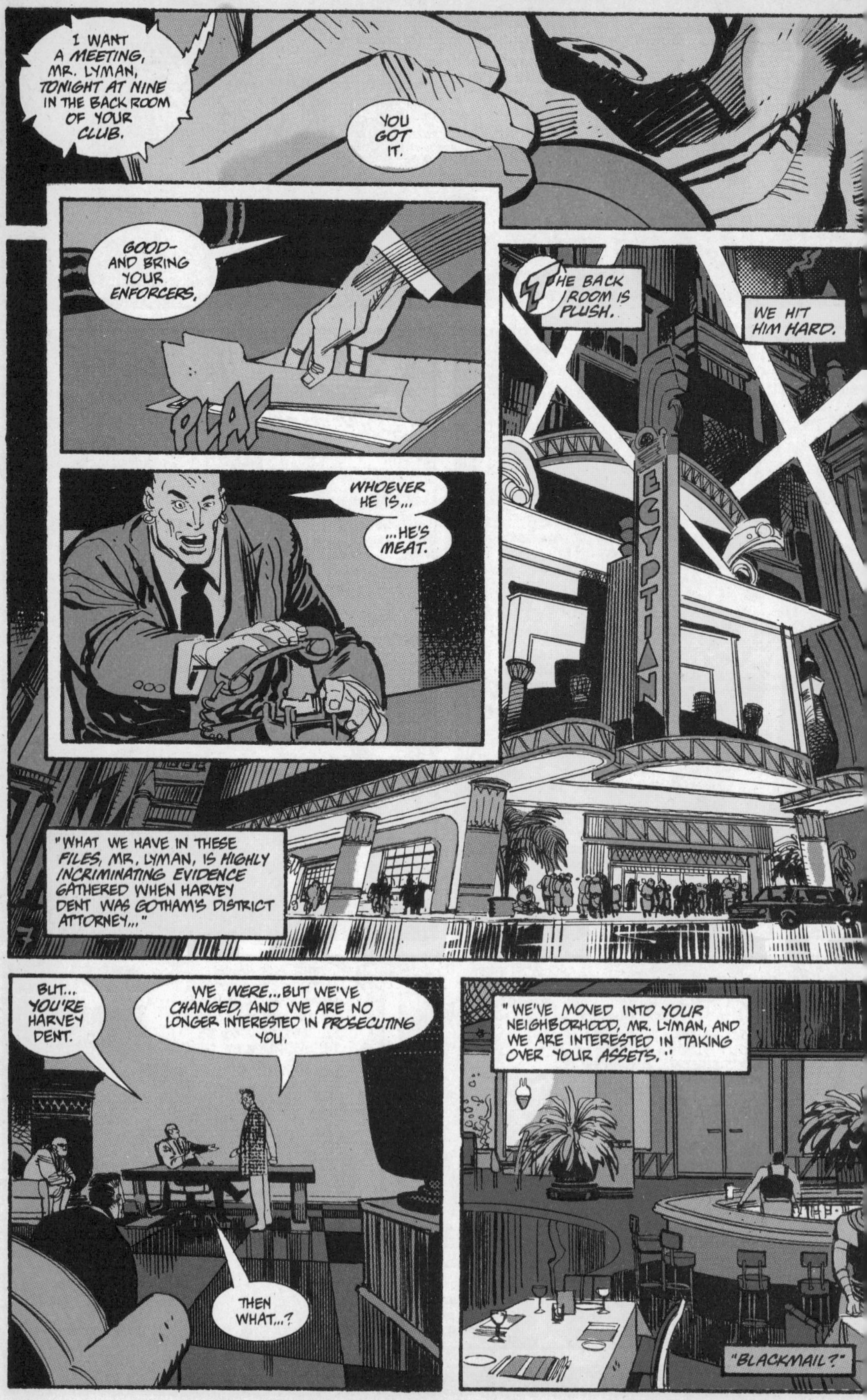
I WANT A MEETING, MR. LYMAN, TONIGHT AT NINE IN THE BACK ROOM OF YOUR CLUB.
YOU GOT IT.
GOOD-AND BRING YOUR ENFORCERS.
PLAF
WHOEVER HE IS...
...HE'S MEAT.
THE BACK ROOM IS PLUSH.
WE HIT HIM HARD.
EGYPTIAN
"WHAT WE HAVE IN THESE FILES, MR. LYMAN, IS HIGHLY INCRIMINATING EVIDENCE GATHERED WHEN HARVEY DENT WAS GOTHAM'S DISTRICT ATTORNEY..."
BUT... YOU'RE HARVEY DENT.
WE WERE...BUT WE'VE CHANGED, AND WE ARE NO LONGER INTERESTED IN PROSECUTING YOU.
THEN WHAT...?
"WE'VE MOVED INTO YOUR NEIGHBORHOOD, MR. LYMAN, AND WE ARE INTERESTED IN TAKING OVER YOUR ASSETS."
"BLACKMAIL?"

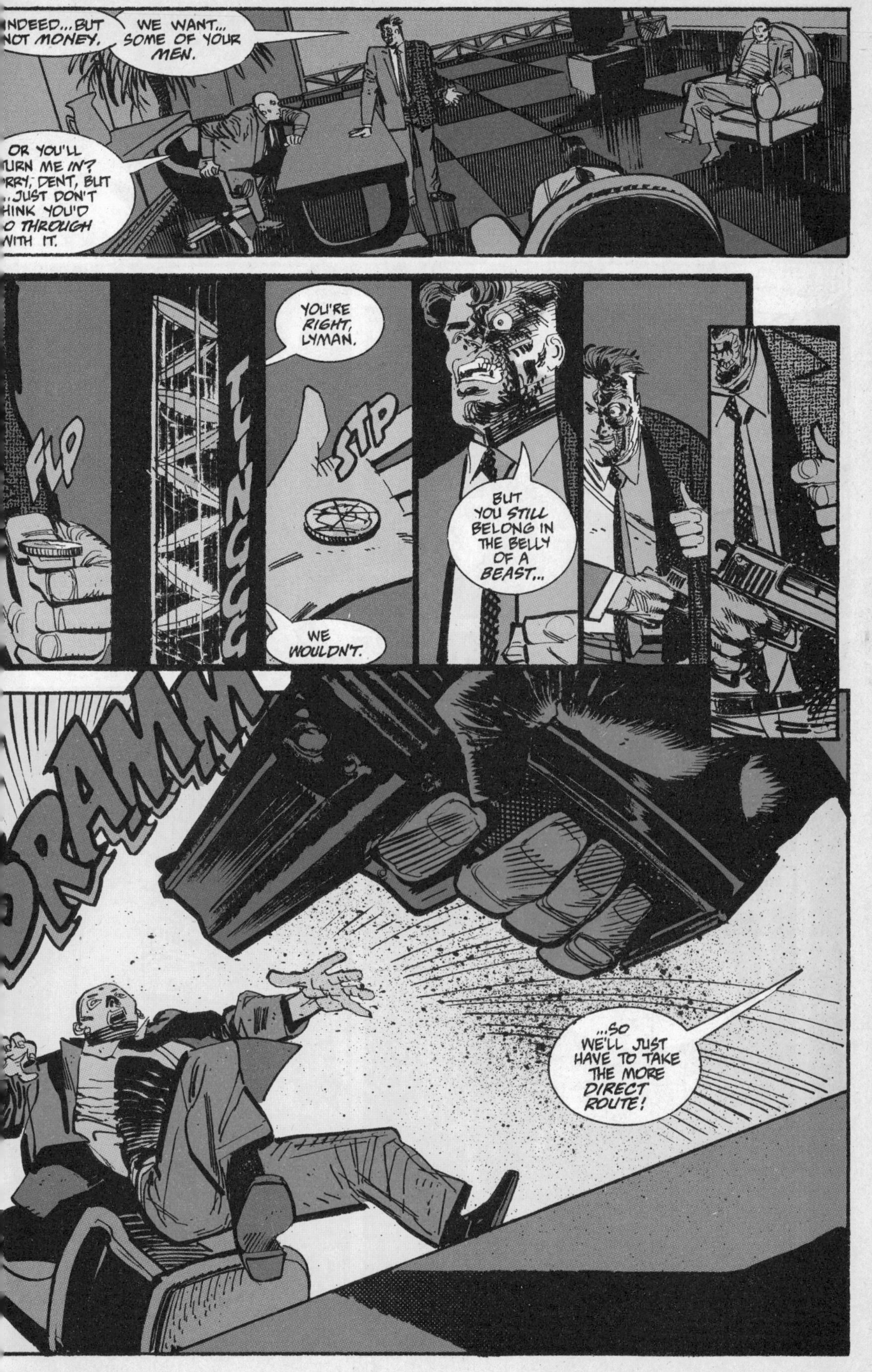
NDEED... BUT NOT MONEY.
WE WANT... SOME OF YOUR MEN.
OR YOU'LL TURN ME IN? RRY, DENT, BUT ..JUST DON'T HINK YOU'D O THROUGH WITH IT.
FLP
TLINGGG
YOU'RE RIGHT, LYMAN.
STP
WE WOULDN'T.
BUT YOU STILL BELONG IN THE BELLY OF A BEAST...
RAMM
...SO WE'LL JUST HAVE TO TAKE THE MORE DIRECT ROUTE!

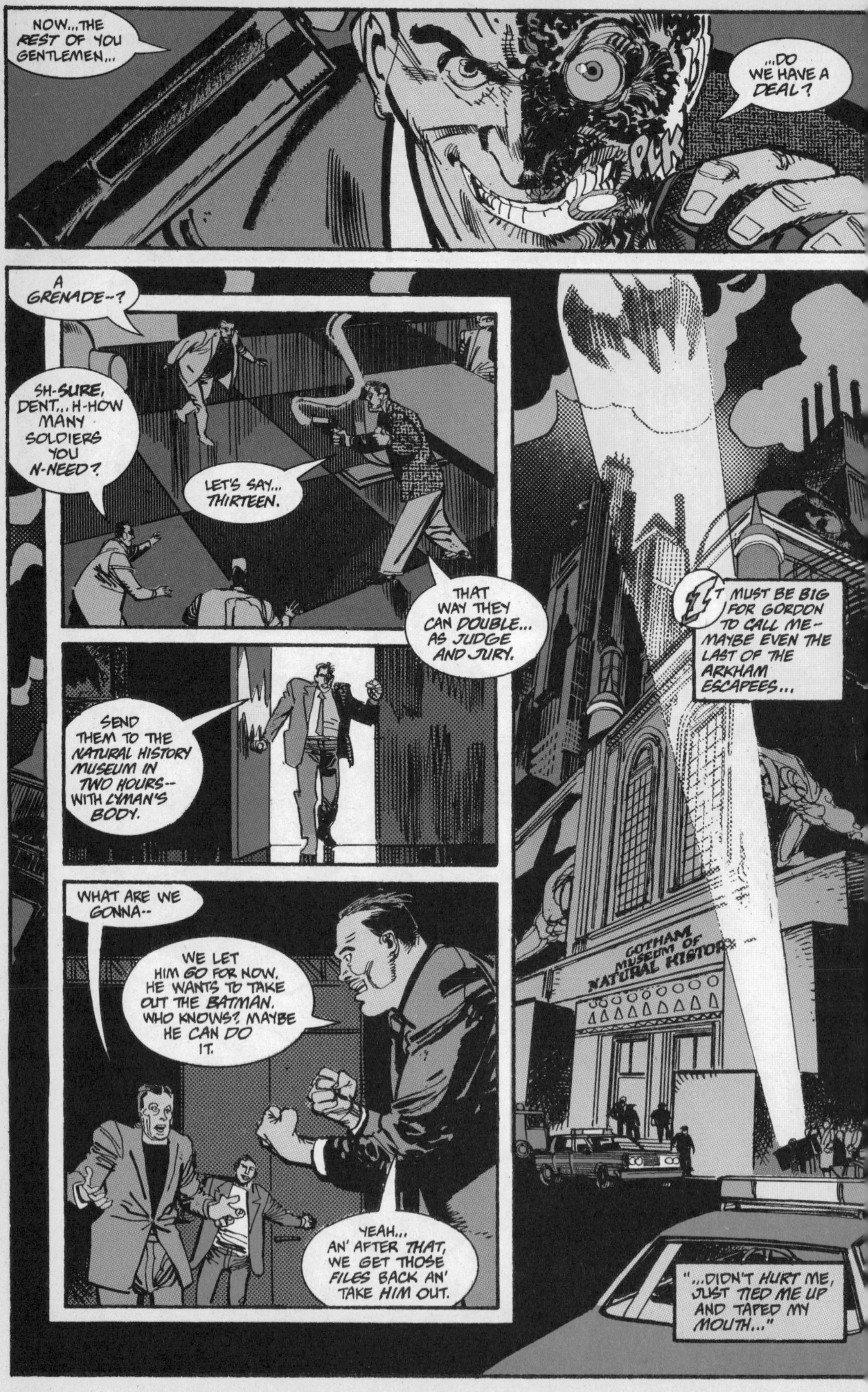

NOW... THE REST OF YOU GENTLEMEN...
...DO WE HAVE A DEAL?
PLK
A GRENADE--?
SH-SURE, DENT... H-HOW MANY SOLDIERS YOU N-NEED?
LET'S SAY... THIRTEEN.
THAT WAY THEY CAN DOUBLE... AS JUDGE AND JURY.
SEND THEM TO THE NATURAL HISTORY MUSEUM IN TWO HOURS-- WITH LYMAN'S BODY.
WHAT ARE WE GONNA--
WE LET HIM GO FOR NOW. HE WANTS TO TAKE OUT THE BATMAN. WHO KNOWS? MAYBE HE CAN DO IT.
YEAH... AN' AFTER THAT, WE GET THOSE FILES BACK AN' TAKE HIM OUT.
IT MUST BE BIG FOR GORDON TO CALL ME-- MAYBE EVEN THE LAST OF THE ARKHAM ESCAPEES...
GOTHAM MUSEUM OF NATURAL HISTORY
"...DIDN'T HURT ME, JUST TIED ME UP AND TAPED MY MOUTH..."

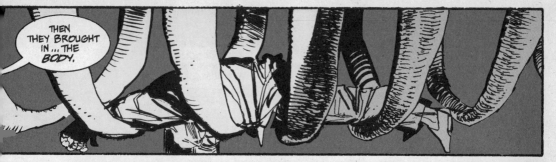

THEN THEY BROUGHT IN ... THE BODY.

MANAGED TO WORK MY HANDS FREE ABOUT A HALF-HOUR AFTER THEY LEFT.

THEN I CALLED YOU GUYS.

BUT EVEN THOUGH THERE WAS NOTHING *UNUSUAL* ABOUT THESE MEN, DO YOU THINK YOU COULD PICK THEM OUT FROM MUGSHO--

EH--?

THP

ALL RIGHT, EVERYBODY TAKE A BREAK-- EXCEPT THE *NIGHT GUARD.*

GUESS HE'S HERE.

IT'S CLEAR.

THEY'RE GONE.

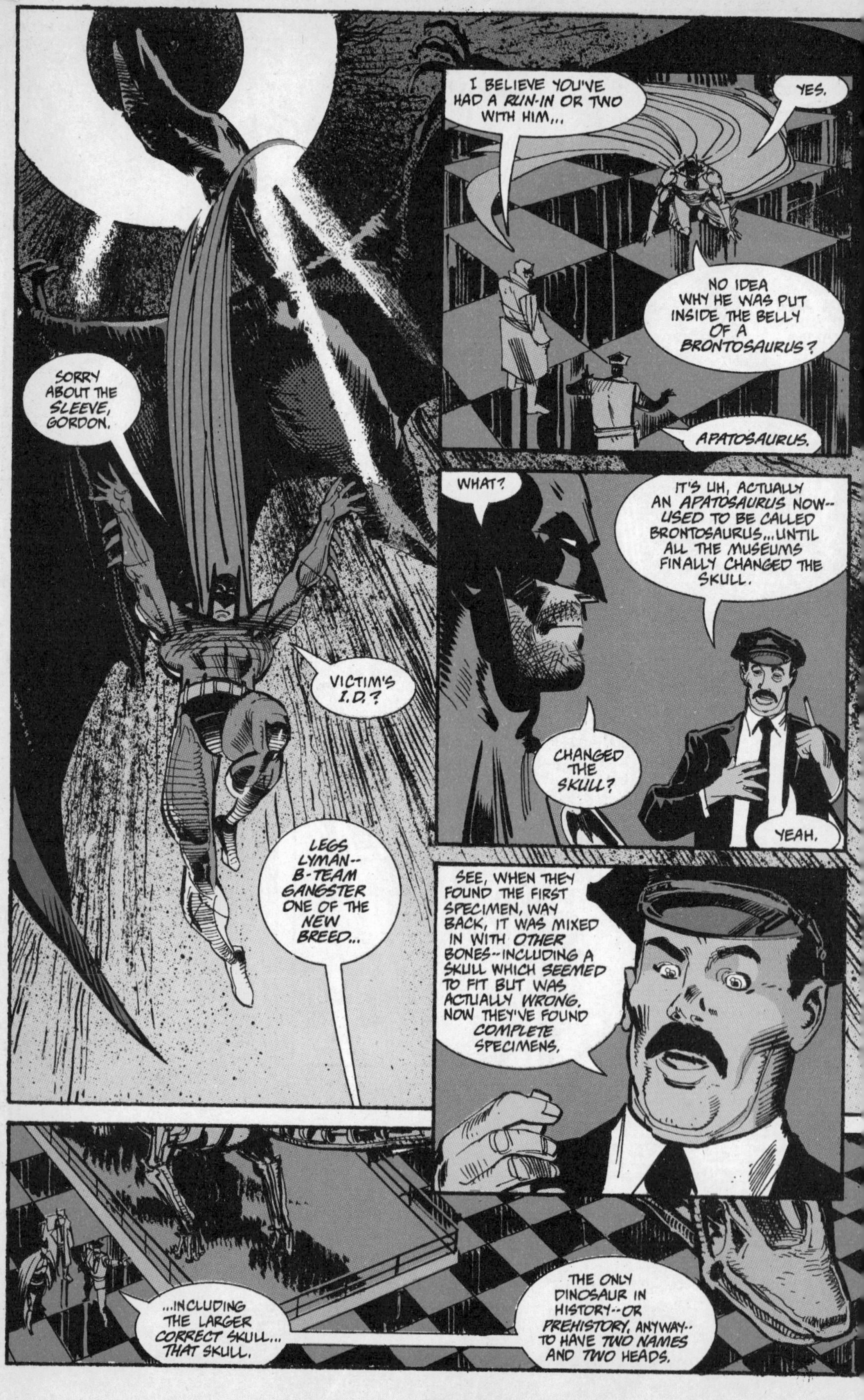
I BELIEVE YOU'VE HAD A RUN-IN OR TWO WITH HIM...
YES.
NO IDEA WHY HE WAS PUT INSIDE THE BELLY OF A BRONTOSAURUS?
APATOSAURUS.
SORRY ABOUT THE SLEEVE, GORDON.
WHAT?
IT'S UH, ACTUALLY AN APATOSAURUS NOW-- USED TO BE CALLED BRONTOSAURUS... UNTIL ALL THE MUSEUMS FINALLY CHANGED THE SKULL.
CHANGED THE SKULL?
YEAH.
VICTIM'S I.D.?
LEGS LYMAN-- B-TEAM GANGSTER ONE OF THE NEW BREED...
SEE, WHEN THEY FOUND THE FIRST SPECIMEN, WAY BACK, IT WAS MIXED IN WITH OTHER BONES--INCLUDING A SKULL WHICH SEEMED TO FIT BUT WAS ACTUALLY WRONG. NOW THEY'VE FOUND COMPLETE SPECIMENS.
...INCLUDING THE LARGER CORRECT SKULL... THAT SKULL.
THE ONLY DINOSAUR IN HISTORY--OR PREHISTORY, ANYWAY-- TO HAVE TWO NAMES AND TWO HEADS.

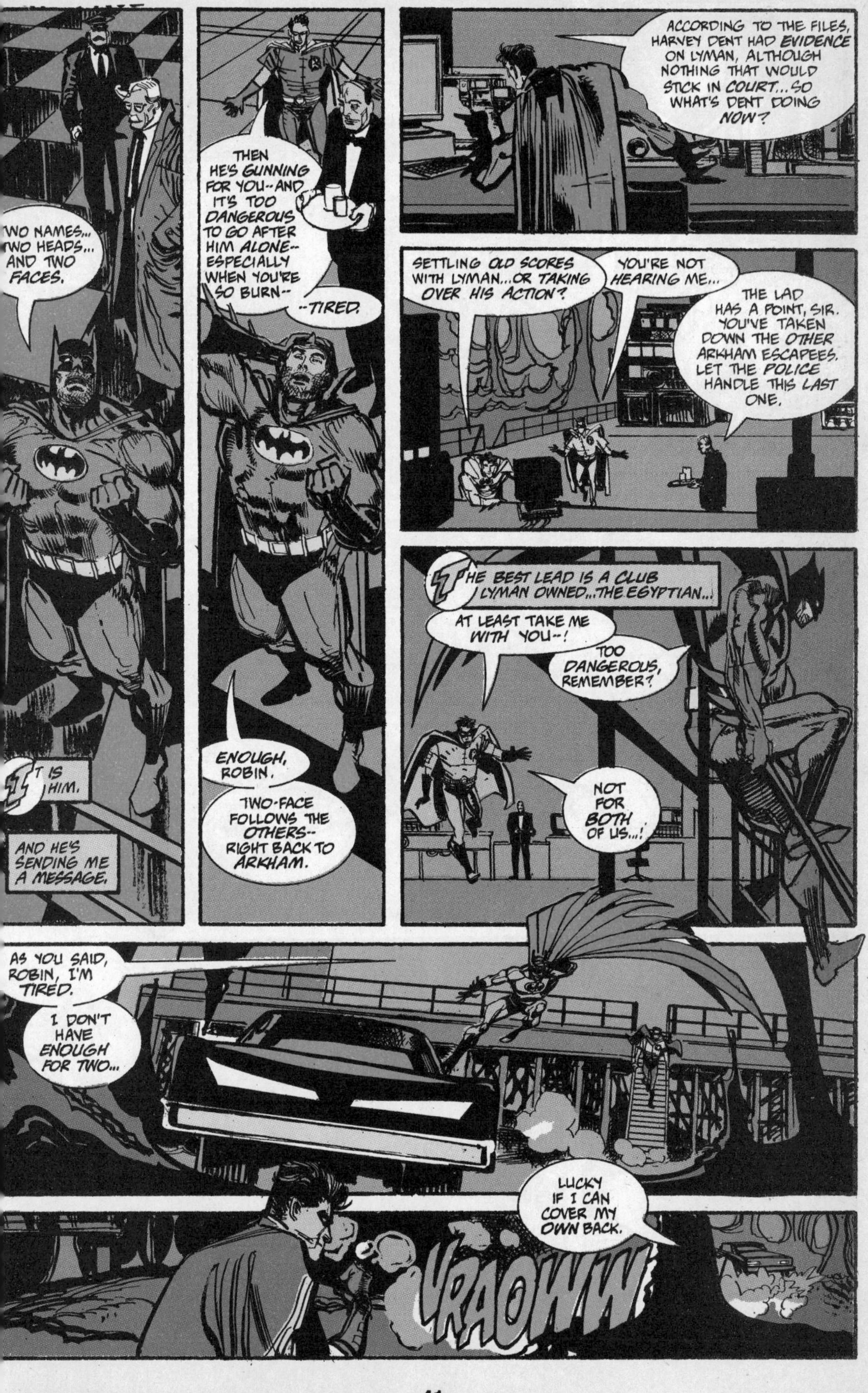

TWO NAMES... TWO HEADS... AND TWO FACES.
THEN HE'S GUNNING FOR YOU--AND IT'S TOO DANGEROUS TO GO AFTER HIM ALONE--ESPECIALLY WHEN YOU'RE SO BURN--
--TIRED.
IT IS HIM.
AND HE'S SENDING ME A MESSAGE.
ENOUGH, ROBIN.
TWO-FACE FOLLOWS THE OTHERS--RIGHT BACK TO ARKHAM.
ACCORDING TO THE FILES, HARVEY DENT HAD EVIDENCE ON LYMAN, ALTHOUGH NOTHING THAT WOULD STICK IN COURT... SO WHAT'S DENT DOING NOW?
SETTLING OLD SCORES WITH LYMAN... OR TAKING OVER HIS ACTION?
YOU'RE NOT HEARING ME...
THE LAD HAS A POINT, SIR. YOU'VE TAKEN DOWN THE OTHER ARKHAM ESCAPEES. LET THE POLICE HANDLE THIS LAST ONE.
THE BEST LEAD IS A CLUB LYMAN OWNED... THE EGYPTIAN...
AT LEAST TAKE ME WITH YOU--!
TOO DANGEROUS, REMEMBER?
NOT FOR BOTH OF US...!
AS YOU SAID, ROBIN, I'M TIRED.
I DON'T HAVE ENOUGH FOR TWO...
LUCKY IF I CAN COVER MY OWN BACK.
VRAOWW

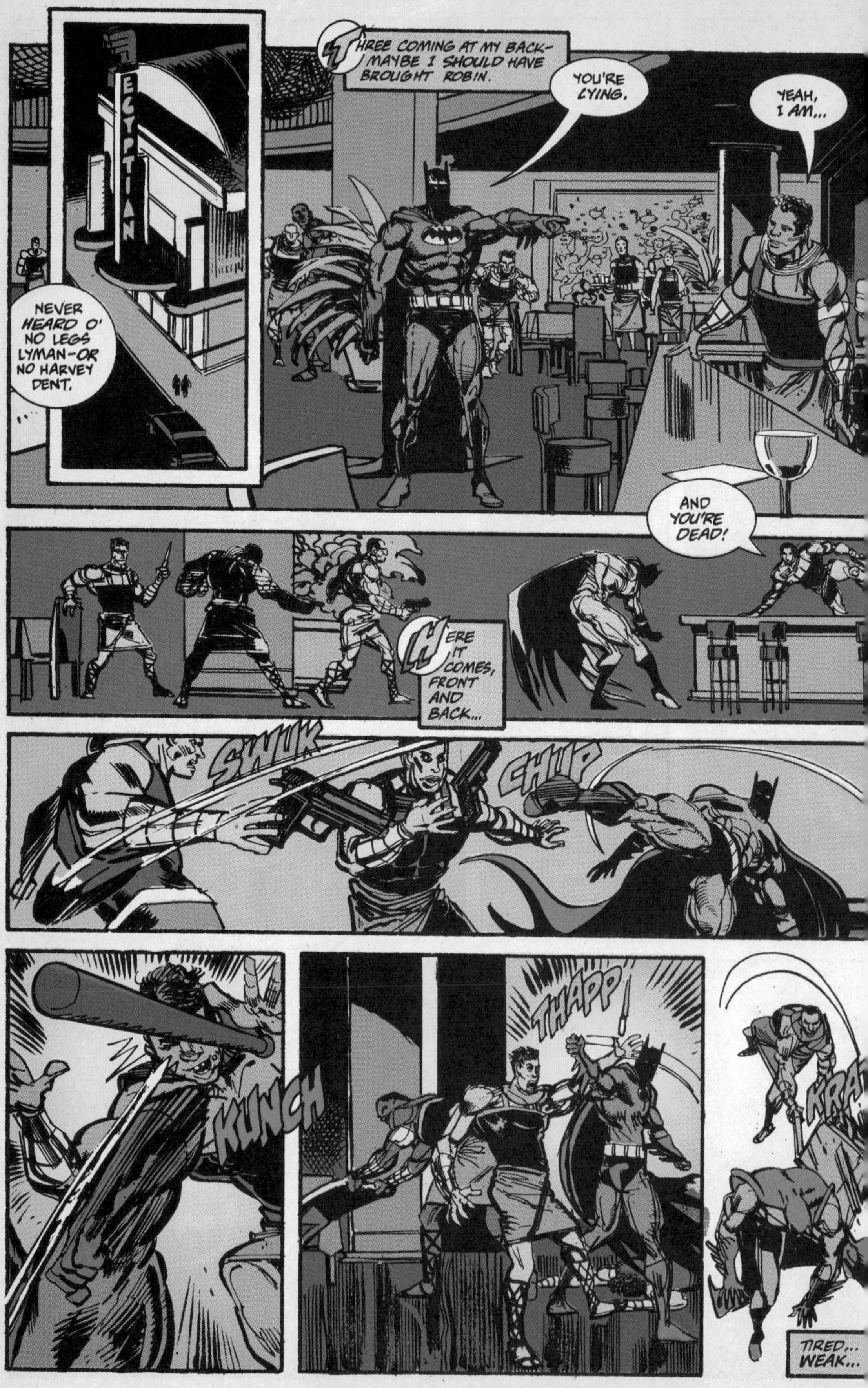
NEVER HEARD O' NO LEGS LYMAN—OR NO HARVEY DENT.
THREE COMING AT MY BACK— MAYBE I SHOULD HAVE BROUGHT ROBIN.
YOU'RE LYING.
YEAH, I AM...
AND YOU'RE DEAD!
HERE IT COMES, FRONT AND BACK...
SHUK
CHUP
KUNCH
THAPP
TIRED... WEAK...

B<sub></sub>Y NOW, ALL FOUR SHOULD BE DOWN TO STAY...

SWOKK

...THE FIGHT FINISHED IN SECONDS...

BUT INSTEAD--

KWUMP

UHN--!

--THEY JUST KEEP COMING...

SNUFF

CHUFF

...BIG AND CLUMSY...

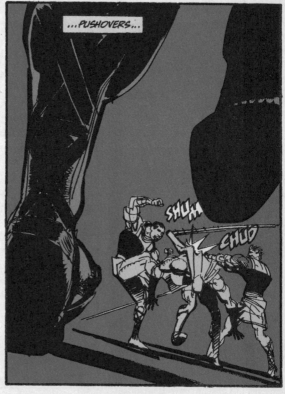

...PUSHOVERS...

SHUM

CHUD

43

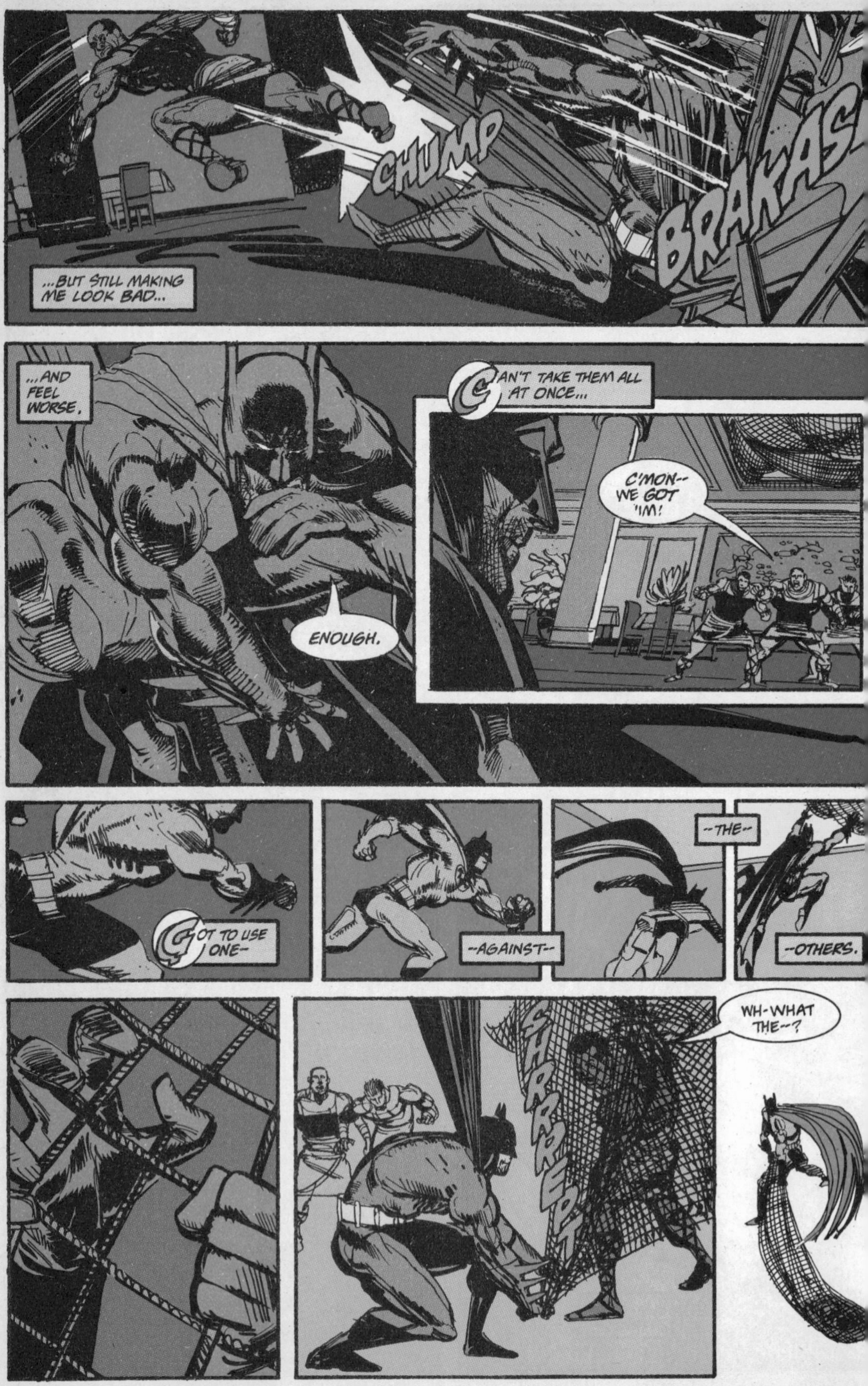
CHUMP
BRAKAS
...BUT STILL MAKING ME LOOK BAD...
...AND FEEL WORSE.
ENOUGH.
CAN'T TAKE THEM ALL AT ONCE...
C'MON-- WE GOT 'IM!
GOT TO USE ONE-
-AGAINST-
--THE--
--OTHERS.
SHRRRUPT
WH-WHAT THE--?

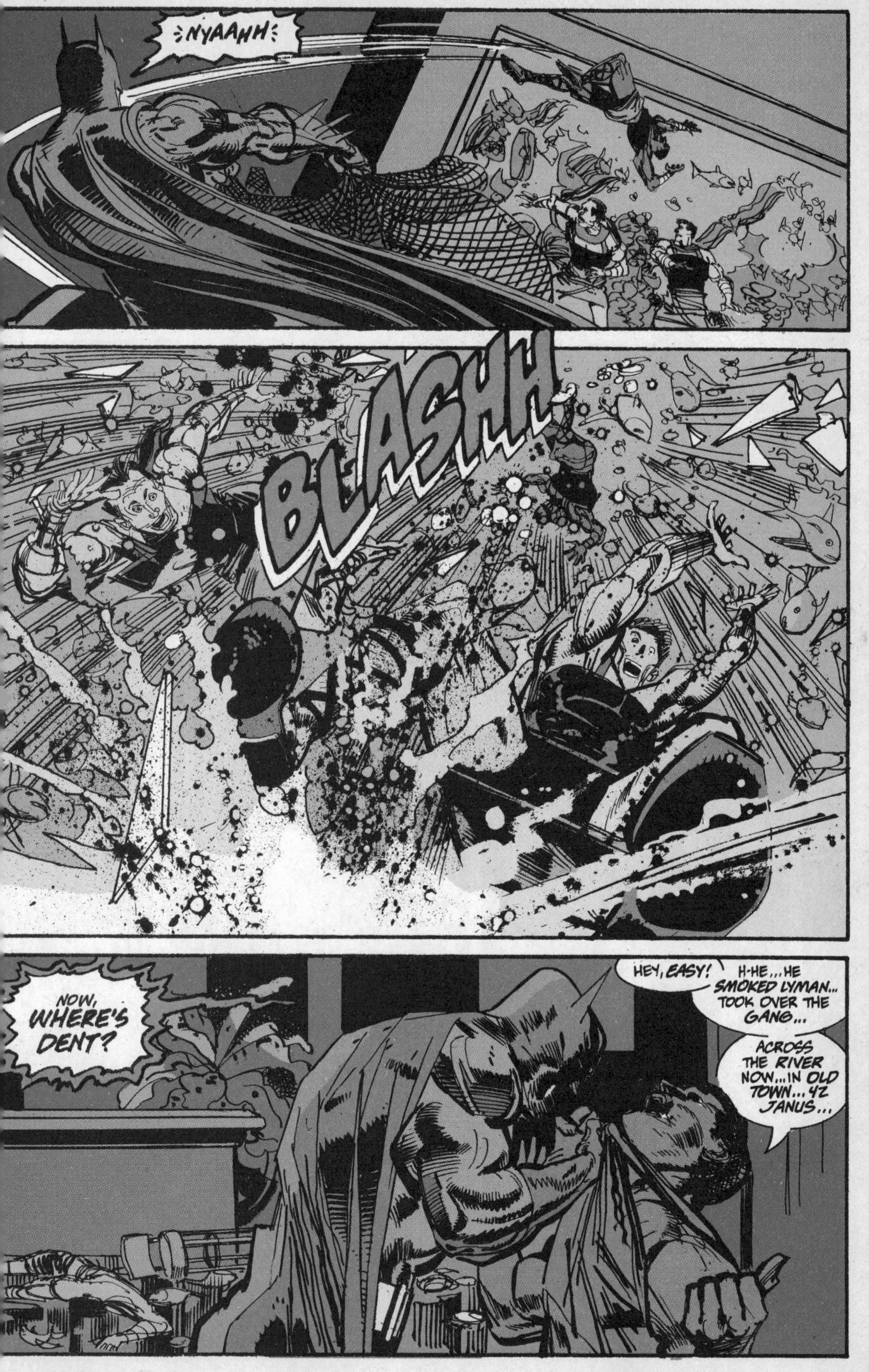
NYAAHH
BLASHH
NOW, WHERE'S DENT?
HEY, EASY!
H-HE,...HE SMOKED LYMAN... TOOK OVER THE GANG...
ACROSS THE RIVER NOW...IN OLD TOWN... 42 JANUS...

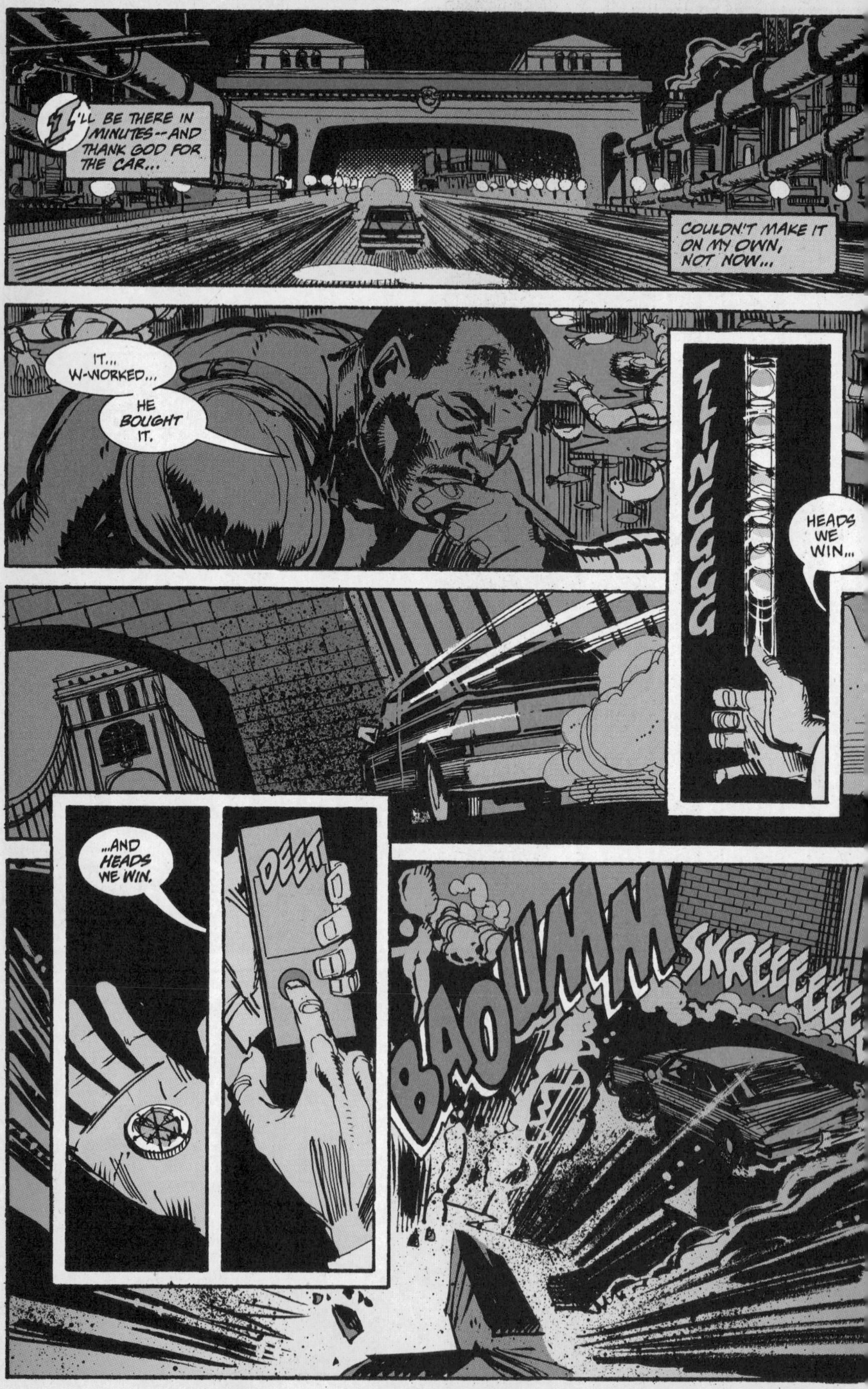
I'LL BE THERE IN MINUTES--AND THANK GOD FOR THE CAR...
COULDN'T MAKE IT ON MY OWN, NOT NOW...
IT... W-WORKED...
HE BOUGHT IT.
TLINGGGG
HEADS WE WIN...
...AND HEADS WE WIN.
DEET
BAOUMM
SKREEEEEE

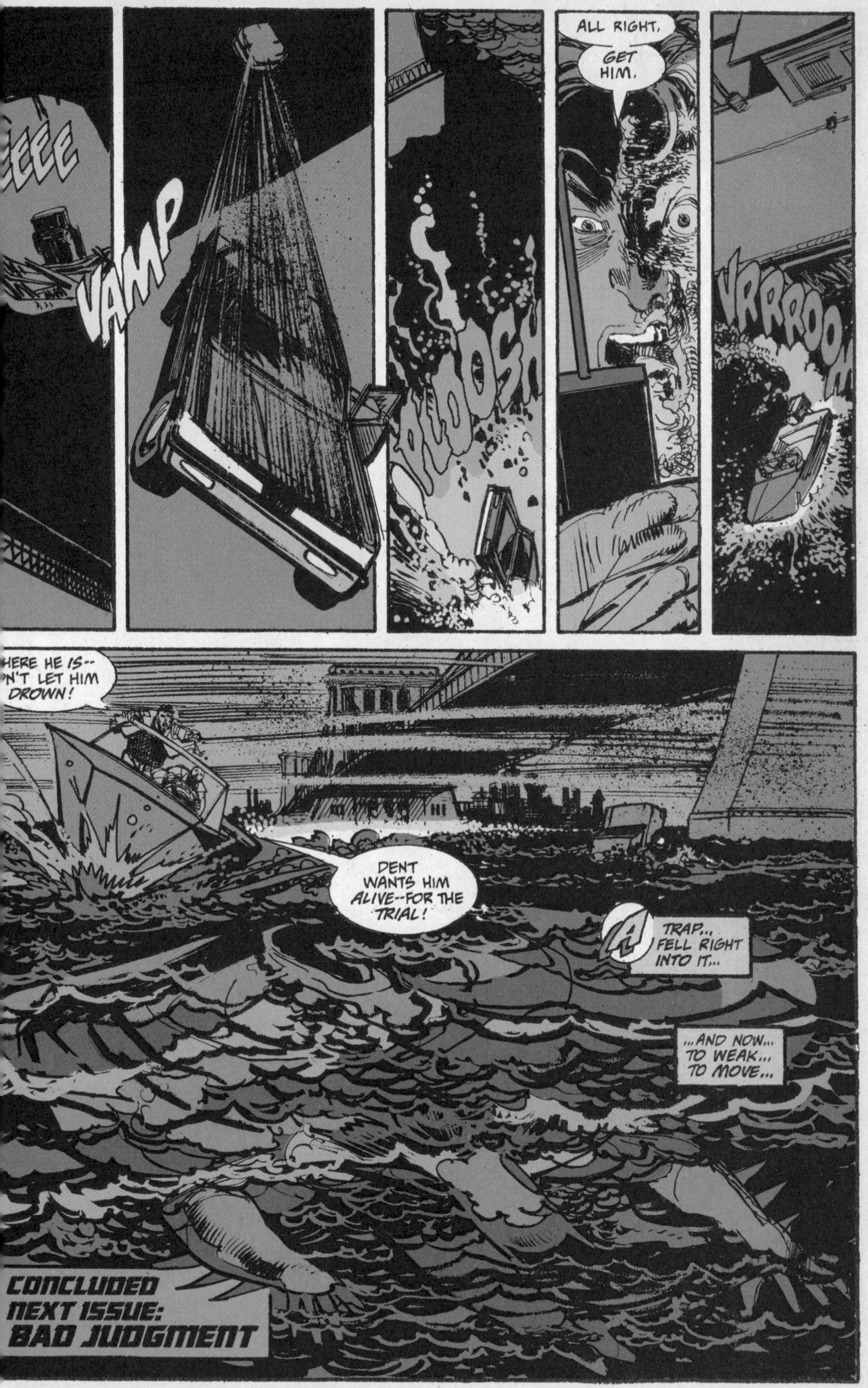

EEEE
VAMP
HOOSH
ALL RIGHT.
GET HIM.
VRRROOM
HERE HE IS-- N'T LET HIM DROWN!
DENT WANTS HIM ALIVE--FOR THE TRIAL!
TRAP... FELL RIGHT INTO IT...
...AND NOW... TO WEAK... TO MOVE...
CONCLUDED NEXT ISSUE: BAD JUDGMENT

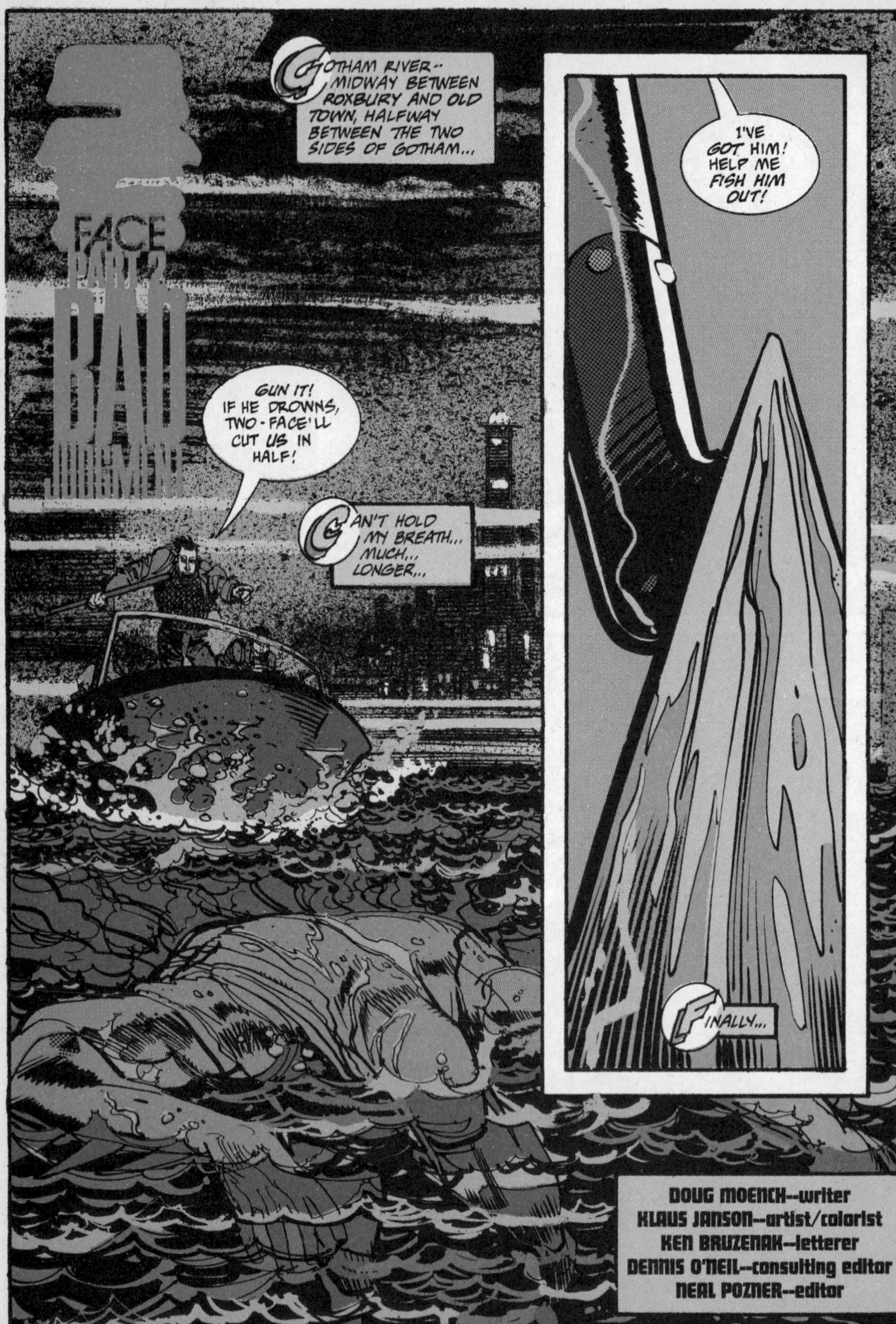

TWO FACE PART 2 BAD JUDGMENT
GOTHAM RIVER-- MIDWAY BETWEEN ROXBURY AND OLD TOWN, HALFWAY BETWEEN THE TWO SIDES OF GOTHAM...
I'VE GOT HIM! HELP ME FISH HIM OUT!
GUN IT! IF HE DROWNS, TWO-FACE'LL CUT US IN HALF!
CAN'T HOLD MY BREATH... MUCH... LONGER...
FINALLY...
DOUG MOENCH--writer
KLAUS JANSON--artist/colorist
KEN BRUZENAK--letterer
DENNIS O'NEIL--consulting editor
NEAL POZNER--editor

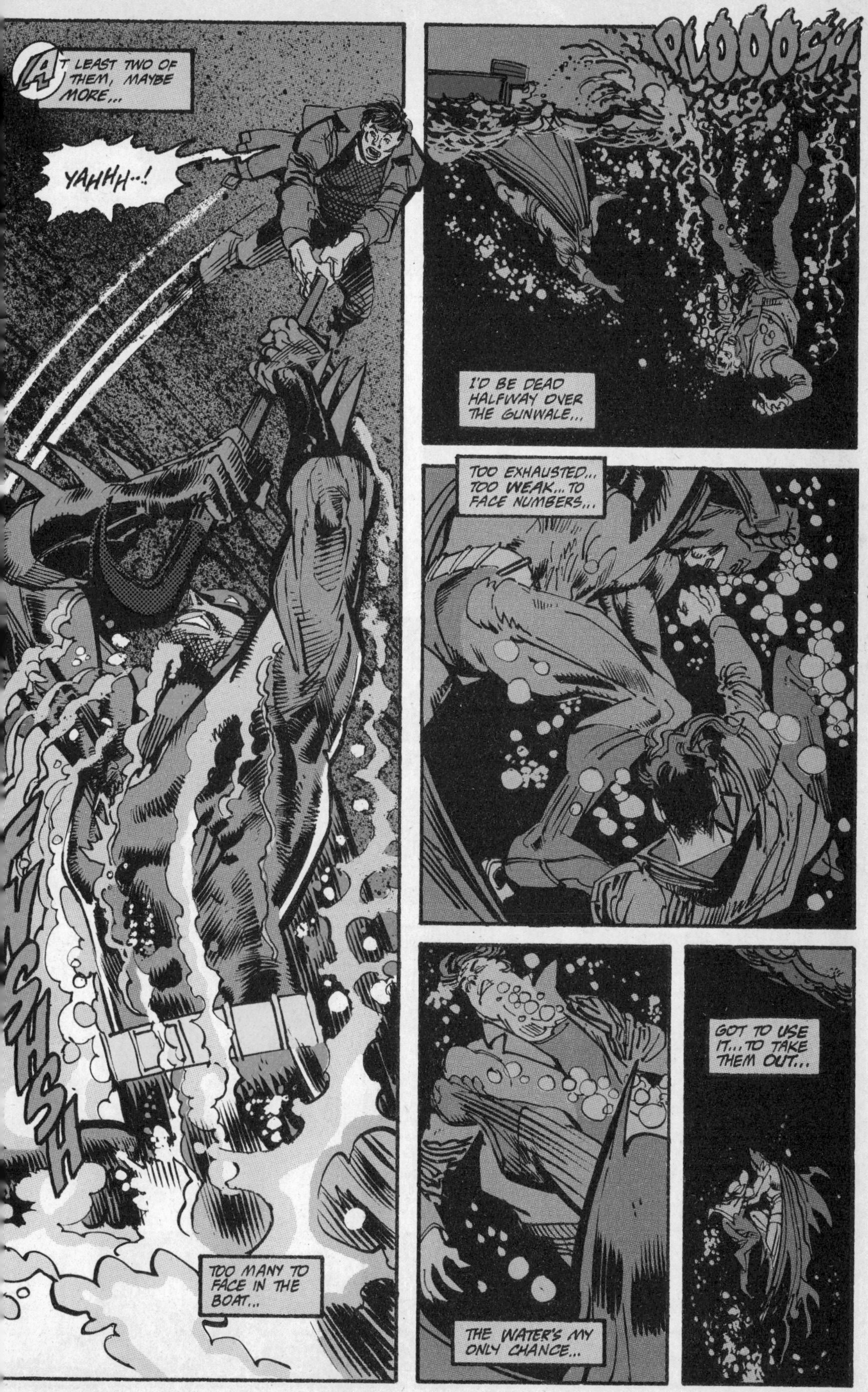
AT LEAST TWO OF THEM, MAYBE MORE...
YAHHH--!
TOO MANY TO FACE IN THE BOAT...
PLOOOSH!
I'D BE DEAD HALFWAY OVER THE GUNWALE...
TOO EXHAUSTED... TOO WEAK... TO FACE NUMBERS...
THE WATER'S MY ONLY CHANCE...
GOT TO USE IT... TO TAKE THEM OUT...

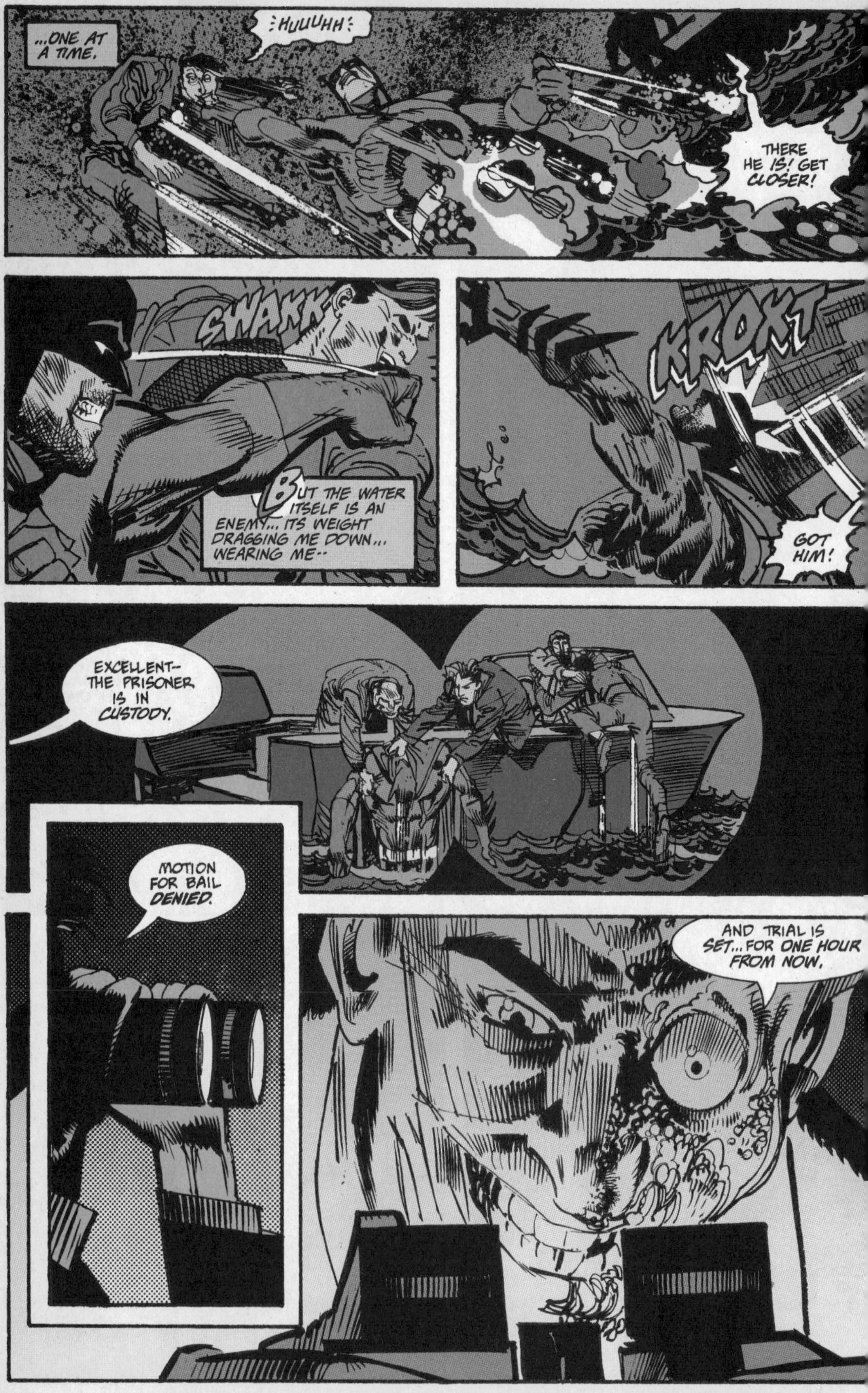
...ONE AT A TIME.
HUUUHH
THERE HE IS! GET CLOSER!
SNAKK
BUT THE WATER ITSELF IS AN ENEMY... ITS WEIGHT DRAGGING ME DOWN... WEARING ME--
KROXT
GOT HIM!
EXCELLENT-- THE PRISONER IS IN CUSTODY.
MOTION FOR BAIL DENIED.
AND TRIAL IS SET... FOR ONE HOUR FROM NOW.

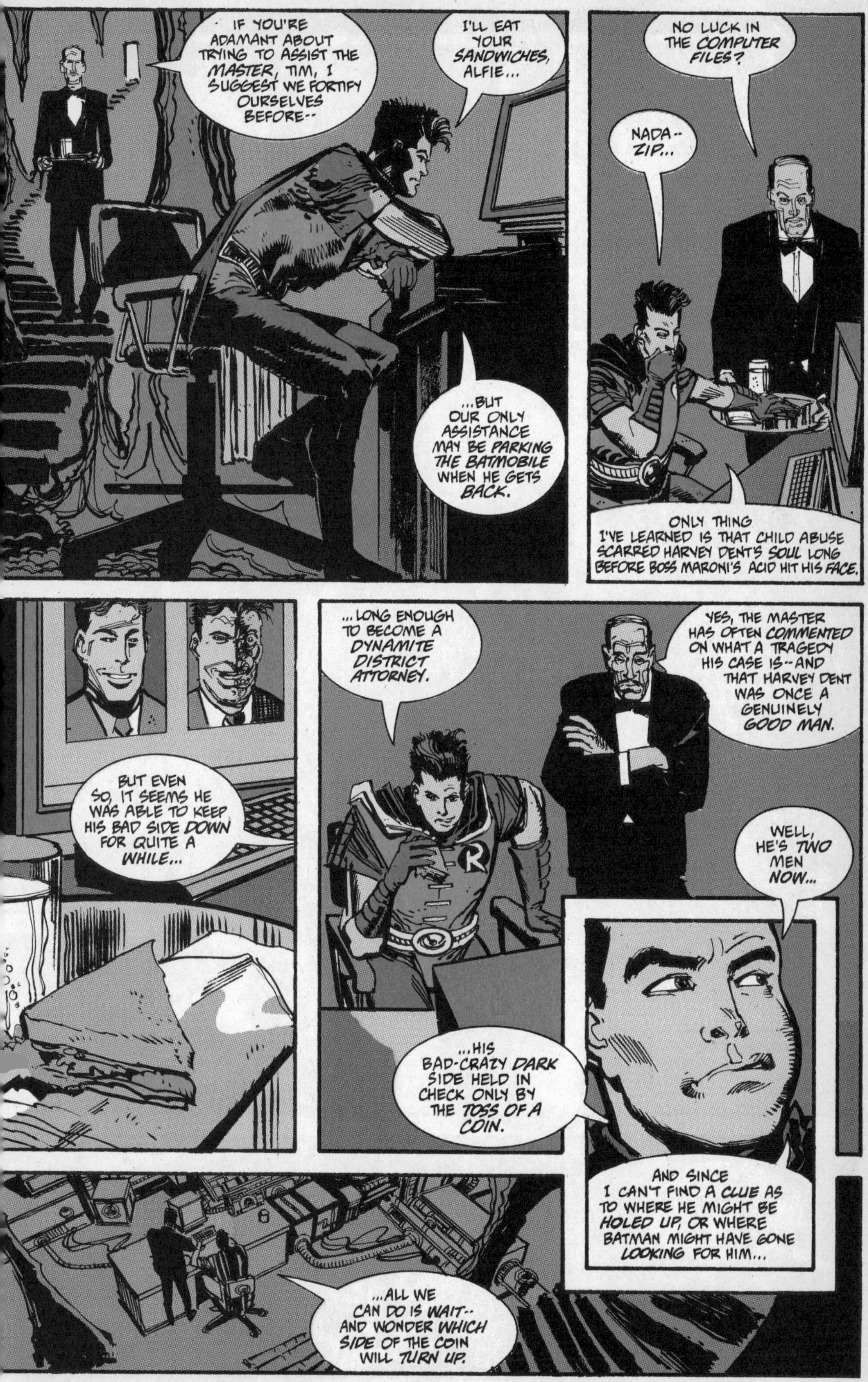
IF YOU'RE ADAMANT ABOUT TRYING TO ASSIST THE MASTER, TIM, I SUGGEST WE FORTIFY OURSELVES BEFORE--
I'LL EAT YOUR SANDWICHES, ALFIE...
...BUT OUR ONLY ASSISTANCE MAY BE PARKING THE BATMOBILE WHEN HE GETS BACK.
NO LUCK IN THE COMPUTER FILES?
NADA-- ZIP...
ONLY THING I'VE LEARNED IS THAT CHILD ABUSE SCARRED HARVEY DENT'S SOUL LONG BEFORE BOSS MARONI'S ACID HIT HIS FACE.
BUT EVEN SO, IT SEEMS HE WAS ABLE TO KEEP HIS BAD SIDE DOWN FOR QUITE A WHILE...
...LONG ENOUGH TO BECOME A DYNAMITE DISTRICT ATTORNEY.
YES, THE MASTER HAS OFTEN COMMENTED ON WHAT A TRAGEDY HIS CASE IS--AND THAT HARVEY DENT WAS ONCE A GENUINELY GOOD MAN.
WELL, HE'S TWO MEN NOW...
...HIS BAD-CRAZY DARK SIDE HELD IN CHECK ONLY BY THE TOSS OF A COIN.
AND SINCE I CAN'T FIND A CLUE AS TO WHERE HE MIGHT BE HOLED UP, OR WHERE BATMAN MIGHT HAVE GONE LOOKING FOR HIM...
...ALL WE CAN DO IS WAIT-- AND WONDER WHICH SIDE OF THE COIN WILL TURN UP.

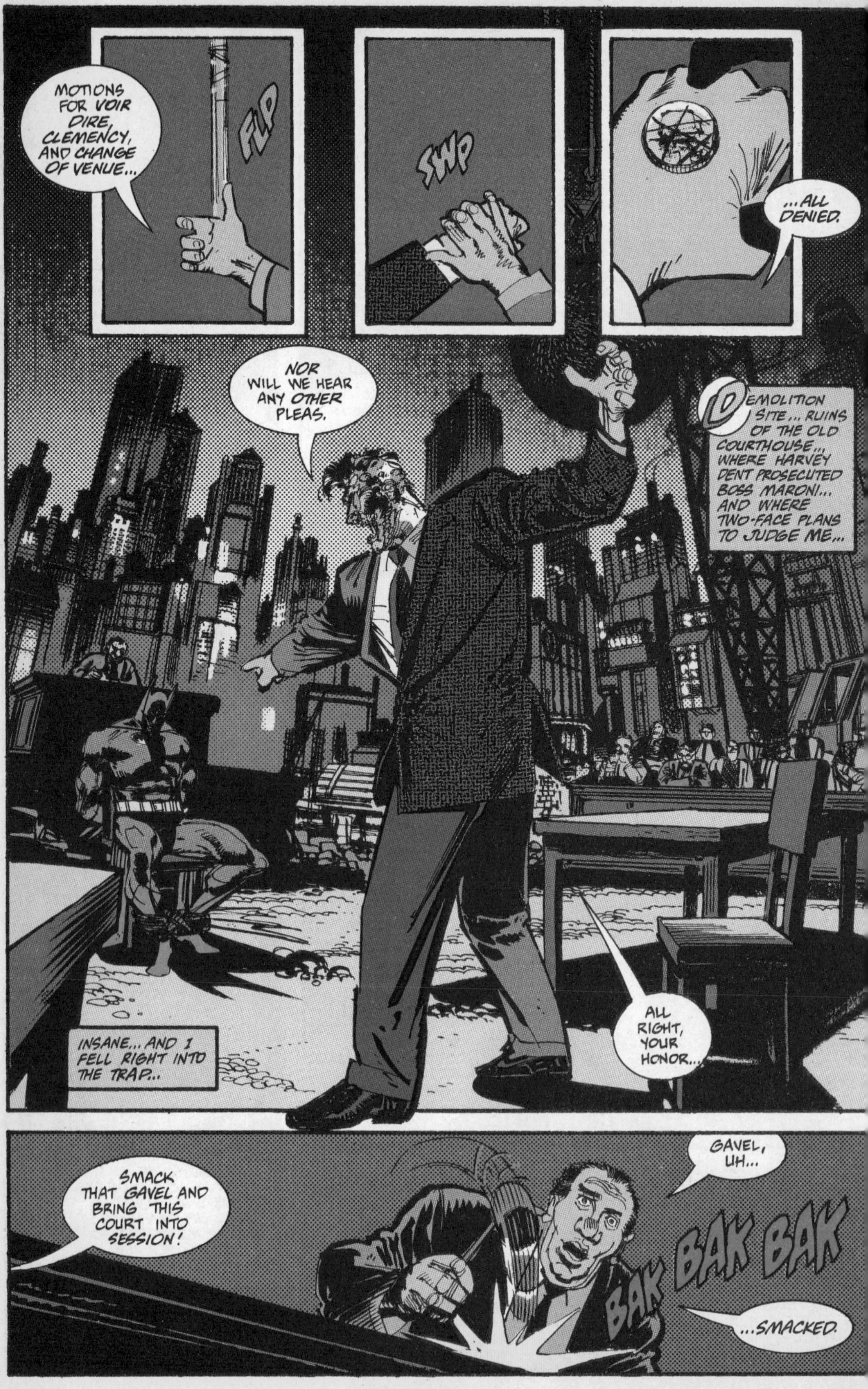
MOTIONS FOR VOIR DIRE, CLEMENCY, AND CHANGE OF VENUE...
FLP
SWP
...ALL DENIED.
NOR WILL WE HEAR ANY OTHER PLEAS.
DEMOLITION SITE... RUINS OF THE OLD COURTHOUSE... WHERE HARVEY DENT PROSECUTED BOSS MARONI... AND WHERE TWO-FACE PLANS TO JUDGE ME...
INSANE... AND I FELL RIGHT INTO THE TRAP...
ALL RIGHT, YOUR HONOR...
SMACK THAT GAVEL AND BRING THIS COURT INTO SESSION!
GAVEL, UH...
BAK BAK BAK
...SMACKED.

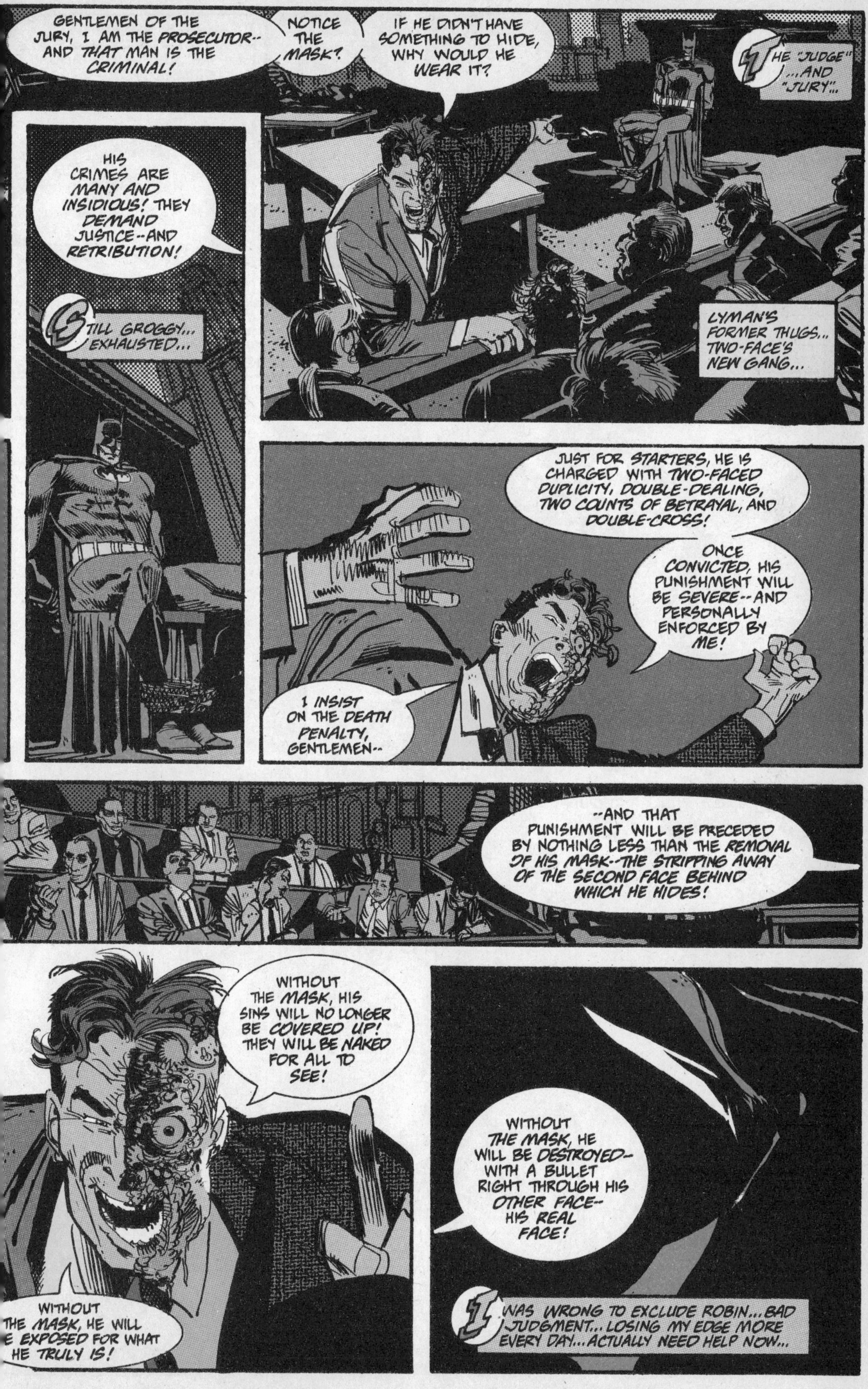

GENTLEMEN OF THE JURY, I AM THE PROSECUTOR-- AND THAT MAN IS THE CRIMINAL!
NOTICE THE MASK?
IF HE DIDN'T HAVE SOMETHING TO HIDE, WHY WOULD HE WEAR IT?
THE "JUDGE" ...AND "JURY"...
HIS CRIMES ARE MANY AND INSIDIOUS! THEY DEMAND JUSTICE--AND RETRIBUTION!
STILL GROGGY... EXHAUSTED...
LYMAN'S FORMER THUGS... TWO-FACE'S NEW GANG...
JUST FOR STARTERS, HE IS CHARGED WITH TWO-FACED DUPLICITY, DOUBLE-DEALING, TWO COUNTS OF BETRAYAL, AND DOUBLE-CROSS!
ONCE CONVICTED, HIS PUNISHMENT WILL BE SEVERE--AND PERSONALLY ENFORCED BY ME!
I INSIST ON THE DEATH PENALTY, GENTLEMEN--
--AND THAT PUNISHMENT WILL BE PRECEDED BY NOTHING LESS THAN THE REMOVAL OF HIS MASK--THE STRIPPING AWAY OF THE SECOND FACE BEHIND WHICH HE HIDES!
WITHOUT THE MASK, HIS SINS WILL NO LONGER BE COVERED UP! THEY WILL BE NAKED FOR ALL TO SEE!
WITHOUT THE MASK, HE WILL BE EXPOSED FOR WHAT HE TRULY IS!
WITHOUT THE MASK, HE WILL BE DESTROYED-- WITH A BULLET RIGHT THROUGH HIS OTHER FACE-- HIS REAL FACE!
I WAS WRONG TO EXCLUDE ROBIN...BAD JUDGMENT... LOSING MY EDGE MORE EVERY DAY...ACTUALLY NEED HELP NOW...

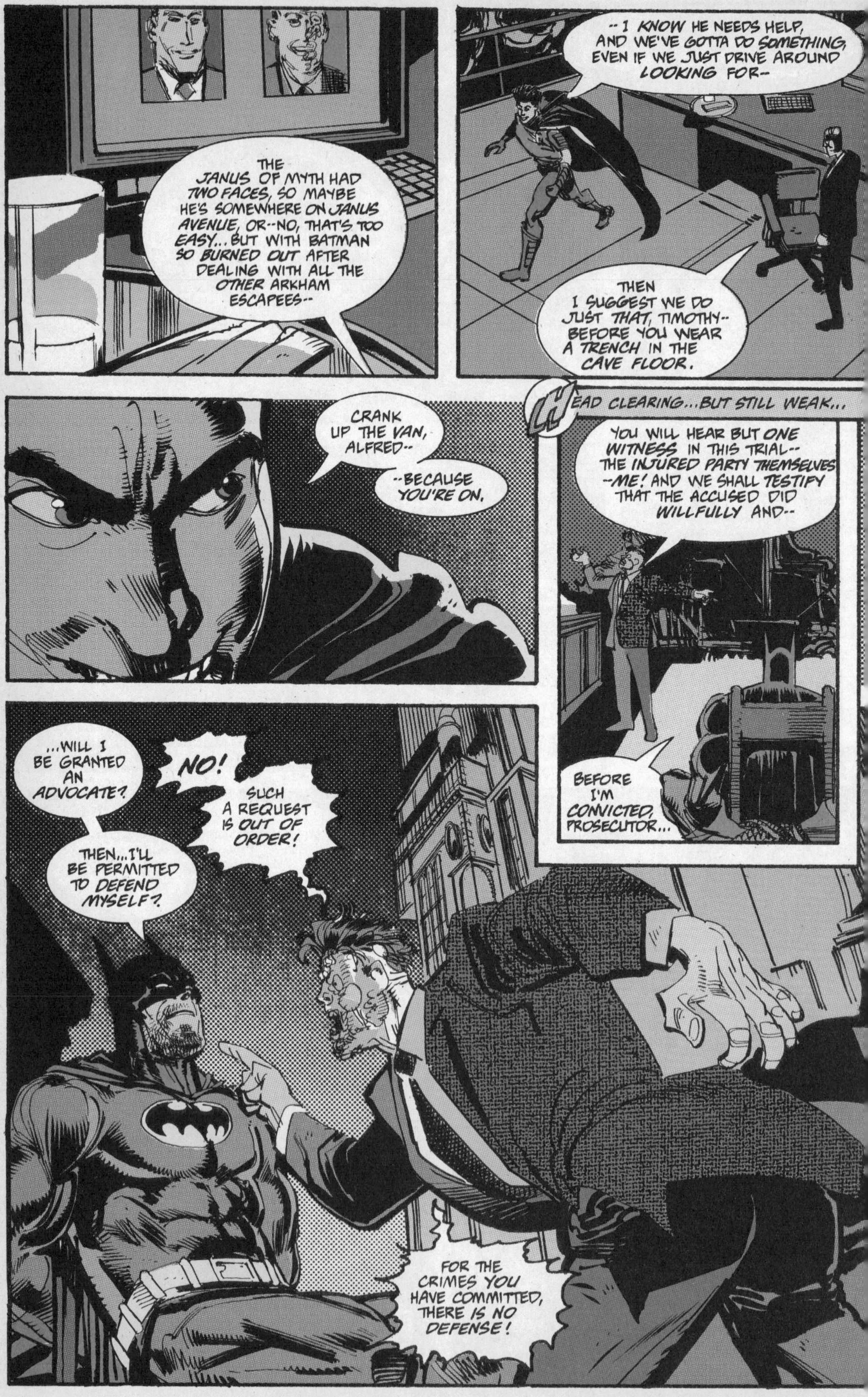
THE JANUS OF MYTH HAD TWO FACES, SO MAYBE HE'S SOMEWHERE ON JANUS AVENUE, OR--NO, THAT'S TOO EASY... BUT WITH BATMAN SO BURNED OUT AFTER DEALING WITH ALL THE OTHER ARKHAM ESCAPEES--
--I KNOW HE NEEDS HELP, AND WE'VE GOTTA DO SOMETHING, EVEN IF WE JUST DRIVE AROUND LOOKING FOR--
THEN I SUGGEST WE DO JUST THAT, TIMOTHY-- BEFORE YOU WEAR A TRENCH IN THE CAVE FLOOR.
CRANK UP THE VAN, ALFRED--
--BECAUSE YOU'RE ON.
HEAD CLEARING... BUT STILL WEAK...
YOU WILL HEAR BUT ONE WITNESS IN THIS TRIAL-- THE INJURED PARTY THEMSELVES --ME! AND WE SHALL TESTIFY THAT THE ACCUSED DID WILLFULLY AND--
BEFORE I'M CONVICTED, PROSECUTOR...
...WILL I BE GRANTED AN ADVOCATE?
NO!
SUCH A REQUEST IS OUT OF ORDER!
THEN...I'LL BE PERMITTED TO DEFEND MYSELF?
FOR THE CRIMES YOU HAVE COMMITTED, THERE IS NO DEFENSE!

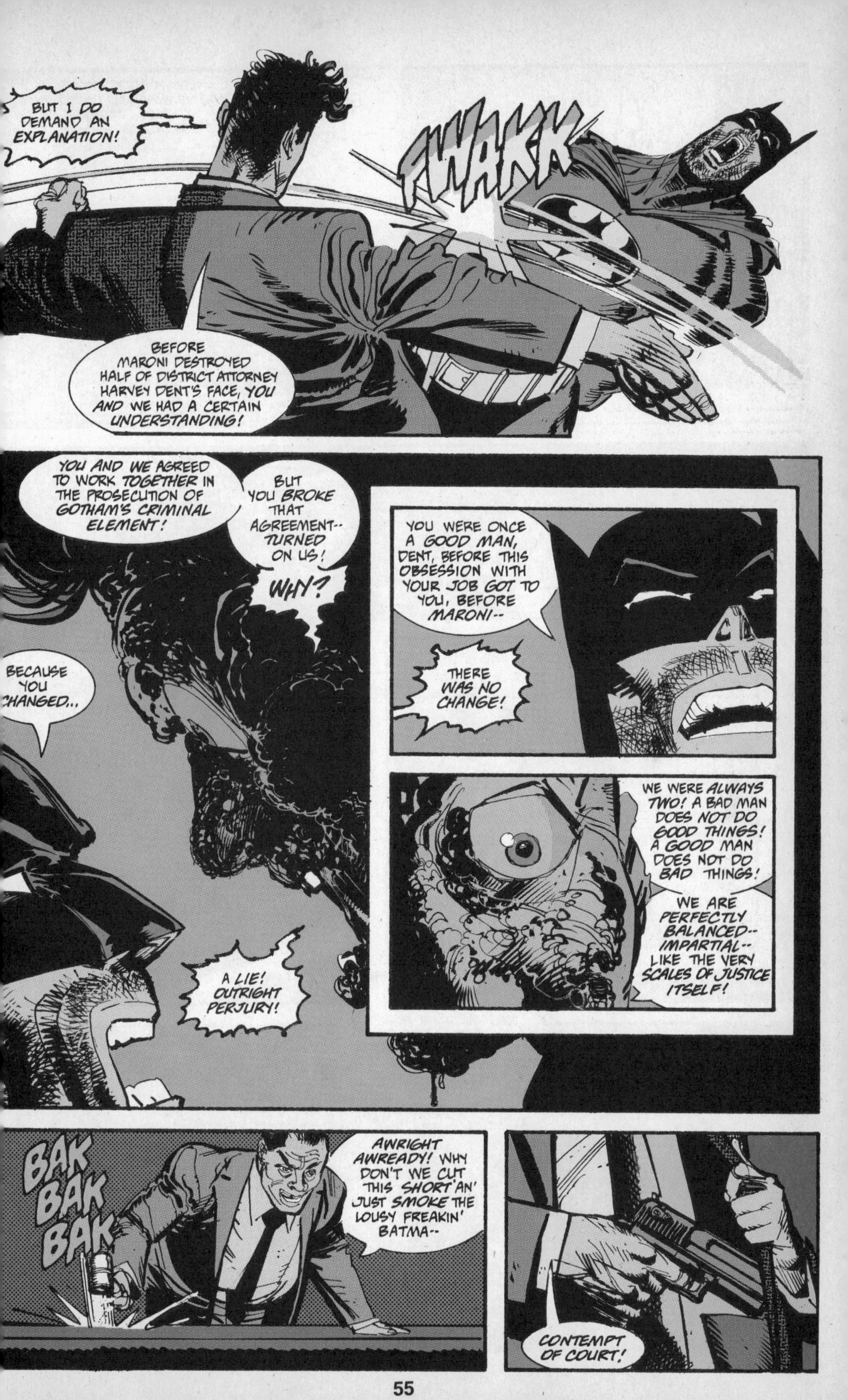
BUT I DO DEMAND AN EXPLANATION!
AWAKK
BEFORE MARONI DESTROYED HALF OF DISTRICT ATTORNEY HARVEY DENT'S FACE, YOU AND WE HAD A CERTAIN UNDERSTANDING!
YOU AND WE AGREED TO WORK TOGETHER IN THE PROSECUTION OF GOTHAM'S CRIMINAL ELEMENT!
BUT YOU BROKE THAT AGREEMENT-- TURNED ON US!
WHY?
BECAUSE YOU CHANGED...
A LIE! OUTRIGHT PERJURY!
YOU WERE ONCE A GOOD MAN, DENT, BEFORE THIS OBSESSION WITH YOUR JOB GOT TO YOU, BEFORE MARONI--
THERE WAS NO CHANGE!
WE WERE ALWAYS TWO! A BAD MAN DOES NOT DO GOOD THINGS! A GOOD MAN DOES NOT DO BAD THINGS!
WE ARE PERFECTLY BALANCED-- IMPARTIAL-- LIKE THE VERY SCALES OF JUSTICE ITSELF!
BAK BAK BAK
AWRIGHT AWREADY! WHY DON'T WE CUT THIS SHORT AN' JUST SMOKE THE LOUSY FREAKIN' BATMA--
CONTEMPT OF COURT!

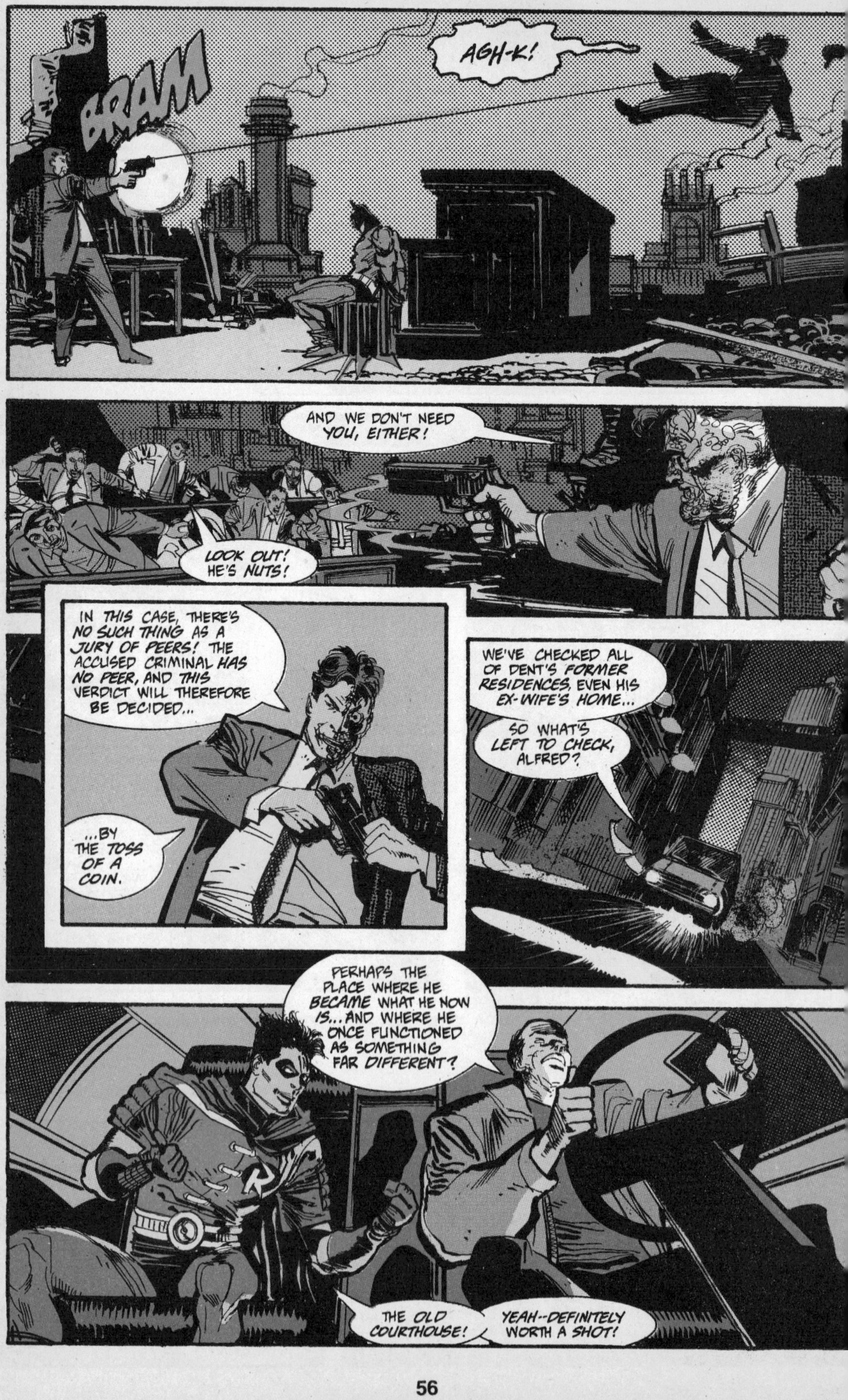
BRAM
AGH-K!
AND WE DON'T NEED YOU, EITHER!
LOOK OUT! HE'S NUTS!
IN THIS CASE, THERE'S NO SUCH THING AS A JURY OF PEERS! THE ACCUSED CRIMINAL HAS NO PEER, AND THIS VERDICT WILL THEREFORE BE DECIDED...
...BY THE TOSS OF A COIN.
WE'VE CHECKED ALL OF DENT'S FORMER RESIDENCES, EVEN HIS EX-WIFE'S HOME...
SO WHAT'S LEFT TO CHECK, ALFRED?
PERHAPS THE PLACE WHERE HE BECAME WHAT HE NOW IS... AND WHERE HE ONCE FUNCTIONED AS SOMETHING FAR DIFFERENT?
THE OLD COURTHOUSE!
YEAH--DEFINITELY WORTH A SHOT!

THE ACCUSED IS HEREBY JUDGED AND FOUND...

...GUILTY.

A BAD MAN DOES NOT DO GOOD THINGS... A BAT MAN CAN ONLY DO BAD THINGS...

...AND YOU ARE BAD!

NO CHOICE NOW...

NO MORE TIME TO GATHER STRENGTH IN MY LEGS...

THE SENTENCE HAS BEEN PASSED!

GOT TO DIG IN...

LET IT BE EXECUTED!

BRAAM

WHAT--?

...AND SHOVE BACK.

KRATCH

57

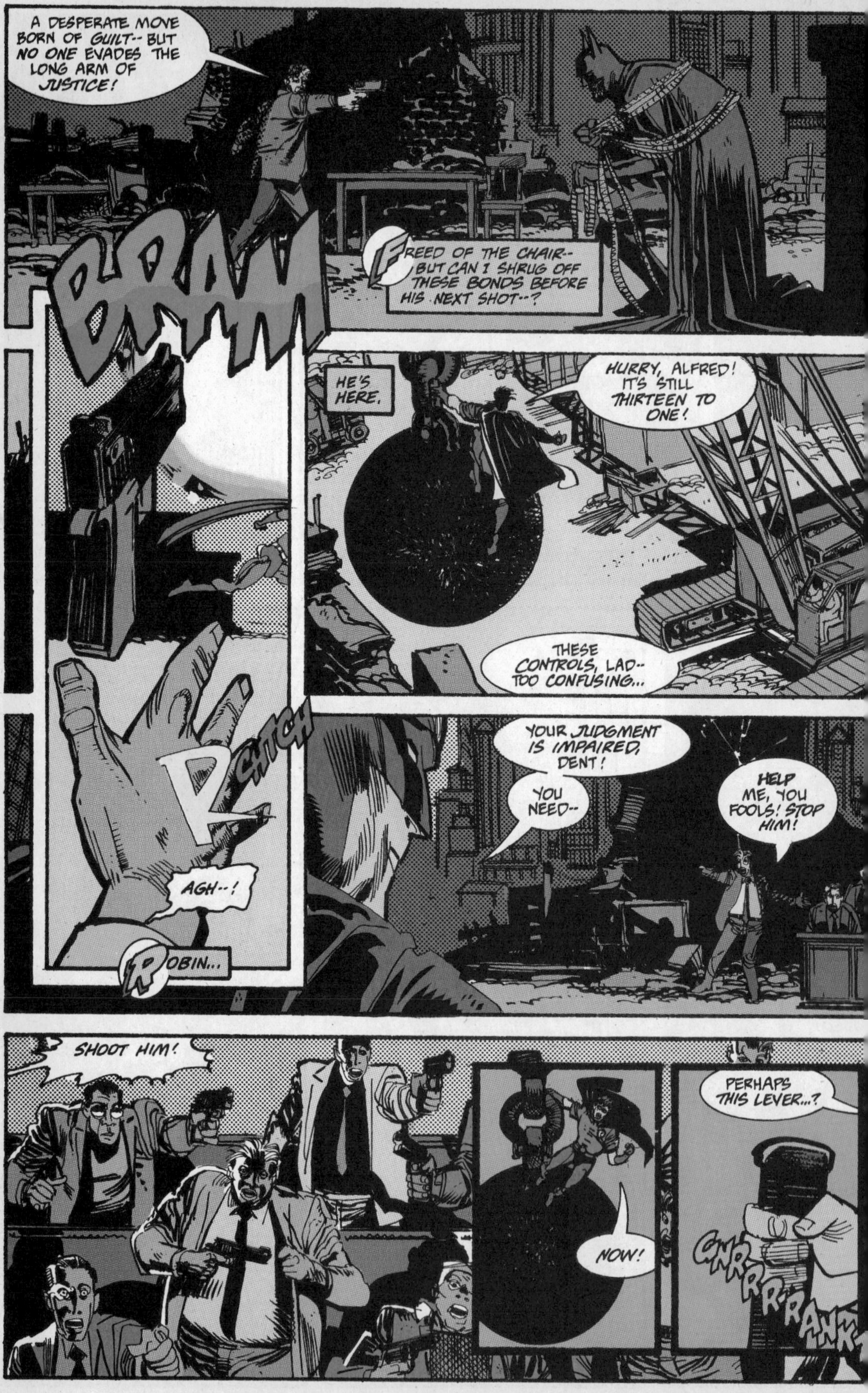
A DESPERATE MOVE BORN OF GUILT-- BUT NO ONE EVADES THE LONG ARM OF JUSTICE!
BRAM
FREED OF THE CHAIR-- BUT CAN I SHRUG OFF THESE BONDS BEFORE HIS NEXT SHOT--?
HE'S HERE.
HURRY, ALFRED! IT'S STILL THIRTEEN TO ONE!
THESE CONTROLS, LAD-- TOO CONFUSING...
RCHTCH
AGH--!
ROBIN...
YOUR JUDGMENT IS IMPAIRED, DENT!
YOU NEED--
HELP ME, YOU FOOLS! STOP HIM!
SHOOT HIM!
NOW!
PERHAPS THIS LEVER...?
GNRRRRRANK

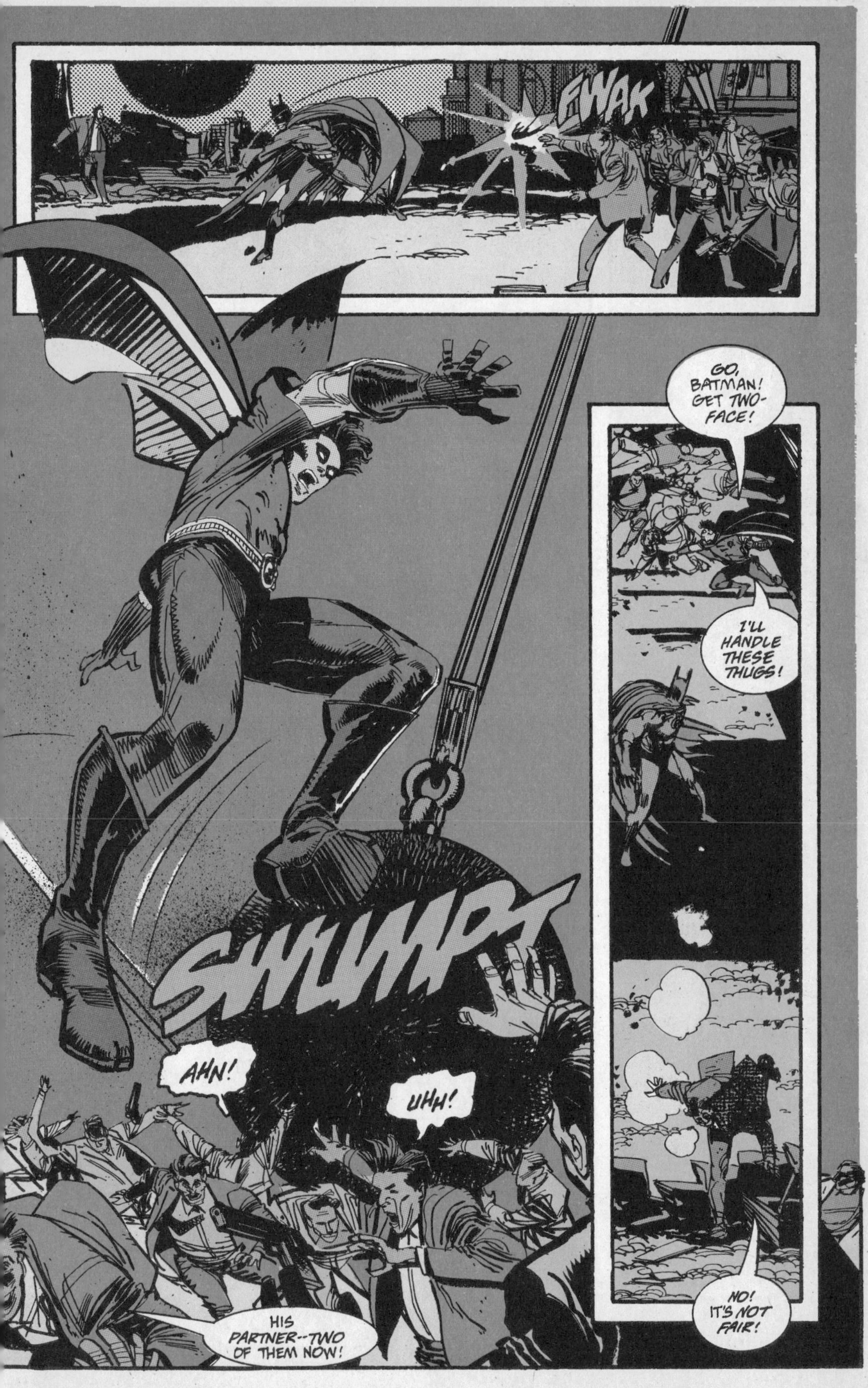

KWAK
GO, BATMAN! GET TWO-FACE!
I'LL HANDLE THESE THUGS!
SHUMP
AHN!
UHH!
HIS PARTNER--TWO OF THEM NOW!
NO! IT'S NOT FAIR!

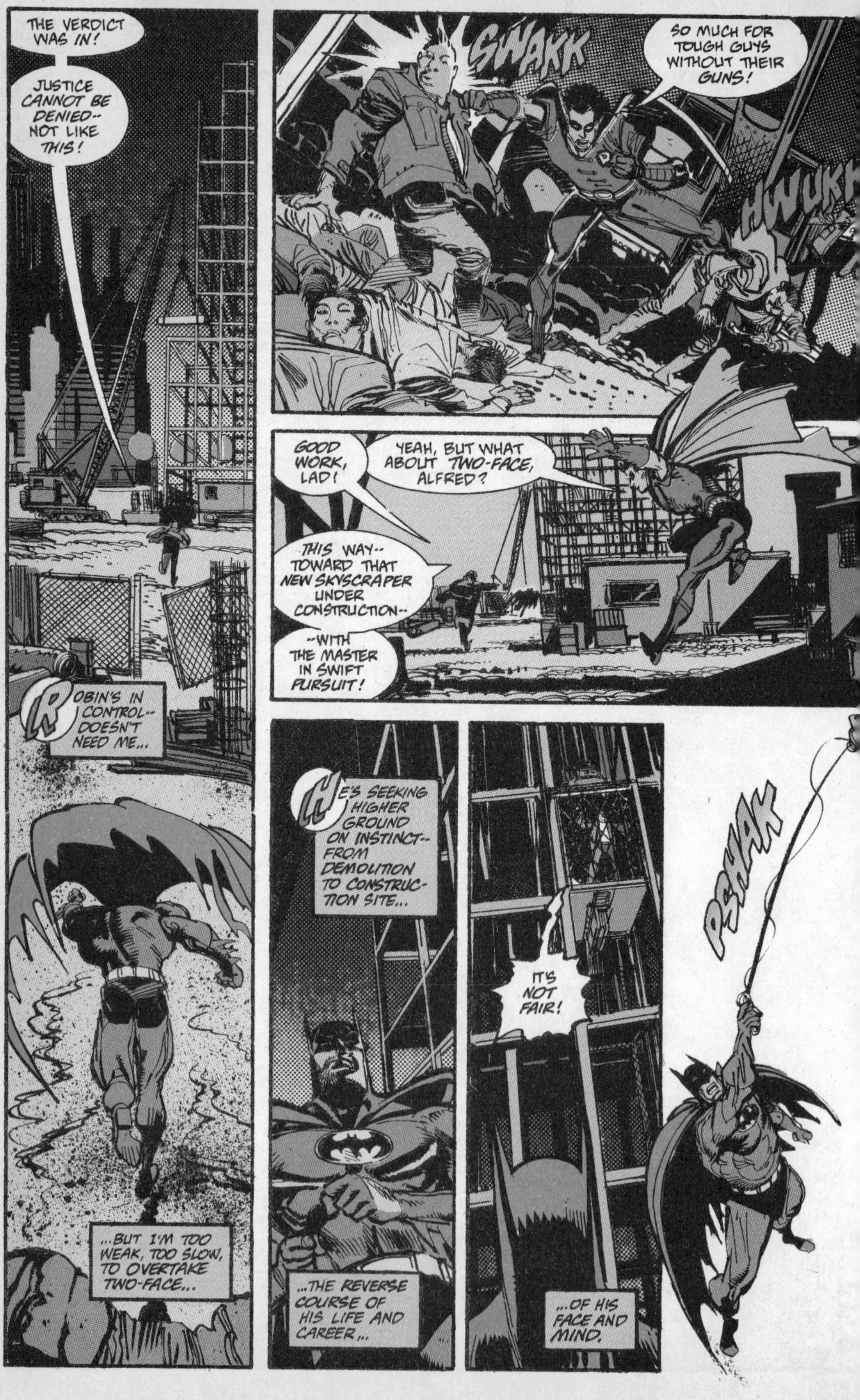
THE VERDICT WAS IN!
JUSTICE CANNOT BE DENIED-- NOT LIKE THIS!
ROBIN'S IN CONTROL-- DOESN'T NEED ME...
...BUT I'M TOO WEAK, TOO SLOW, TO OVERTAKE TWO-FACE...
SWAKK
SO MUCH FOR TOUGH GUYS WITHOUT THEIR GUNS!
HWUKK
GOOD WORK, LAD!
YEAH, BUT WHAT ABOUT TWO-FACE, ALFRED?
THIS WAY-- TOWARD THAT NEW SKYSCRAPER UNDER CONSTRUCTION--
--WITH THE MASTER IN SWIFT PURSUIT!
HE'S SEEKING HIGHER GROUND ON INSTINCT-- FROM DEMOLITION TO CONSTRUCTION SITE...
...THE REVERSE COURSE OF HIS LIFE AND CAREER...
IT'S NOT FAIR!
...OF HIS FACE AND MIND.
PSHAK

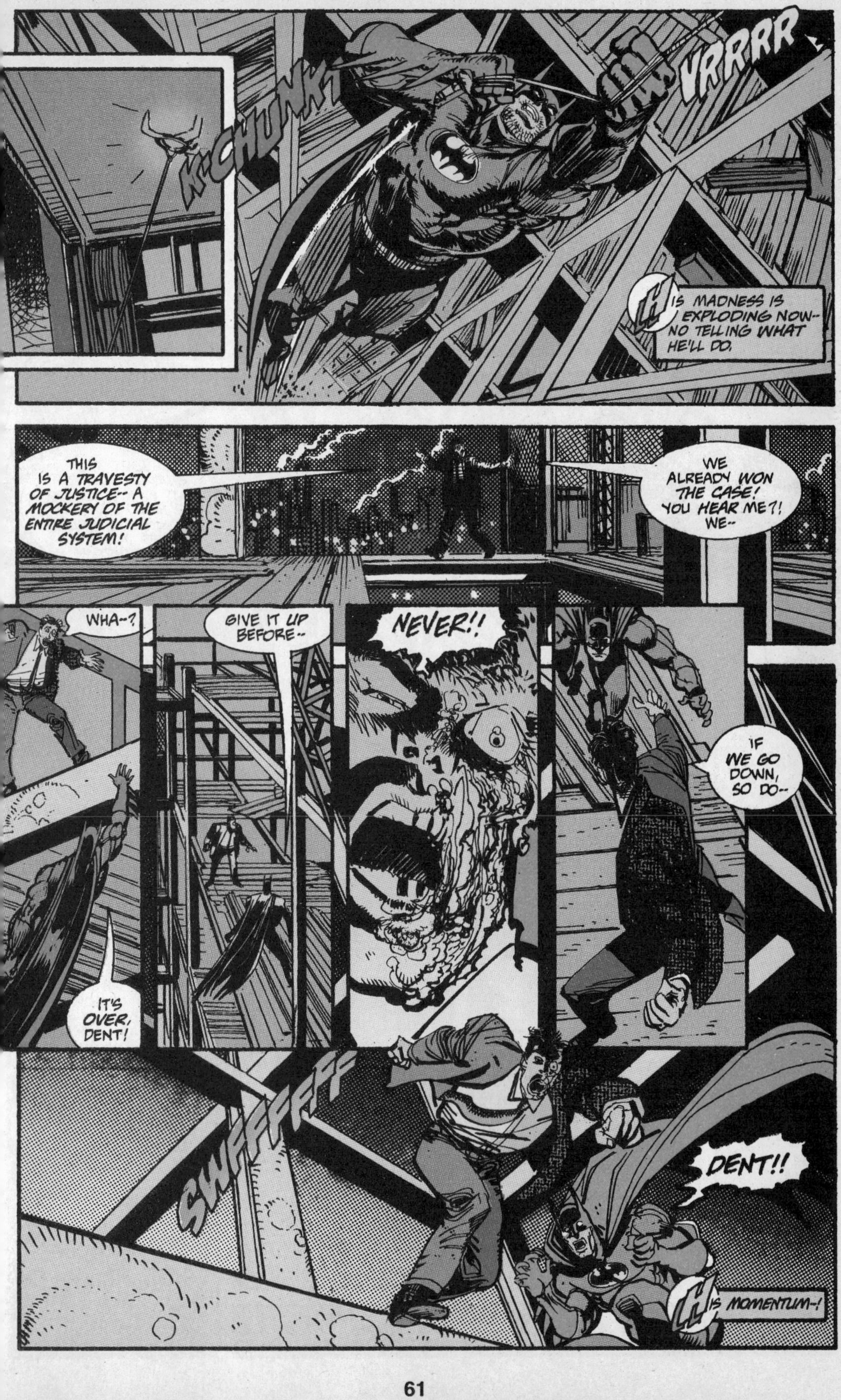

K-CHUNK!
VRRRR
HIS MADNESS IS EXPLODING NOW-- NO TELLING WHAT HE'LL DO.
THIS IS A TRAVESTY OF JUSTICE-- A MOCKERY OF THE ENTIRE JUDICIAL SYSTEM!
WE ALREADY WON THE CASE! YOU HEAR ME?! WE--
WHA--?
IT'S OVER, DENT!
GIVE IT UP BEFORE--
NEVER!!
IF WE GO DOWN, SO DO--
SWFFFFF
DENT!!
HIS MOMENTUM--!

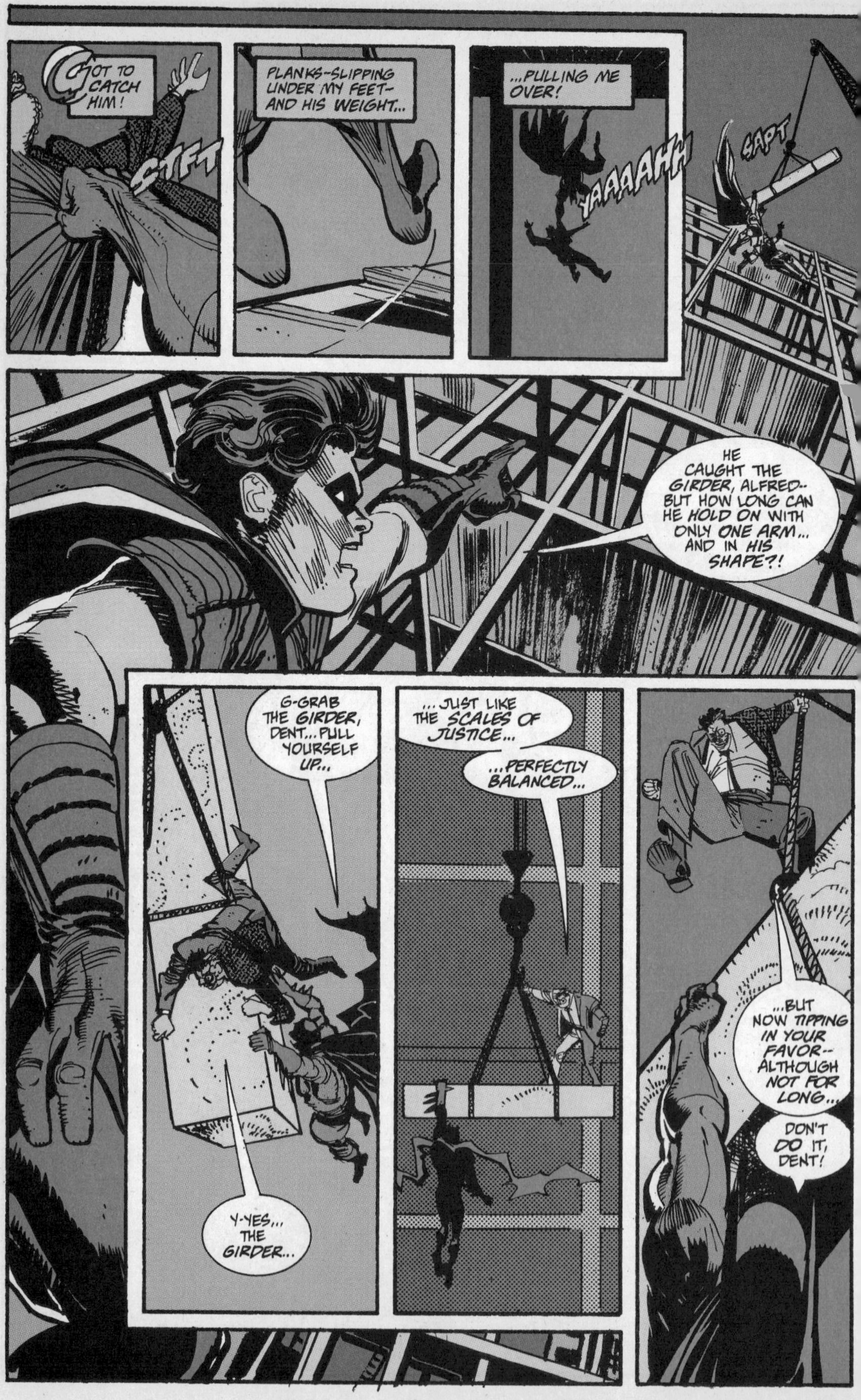
GOT TO CATCH HIM!
STFT
PLANKS--SLIPPING UNDER MY FEET-- AND HIS WEIGHT...
...PULLING ME OVER!
YAAAAHH
SAPT
HE CAUGHT THE GIRDER, ALFRED-- BUT HOW LONG CAN HE HOLD ON WITH ONLY ONE ARM... AND IN HIS SHAPE?!
G-GRAB THE GIRDER, DENT... PULL YOURSELF UP...
Y-YES... THE GIRDER...
...JUST LIKE THE SCALES OF JUSTICE...
...PERFECTLY BALANCED...
...BUT NOW TIPPING IN YOUR FAVOR-- ALTHOUGH NOT FOR LONG...
DON'T DO IT, DENT!

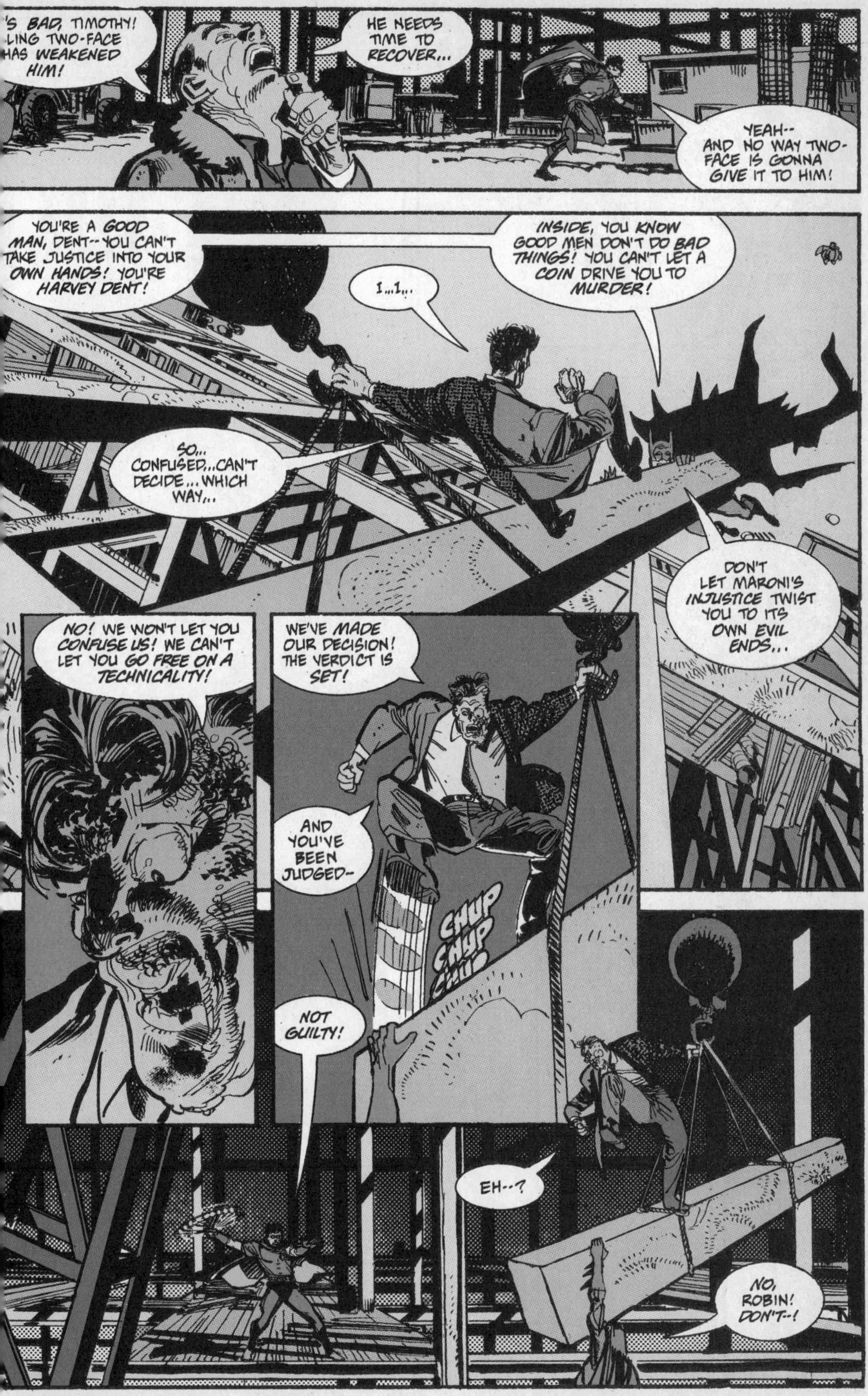
'S BAD, TIMOTHY! -LING TWO-FACE HAS WEAKENED HIM!
HE NEEDS TIME TO RECOVER...
YEAH-- AND NO WAY TWO-FACE IS GONNA GIVE IT TO HIM!
YOU'RE A GOOD MAN, DENT-- YOU CAN'T TAKE JUSTICE INTO YOUR OWN HANDS! YOU'RE HARVEY DENT!
INSIDE, YOU KNOW GOOD MEN DON'T DO BAD THINGS! YOU CAN'T LET A COIN DRIVE YOU TO MURDER!
I...I...
SO... CONFUSED...CAN'T DECIDE... WHICH WAY...
DON'T LET MARONI'S INJUSTICE TWIST YOU TO ITS OWN EVIL ENDS...
NO! WE WON'T LET YOU CONFUSE US! WE CAN'T LET YOU GO FREE ON A TECHNICALITY!
WE'VE MADE OUR DECISION! THE VERDICT IS SET!
AND YOU'VE BEEN JUDGED--
CHUP CHUP CHUP
NOT GUILTY!
EH--?
NO, ROBIN! DON'T--!

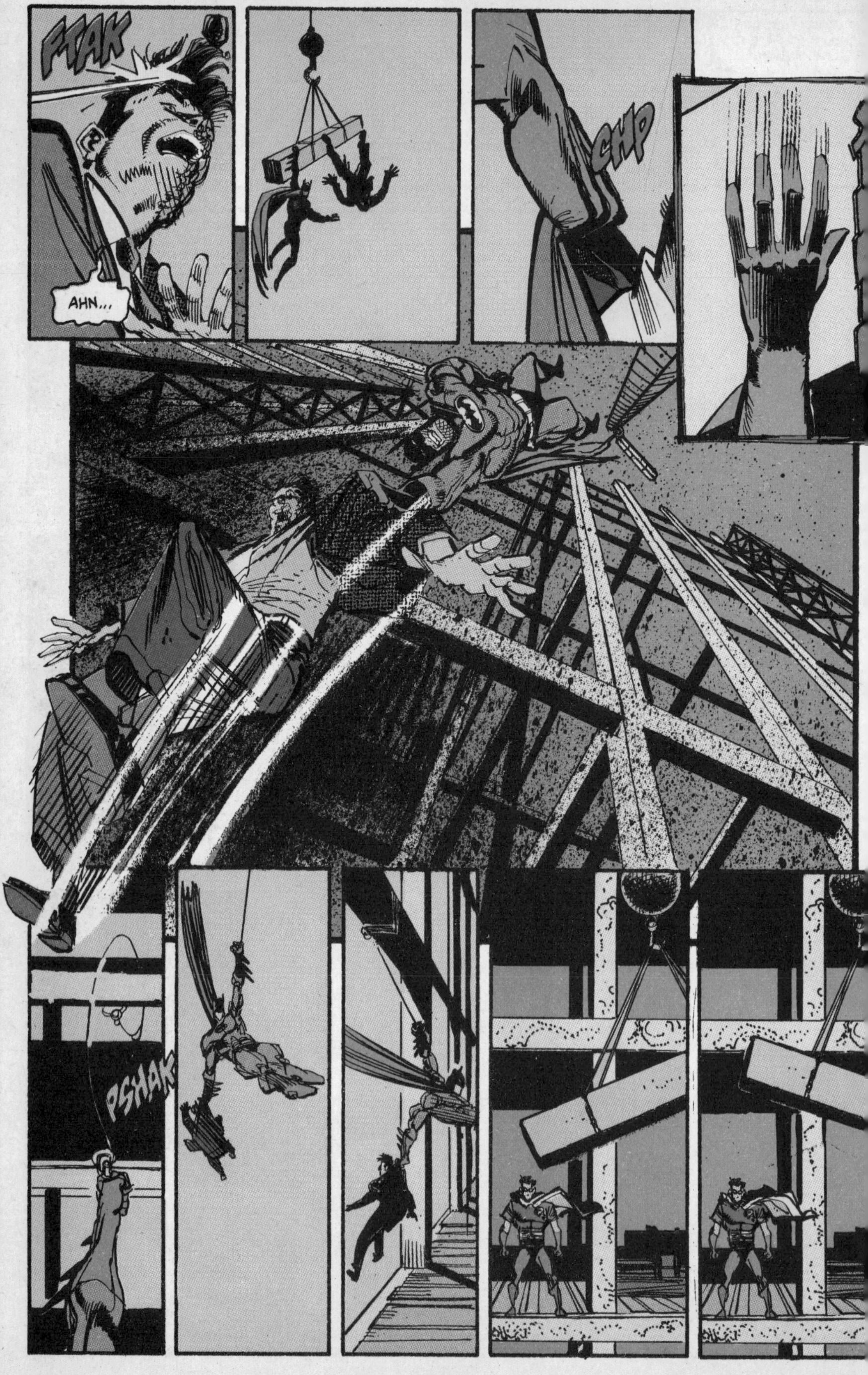
FTAK
AHN...
CHP
PSHAK

"IT WAS A *BAD* MOVE, PLAIN AND SIMPLE..."

AND YOU NEVER SHOULD HAVE *MADE* IT!

BUT HE WAS TRYING TO KILL YOU!

IT DOESN'T *MATTER!* WHAT YOU DID COULD HAVE *KILLED* HIM!

HEY, I COULDN'T JUST STAND BY AND DO *NOTHING!*

THERE WAS NO WAY YOU COULD KNOW I'D *CATCH* HIM!

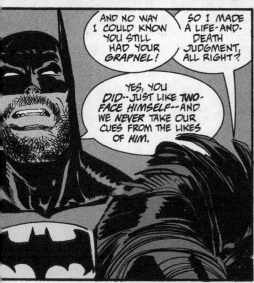

AND NO WAY I COULD KNOW YOU *STILL* HAD YOUR GRAPNEL!

SO I MADE A LIFE-AND-DEATH JUDGMENT, ALL RIGHT?

YES, YOU *DID*--JUST LIKE *TWO-FACE* HIMSELF--AND WE *NEVER* TAKE OUR CUES FROM THE LIKES OF HIM.

G-GUILTY...

...N-NOT... GUILTY...

IT RESULTS IN NOTHING BUT *CONFUSION* AND *CHAOS*--

--AND *BAD* JUDGMENT *EVERY* TIME!

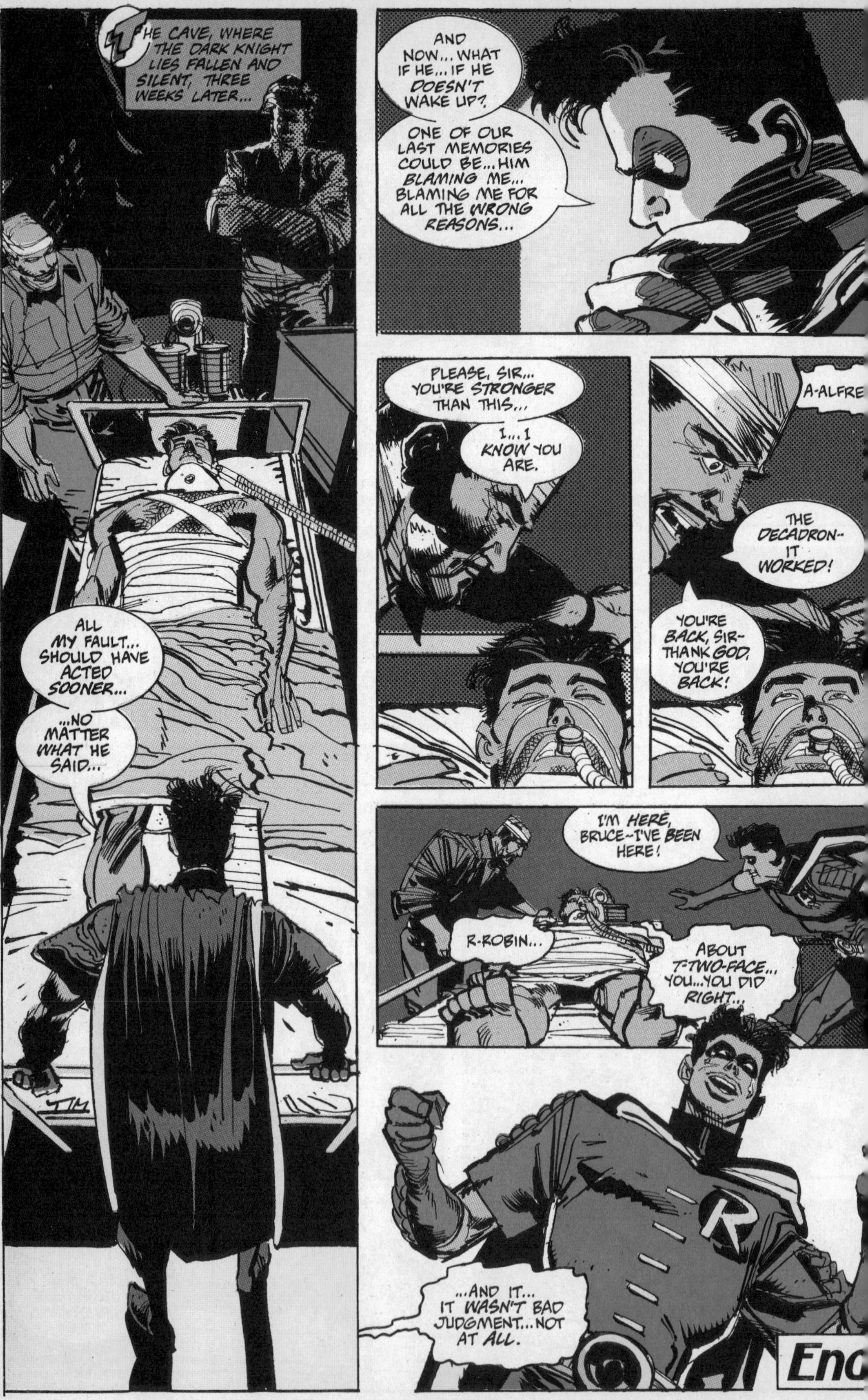
THE CAVE, WHERE THE DARK KNIGHT LIES FALLEN AND SILENT, THREE WEEKS LATER...
ALL MY FAULT... SHOULD HAVE ACTED SOONER...
...NO MATTER WHAT HE SAID...
AND NOW... WHAT IF HE... IF HE DOESN'T WAKE UP?
ONE OF OUR LAST MEMORIES COULD BE... HIM BLAMING ME... BLAMING ME FOR ALL THE WRONG REASONS...
PLEASE, SIR... YOU'RE STRONGER THAN THIS...
I... I KNOW YOU ARE.
A-ALFRE
THE DECADRON-- IT WORKED!
YOU'RE BACK, SIR-- THANK GOD, YOU'RE BACK!
I'M HERE, BRUCE--I'VE BEEN HERE!
R-ROBIN...
ABOUT T-TWO-FACE... YOU...YOU DID RIGHT...
...AND IT... IT WASN'T BAD JUDGMENT...NOT AT ALL.
Enc

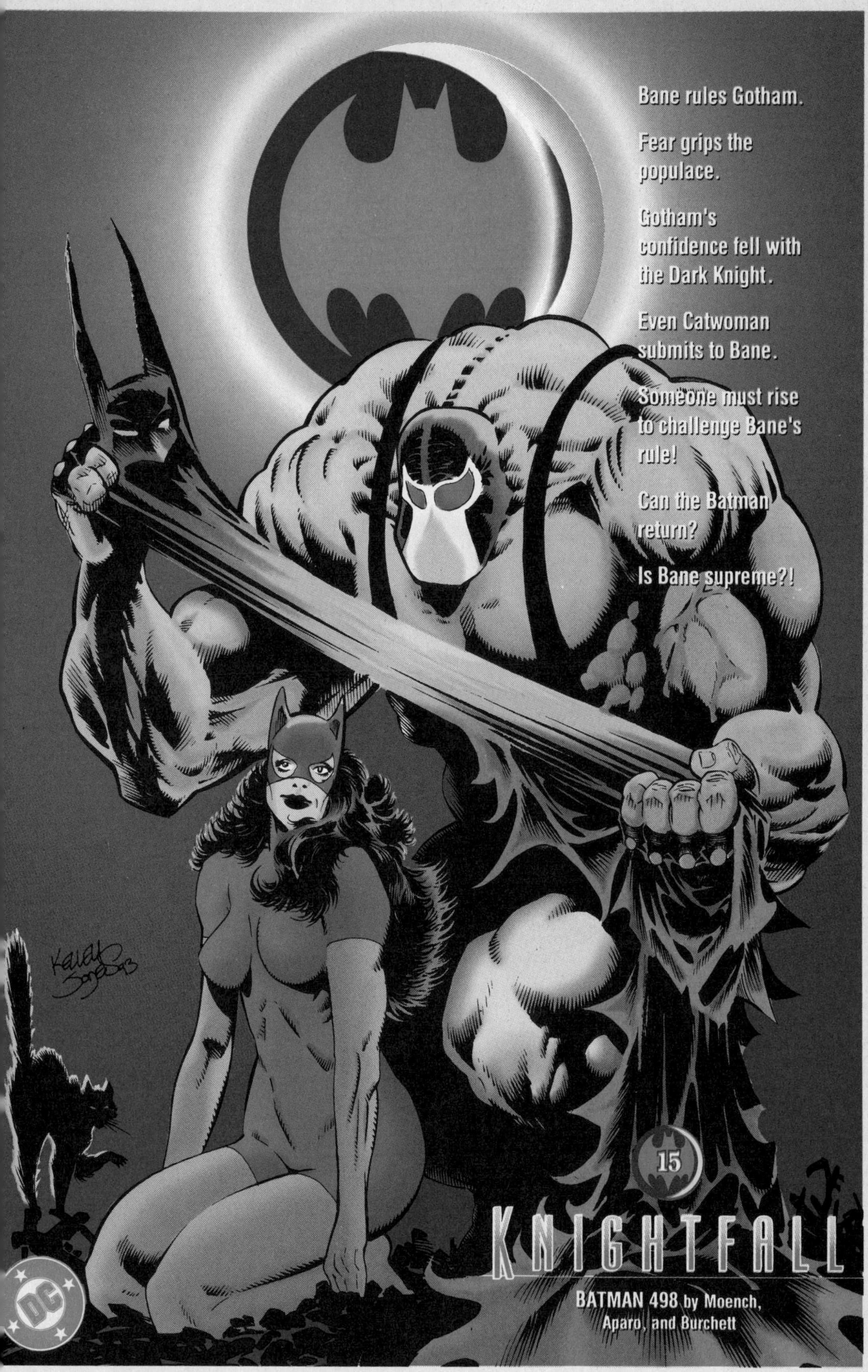

Bane rules Gotham.

Fear grips the populace.

Gotham's confidence fell with the Dark Knight.

Even Catwoman submits to Bane.

Someone must rise to challenge Bane's rule!

Can the Batman return?

Is Bane supreme?!

15

# KNIGHTFALL

BATMAN 498 by Moench, Aparo, and Burchett

All titles, characters and related indicia are trademarks of DC Comics. © 1993. All Rights Reserved.

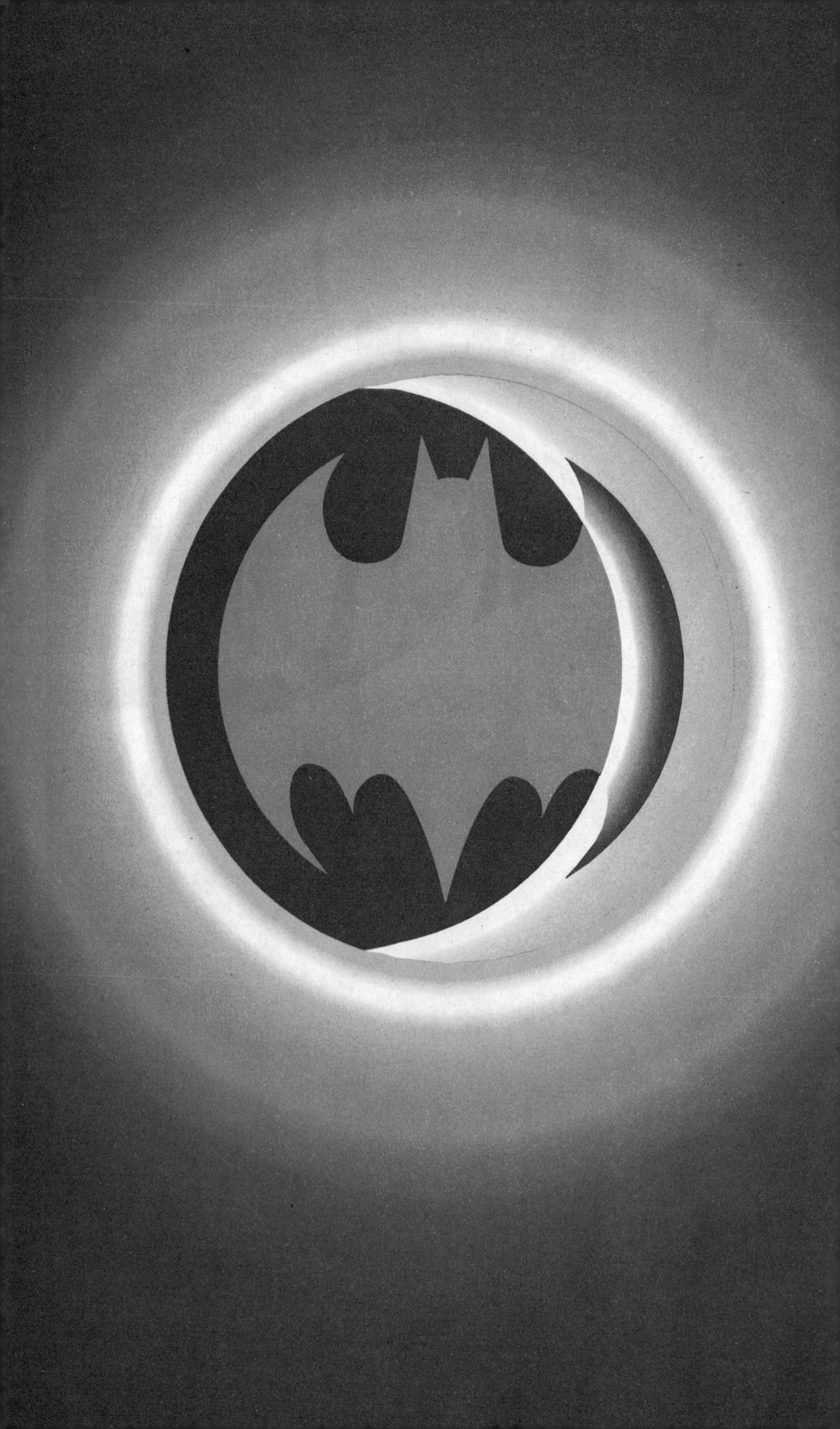

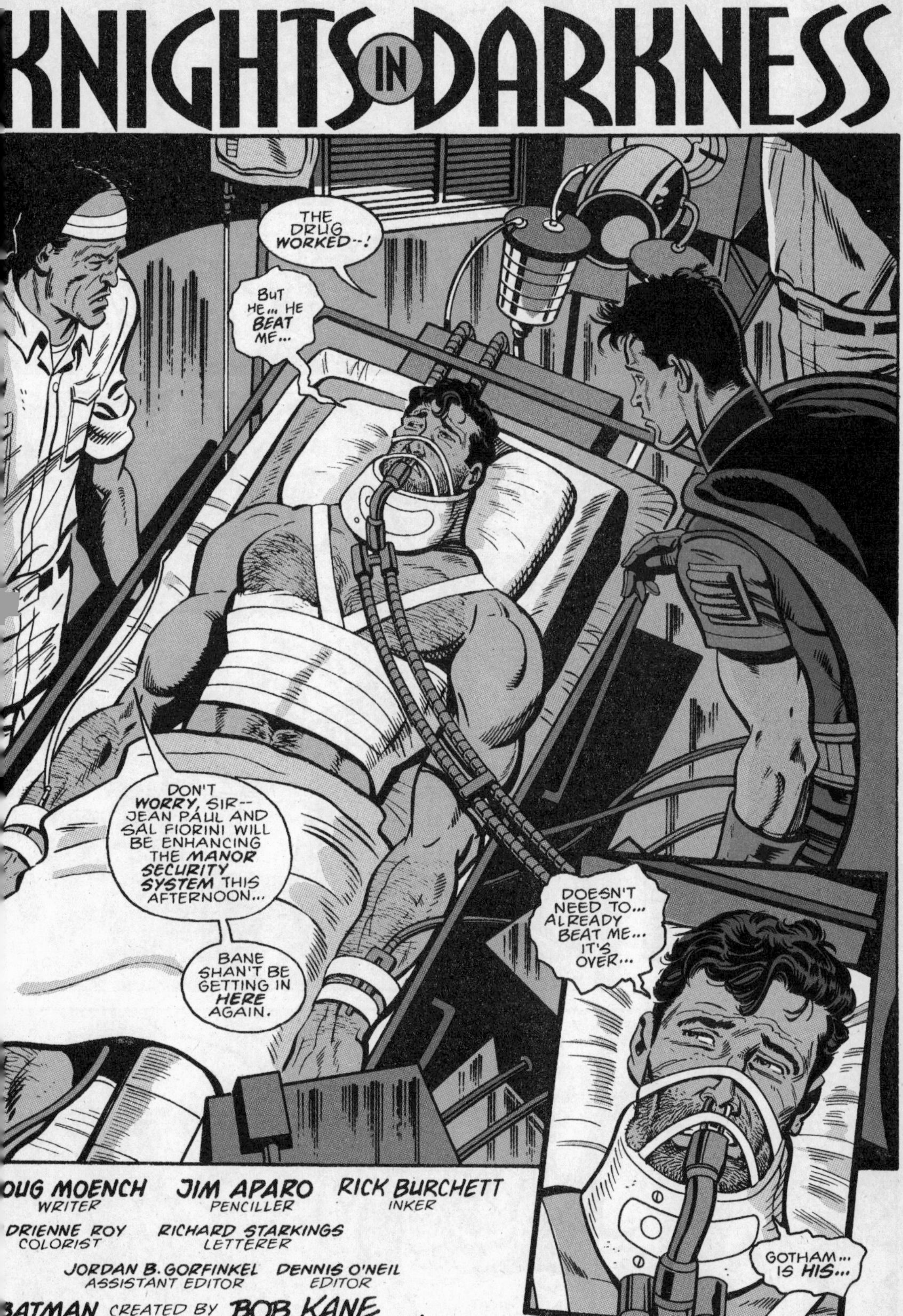
KNIGHTS IN DARKNESS
THE DRUG WORKED--!
BUT HE... HE BEAT ME...
DON'T WORRY, SIR-- JEAN PAUL AND SAL FIORINI WILL BE ENHANCING THE MANOR SECURITY SYSTEM THIS AFTERNOON...
BANE SHAN'T BE GETTING IN HERE AGAIN.
DOESN'T NEED TO... ALREADY BEAT ME... IT'S OVER...
GOTHAM... IS HIS...
OUG MOENCH WRITER
JIM APARO PENCILLER
RICK BURCHETT INKER
DRIENNE ROY COLORIST
RICHARD STARKINGS LETTERER
JORDAN B. GORFINKEL ASSISTANT EDITOR
DENNIS O'NEIL EDITOR
ATMAN CREATED BY BOB KANE

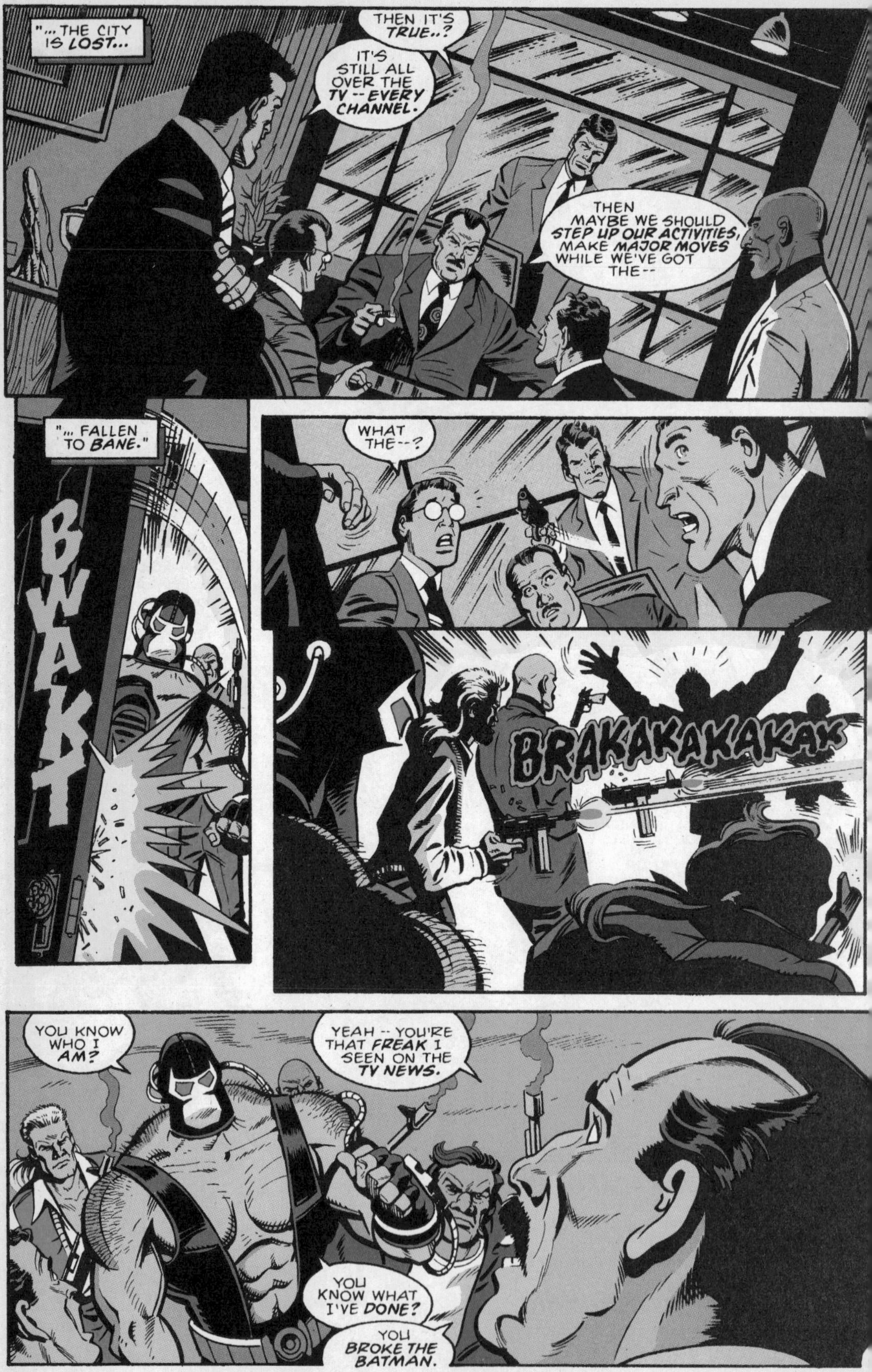
"... THE CITY IS LOST...
THEN IT'S TRUE..?
IT'S STILL ALL OVER THE TV -- EVERY CHANNEL.
THEN MAYBE WE SHOULD STEP UP OUR ACTIVITIES, MAKE MAJOR MOVES WHILE WE'VE GOT THE--
"... FALLEN TO BANE."
BWAKT
WHAT THE--?
BRAKAKAKAKAKAK
YOU KNOW WHO I AM?
YEAH -- YOU'RE THAT FREAK I SEEN ON THE TV NEWS.
YOU KNOW WHAT I'VE DONE?
YOU BROKE THE BATMAN.

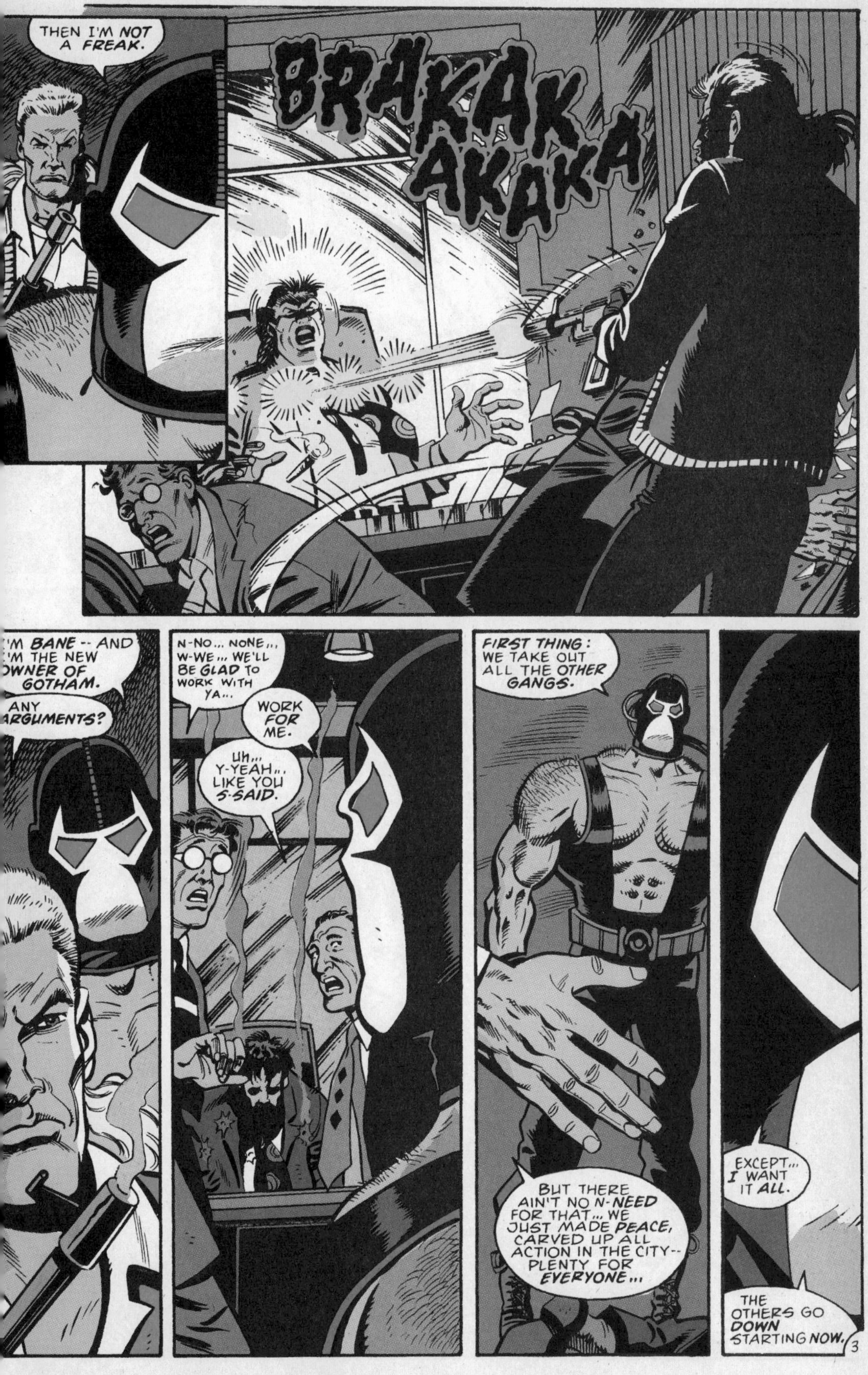
THEN I'M NOT A FREAK.
BRAKAK AKAKA
I'M BANE -- AND I'M THE NEW OWNER OF GOTHAM.
ANY ARGUMENTS?
N-NO... NONE... W-WE... WE'LL BE GLAD TO WORK WITH YA...
WORK FOR ME.
UH... Y-YEAH... LIKE YOU S-SAID.
FIRST THING: WE TAKE OUT ALL THE OTHER GANGS.
BUT THERE AIN'T NO N-NEED FOR THAT... WE JUST MADE PEACE, CARVED UP ALL ACTION IN THE CITY-- PLENTY FOR EVERYONE...
EXCEPT... I WANT IT ALL.
THE OTHERS GO DOWN STARTING NOW.
3

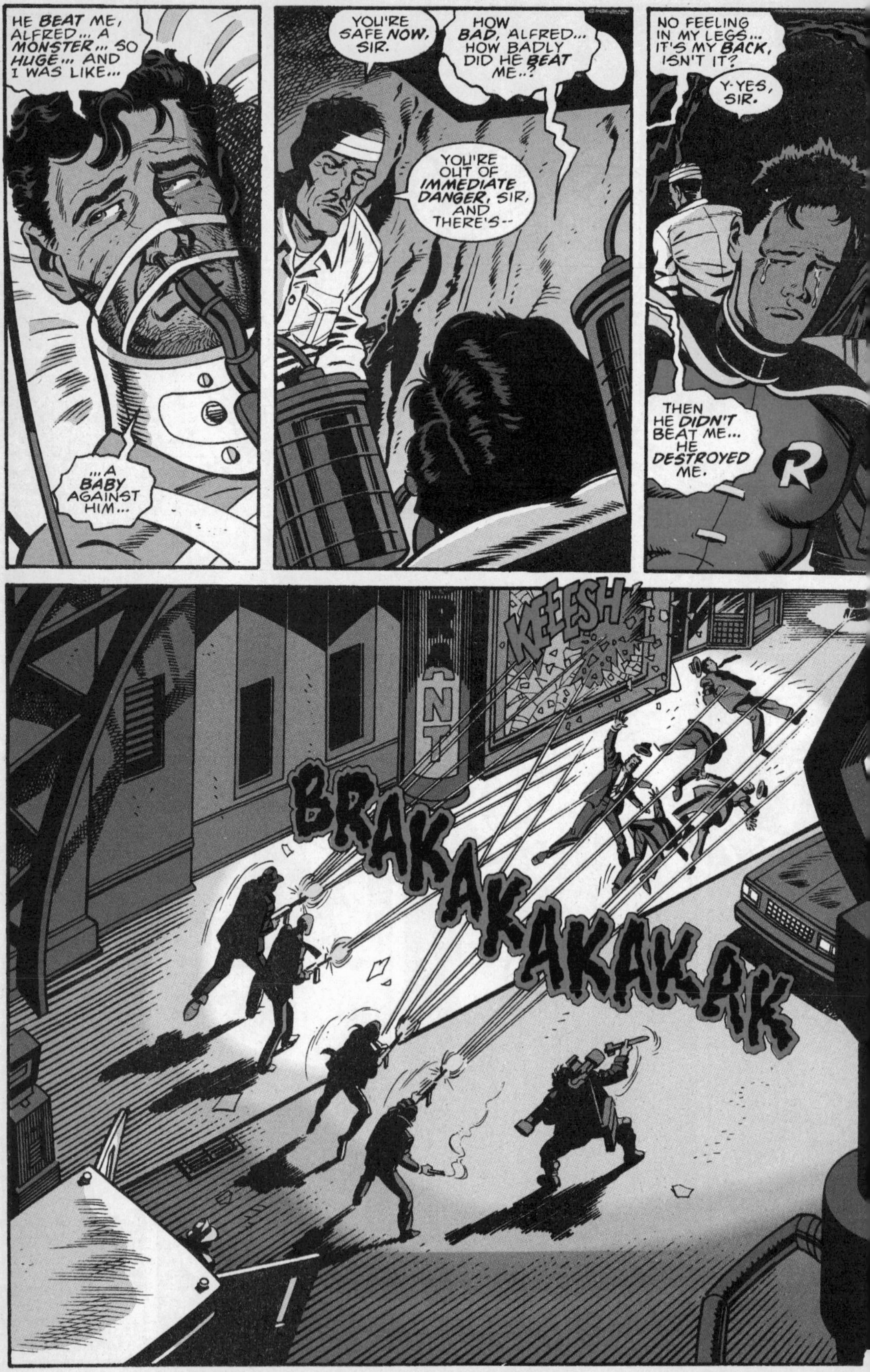
HE BEAT ME, ALFRED... A MONSTER... SO HUGE... AND I WAS LIKE...
...A BABY AGAINST HIM...
YOU'RE SAFE NOW, SIR.
HOW BAD, ALFRED... HOW BADLY DID HE BEAT ME...?
YOU'RE OUT OF IMMEDIATE DANGER, SIR, AND THERE'S--
NO FEELING IN MY LEGS... IT'S MY BACK, ISN'T IT?
Y-YES, SIR.
THEN HE DIDN'T BEAT ME... HE DESTROYED ME.
KEEESH
BRAKAKAKAKAKAK

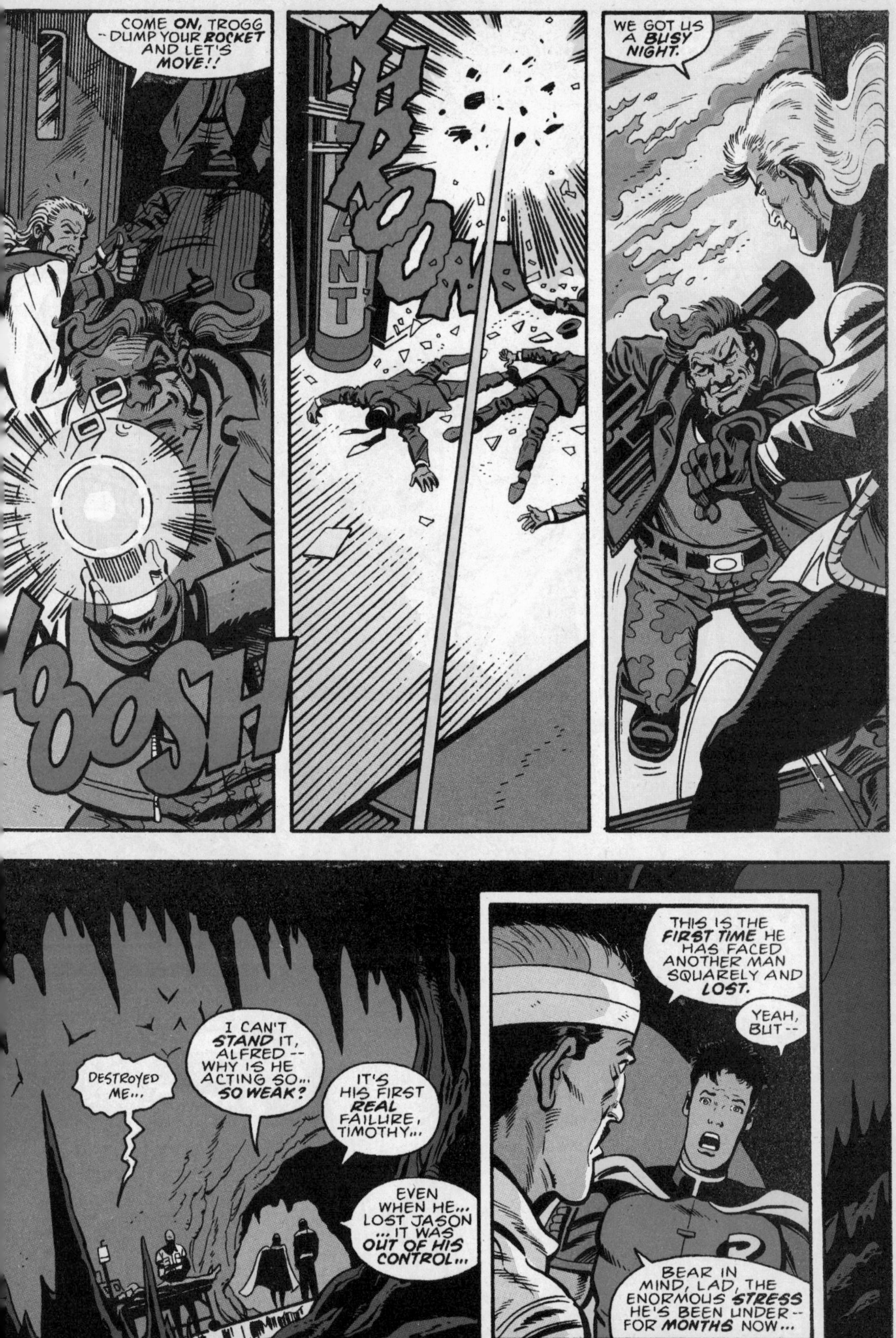
COME ON, TROGG -- DUMP YOUR ROCKET AND LET'S MOVE!!
WOOSH
KA-BOOM
WE GOT US A BUSY NIGHT.
DESTROYED ME...
I CAN'T STAND IT, ALFRED -- WHY IS HE ACTING SO... SO WEAK?
IT'S HIS FIRST REAL FAILURE, TIMOTHY...
EVEN WHEN HE... LOST JASON ... IT WAS OUT OF HIS CONTROL...
THIS IS THE FIRST TIME HE HAS FACED ANOTHER MAN SQUARELY AND LOST.
YEAH, BUT--
BEAR IN MIND, LAD, THE ENORMOUS STRESS HE'S BEEN UNDER -- FOR MONTHS NOW...
5

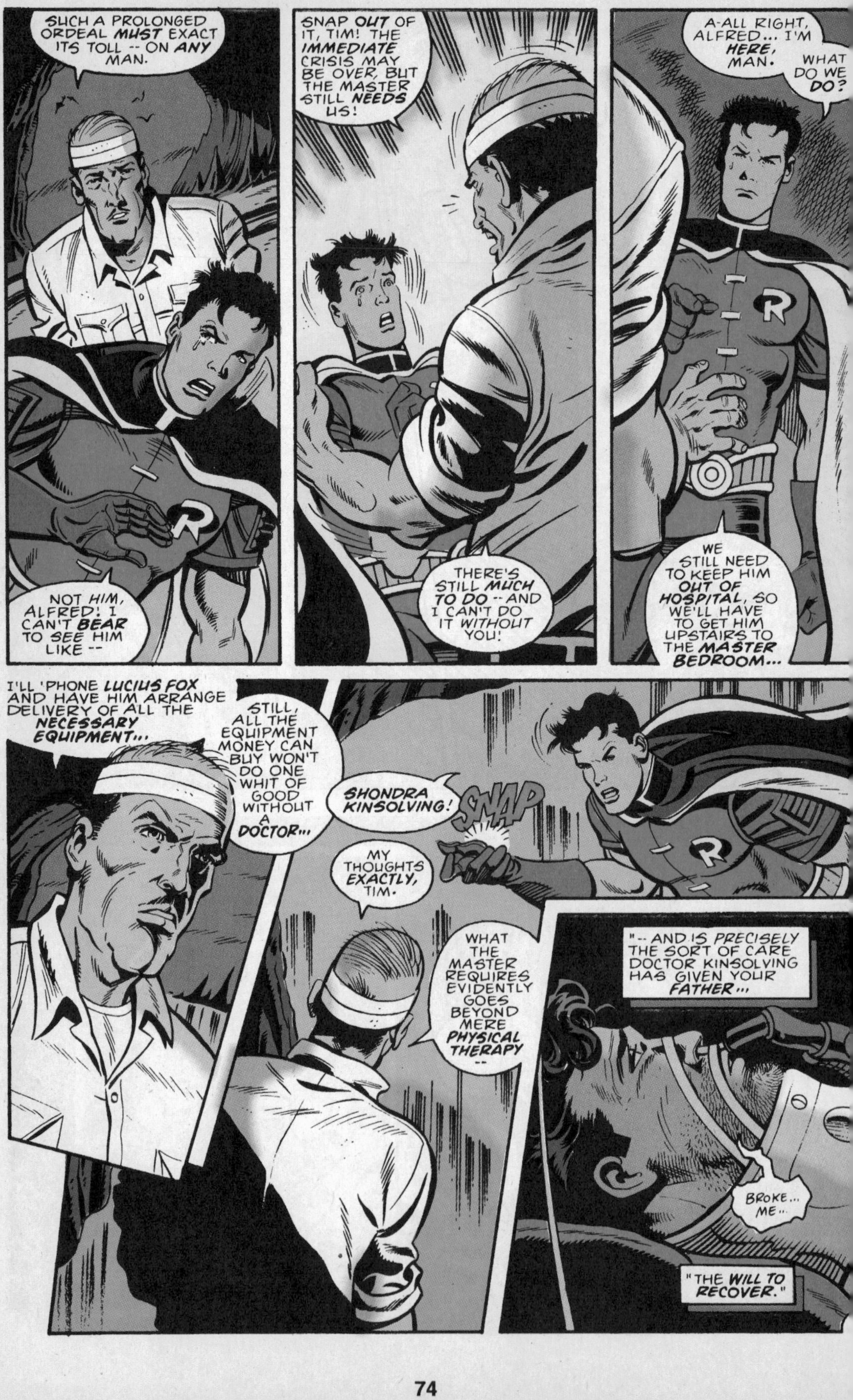
SUCH A PROLONGED ORDEAL MUST EXACT ITS TOLL -- ON ANY MAN.
NOT HIM, ALFRED! I CAN'T BEAR TO SEE HIM LIKE --
SNAP OUT OF IT, TIM! THE IMMEDIATE CRISIS MAY BE OVER, BUT THE MASTER STILL NEEDS US!
THERE'S STILL MUCH TO DO -- AND I CAN'T DO IT WITHOUT YOU!
A-ALL RIGHT, ALFRED... I'M HERE, MAN.
WHAT DO WE DO?
WE STILL NEED TO KEEP HIM OUT OF HOSPITAL, SO WE'LL HAVE TO GET HIM UPSTAIRS TO THE MASTER BEDROOM...
I'LL 'PHONE LUCIUS FOX AND HAVE HIM ARRANGE DELIVERY OF ALL THE NECESSARY EQUIPMENT...
STILL, ALL THE EQUIPMENT MONEY CAN BUY WON'T DO ONE WHIT OF GOOD WITHOUT A DOCTOR...
SHONDRA KINSOLVING!
SNAP
MY THOUGHTS EXACTLY, TIM.
WHAT THE MASTER REQUIRES EVIDENTLY GOES BEYOND MERE PHYSICAL THERAPY --
"-- AND IS PRECISELY THE SORT OF CARE DOCTOR KINSOLVING HAS GIVEN YOUR FATHER...
BROKE... ME...
"THE WILL TO RECOVER."

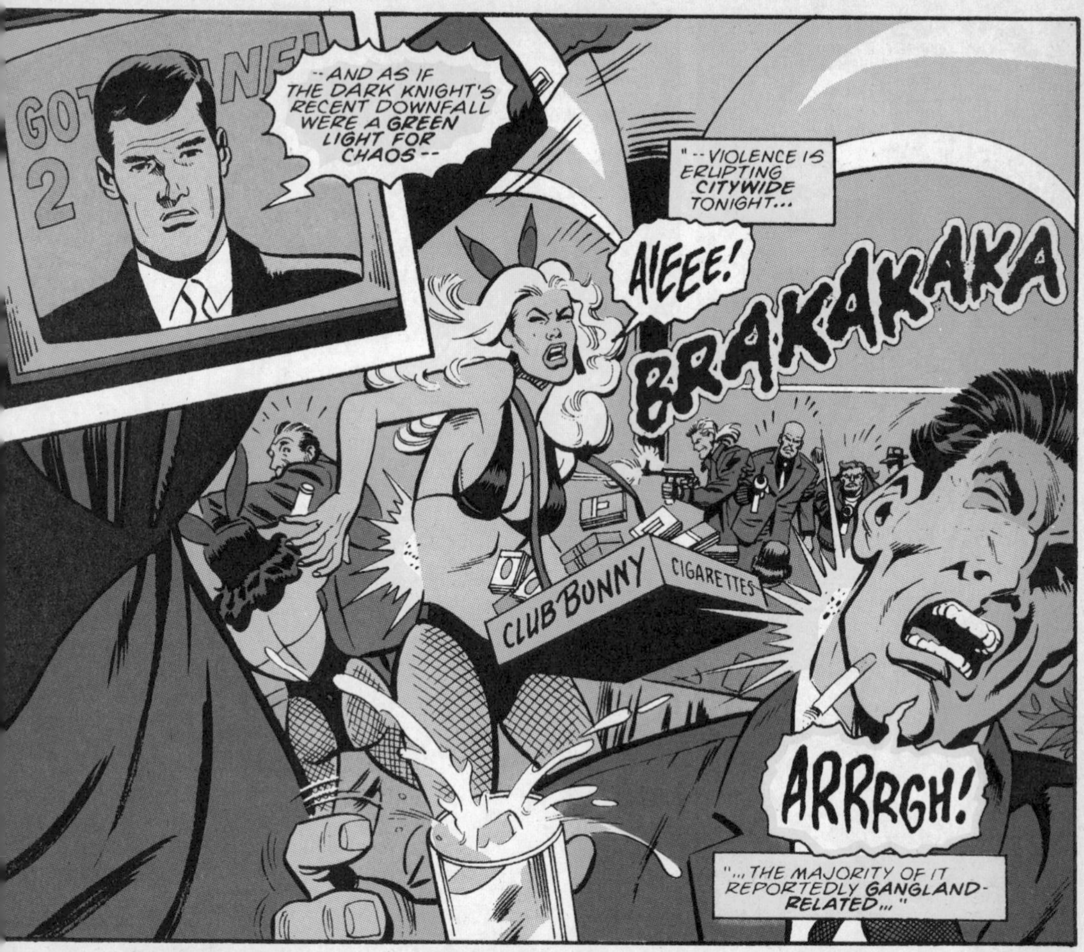
GOT
2
--AND AS IF THE DARK KNIGHT'S RECENT DOWNFALL WERE A GREEN LIGHT FOR CHAOS--
"--VIOLENCE IS ERUPTING CITYWIDE TONIGHT...
AIEEE!
BRAKAKAKA
CLUB BUNNY
CIGARETTES
ARRRGH!
"...THE MAJORITY OF IT REPORTEDLY GANGLAND-RELATED..."

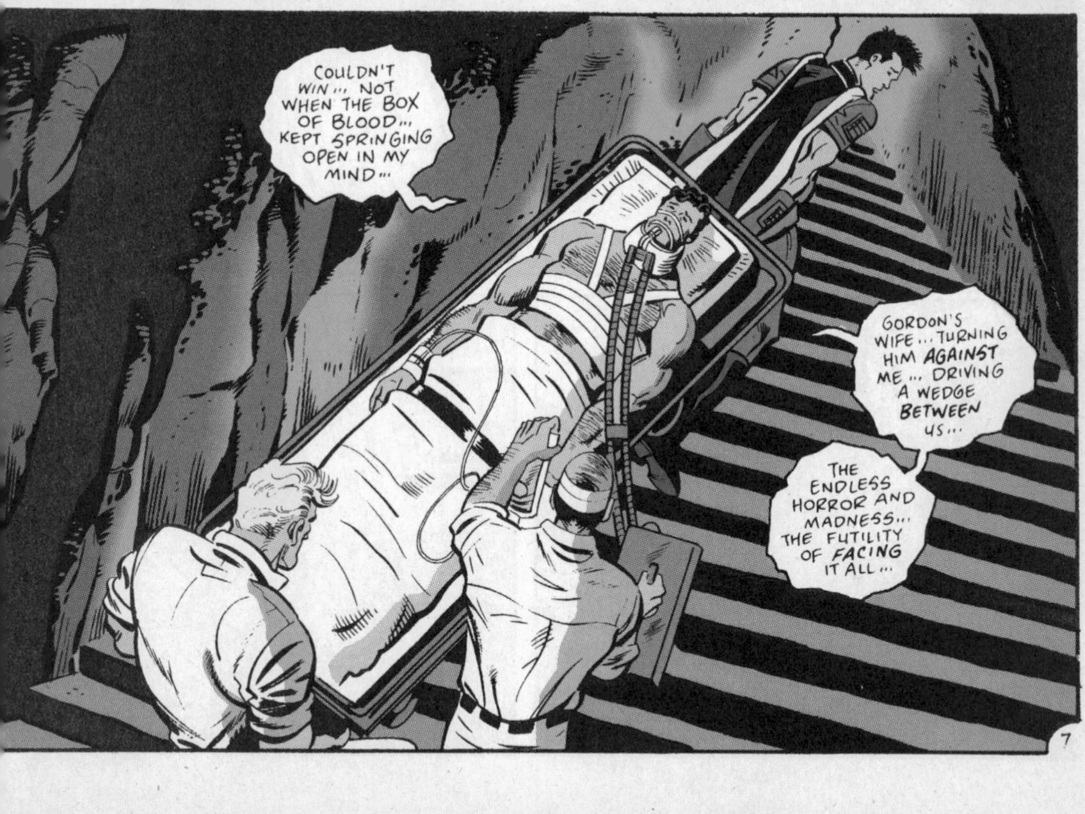
COULDN'T WIN... NOT WHEN THE BOX OF BLOOD... KEPT SPRINGING OPEN IN MY MIND...
GORDON'S WIFE... TURNING HIM AGAINST ME... DRIVING A WEDGE BETWEEN US...
THE ENDLESS HORROR AND MADNESS... THE FUTILITY OF FACING IT ALL...
7

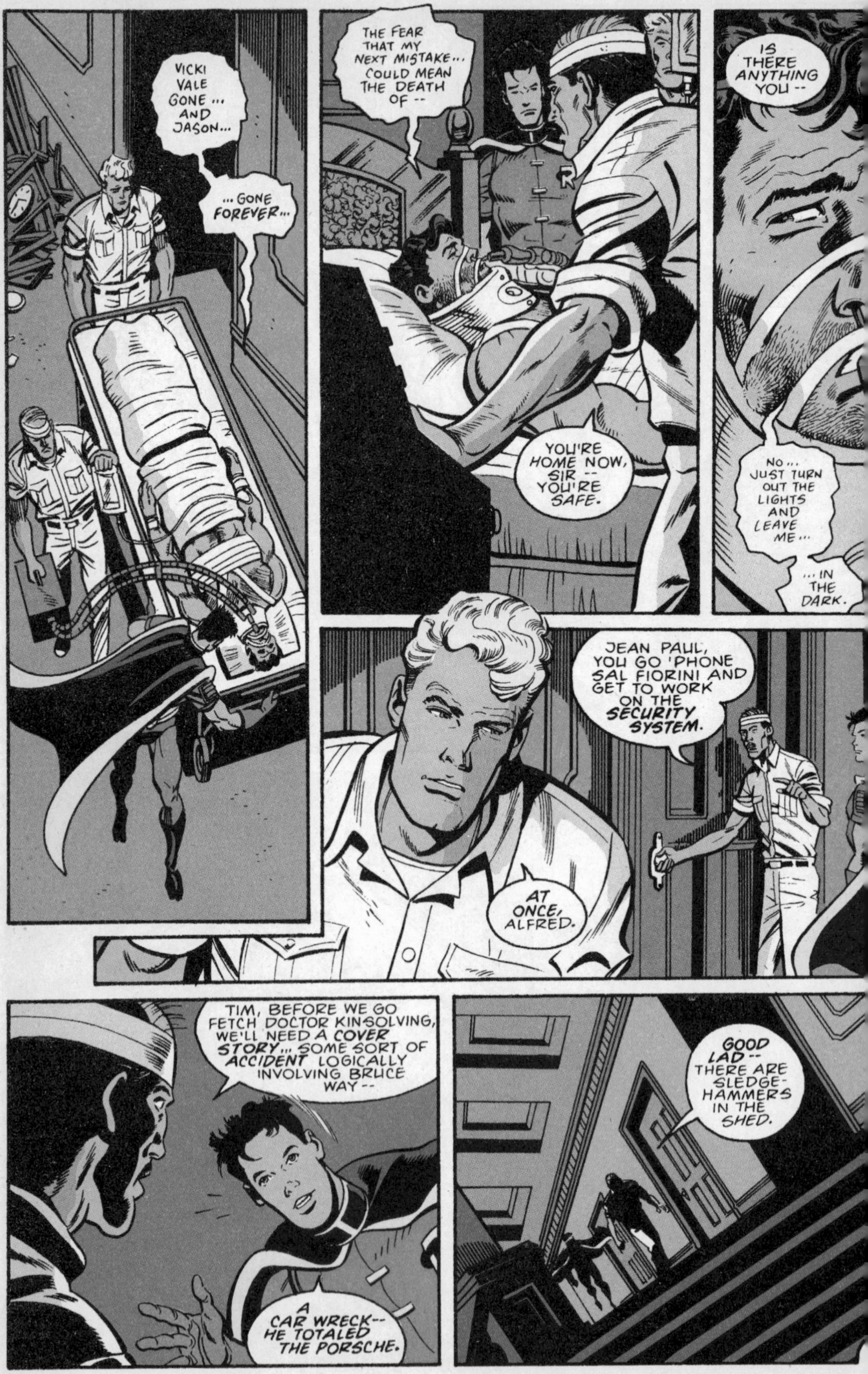
VICKI VALE GONE... AND JASON...
...GONE FOREVER...
THE FEAR THAT MY NEXT MISTAKE... COULD MEAN THE DEATH OF --
YOU'RE HOME NOW, SIR -- YOU'RE SAFE.
IS THERE ANYTHING YOU --
NO... JUST TURN OUT THE LIGHTS AND LEAVE ME...
...IN THE DARK.
JEAN PAUL, YOU GO 'PHONE SAL FIORINI AND GET TO WORK ON THE SECURITY SYSTEM.
AT ONCE, ALFRED.
TIM, BEFORE WE GO FETCH DOCTOR KINSOLVING, WE'LL NEED A COVER STORY... SOME SORT OF ACCIDENT LOGICALLY INVOLVING BRUCE WAY --
A CAR WRECK-- HE TOTALED THE PORSCHE.
GOOD LAD -- THERE ARE SLEDGE-HAMMERS IN THE SHED.

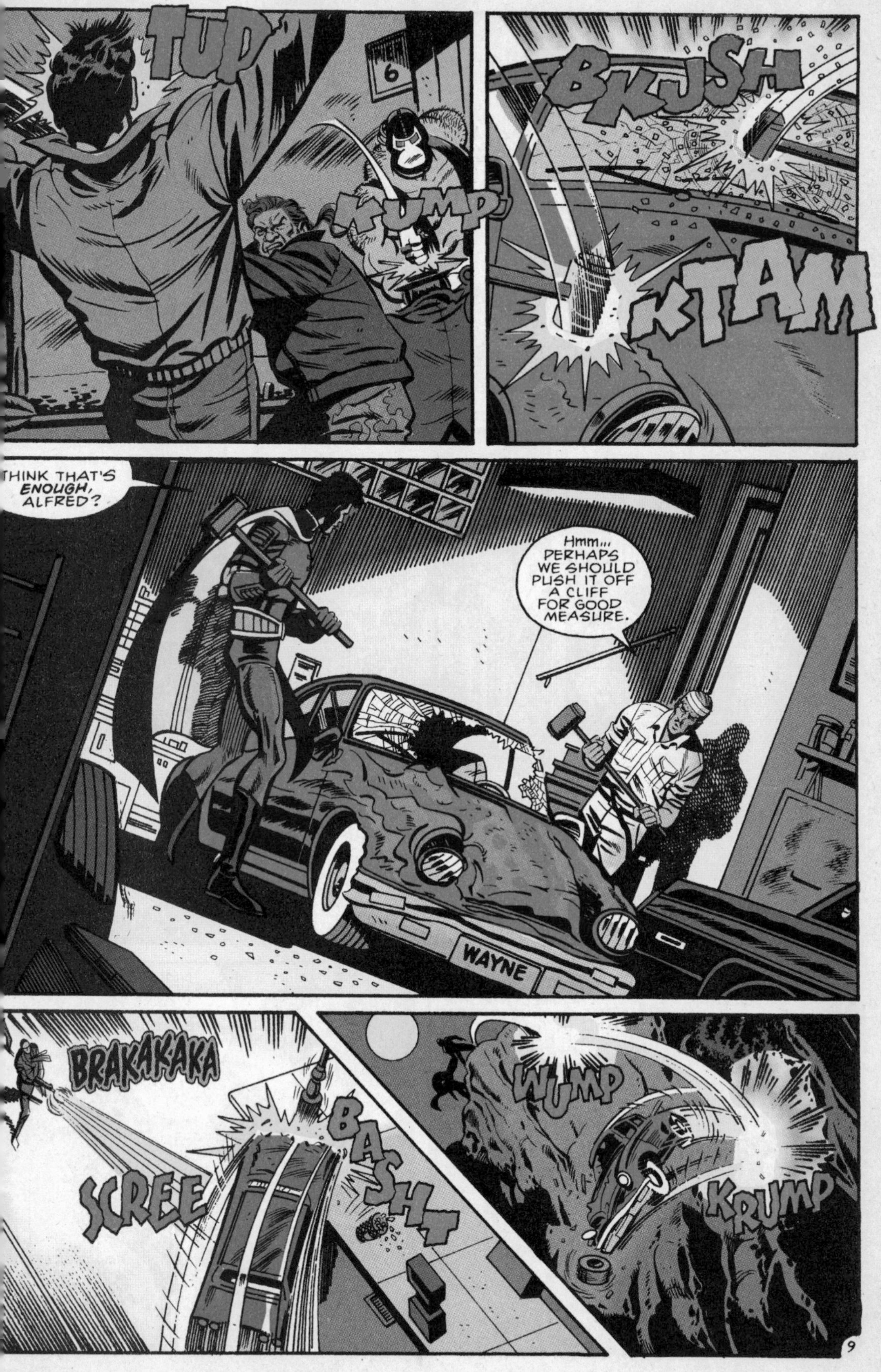
TUD
6
KUMP
BKJSH
KTAM
THINK THAT'S ENOUGH, ALFRED?
Hmm... PERHAPS WE SHOULD PUSH IT OFF A CLIFF FOR GOOD MEASURE.
WAYNE
BRAKAKAKA
SCREE
BASHT
WUMP
KRUMP
9

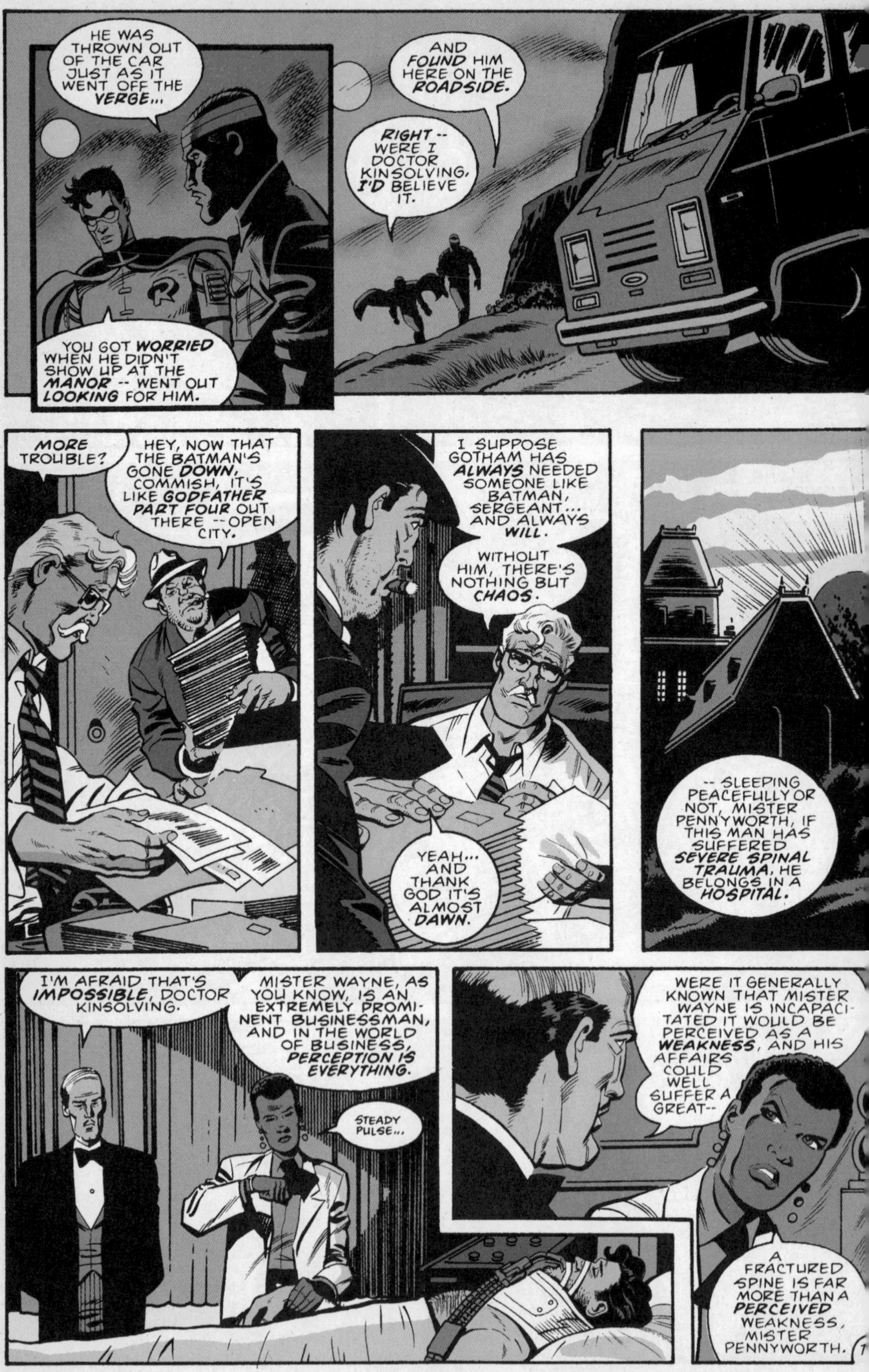
HE WAS THROWN OUT OF THE CAR JUST AS IT WENT OFF THE VERGE...
AND FOUND HIM HERE ON THE ROADSIDE.
RIGHT -- WERE I DOCTOR KINSOLVING, I'D BELIEVE IT.
YOU GOT WORRIED WHEN HE DIDN'T SHOW UP AT THE MANOR -- WENT OUT LOOKING FOR HIM.
MORE TROUBLE?
HEY, NOW THAT THE BATMAN'S GONE DOWN, COMMISH, IT'S LIKE GODFATHER PART FOUR OUT THERE -- OPEN CITY.
I SUPPOSE GOTHAM HAS ALWAYS NEEDED SOMEONE LIKE BATMAN, SERGEANT... AND ALWAYS WILL.
WITHOUT HIM, THERE'S NOTHING BUT CHAOS.
YEAH... AND THANK GOD IT'S ALMOST DAWN.
-- SLEEPING PEACEFULLY OR NOT, MISTER PENNYWORTH, IF THIS MAN HAS SUFFERED SEVERE SPINAL TRAUMA, HE BELONGS IN A HOSPITAL.
I'M AFRAID THAT'S IMPOSSIBLE, DOCTOR KINSOLVING.
MISTER WAYNE, AS YOU KNOW, IS AN EXTREMELY PROMINENT BUSINESSMAN, AND IN THE WORLD OF BUSINESS, PERCEPTION IS EVERYTHING.
STEADY PULSE...
WERE IT GENERALLY KNOWN THAT MISTER WAYNE IS INCAPACITATED IT WOULD BE PERCEIVED AS A WEAKNESS, AND HIS AFFAIRS COULD WELL SUFFER A GREAT--
A FRACTURED SPINE IS FAR MORE THAN A PERCEIVED WEAKNESS, MISTER PENNYWORTH.

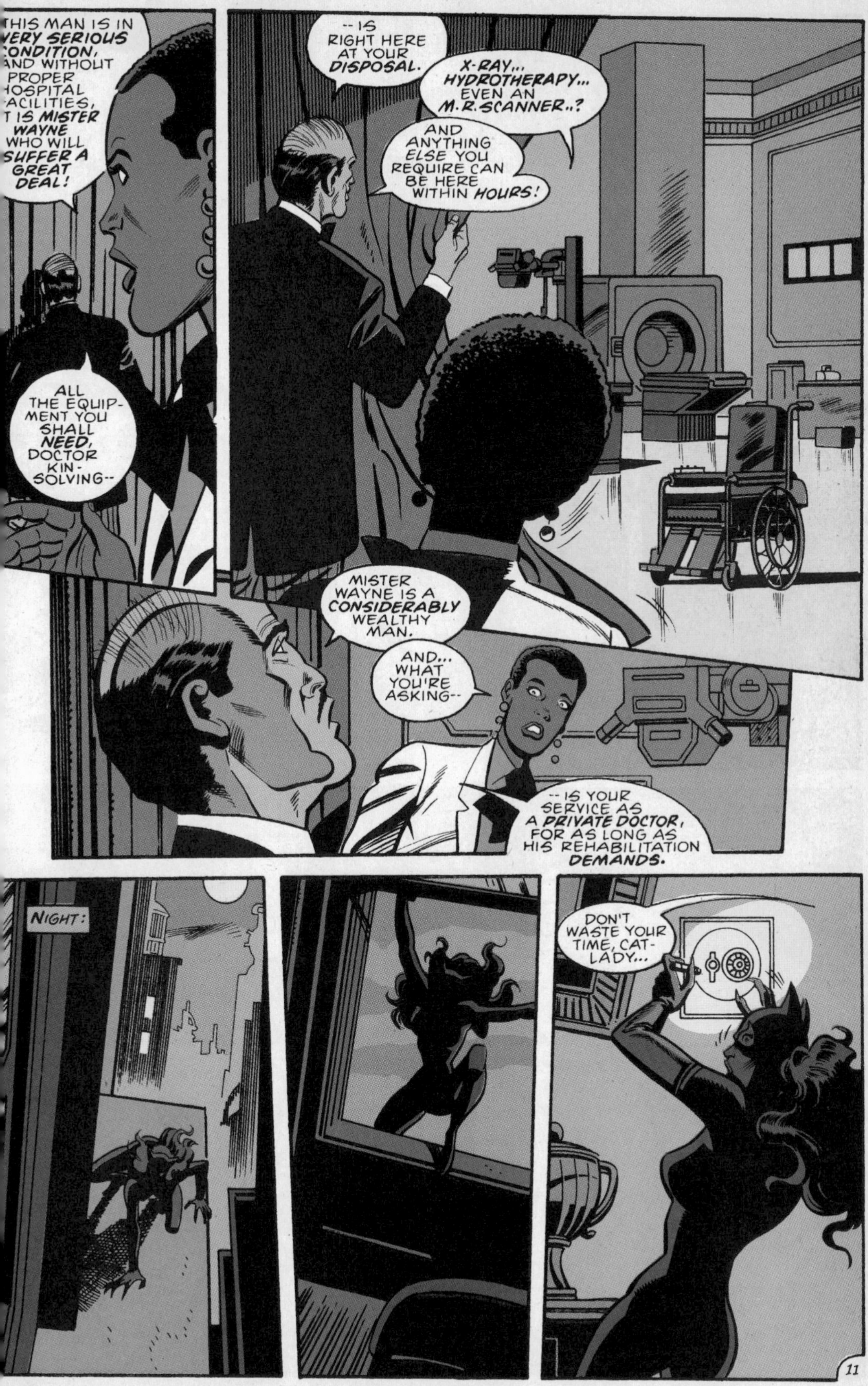
THIS MAN IS IN VERY SERIOUS CONDITION, AND WITHOUT PROPER HOSPITAL FACILITIES, IT IS MISTER WAYNE WHO WILL SUFFER A GREAT DEAL!
ALL THE EQUIPMENT YOU SHALL NEED, DOCTOR KINSOLVING--
--IS RIGHT HERE AT YOUR DISPOSAL.
X-RAY... HYDROTHERAPY... EVEN AN M.R. SCANNER..?
AND ANYTHING ELSE YOU REQUIRE CAN BE HERE WITHIN HOURS!
MISTER WAYNE IS A CONSIDERABLY WEALTHY MAN.
AND... WHAT YOU'RE ASKING--
--IS YOUR SERVICE AS A PRIVATE DOCTOR, FOR AS LONG AS HIS REHABILITATION DEMANDS.
NIGHT:
DON'T WASTE YOUR TIME, CAT-LADY...
11

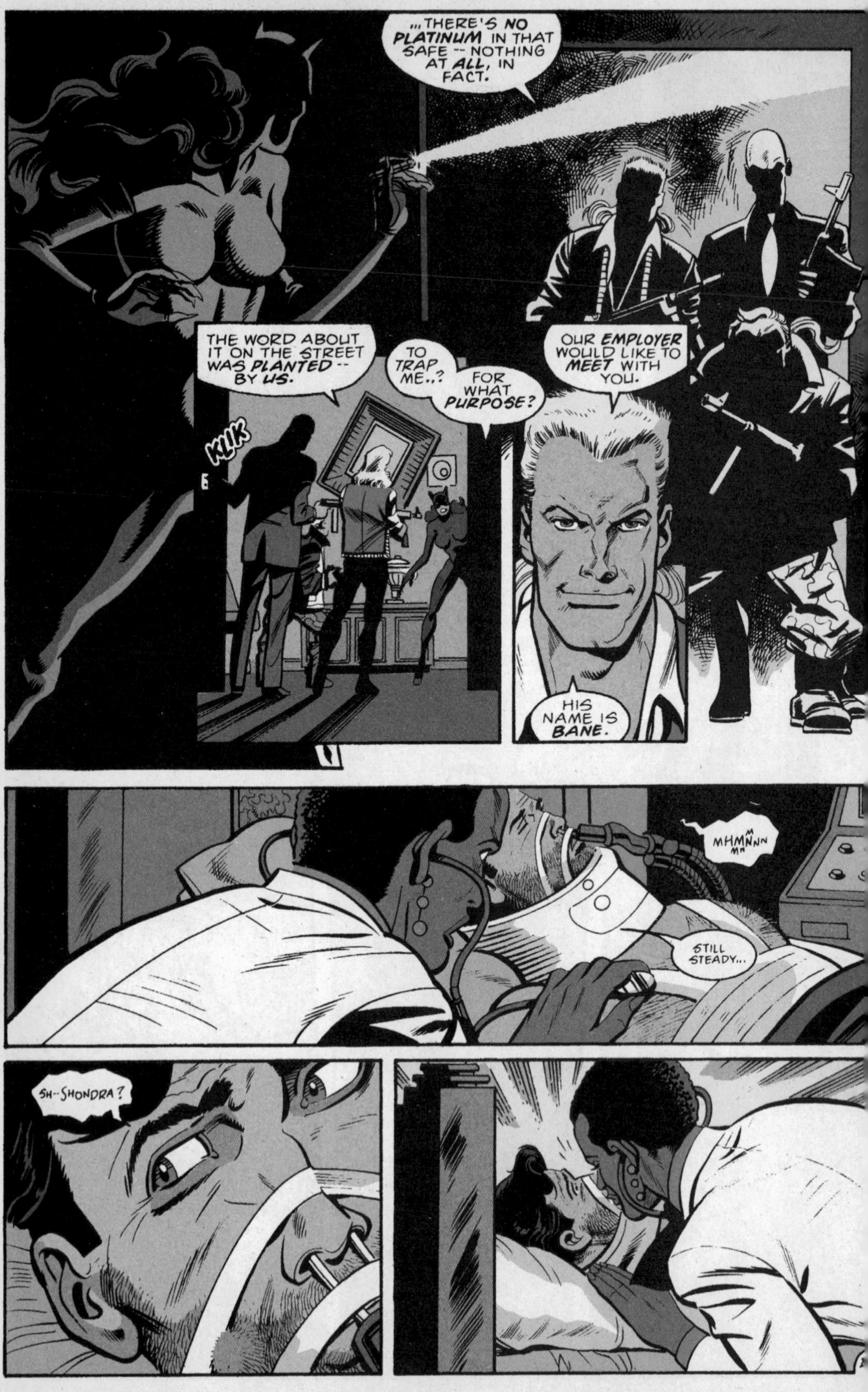
...THERE'S NO PLATINUM IN THAT SAFE -- NOTHING AT ALL, IN FACT.
THE WORD ABOUT IT ON THE STREET WAS PLANTED -- BY US.
TO TRAP ME..?
FOR WHAT PURPOSE?
OUR EMPLOYER WOULD LIKE TO MEET WITH YOU.
HIS NAME IS BANE.
KLIK
MHMMNNN
STILL STEADY...
SH--SHONDRA?

STILL NO WORD ON WHERE HE *IS*, COMMISH?

NO.

GOIN' UP TO THE *ROOF*?

IT CAN'T *HURT*, SERGEANT, TO *TRY*.

DONUT HO

ABOUT WHAT HAPPENED WHEN YOU *WOKE* UP, BRUCE, I... WELL, I CAN'T REALLY *EXPLAIN* IT...

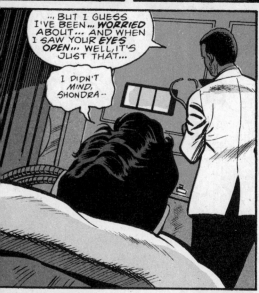

...BUT I GUESS I'VE BEEN... *WORRIED* ABOUT... AND WHEN I SAW YOUR *EYES* OPEN... WELL, IT'S JUST THAT...

I DIDN'T *MIND*, SHONDRA--

YOU *DIDN'T*?

OTHER THAN... *WEAKNESS* AND *PAIN*... IT WAS THE FIRST TIME, IN FAR TOO LONG, THAT I'VE FELT *ANYTHING*.

YES, ALFRED AND TIMOTHY TOLD ME YOU'RE EXPERIENCING SOME *DEPRESSION*...

'VE SUFFERED A... *LOSS*... EYOND THE *INJURY*...

I HOPE YOU'RE NOT TALKING ABOUT A MERE *CAR*.

*CAR?!?*

AHEM...

THE *PORSCHE*, SIR.

YOU WERE IN *SHOCK* WHEN I FOUND YOU BY THE *ROADSIDE*, REMEMBER -- WITH LITTLE OR NO *MEMORY* OF YOUR *ACCIDENT*.

13

IT MAY *TAKE* A WHILE, DOCTOR, FOR MISTER WAYNE TO --

IF ANYONE CAN HEAL HIM, MISTER PENNYWORTH, *I WILL.*

MIGHTY *CONFIDENT...*

EXACTLY, BRUCE, AND THAT'S WHAT YOU MUST BE -- *BOTH OF US* -- TOGETHER.

FROM WHAT I *KNOW* OF YOU, YOU'RE NOT THE TYPE WHO *QUITS...* EVEN IF YOU ARE CAPABLE OF *LYING.*

*LYING..?*

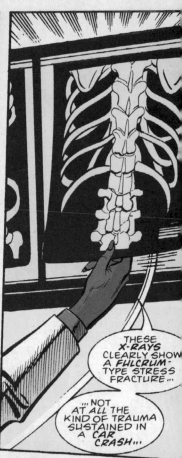

THESE *X-RAYS* CLEARLY SHOW A *FULCRUM-* TYPE STRESS FRACTURE...

...NOT AT ALL THE KIND OF TRAUMA SUSTAINED IN A *CAR CRASH...*

...WHICH, IN ANY CASE, WOULD HAVE *SHATTERED* YOUR *LEGS* BEFORE AFFECTING YOUR *BACK.*

I...

HE WAS *THROWN* FROM THE CAR -- BEFORE IT WENT OVER THE *VERGE* -- LANDED ON A *LARGE ROCK.*

THAT'S ALL RIGHT -- I *LIKE* IT.

YOU... *DO?!*

YOU'RE A *MYSTERY* TO ME, BRUCE -- AND THE FACT THAT YOU'RE *CLINGING* TO YOUR MYSTERY PROVES YOU *HAVEN'T* GIVEN UP!

BESIDES, TH— DIAGNOSTICIA— IN ME ENJOYS PEELING MYSTERIES *OPEN...* ONE LAYER AT A *TIME.*

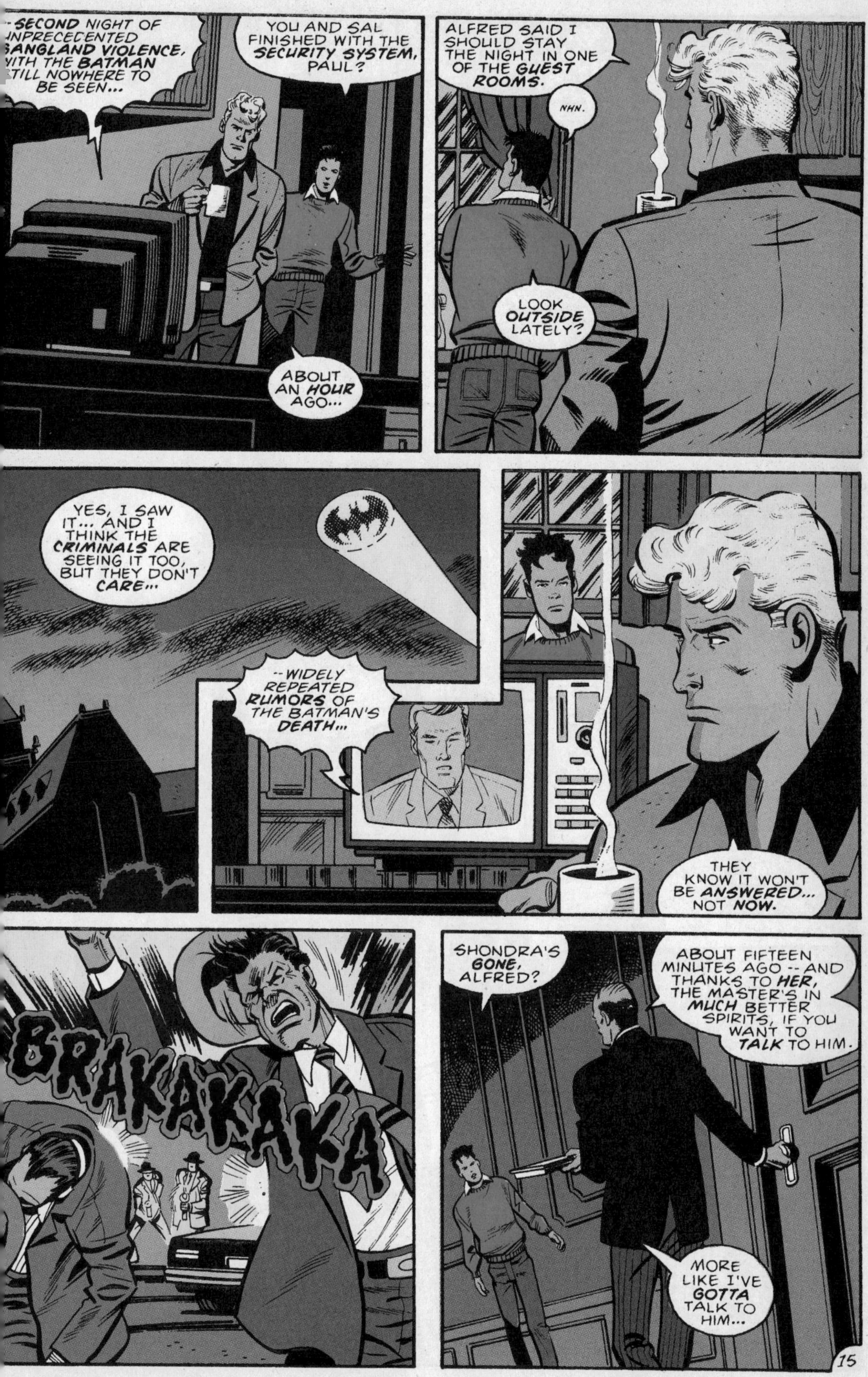
--SECOND NIGHT OF UNPRECEDENTED GANGLAND VIOLENCE, WITH THE BATMAN STILL NOWHERE TO BE SEEN...
YOU AND SAL FINISHED WITH THE SECURITY SYSTEM, PAUL?
ABOUT AN HOUR AGO...
ALFRED SAID I SHOULD STAY THE NIGHT IN ONE OF THE GUEST ROOMS.
NHN.
LOOK OUTSIDE LATELY?
YES, I SAW IT... AND I THINK THE CRIMINALS ARE SEEING IT TOO, BUT THEY DON'T CARE...
--WIDELY REPEATED RUMORS OF THE BATMAN'S DEATH...
THEY KNOW IT WON'T BE ANSWERED... NOT NOW.
BRAKAKAKAKA
SHONDRA'S GONE, ALFRED?
ABOUT FIFTEEN MINUTES AGO -- AND THANKS TO HER, THE MASTER'S IN MUCH BETTER SPIRITS, IF YOU WANT TO TALK TO HIM.
MORE LIKE I'VE GOTTA TALK TO HIM...
15

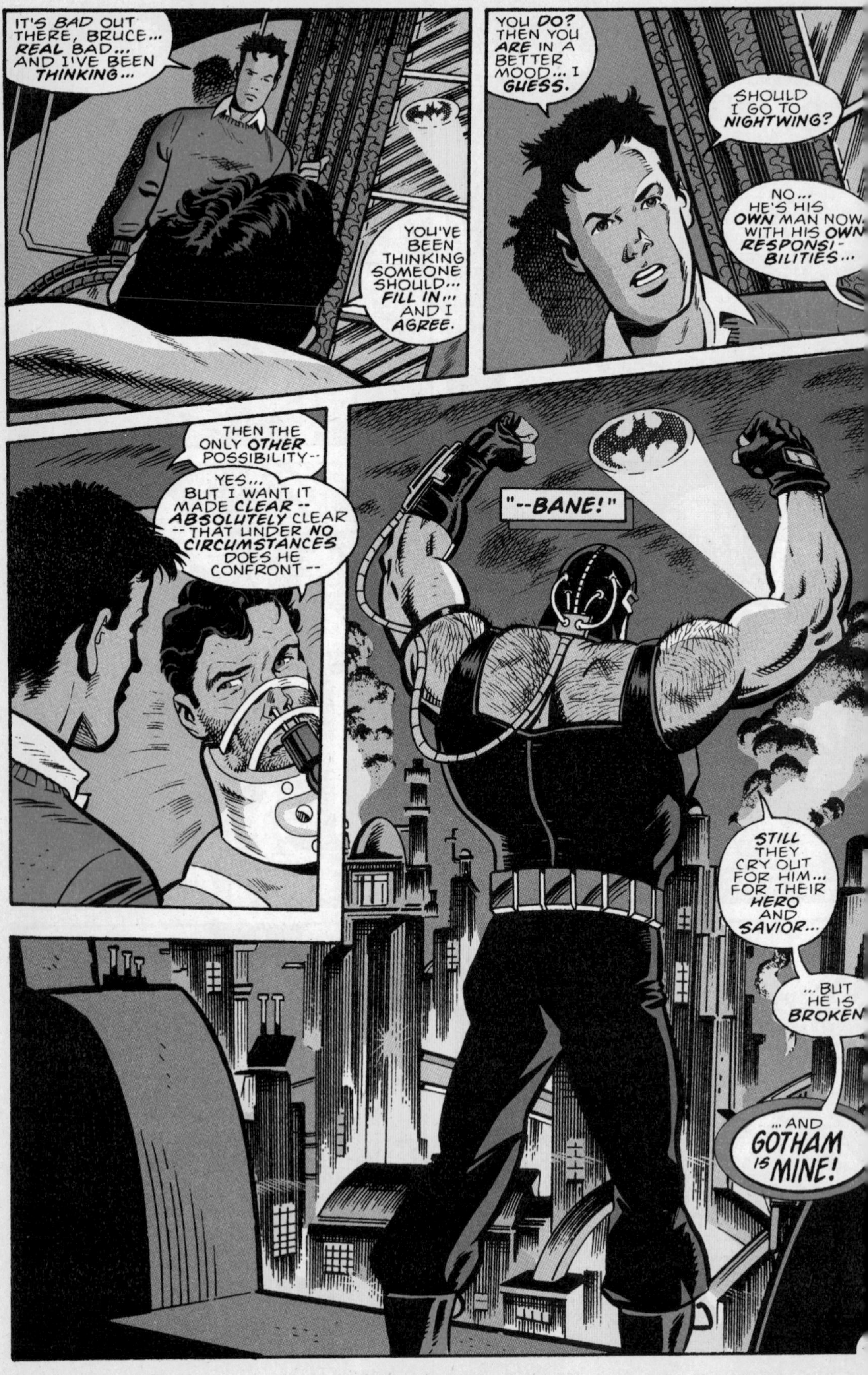
IT'S BAD OUT THERE, BRUCE... REAL BAD... AND I'VE BEEN THINKING...
YOU'VE BEEN THINKING SOMEONE SHOULD... FILL IN... AND I AGREE.
YOU DO? THEN YOU ARE IN A BETTER MOOD... I GUESS.
SHOULD I GO TO NIGHTWING?
NO... HE'S HIS OWN MAN NOW, WITH HIS OWN RESPONSI-BILITIES...
THEN THE ONLY OTHER POSSIBILITY--
YES... BUT I WANT IT MADE CLEAR -- ABSOLUTELY CLEAR -- THAT UNDER NO CIRCUMSTANCES DOES HE CONFRONT --
"--BANE!"
STILL THEY CRY OUT FOR HIM... FOR THEIR HERO AND SAVIOR...
...BUT HE IS BROKEN
...AND GOTHAM IS MINE!

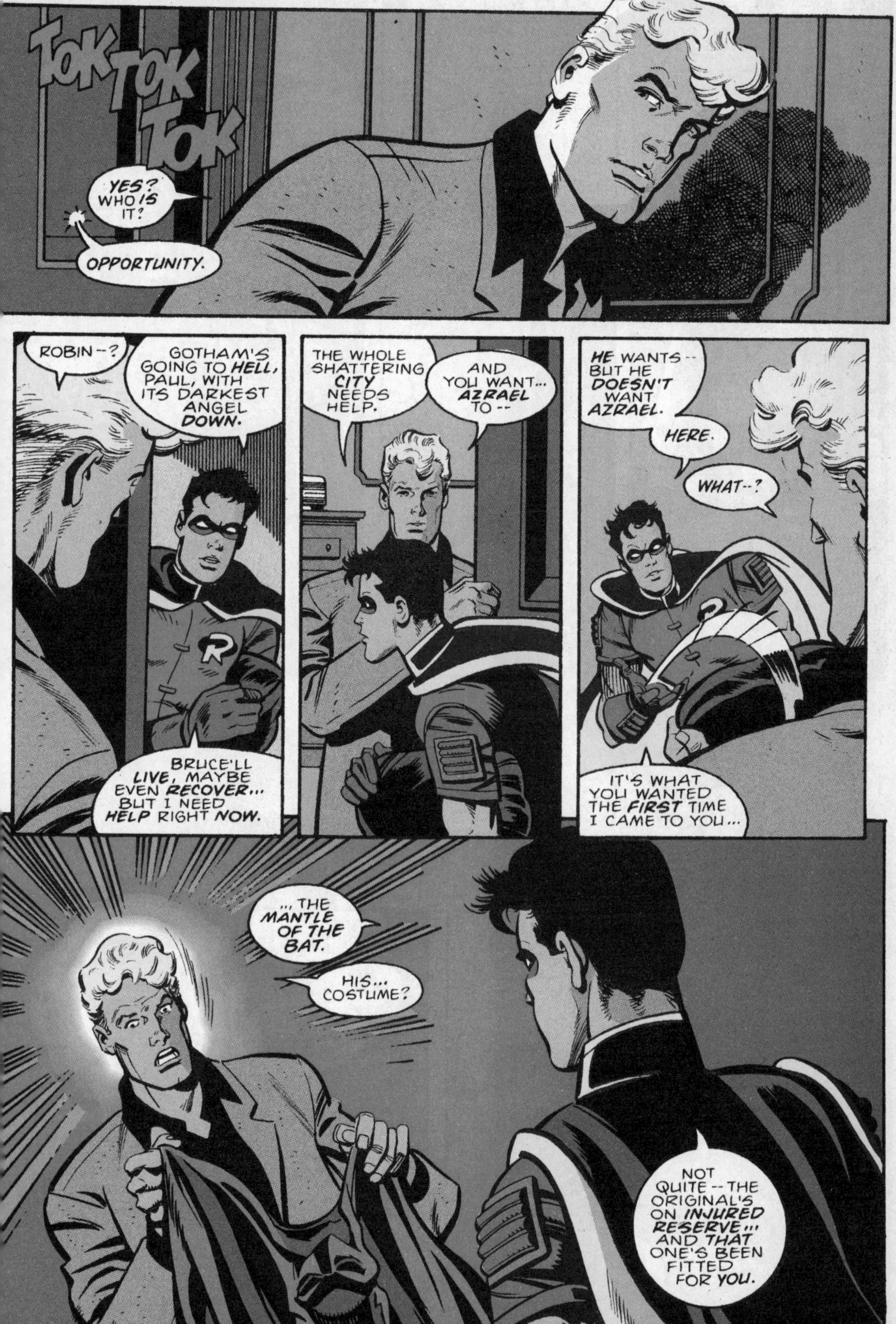
TOK TOK TOK
YES? WHO IS IT?
OPPORTUNITY.
ROBIN--?
GOTHAM'S GOING TO HELL, PAUL, WITH ITS DARKEST ANGEL DOWN.
BRUCE'LL LIVE, MAYBE EVEN RECOVER... BUT I NEED HELP RIGHT NOW.
THE WHOLE SHATTERING CITY NEEDS HELP.
AND YOU WANT... AZRAEL TO --
HE WANTS -- BUT HE DOESN'T WANT AZRAEL.
HERE.
WHAT--?
IT'S WHAT YOU WANTED THE FIRST TIME I CAME TO YOU...
... THE MANTLE OF THE BAT.
HIS... COSTUME?
NOT QUITE -- THE ORIGINAL'S ON INJURED RESERVE... AND THAT ONE'S BEEN FITTED FOR YOU.
17

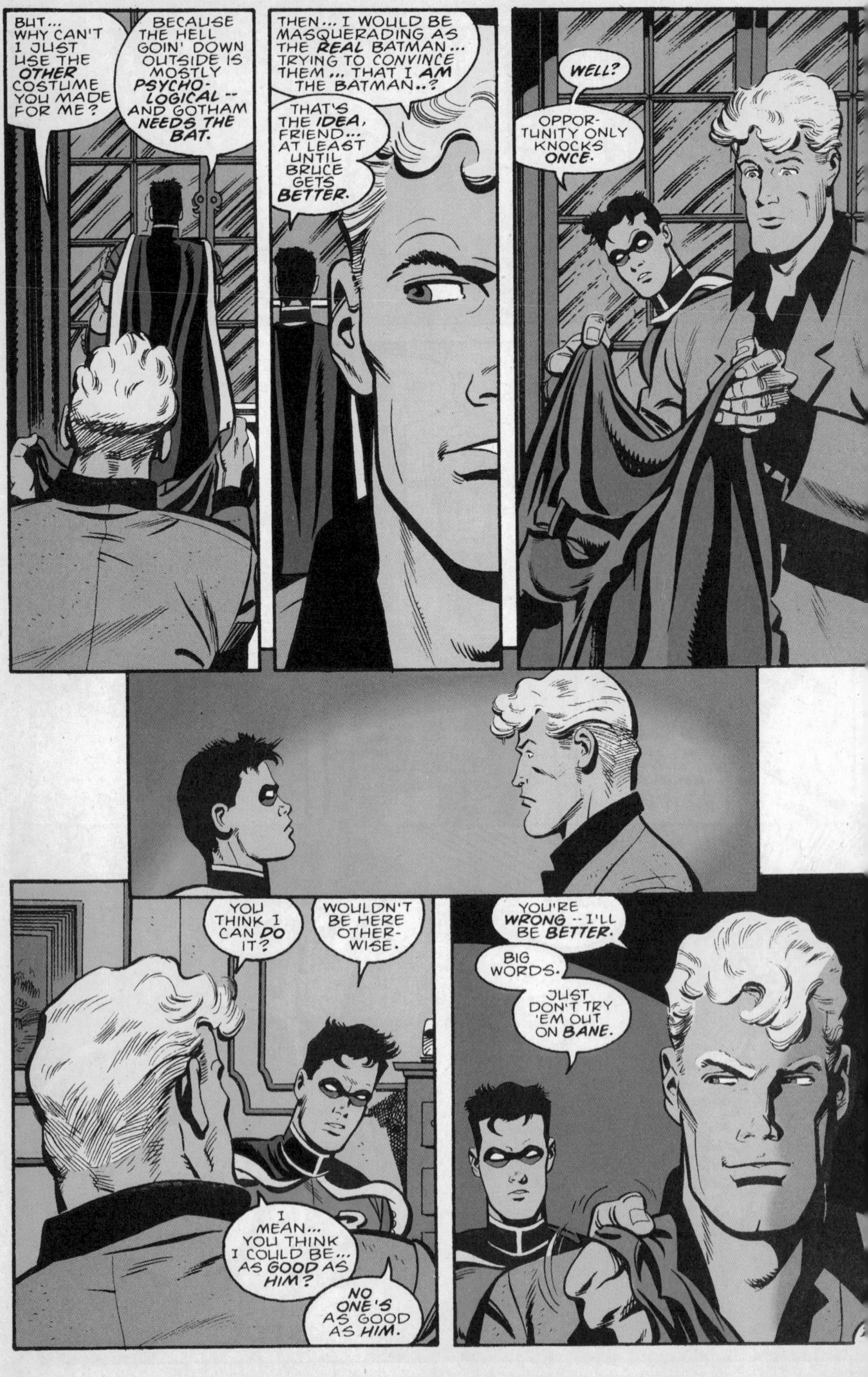
BUT... WHY CAN'T I JUST USE THE OTHER COSTUME YOU MADE FOR ME?
BECAUSE THE HELL GOIN' DOWN OUTSIDE IS MOSTLY PSYCHO-LOGICAL -- AND GOTHAM NEEDS THE BAT.
THEN... I WOULD BE MASQUERADING AS THE REAL BATMAN... TRYING TO CONVINCE THEM... THAT I AM THE BATMAN..?
THAT'S THE IDEA, FRIEND... AT LEAST UNTIL BRUCE GETS BETTER.
WELL?
OPPOR-TUNITY ONLY KNOCKS ONCE.
YOU THINK I CAN DO IT?
WOULDN'T BE HERE OTHER-WISE.
I MEAN... YOU THINK I COULD BE... AS GOOD AS HIM?
NO ONE'S AS GOOD AS HIM.
YOU'RE WRONG -- I'LL BE BETTER.
BIG WORDS.
JUST DON'T TRY 'EM OUT ON BANE.

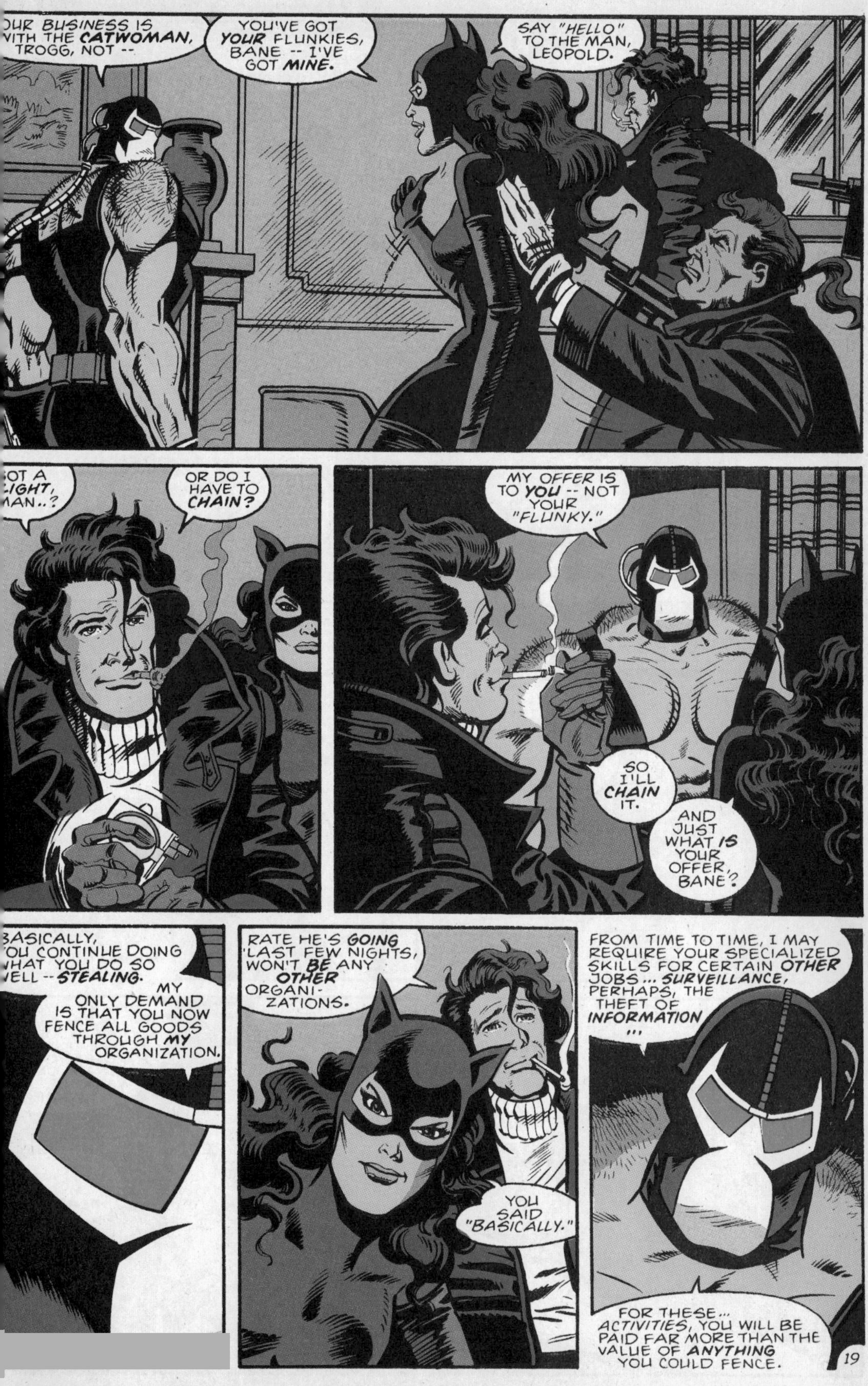
OUR BUSINESS IS WITH THE CATWOMAN, TROGG, NOT --
YOU'VE GOT YOUR FLUNKIES, BANE -- I'VE GOT MINE.
SAY "HELLO" TO THE MAN, LEOPOLD.
GOT A LIGHT, MAN..?
OR DO I HAVE TO CHAIN?
MY OFFER IS TO YOU -- NOT YOUR "FLUNKY."
SO I'LL CHAIN IT.
AND JUST WHAT IS YOUR OFFER, BANE?
BASICALLY, YOU CONTINUE DOING WHAT YOU DO SO WELL -- STEALING.
MY ONLY DEMAND IS THAT YOU NOW FENCE ALL GOODS THROUGH MY ORGANIZATION.
RATE HE'S GOING LAST FEW NIGHTS, WON'T BE ANY OTHER ORGANI-ZATIONS.
YOU SAID "BASICALLY."
FROM TIME TO TIME, I MAY REQUIRE YOUR SPECIALIZED SKILLS FOR CERTAIN OTHER JOBS... SURVEILLANCE, PERHAPS, THE THEFT OF INFORMATION...
FOR THESE... ACTIVITIES, YOU WILL BE PAID FAR MORE THAN THE VALUE OF ANYTHING YOU COULD FENCE.
19

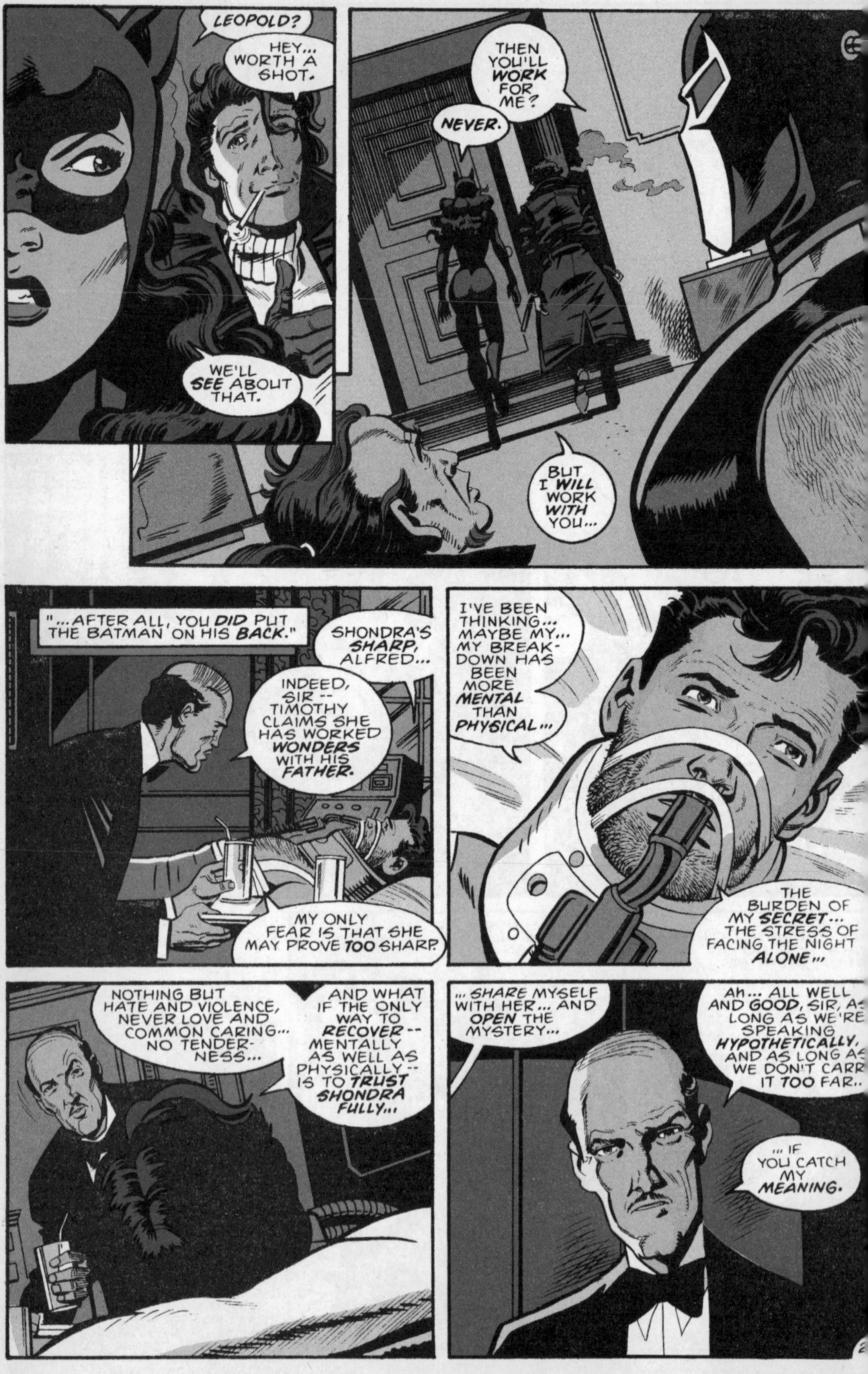
LEOPOLD?
HEY... WORTH A SHOT.
WE'LL SEE ABOUT THAT.
THEN YOU'LL WORK FOR ME?
NEVER.
BUT I WILL WORK WITH YOU...
"...AFTER ALL, YOU DID PUT THE BATMAN ON HIS BACK."
SHONDRA'S SHARP, ALFRED...
INDEED, SIR -- TIMOTHY CLAIMS SHE HAS WORKED WONDERS WITH HIS FATHER.
MY ONLY FEAR IS THAT SHE MAY PROVE TOO SHARP.
I'VE BEEN THINKING... MAYBE MY... MY BREAK-DOWN HAS BEEN MORE MENTAL THAN PHYSICAL...
THE BURDEN OF MY SECRET... THE STRESS OF FACING THE NIGHT ALONE...
NOTHING BUT HATE AND VIOLENCE, NEVER LOVE AND COMMON CARING... NO TENDER-NESS...
AND WHAT IF THE ONLY WAY TO RECOVER -- MENTALLY AS WELL AS PHYSICALLY -- IS TO TRUST SHONDRA FULLY...
...SHARE MYSELF WITH HER... AND OPEN THE MYSTERY...
Ah... ALL WELL AND GOOD, SIR, AS LONG AS WE'RE SPEAKING HYPOTHETICALLY, AND AS LONG AS WE DON'T CARR IT TOO FAR...
...IF YOU CATCH MY MEANING.

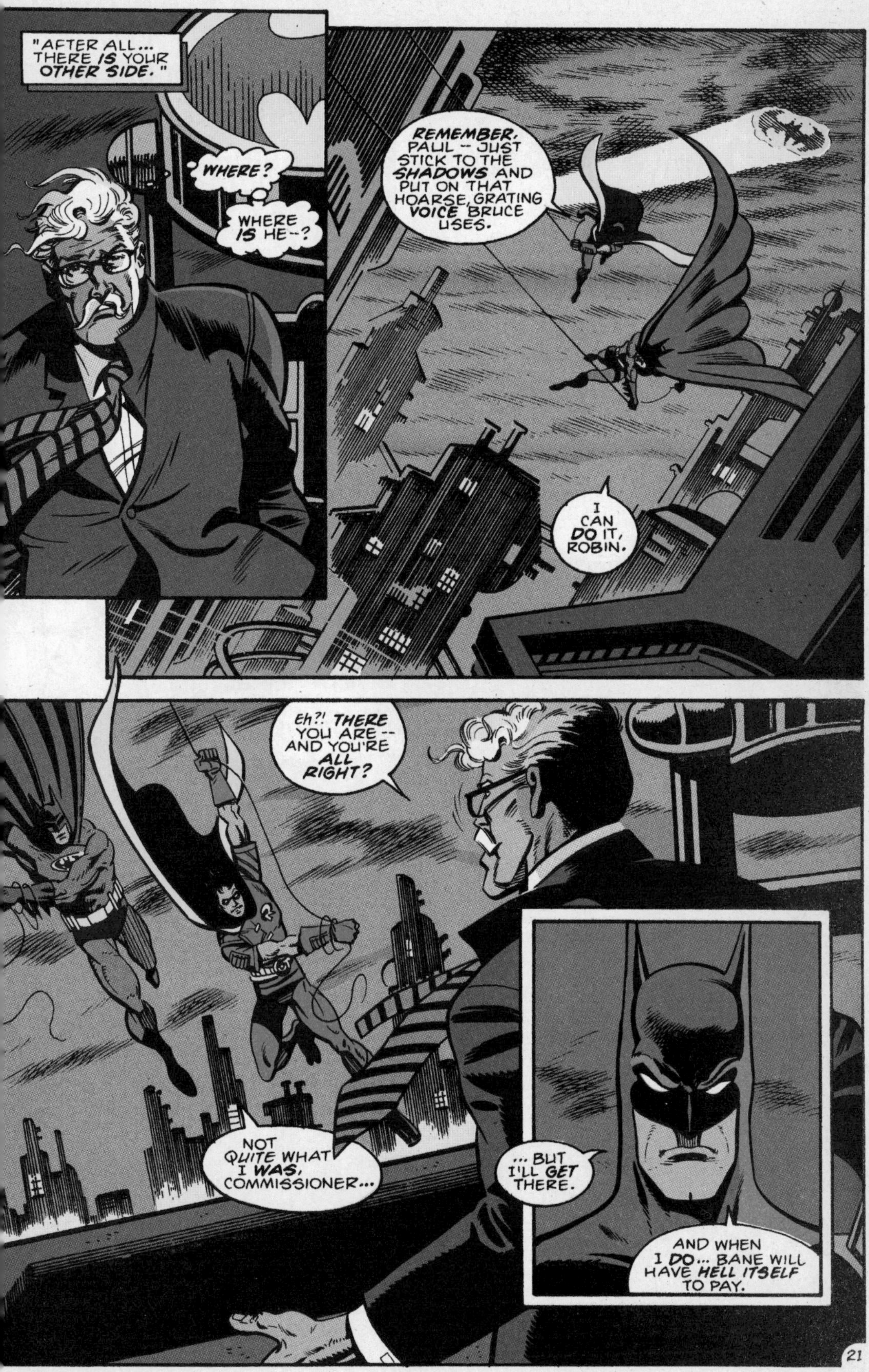
"AFTER ALL... THERE IS YOUR OTHER SIDE."
WHERE?
WHERE IS HE--?
REMEMBER, PAUL -- JUST STICK TO THE SHADOWS AND PUT ON THAT HOARSE, GRATING VOICE BRUCE USES.
I CAN DO IT, ROBIN.
Eh?! THERE YOU ARE -- AND YOU'RE ALL RIGHT?
NOT QUITE WHAT I WAS, COMMISSIONER...
...BUT I'LL GET THERE.
AND WHEN I DO... BANE WILL HAVE HELL ITSELF TO PAY.
21

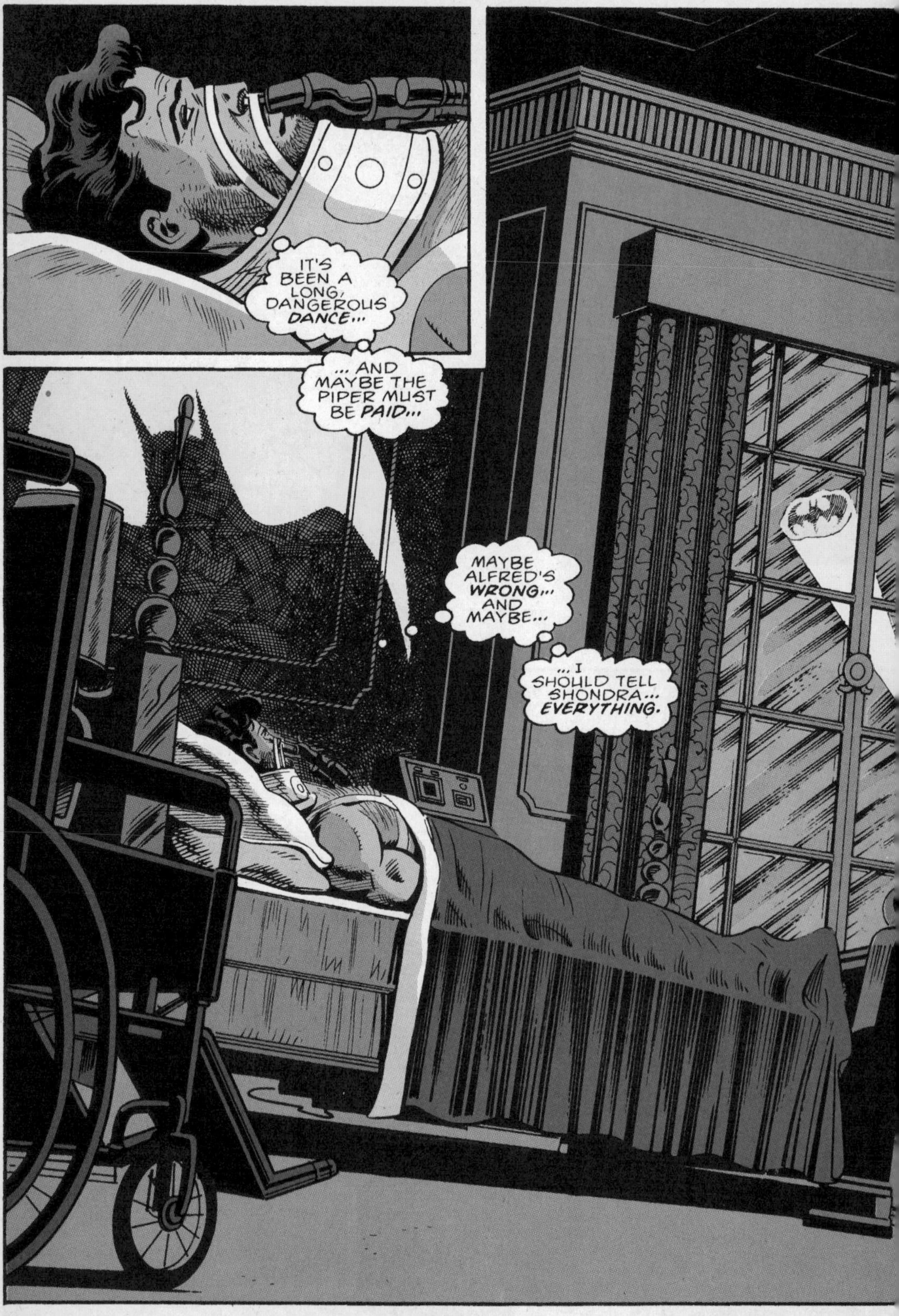
IT'S BEEN A LONG, DANGEROUS DANCE...
... AND MAYBE THE PIPER MUST BE PAID...
MAYBE ALFRED'S WRONG... AND MAYBE...
... I SHOULD TELL SHONDRA... EVERYTHING.

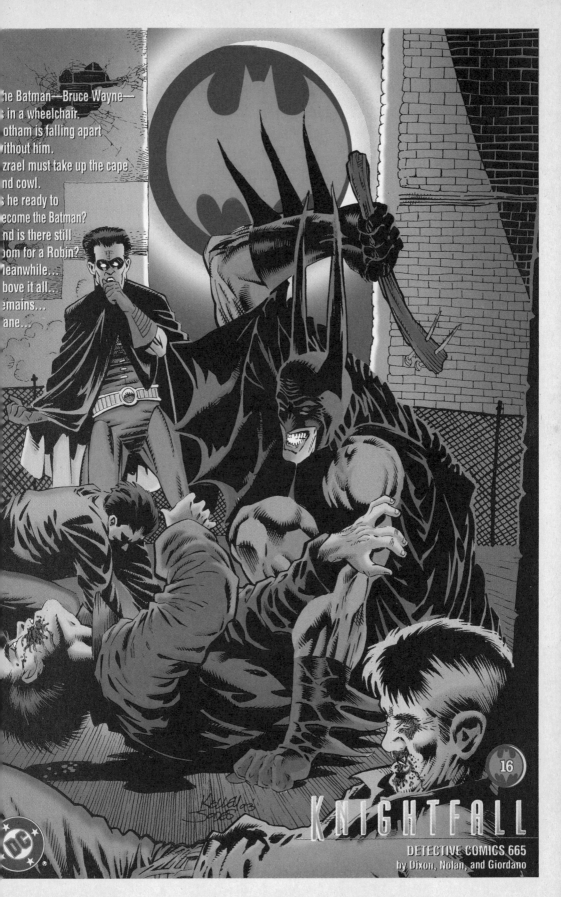

he Batman—Bruce Wayne—
s in a wheelchair.
otham is falling apart
ithout him.
zrael must take up the cape
nd cowl.
s he ready to
ecome the Batman?
nd is there still
om for a Robin?
Meanwhile…
bove it all…
emains…
ane…

16

KNIGHTFALL

DETECTIVE COMICS 665
by Dixon, Nolan, and Giordano

All titles, characters and related indicia are trademarks of DC Comics Inc. © 1993. All Rights Reserved.

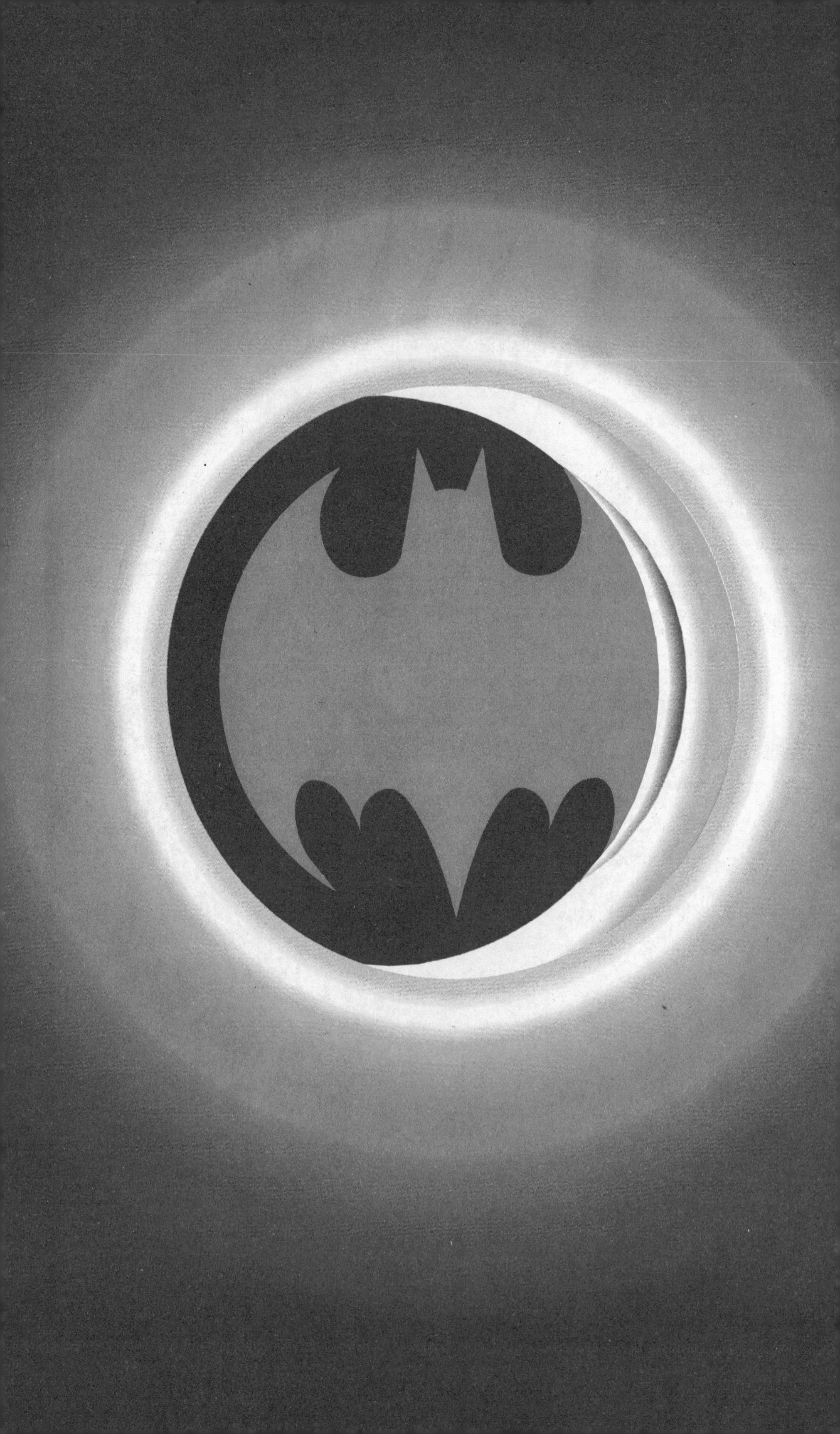

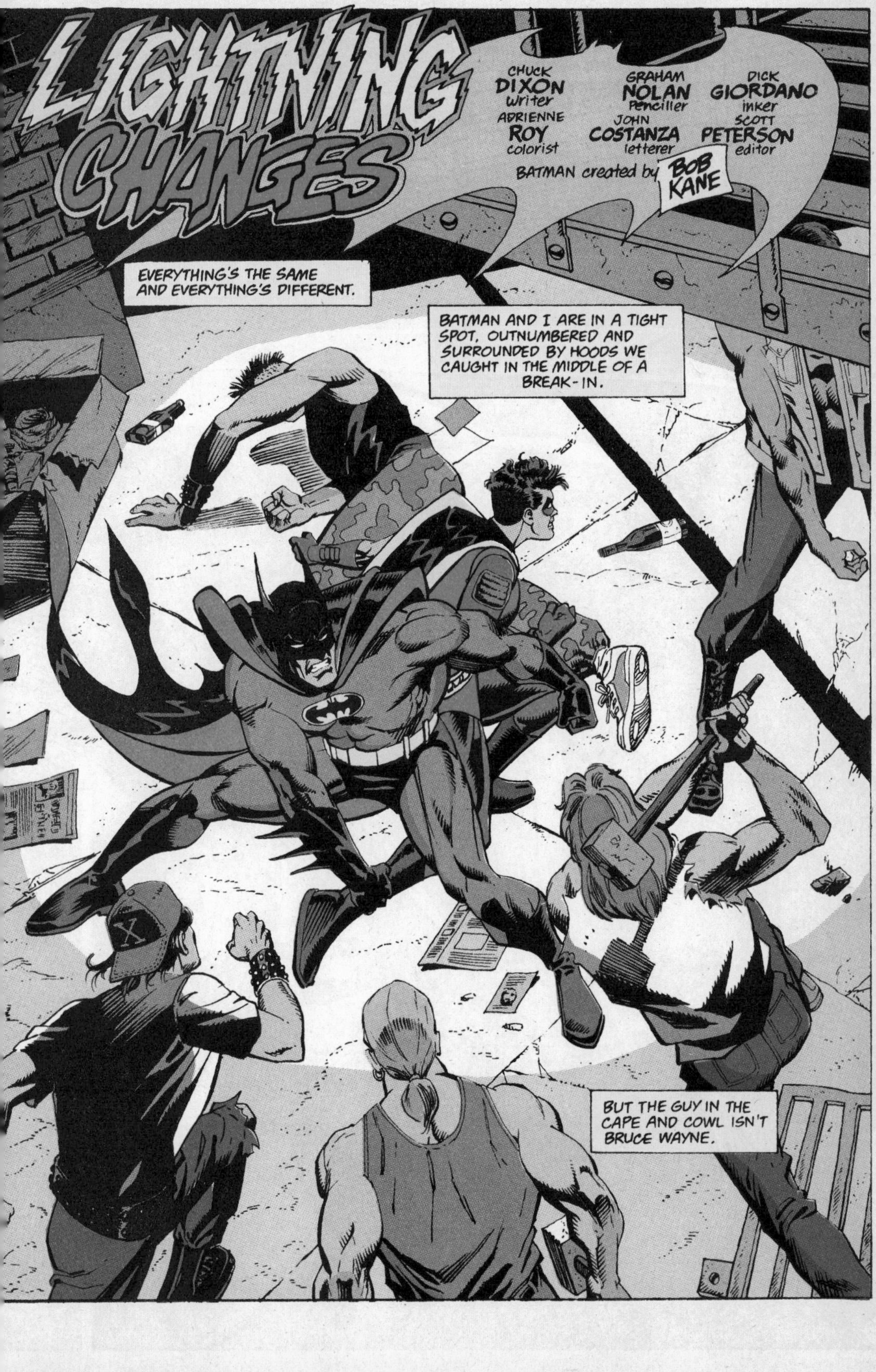
LIGHTNING CHANGES
CHUCK DIXON writer
GRAHAM NOLAN penciller
DICK GIORDANO inker
ADRIENNE ROY colorist
JOHN COSTANZA letterer
SCOTT PETERSON editor
BATMAN created by BOB KANE
EVERYTHING'S THE SAME AND EVERYTHING'S DIFFERENT.
BATMAN AND I ARE IN A TIGHT SPOT, OUTNUMBERED AND SURROUNDED BY HOODS WE CAUGHT IN THE MIDDLE OF A BREAK-IN.
BUT THE GUY IN THE CAPE AND COWL ISN'T BRUCE WAYNE.

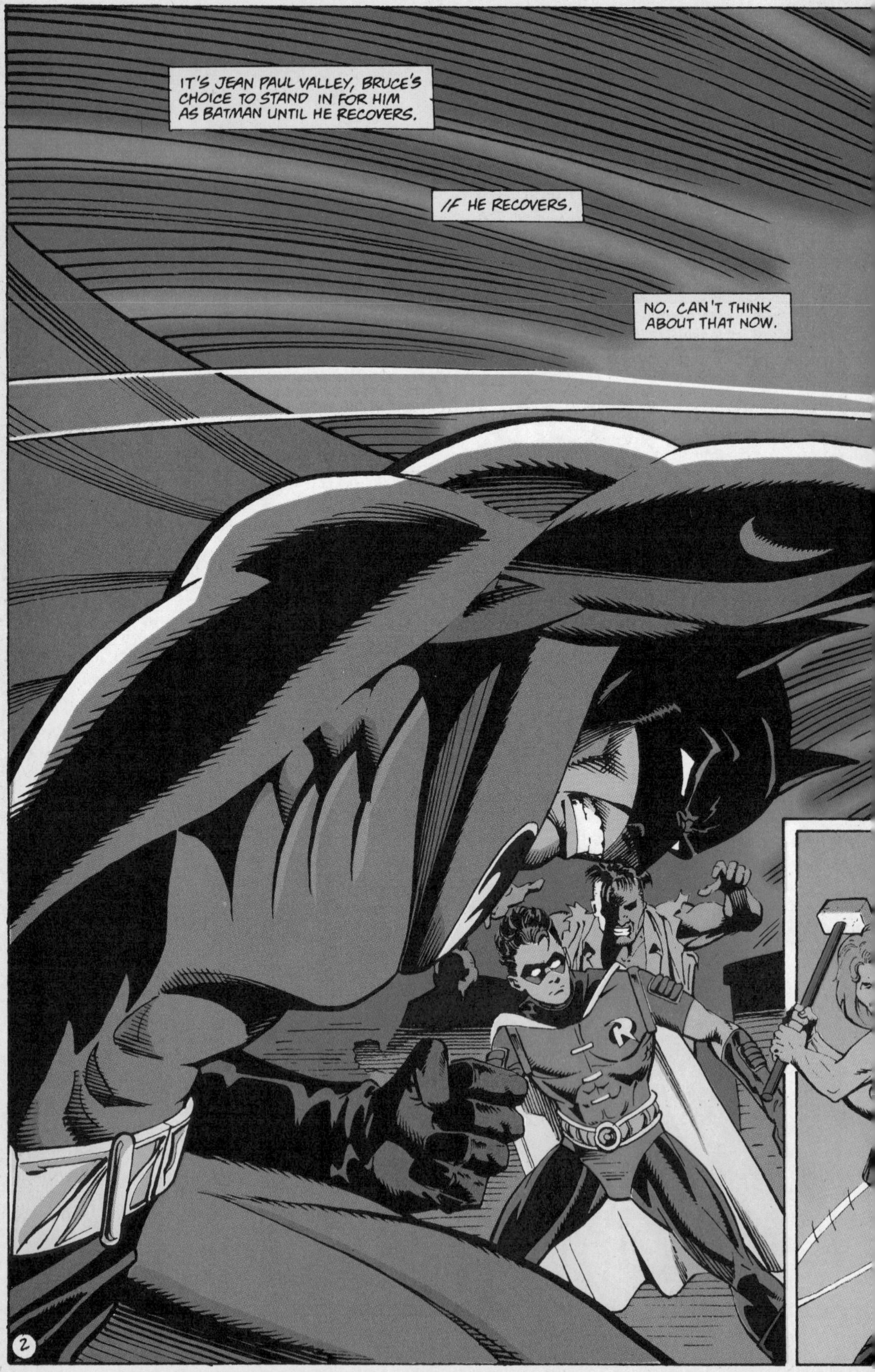

IT'S JEAN PAUL VALLEY, BRUCE'S CHOICE TO STAND IN FOR HIM AS BATMAN UNTIL HE RECOVERS.
IF HE RECOVERS.
NO. CAN'T THINK ABOUT THAT NOW.
2

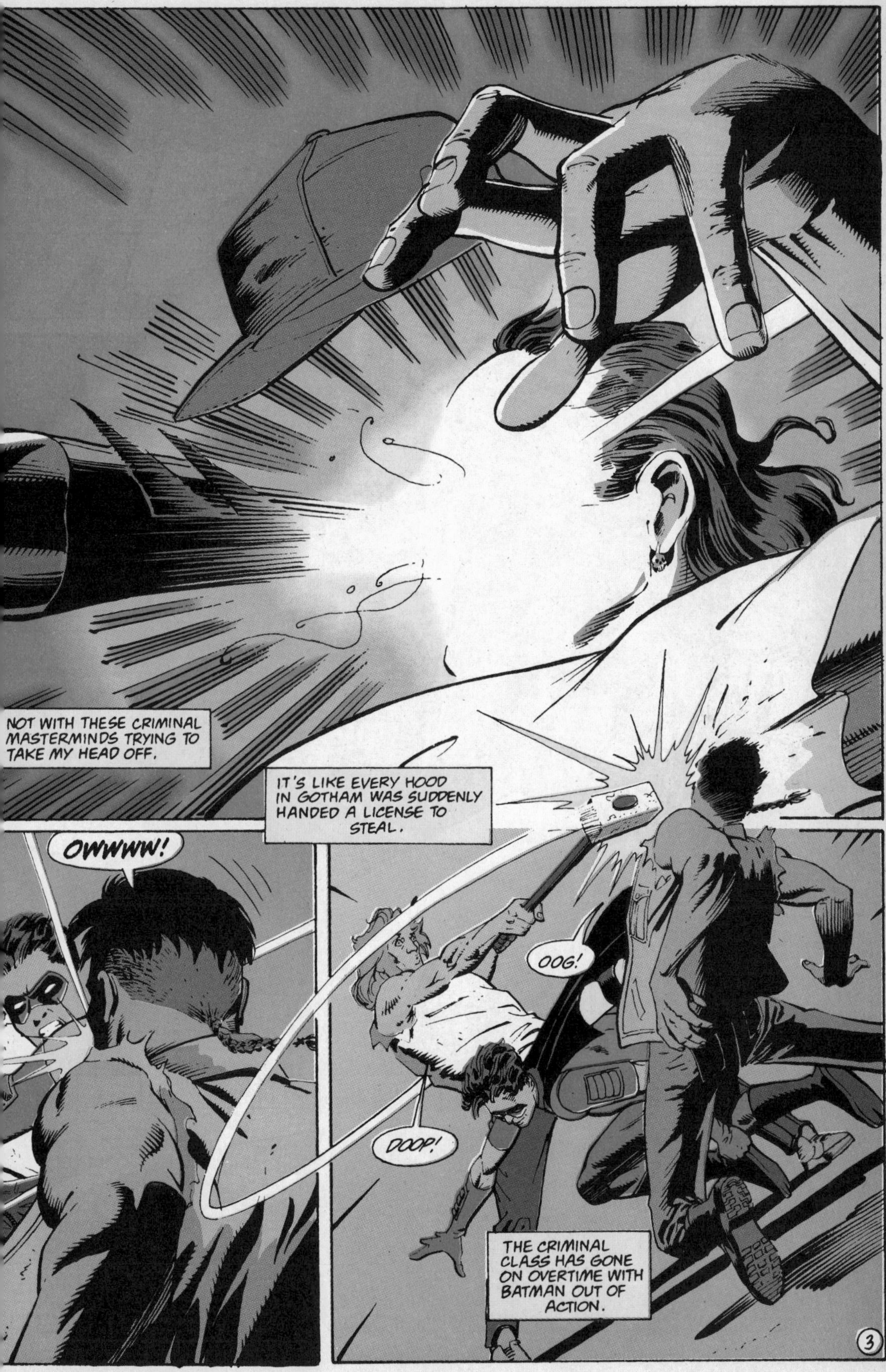
NOT WITH THESE CRIMINAL MASTERMINDS TRYING TO TAKE MY HEAD OFF.
IT'S LIKE EVERY HOOD IN GOTHAM WAS SUDDENLY HANDED A LICENSE TO STEAL.
OWWWW!
OOG!
DOOP!
THE CRIMINAL CLASS HAS GONE ON OVERTIME WITH BATMAN OUT OF ACTION.
3

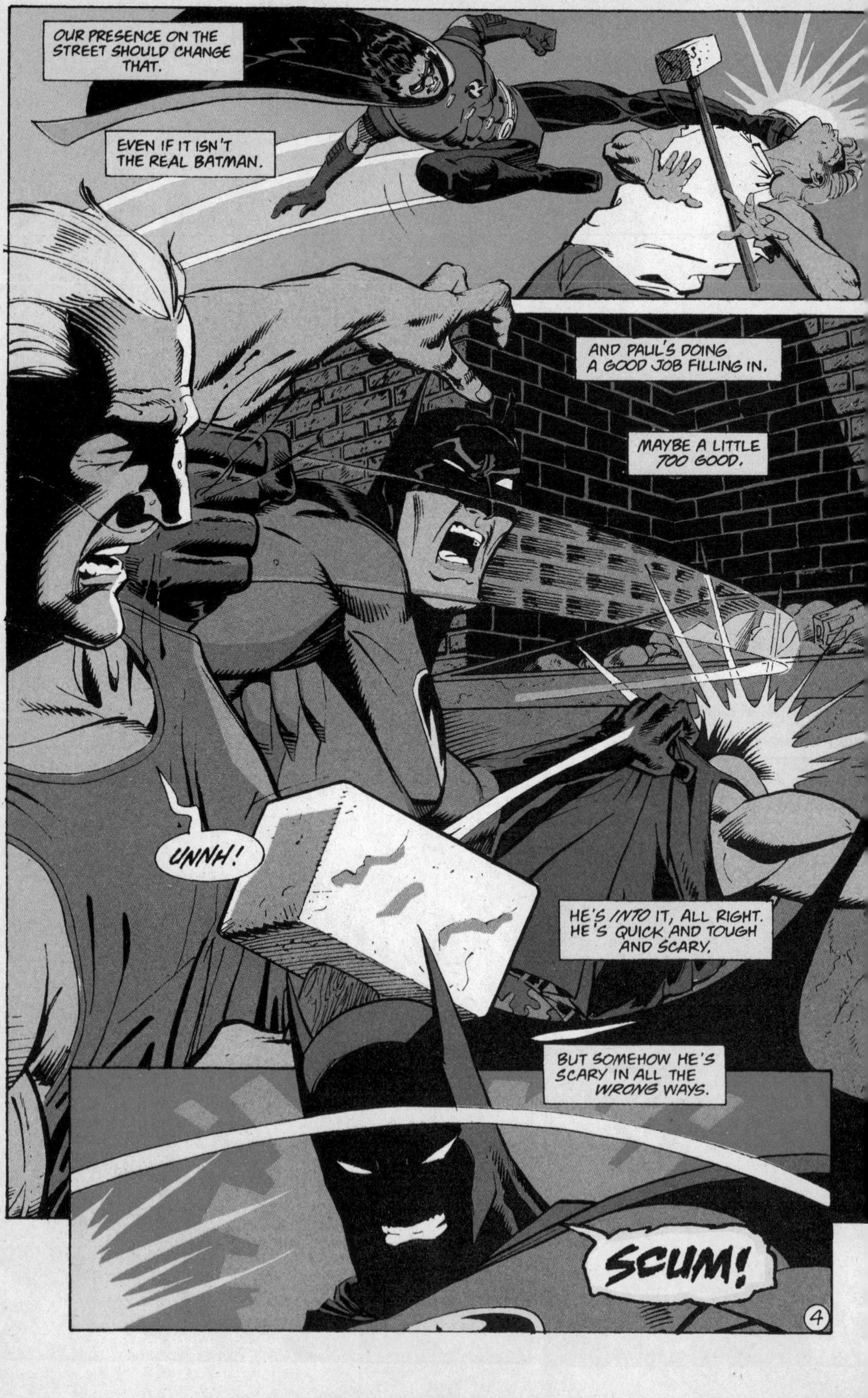
OUR PRESENCE ON THE STREET SHOULD CHANGE THAT.
EVEN IF IT ISN'T THE REAL BATMAN.
AND PAUL'S DOING A GOOD JOB FILLING IN.
MAYBE A LITTLE TOO GOOD.
UNNH!
HE'S INTO IT, ALL RIGHT. HE'S QUICK AND TOUGH AND SCARY.
BUT SOMEHOW HE'S SCARY IN ALL THE WRONG WAYS.
SCUM!
4

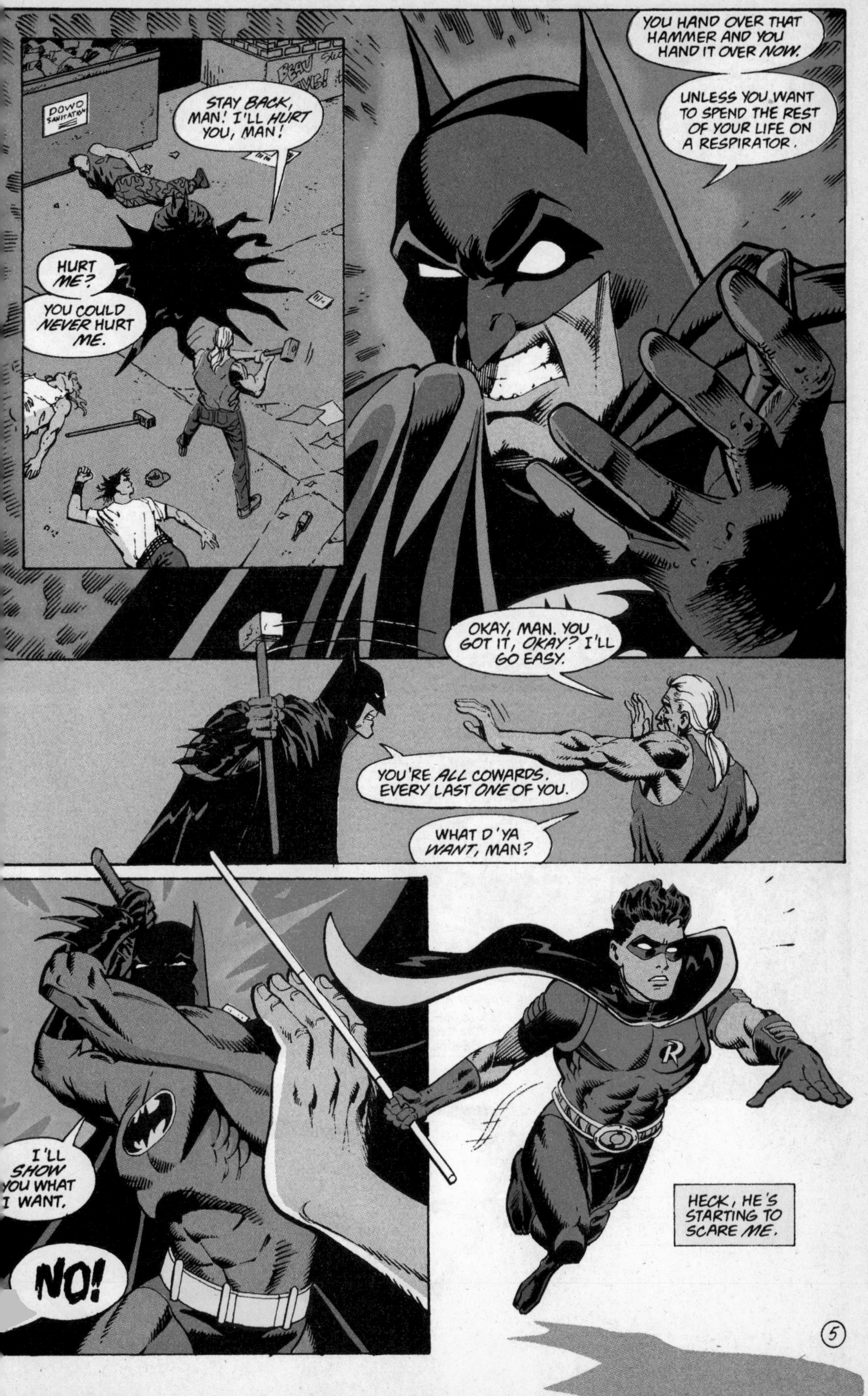
DOWO SANITATION
STAY BACK, MAN! I'LL HURT YOU, MAN!
HURT ME?
YOU COULD NEVER HURT ME.
YOU HAND OVER THAT HAMMER AND YOU HAND IT OVER NOW.
UNLESS YOU WANT TO SPEND THE REST OF YOUR LIFE ON A RESPIRATOR.
OKAY, MAN. YOU GOT IT, OKAY? I'LL GO EASY.
YOU'RE ALL COWARDS. EVERY LAST ONE OF YOU.
WHAT D'YA WANT, MAN?
I'LL SHOW YOU WHAT I WANT.
NO!
HECK, HE'S STARTING TO SCARE ME.
5

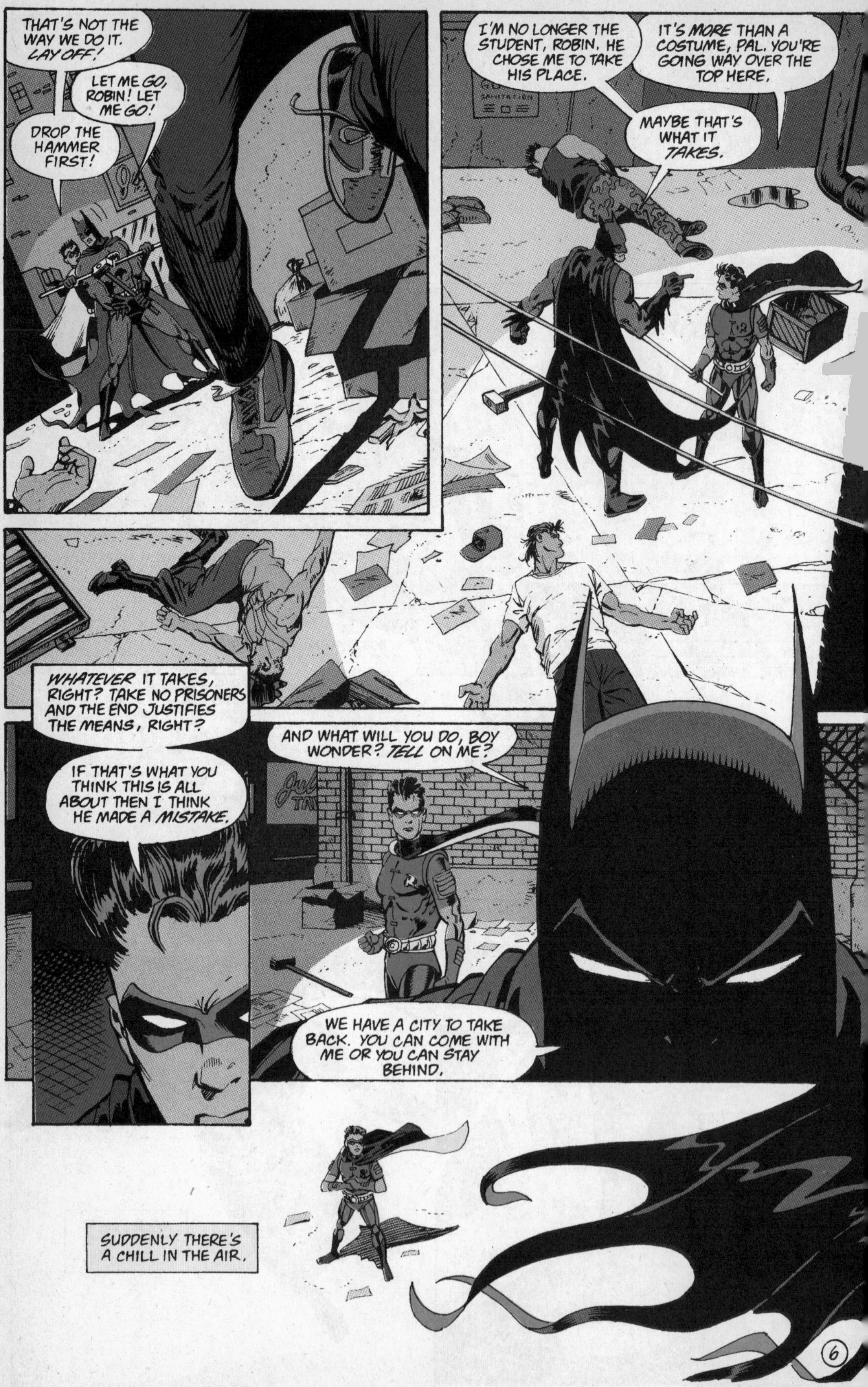
THAT'S NOT THE WAY WE DO IT. LAY OFF!
LET ME GO, ROBIN! LET ME GO!
DROP THE HAMMER FIRST!
I'M NO LONGER THE STUDENT, ROBIN. HE CHOSE ME TO TAKE HIS PLACE.
IT'S MORE THAN A COSTUME, PAL. YOU'RE GOING WAY OVER THE TOP HERE.
MAYBE THAT'S WHAT IT TAKES.
WHATEVER IT TAKES, RIGHT? TAKE NO PRISONERS AND THE END JUSTIFIES THE MEANS, RIGHT?
IF THAT'S WHAT YOU THINK THIS IS ALL ABOUT THEN I THINK HE MADE A MISTAKE.
AND WHAT WILL YOU DO, BOY WONDER? TELL ON ME?
WE HAVE A CITY TO TAKE BACK. YOU CAN COME WITH ME OR YOU CAN STAY BEHIND.
SUDDENLY THERE'S A CHILL IN THE AIR.
6

AND THE NIGHT GETS A LITTLE DARKER.

AND COULD YOU TELL ME WHERE SHE'S GONE?

WELL, I AM A PATIENT BUT IT'S MORE IN THE LINE OF A PERSONAL MATTER.

IF YOU COULD JUST TELL ME WHERE DR. KINSOLVING IS. OR AT LEAST TELL HER TO CONTACT BRUCE WAYNE AT HER EARLIEST--

OH, MR. WAYNE. THE DOCTOR HAS LEFT SPECIFIC INSTRUCTIONS THAT YOU BE TOLD WHERE TO REACH HER AT ANY TIME.

SHE'S MAKING A HOUSE CALL AT THE MOMENT...

...OVER IN BRISTOL. THE PATIENT IS A MR. DRAKE.

JACK DRAKE, TIM'S FATHER. THAT'S NEXT DOOR.

THANK YOU VERY MUCH, HAVE A GOOD EVENING.

JACK HAS BEEN A PATIENT OF SHONDRA'S SINCE HE REVIVED FROM HIS COMA. I COULD GET ALFRED TO DRIVE ME OVER.

BUT THIS IS THE FIRST DECENT SLEEP HE'S HAD IN DAYS.

LET HIM BE.

⑦

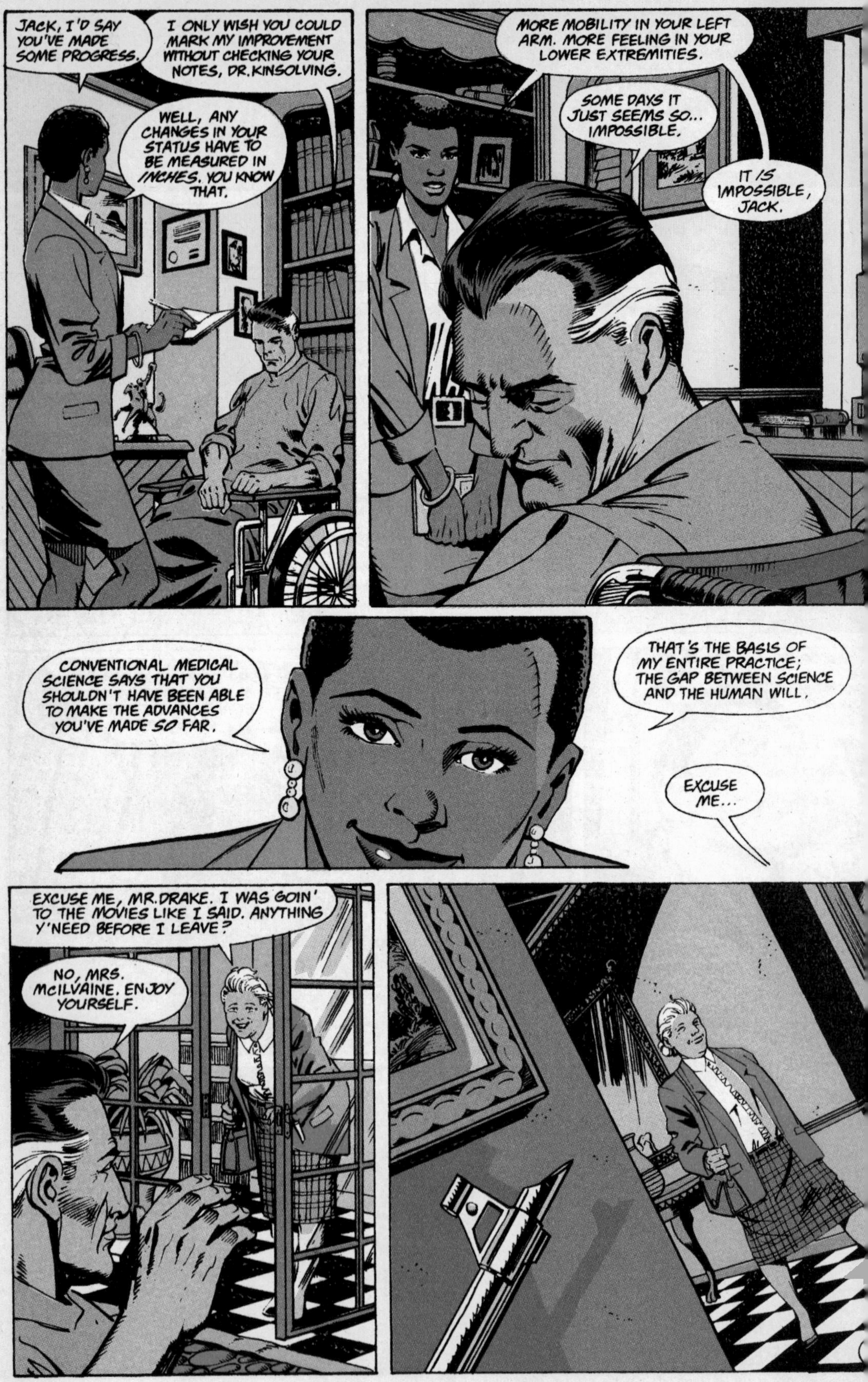
JACK, I'D SAY YOU'VE MADE SOME PROGRESS.
I ONLY WISH YOU COULD MARK MY IMPROVEMENT WITHOUT CHECKING YOUR NOTES, DR. KINSOLVING.
WELL, ANY CHANGES IN YOUR STATUS HAVE TO BE MEASURED IN INCHES. YOU KNOW THAT.
MORE MOBILITY IN YOUR LEFT ARM. MORE FEELING IN YOUR LOWER EXTREMITIES.
SOME DAYS IT JUST SEEMS SO... IMPOSSIBLE.
IT IS IMPOSSIBLE, JACK.
CONVENTIONAL MEDICAL SCIENCE SAYS THAT YOU SHOULDN'T HAVE BEEN ABLE TO MAKE THE ADVANCES YOU'VE MADE SO FAR.
THAT'S THE BASIS OF MY ENTIRE PRACTICE; THE GAP BETWEEN SCIENCE AND THE HUMAN WILL.
EXCUSE ME...
EXCUSE ME, MR. DRAKE. I WAS GOIN' TO THE MOVIES LIKE I SAID. ANYTHING Y'NEED BEFORE I LEAVE?
NO, MRS. MCILVAINE. ENJOY YOURSELF.

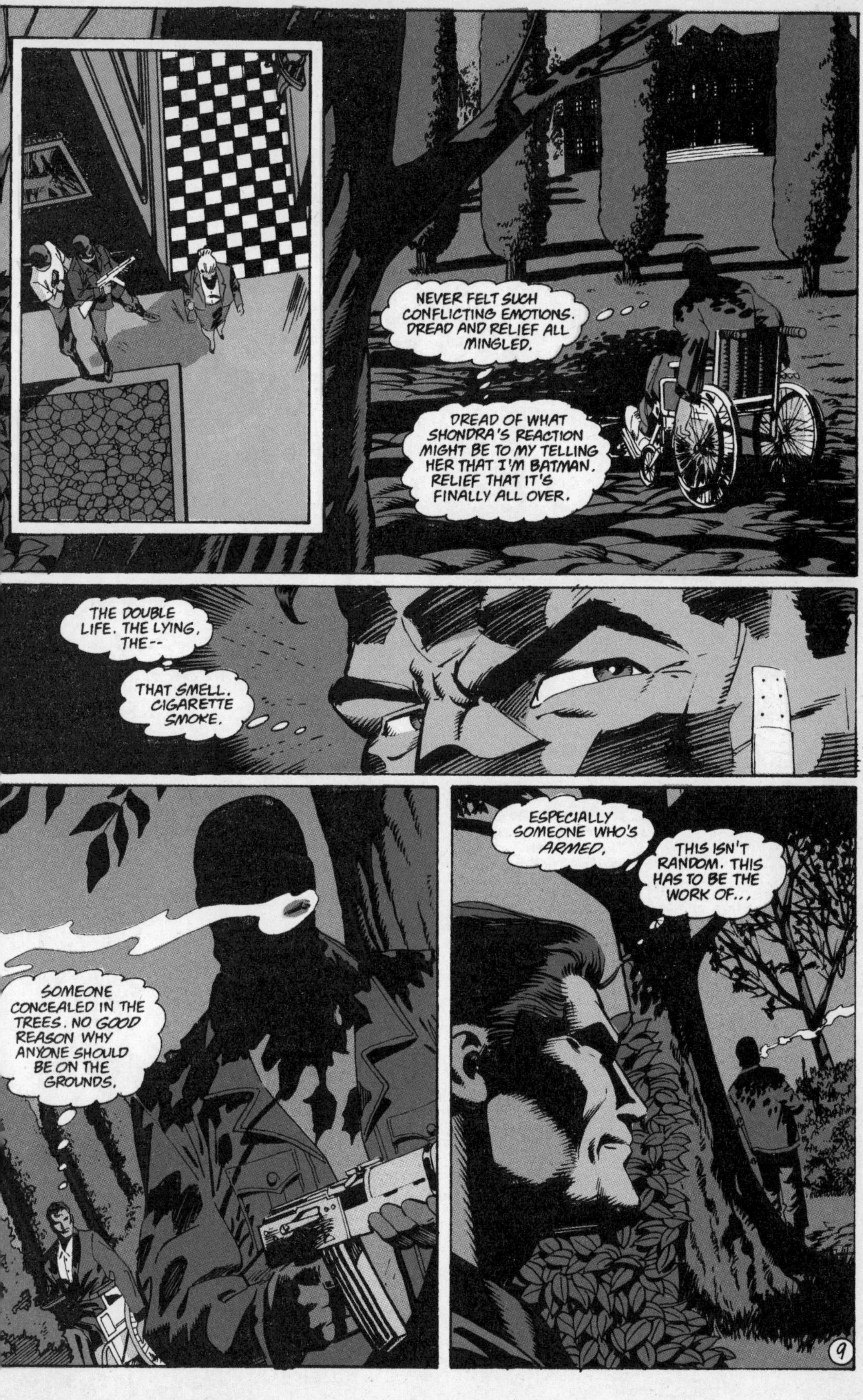

NEVER FELT SUCH CONFLICTING EMOTIONS. DREAD AND RELIEF ALL MINGLED.
DREAD OF WHAT SHONDRA'S REACTION MIGHT BE TO MY TELLING HER THAT I'M BATMAN. RELIEF THAT IT'S FINALLY ALL OVER.
THE DOUBLE LIFE. THE LYING, THE--
THAT SMELL. CIGARETTE SMOKE.
SOMEONE CONCEALED IN THE TREES. NO *GOOD* REASON WHY ANYONE SHOULD BE ON THE GROUNDS.
ESPECIALLY SOMEONE WHO'S *ARMED*.
THIS ISN'T RANDOM. THIS HAS TO BE THE WORK OF...
9

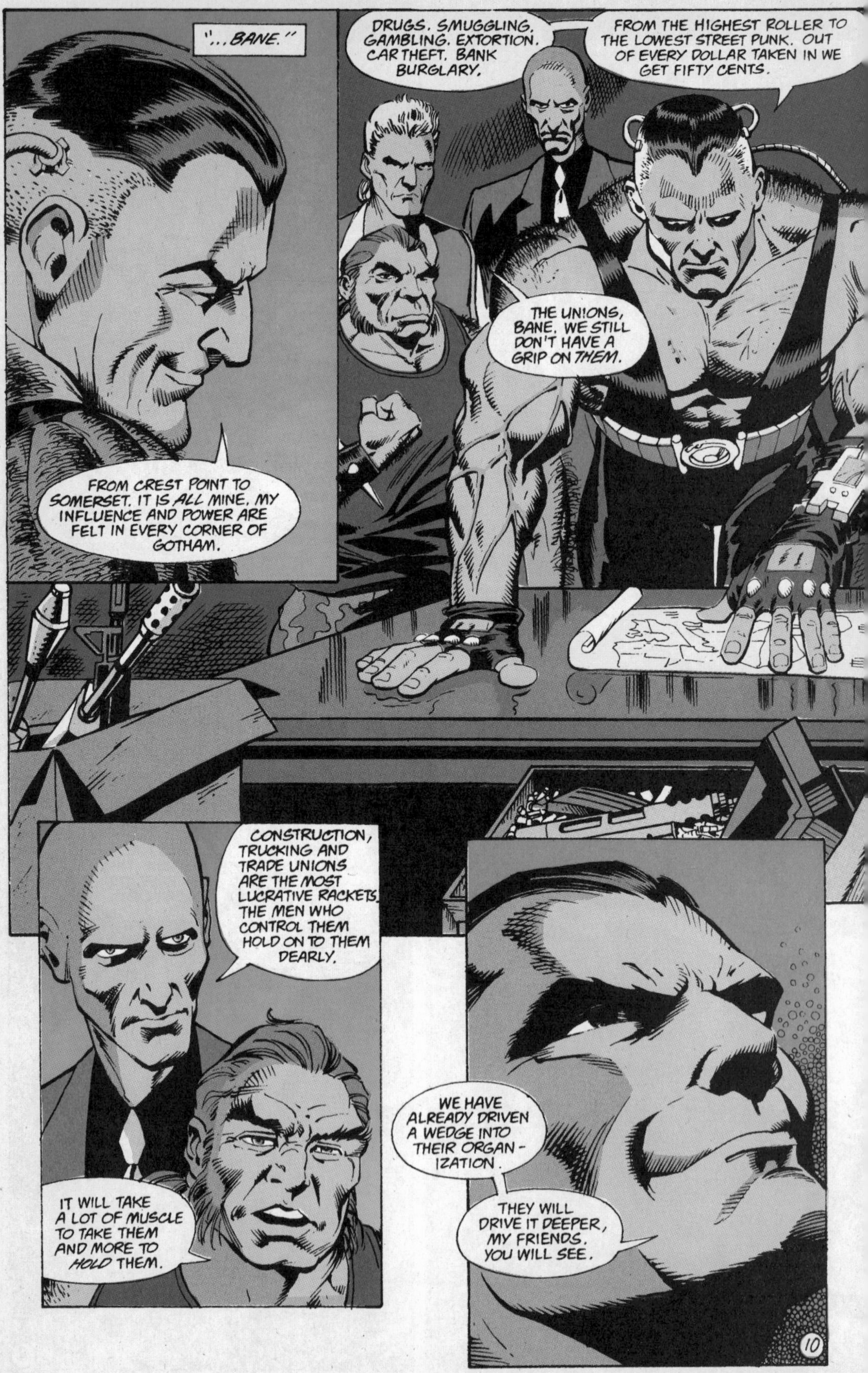

"...BANE."
FROM CREST POINT TO SOMERSET. IT IS ALL MINE. MY INFLUENCE AND POWER ARE FELT IN EVERY CORNER OF GOTHAM.
DRUGS. SMUGGLING. GAMBLING. EXTORTION. CAR THEFT. BANK BURGLARY.
FROM THE HIGHEST ROLLER TO THE LOWEST STREET PUNK. OUT OF EVERY DOLLAR TAKEN IN WE GET FIFTY CENTS.
THE UNIONS, BANE. WE STILL DON'T HAVE A GRIP ON THEM.
CONSTRUCTION, TRUCKING AND TRADE UNIONS ARE THE MOST LUCRATIVE RACKETS. THE MEN WHO CONTROL THEM HOLD ON TO THEM DEARLY.
IT WILL TAKE A LOT OF MUSCLE TO TAKE THEM AND MORE TO HOLD THEM.
WE HAVE ALREADY DRIVEN A WEDGE INTO THEIR ORGAN - IZATION.
THEY WILL DRIVE IT DEEPER, MY FRIENDS. YOU WILL SEE.
10

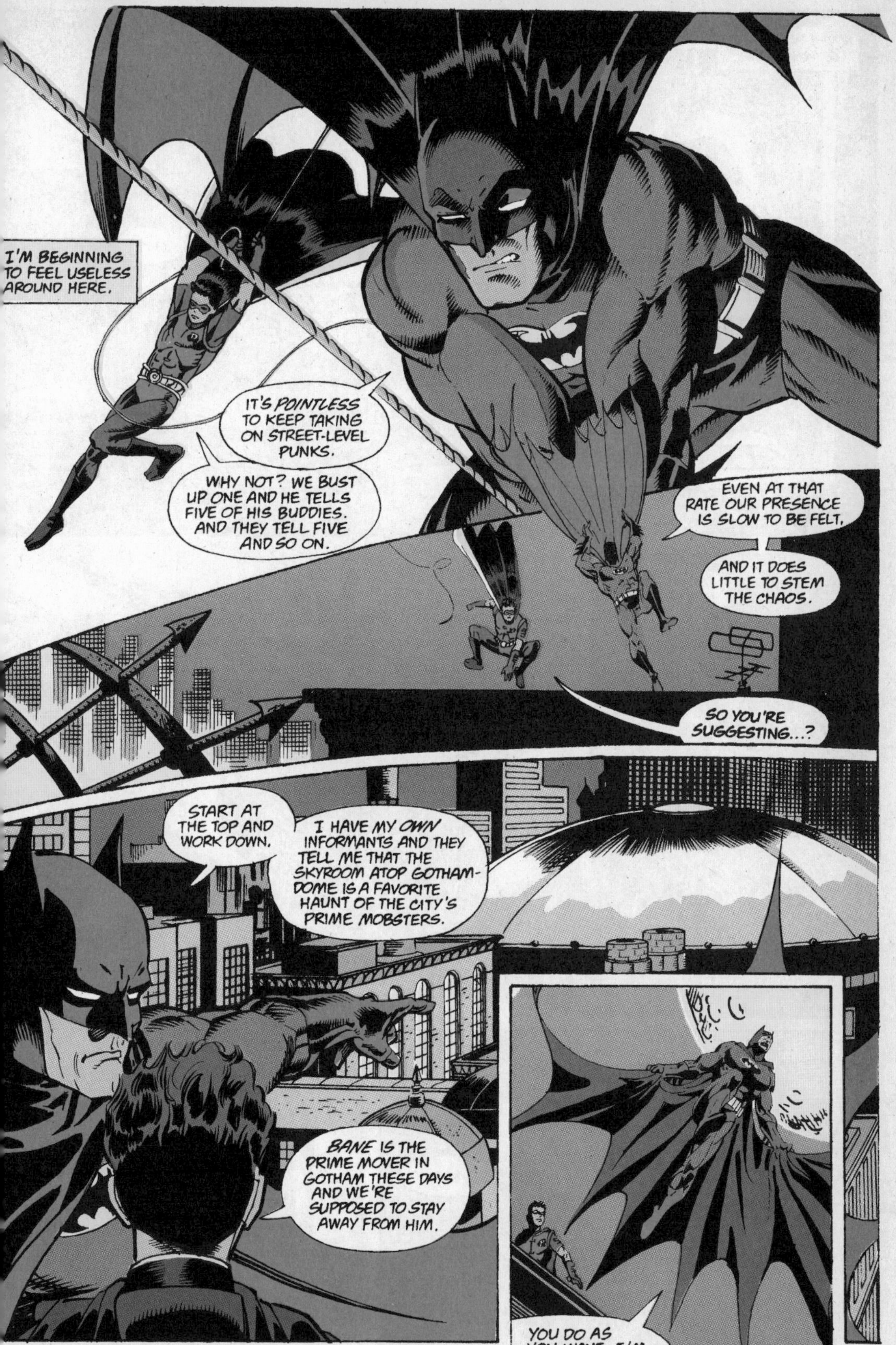
I'M BEGINNING TO FEEL USELESS AROUND HERE.
IT'S POINTLESS TO KEEP TAKING ON STREET-LEVEL PUNKS.
WHY NOT? WE BUST UP ONE AND HE TELLS FIVE OF HIS BUDDIES. AND THEY TELL FIVE AND SO ON.
EVEN AT THAT RATE OUR PRESENCE IS SLOW TO BE FELT.
AND IT DOES LITTLE TO STEM THE CHAOS.
SO YOU'RE SUGGESTING...?
START AT THE TOP AND WORK DOWN.
I HAVE MY OWN INFORMANTS AND THEY TELL ME THAT THE SKYROOM ATOP GOTHAM-DOME IS A FAVORITE HAUNT OF THE CITY'S PRIME MOBSTERS.
BANE IS THE PRIME MOVER IN GOTHAM THESE DAYS AND WE'RE SUPPOSED TO STAY AWAY FROM HIM.
YOU DO AS YOU WANT. I'M GOING TO THE TOP OF THE DOME.
11

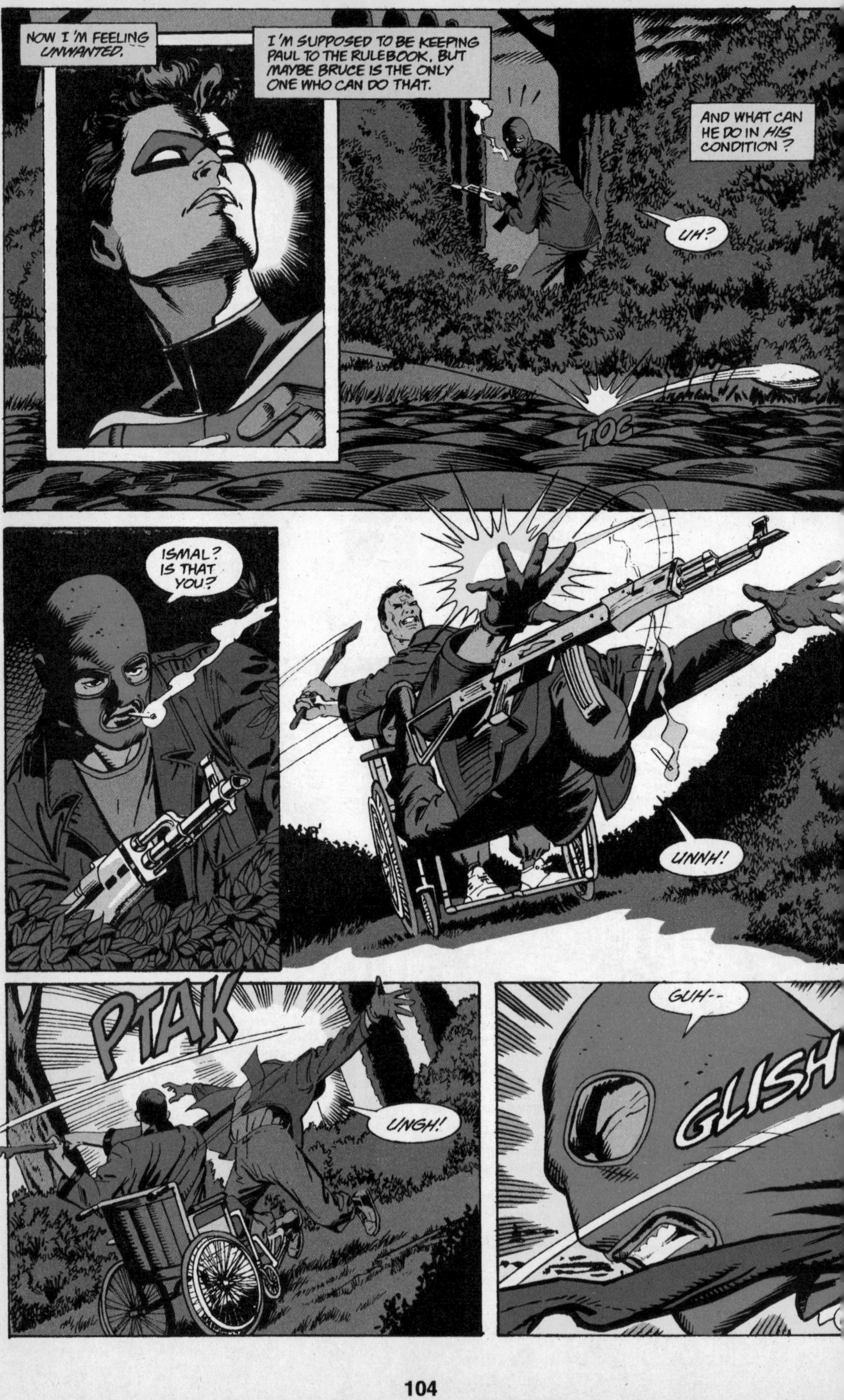
NOW I'M FEELING UNWANTED.
I'M SUPPOSED TO BE KEEPING PAUL TO THE RULEBOOK. BUT MAYBE BRUCE IS THE ONLY ONE WHO CAN DO THAT.
AND WHAT CAN HE DO IN HIS CONDITION?
UH?
TOC
ISMAL? IS THAT YOU?
UNNH!
PTAK
UNGH!
GUH--
GLISH

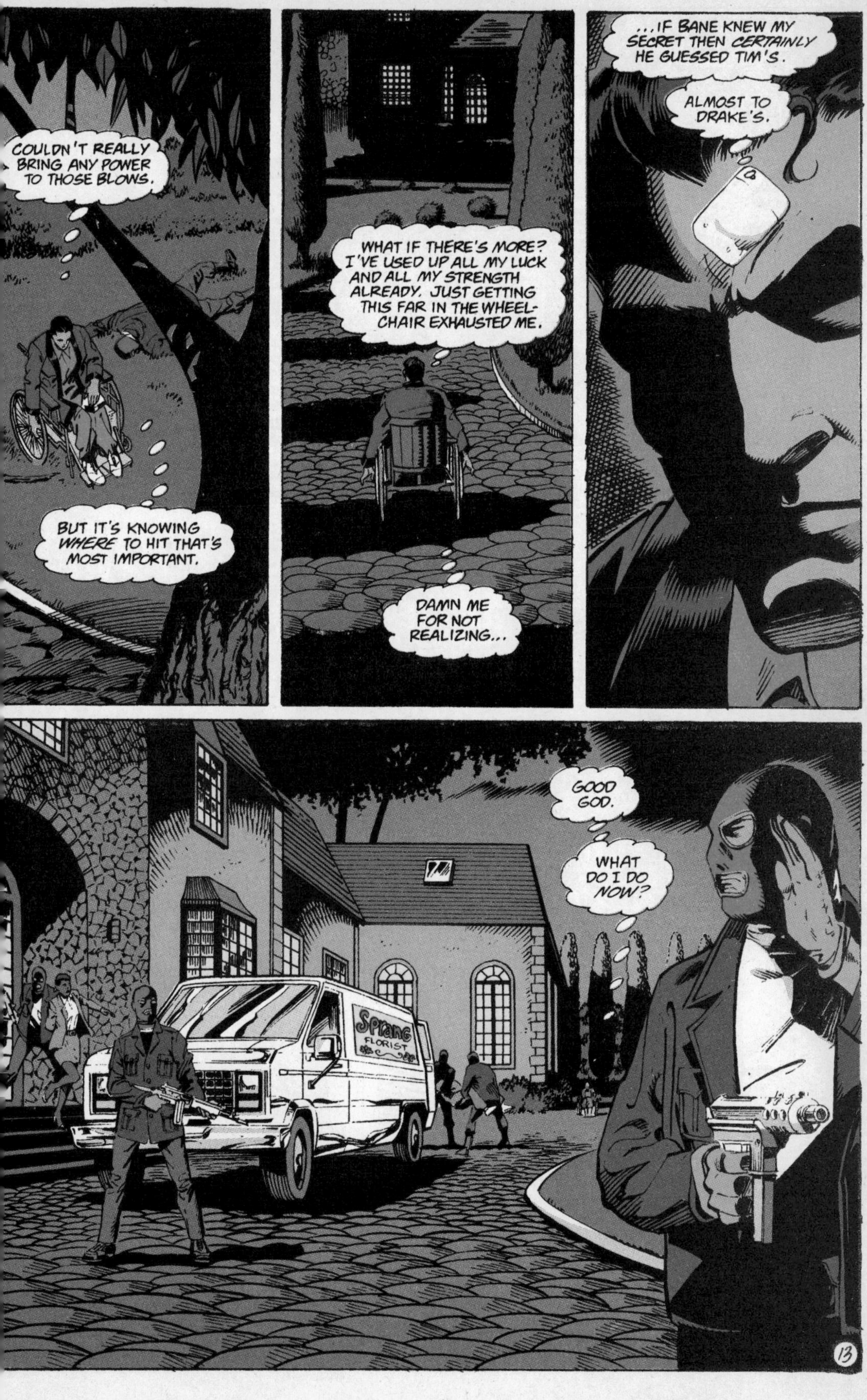
COULDN'T REALLY BRING ANY POWER TO THOSE BLOWS.
BUT IT'S KNOWING *WHERE* TO HIT THAT'S MOST IMPORTANT.
WHAT IF THERE'S *MORE*? I'VE USED UP ALL MY LUCK AND ALL MY STRENGTH ALREADY. JUST GETTING THIS FAR IN THE WHEEL-CHAIR EXHAUSTED ME.
DAMN ME FOR NOT REALIZING...
...IF BANE KNEW MY SECRET THEN *CERTAINLY* HE GUESSED TIM'S.
ALMOST TO DRAKE'S.
Sprang FLORIST
GOOD GOD.
WHAT DO I DO *NOW*?
13

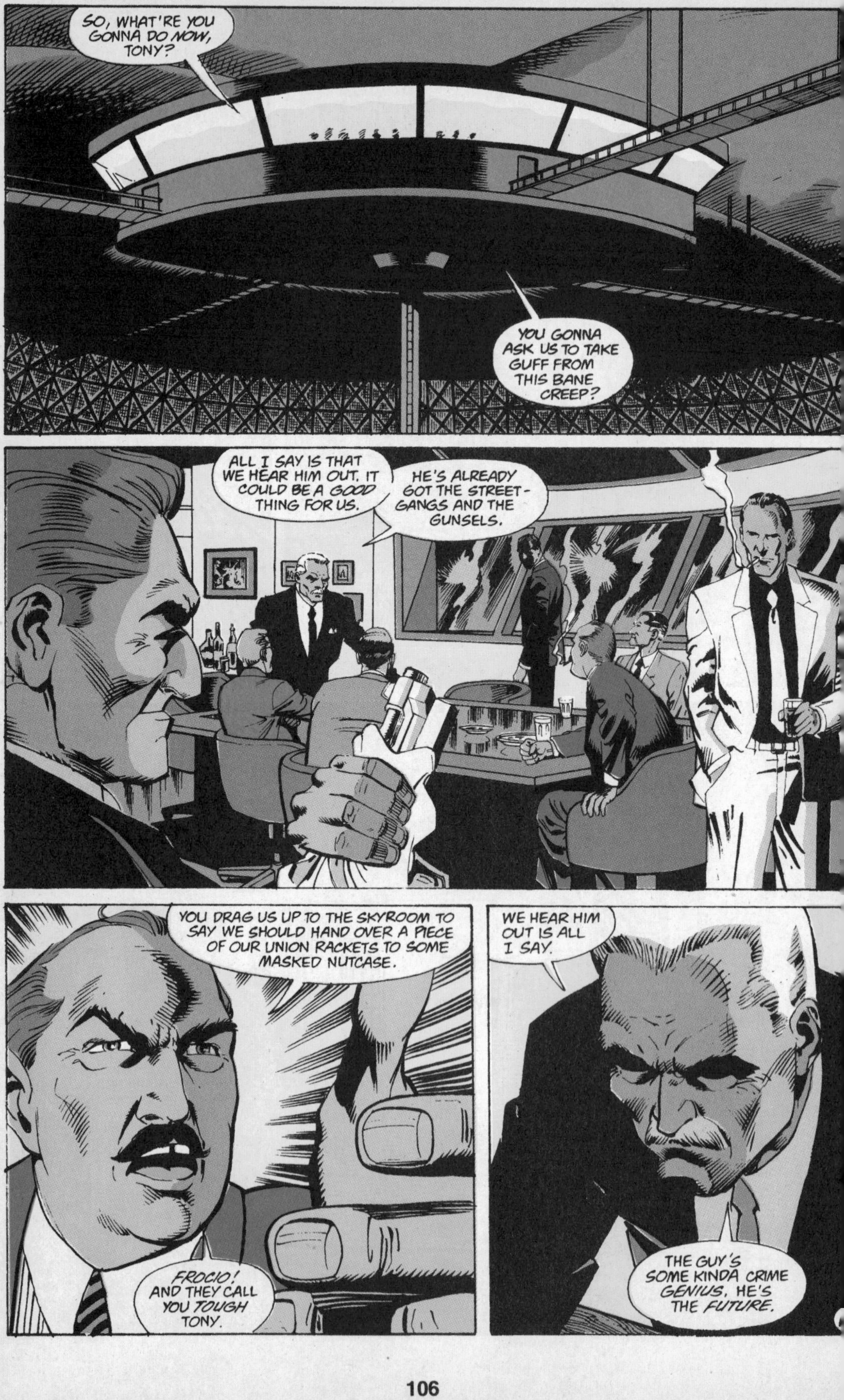
SO, WHAT'RE YOU GONNA DO NOW, TONY?
YOU GONNA ASK US TO TAKE GUFF FROM THIS BANE CREEP?
ALL I SAY IS THAT WE HEAR HIM OUT. IT COULD BE A GOOD THING FOR US.
HE'S ALREADY GOT THE STREET-GANGS AND THE GUNSELS.
YOU DRAG US UP TO THE SKYROOM TO SAY WE SHOULD HAND OVER A PIECE OF OUR UNION RACKETS TO SOME MASKED NUTCASE.
FROCIO! AND THEY CALL YOU TOUGH TONY.
WE HEAR HIM OUT IS ALL I SAY.
THE GUY'S SOME KINDA CRIME GENIUS. HE'S THE FUTURE.

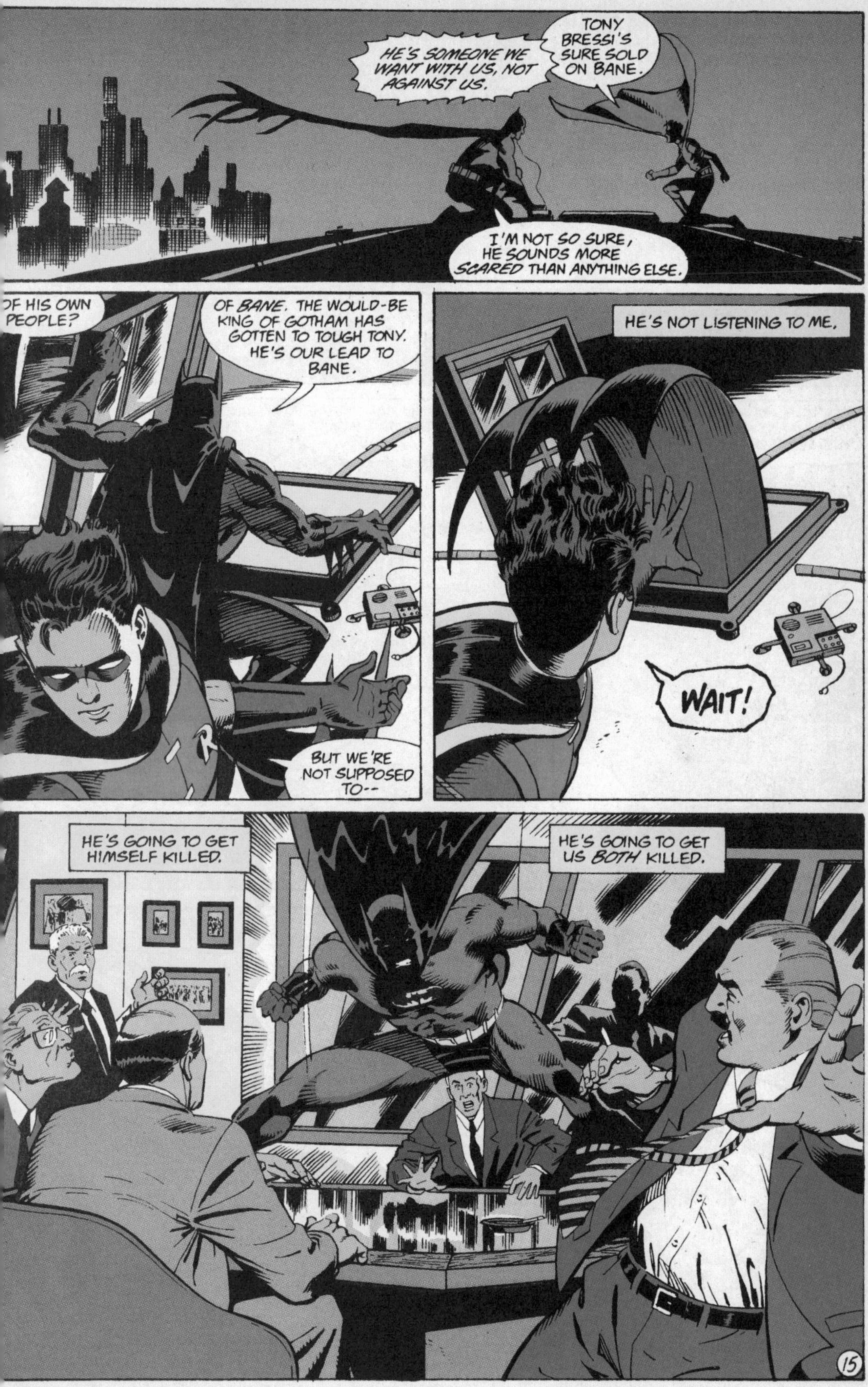
TONY BRESSI'S SURE SOLD ON BANE.
HE'S SOMEONE WE WANT WITH US, NOT AGAINST US.
I'M NOT SO SURE, HE SOUNDS MORE SCARED THAN ANYTHING ELSE.
OF HIS OWN PEOPLE?
OF BANE. THE WOULD-BE KING OF GOTHAM HAS GOTTEN TO TOUGH TONY. HE'S OUR LEAD TO BANE.
BUT WE'RE NOT SUPPOSED TO--
HE'S NOT LISTENING TO ME.
WAIT!
HE'S GOING TO GET HIMSELF KILLED.
HE'S GOING TO GET US BOTH KILLED.
15

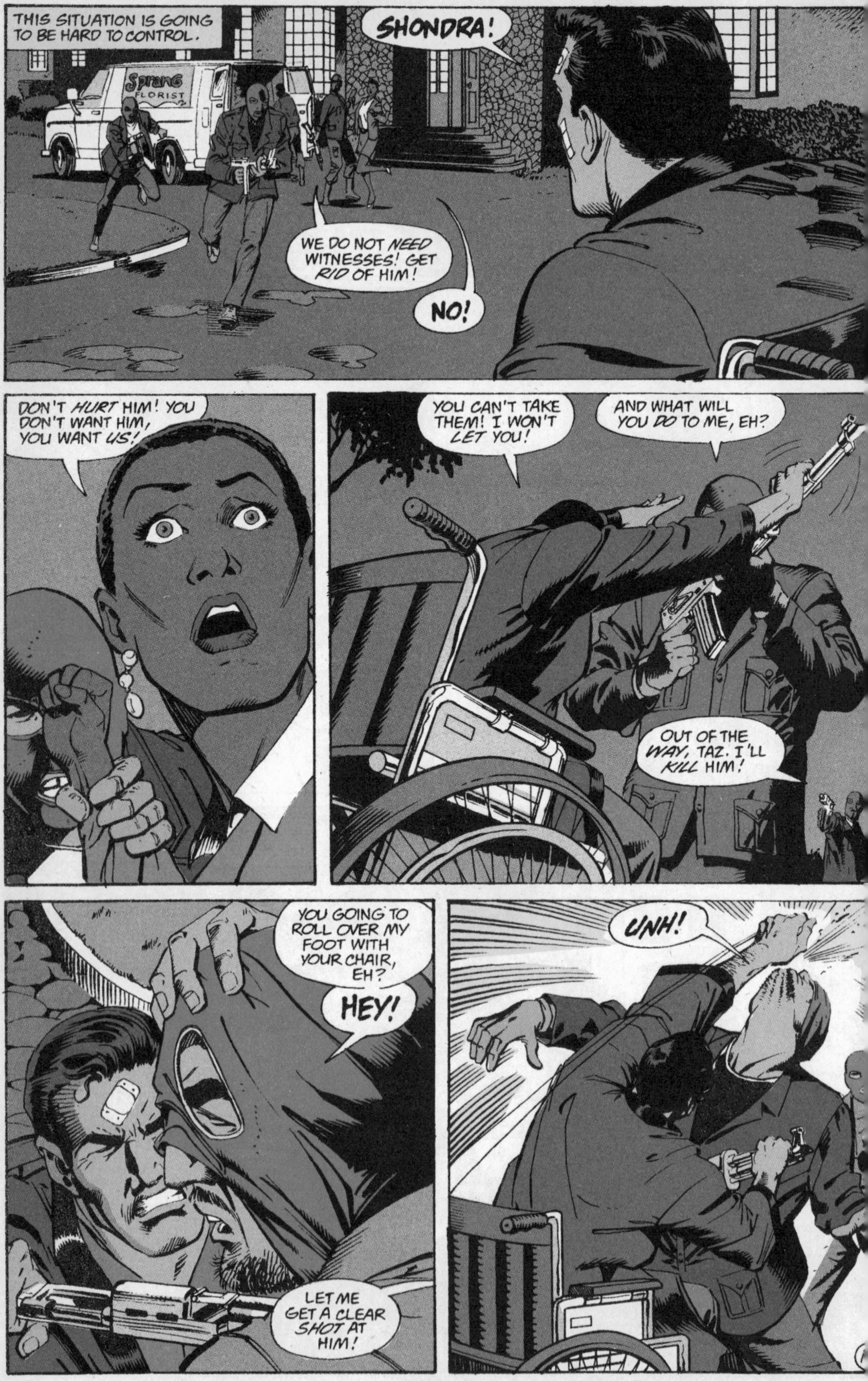
THIS SITUATION IS GOING TO BE HARD TO CONTROL.
SHONDRA!
SPRANG FLORIST
WE DO NOT NEED WITNESSES! GET RID OF HIM!
NO!
DON'T HURT HIM! YOU DON'T WANT HIM, YOU WANT US!
YOU CAN'T TAKE THEM! I WON'T LET YOU!
AND WHAT WILL YOU DO TO ME, EH?
OUT OF THE WAY, TAZ. I'LL KILL HIM!
YOU GOING TO ROLL OVER MY FOOT WITH YOUR CHAIR, EH?
HEY!
LET ME GET A CLEAR SHOT AT HIM!
UNH!

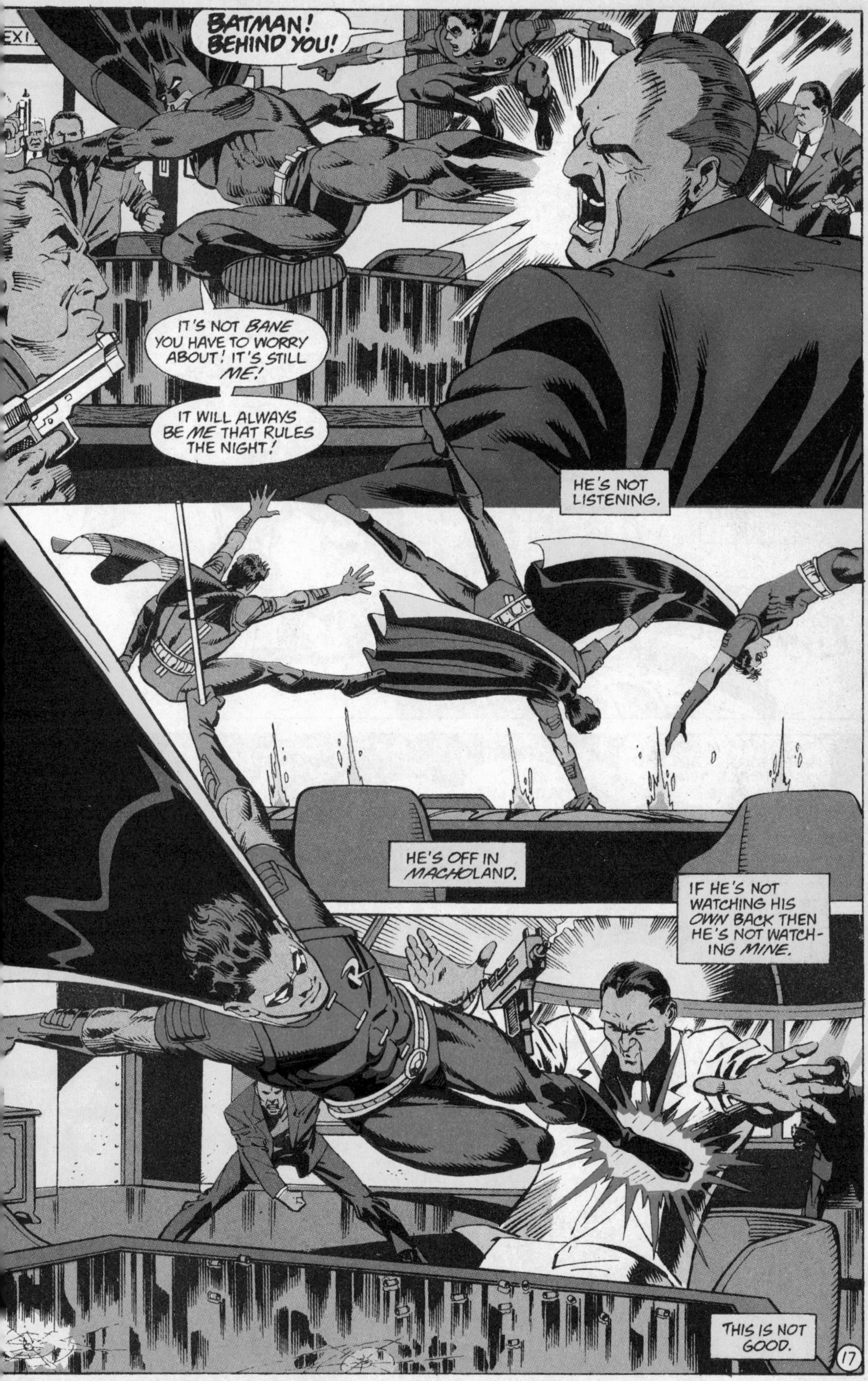

BATMAN! BEHIND YOU!
IT'S NOT BANE YOU HAVE TO WORRY ABOUT! IT'S STILL ME!
IT WILL ALWAYS BE ME THAT RULES THE NIGHT!
HE'S NOT LISTENING.
HE'S OFF IN MACHOLAND.
IF HE'S NOT WATCHING HIS OWN BACK THEN HE'S NOT WATCHING MINE.
THIS IS NOT GOOD.
17

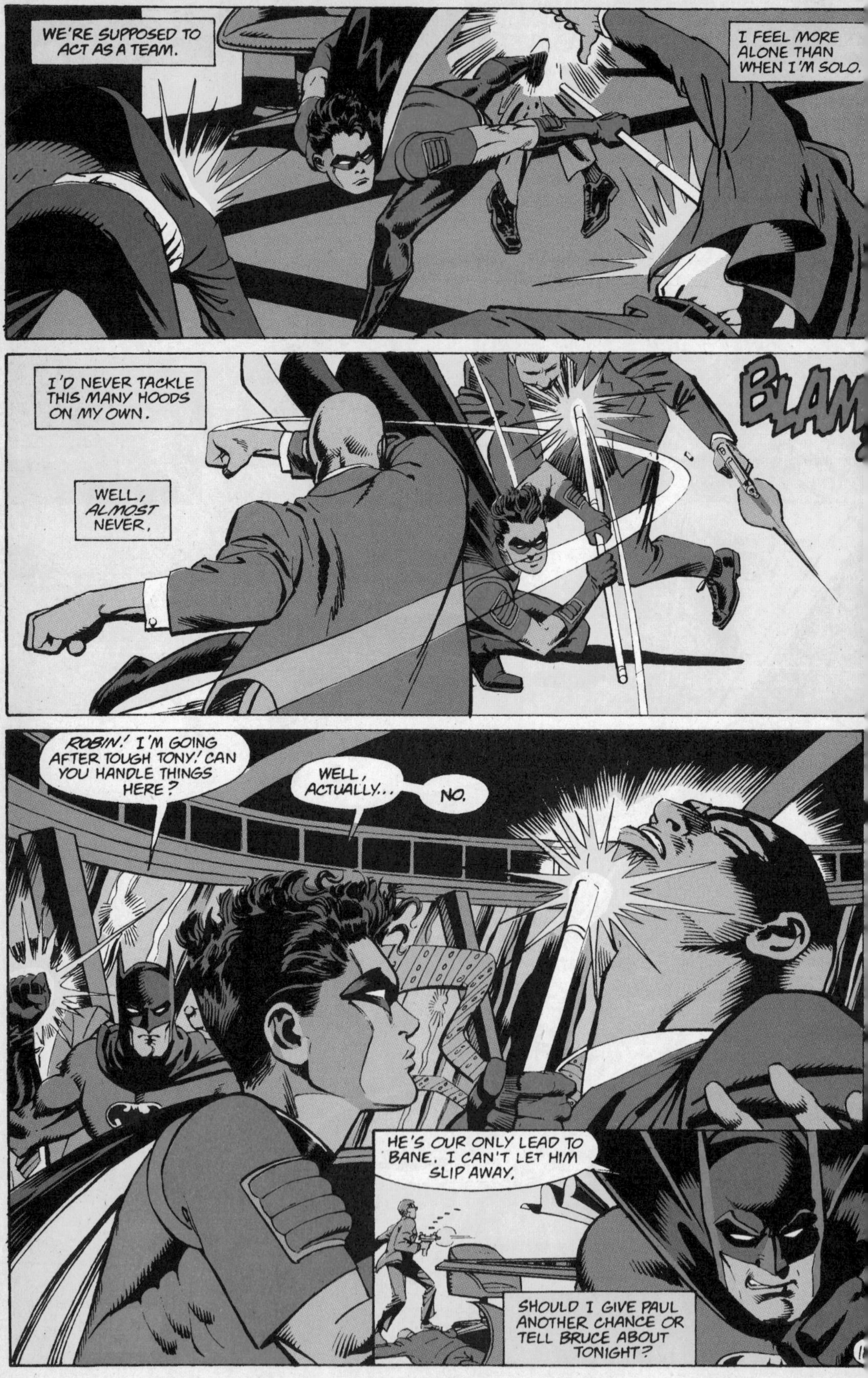

WE'RE SUPPOSED TO ACT AS A TEAM.
I FEEL MORE ALONE THAN WHEN I'M SOLO.
I'D NEVER TACKLE THIS MANY HOODS ON MY OWN.
WELL, ALMOST NEVER.
BLAM
ROBIN! I'M GOING AFTER TOUGH TONY! CAN YOU HANDLE THINGS HERE?
WELL, ACTUALLY...
NO.
HE'S OUR ONLY LEAD TO BANE. I CAN'T LET HIM SLIP AWAY.
SHOULD I GIVE PAUL ANOTHER CHANCE OR TELL BRUCE ABOUT TONIGHT?

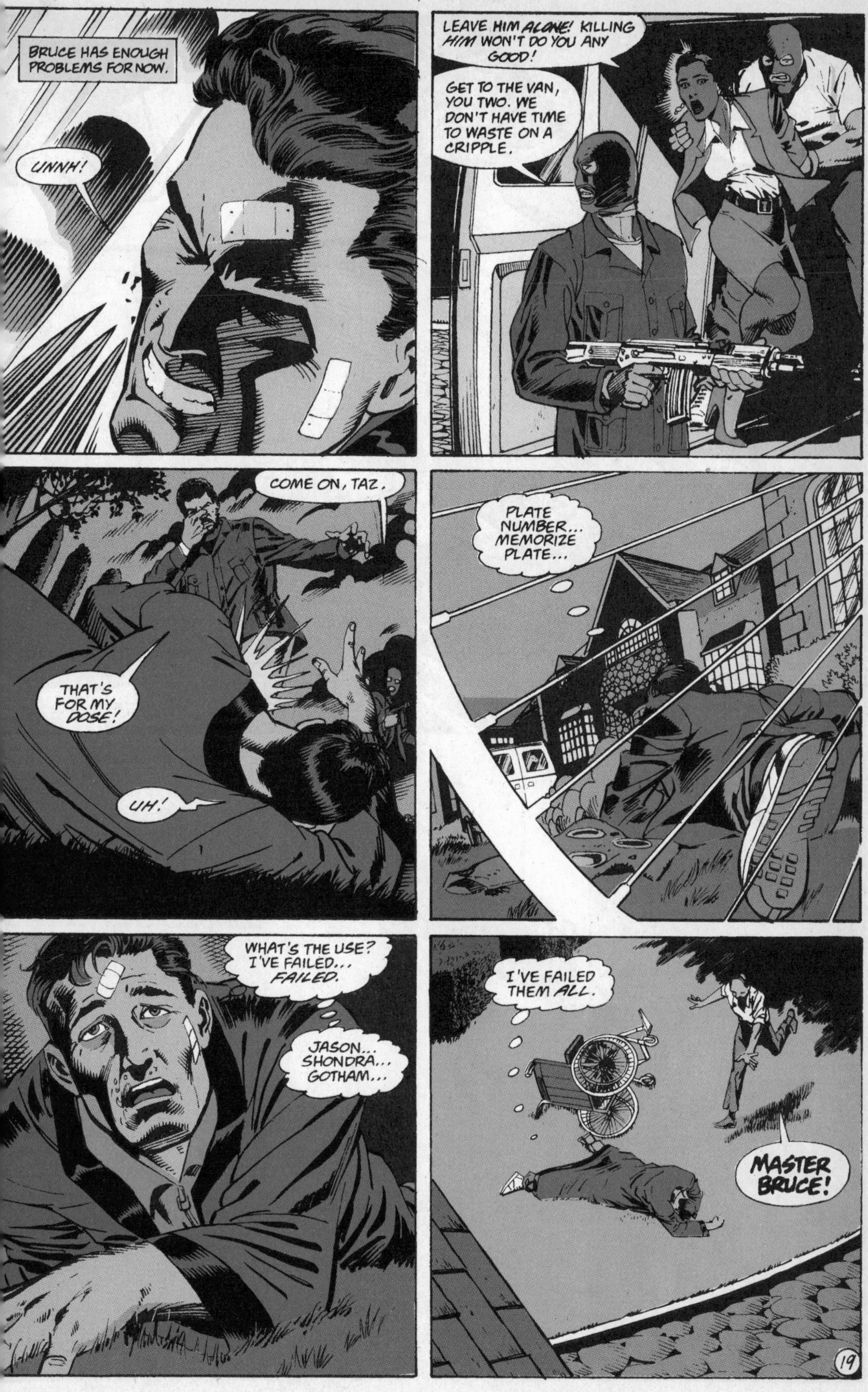
BRUCE HAS ENOUGH PROBLEMS FOR NOW.
UNNH!
LEAVE HIM ALONE! KILLING HIM WON'T DO YOU ANY GOOD!
GET TO THE VAN, YOU TWO. WE DON'T HAVE TIME TO WASTE ON A CRIPPLE.
COME ON, TAZ.
THAT'S FOR MY DOSE!
UH!
PLATE NUMBER... MEMORIZE PLATE...
WHAT'S THE USE? I'VE FAILED... FAILED.
JASON... SHONDRA... GOTHAM...
I'VE FAILED THEM ALL.
MASTER BRUCE!
19

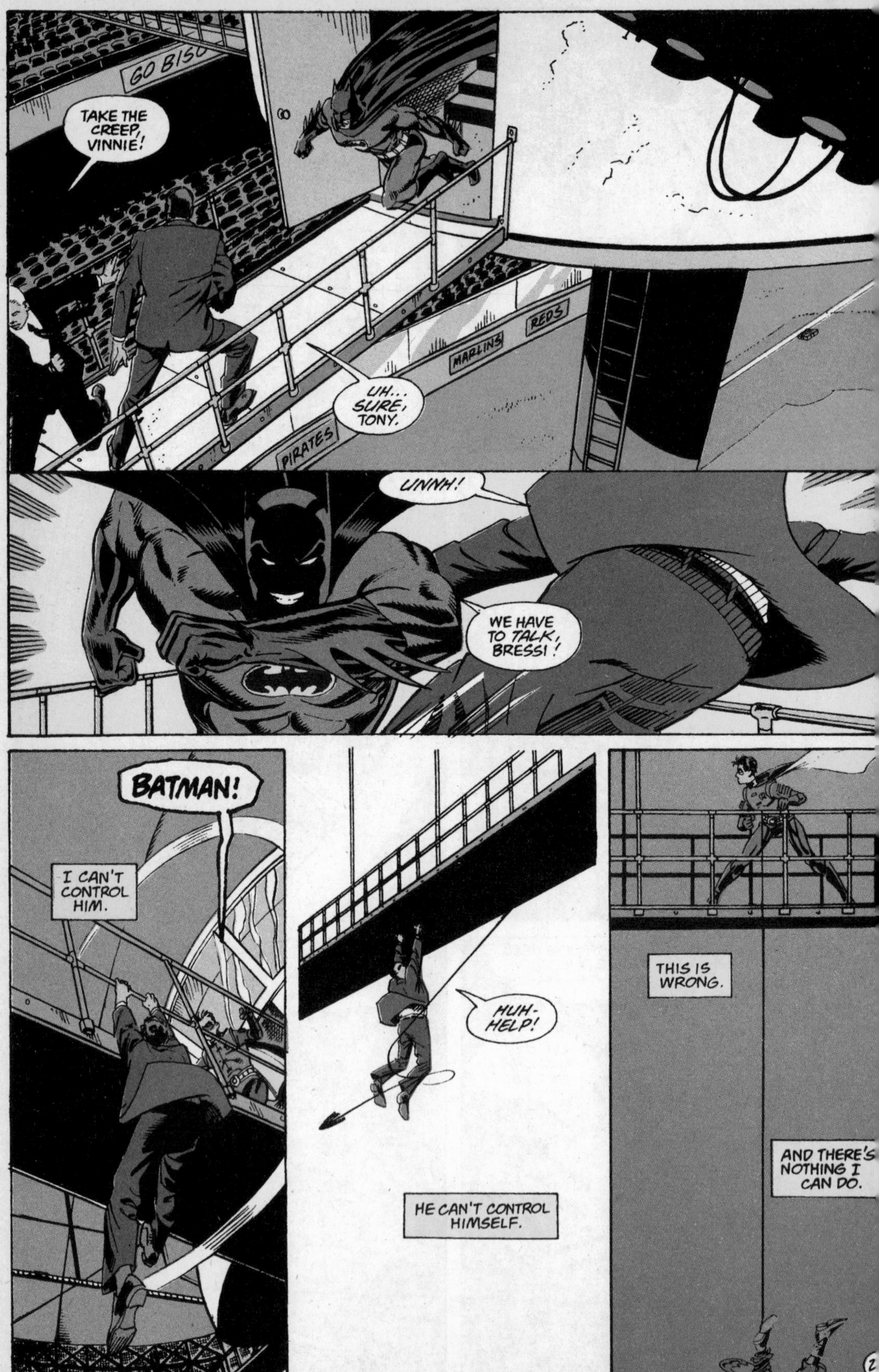
GO BISO
TAKE THE CREEP, VINNIE!
MARLINS
REDS
PIRATES
UH... SURE, TONY.
UNNH!
WE HAVE TO TALK, BRESSI!
BATMAN!
I CAN'T CONTROL HIM.
HUH-HELP!
HE CAN'T CONTROL HIMSELF.
THIS IS WRONG.
AND THERE'S NOTHING I CAN DO.

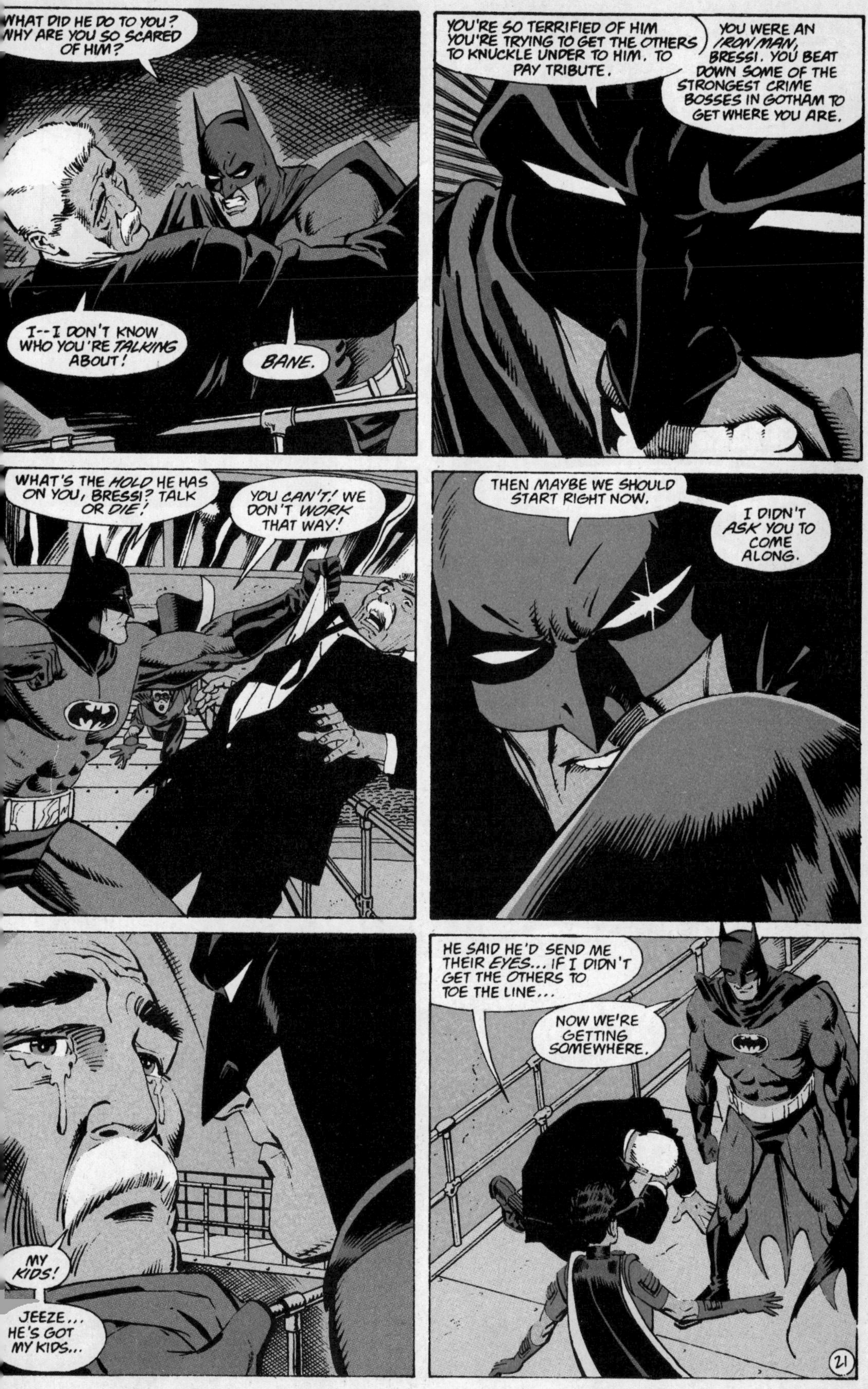

WHAT DID HE DO TO YOU? WHY ARE YOU SO SCARED OF HIM?
I--I DON'T KNOW WHO YOU'RE TALKING ABOUT!
BANE.
YOU'RE SO TERRIFIED OF HIM YOU'RE TRYING TO GET THE OTHERS TO KNUCKLE UNDER TO HIM. TO PAY TRIBUTE.
YOU WERE AN IRON MAN, BRESSI. YOU BEAT DOWN SOME OF THE STRONGEST CRIME BOSSES IN GOTHAM TO GET WHERE YOU ARE.
WHAT'S THE HOLD HE HAS ON YOU, BRESSI? TALK OR DIE!
YOU CAN'T! WE DON'T WORK THAT WAY!
THEN MAYBE WE SHOULD START RIGHT NOW.
I DIDN'T ASK YOU TO COME ALONG.
MY KIDS!
JEEZE... HE'S GOT MY KIDS...
HE SAID HE'D SEND ME THEIR EYES... IF I DIDN'T GET THE OTHERS TO TOE THE LINE...
NOW WE'RE GETTING SOMEWHERE.
21

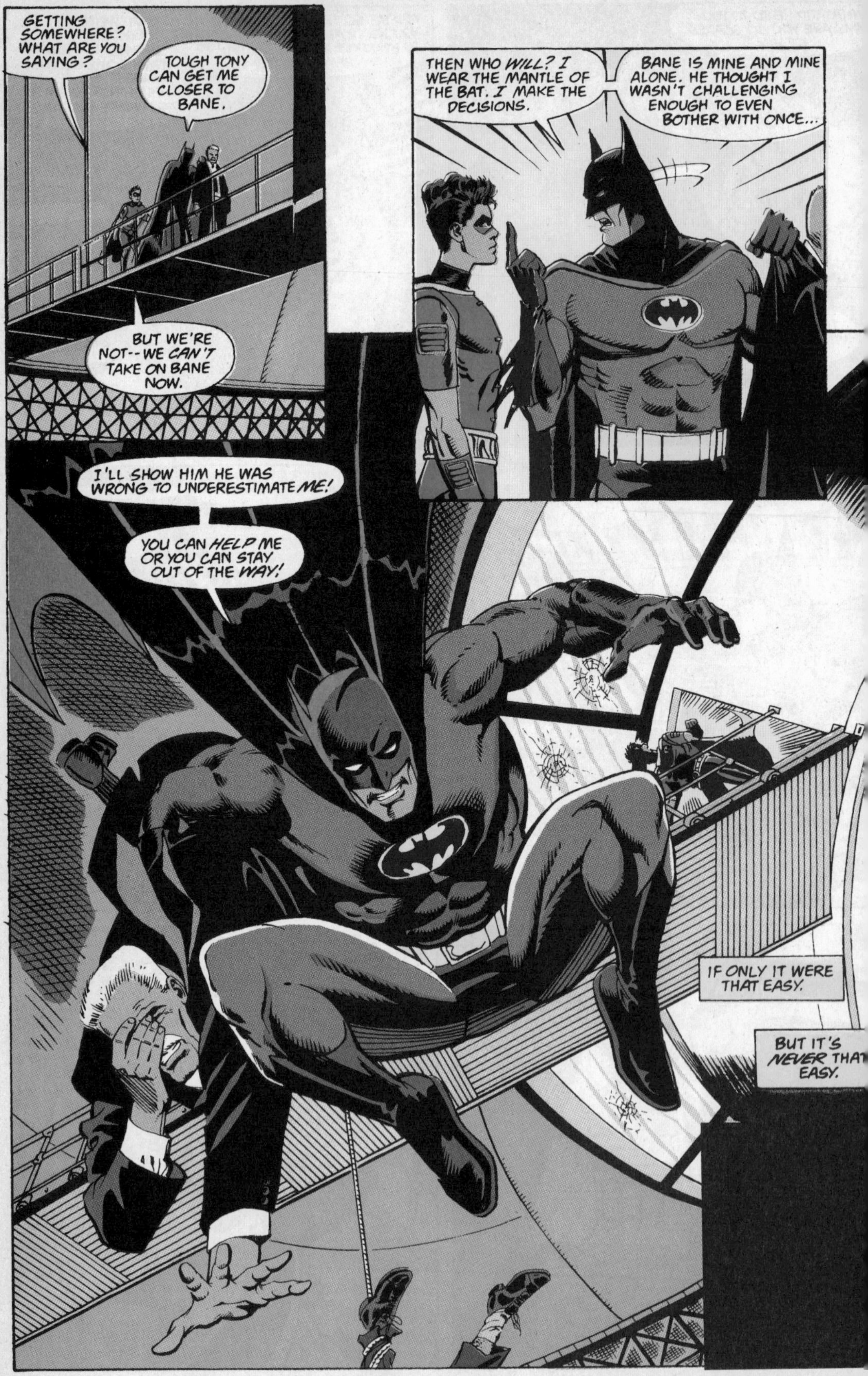
GETTING SOMEWHERE? WHAT ARE YOU SAYING?
TOUGH TONY CAN GET ME CLOSER TO BANE.
BUT WE'RE NOT--WE CAN'T TAKE ON BANE NOW.
THEN WHO WILL? I WEAR THE MANTLE OF THE BAT. I MAKE THE DECISIONS.
BANE IS MINE AND MINE ALONE. HE THOUGHT I WASN'T CHALLENGING ENOUGH TO EVEN BOTHER WITH ONCE...
I'LL SHOW HIM HE WAS WRONG TO UNDERESTIMATE ME!
YOU CAN HELP ME OR YOU CAN STAY OUT OF THE WAY!
IF ONLY IT WERE THAT EASY.
BUT IT'S NEVER THAT EASY.

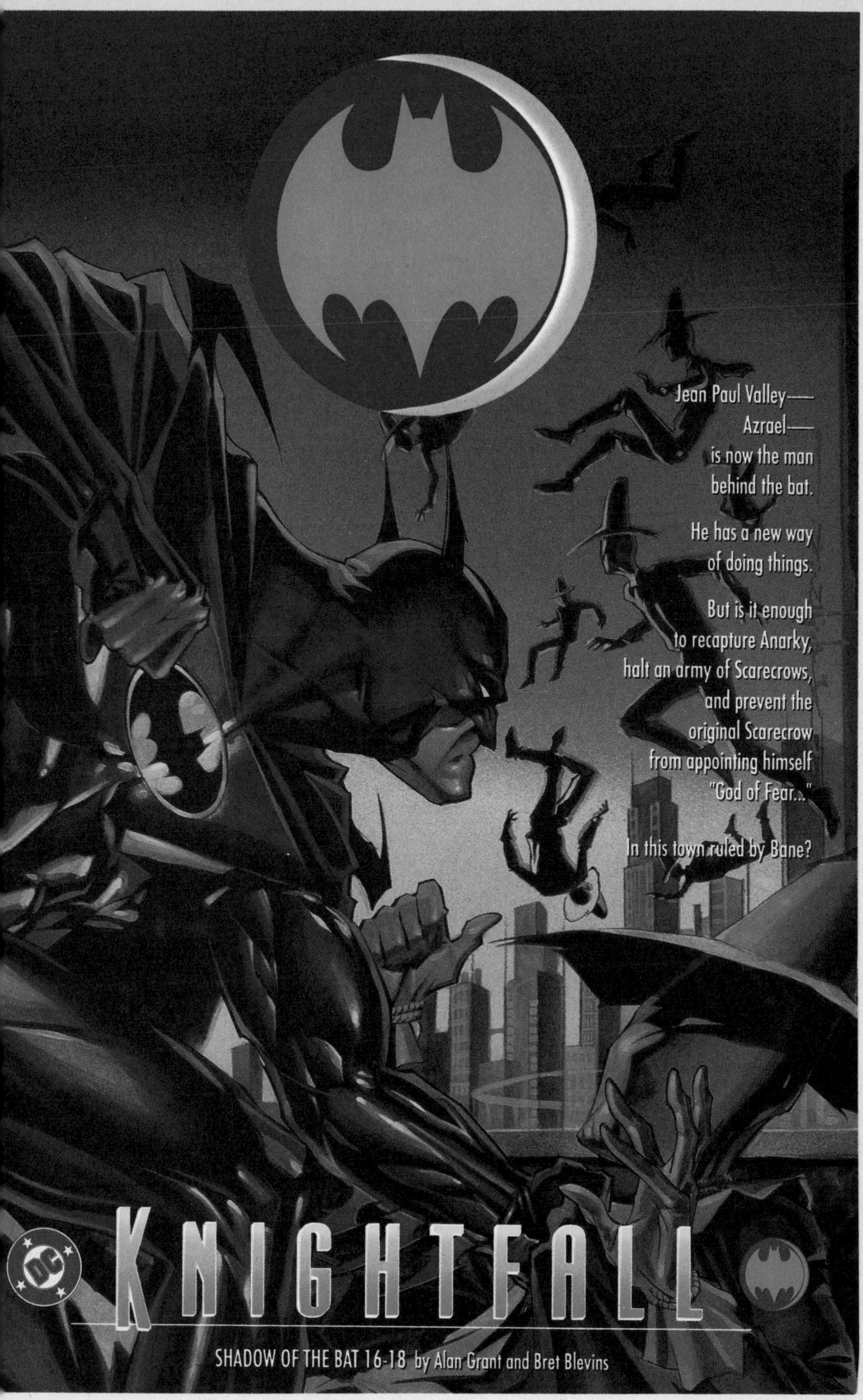
Jean Paul Valley—
Azrael—
is now the man
behind the bat.
He has a new way
of doing things.
But is it enough
to recapture Anarky,
halt an army of Scarecrows,
and prevent the
original Scarecrow
from appointing himself
"God of Fear..."
In this town ruled by Bane?
DC
KNIGHTFALL
SHADOW OF THE BAT 16-18 by Alan Grant and Bret Blevins

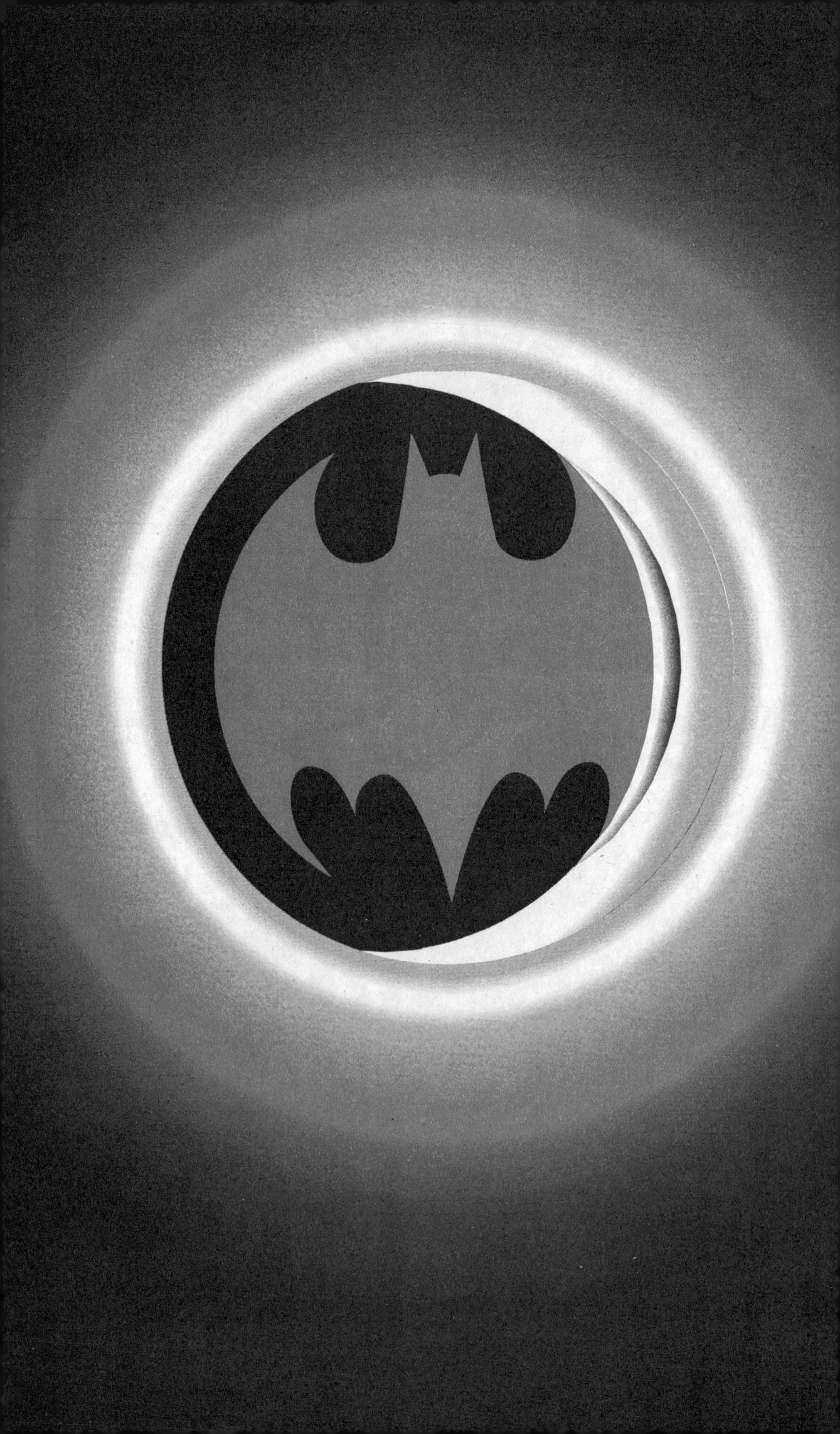

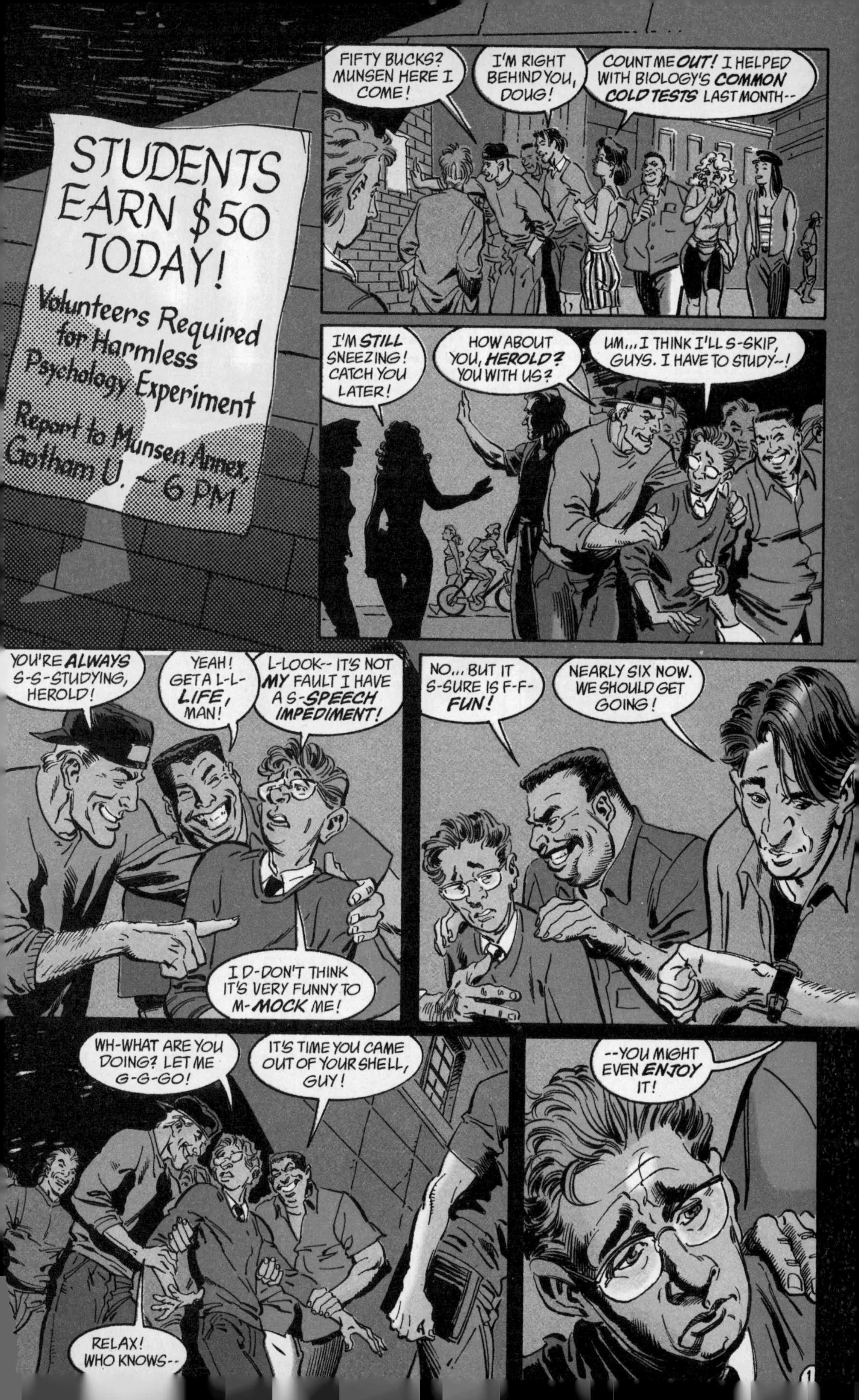
STUDENTS EARN $50 TODAY!
Volunteers Required for Harmless Psychology Experiment
Report to Munsen Annex, Gotham U. ~ 6 PM
FIFTY BUCKS? MUNSEN HERE I COME!
I'M RIGHT BEHIND YOU, DOUG!
COUNT ME OUT! I HELPED WITH BIOLOGY'S COMMON COLD TESTS LAST MONTH--
I'M STILL SNEEZING! CATCH YOU LATER!
HOW ABOUT YOU, HEROLD? YOU WITH US?
UM... I THINK I'LL S-SKIP, GUYS. I HAVE TO STUDY--!
YOU'RE ALWAYS S-S-STUDYING, HEROLD!
YEAH! GET A L-L-LIFE, MAN!
L-LOOK-- IT'S NOT MY FAULT I HAVE A S-SPEECH IMPEDIMENT!
I D-DON'T THINK IT'S VERY FUNNY TO M-MOCK ME!
NO... BUT IT S-SURE IS F-F-FUN!
NEARLY SIX NOW. WE SHOULD GET GOING!
WH-WHAT ARE YOU DOING? LET ME G-G-GO!
IT'S TIME YOU CAME OUT OF YOUR SHELL, GUY!
RELAX! WHO KNOWS--
--YOU MIGHT EVEN ENJOY IT!

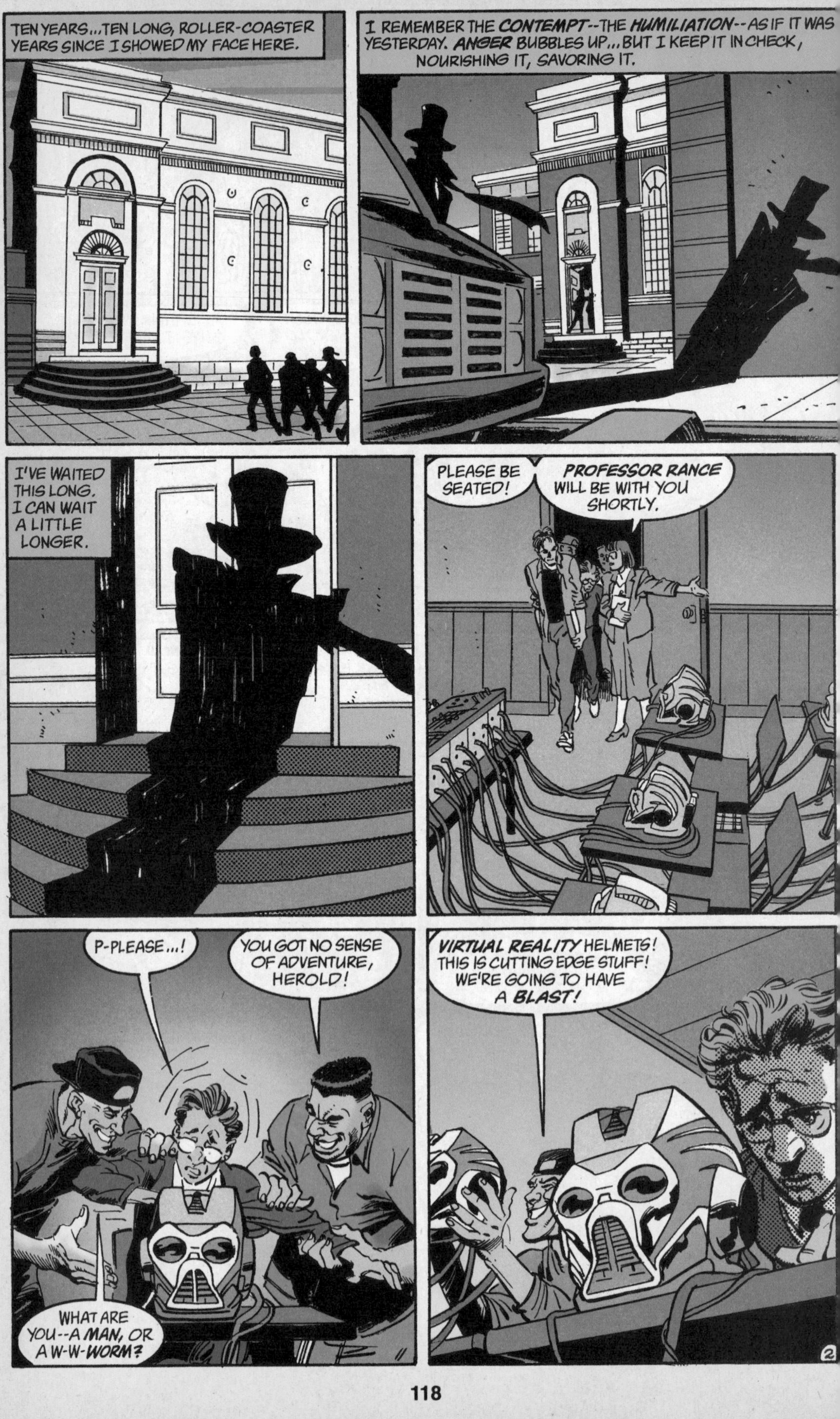
TEN YEARS...TEN LONG, ROLLER-COASTER YEARS SINCE I SHOWED MY FACE HERE.
I REMEMBER THE CONTEMPT--THE HUMILIATION--AS IF IT WAS YESTERDAY. ANGER BUBBLES UP...BUT I KEEP IT IN CHECK, NOURISHING IT, SAVORING IT.
I'VE WAITED THIS LONG. I CAN WAIT A LITTLE LONGER.
PLEASE BE SEATED!
PROFESSOR RANCE WILL BE WITH YOU SHORTLY.
P-PLEASE...!
YOU GOT NO SENSE OF ADVENTURE, HEROLD!
WHAT ARE YOU--A MAN, OR A W-W-WORM?
VIRTUAL REALITY HELMETS! THIS IS CUTTING EDGE STUFF! WE'RE GOING TO HAVE A BLAST!
2

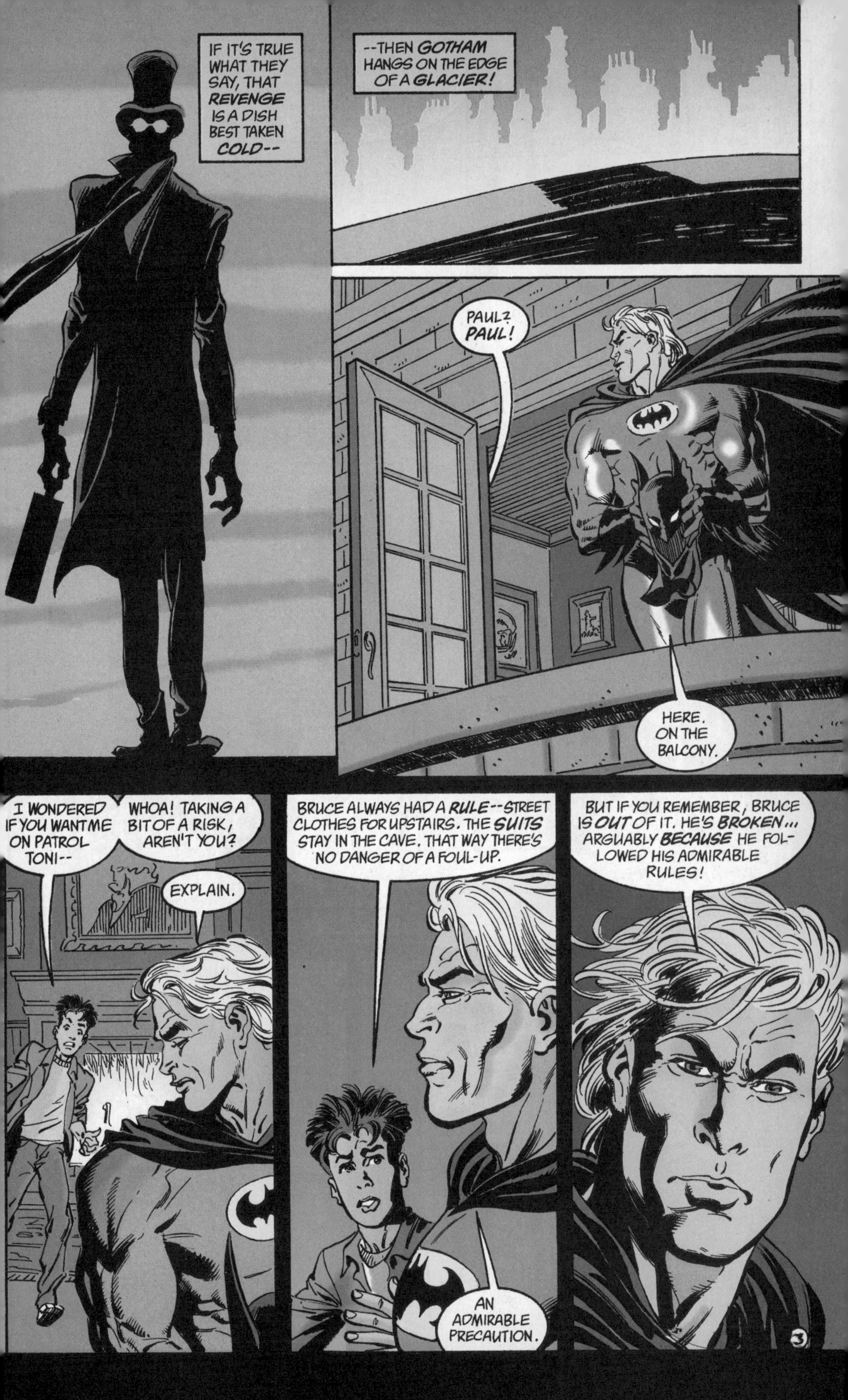
IF IT'S TRUE WHAT THEY SAY, THAT REVENGE IS A DISH BEST TAKEN COLD--
--THEN GOTHAM HANGS ON THE EDGE OF A GLACIER!
PAUL? PAUL!
HERE. ON THE BALCONY.
I WONDERED IF YOU WANT ME ON PATROL TONI--
WHOA! TAKING A BIT OF A RISK, AREN'T YOU?
EXPLAIN.
BRUCE ALWAYS HAD A RULE--STREET CLOTHES FOR UPSTAIRS. THE SUITS STAY IN THE CAVE. THAT WAY THERE'S NO DANGER OF A FOUL-UP.
AN ADMIRABLE PRECAUTION.
BUT IF YOU REMEMBER, BRUCE IS OUT OF IT. HE'S BROKEN... ARGUABLY BECAUSE HE FOLLOWED HIS ADMIRABLE RULES!
3

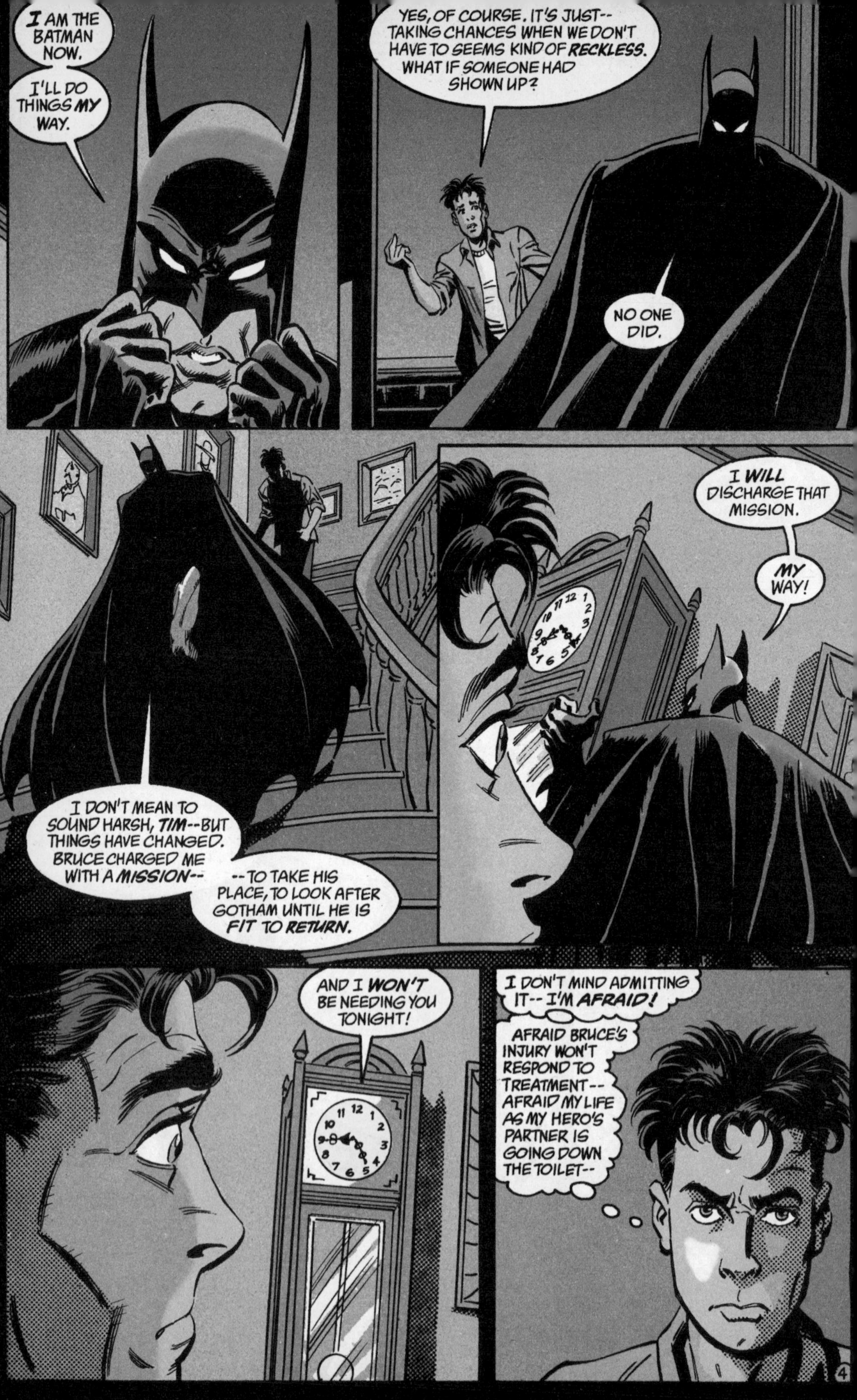
I AM THE BATMAN NOW.
I'LL DO THINGS MY WAY.
YES, OF COURSE. IT'S JUST-- TAKING CHANCES WHEN WE DON'T HAVE TO SEEMS KIND OF RECKLESS. WHAT IF SOMEONE HAD SHOWN UP?
NO ONE DID.
I DON'T MEAN TO SOUND HARSH, TIM--BUT THINGS HAVE CHANGED. BRUCE CHARGED ME WITH A MISSION--
--TO TAKE HIS PLACE, TO LOOK AFTER GOTHAM UNTIL HE IS FIT TO RETURN.
I WILL DISCHARGE THAT MISSION.
MY WAY!
AND I WON'T BE NEEDING YOU TONIGHT!
I DON'T MIND ADMITTING IT-- I'M AFRAID!
AFRAID BRUCE'S INJURY WON'T RESPOND TO TREATMENT-- AFRAID MY LIFE AS MY HERO'S PARTNER IS GOING DOWN THE TOILET--
4

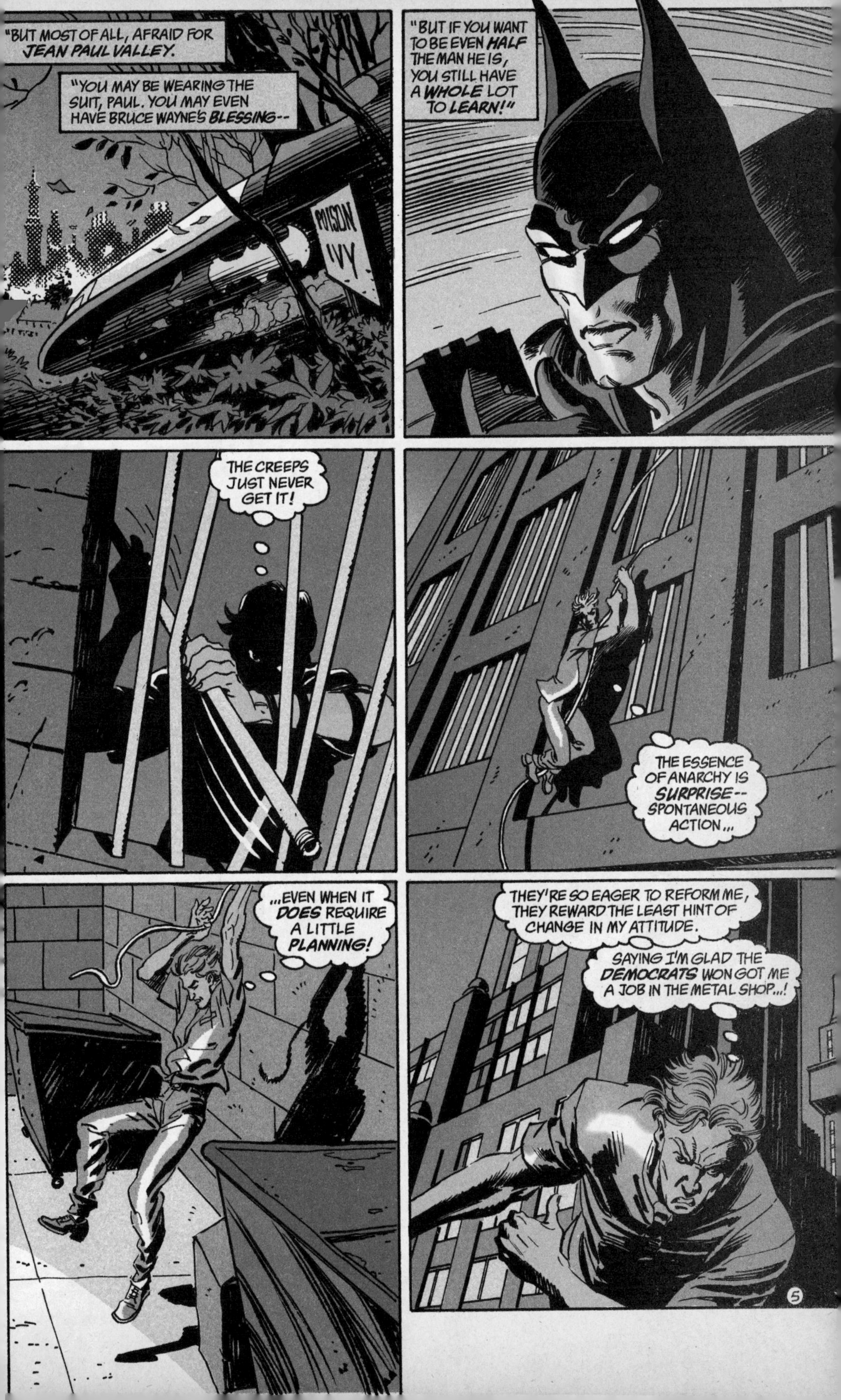
"BUT MOST OF ALL, AFRAID FOR JEAN PAUL VALLEY.
"YOU MAY BE WEARING THE SUIT, PAUL. YOU MAY EVEN HAVE BRUCE WAYNE'S BLESSING--
POISON IVY
"BUT IF YOU WANT TO BE EVEN HALF THE MAN HE IS, YOU STILL HAVE A WHOLE LOT TO LEARN!"
THE CREEPS JUST NEVER GET IT!
THE ESSENCE OF ANARCHY IS SURPRISE-- SPONTANEOUS ACTION...
...EVEN WHEN IT DOES REQUIRE A LITTLE PLANNING!
THEY'RE SO EAGER TO REFORM ME, THEY REWARD THE LEAST HINT OF CHANGE IN MY ATTITUDE.
SAYING I'M GLAD THE DEMOCRATS WON GOT ME A JOB IN THE METAL SHOP...!
5

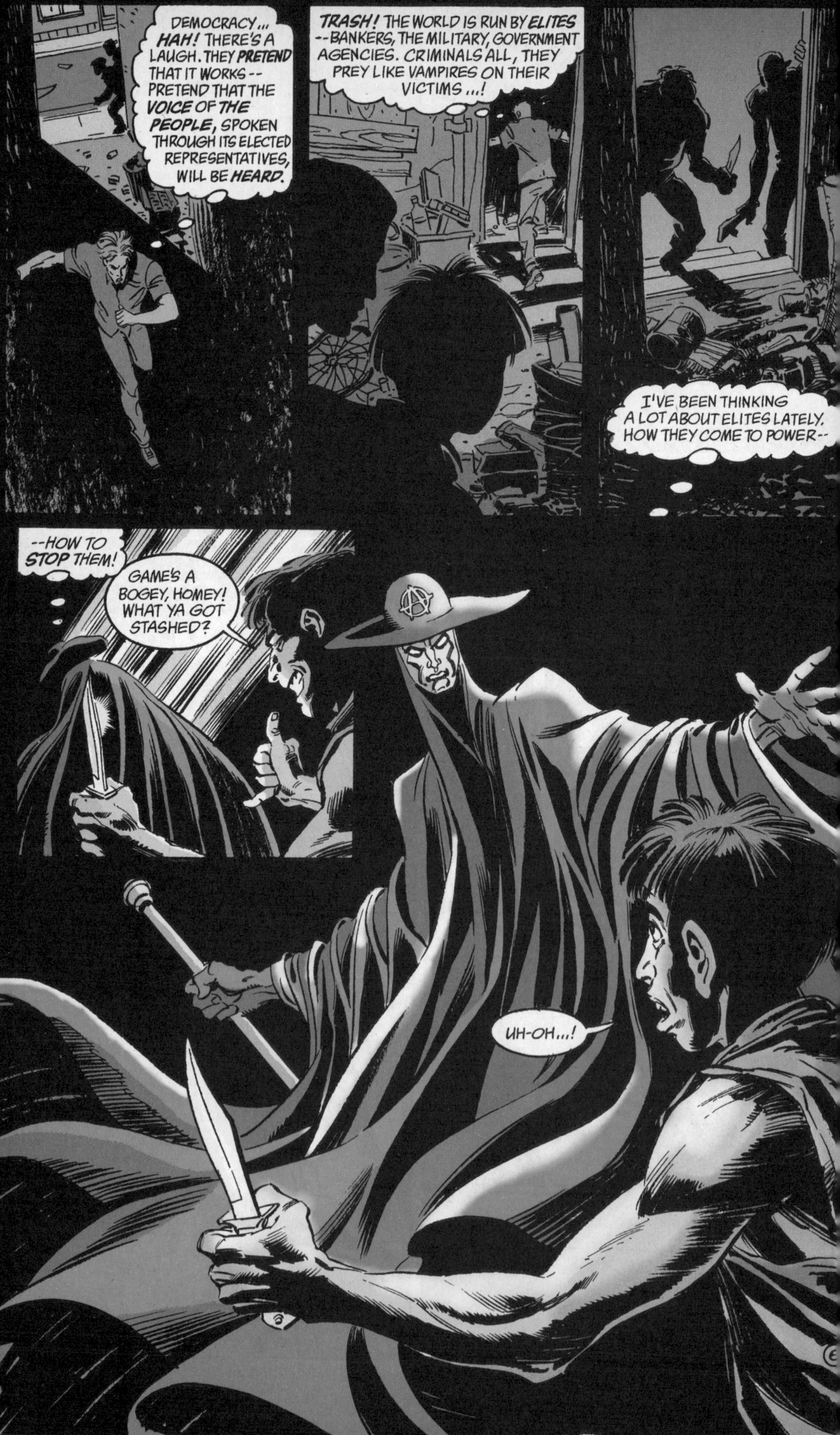

DEMOCRACY... HAH! THERE'S A LAUGH. THEY PRETEND THAT IT WORKS -- PRETEND THAT THE VOICE OF THE PEOPLE, SPOKEN THROUGH ITS ELECTED REPRESENTATIVES, WILL BE HEARD.
TRASH! THE WORLD IS RUN BY ELITES --BANKERS, THE MILITARY, GOVERNMENT AGENCIES. CRIMINALS ALL, THEY PREY LIKE VAMPIRES ON THEIR VICTIMS...!
I'VE BEEN THINKING A LOT ABOUT ELITES LATELY. HOW THEY COME TO POWER--
--HOW TO STOP THEM!
GAME'S A BOGEY, HOMEY! WHAT YA GOT STASHED?
UH-OH...!

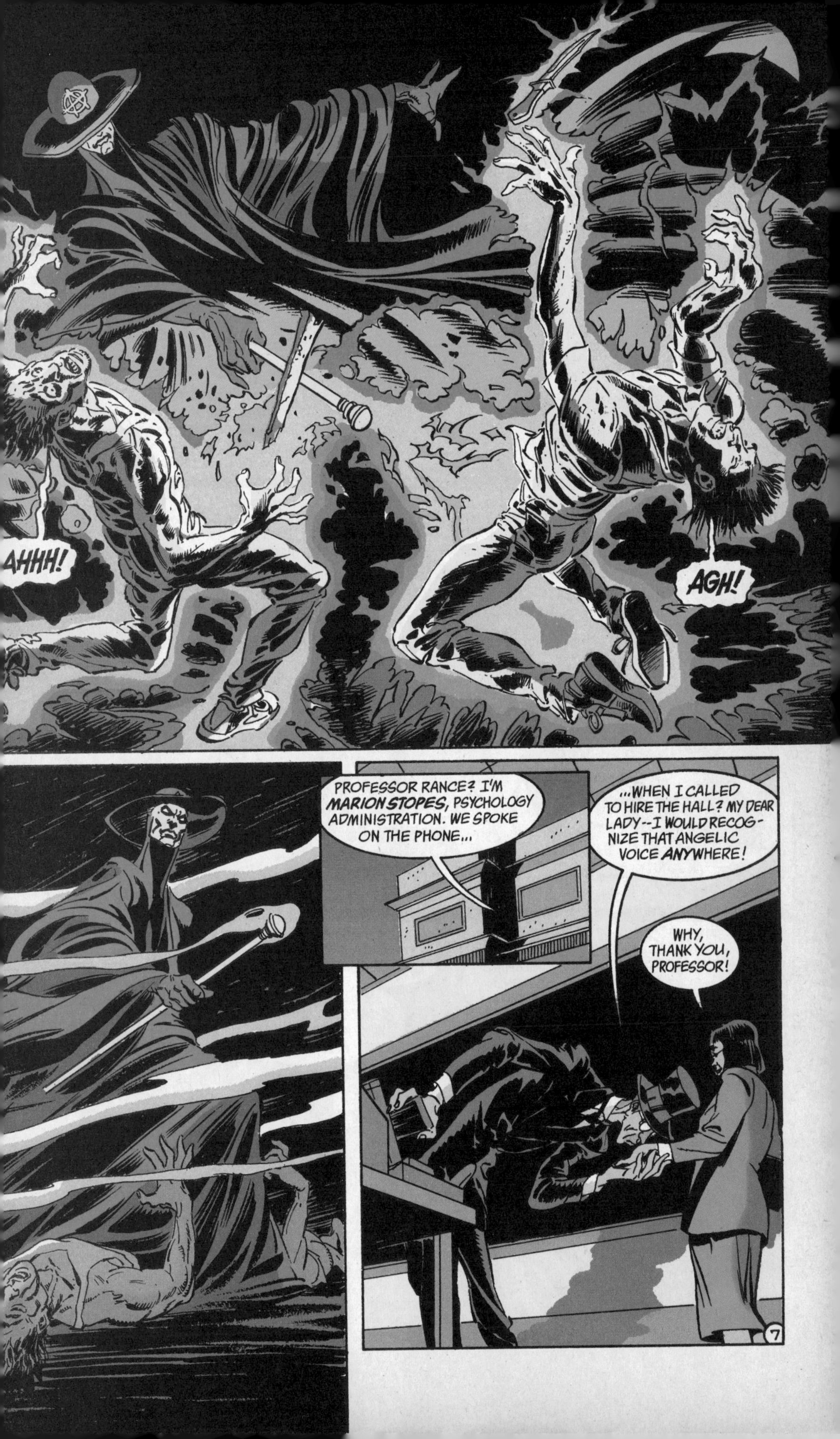

AHHH!
AGH!
PROFESSOR RANCE? I'M **MARION STOPES**, PSYCHOLOGY ADMINISTRATION. WE SPOKE ON THE PHONE...
...WHEN I CALLED TO HIRE THE HALL? MY DEAR LADY--I WOULD RECOGNIZE THAT ANGELIC VOICE **ANY**WHERE!
WHY, THANK YOU, PROFESSOR!
7

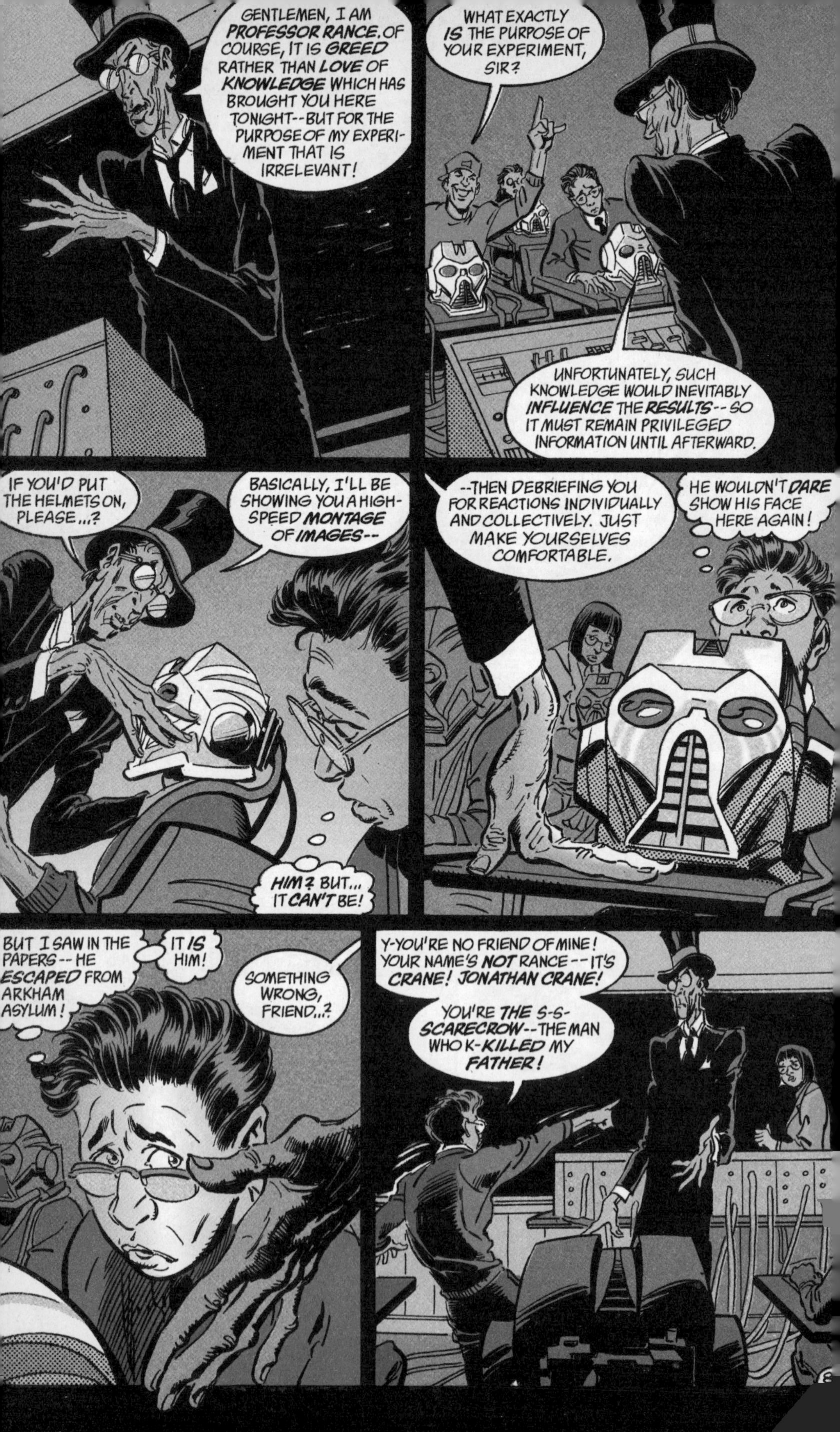

GENTLEMEN, I AM PROFESSOR RANCE. OF COURSE, IT IS GREED RATHER THAN LOVE OF KNOWLEDGE WHICH HAS BROUGHT YOU HERE TONIGHT--BUT FOR THE PURPOSE OF MY EXPERIMENT THAT IS IRRELEVANT!
WHAT EXACTLY IS THE PURPOSE OF YOUR EXPERIMENT, SIR?
UNFORTUNATELY, SUCH KNOWLEDGE WOULD INEVITABLY INFLUENCE THE RESULTS--SO IT MUST REMAIN PRIVILEGED INFORMATION UNTIL AFTERWARD.
IF YOU'D PUT THE HELMETS ON, PLEASE...?
BASICALLY, I'LL BE SHOWING YOU A HIGH-SPEED MONTAGE OF IMAGES--
HIM? BUT... IT CAN'T BE!
--THEN DEBRIEFING YOU FOR REACTIONS INDIVIDUALLY AND COLLECTIVELY. JUST MAKE YOURSELVES COMFORTABLE.
HE WOULDN'T DARE SHOW HIS FACE HERE AGAIN!
BUT I SAW IN THE PAPERS--HE ESCAPED FROM ARKHAM ASYLUM!
IT IS HIM!
SOMETHING WRONG, FRIEND...?
Y-YOU'RE NO FRIEND OF MINE! YOUR NAME'S NOT RANCE--IT'S CRANE! JONATHAN CRANE!
YOU'RE THE S-S-SCARECROW--THE MAN WHO K-KILLED MY FATHER!

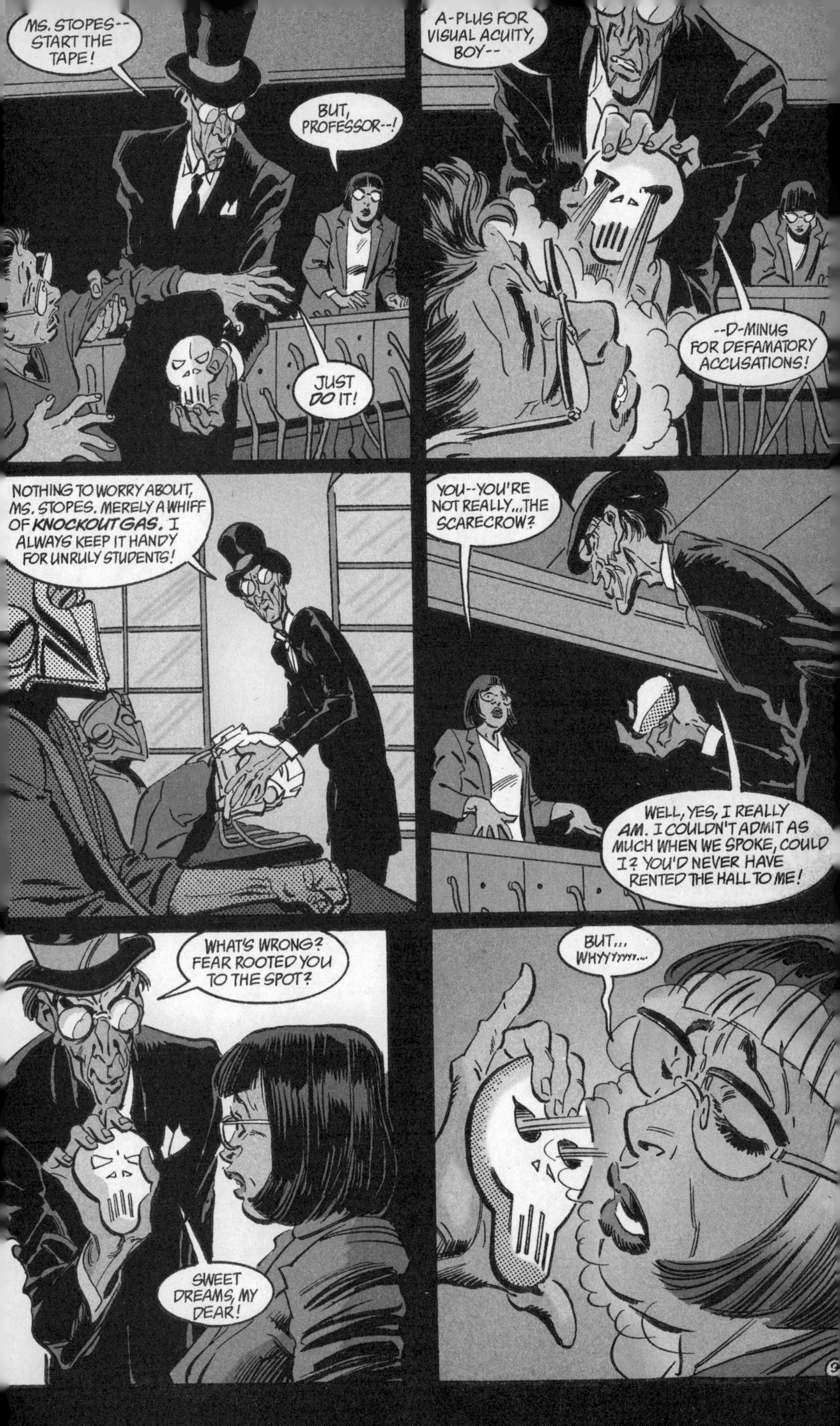
MS. STOPES-- START THE TAPE!
BUT, PROFESSOR--!
JUST DO IT!
A-PLUS FOR VISUAL ACUITY, BOY--
--D-MINUS FOR DEFAMATORY ACCUSATIONS!
NOTHING TO WORRY ABOUT, MS. STOPES. MERELY A WHIFF OF KNOCKOUT GAS. I ALWAYS KEEP IT HANDY FOR UNRULY STUDENTS!
YOU--YOU'RE NOT REALLY...THE SCARECROW?
WELL, YES, I REALLY AM. I COULDN'T ADMIT AS MUCH WHEN WE SPOKE, COULD I? YOU'D NEVER HAVE RENTED THE HALL TO ME!
WHAT'S WRONG? FEAR ROOTED YOU TO THE SPOT?
SWEET DREAMS, MY DEAR!
BUT... WHYYyyyy....

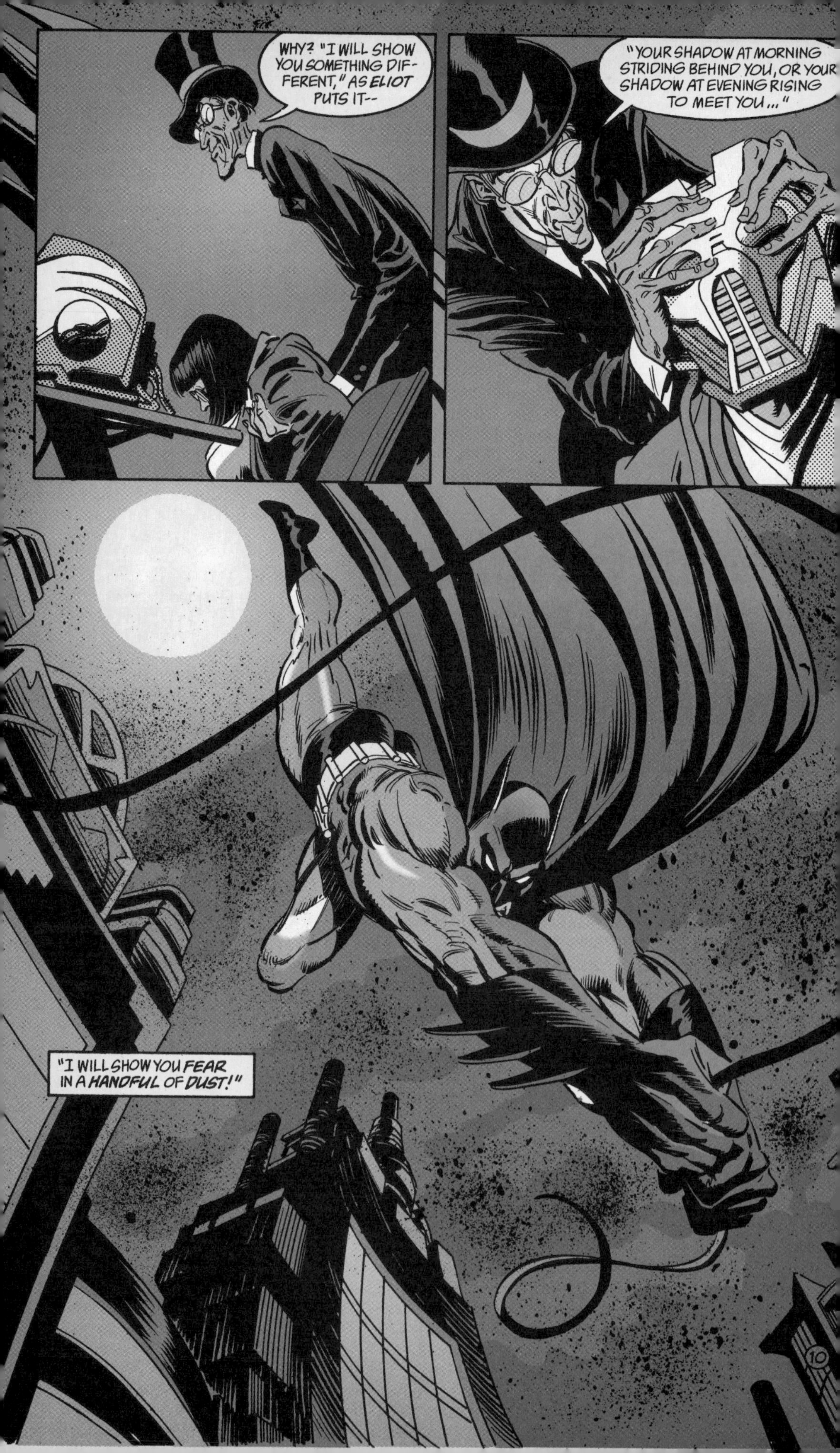
WHY? "I WILL SHOW YOU SOMETHING DIF-FERENT," AS ELIOT PUTS IT--
"YOUR SHADOW AT MORNING STRIDING BEHIND YOU, OR YOUR SHADOW AT EVENING RISING TO MEET YOU..."
"I WILL SHOW YOU FEAR IN A HANDFUL OF DUST!"
10

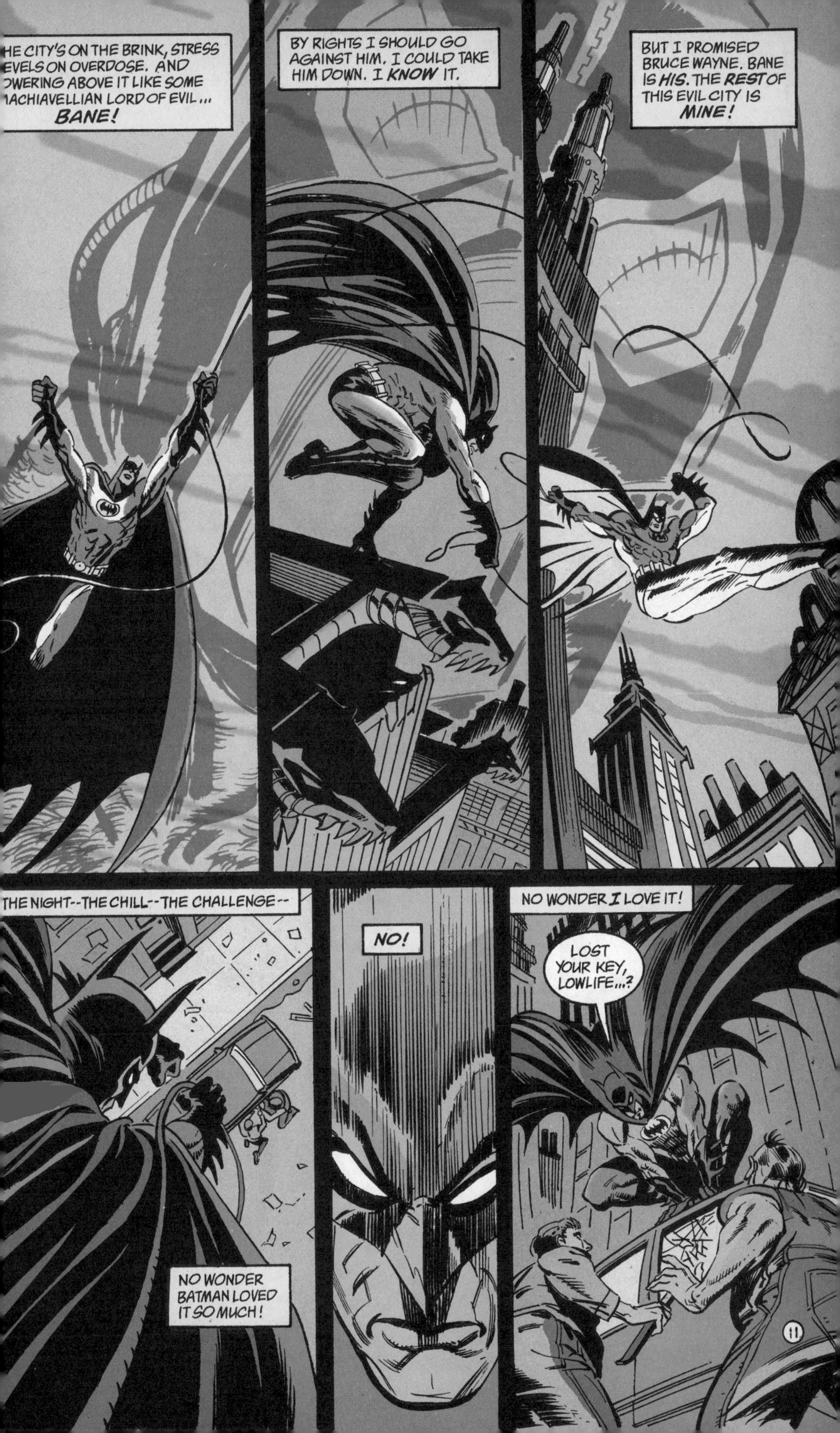
HE CITY'S ON THE BRINK, STRESS EVELS ON OVERDOSE. AND OWERING ABOVE IT LIKE SOME ACHIAVELLIAN LORD OF EVIL... BANE!
BY RIGHTS I SHOULD GO AGAINST HIM. I COULD TAKE HIM DOWN. I KNOW IT.
BUT I PROMISED BRUCE WAYNE. BANE IS HIS. THE REST OF THIS EVIL CITY IS MINE!
THE NIGHT--THE CHILL--THE CHALLENGE--
NO WONDER BATMAN LOVED IT SO MUCH!
NO!
NO WONDER I LOVE IT!
LOST YOUR KEY, LOWLIFE...?
11

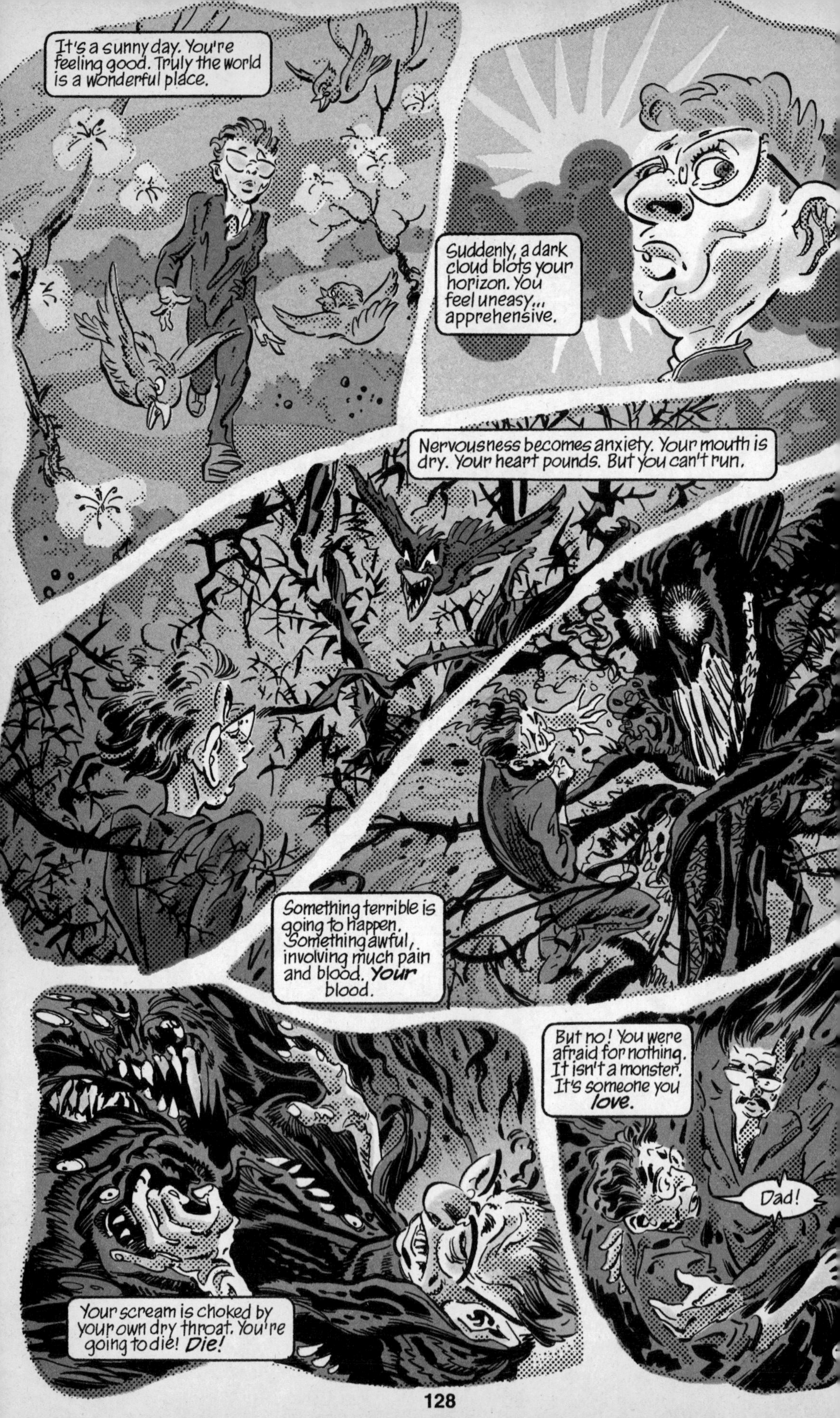
It's a sunny day. You're feeling good. Truly the world is a wonderful place.
Suddenly, a dark cloud blots your horizon. You feel uneasy... apprehensive.
Nervousness becomes anxiety. Your mouth is dry. Your heart pounds. But you can't run.
Something terrible is going to happen. Something awful, involving much pain and blood. *Your* blood.
Your scream is choked by your own dry throat. You're going to die! *Die!*
But no! You were afraid for nothing. It isn't a monster. It's someone you *love*.
Dad!

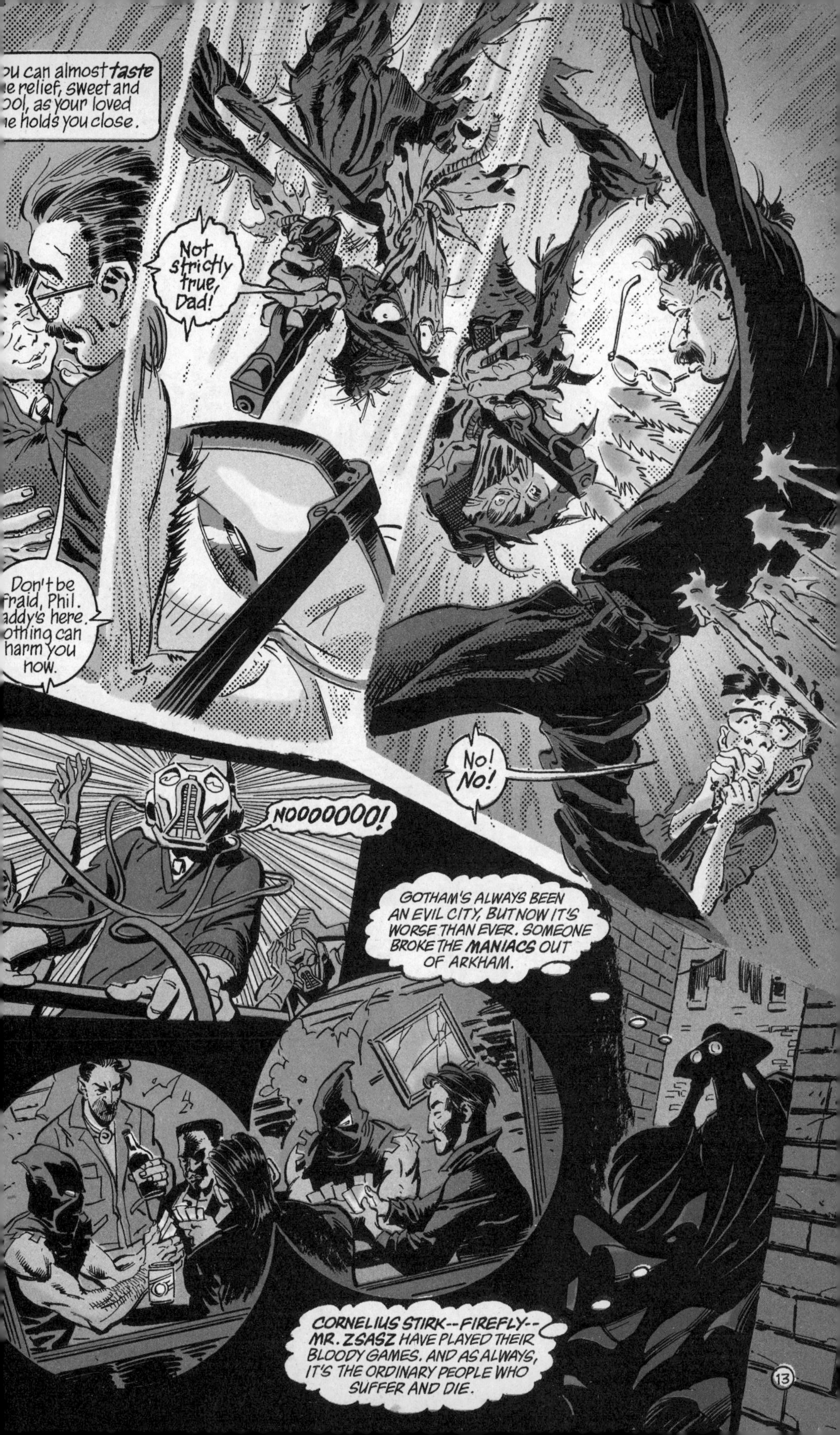
ou can almost taste
e relief, sweet and
ool, as your loved
e holds you close.
Not strictly true, Dad!
Don't be
fraid, Phil.
addy's here.
othing can
harm you
now.
No! No!
NOOOOOOO!
GOTHAM'S ALWAYS BEEN AN EVIL CITY, BUT NOW IT'S WORSE THAN EVER. SOMEONE BROKE THE MANIACS OUT OF ARKHAM.
CORNELIUS STIRK--FIREFLY--MR. ZSASZ HAVE PLAYED THEIR BLOODY GAMES. AND AS ALWAYS, IT'S THE ORDINARY PEOPLE WHO SUFFER AND DIE.
13

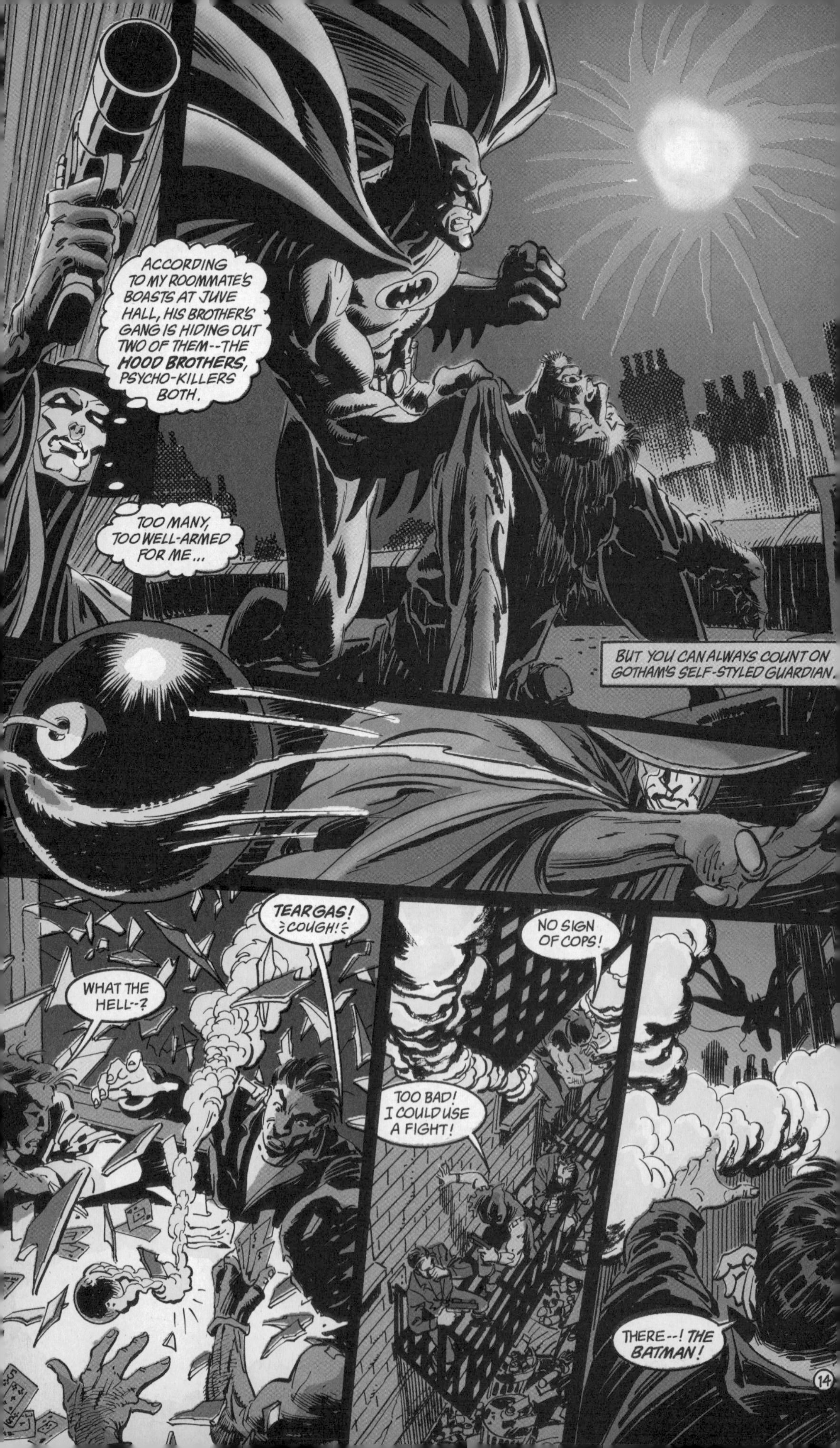
ACCORDING TO MY ROOMMATE'S BOASTS AT JUVE HALL, HIS BROTHER'S GANG IS HIDING OUT TWO OF THEM--THE HOOD BROTHERS, PSYCHO-KILLERS BOTH.
TOO MANY, TOO WELL-ARMED FOR ME...
BUT YOU CAN ALWAYS COUNT ON GOTHAM'S SELF-STYLED GUARDIAN.
WHAT THE HELL--?
TEARGAS! COUGH!
NO SIGN OF COPS!
TOO BAD! I COULD USE A FIGHT!
THERE--! THE BATMAN!
14

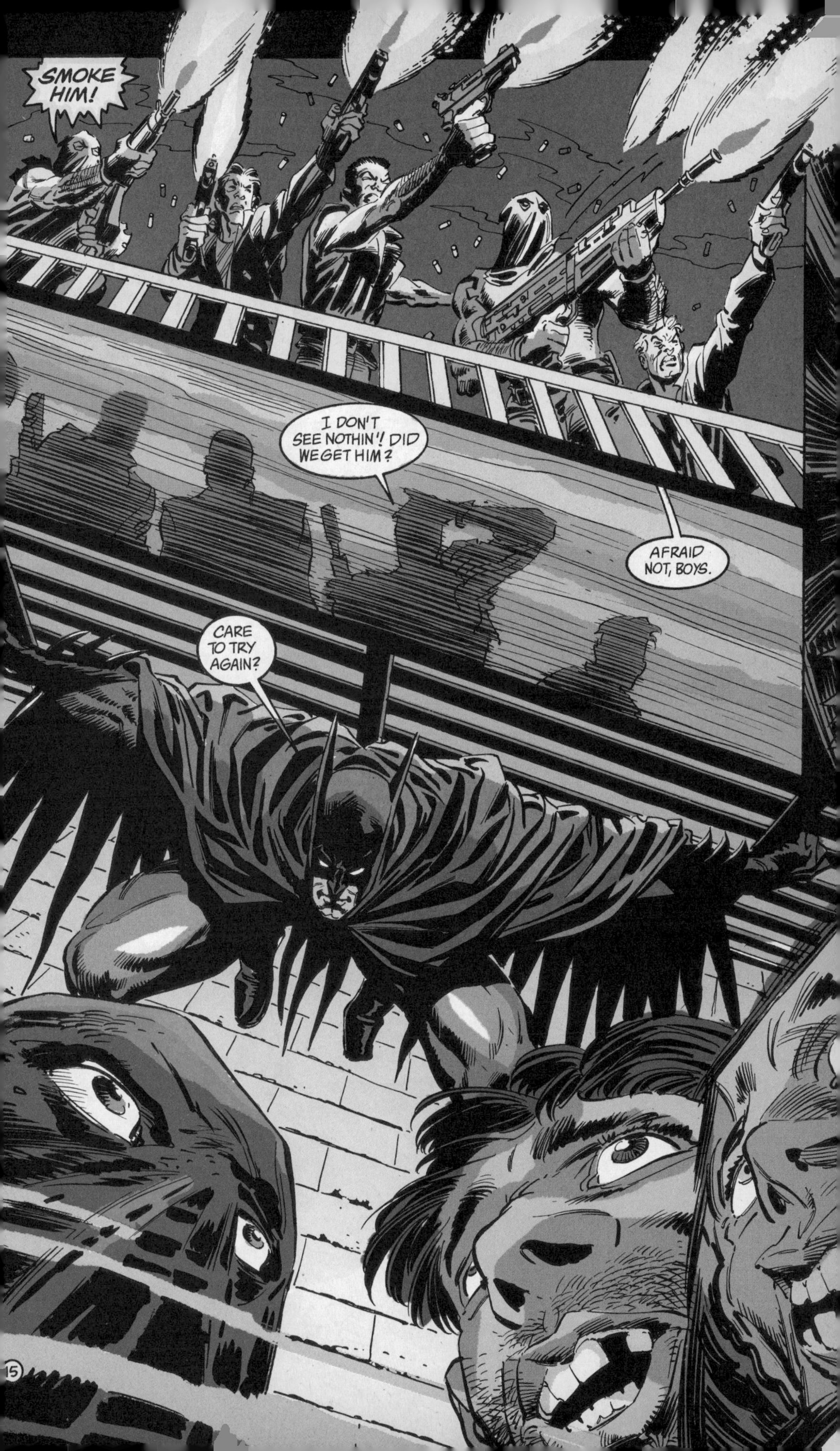
SMOKE HIM!
I DON'T SEE NOTHIN'! DID WE GET HIM?
AFRAID NOT, BOYS.
CARE TO TRY AGAIN?

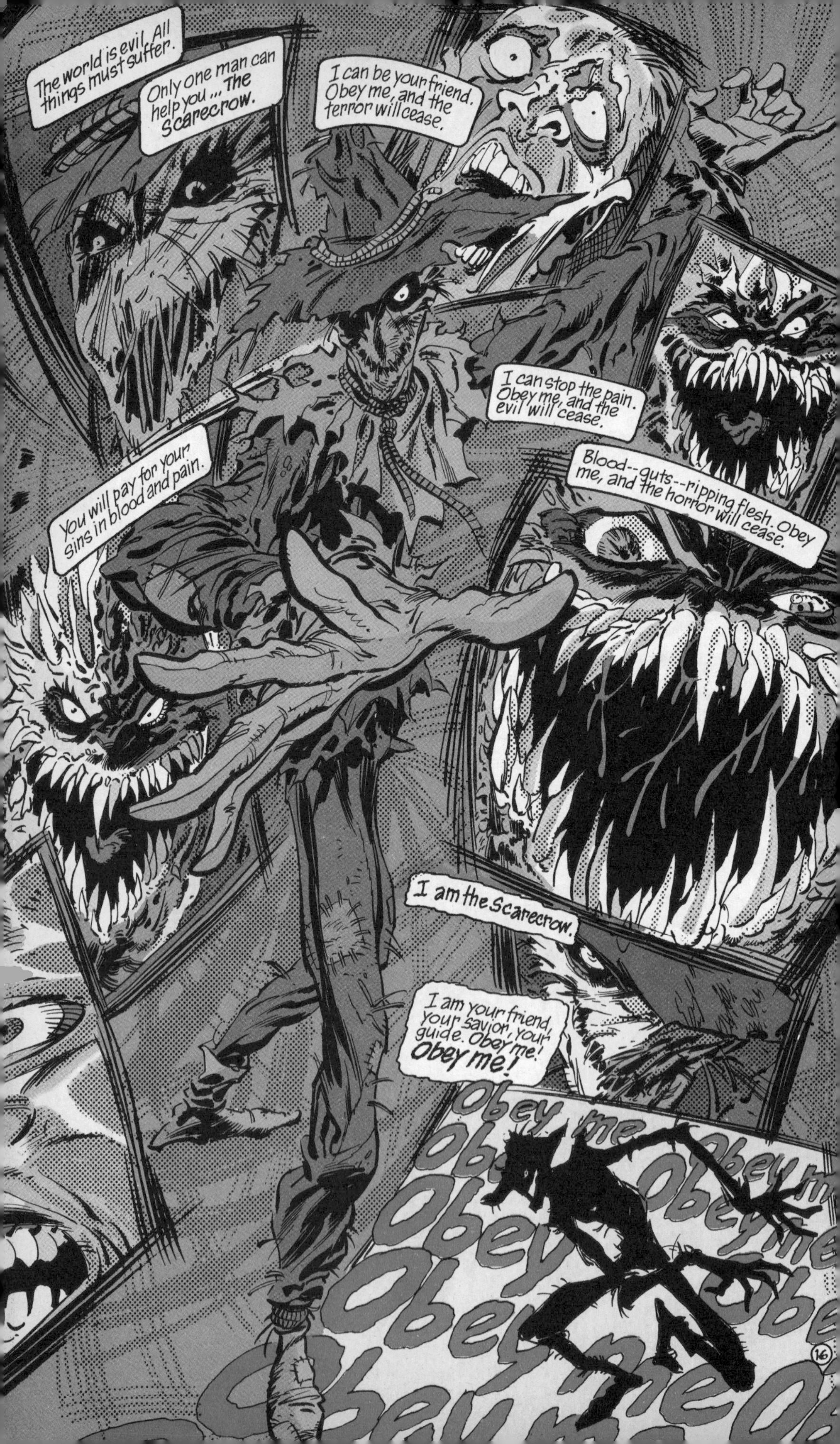
The world is evil. All things must suffer.
Only one man can help you ... The Scarecrow.
I can be your friend. Obey me, and the terror will cease.
I can stop the pain. Obey me, and the evil will cease.
You will pay for your sins in blood and pain.
Blood--guts--ripping flesh. Obey me, and the horror will cease.
I am the Scarecrow.
I am your friend, your savior, your guide. Obey me! Obey me!
Obey me

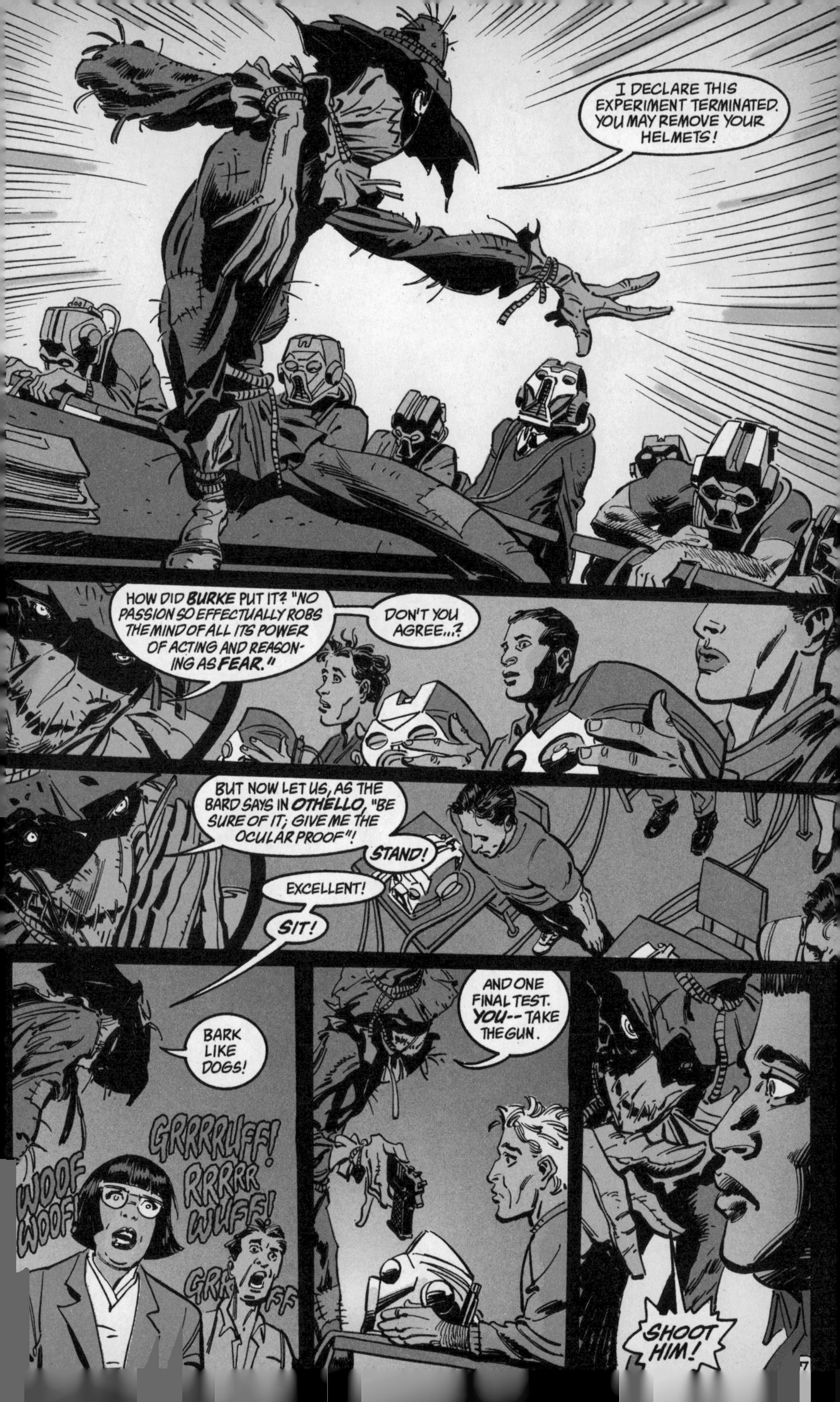
I DECLARE THIS EXPERIMENT TERMINATED. YOU MAY REMOVE YOUR HELMETS!
HOW DID BURKE PUT IT? "NO PASSION SO EFFECTUALLY ROBS THE MIND OF ALL ITS POWER OF ACTING AND REASONING AS FEAR."
DON'T YOU AGREE...?
BUT NOW LET US, AS THE BARD SAYS IN OTHELLO, "BE SURE OF IT; GIVE ME THE OCULAR PROOF"!
STAND!
EXCELLENT!
SIT!
BARK LIKE DOGS!
GRRRRUFF! RRRRR WUFF!
WOOF WOOF!
GRRFF
AND ONE FINAL TEST. YOU-- TAKE THE GUN.
SHOOT HIM!

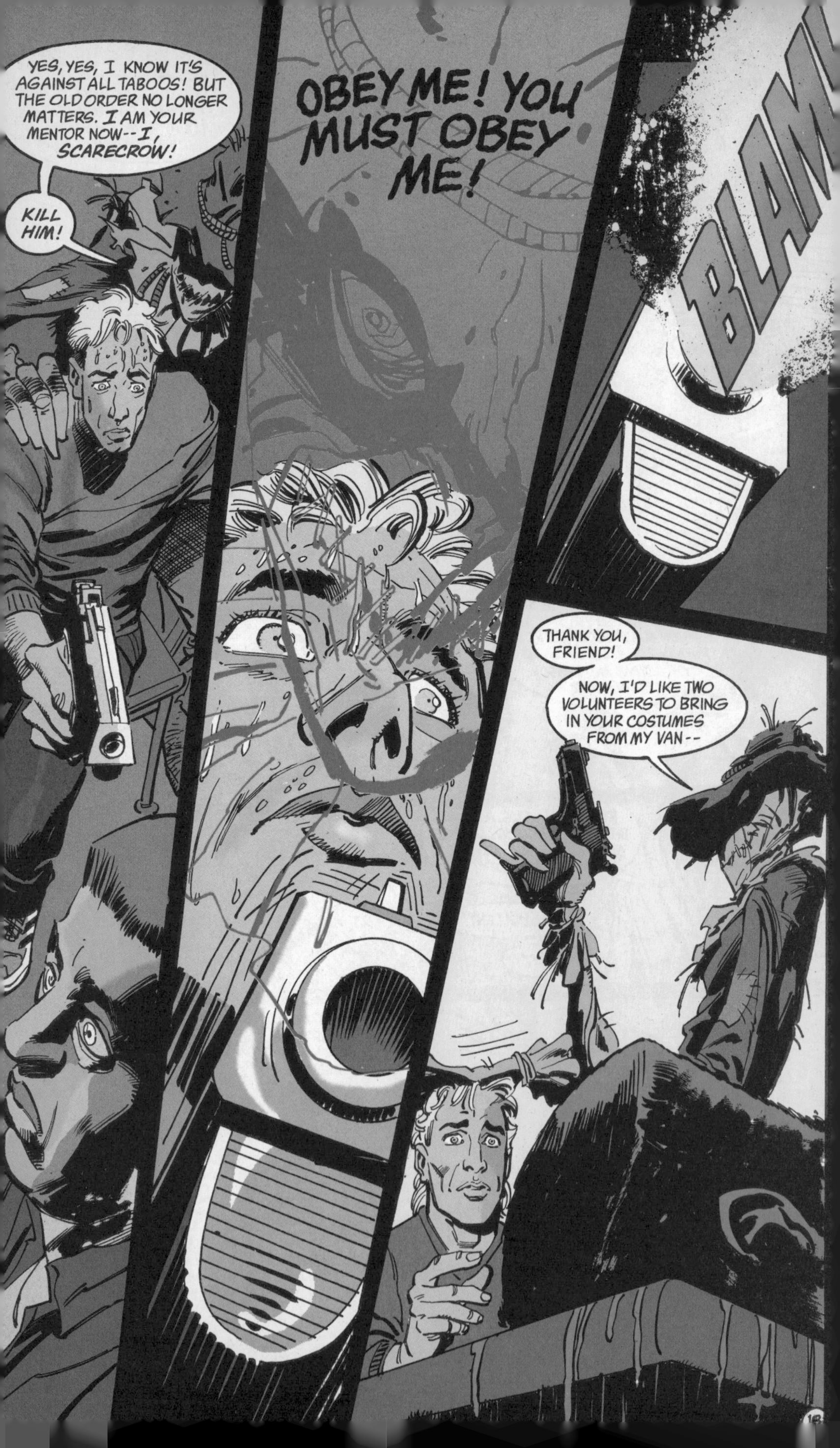
YES, YES, I KNOW IT'S AGAINST ALL TABOOS! BUT THE OLD ORDER NO LONGER MATTERS. I AM YOUR MENTOR NOW--I, SCARECROW!
KILL HIM!
OBEY ME! YOU MUST OBEY ME!
THANK YOU, FRIEND!
NOW, I'D LIKE TWO VOLUNTEERS TO BRING IN YOUR COSTUMES FROM MY VAN--

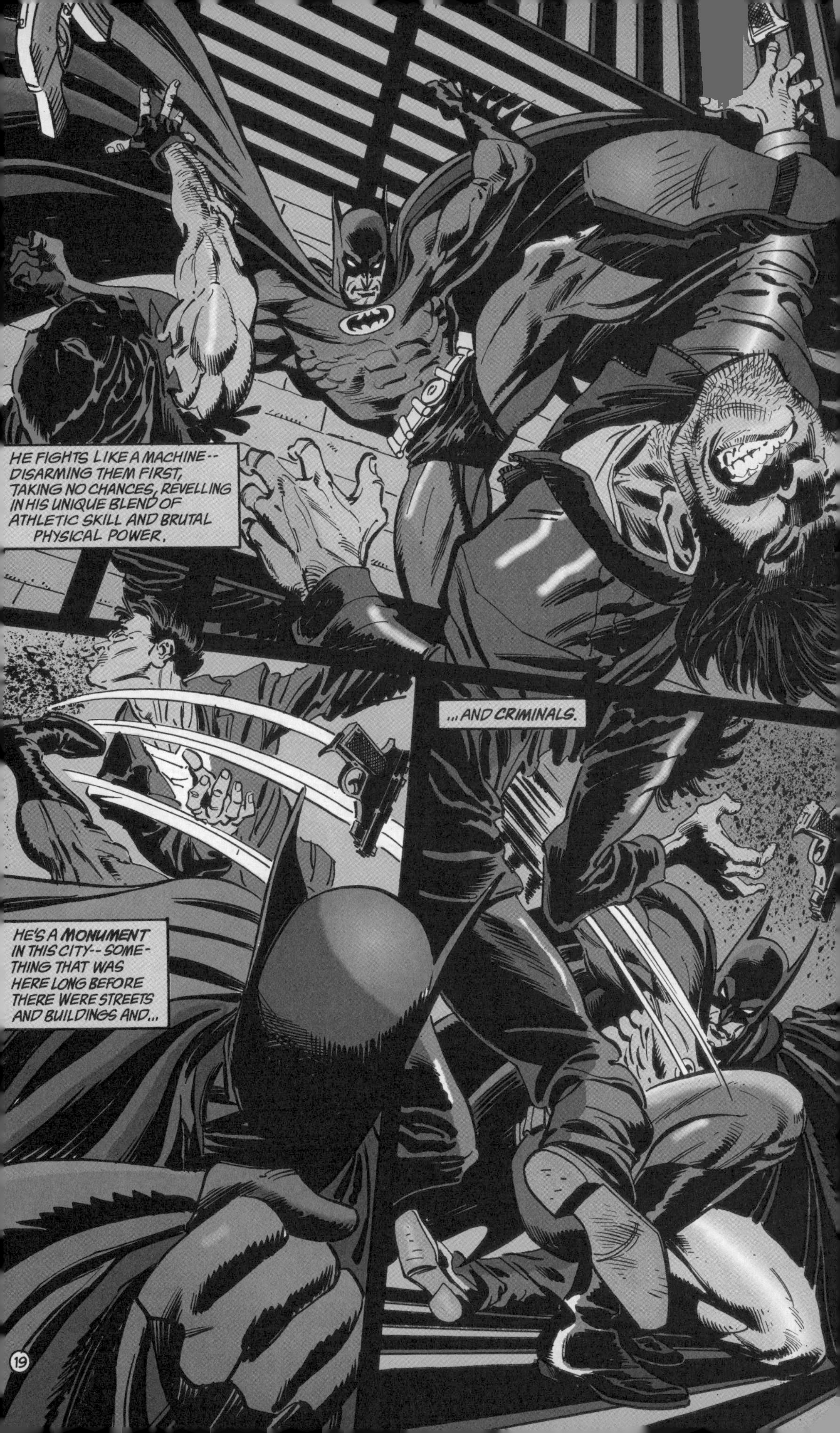
HE FIGHTS LIKE A MACHINE-- DISARMING THEM FIRST, TAKING NO CHANCES, REVELLING IN HIS UNIQUE BLEND OF ATHLETIC SKILL AND BRUTAL PHYSICAL POWER.
...AND CRIMINALS.
HE'S A MONUMENT IN THIS CITY-- SOMETHING THAT WAS HERE LONG BEFORE THERE WERE STREETS AND BUILDINGS AND...
19

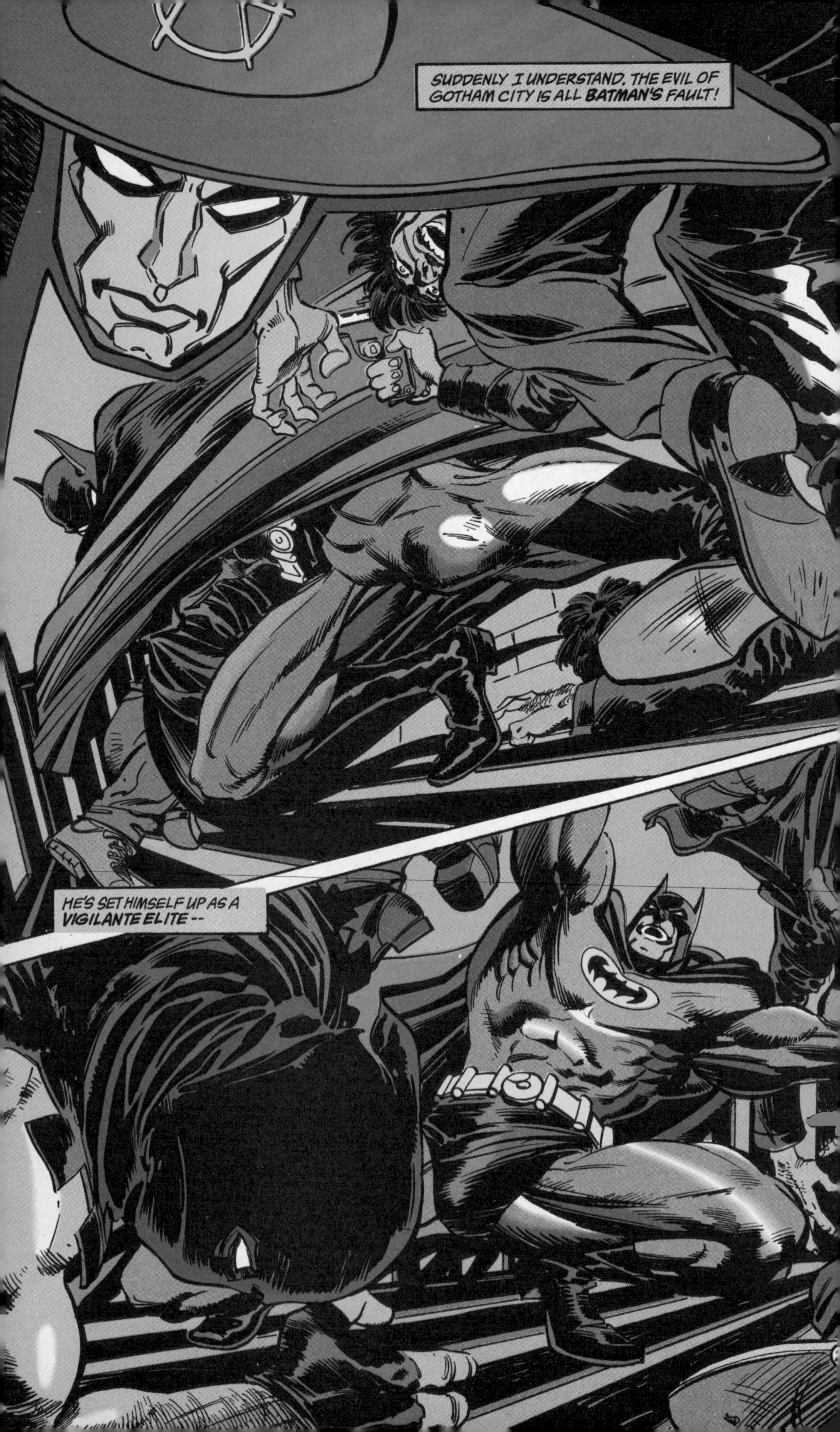
SUDDENLY I UNDERSTAND. THE EVIL OF GOTHAM CITY IS ALL BATMAN'S FAULT!
HE'S SET HIMSELF UP AS A VIGILANTE ELITE --

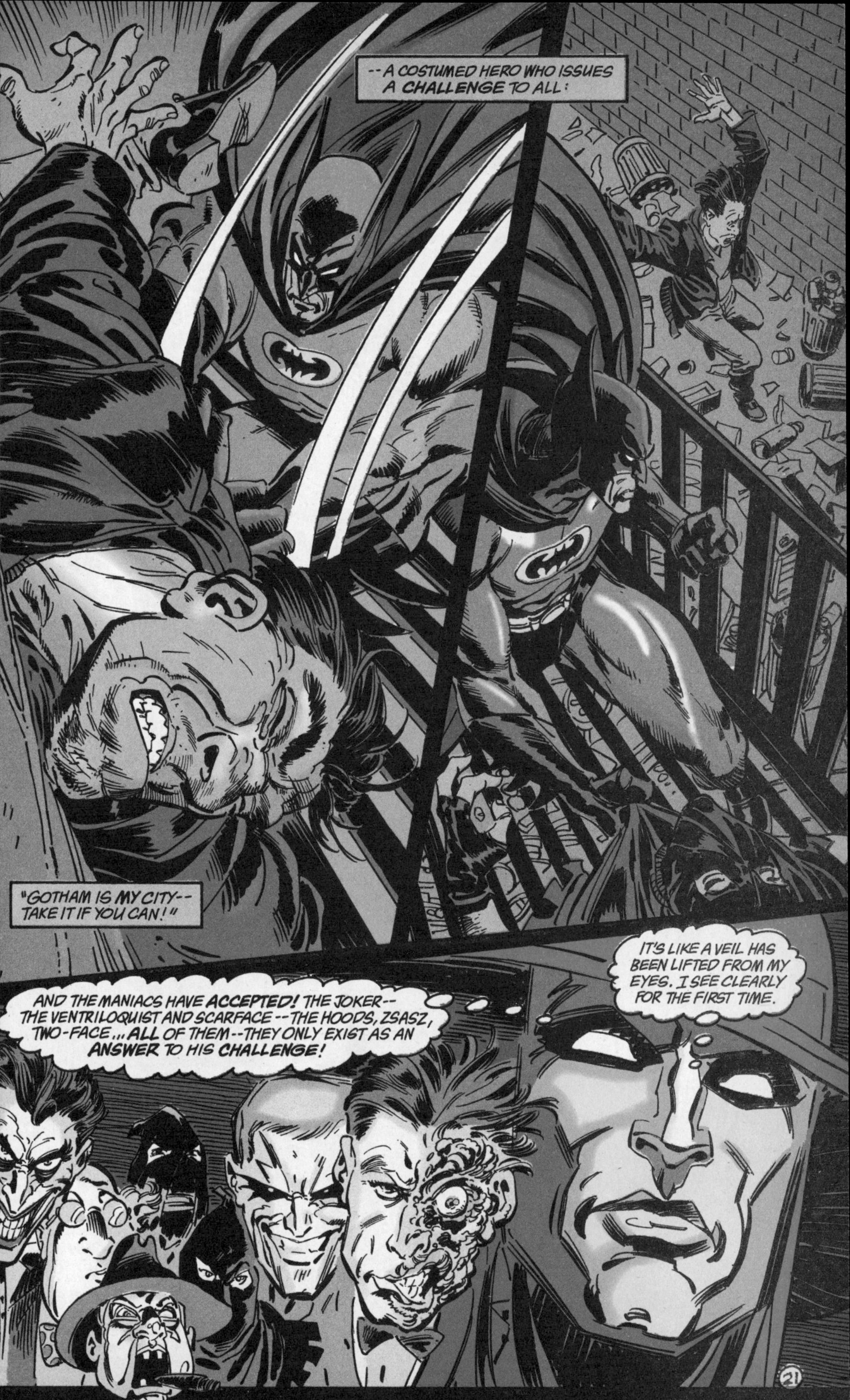

--A COSTUMED HERO WHO ISSUES A CHALLENGE TO ALL:
"GOTHAM IS MY CITY-- TAKE IT IF YOU CAN!"
IT'S LIKE A VEIL HAS BEEN LIFTED FROM MY EYES. I SEE CLEARLY FOR THE FIRST TIME.
AND THE MANIACS HAVE ACCEPTED! THE JOKER-- THE VENTRILOQUIST AND SCARFACE --THE HOODS, ZSASZ, TWO-FACE ... ALL OF THEM--THEY ONLY EXIST AS AN ANSWER TO HIS CHALLENGE!

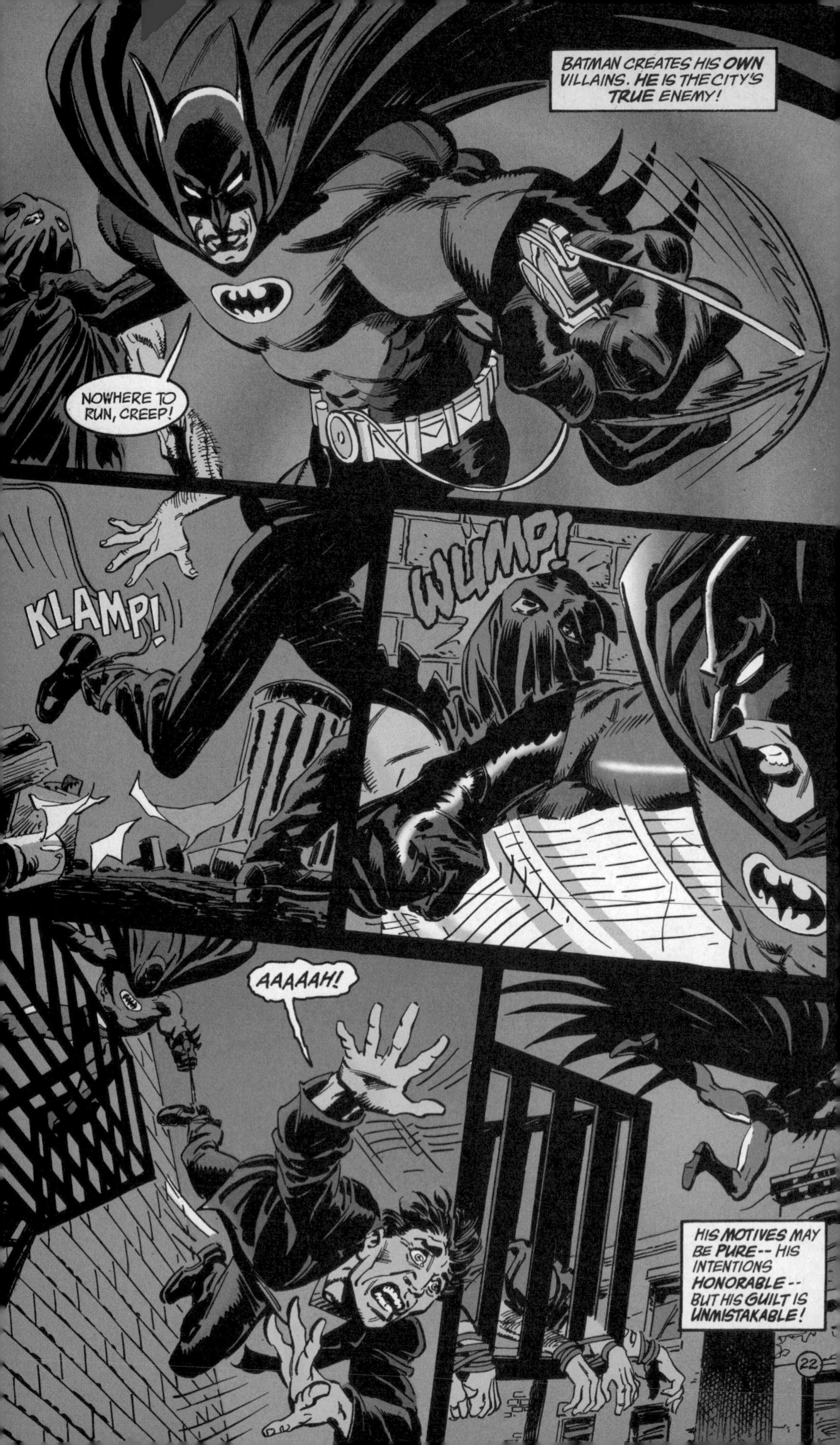

BATMAN CREATES HIS OWN VILLAINS. HE IS THE CITY'S TRUE ENEMY!
NOWHERE TO RUN, CREEP!
KLAMP!
WUMP!
AAAAAH!
HIS MOTIVES MAY BE PURE-- HIS INTENTIONS HONORABLE-- BUT HIS GUILT IS UNMISTAKABLE!

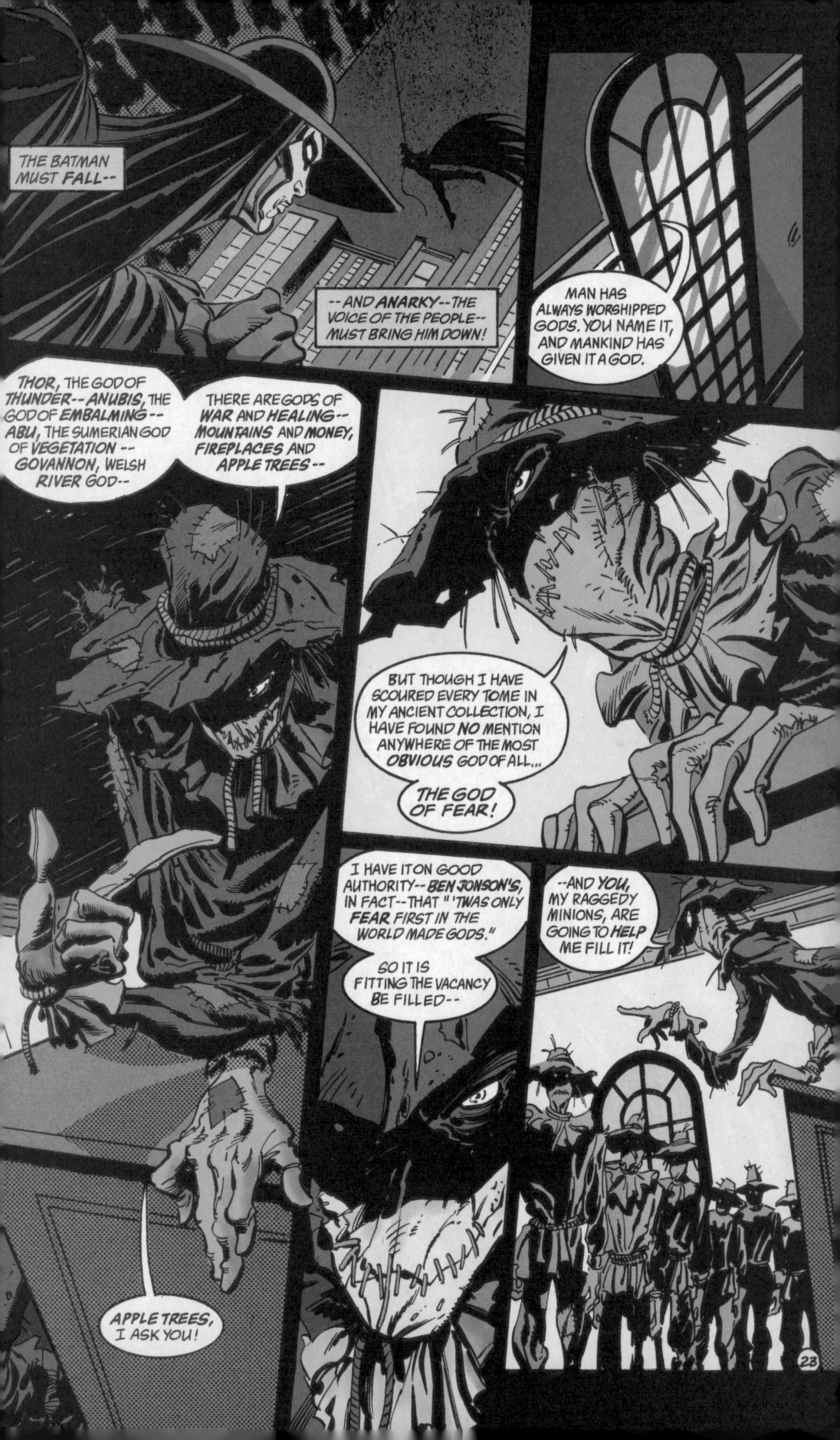

THE BATMAN MUST FALL--
--AND ANARKY--THE VOICE OF THE PEOPLE--MUST BRING HIM DOWN!
MAN HAS ALWAYS WORSHIPPED GODS. YOU NAME IT, AND MANKIND HAS GIVEN IT A GOD.
THOR, THE GOD OF THUNDER--ANUBIS, THE GOD OF EMBALMING--ABU, THE SUMERIAN GOD OF VEGETATION--GOVANNON, WELSH RIVER GOD--
THERE ARE GODS OF WAR AND HEALING--MOUNTAINS AND MONEY, FIREPLACES AND APPLE TREES--
BUT THOUGH I HAVE SCOURED EVERY TOME IN MY ANCIENT COLLECTION, I HAVE FOUND NO MENTION ANYWHERE OF THE MOST OBVIOUS GOD OF ALL...
THE GOD OF FEAR!
APPLE TREES, I ASK YOU!
I HAVE IT ON GOOD AUTHORITY--BEN JONSON'S, IN FACT--THAT " 'TWAS ONLY FEAR FIRST IN THE WORLD MADE GODS."
SO IT IS FITTING THE VACANCY BE FILLED--
--AND YOU, MY RAGGEDY MINIONS, ARE GOING TO HELP ME FILL IT!

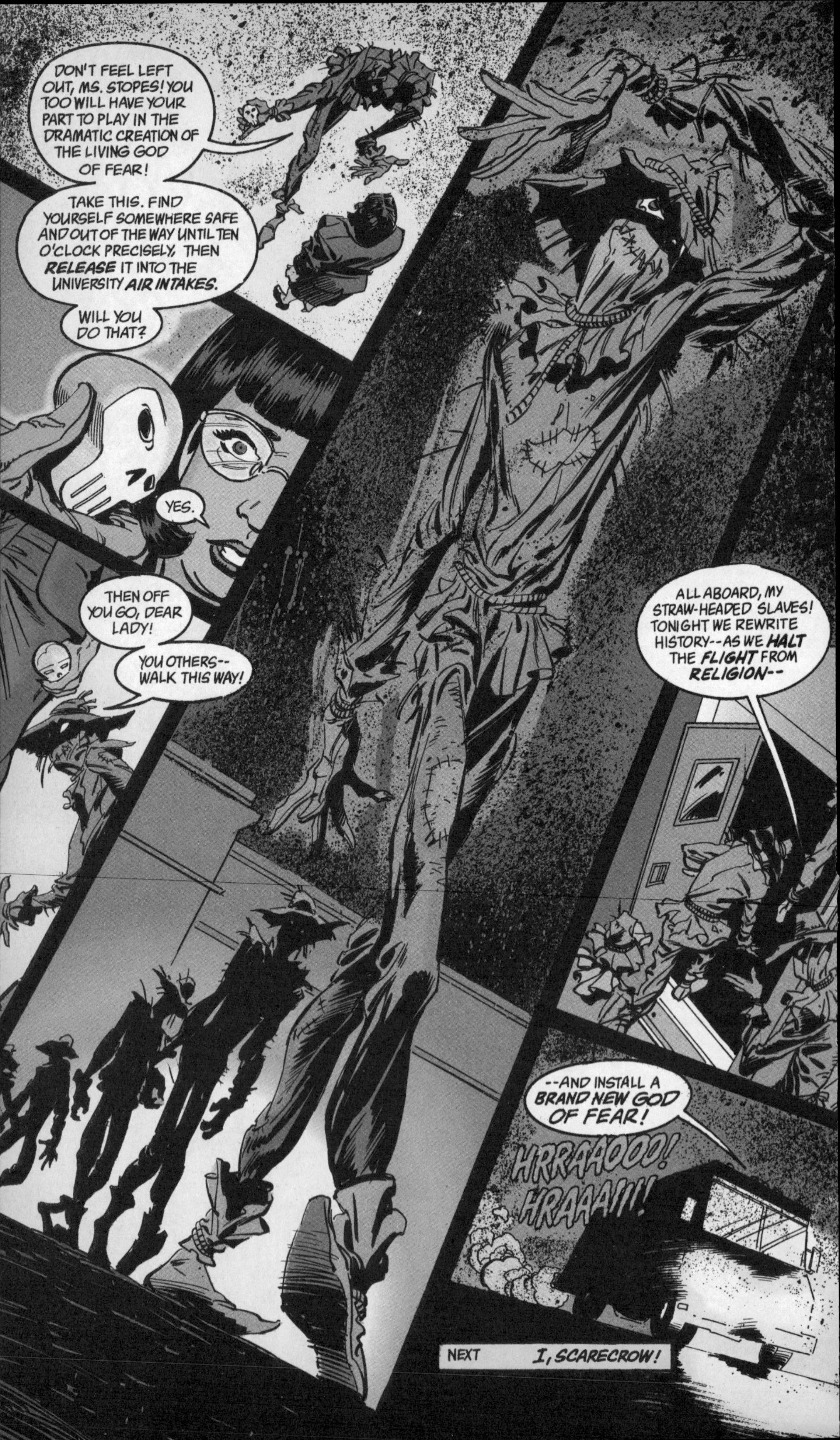
DON'T FEEL LEFT OUT, MS. STOPES! YOU TOO WILL HAVE YOUR PART TO PLAY IN THE DRAMATIC CREATION OF THE LIVING GOD OF FEAR!
TAKE THIS. FIND YOURSELF SOMEWHERE SAFE AND OUT OF THE WAY UNTIL TEN O'CLOCK PRECISELY, THEN RELEASE IT INTO THE UNIVERSITY AIR INTAKES.
WILL YOU DO THAT?
YES.
THEN OFF YOU GO, DEAR LADY!
YOU OTHERS--WALK THIS WAY!
ALL ABOARD, MY STRAW-HEADED SLAVES! TONIGHT WE REWRITE HISTORY--AS WE HALT THE FLIGHT FROM RELIGION--
--AND INSTALL A BRAND NEW GOD OF FEAR!
HRRAAOOO! HRAAAII!
NEXT I, SCARECROW!

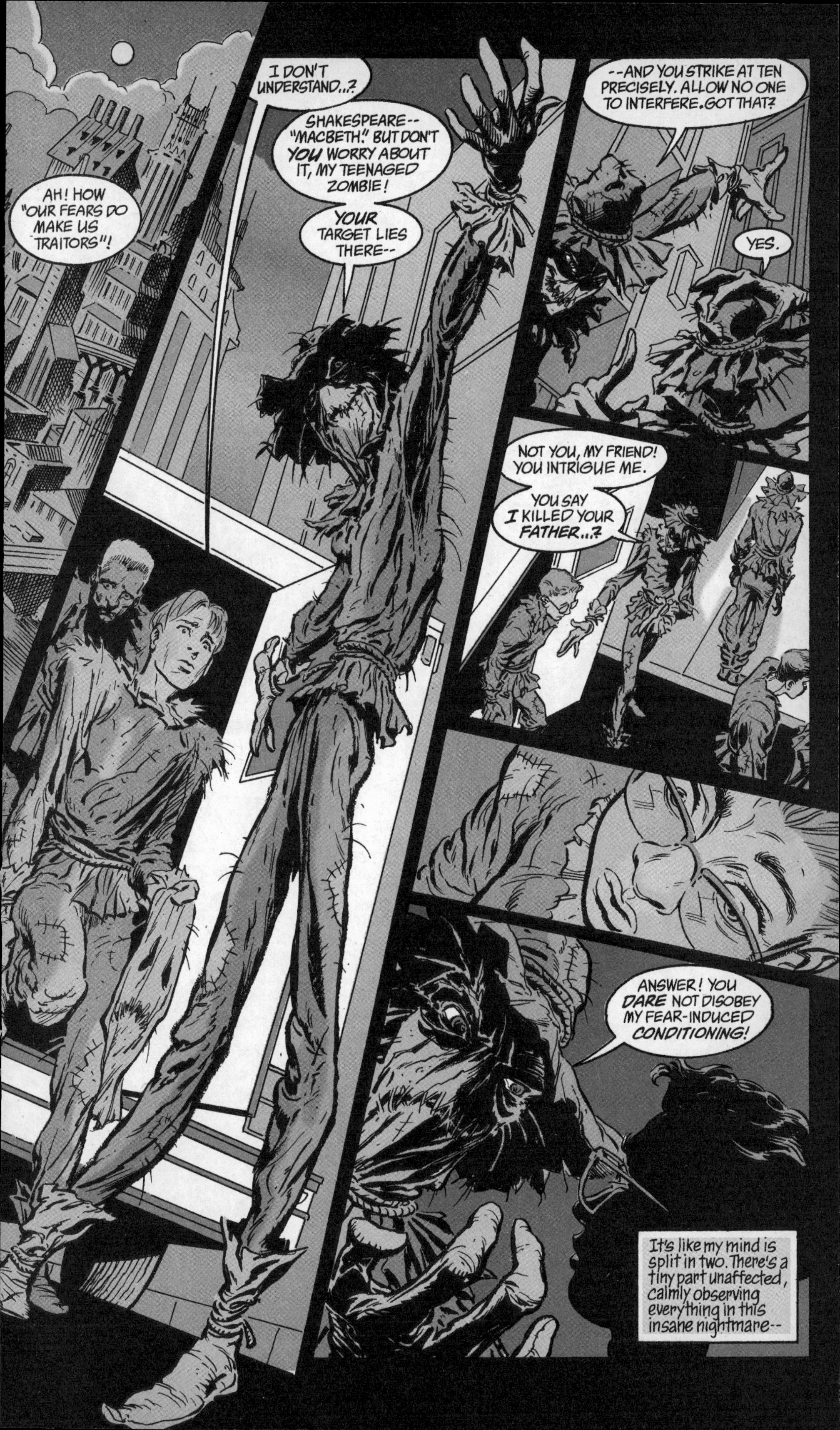
AH! HOW "OUR FEARS DO MAKE US TRAITORS"!
I DON'T UNDERSTAND...?
SHAKESPEARE-- "MACBETH." BUT DON'T YOU WORRY ABOUT IT, MY TEENAGED ZOMBIE!
YOUR TARGET LIES THERE--
--AND YOU STRIKE AT TEN PRECISELY. ALLOW NO ONE TO INTERFERE. GOT THAT?
YES.
NOT YOU, MY FRIEND! YOU INTRIGUE ME.
YOU SAY I KILLED YOUR FATHER...?
ANSWER! YOU DARE NOT DISOBEY MY FEAR-INDUCED CONDITIONING!
It's like my mind is split in two. There's a tiny part unaffected, calmly observing everything in this insane nightmare--

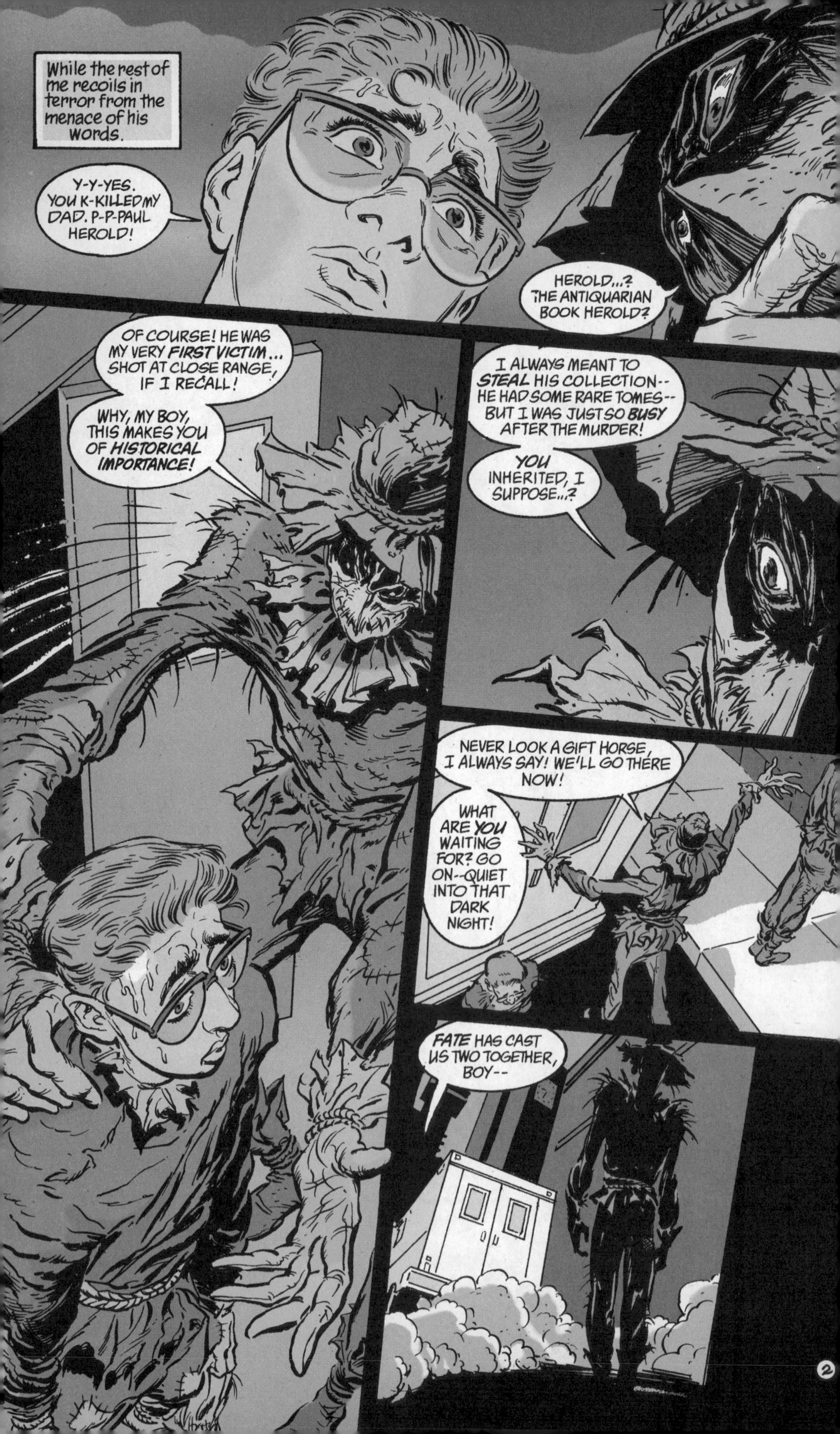
While the rest of me recoils in terror from the menace of his words.
Y-Y-YES. YOU K-KILLED MY DAD. P-P-PAUL HEROLD!
HEROLD...? THE ANTIQUARIAN BOOK HEROLD?
OF COURSE! HE WAS MY VERY FIRST VICTIM... SHOT AT CLOSE RANGE, IF I RECALL!
WHY, MY BOY, THIS MAKES YOU OF HISTORICAL IMPORTANCE!
I ALWAYS MEANT TO STEAL HIS COLLECTION-- HE HAD SOME RARE TOMES-- BUT I WAS JUST SO BUSY AFTER THE MURDER!
YOU INHERITED, I SUPPOSE...?
NEVER LOOK A GIFT HORSE, I ALWAYS SAY! WE'LL GO THERE NOW!
WHAT ARE YOU WAITING FOR? GO ON--QUIET INTO THAT DARK NIGHT!
FATE HAS CAST US TWO TOGETHER, BOY--

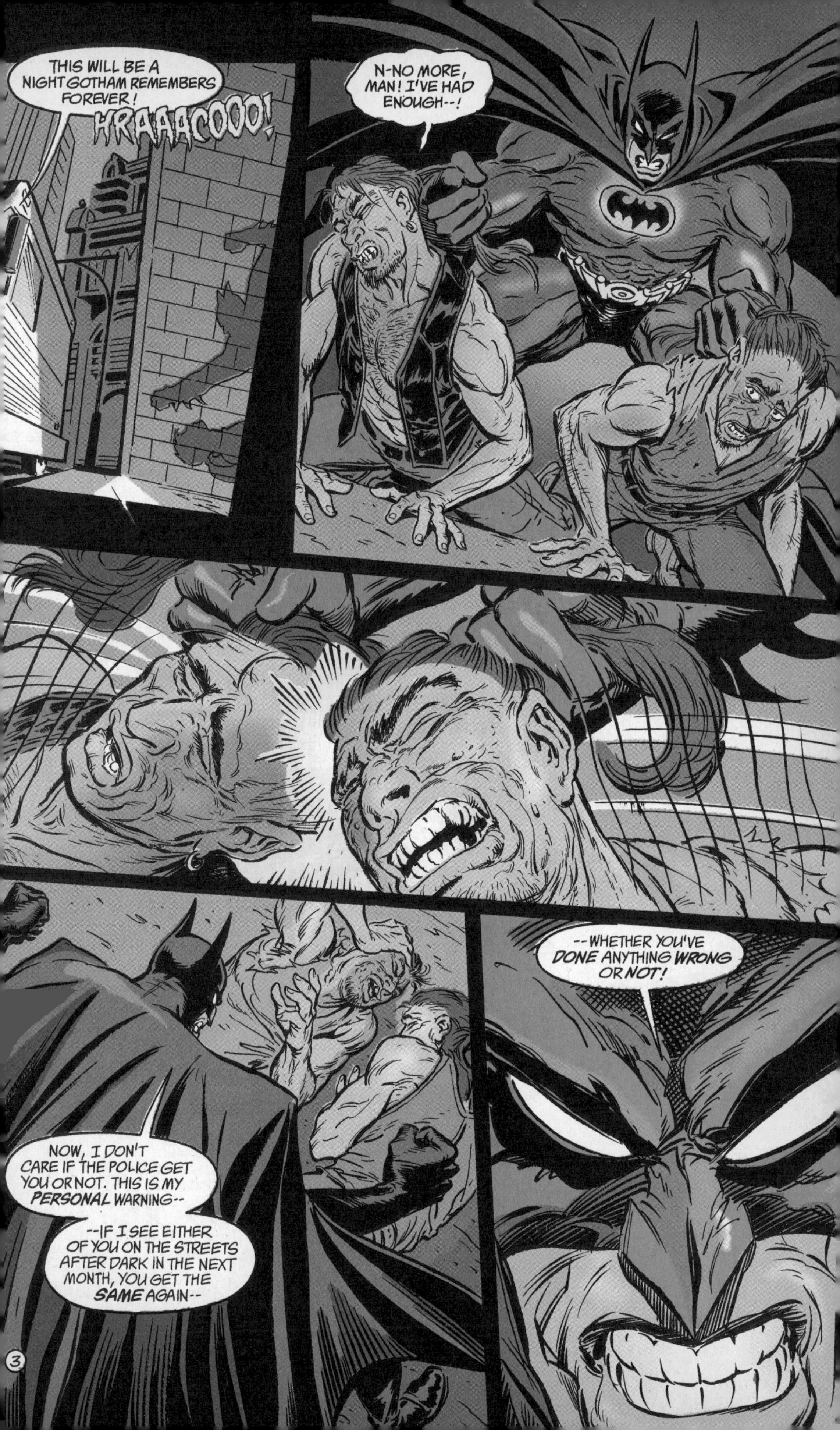
THIS WILL BE A NIGHT GOTHAM REMEMBERS FOREVER!
HRAAACOOO!
N-NO MORE, MAN! I'VE HAD ENOUGH--!
NOW, I DON'T CARE IF THE POLICE GET YOU OR NOT. THIS IS MY PERSONAL WARNING--
--IF I SEE EITHER OF YOU ON THE STREETS AFTER DARK IN THE NEXT MONTH, YOU GET THE SAME AGAIN--
--WHETHER YOU'VE DONE ANYTHING WRONG OR NOT!
3

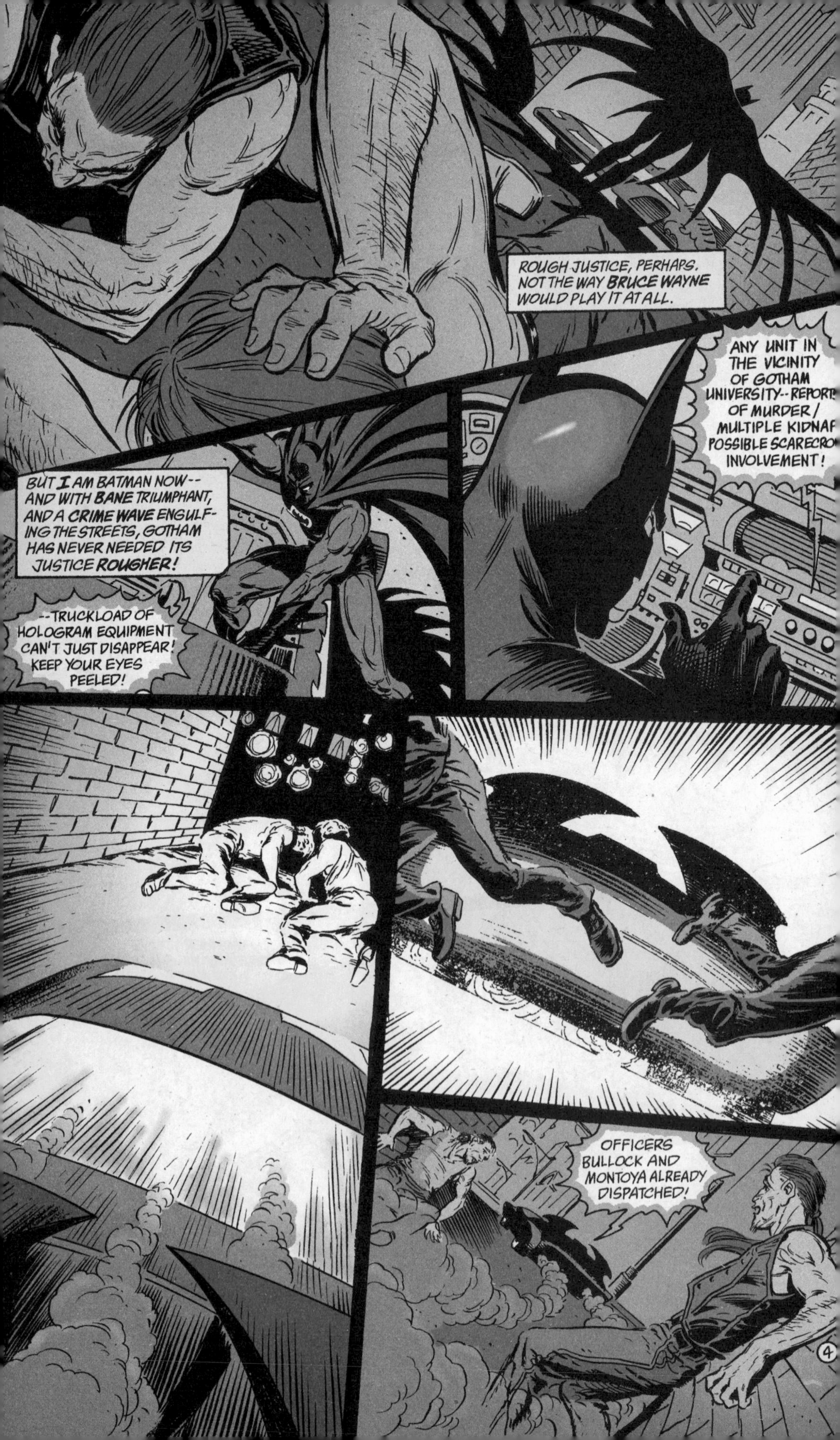

ROUGH JUSTICE, PERHAPS. NOT THE WAY BRUCE WAYNE WOULD PLAY IT AT ALL.
BUT I AM BATMAN NOW-- AND WITH BANE TRIUMPHANT, AND A CRIME WAVE ENGULFING THE STREETS, GOTHAM HAS NEVER NEEDED ITS JUSTICE ROUGHER!
--TRUCKLOAD OF HOLOGRAM EQUIPMENT CAN'T JUST DISAPPEAR! KEEP YOUR EYES PEELED!
ANY UNIT IN THE VICINITY OF GOTHAM UNIVERSITY--REPORT OF MURDER/ MULTIPLE KIDNAP POSSIBLE SCARECRO INVOLVEMENT!
OFFICERS BULLOCK AND MONTOYA ALREADY DISPATCHED!
4

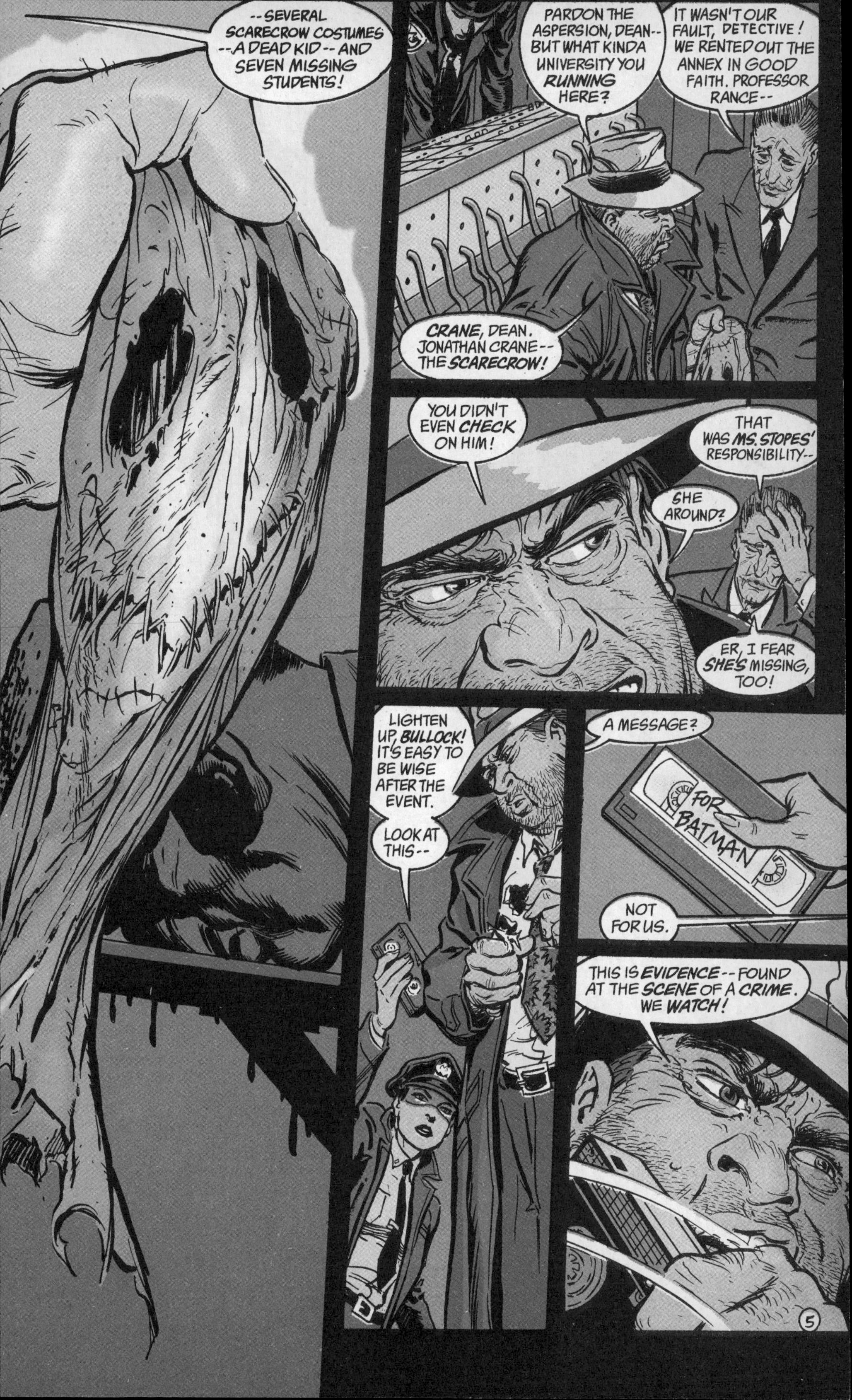
--SEVERAL SCARECROW COSTUMES --A DEAD KID-- AND SEVEN MISSING STUDENTS!
PARDON THE ASPERSION, DEAN-- BUT WHAT KINDA UNIVERSITY YOU RUNNING HERE?
IT WASN'T OUR FAULT, DETECTIVE! WE RENTED OUT THE ANNEX IN GOOD FAITH. PROFESSOR RANCE--
CRANE, DEAN. JONATHAN CRANE-- THE SCARECROW!
YOU DIDN'T EVEN CHECK ON HIM!
THAT WAS MS. STOPES' RESPONSIBILITY--
SHE AROUND?
ER, I FEAR SHE'S MISSING, TOO!
LIGHTEN UP, BULLOCK! IT'S EASY TO BE WISE AFTER THE EVENT.
LOOK AT THIS--
A MESSAGE?
FOR BATMAN
NOT FOR US.
THIS IS EVIDENCE-- FOUND AT THE SCENE OF A CRIME. WE WATCH!
5

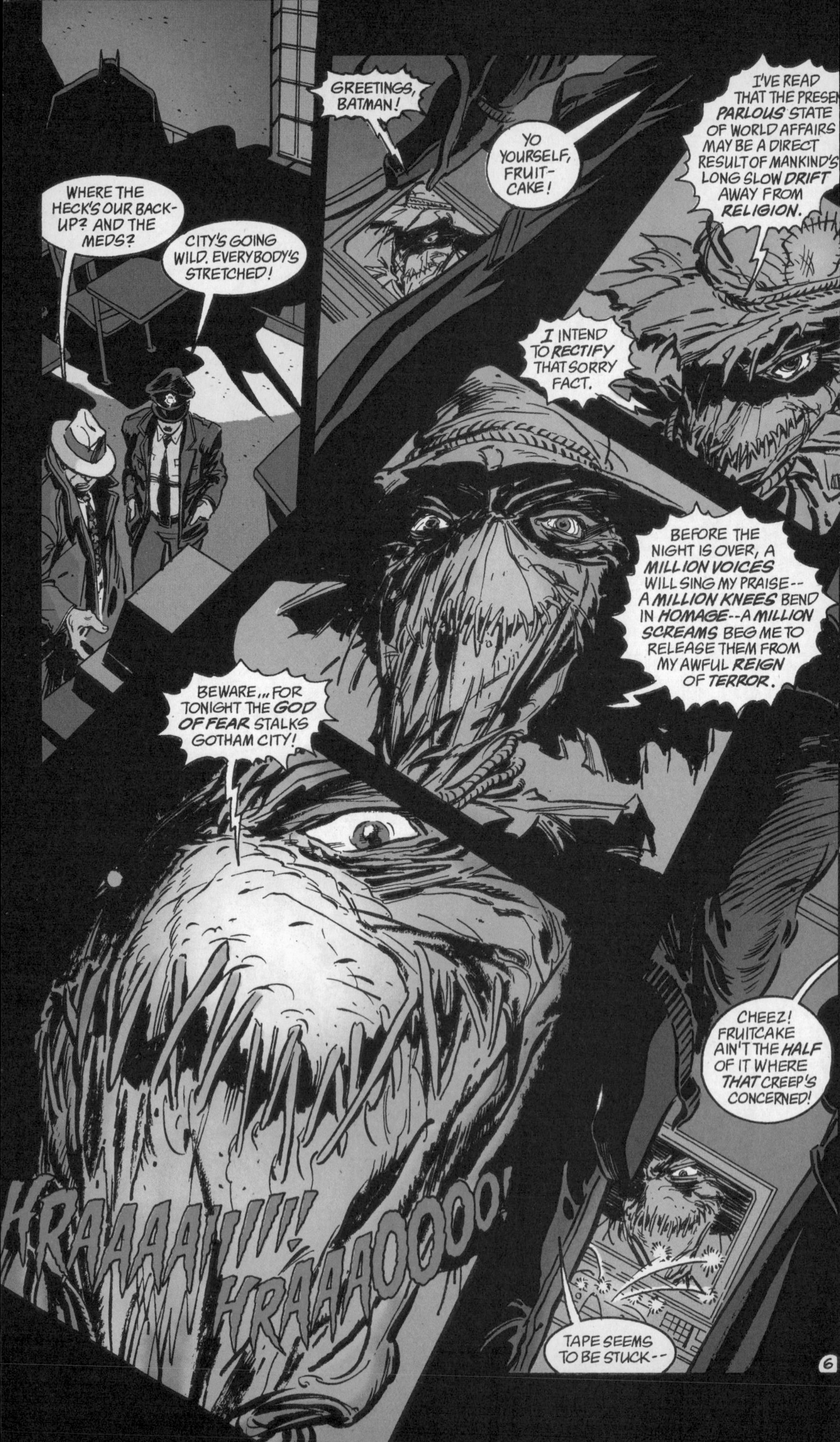
WHERE THE HECK'S OUR BACK-UP? AND THE MEDS?
CITY'S GOING WILD. EVERYBODY'S STRETCHED!
GREETINGS, BATMAN!
YO YOURSELF, FRUIT-CAKE!
I'VE READ THAT THE PRESEN PARLOUS STATE OF WORLD AFFAIRS MAY BE A DIRECT RESULT OF MANKIND'S LONG SLOW DRIFT AWAY FROM RELIGION.
I INTEND TO RECTIFY THAT SORRY FACT.
BEFORE THE NIGHT IS OVER, A MILLION VOICES WILL SING MY PRAISE-- A MILLION KNEES BEND IN HOMAGE--A MILLION SCREAMS BEG ME TO RELEASE THEM FROM MY AWFUL REIGN OF TERROR.
BEWARE... FOR TONIGHT THE GOD OF FEAR STALKS GOTHAM CITY!
CHEEZ! FRUITCAKE AIN'T THE HALF OF IT WHERE THAT CREEP'S CONCERNED!
HRAAAAIII!
HRAAAOOOO!
TAPE SEEMS TO BE STUCK--

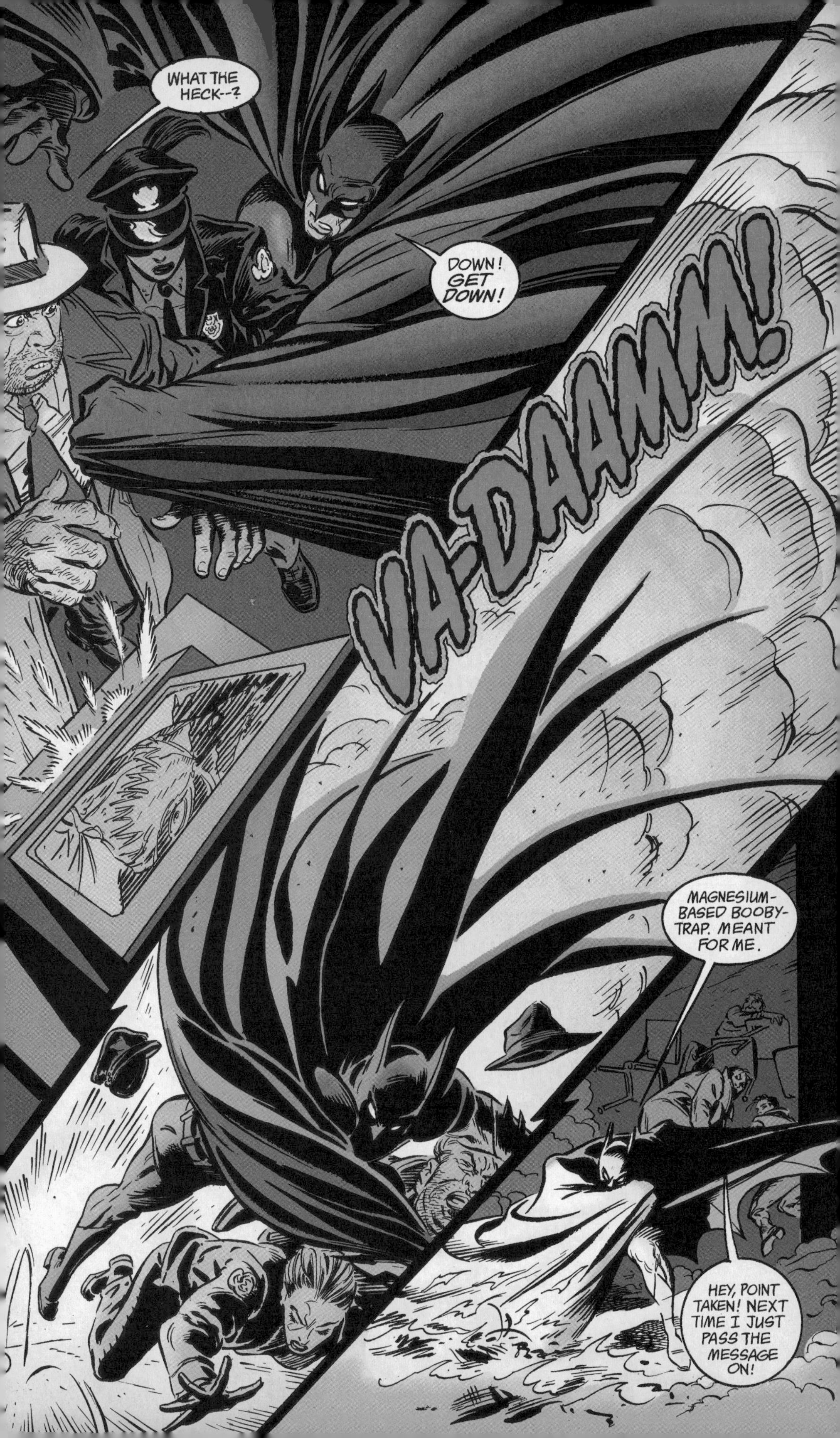
WHAT THE HECK--?
DOWN! GET DOWN!
VA-DAAMM!
MAGNESIUM-BASED BOOBY-TRAP. MEANT FOR ME.
HEY, POINT TAKEN! NEXT TIME I JUST PASS THE MESSAGE ON!

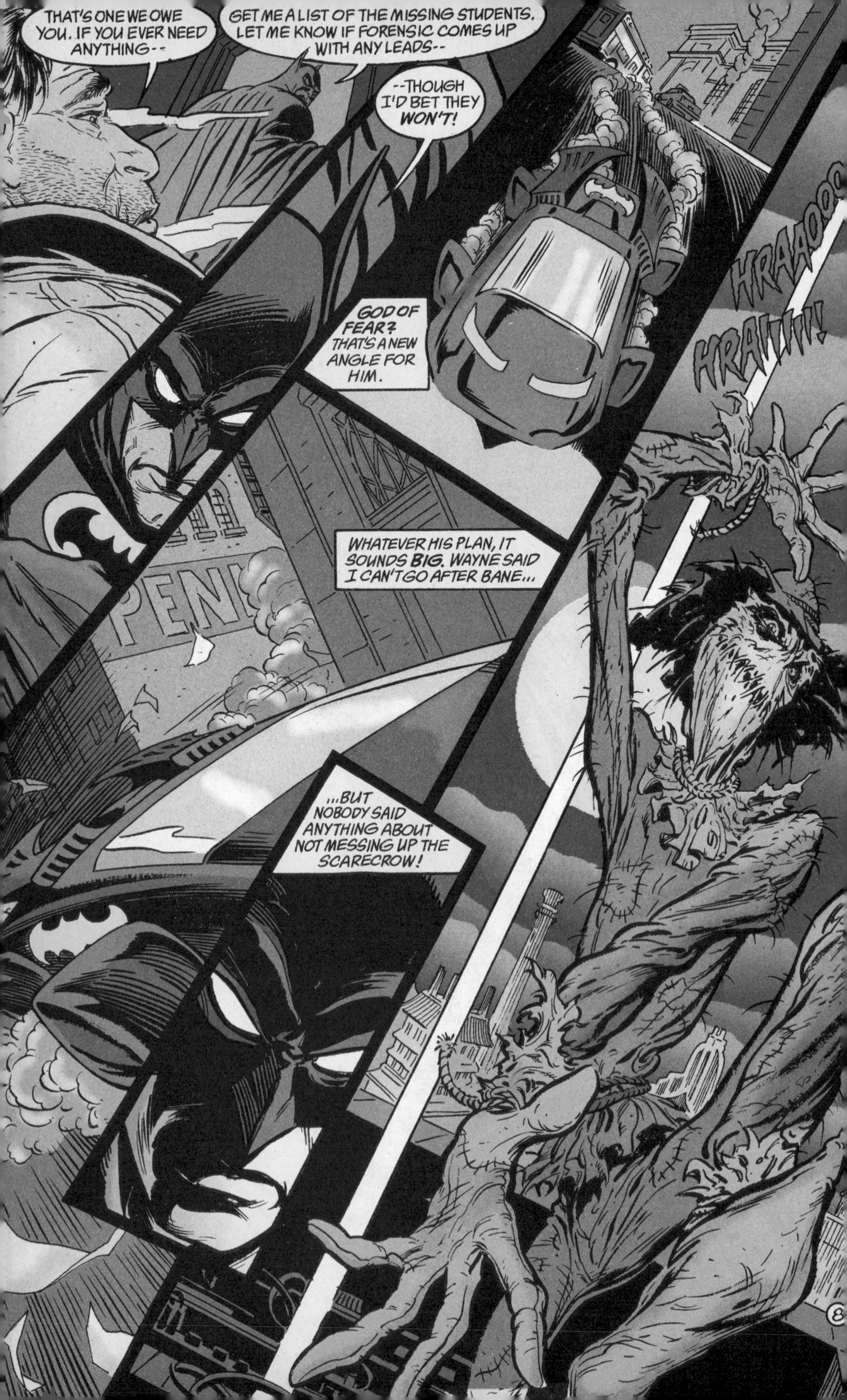

THAT'S ONE WE OWE YOU. IF YOU EVER NEED ANYTHING--
GET ME A LIST OF THE MISSING STUDENTS. LET ME KNOW IF FORENSIC COMES UP WITH ANY LEADS--
--THOUGH I'D BET THEY WON'T!
GOD OF FEAR? THAT'S A NEW ANGLE FOR HIM.
WHATEVER HIS PLAN, IT SOUNDS BIG. WAYNE SAID I CAN'T GO AFTER BANE...
PENN
...BUT NOBODY SAID ANYTHING ABOUT NOT MESSING UP THE SCARECROW!
HRAAOOO
HRAIIIII!
8

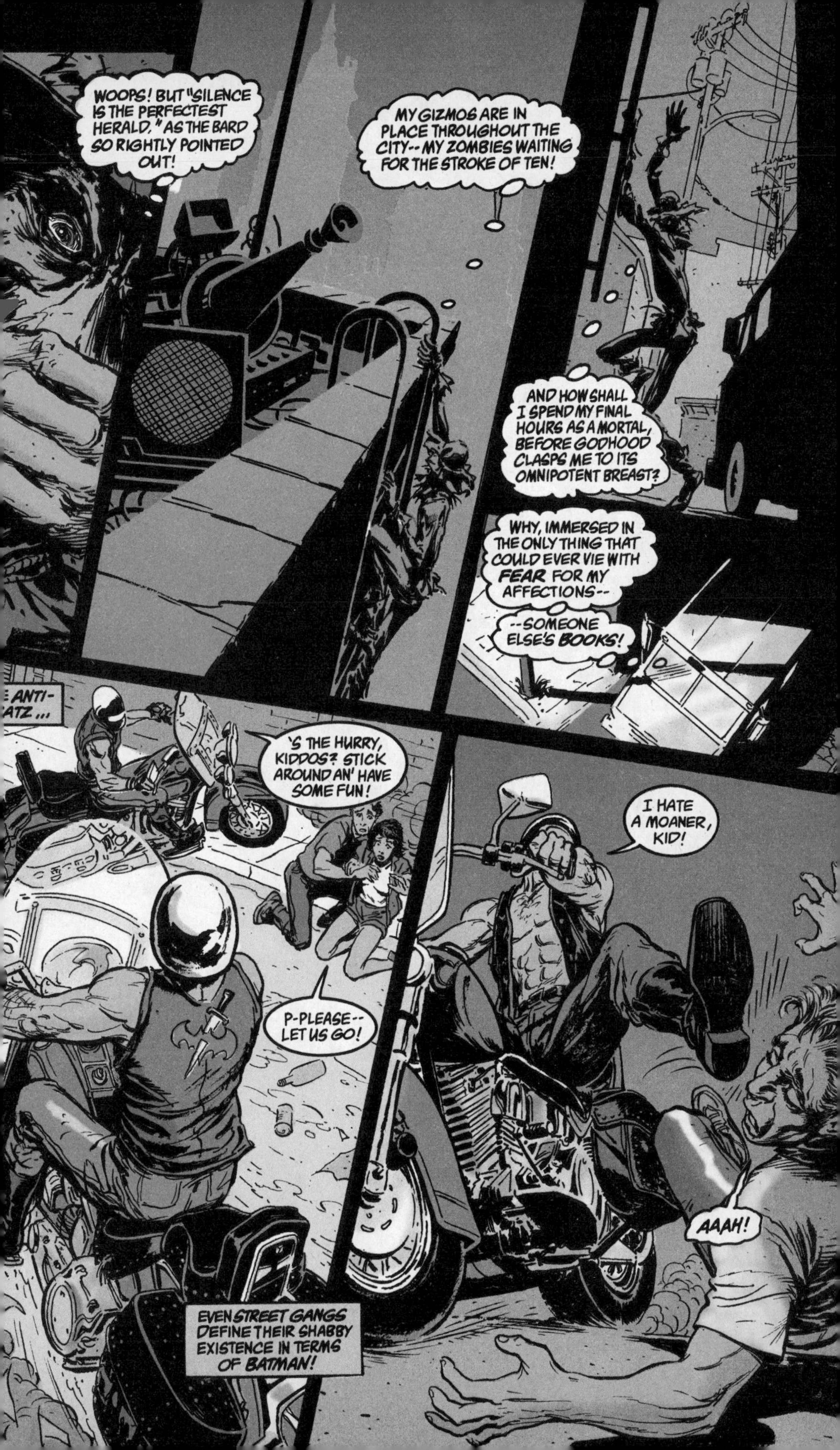
WOOPS! BUT "SILENCE IS THE PERFECTEST HERALD," AS THE BARD SO RIGHTLY POINTED OUT!
MY GIZMOS ARE IN PLACE THROUGHOUT THE CITY-- MY ZOMBIES WAITING FOR THE STROKE OF TEN!
AND HOW SHALL I SPEND MY FINAL HOURS AS A MORTAL, BEFORE GODHOOD CLASPS ME TO ITS OMNIPOTENT BREAST?
WHY, IMMERSED IN THE ONLY THING THAT COULD EVER VIE WITH FEAR FOR MY AFFECTIONS--
--SOMEONE ELSE'S BOOKS!
'S THE HURRY, KIDDOS? STICK AROUND AN' HAVE SOME FUN!
P-PLEASE-- LET US GO!
EVEN STREET GANGS DEFINE THEIR SHABBY EXISTENCE IN TERMS OF BATMAN!
I HATE A MOANER, KID!
AAAH!

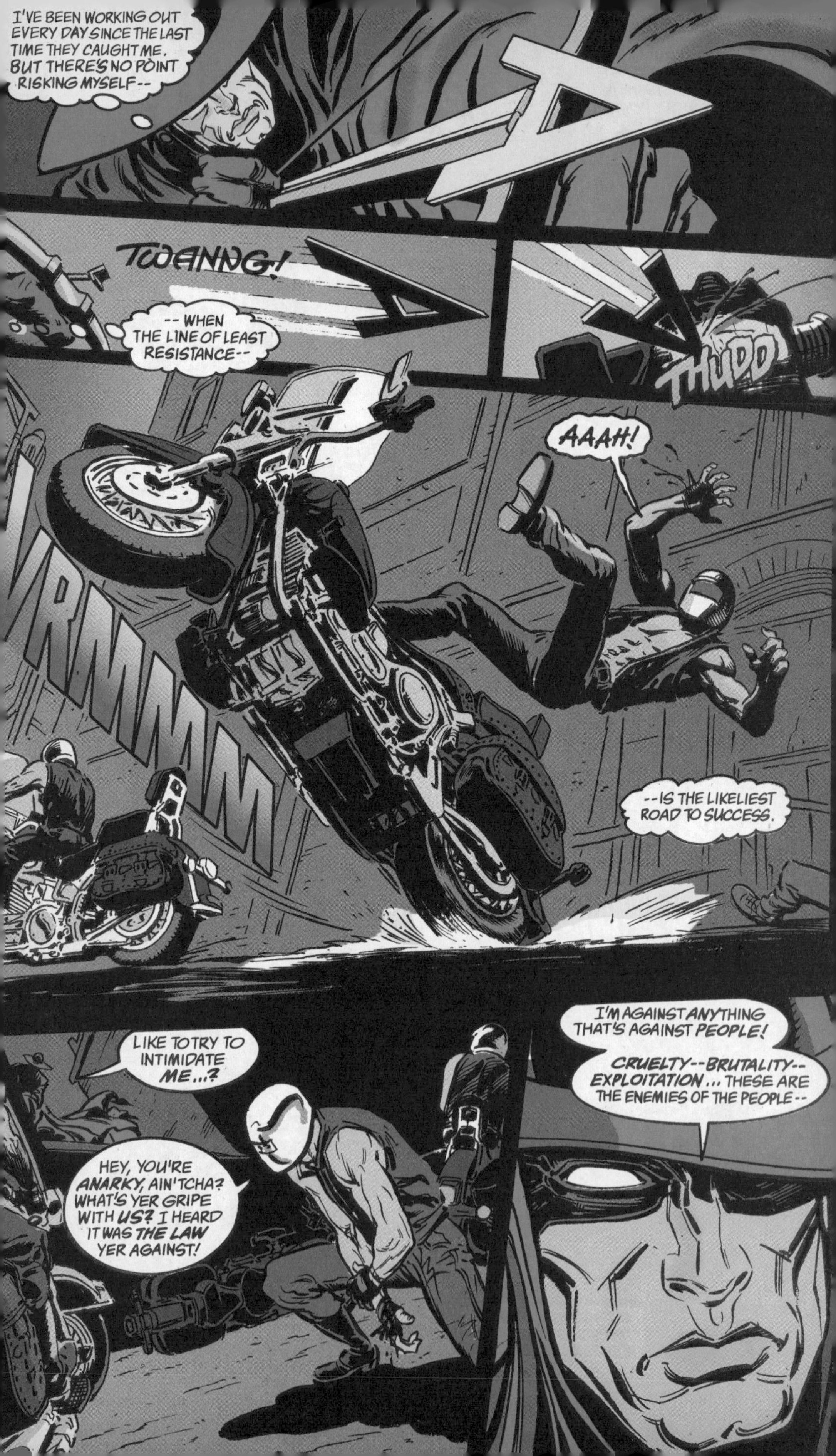

I'VE BEEN WORKING OUT EVERY DAY SINCE THE LAST TIME THEY CAUGHT ME. BUT THERE'S NO POINT RISKING MYSELF--
TWANNG!
-- WHEN THE LINE OF LEAST RESISTANCE--
THUDD
AAAH!
VRMMMM
--IS THE LIKELIEST ROAD TO SUCCESS.
LIKE TO TRY TO INTIMIDATE ME...?
HEY, YOU'RE ANARKY, AIN'TCHA? WHAT'S YER GRIPE WITH US? I HEARD IT WAS THE LAW YER AGAINST!
I'M AGAINST ANYTHING THAT'S AGAINST PEOPLE!
CRUELTY--BRUTALITY--EXPLOITATION... THESE ARE THE ENEMIES OF THE PEOPLE--

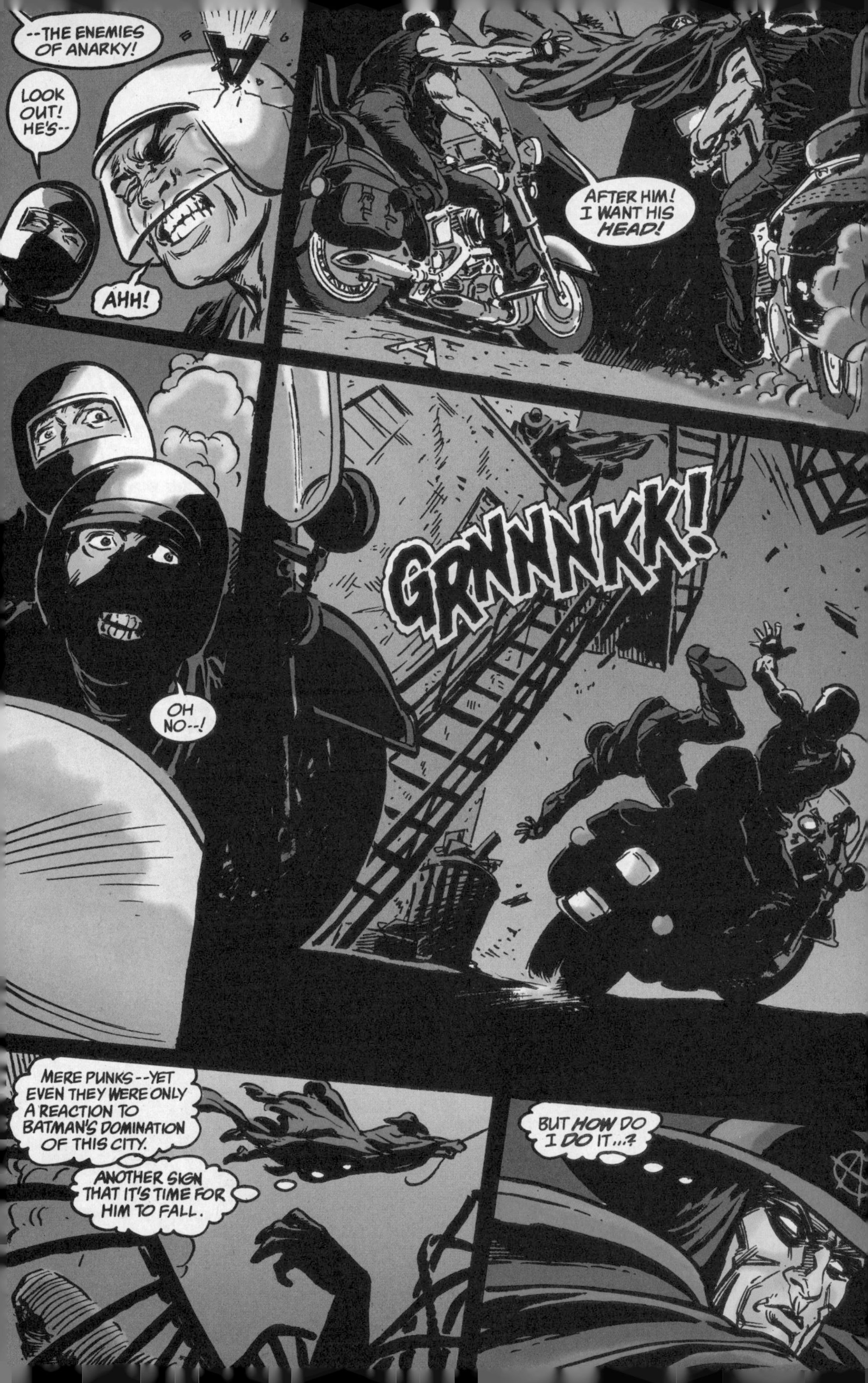
--THE ENEMIES OF ANARKY!
LOOK OUT! HE'S--
AHH!
AFTER HIM! I WANT HIS HEAD!
OH NO--!
GRNNNKK!
MERE PUNKS--YET EVEN THEY WERE ONLY A REACTION TO BATMAN'S DOMINATION OF THIS CITY.
ANOTHER SIGN THAT IT'S TIME FOR HIM TO FALL.
BUT HOW DO I DO IT...?

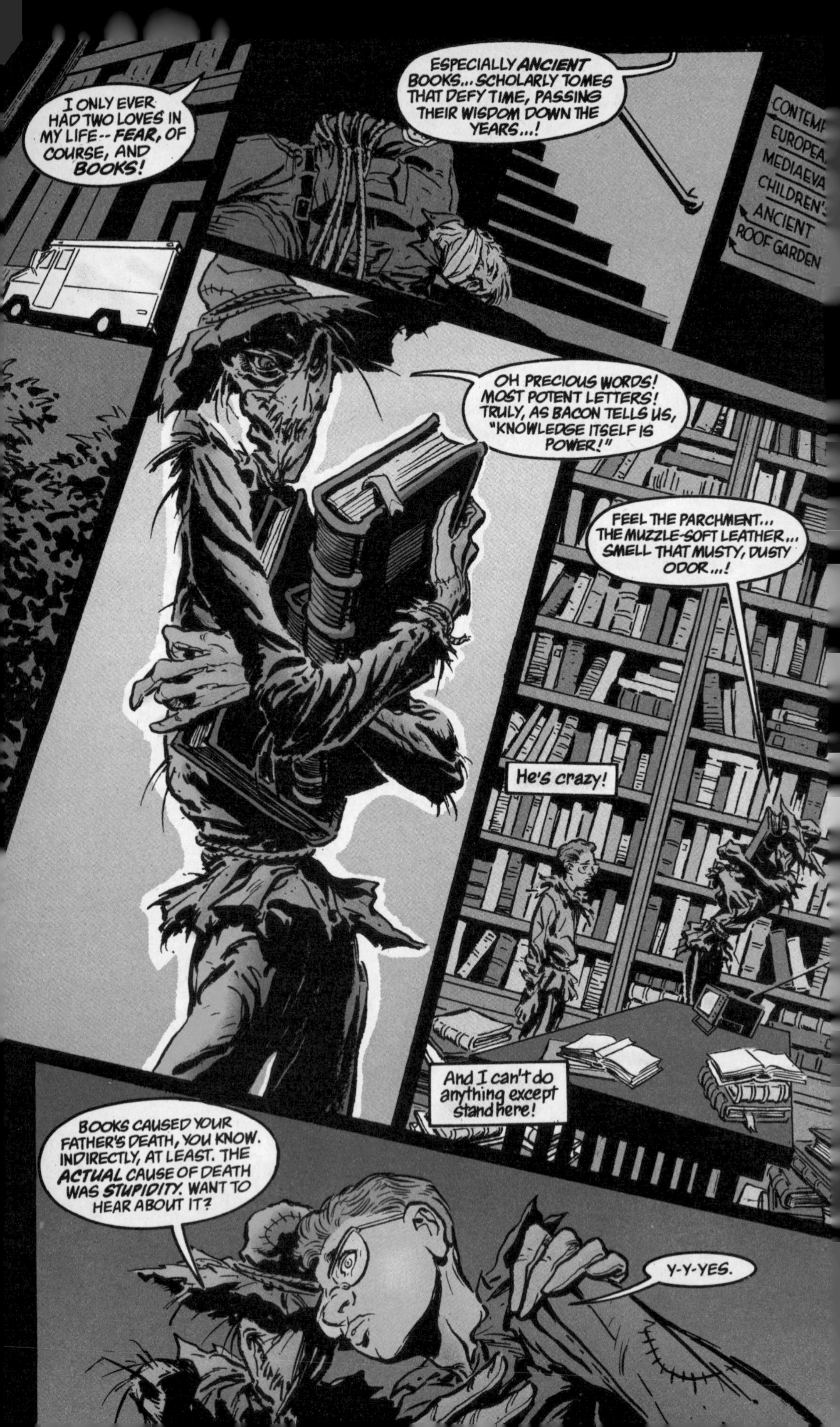
I ONLY EVER HAD TWO LOVES IN MY LIFE-- FEAR, OF COURSE, AND BOOKS!
ESPECIALLY ANCIENT BOOKS... SCHOLARLY TOMES THAT DEFY TIME, PASSING THEIR WISDOM DOWN THE YEARS...!
CONTEMP
EUROPEA
MEDIAEVA
CHILDREN'S
ANCIENT
ROOF GARDEN
OH PRECIOUS WORDS! MOST POTENT LETTERS! TRULY, AS BACON TELLS US, "KNOWLEDGE ITSELF IS POWER!"
FEEL THE PARCHMENT... THE MUZZLE-SOFT LEATHER... SMELL THAT MUSTY, DUSTY ODOR...!
He's crazy!
And I can't do anything except stand here!
BOOKS CAUSED YOUR FATHER'S DEATH, YOU KNOW. INDIRECTLY, AT LEAST. THE ACTUAL CAUSE OF DEATH WAS STUPIDITY. WANT TO HEAR ABOUT IT?
Y-Y-YES.

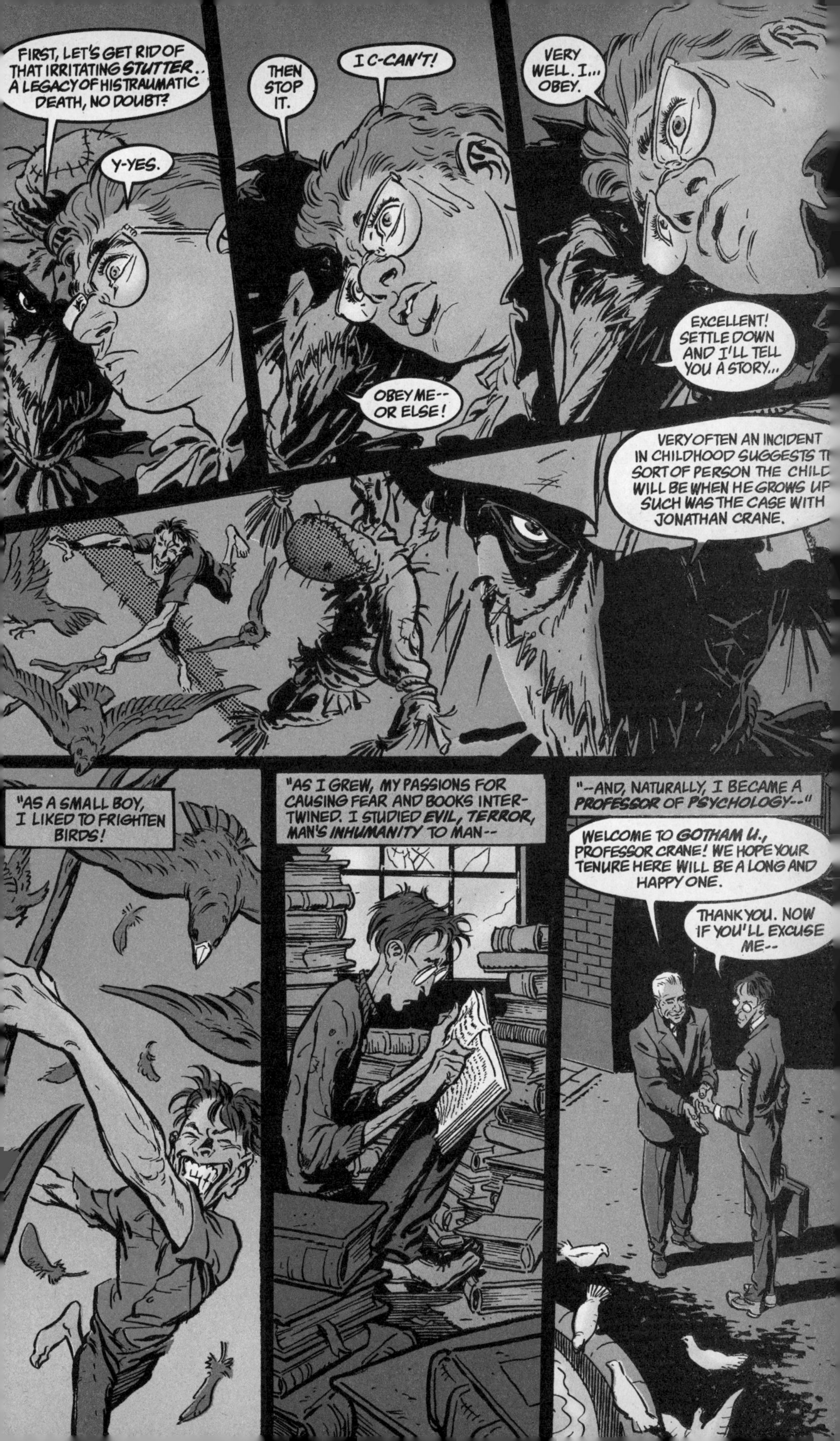
FIRST, LET'S GET RID OF THAT IRRITATING STUTTER.. A LEGACY OF HIS TRAUMATIC DEATH, NO DOUBT?
Y-YES.
THEN STOP IT.
I C-CAN'T!
OBEY ME-- OR ELSE!
VERY WELL. I... OBEY.
EXCELLENT! SETTLE DOWN AND I'LL TELL YOU A STORY...
VERY OFTEN AN INCIDENT IN CHILDHOOD SUGGESTS TH SORT OF PERSON THE CHILD WILL BE WHEN HE GROWS UP SUCH WAS THE CASE WITH JONATHAN CRANE.
"AS A SMALL BOY, I LIKED TO FRIGHTEN BIRDS!
"AS I GREW, MY PASSIONS FOR CAUSING FEAR AND BOOKS INTER-TWINED. I STUDIED EVIL, TERROR, MAN'S INHUMANITY TO MAN--
"--AND, NATURALLY, I BECAME A PROFESSOR OF PSYCHOLOGY--"
WELCOME TO GOTHAM U., PROFESSOR CRANE! WE HOPE YOUR TENURE HERE WILL BE A LONG AND HAPPY ONE.
THANK YOU. NOW IF YOU'LL EXCUSE ME--

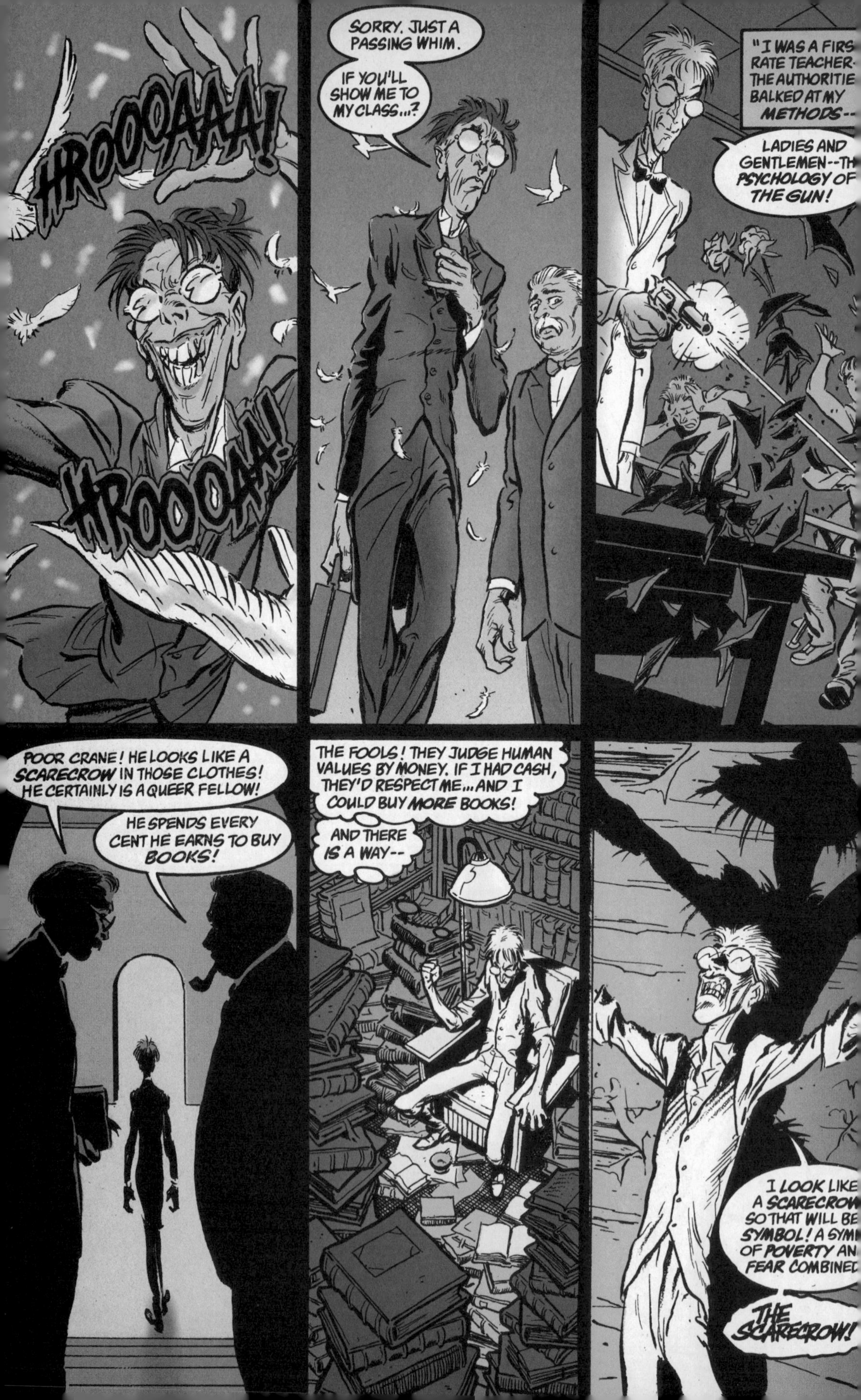
HROOOAAA!
HROOOAA!
SORRY. JUST A PASSING WHIM.
IF YOU'LL SHOW ME TO MY CLASS...?
"I WAS A FIRS RATE TEACHER THE AUTHORITIE BALKED AT MY METHODS--
LADIES AND GENTLEMEN--TH PSYCHOLOGY OF THE GUN!
POOR CRANE! HE LOOKS LIKE A SCARECROW IN THOSE CLOTHES! HE CERTAINLY IS A QUEER FELLOW!
HE SPENDS EVERY CENT HE EARNS TO BUY BOOKS!
THE FOOLS! THEY JUDGE HUMAN VALUES BY MONEY. IF I HAD CASH, THEY'D RESPECT ME... AND I COULD BUY MORE BOOKS!
AND THERE IS A WAY--
I LOOK LIKE A SCARECROW SO THAT WILL BE SYMBOL! A SYM OF POVERTY AN FEAR COMBINED
THE SCARECROW!

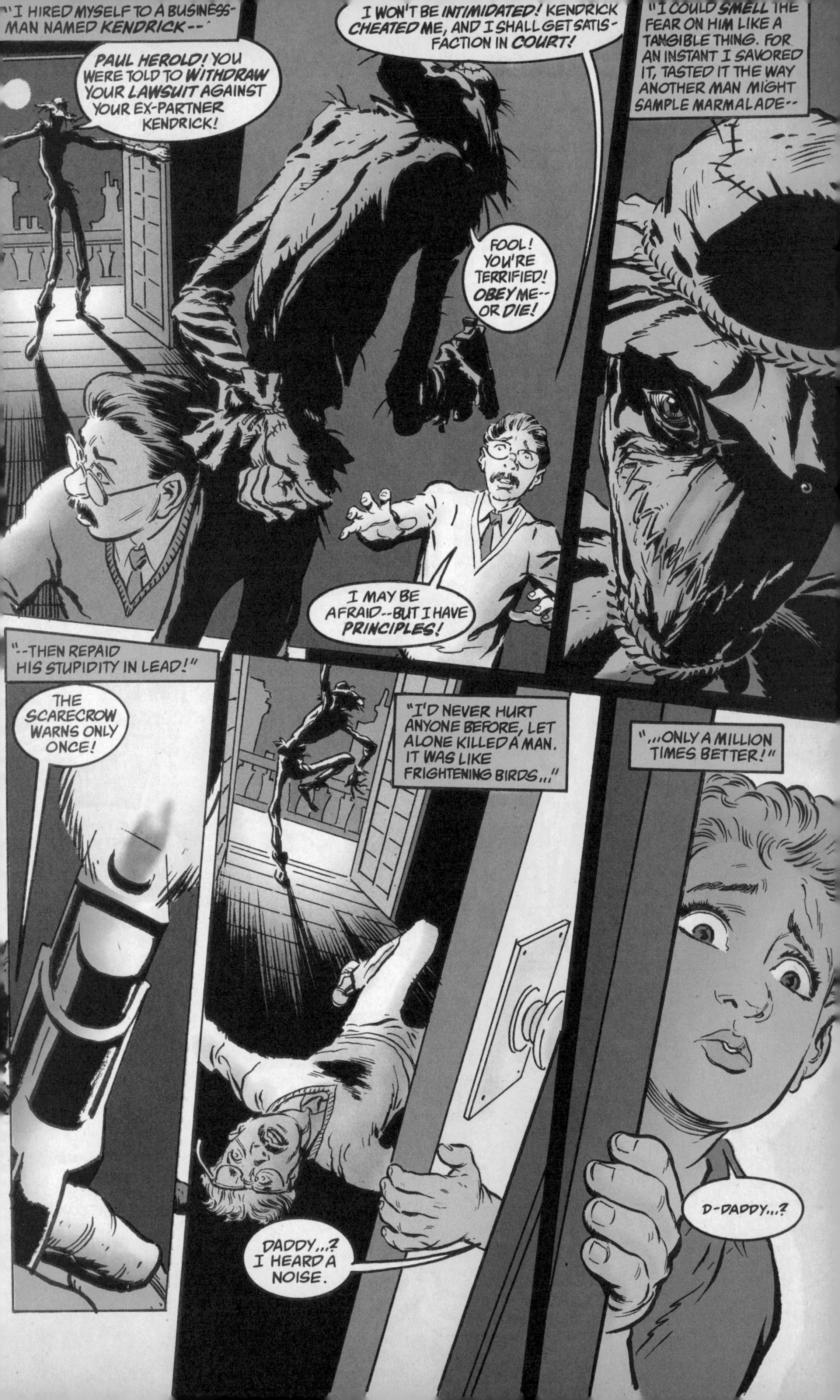
"I HIRED MYSELF TO A BUSINESSMAN NAMED KENDRICK--
PAUL HEROLD! YOU WERE TOLD TO WITHDRAW YOUR LAWSUIT AGAINST YOUR EX-PARTNER KENDRICK!
I WON'T BE INTIMIDATED! KENDRICK CHEATED ME, AND I SHALL GET SATISFACTION IN COURT!
FOOL! YOU'RE TERRIFIED! OBEY ME-- OR DIE!
I MAY BE AFRAID--BUT I HAVE PRINCIPLES!
"I COULD SMELL THE FEAR ON HIM LIKE A TANGIBLE THING. FOR AN INSTANT I SAVORED IT, TASTED IT THE WAY ANOTHER MAN MIGHT SAMPLE MARMALADE--
"--THEN REPAID HIS STUPIDITY IN LEAD!"
THE SCARECROW WARNS ONLY ONCE!
"I'D NEVER HURT ANYONE BEFORE, LET ALONE KILLED A MAN. IT WAS LIKE FRIGHTENING BIRDS..."
DADDY...? I HEARD A NOISE.
"...ONLY A MILLION TIMES BETTER!"
D-DADDY...?

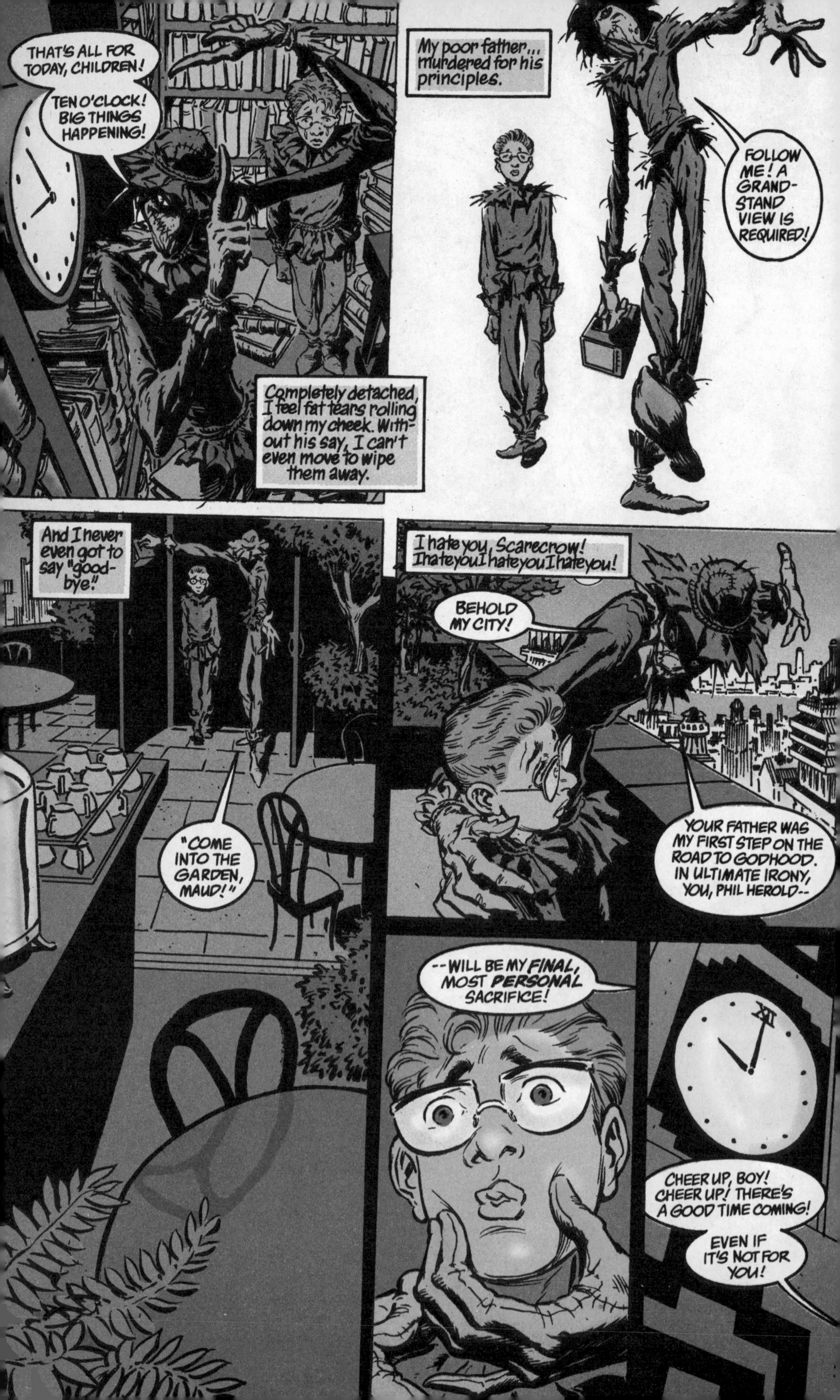
THAT'S ALL FOR TODAY, CHILDREN!
TEN O'CLOCK! BIG THINGS HAPPENING!
Completely detached, I feel fat tears rolling down my cheek. Without his say, I can't even move to wipe them away.
My poor father... murdered for his principles.
FOLLOW ME! A GRAND-STAND VIEW IS REQUIRED!
And I never even got to say "good-bye."
"COME INTO THE GARDEN, MAUD!"
I hate you, Scarecrow! I hate you I hate you I hate you!
BEHOLD MY CITY!
YOUR FATHER WAS MY FIRST STEP ON THE ROAD TO GODHOOD. IN ULTIMATE IRONY, YOU, PHIL HEROLD--
--WILL BE MY FINAL, MOST PERSONAL SACRIFICE!
CHEER UP, BOY! CHEER UP! THERE'S A GOOD TIME COMING!
EVEN IF IT'S NOT FOR YOU!

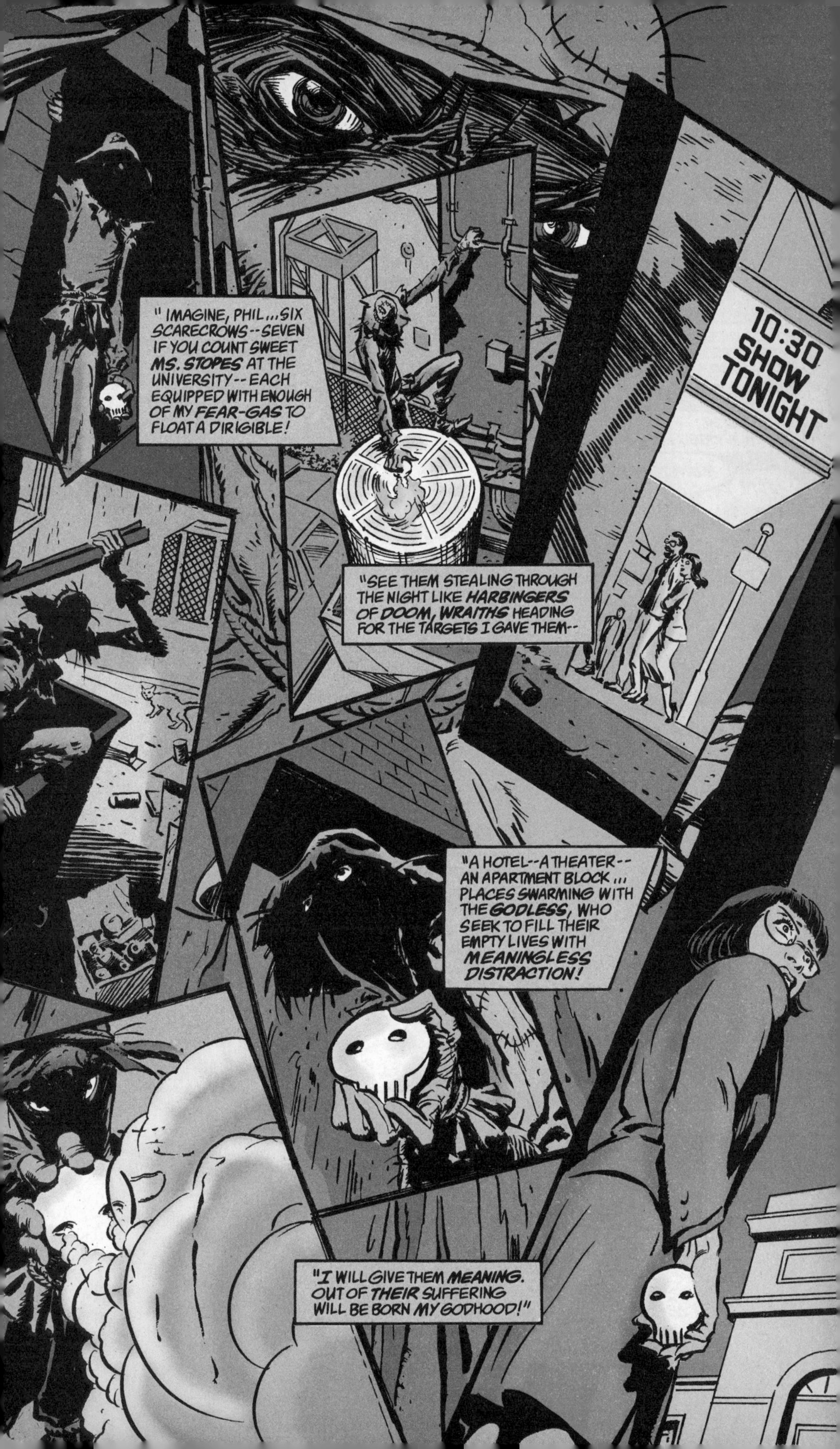
"IMAGINE, PHIL...SIX SCARECROWS--SEVEN IF YOU COUNT SWEET MS. STOPES AT THE UNIVERSITY--EACH EQUIPPED WITH ENOUGH OF MY FEAR-GAS TO FLOAT A DIRIGIBLE!
10:30 SHOW TONIGHT
"SEE THEM STEALING THROUGH THE NIGHT LIKE HARBINGERS OF DOOM, WRAITHS HEADING FOR THE TARGETS I GAVE THEM--
"A HOTEL--A THEATER--AN APARTMENT BLOCK... PLACES SWARMING WITH THE GODLESS, WHO SEEK TO FILL THEIR EMPTY LIVES WITH MEANINGLESS DISTRACTION!
"I WILL GIVE THEM MEANING. OUT OF THEIR SUFFERING WILL BE BORN MY GODHOOD!"

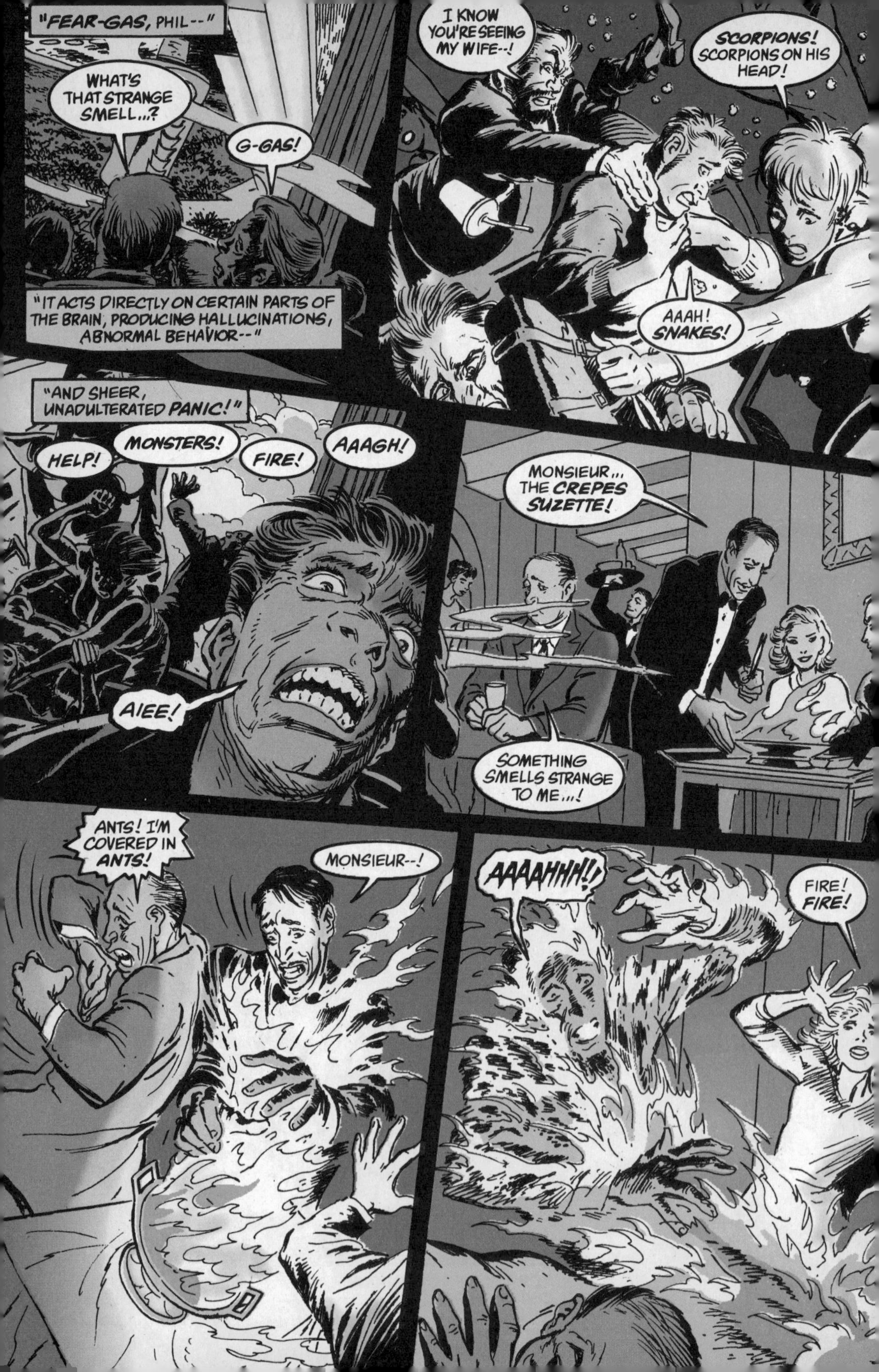
"FEAR-GAS, PHIL--"
WHAT'S THAT STRANGE SMELL...?
G-GAS!
"IT ACTS DIRECTLY ON CERTAIN PARTS OF THE BRAIN, PRODUCING HALLUCINATIONS, ABNORMAL BEHAVIOR--"
I KNOW YOU'RE SEEING MY WIFE--!
SCORPIONS! SCORPIONS ON HIS HEAD!
AAAH! SNAKES!
"AND SHEER, UNADULTERATED PANIC!"
HELP!
MONSTERS!
FIRE!
AAAGH!
AIEE!
MONSIEUR... THE CREPES SUZETTE!
SOMETHING SMELLS STRANGE TO ME...!
ANTS! I'M COVERED IN ANTS!
MONSIEUR--!
AAAAHHH!!
FIRE! FIRE!

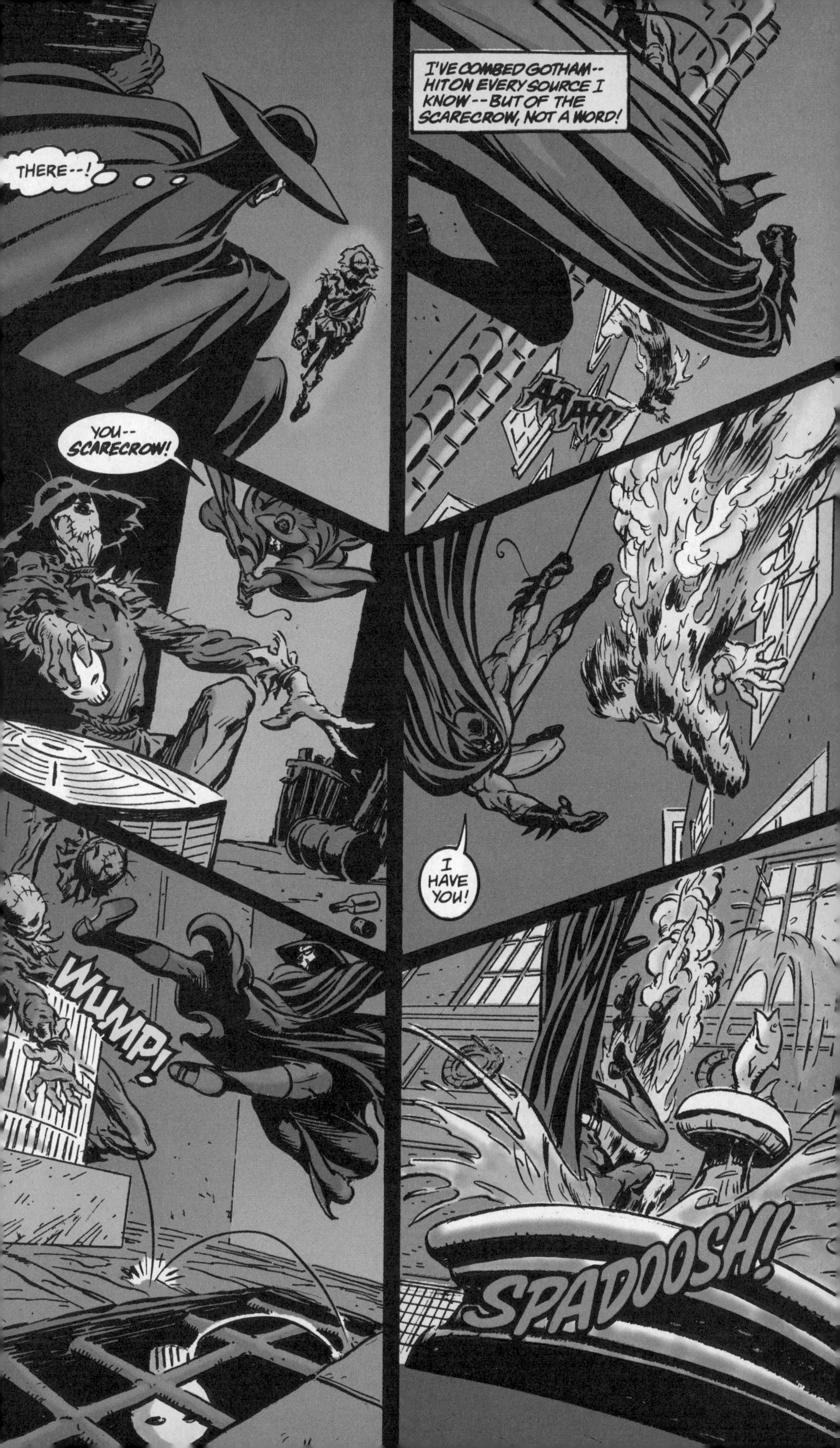
THERE--!
I'VE COMBED GOTHAM--HIT ON EVERY SOURCE I KNOW--BUT OF THE SCARECROW, NOT A WORD!
AAAH!
YOU--SCARECROW!
I HAVE YOU!
WUMP!
SPADOOSH!

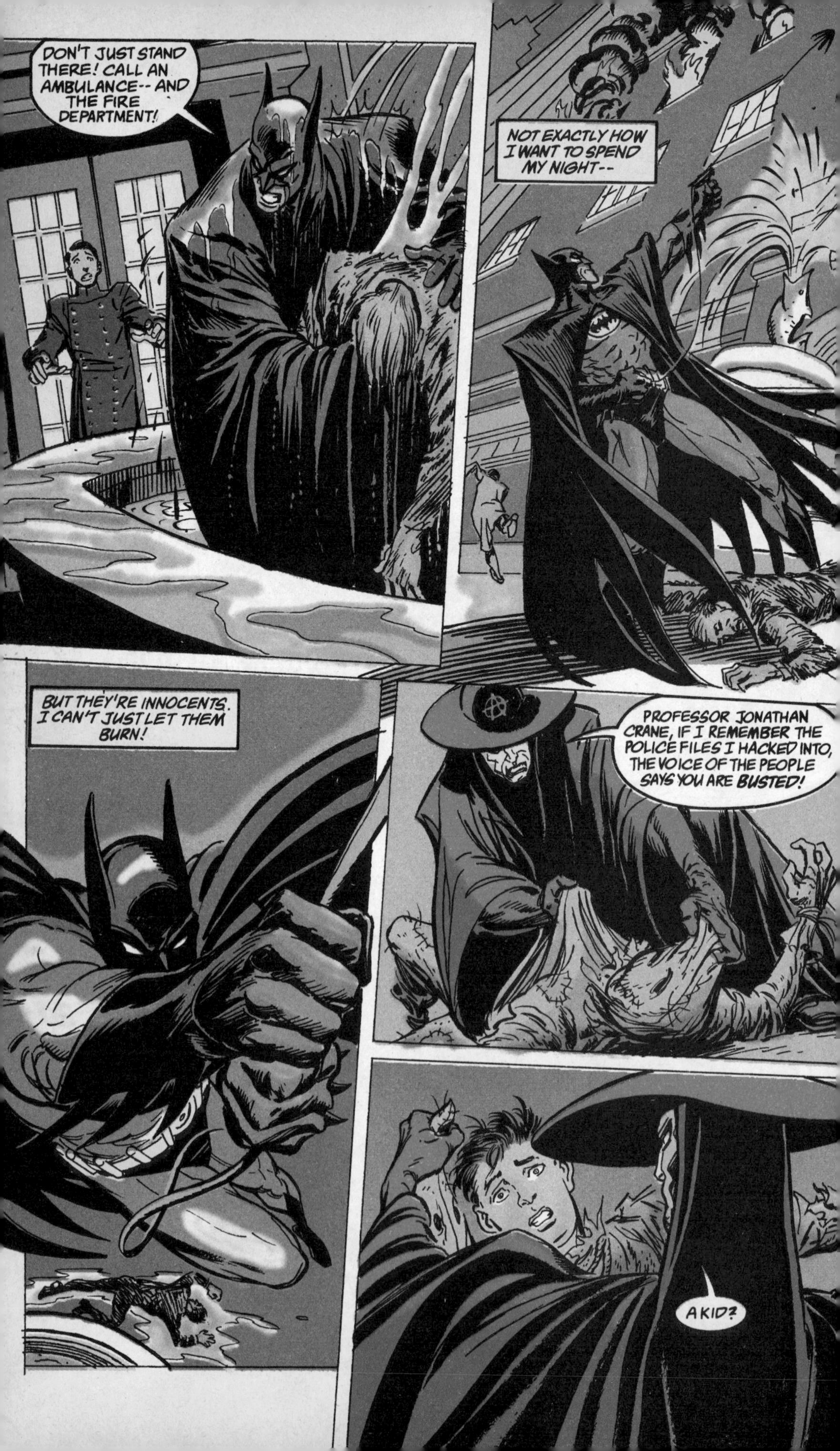
DON'T JUST STAND THERE! CALL AN AMBULANCE-- AND THE FIRE DEPARTMENT!
NOT EXACTLY HOW I WANT TO SPEND MY NIGHT--
BUT THEY'RE INNOCENTS. I CAN'T JUST LET THEM BURN!
PROFESSOR JONATHAN CRANE, IF I REMEMBER THE POLICE FILES I HACKED INTO, THE VOICE OF THE PEOPLE SAYS YOU ARE BUSTED!
A KID?

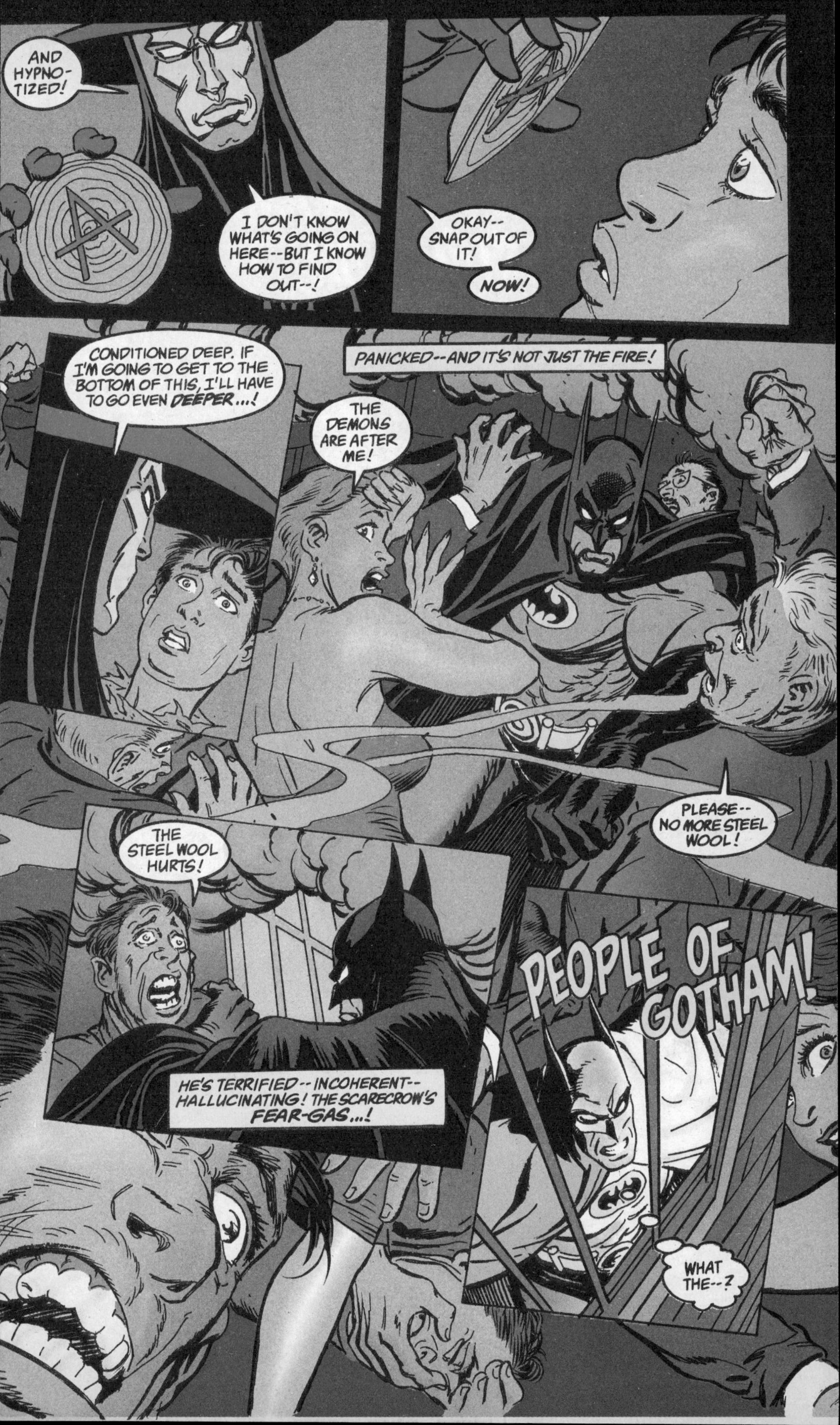
AND HYPNO-TIZED!
I DON'T KNOW WHAT'S GOING ON HERE--BUT I KNOW HOW TO FIND OUT--!
OKAY-- SNAP OUT OF IT!
NOW!
CONDITIONED DEEP. IF I'M GOING TO GET TO THE BOTTOM OF THIS, I'LL HAVE TO GO EVEN DEEPER...!
PANICKED--AND IT'S NOT JUST THE FIRE!
THE DEMONS ARE AFTER ME!
PLEASE-- NO MORE STEEL WOOL!
THE STEEL WOOL HURTS!
HE'S TERRIFIED--INCOHERENT--HALLUCINATING! THE SCARECROW'S FEAR-GAS...!
PEOPLE OF GOTHAM!
WHAT THE--?

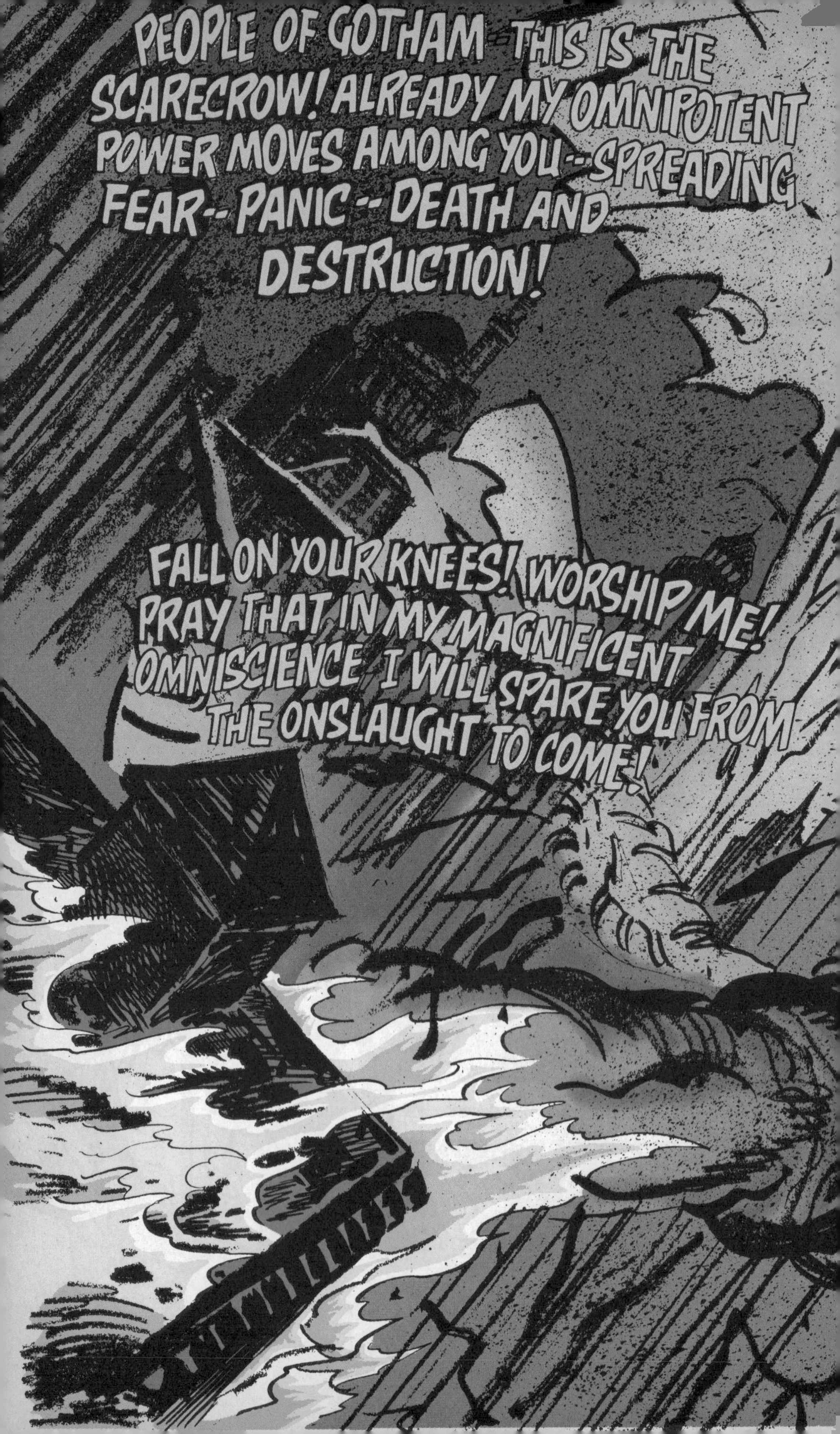
PEOPLE OF GOTHAM--THIS IS THE SCARECROW! ALREADY MY OMNIPOTENT POWER MOVES AMONG YOU--SPREADING FEAR--PANIC--DEATH AND DESTRUCTION!
FALL ON YOUR KNEES! WORSHIP ME! PRAY THAT IN MY MAGNIFICENT OMNISCIENCE I WILL SPARE YOU FROM THE ONSLAUGHT TO COME!

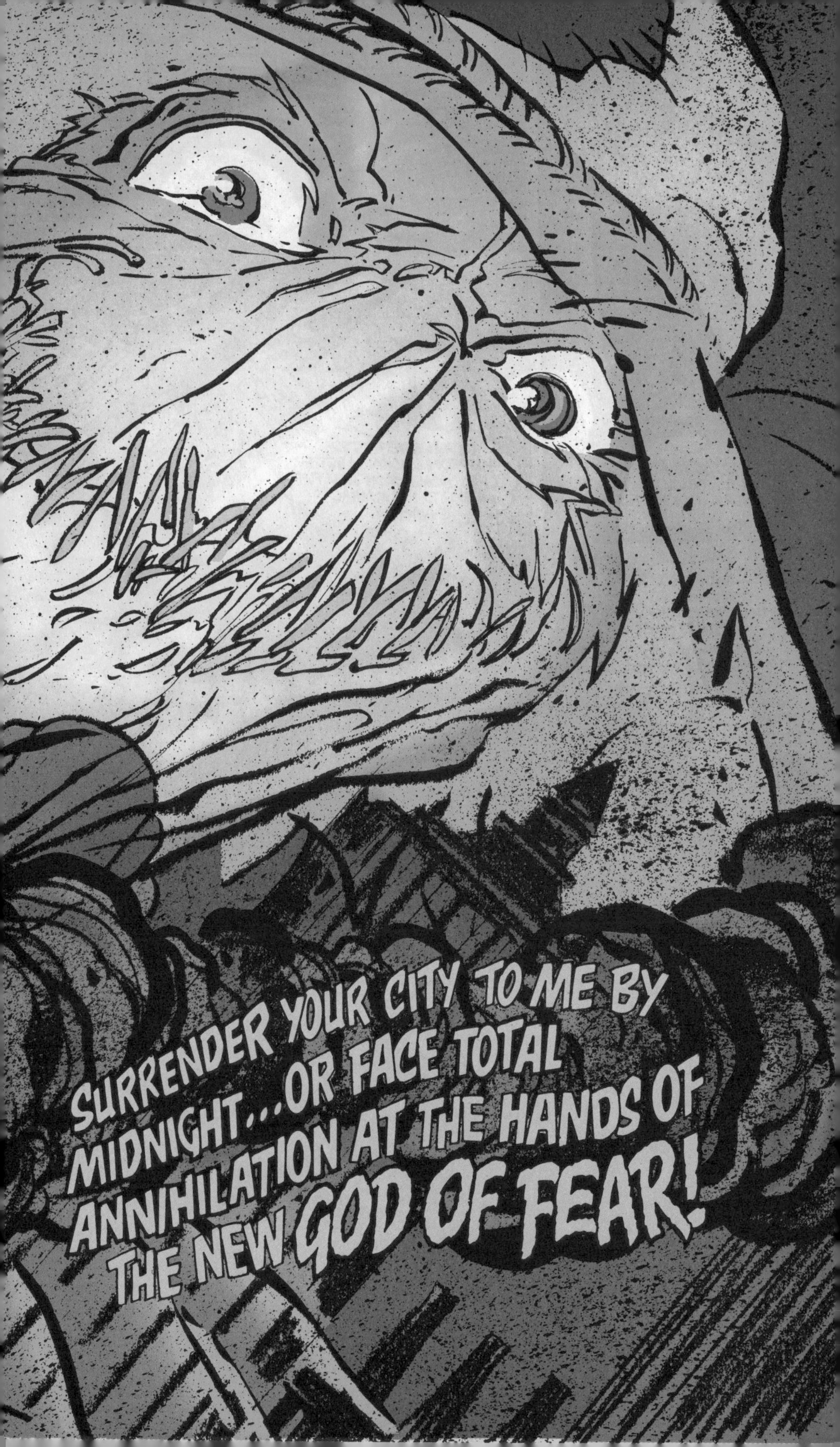
SURRENDER YOUR CITY TO ME BY MIDNIGHT...OR FACE TOTAL ANNIHILATION AT THE HANDS OF THE NEW GOD OF FEAR!

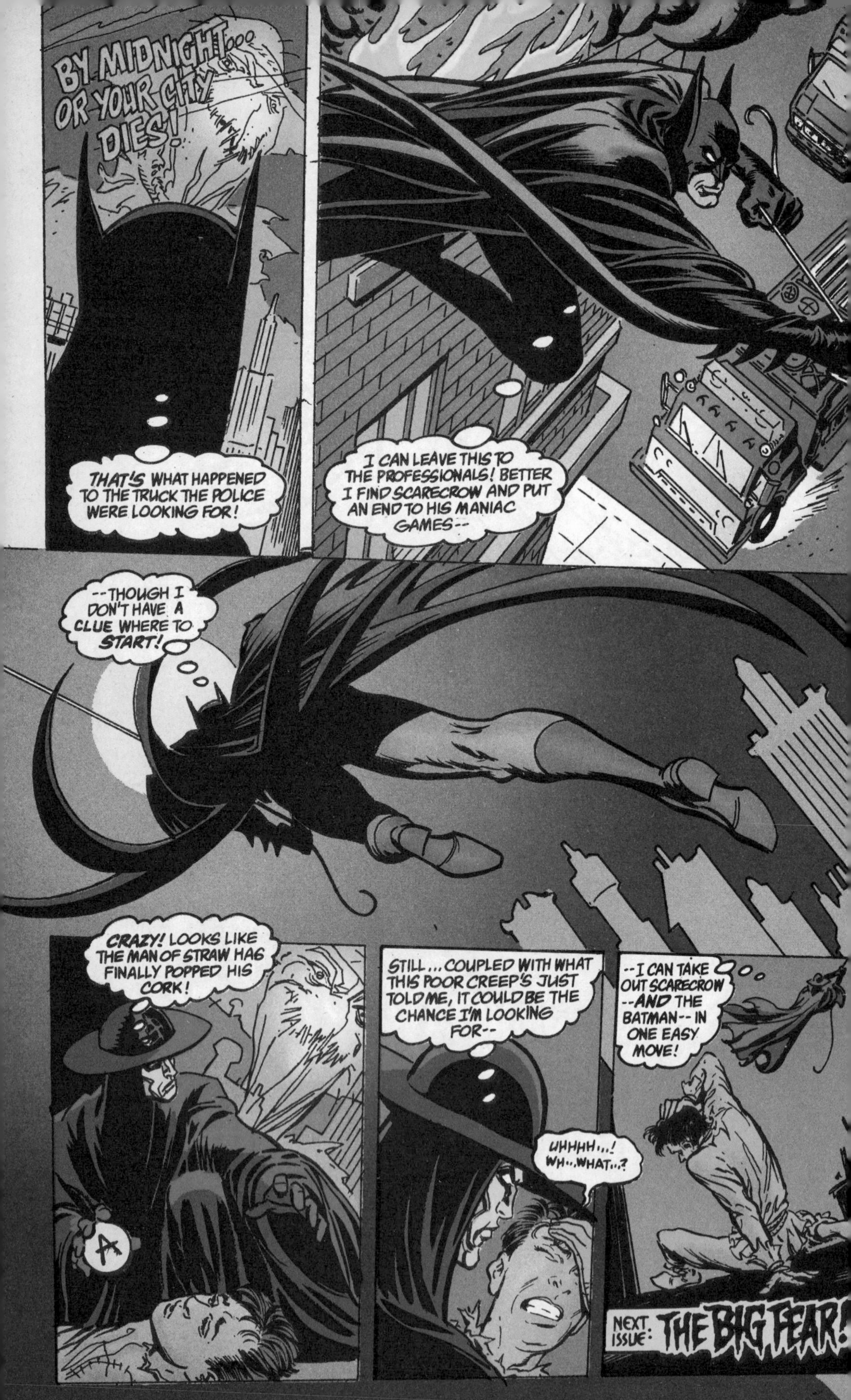
BY MIDNIGHT... OR YOUR CITY DIES!
THAT'S WHAT HAPPENED TO THE TRUCK THE POLICE WERE LOOKING FOR!
I CAN LEAVE THIS TO THE PROFESSIONALS! BETTER I FIND SCARECROW AND PUT AN END TO HIS MANIAC GAMES--
--THOUGH I DON'T HAVE A CLUE WHERE TO START!
CRAZY! LOOKS LIKE THE MAN OF STRAW HAS FINALLY POPPED HIS CORK!
STILL... COUPLED WITH WHAT THIS POOR CREEP'S JUST TOLD ME, IT COULD BE THE CHANCE I'M LOOKING FOR--
UHHHH...! WH...WHAT...?
--I CAN TAKE OUT SCARECROW --AND THE BATMAN-- IN ONE EASY MOVE!
NEXT ISSUE: THE BIG FEAR!

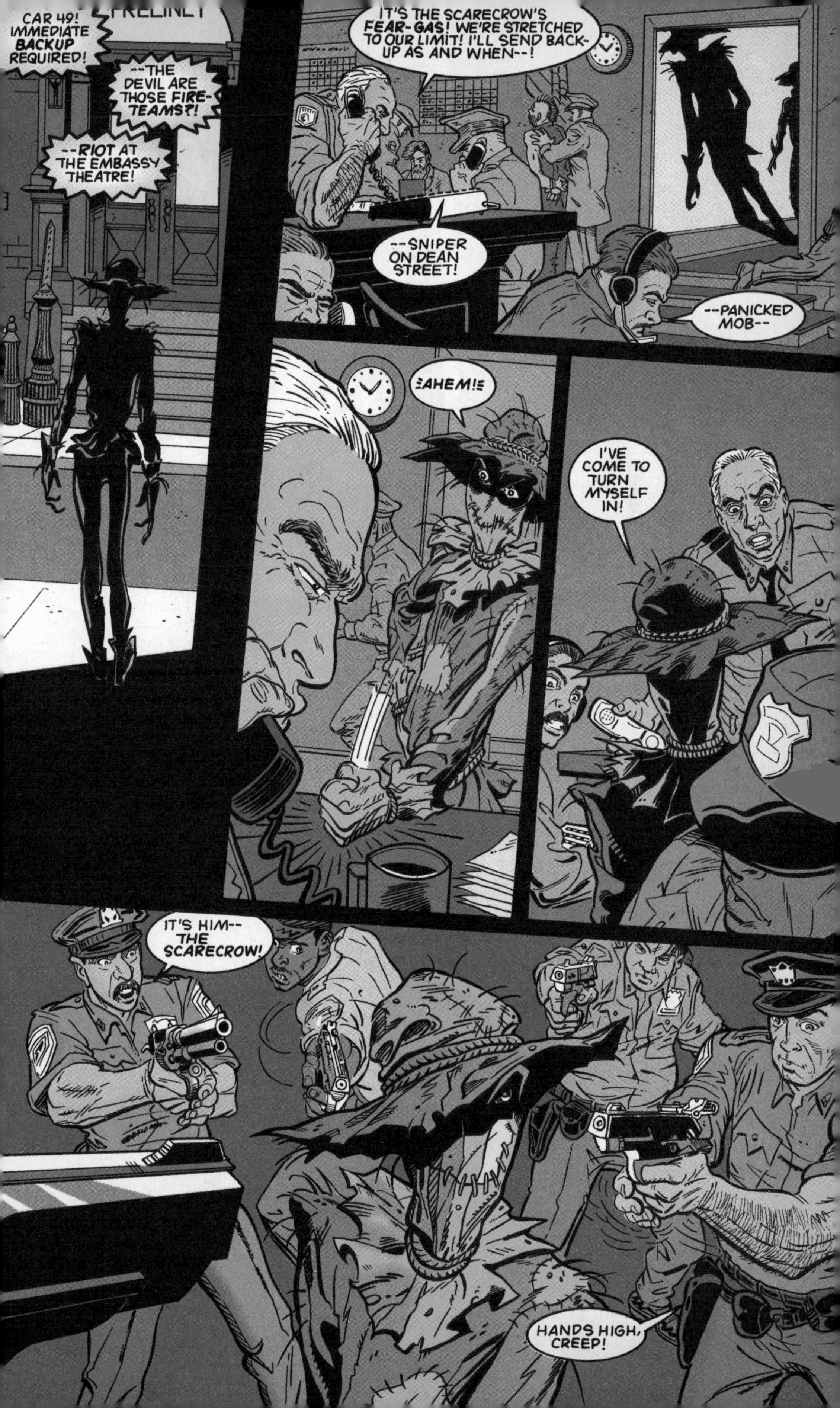
CAR 49! IMMEDIATE BACKUP REQUIRED!
--THE DEVIL ARE THOSE FIRE-TEAMS?!
--RIOT AT THE EMBASSY THEATRE!
IT'S THE SCARECROW'S FEAR-GAS! WE'RE STRETCHED TO OUR LIMIT! I'LL SEND BACK-UP AS AND WHEN--!
--SNIPER ON DEAN STREET!
--PANICKED MOB--
AHEM!
I'VE COME TO TURN MYSELF IN!
IT'S HIM-- THE SCARECROW!
HANDS HIGH, CREEP!

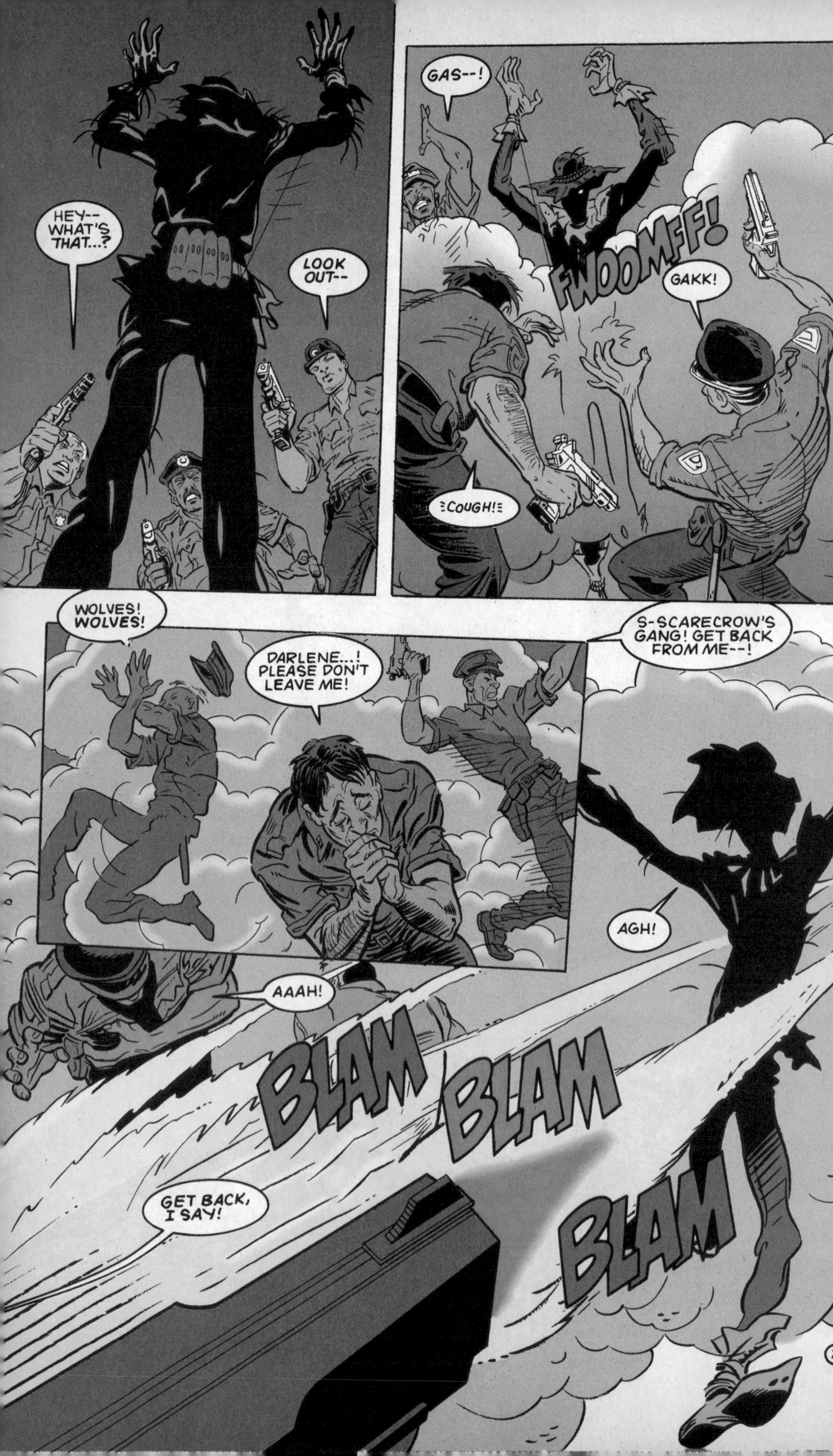
HEY-- WHAT'S THAT...?
LOOK OUT--
GAS--!
FWOOMFF!
GAKK!
COUGH!
WOLVES! WOLVES!
DARLENE...! PLEASE DON'T LEAVE ME!
S-SCARECROW'S GANG! GET BACK FROM ME--!
AGH!
AAAH!
BLAM
BLAM
BLAM
GET BACK, I SAY!

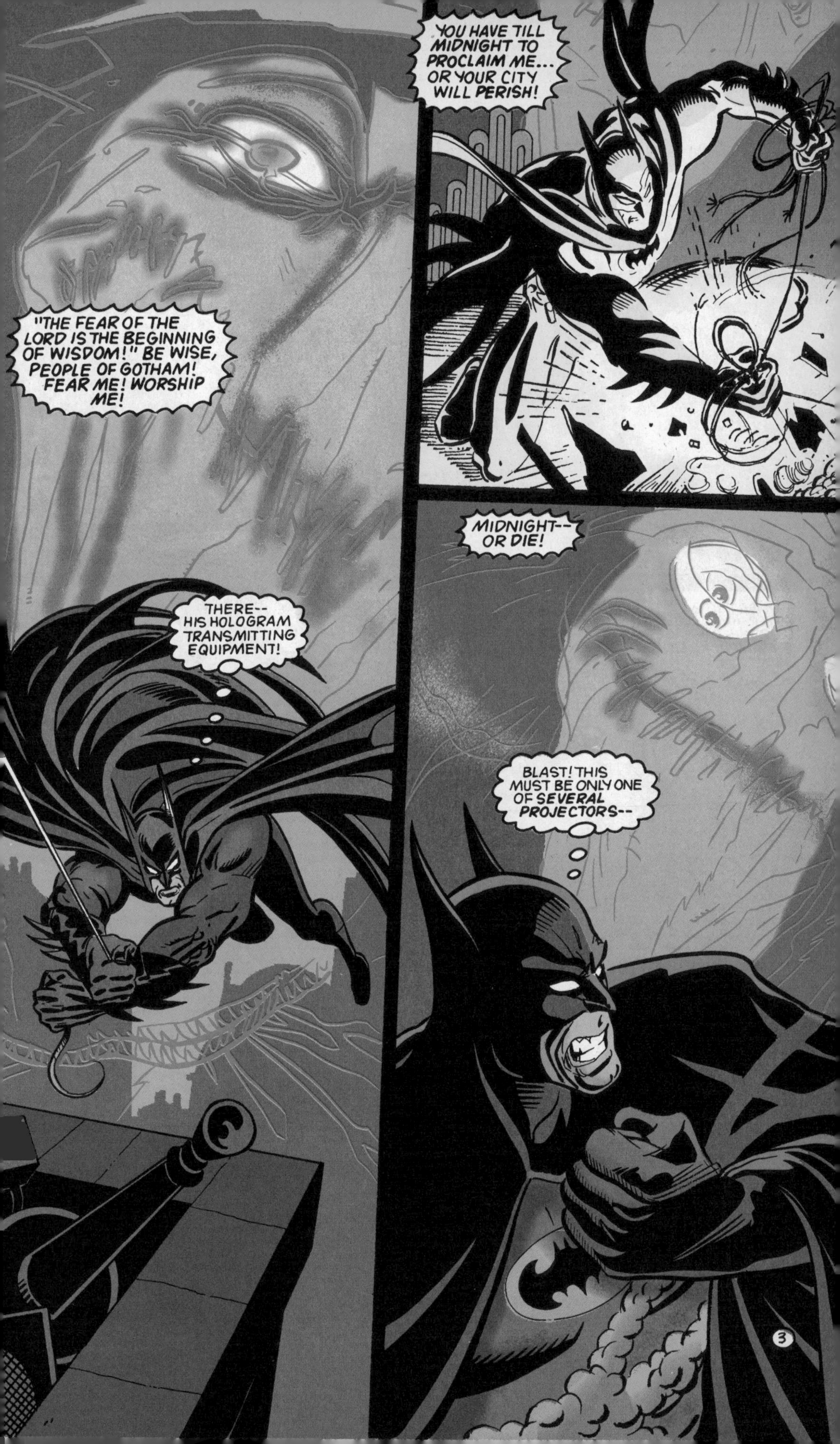
"THE FEAR OF THE LORD IS THE BEGINNING OF WISDOM!" BE WISE, PEOPLE OF GOTHAM! FEAR ME! WORSHIP ME!
YOU HAVE TILL MIDNIGHT TO PROCLAIM ME... OR YOUR CITY WILL PERISH!
THERE-- HIS HOLOGRAM TRANSMITTING EQUIPMENT!
MIDNIGHT-- OR DIE!
BLAST! THIS MUST BE ONLY ONE OF SEVERAL PROJECTORS--
3

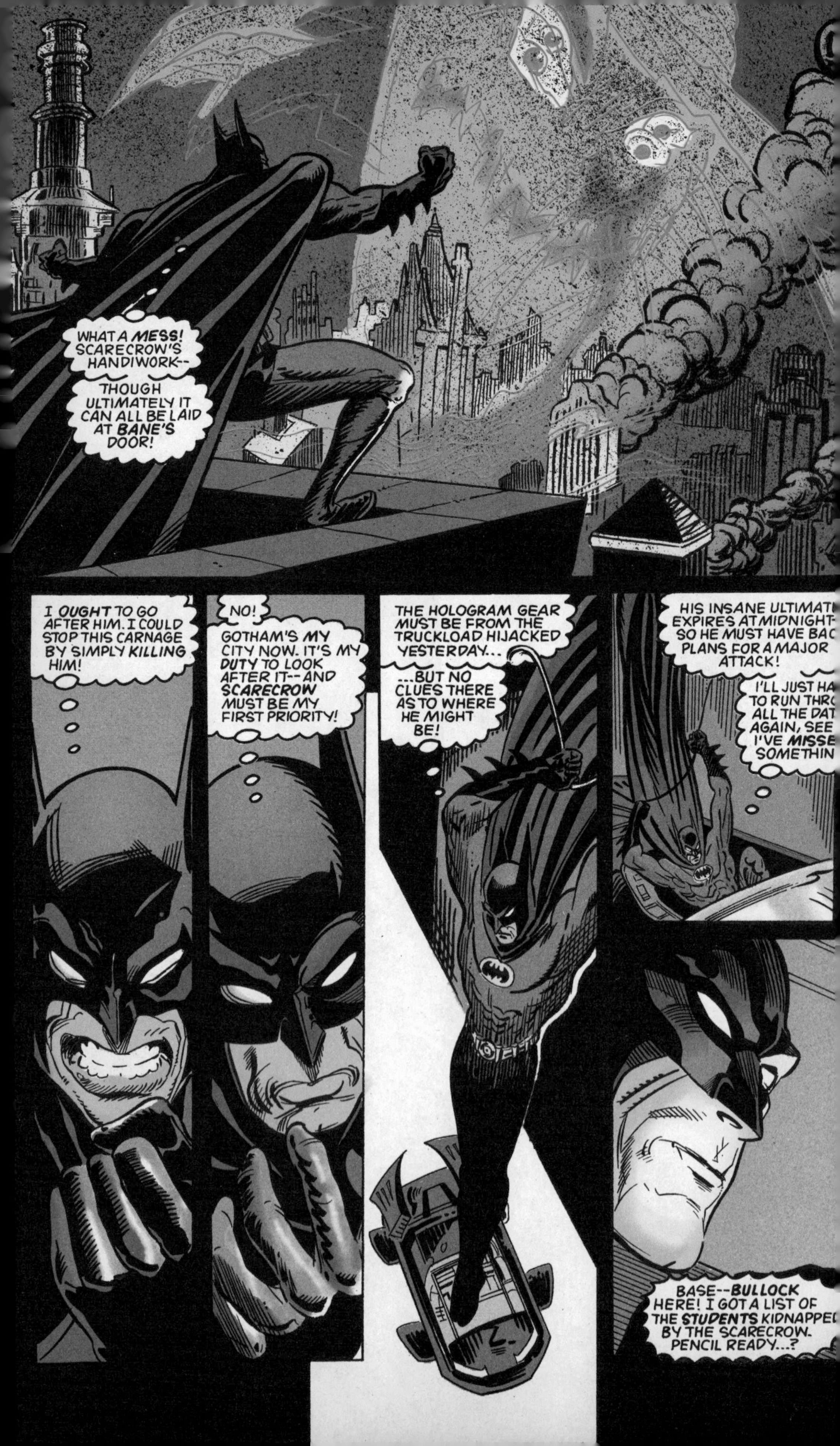

WHAT A MESS! SCARECROW'S HANDIWORK--
THOUGH ULTIMATELY IT CAN ALL BE LAID AT BANE'S DOOR!
I OUGHT TO GO AFTER HIM. I COULD STOP THIS CARNAGE BY SIMPLY KILLING HIM!
NO!
GOTHAM'S MY CITY NOW. IT'S MY DUTY TO LOOK AFTER IT--AND SCARECROW MUST BE MY FIRST PRIORITY!
THE HOLOGRAM GEAR MUST BE FROM THE TRUCKLOAD HIJACKED YESTERDAY...
...BUT NO CLUES THERE AS TO WHERE HE MIGHT BE!
HIS INSANE ULTIMAT EXPIRES AT MIDNIGHT- SO HE MUST HAVE BAC PLANS FOR A MAJOR ATTACK!
I'LL JUST HA TO RUN THRO ALL THE DAT AGAIN, SEE I'VE MISSE SOMETHIN
BASE--BULLOCK HERE! I GOT A LIST OF THE STUDENTS KIDNAPPEL BY THE SCARECROW. PENCIL READY...?

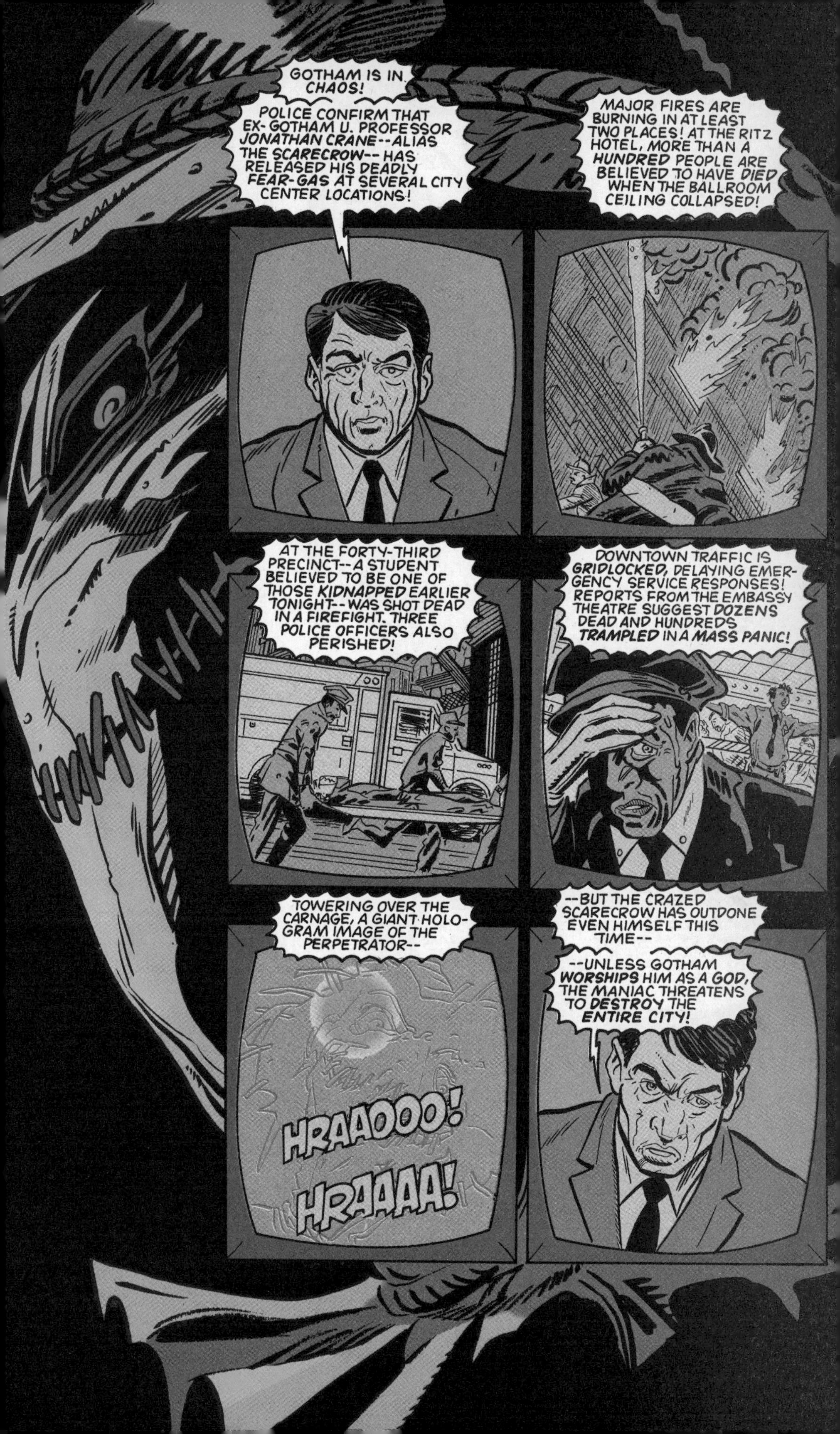
GOTHAM IS IN CHAOS!
POLICE CONFIRM THAT EX-GOTHAM U. PROFESSOR JONATHAN CRANE--ALIAS THE SCARECROW--HAS RELEASED HIS DEADLY FEAR-GAS AT SEVERAL CITY CENTER LOCATIONS!
MAJOR FIRES ARE BURNING IN AT LEAST TWO PLACES! AT THE RITZ HOTEL, MORE THAN A HUNDRED PEOPLE ARE BELIEVED TO HAVE DIED WHEN THE BALLROOM CEILING COLLAPSED!
AT THE FORTY-THIRD PRECINCT--A STUDENT BELIEVED TO BE ONE OF THOSE KIDNAPPED EARLIER TONIGHT--WAS SHOT DEAD IN A FIREFIGHT. THREE POLICE OFFICERS ALSO PERISHED!
DOWNTOWN TRAFFIC IS GRIDLOCKED, DELAYING EMERGENCY SERVICE RESPONSES! REPORTS FROM THE EMBASSY THEATRE SUGGEST DOZENS DEAD AND HUNDREDS TRAMPLED IN A MASS PANIC!
TOWERING OVER THE CARNAGE, A GIANT HOLOGRAM IMAGE OF THE PERPETRATOR--
HRAAOOO!
HRAAAAA!
--BUT THE CRAZED SCARECROW HAS OUTDONE EVEN HIMSELF THIS TIME--
--UNLESS GOTHAM WORSHIPS HIM AS A GOD, THE MANIAC THREATENS TO DESTROY THE ENTIRE CITY!

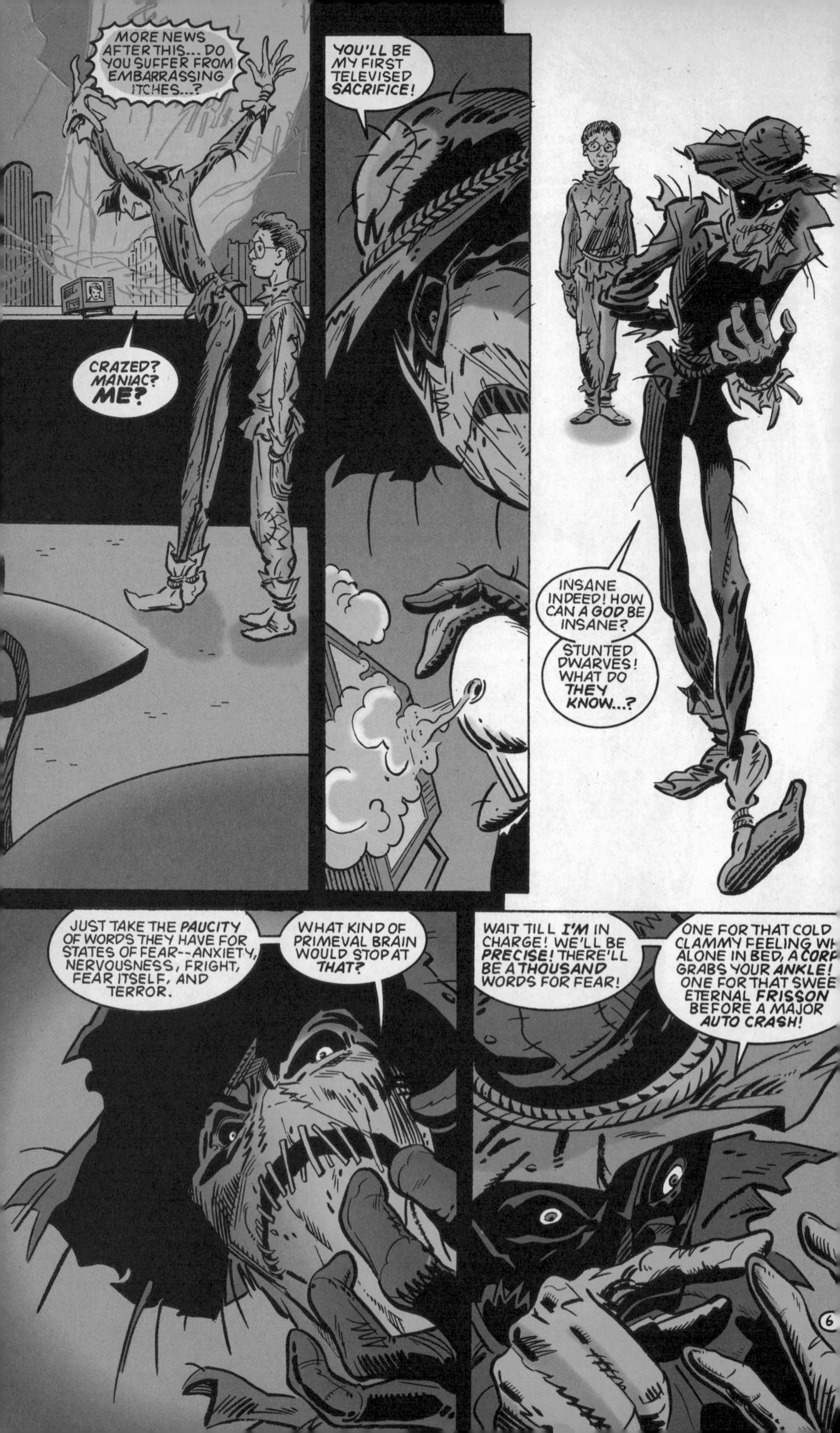
MORE NEWS AFTER THIS... DO YOU SUFFER FROM EMBARRASSING ITCHES...?
CRAZED? MANIAC? ME?
YOU'LL BE MY FIRST TELEVISED SACRIFICE!
INSANE INDEED! HOW CAN A GOD BE INSANE?
STUNTED DWARVES! WHAT DO THEY KNOW...?
JUST TAKE THE PAUCITY OF WORDS THEY HAVE FOR STATES OF FEAR--ANXIETY, NERVOUSNESS, FRIGHT, FEAR ITSELF, AND TERROR.
WHAT KIND OF PRIMEVAL BRAIN WOULD STOP AT THAT?
WAIT TILL I'M IN CHARGE! WE'LL BE PRECISE! THERE'LL BE A THOUSAND WORDS FOR FEAR!
ONE FOR THAT COLD CLAMMY FEELING WH ALONE IN BED, A CORP GRABS YOUR ANKLE! ONE FOR THAT SWEE ETERNAL FRISSON BEFORE A MAJOR AUTO CRASH!
6

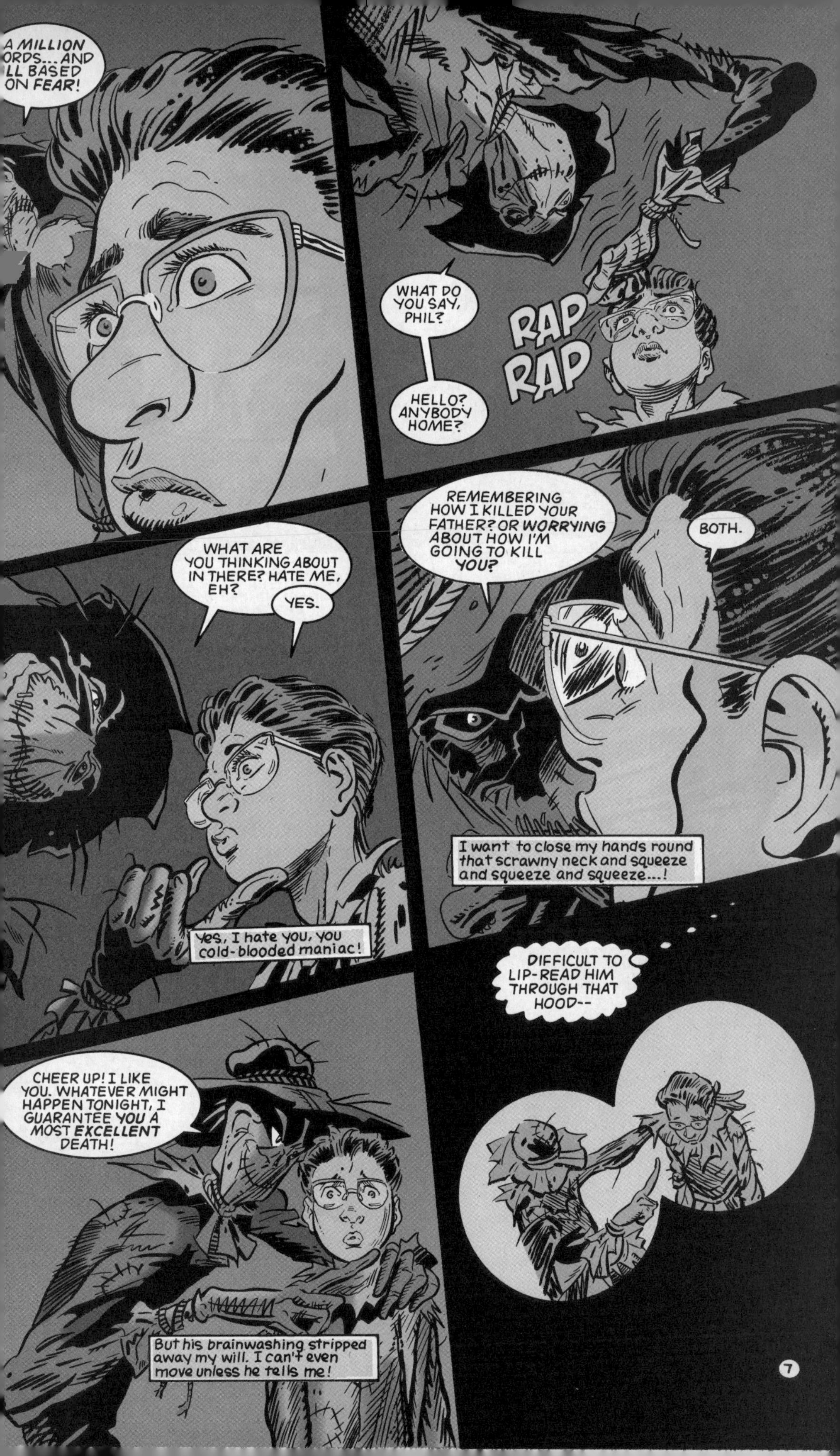
A MILLION ORDS... AND LL BASED ON FEAR!
WHAT DO YOU SAY, PHIL?
HELLO? ANYBODY HOME?
RAP RAP
WHAT ARE YOU THINKING ABOUT IN THERE? HATE ME, EH?
YES.
Yes, I hate you, you cold-blooded maniac!
REMEMBERING HOW I KILLED YOUR FATHER? OR WORRYING ABOUT HOW I'M GOING TO KILL YOU?
BOTH.
I want to close my hands round that scrawny neck and squeeze and squeeze and squeeze...!
CHEER UP! I LIKE YOU. WHATEVER MIGHT HAPPEN TONIGHT, I GUARANTEE YOU A MOST EXCELLENT DEATH!
But his brainwashing stripped away my will. I can't even move unless he tells me!
DIFFICULT TO LIP-READ HIM THROUGH THAT HOOD--

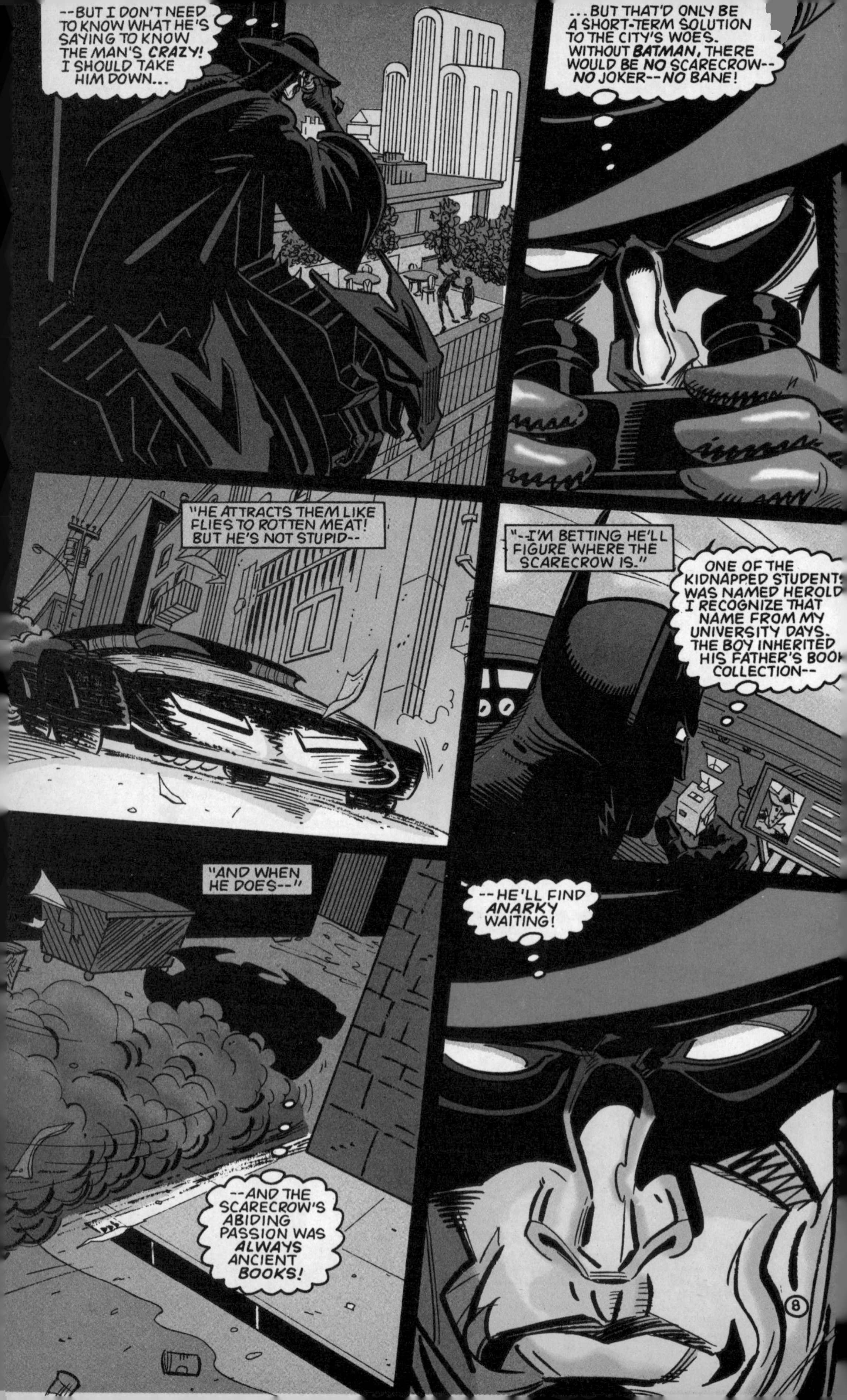
--BUT I DON'T NEED TO KNOW WHAT HE'S SAYING TO KNOW THE MAN'S CRAZY! I SHOULD TAKE HIM DOWN...
...BUT THAT'D ONLY BE A SHORT-TERM SOLUTION TO THE CITY'S WOES. WITHOUT BATMAN, THERE WOULD BE NO SCARECROW--NO JOKER--NO BANE!
"HE ATTRACTS THEM LIKE FLIES TO ROTTEN MEAT! BUT HE'S NOT STUPID--
"--I'M BETTING HE'LL FIGURE WHERE THE SCARECROW IS."
ONE OF THE KIDNAPPED STUDENTS WAS NAMED HEROLD. I RECOGNIZE THAT NAME FROM MY UNIVERSITY DAYS. THE BOY INHERITED HIS FATHER'S BOOK COLLECTION--
"AND WHEN HE DOES--"
--AND THE SCARECROW'S ABIDING PASSION WAS ALWAYS ANCIENT BOOKS!
--HE'LL FIND ANARKY WAITING!
8

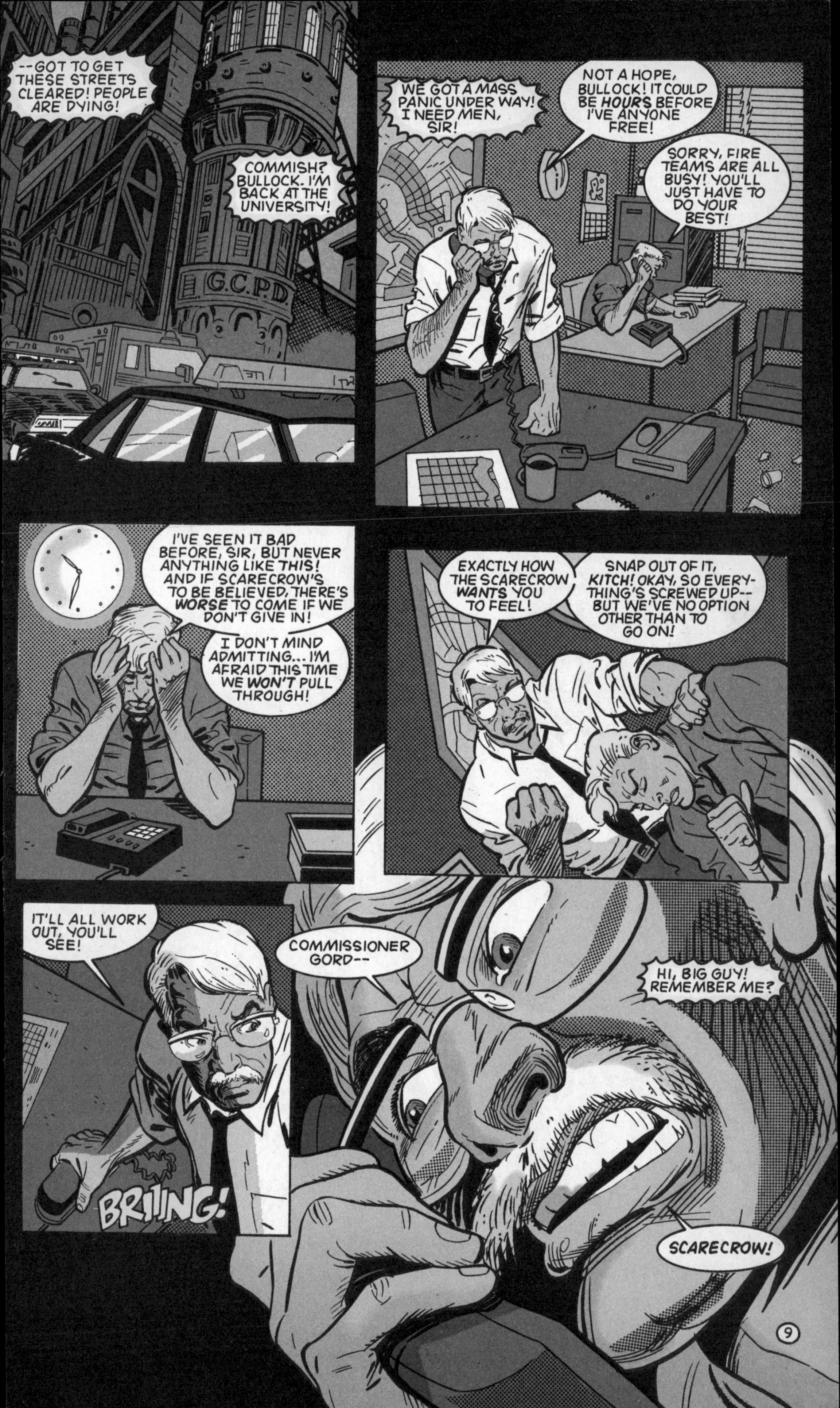
--GOT TO GET THESE STREETS CLEARED! PEOPLE ARE DYING!
COMMISH? BULLOCK. I'M BACK AT THE UNIVERSITY!
G.C.P.D
WE GOT A MASS PANIC UNDER WAY! I NEED MEN, SIR!
NOT A HOPE, BULLOCK! IT COULD BE HOURS BEFORE I'VE ANYONE FREE!
SORRY, FIRE TEAMS ARE ALL BUSY! YOU'LL JUST HAVE TO DO YOUR BEST!
I'VE SEEN IT BAD BEFORE, SIR, BUT NEVER ANYTHING LIKE THIS! AND IF SCARECROW'S TO BE BELIEVED, THERE'S WORSE TO COME IF WE DON'T GIVE IN!
I DON'T MIND ADMITTING... I'M AFRAID THIS TIME WE WON'T PULL THROUGH!
EXACTLY HOW THE SCARECROW WANTS YOU TO FEEL!
SNAP OUT OF IT, KITCH! OKAY, SO EVERYTHING'S SCREWED UP-- BUT WE'VE NO OPTION OTHER THAN TO GO ON!
IT'LL ALL WORK OUT, YOU'LL SEE!
BRIIING!
COMMISSIONER GORD--
HI, BIG GUY! REMEMBER ME?
SCARECROW!

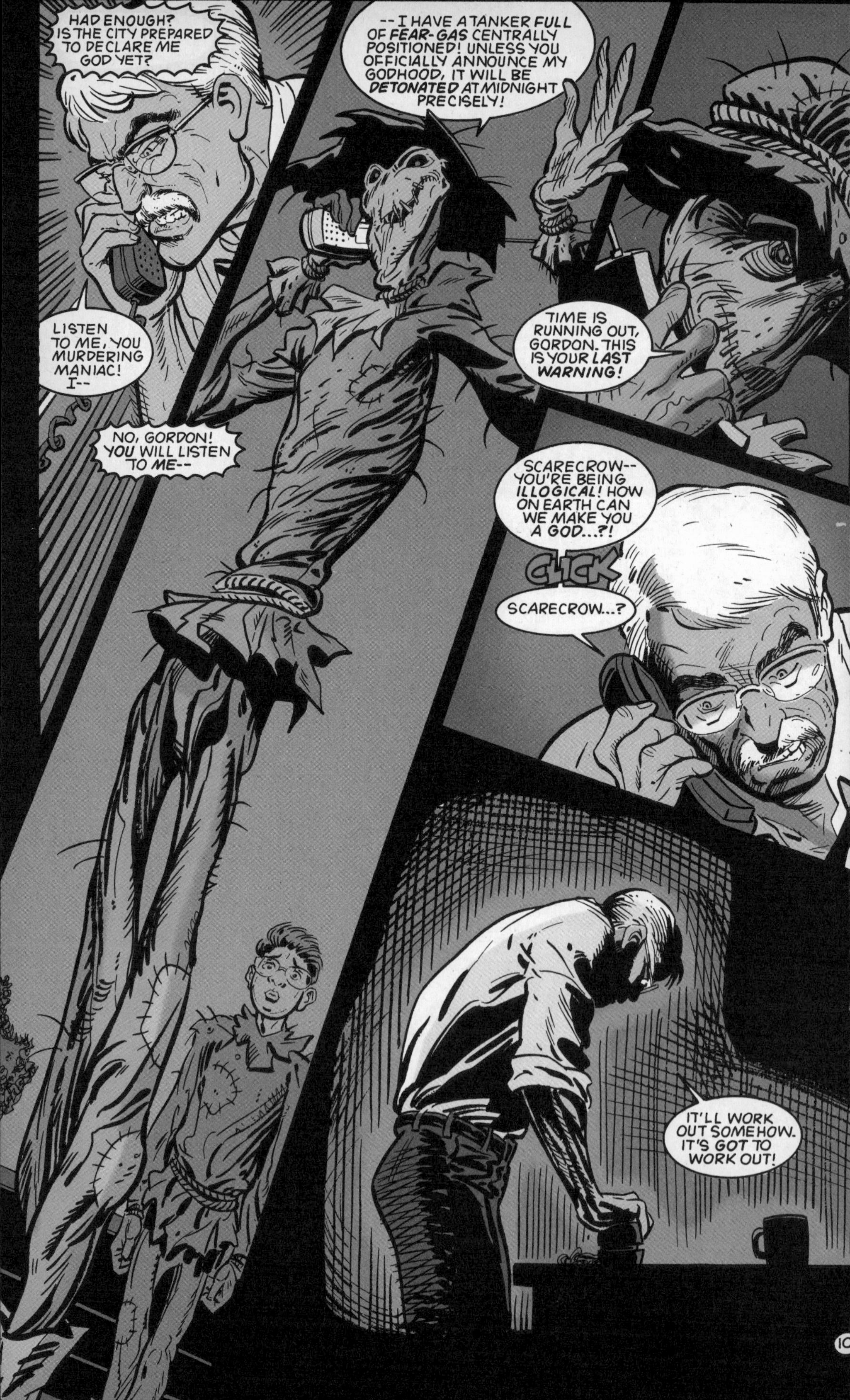
HAD ENOUGH? IS THE CITY PREPARED TO DECLARE ME GOD YET?
LISTEN TO ME, YOU MURDERING MANIAC! I--
NO, GORDON! YOU WILL LISTEN TO ME--
-- I HAVE A TANKER FULL OF FEAR-GAS CENTRALLY POSITIONED! UNLESS YOU OFFICIALLY ANNOUNCE MY GODHOOD, IT WILL BE DETONATED AT MIDNIGHT PRECISELY!
TIME IS RUNNING OUT, GORDON. THIS IS YOUR LAST WARNING!
SCARECROW-- YOU'RE BEING ILLOGICAL! HOW ON EARTH CAN WE MAKE YOU A GOD...?!
CLICK
SCARECROW...?
IT'LL WORK OUT SOMEHOW. IT'S GOT TO WORK OUT!

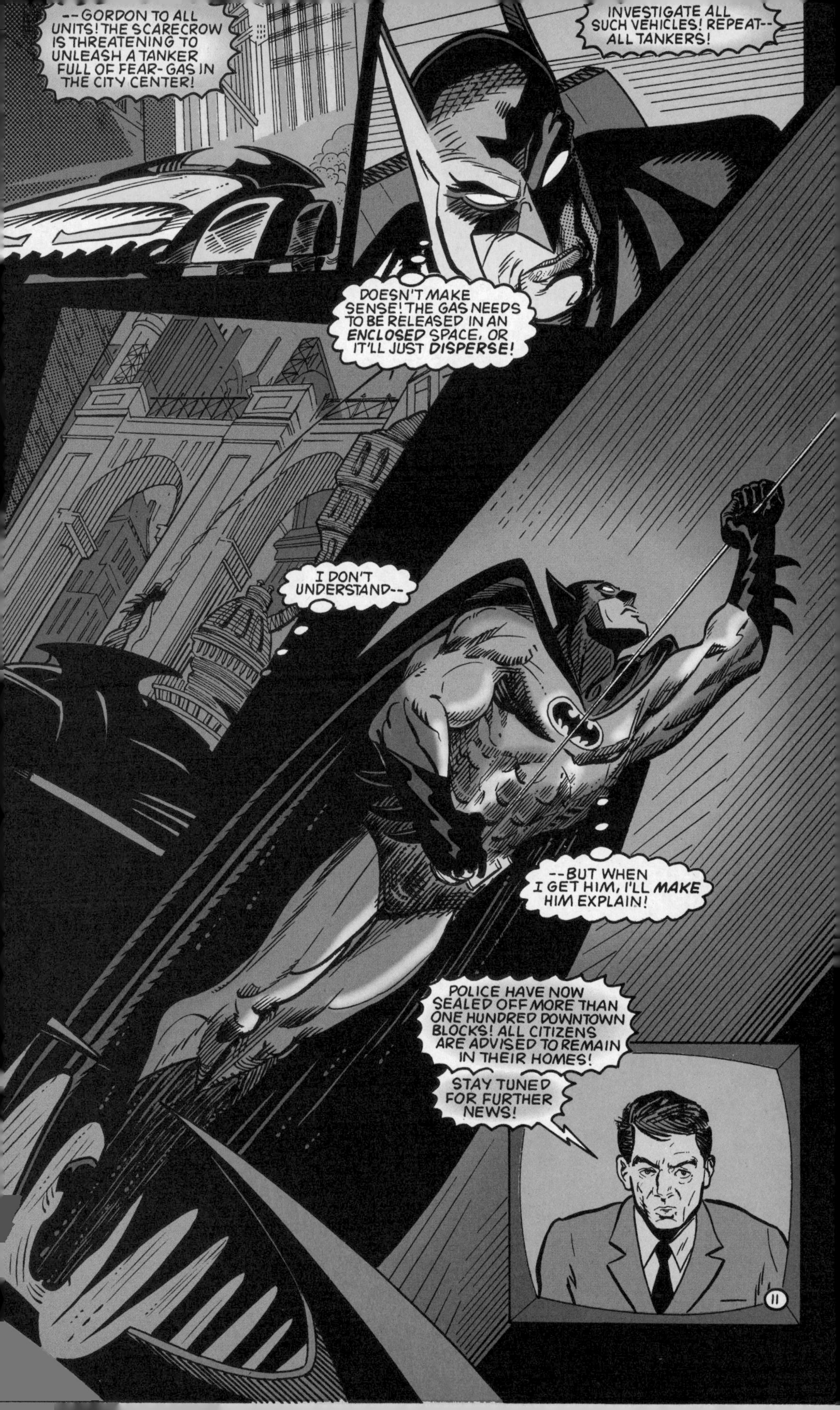
--GORDON TO ALL UNITS! THE SCARECROW IS THREATENING TO UNLEASH A TANKER FULL OF FEAR-GAS IN THE CITY CENTER!
INVESTIGATE ALL SUCH VEHICLES! REPEAT--ALL TANKERS!
DOESN'T MAKE SENSE! THE GAS NEEDS TO BE RELEASED IN AN ENCLOSED SPACE, OR IT'LL JUST DISPERSE!
I DON'T UNDERSTAND--
--BUT WHEN I GET HIM, I'LL MAKE HIM EXPLAIN!
POLICE HAVE NOW SEALED OFF MORE THAN ONE HUNDRED DOWNTOWN BLOCKS! ALL CITIZENS ARE ADVISED TO REMAIN IN THEIR HOMES!
STAY TUNED FOR FURTHER NEWS!
11

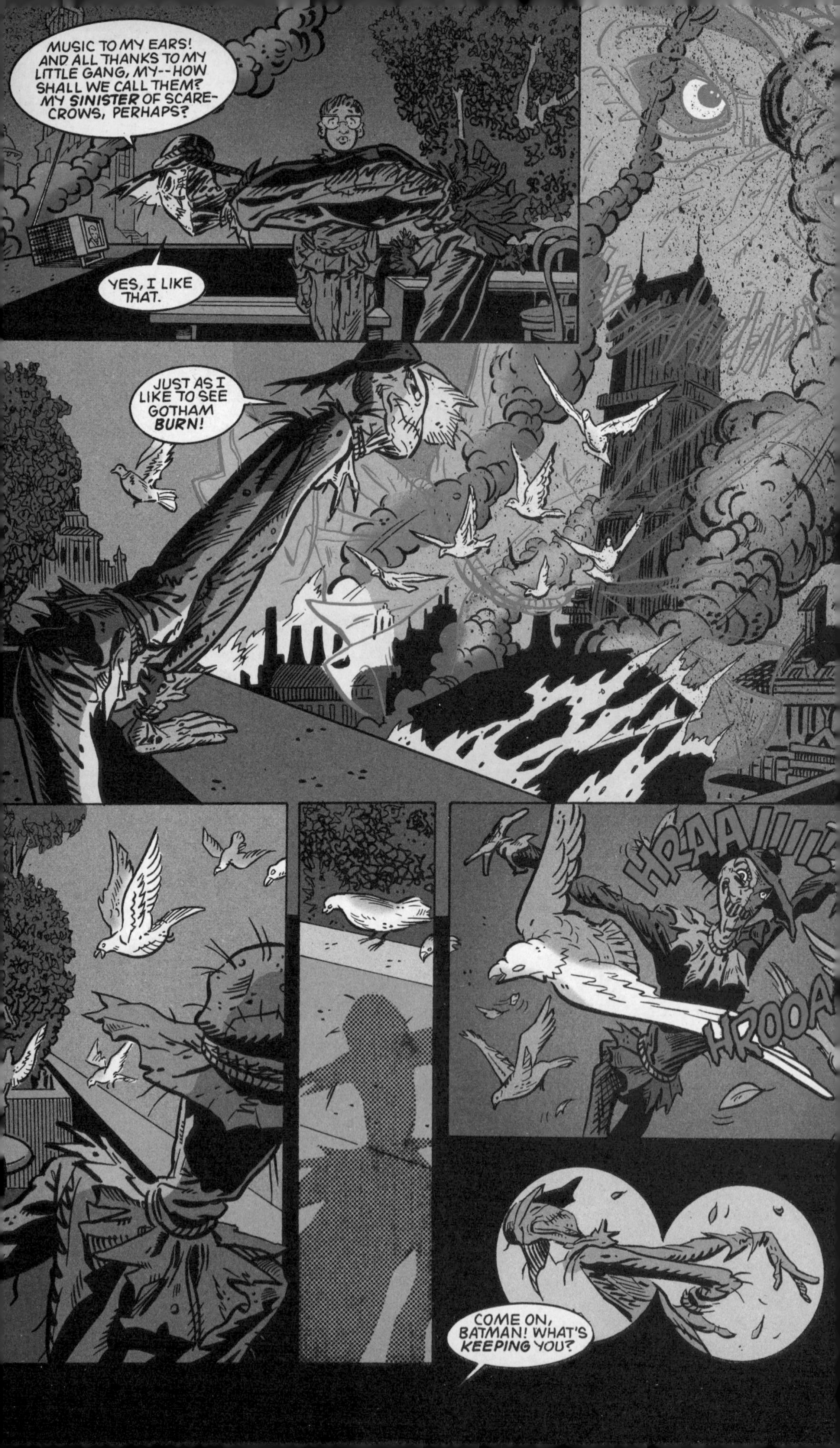
MUSIC TO MY EARS! AND ALL THANKS TO MY LITTLE GANG, MY--HOW SHALL WE CALL THEM? MY SINISTER OF SCARE-CROWS, PERHAPS?
YES, I LIKE THAT.
JUST AS I LIKE TO SEE GOTHAM BURN!
HRAAIIII
HROOA
COME ON, BATMAN! WHAT'S KEEPING YOU?

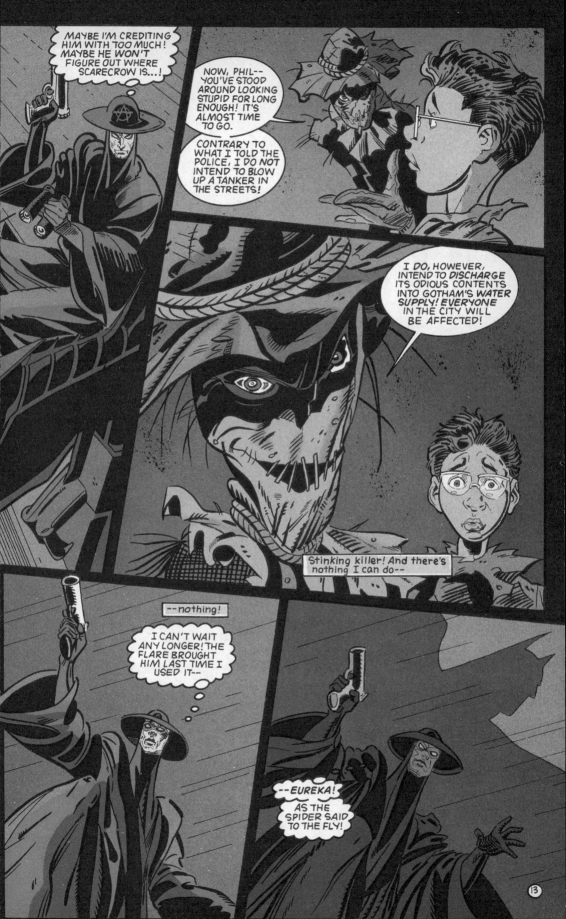

MAYBE I'M CREDITING HIM WITH TOO MUCH! MAYBE HE WON'T FIGURE OUT WHERE SCARECROW IS...!

NOW, PHIL-- YOU'VE STOOD AROUND LOOKING STUPID FOR LONG ENOUGH! IT'S ALMOST TIME TO GO.

CONTRARY TO WHAT I TOLD THE POLICE, I DO NOT INTEND TO BLOW UP A TANKER IN THE STREETS!

I DO, HOWEVER, INTEND TO *DISCHARGE* ITS ODIOUS CONTENTS INTO GOTHAM'S *WATER SUPPLY!* EVERYONE IN THE CITY WILL BE AFFECTED!

Stinking killer! And there's nothing I can do--

--nothing!

I CAN'T WAIT ANY LONGER! THE FLARE BROUGHT HIM LAST TIME I USED IT--

--EUREKA! AS THE SPIDER SAID TO THE FLY!

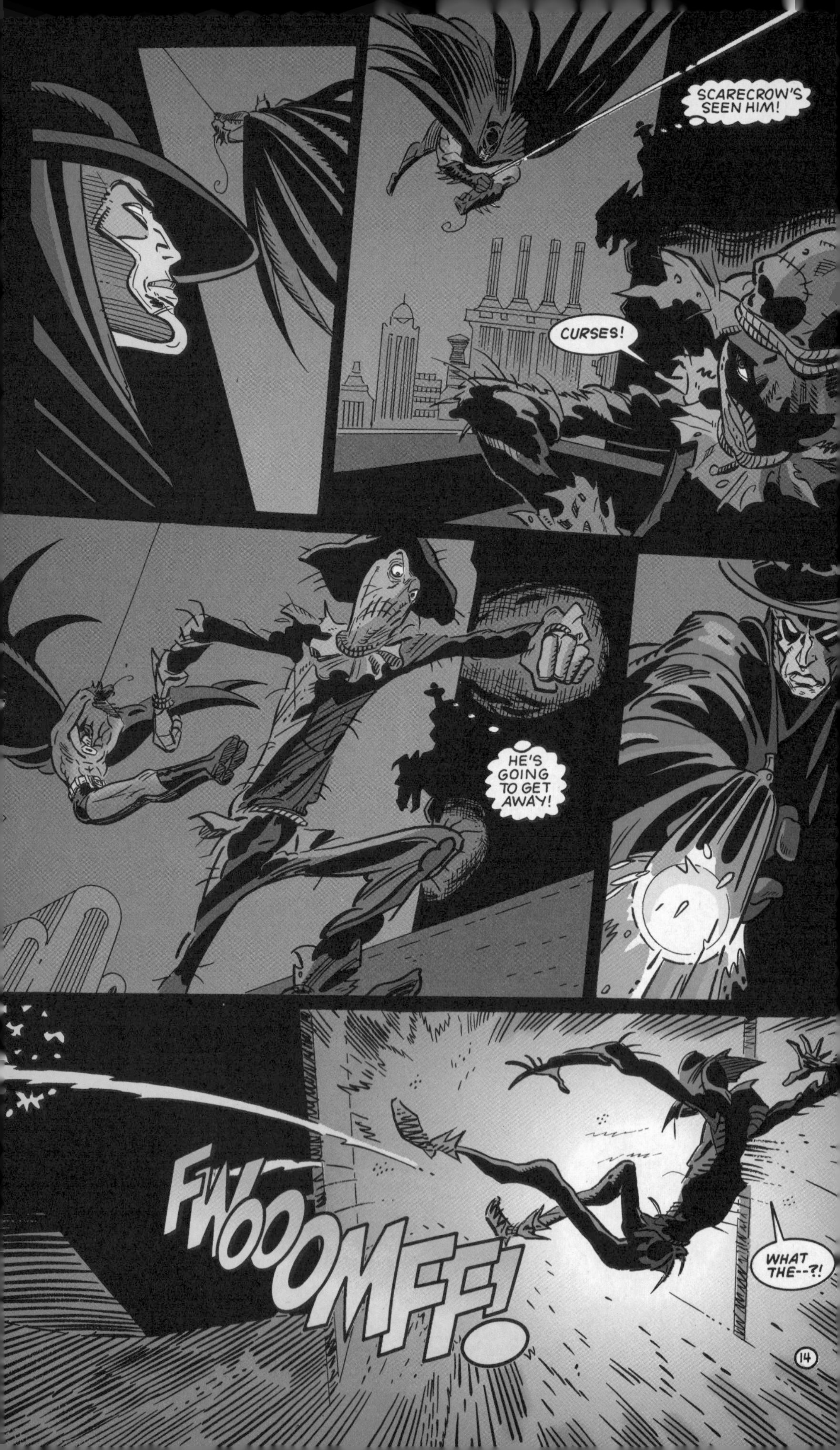
SCARECROW'S SEEN HIM!
CURSES!
HE'S GOING TO GET AWAY!
FWOOOMFF!
WHAT THE--?!
14

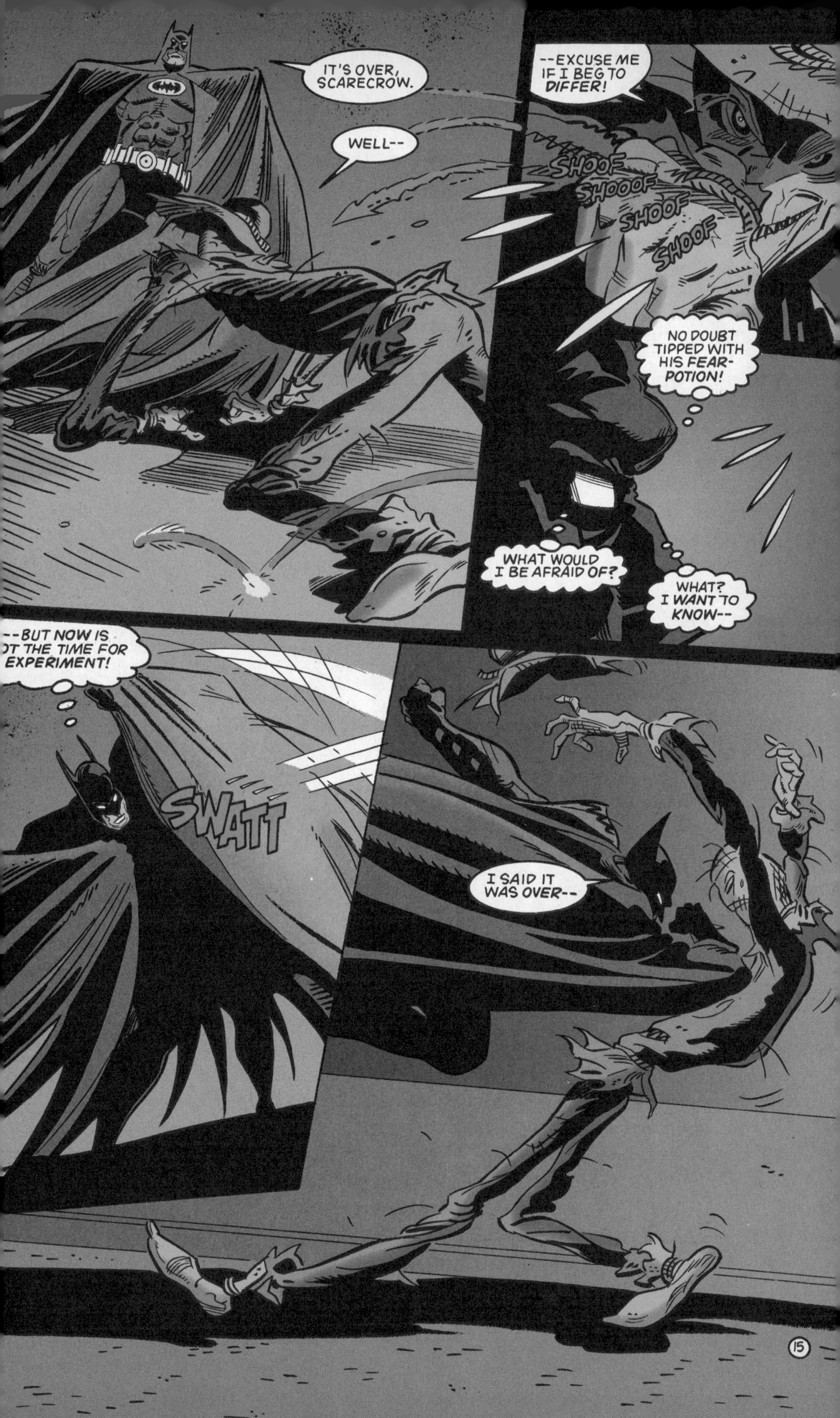
IT'S OVER, SCARECROW.
WELL--
--EXCUSE ME IF I BEG TO DIFFER!
SHOOF
SHOOOF
SHOOF
SHOOF
NO DOUBT TIPPED WITH HIS FEAR-POTION!
WHAT WOULD I BE AFRAID OF?
WHAT? I WANT TO KNOW--
--BUT NOW IS OT THE TIME FOR EXPERIMENT!
SWATT
I SAID IT WAS OVER--

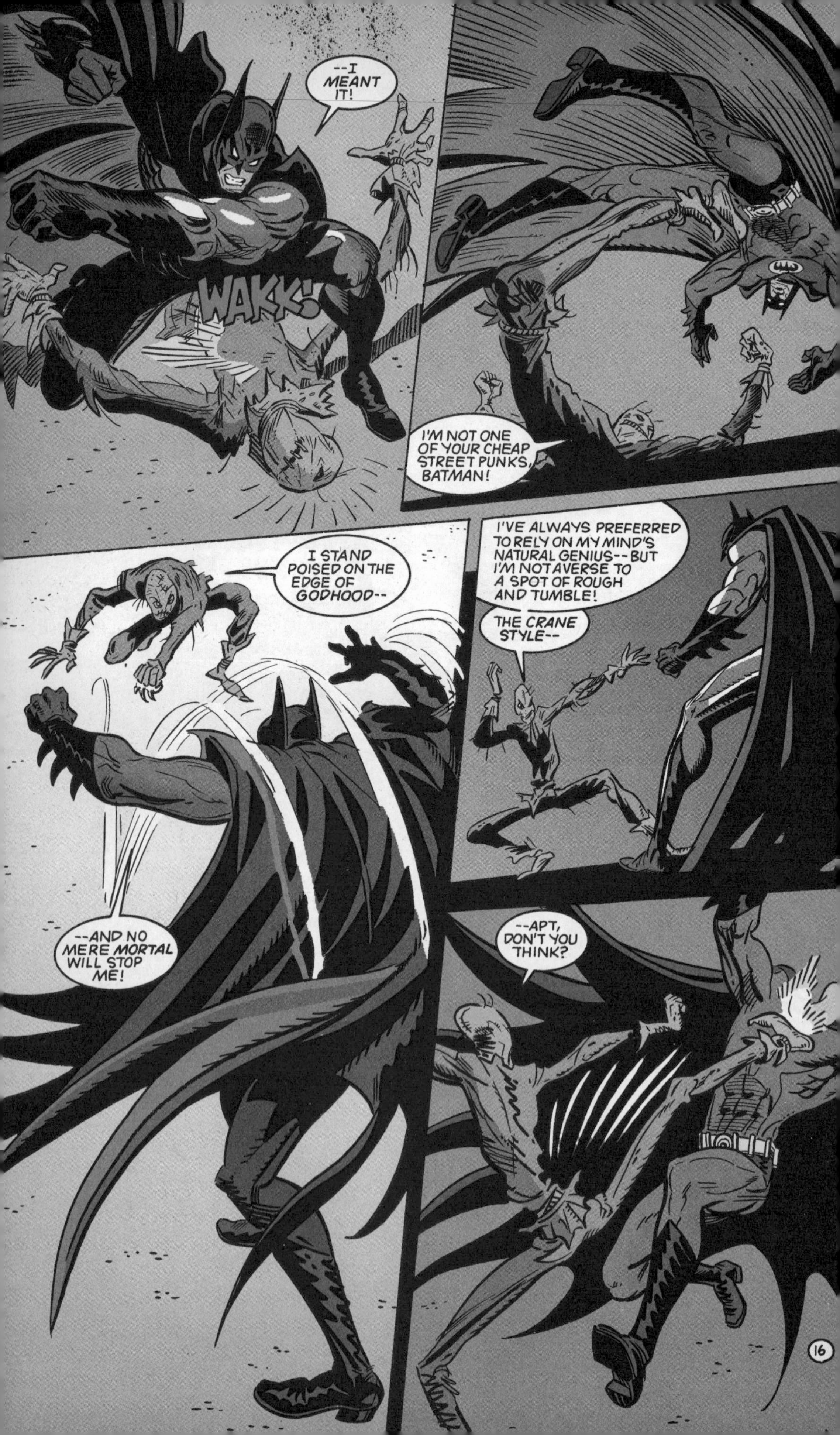
--I MEANT IT!
WAKK!
I'M NOT ONE OF YOUR CHEAP STREET PUNKS, BATMAN!
I STAND POISED ON THE EDGE OF GODHOOD--
--AND NO MERE MORTAL WILL STOP ME!
I'VE ALWAYS PREFERRED TO RELY ON MY MIND'S NATURAL GENIUS--BUT I'M NOT AVERSE TO A SPOT OF ROUGH AND TUMBLE!
THE CRANE STYLE--
--APT, DON'T YOU THINK?

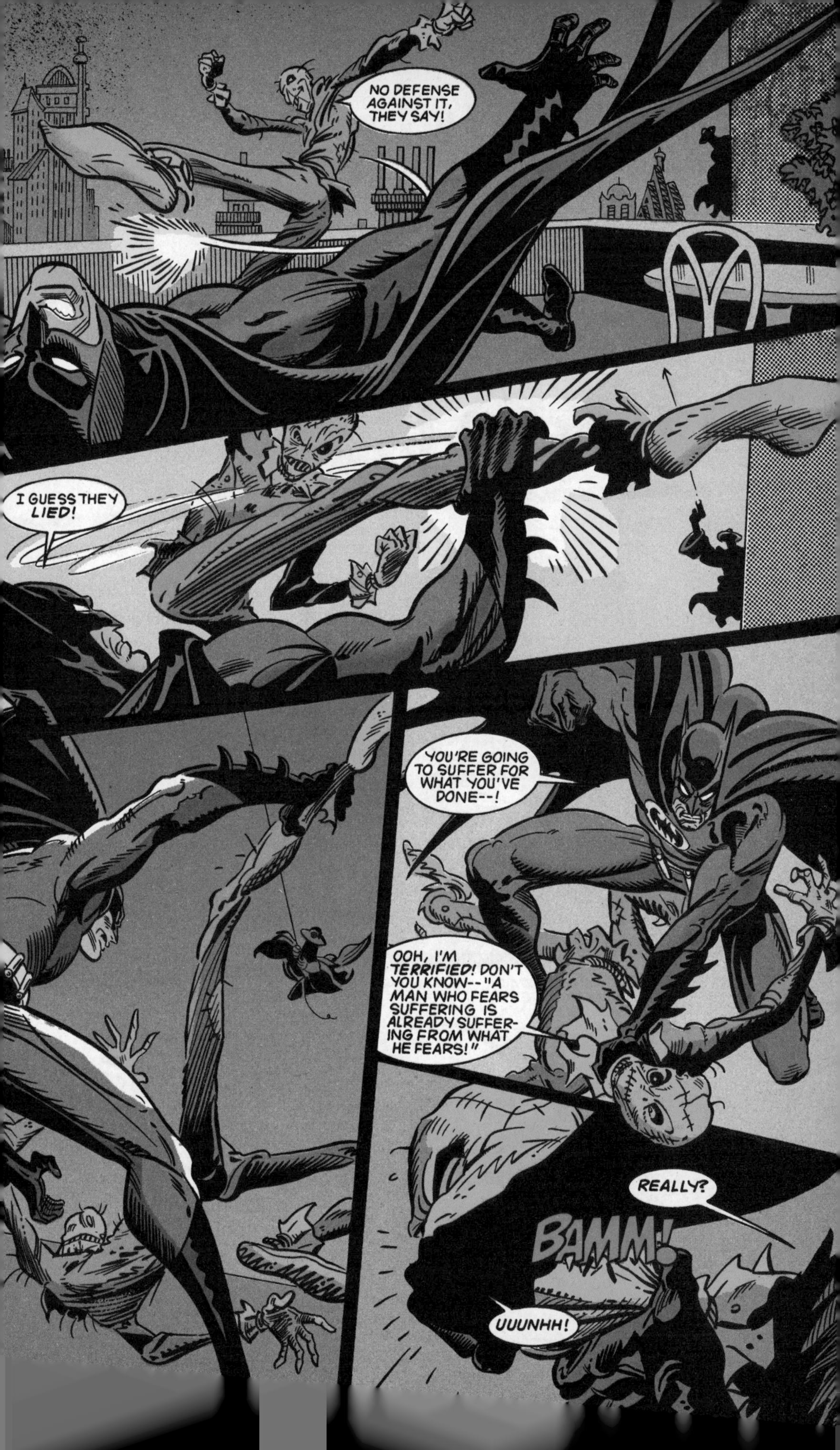
NO DEFENSE AGAINST IT, THEY SAY!
I GUESS THEY LIED!
YOU'RE GOING TO SUFFER FOR WHAT YOU'VE DONE--!
OOH, I'M TERRIFIED! DON'T YOU KNOW--"A MAN WHO FEARS SUFFERING IS ALREADY SUFFERING FROM WHAT HE FEARS!"
REALLY?
BAMM!
UUUNHH!

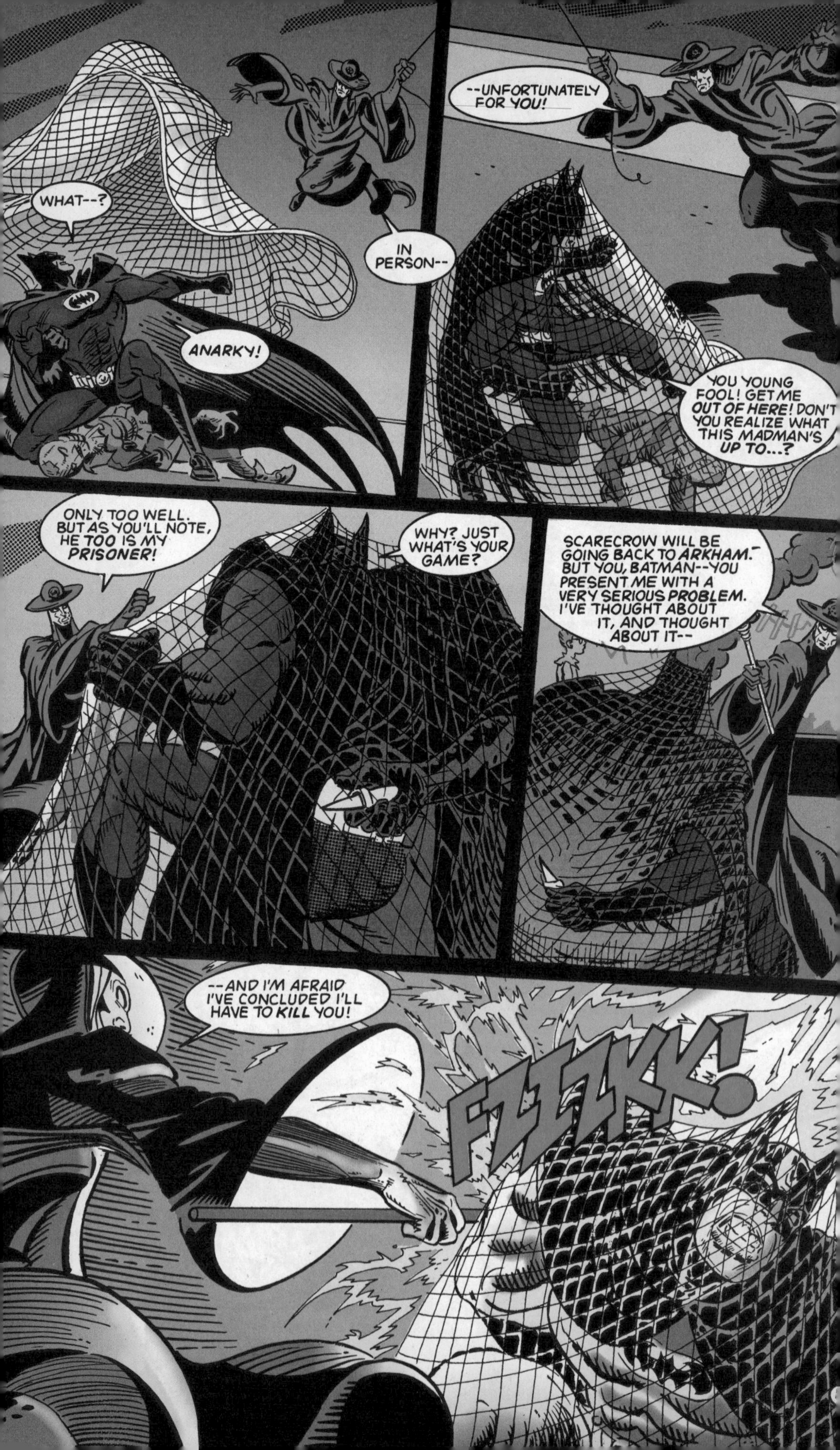
WHAT--?
IN PERSON--
ANARKY!
--UNFORTUNATELY FOR YOU!
YOU YOUNG FOOL! GET ME OUT OF HERE! DON'T YOU REALIZE WHAT THIS MADMAN'S UP TO...?
ONLY TOO WELL. BUT AS YOU'LL NOTE, HE TOO IS MY PRISONER!
WHY? JUST WHAT'S YOUR GAME?
SCARECROW WILL BE GOING BACK TO ARKHAM. BUT YOU, BATMAN--YOU PRESENT ME WITH A VERY SERIOUS PROBLEM. I'VE THOUGHT ABOUT IT, AND THOUGHT ABOUT IT--
--AND I'M AFRAID I'VE CONCLUDED I'LL HAVE TO KILL YOU!
FZZKK!

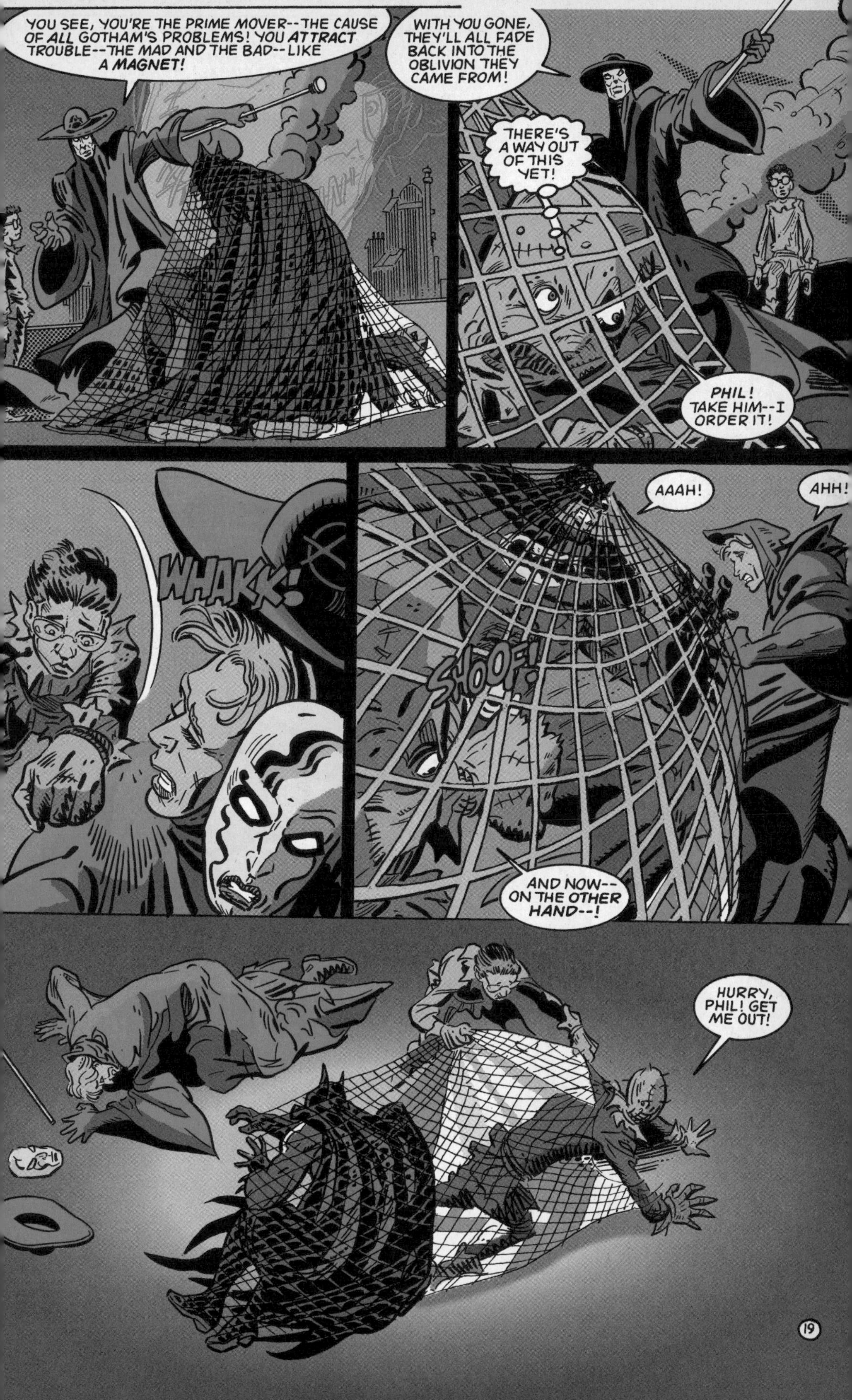
YOU SEE, YOU'RE THE PRIME MOVER--THE CAUSE OF ALL GOTHAM'S PROBLEMS! YOU ATTRACT TROUBLE--THE MAD AND THE BAD--LIKE A MAGNET!
WITH YOU GONE, THEY'LL ALL FADE BACK INTO THE OBLIVION THEY CAME FROM!
THERE'S A WAY OUT OF THIS YET!
PHIL! TAKE HIM--I ORDER IT!
WHAKK!
AAAH!
AHH!
SHOOF!
AND NOW--ON THE OTHER HAND--!
HURRY, PHIL! GET ME OUT!

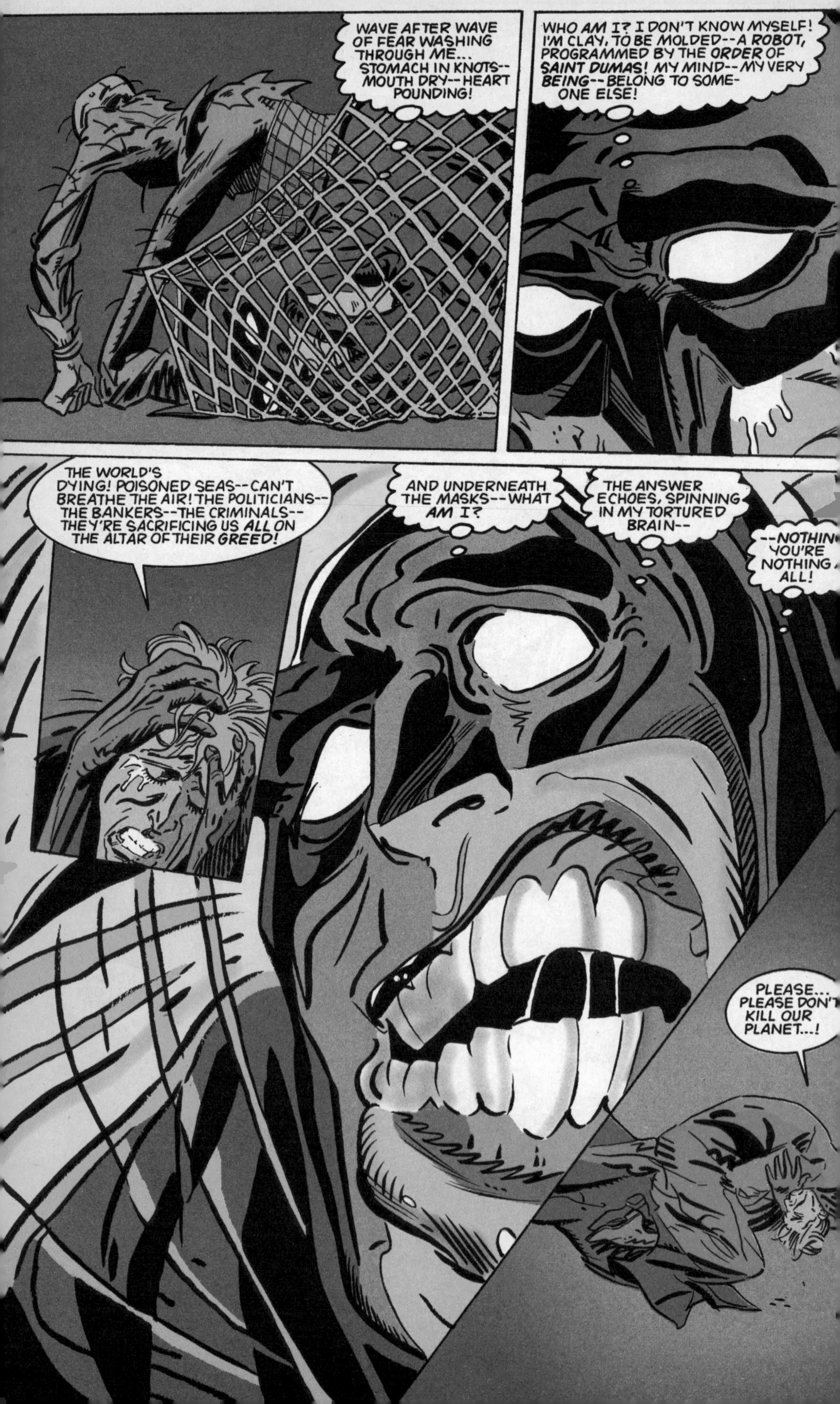

WAVE AFTER WAVE OF FEAR WASHING THROUGH ME... STOMACH IN KNOTS--MOUTH DRY--HEART POUNDING!
WHO AM I? I DON'T KNOW MYSELF! I'M CLAY, TO BE MOLDED--A ROBOT, PROGRAMMED BY THE ORDER OF SAINT DUMAS! MY MIND--MY VERY BEING--BELONG TO SOME-ONE ELSE!
THE WORLD'S DYING! POISONED SEAS--CAN'T BREATHE THE AIR! THE POLITICIANS--THE BANKERS--THE CRIMINALS--THEY'RE SACRIFICING US ALL ON THE ALTAR OF THEIR GREED!
AND UNDERNEATH THE MASKS--WHAT AM I?
THE ANSWER ECHOES, SPINNING IN MY TORTURED BRAIN--
--NOTHIN YOU'RE NOTHING ALL!
PLEASE... PLEASE DON'T KILL OUR PLANET...!

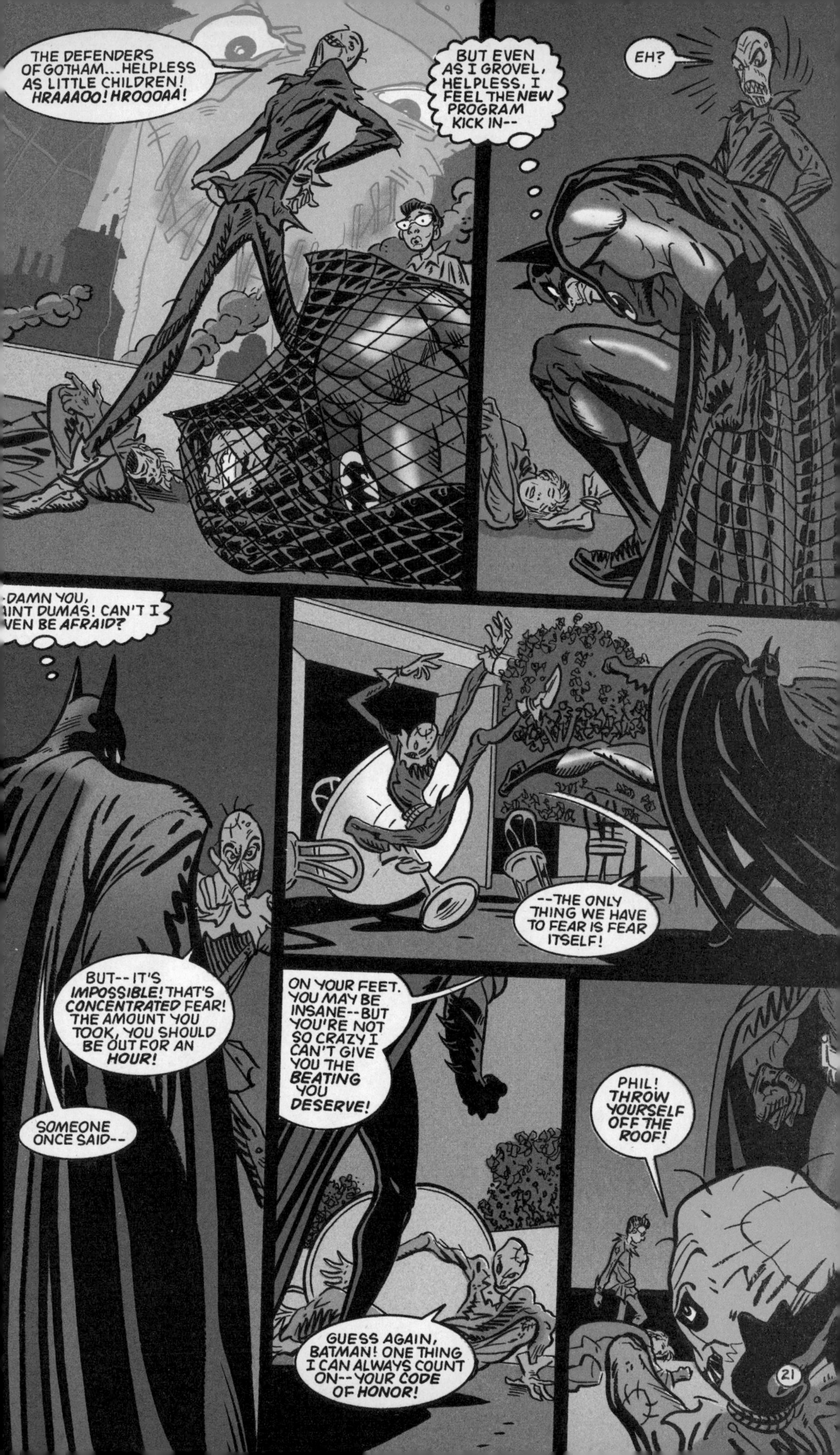
THE DEFENDERS OF GOTHAM...HELPLESS AS LITTLE CHILDREN! HRAAAOO! HROOOAA!
BUT EVEN AS I GROVEL, HELPLESS, I FEEL THE NEW PROGRAM KICK IN--
EH?
-DAMN YOU, AINT DUMAS! CAN'T I VEN BE AFRAID?
BUT--IT'S IMPOSSIBLE! THAT'S CONCENTRATED FEAR! THE AMOUNT YOU TOOK, YOU SHOULD BE OUT FOR AN HOUR!
SOMEONE ONCE SAID--
--THE ONLY THING WE HAVE TO FEAR IS FEAR ITSELF!
ON YOUR FEET. YOU MAY BE INSANE--BUT YOU'RE NOT SO CRAZY I CAN'T GIVE YOU THE BEATING YOU DESERVE!
GUESS AGAIN, BATMAN! ONE THING I CAN ALWAYS COUNT ON--YOUR CODE OF HONOR!
PHIL! THROW YOURSELF OFF THE ROOF!
21

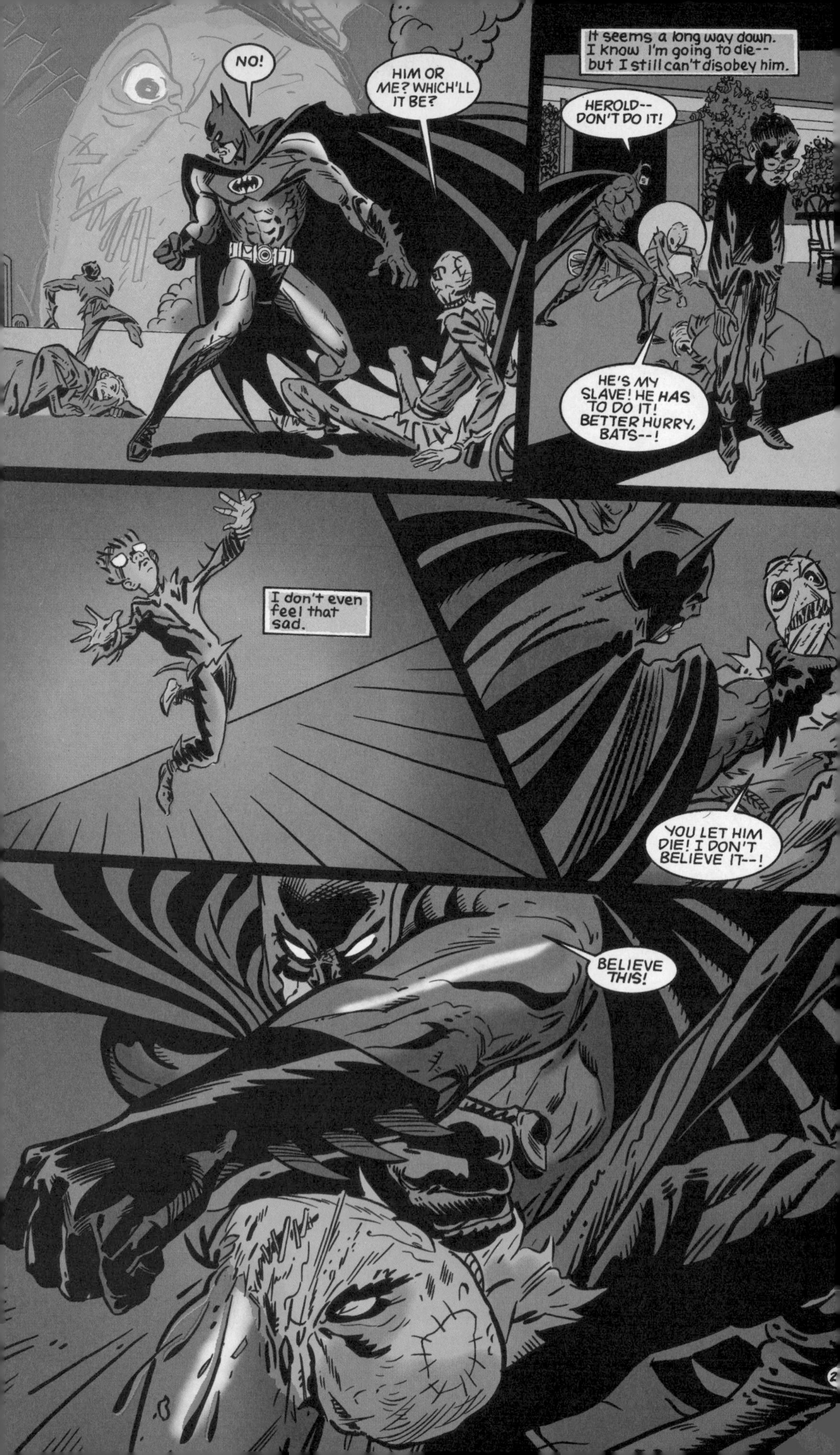

NO!
HIM OR ME? WHICH'LL IT BE?
It seems a long way down. I know I'm going to die-- but I still can't disobey him.
HEROLD-- DON'T DO IT!
HE'S MY SLAVE! HE HAS TO DO IT! BETTER HURRY, BATS--!
I don't even feel that sad.
YOU LET HIM DIE! I DON'T BELIEVE IT--!
BELIEVE THIS!

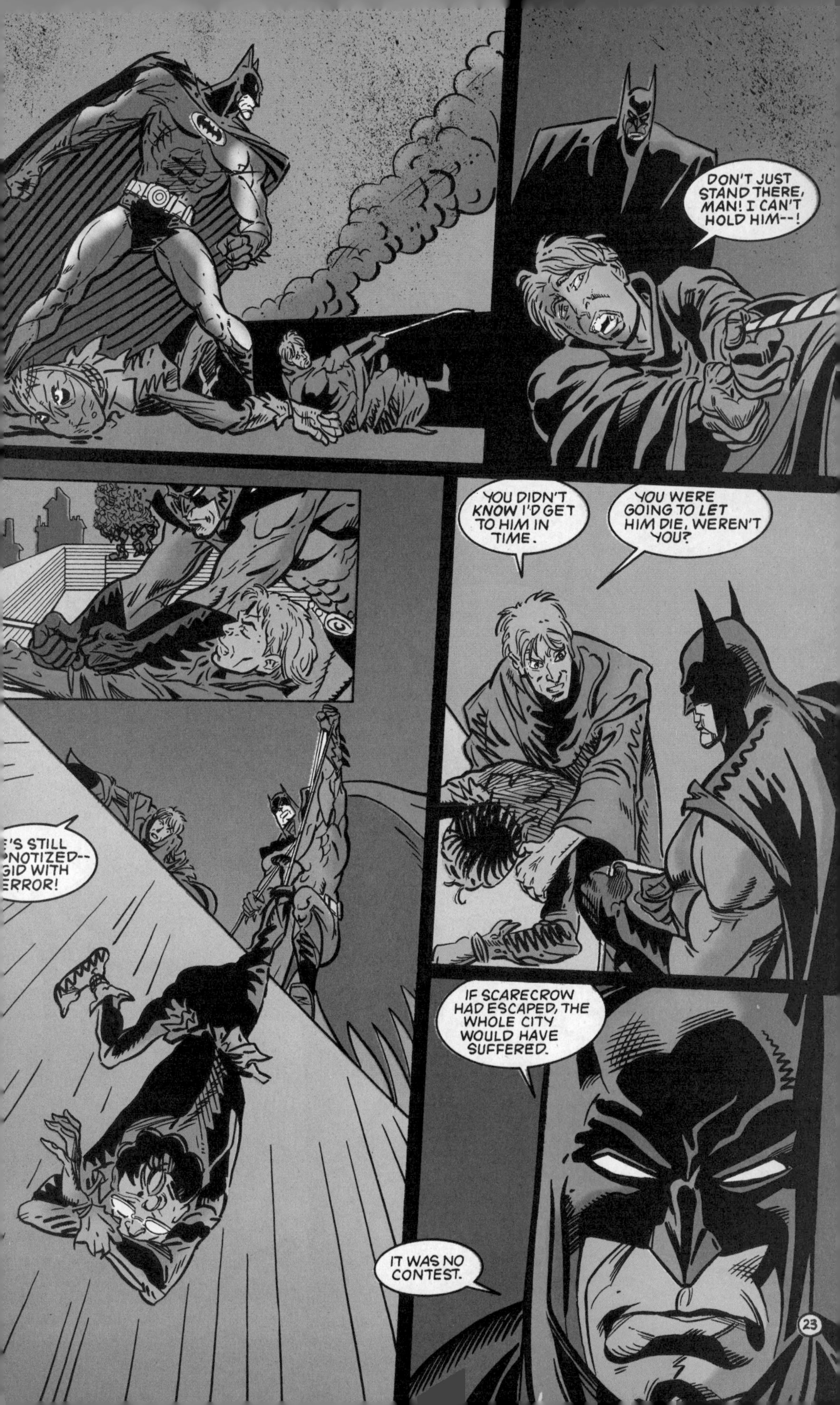
DON'T JUST STAND THERE, MAN! I CAN'T HOLD HIM--!
E'S STILL PNOTIZED-- GID WITH ERROR!
YOU DIDN'T KNOW I'D GET TO HIM IN TIME.
YOU WERE GOING TO LET HIM DIE, WEREN'T YOU?
IF SCARECROW HAD ESCAPED, THE WHOLE CITY WOULD HAVE SUFFERED.
IT WAS NO CONTEST.

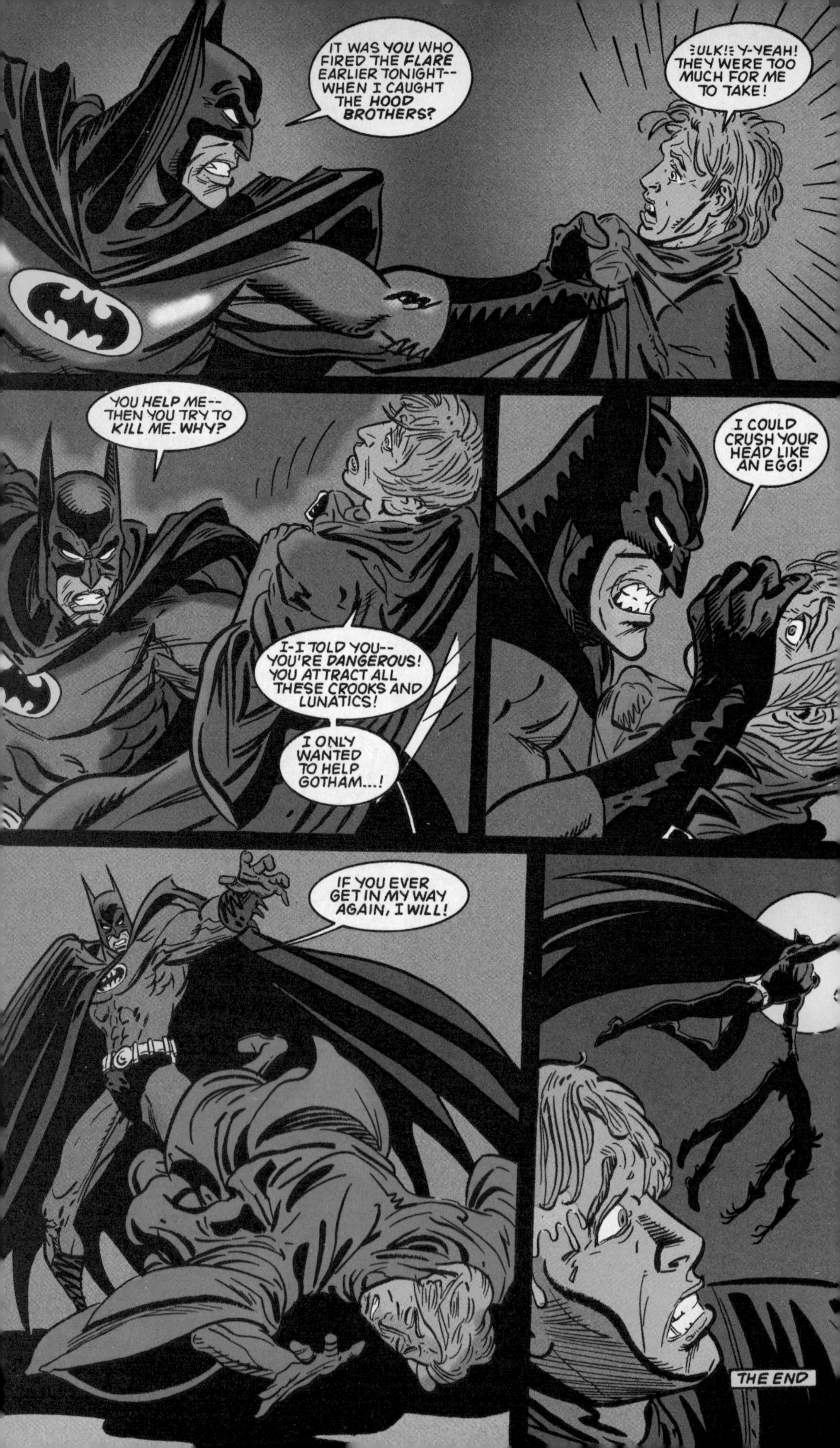
IT WAS YOU WHO FIRED THE FLARE EARLIER TONIGHT-- WHEN I CAUGHT THE HOOD BROTHERS?
ULK! Y-YEAH! THEY WERE TOO MUCH FOR ME TO TAKE!
YOU HELP ME-- THEN YOU TRY TO KILL ME. WHY?
I-I TOLD YOU-- YOU'RE DANGEROUS! YOU ATTRACT ALL THESE CROOKS AND LUNATICS!
I ONLY WANTED TO HELP GOTHAM...!
I COULD CRUSH YOUR HEAD LIKE AN EGG!
IF YOU EVER GET IN MY WAY AGAIN, I WILL!
THE END

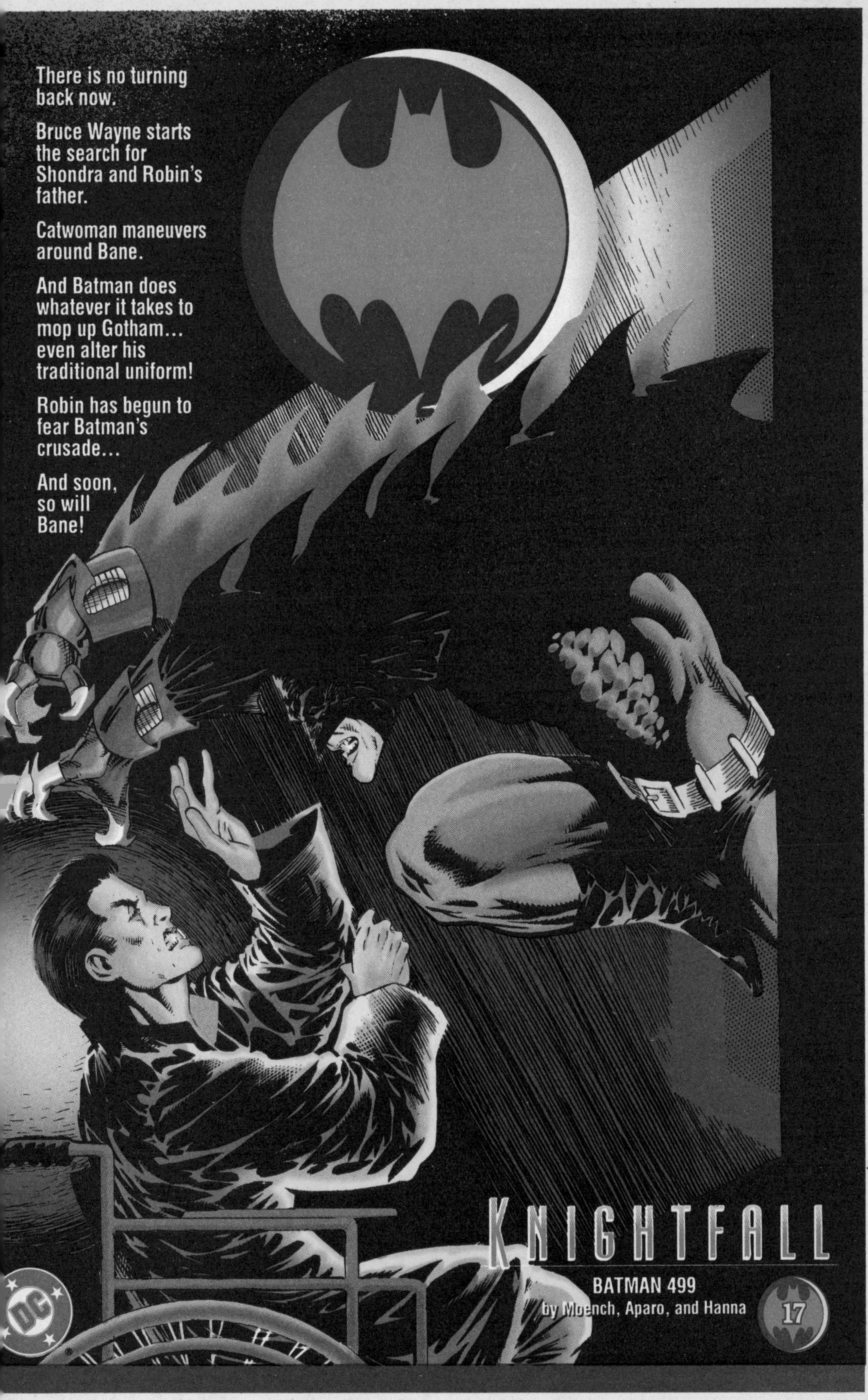
There is no turning back now.
Bruce Wayne starts the search for Shondra and Robin's father.
Catwoman maneuvers around Bane.
And Batman does whatever it takes to mop up Gotham... even alter his traditional uniform!
Robin has begun to fear Batman's crusade...
And soon, so will Bane!
KNIGHTFALL
BATMAN 499
by Moench, Aparo, and Hanna
17

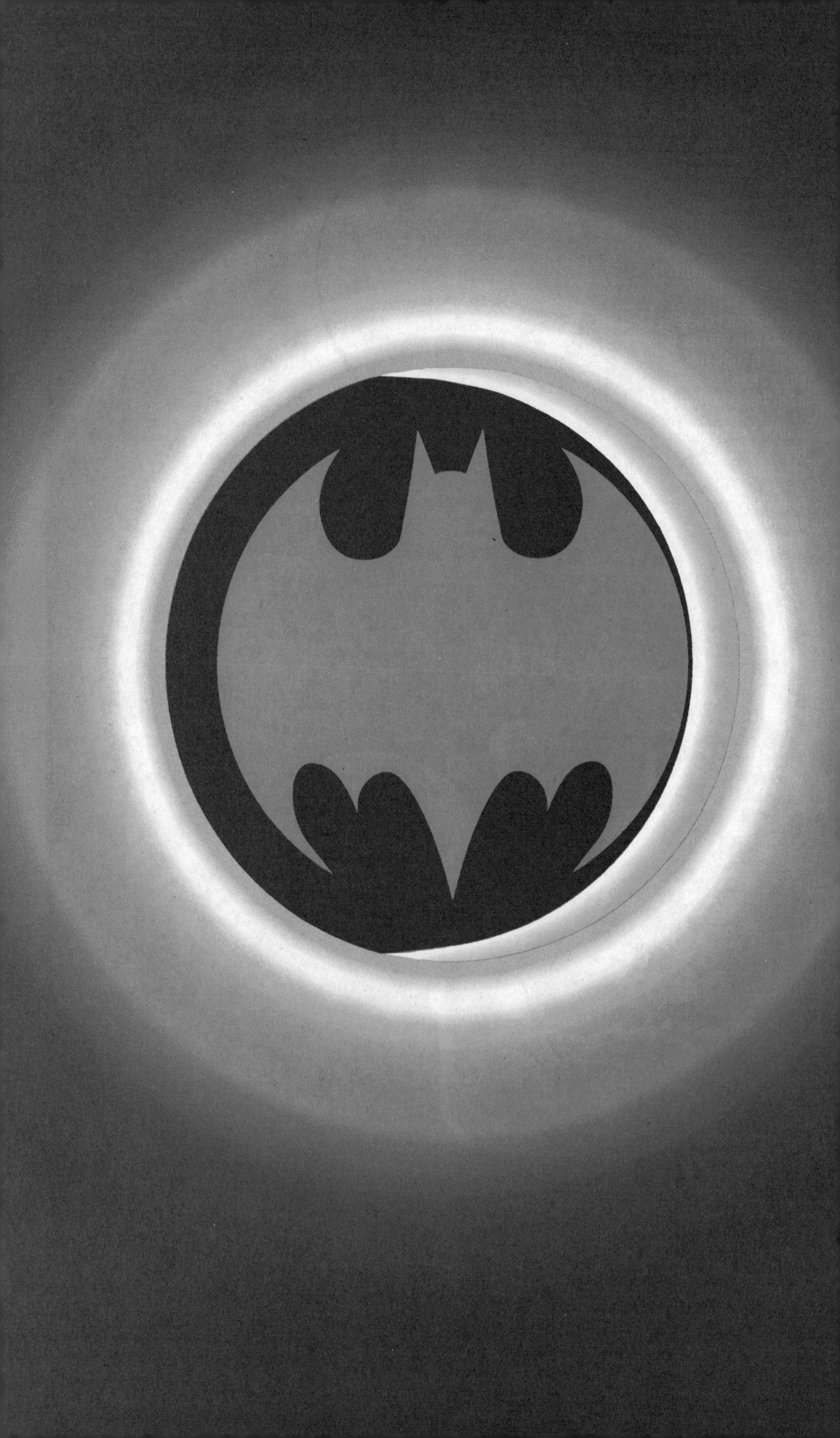

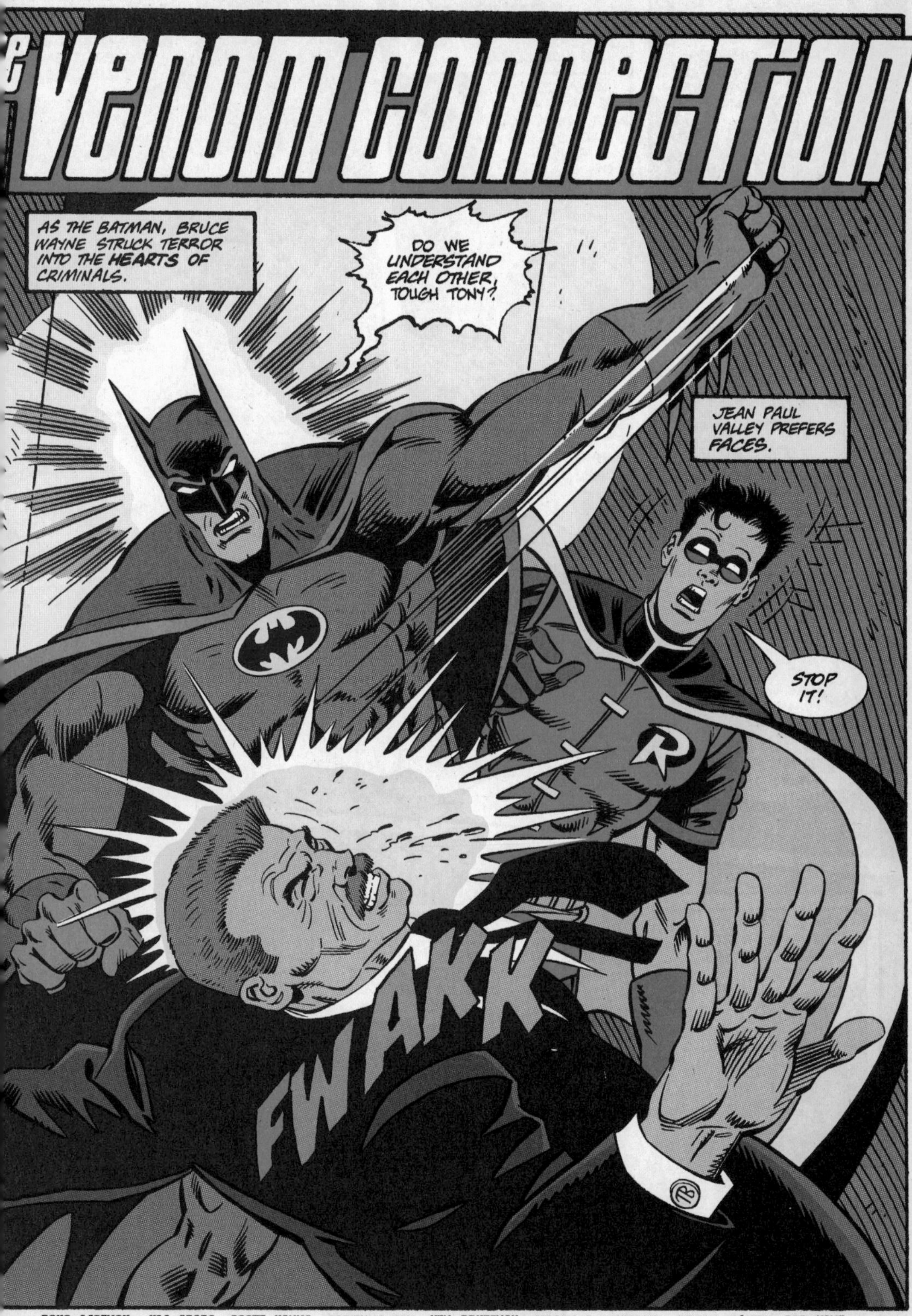

VENOM CONNECTION
AS THE BATMAN, BRUCE WAYNE STRUCK TERROR INTO THE HEARTS OF CRIMINALS.
DO WE UNDERSTAND EACH OTHER, TOUGH TONY?
JEAN PAUL VALLEY PREFERS FACES.
STOP IT!
FWAKK


DOUG MOENCH--JIM APARO--SCOTT HANNA--ADRIENNE ROY--KEN BRUZENAK--JORDAN B. GORFINKEL--DENNIS O'NEIL--BOB KANE

writer, artist, inker, colorist, letterer, vaccine creator, editor, Batman creator

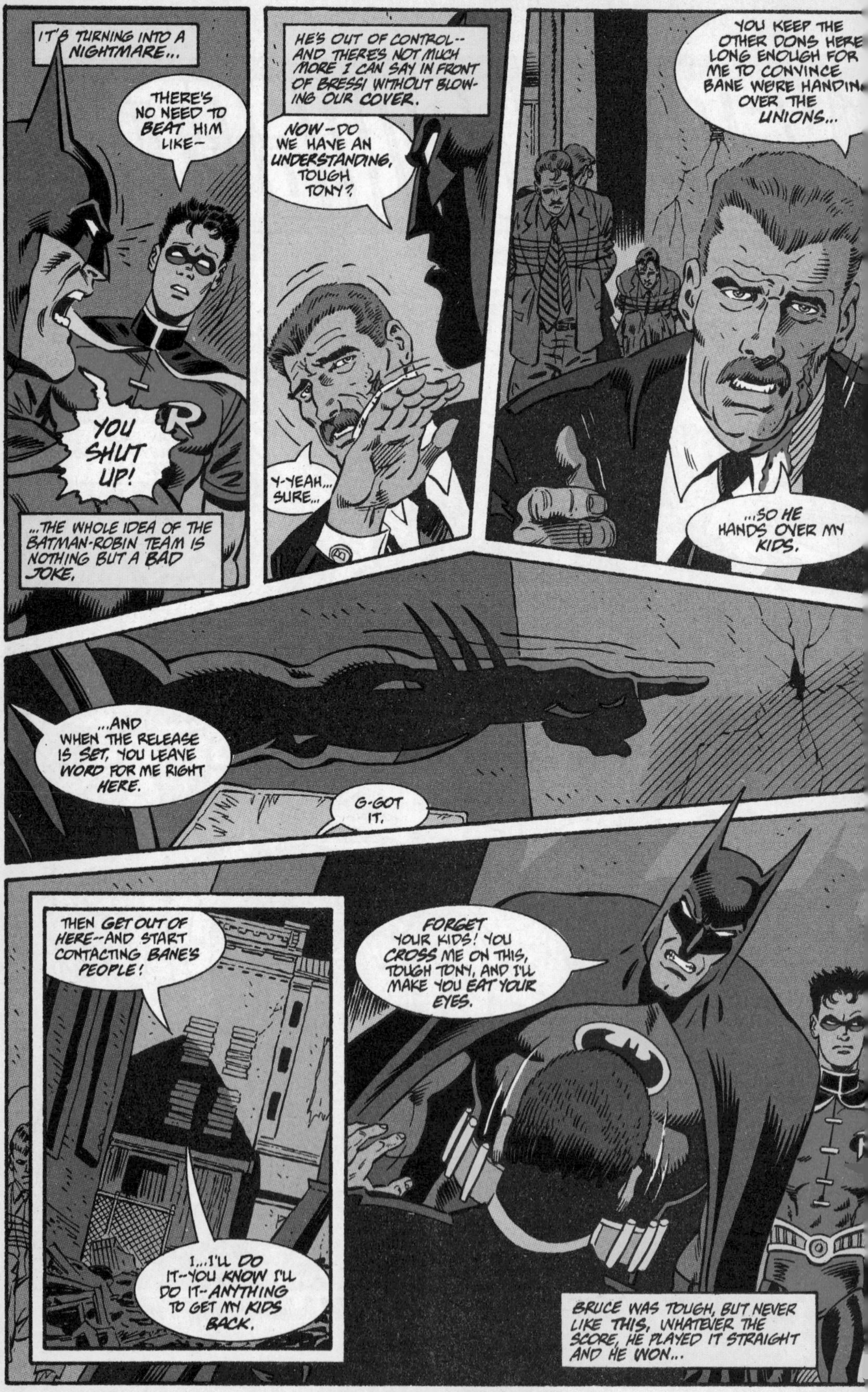
IT'S TURNING INTO A NIGHTMARE...
THERE'S NO NEED TO BEAT HIM LIKE--
YOU SHUT UP!
...THE WHOLE IDEA OF THE BATMAN-ROBIN TEAM IS NOTHING BUT A BAD JOKE.
HE'S OUT OF CONTROL-- AND THERE'S NOT MUCH MORE I CAN SAY IN FRONT OF BRESSI WITHOUT BLOWING OUR COVER.
NOW--DO WE HAVE AN UNDERSTANDING, TOUGH TONY?
Y-YEAH... SURE...
YOU KEEP THE OTHER DONS HERE LONG ENOUGH FOR ME TO CONVINCE BANE WE'RE HANDING OVER THE UNIONS...
...SO HE HANDS OVER MY KIDS.
...AND WHEN THE RELEASE IS SET, YOU LEAVE WORD FOR ME RIGHT HERE.
G-GOT IT.
THEN GET OUT OF HERE--AND START CONTACTING BANE'S PEOPLE!
FORGET YOUR KIDS! YOU CROSS ME ON THIS, TOUGH TONY, AND I'LL MAKE YOU EAT YOUR EYES.
I...I'LL DO IT--YOU KNOW I'LL DO IT--ANYTHING TO GET MY KIDS BACK.
BRUCE WAS TOUGH, BUT NEVER LIKE THIS. WHATEVER THE SCORE, HE PLAYED IT STRAIGHT AND HE WON...

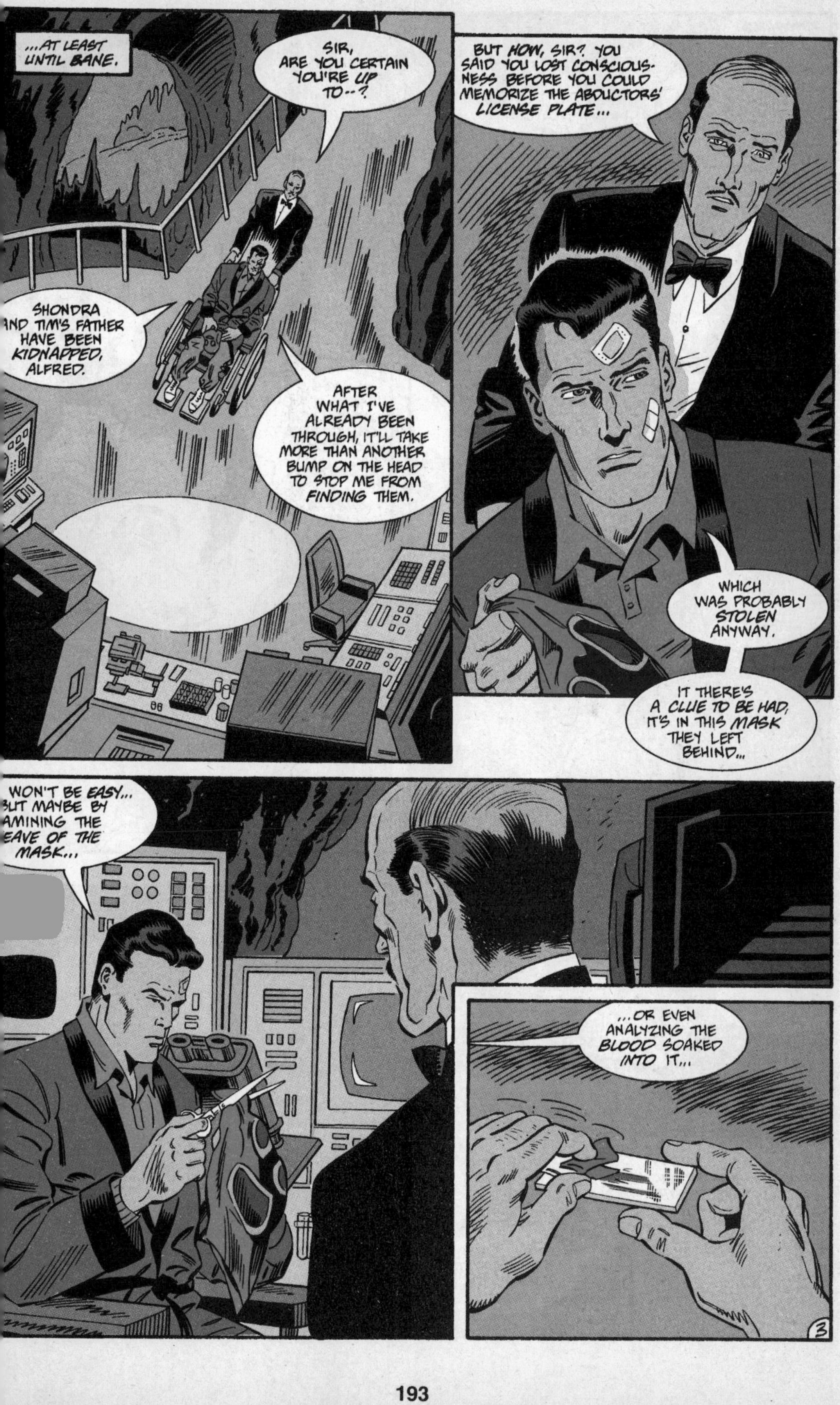
...AT LEAST UNTIL BANE.
SIR, ARE YOU CERTAIN YOU'RE UP TO--?
SHONDRA AND TIM'S FATHER HAVE BEEN KIDNAPPED, ALFRED.
AFTER WHAT I'VE ALREADY BEEN THROUGH, IT'LL TAKE MORE THAN ANOTHER BUMP ON THE HEAD TO STOP ME FROM FINDING THEM.
BUT HOW, SIR? YOU SAID YOU LOST CONSCIOUSNESS BEFORE YOU COULD MEMORIZE THE ABDUCTORS' LICENSE PLATE...
WHICH WAS PROBABLY STOLEN ANYWAY.
IT THERE'S A CLUE TO BE HAD, IT'S IN THIS MASK THEY LEFT BEHIND...
WON'T BE EASY... BUT MAYBE BY AMINING THE EAVE OF THE MASK...
...OR EVEN ANALYZING THE BLOOD SOAKED INTO IT...
3

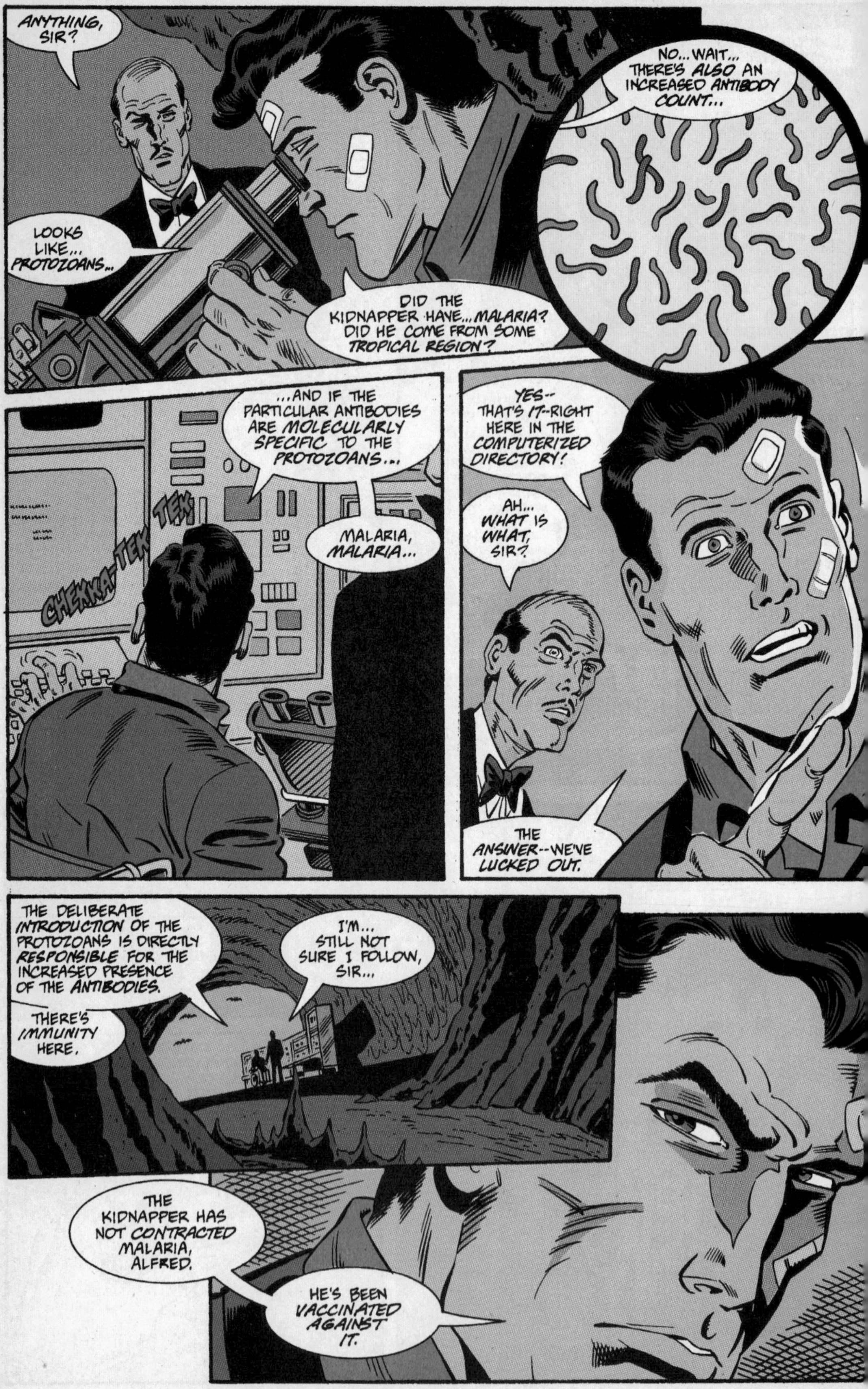

ANYTHING, SIR?
LOOKS LIKE... PROTOZOANS...
NO... WAIT... THERE'S ALSO AN INCREASED ANTIBODY COUNT...
DID THE KIDNAPPER HAVE... MALARIA? DID HE COME FROM SOME TROPICAL REGION?
...AND IF THE PARTICULAR ANTIBODIES ARE MOLECULARLY SPECIFIC TO THE PROTOZOANS...
CHEKKA-TEK TEK
MALARIA, MALARIA...
YES-- THAT'S IT--RIGHT HERE IN THE COMPUTERIZED DIRECTORY!
AH... WHAT IS WHAT, SIR?
THE ANSWER--WE'VE LUCKED OUT.
THE DELIBERATE INTRODUCTION OF THE PROTOZOANS IS DIRECTLY RESPONSIBLE FOR THE INCREASED PRESENCE OF THE ANTIBODIES.
THERE'S IMMUNITY HERE.
I'M... STILL NOT SURE I FOLLOW, SIR...
THE KIDNAPPER HAS NOT CONTRACTED MALARIA, ALFRED.
HE'S BEEN VACCINATED AGAINST IT.

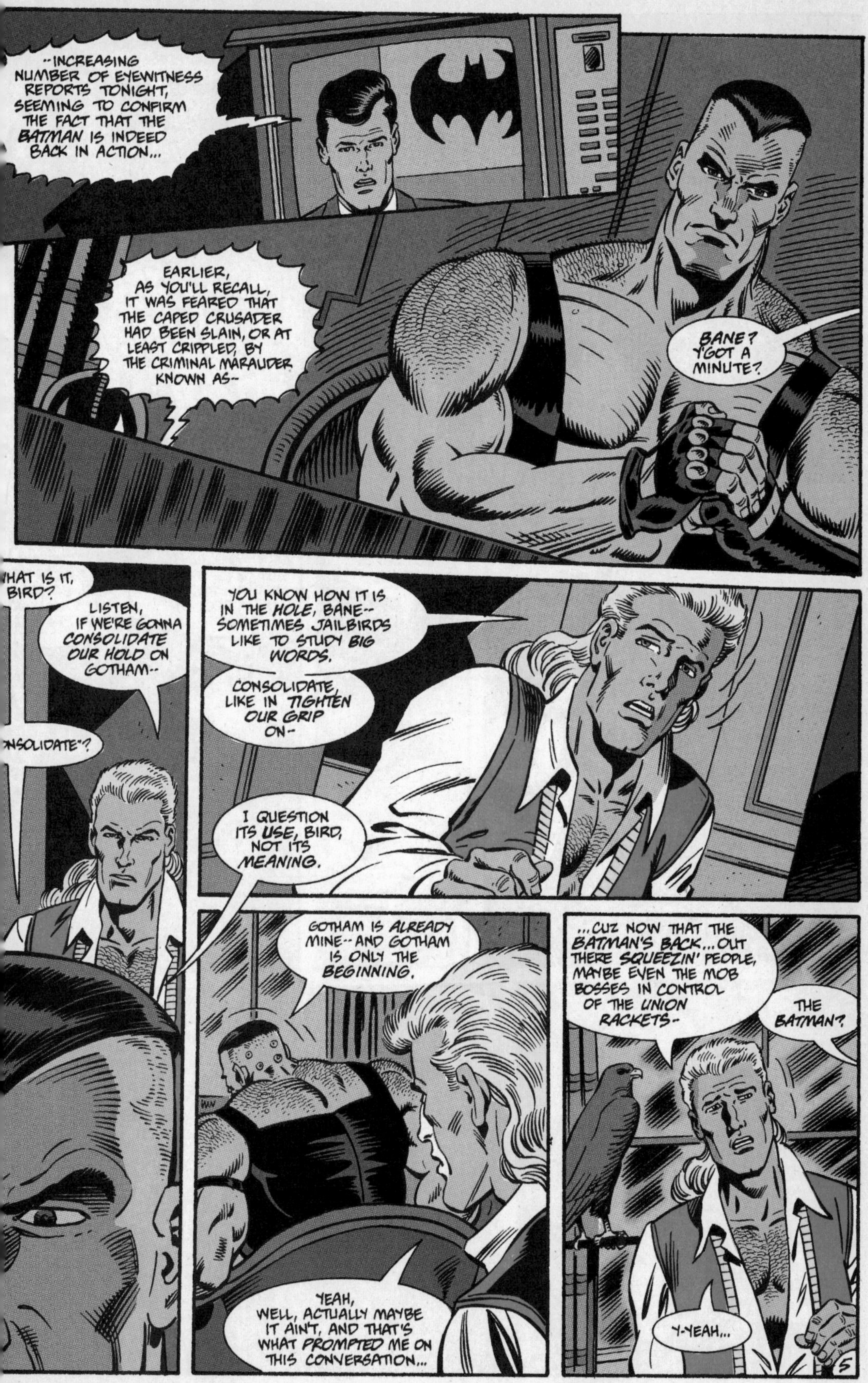
--INCREASING NUMBER OF EYEWITNESS REPORTS TONIGHT, SEEMING TO CONFIRM THE FACT THAT THE BATMAN IS INDEED BACK IN ACTION...
EARLIER, AS YOU'LL RECALL, IT WAS FEARED THAT THE CAPED CRUSADER HAD BEEN SLAIN, OR AT LEAST CRIPPLED, BY THE CRIMINAL MARAUDER KNOWN AS--
BANE? Y'GOT A MINUTE?
WHAT IS IT, BIRD?
LISTEN, IF WE'RE GONNA CONSOLIDATE OUR HOLD ON GOTHAM--
NSOLIDATE"?
YOU KNOW HOW IT IS IN THE HOLE, BANE-- SOMETIMES JAILBIRDS LIKE TO STUDY BIG WORDS.
CONSOLIDATE, LIKE IN TIGHTEN OUR GRIP ON--
I QUESTION ITS USE, BIRD, NOT ITS MEANING.
GOTHAM IS ALREADY MINE-- AND GOTHAM IS ONLY THE BEGINNING.
YEAH, WELL, ACTUALLY MAYBE IT AIN'T, AND THAT'S WHAT PROMPTED ME ON THIS CONVERSATION...
...CUZ NOW THAT THE BATMAN'S BACK... OUT THERE SQUEEZIN' PEOPLE, MAYBE EVEN THE MOB BOSSES IN CONTROL OF THE UNION RACKETS--
THE BATMAN?
Y-YEAH...
5

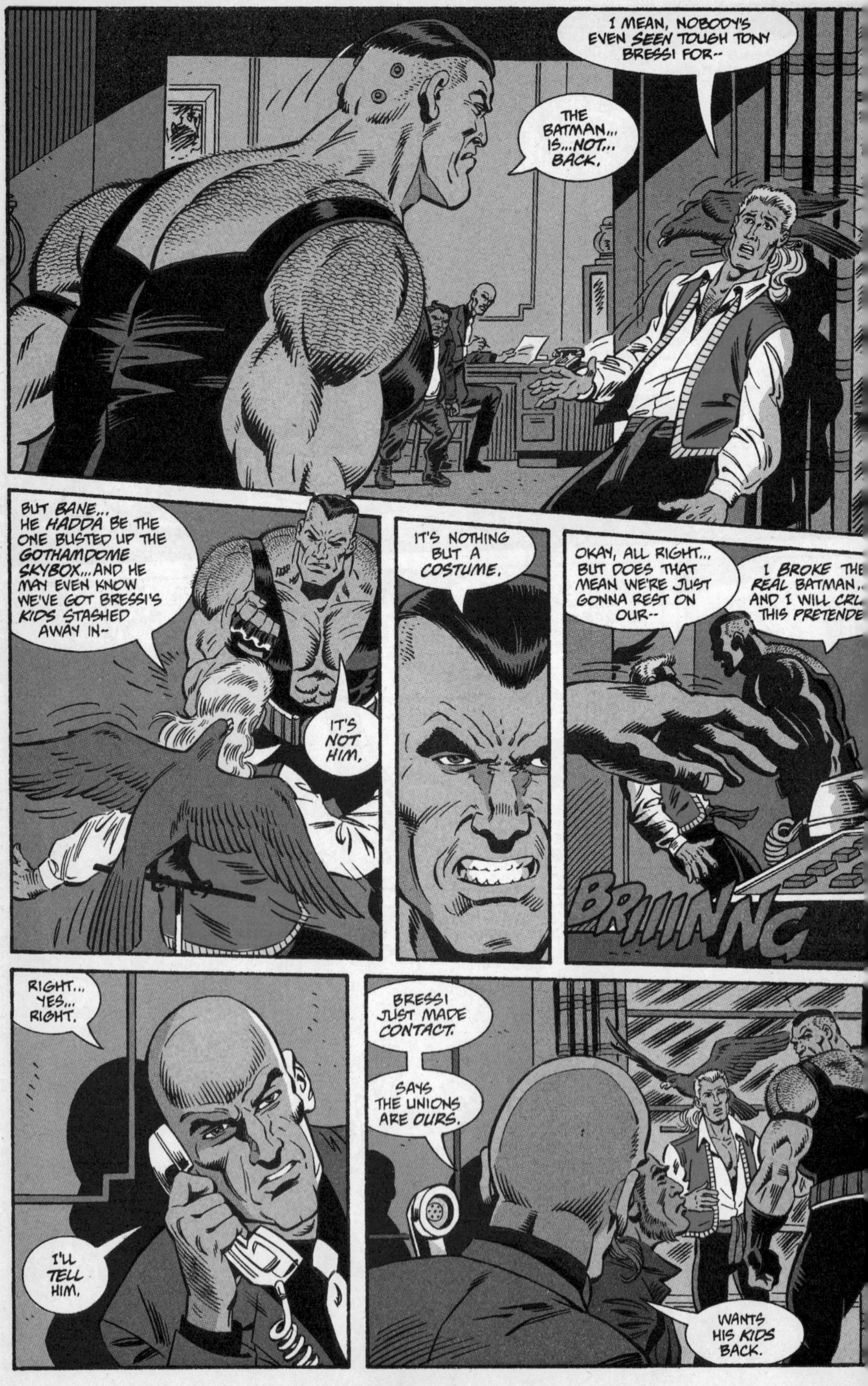
I MEAN, NOBODY'S EVEN SEEN TOUGH TONY BRESSI FOR--
THE BATMAN... IS...NOT... BACK.
BUT BANE... HE HADDA BE THE ONE BUSTED UP THE GOTHAMDOME SKYBOX...AND HE MAY EVEN KNOW WE'VE GOT BRESSI'S KIDS STASHED AWAY IN--
IT'S NOT HIM.
IT'S NOTHING BUT A COSTUME.
OKAY, ALL RIGHT... BUT DOES THAT MEAN WE'RE JUST GONNA REST ON OUR--
I BROKE THE REAL BATMAN... AND I WILL CRU THIS PRETENDE
BRIIINNG
RIGHT... YES... RIGHT.
I'LL TELL HIM.
BRESSI JUST MADE CONTACT.
SAYS THE UNIONS ARE OURS.
WANTS HIS KIDS BACK.

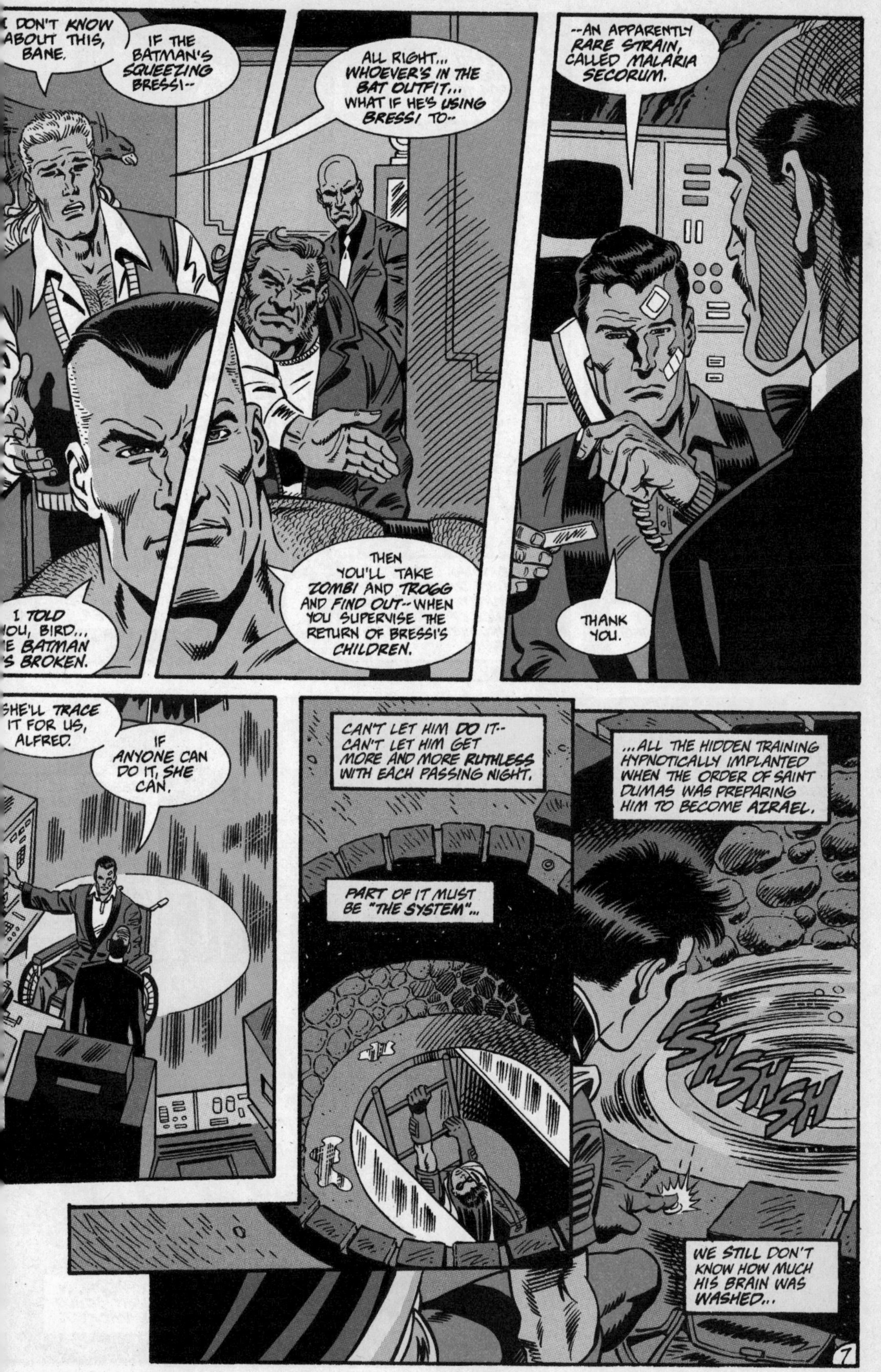
I DON'T KNOW ABOUT THIS, BANE.
IF THE BATMAN'S SQUEEZING BRESSI--
ALL RIGHT... WHOEVER'S IN THE BAT OUTFIT... WHAT IF HE'S USING BRESSI TO--
I TOLD YOU, BIRD... THE BATMAN IS BROKEN.
THEN YOU'LL TAKE ZOMBI AND TROGG AND FIND OUT--WHEN YOU SUPERVISE THE RETURN OF BRESSI'S CHILDREN.
--AN APPARENTLY RARE STRAIN, CALLED MALARIA SECORUM.
THANK YOU.
SHE'LL TRACE IT FOR US, ALFRED.
IF ANYONE CAN DO IT, SHE CAN.
CAN'T LET HIM DO IT-- CAN'T LET HIM GET MORE AND MORE RUTHLESS WITH EACH PASSING NIGHT.
PART OF IT MUST BE "THE SYSTEM"...
...ALL THE HIDDEN TRAINING HYPNOTICALLY IMPLANTED WHEN THE ORDER OF SAINT DUMAS WAS PREPARING HIM TO BECOME AZRAEL.
SHSHSH
WE STILL DON'T KNOW HOW MUCH HIS BRAIN WAS WASHED...
7

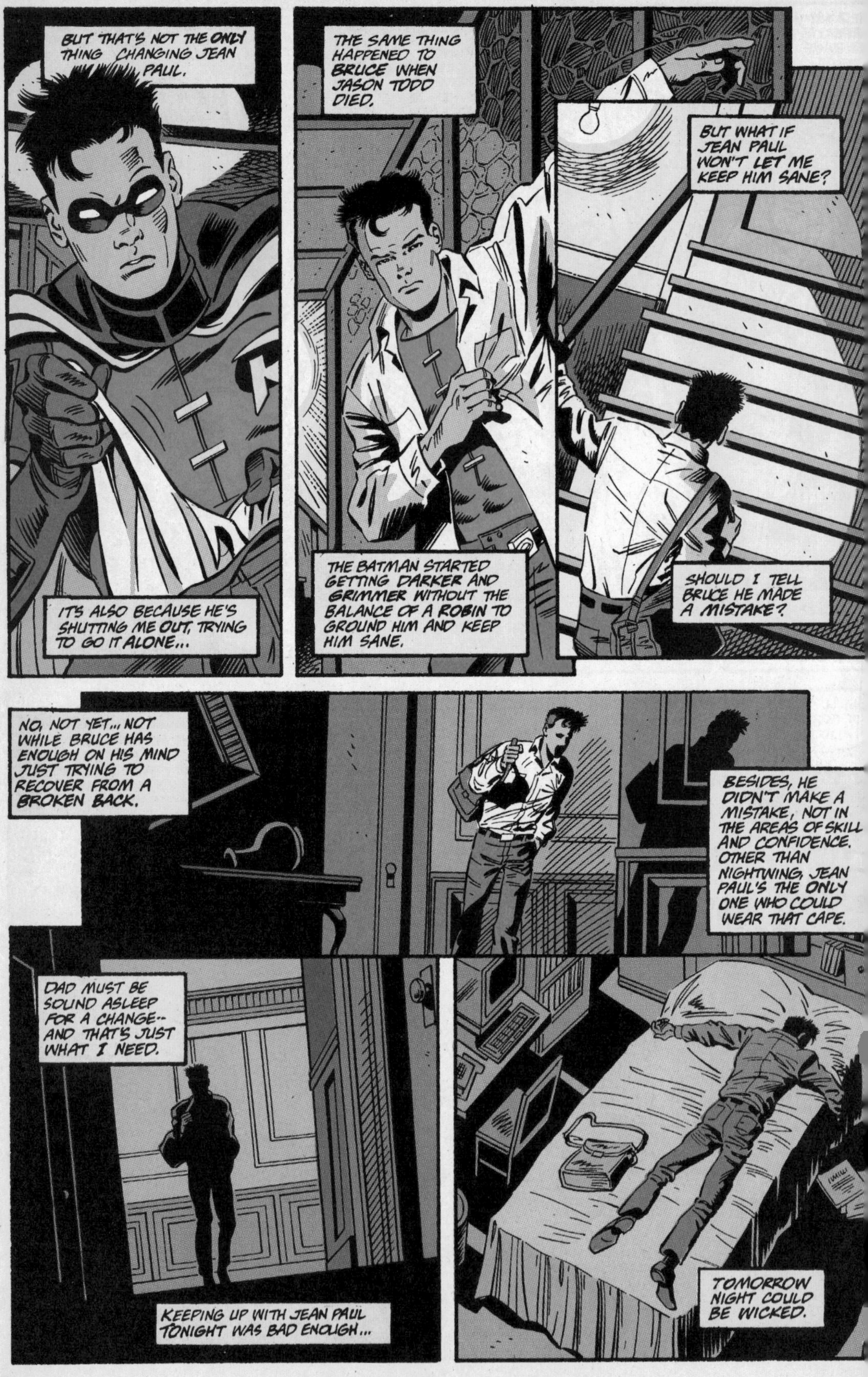

BUT THAT'S NOT THE ONLY THING CHANGING JEAN PAUL.
IT'S ALSO BECAUSE HE'S SHUTTING ME OUT, TRYING TO GO IT ALONE...
THE SAME THING HAPPENED TO BRUCE WHEN JASON TODD DIED.
THE BATMAN STARTED GETTING DARKER AND GRIMMER WITHOUT THE BALANCE OF A ROBIN TO GROUND HIM AND KEEP HIM SANE.
BUT WHAT IF JEAN PAUL WON'T LET ME KEEP HIM SANE?
SHOULD I TELL BRUCE HE MADE A MISTAKE?
NO, NOT YET... NOT WHILE BRUCE HAS ENOUGH ON HIS MIND JUST TRYING TO RECOVER FROM A BROKEN BACK.
BESIDES, HE DIDN'T MAKE A MISTAKE, NOT IN THE AREAS OF SKILL AND CONFIDENCE. OTHER THAN NIGHTWING, JEAN PAUL'S THE ONLY ONE WHO COULD WEAR THAT CAPE.
DAD MUST BE SOUND ASLEEP FOR A CHANGE-- AND THAT'S JUST WHAT I NEED.
KEEPING UP WITH JEAN PAUL TONIGHT WAS BAD ENOUGH...
TOMORROW NIGHT COULD BE WICKED.

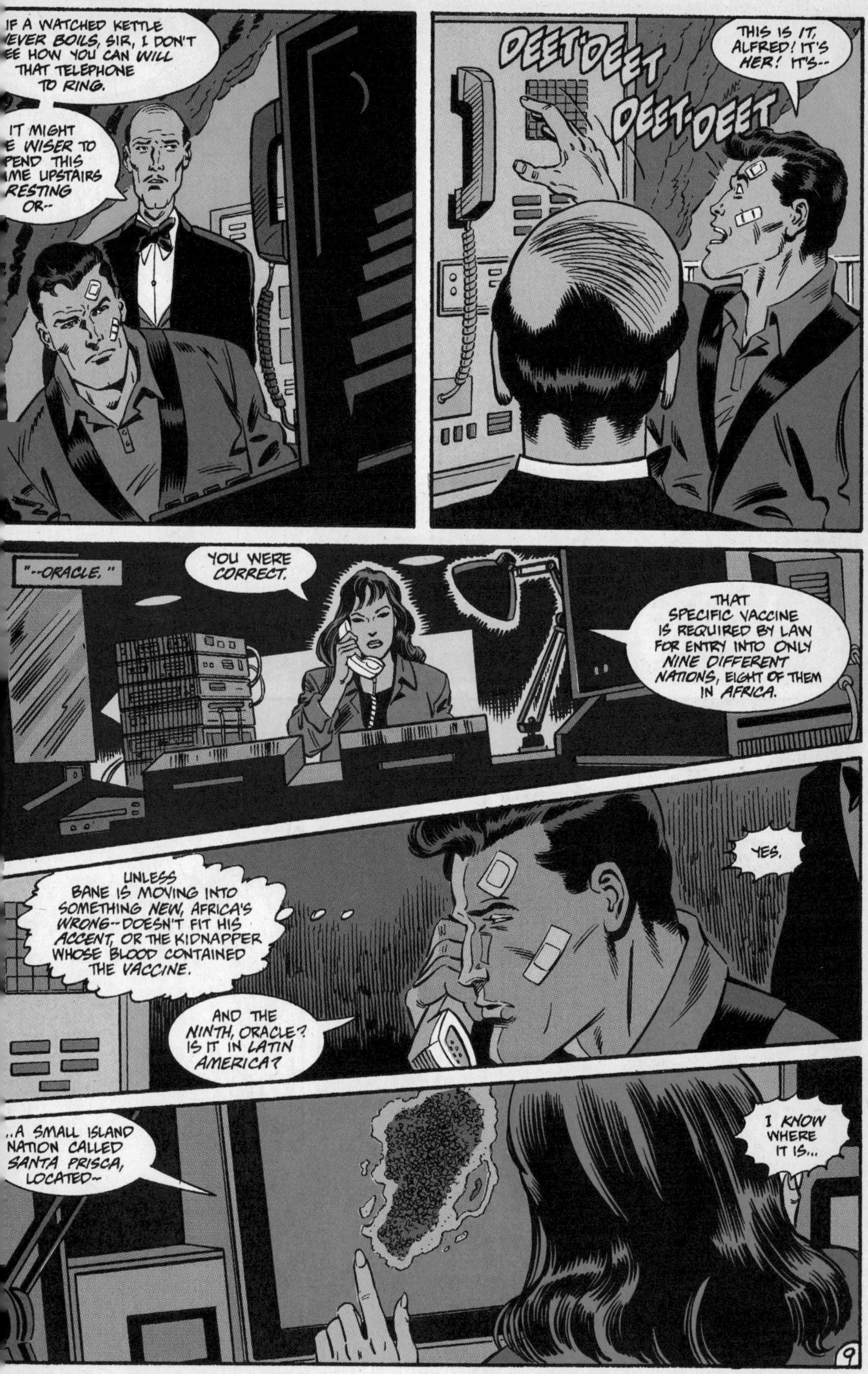
IF A WATCHED KETTLE NEVER BOILS, SIR, I DON'T SEE HOW YOU CAN WILL THAT TELEPHONE TO RING.
IT MIGHT BE WISER TO SPEND THIS TIME UPSTAIRS RESTING OR--
DEET DEET DEET DEET
THIS IS IT, ALFRED! IT'S HER! IT'S--
"--ORACLE."
YOU WERE CORRECT.
THAT SPECIFIC VACCINE IS REQUIRED BY LAW FOR ENTRY INTO ONLY NINE DIFFERENT NATIONS, EIGHT OF THEM IN AFRICA.
YES.
UNLESS BANE IS MOVING INTO SOMETHING NEW, AFRICA'S WRONG--DOESN'T FIT HIS ACCENT, OR THE KIDNAPPER WHOSE BLOOD CONTAINED THE VACCINE.
AND THE NINTH, ORACLE? IS IT IN LATIN AMERICA?
..A SMALL ISLAND NATION CALLED SANTA PRISCA, LOCATED--
I KNOW WHERE IT IS...
9

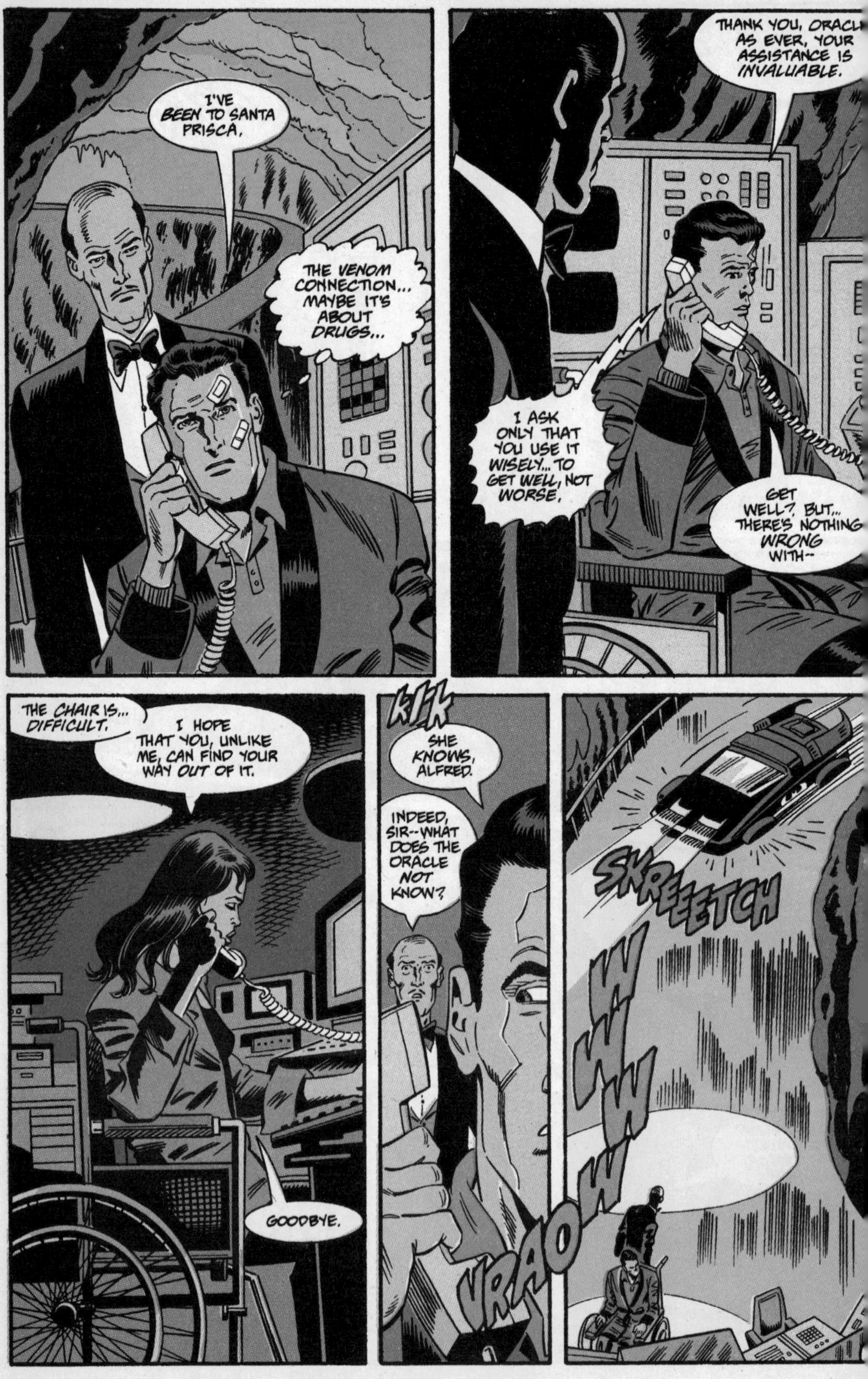
I'VE BEEN TO SANTA PRISCA.
THE VENOM CONNECTION... MAYBE IT'S ABOUT DRUGS...
THANK YOU, ORACLE AS EVER, YOUR ASSISTANCE IS INVALUABLE.
I ASK ONLY THAT YOU USE IT WISELY... TO GET WELL, NOT WORSE.
GET WELL? BUT... THERE'S NOTHING WRONG WITH--
THE CHAIR IS... DIFFICULT.
I HOPE THAT YOU, UNLIKE ME, CAN FIND YOUR WAY OUT OF IT.
GOODBYE.
KLIK
SHE KNOWS, ALFRED.
INDEED, SIR--WHAT DOES THE ORACLE NOT KNOW?
SKREEETCH
VRAOWWWWWWW

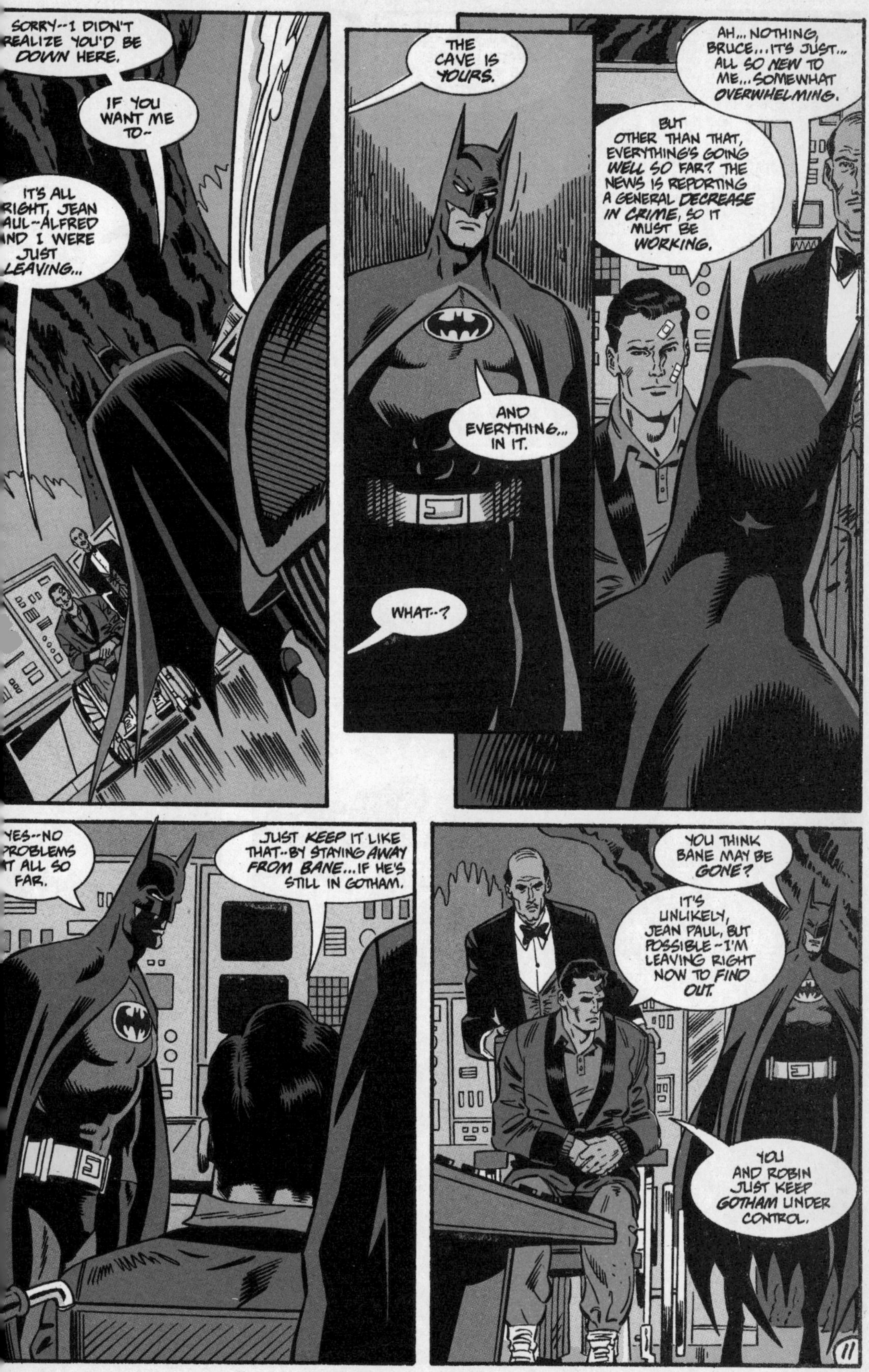
SORRY--I DIDN'T REALIZE YOU'D BE DOWN HERE.
IF YOU WANT ME TO--
IT'S ALL RIGHT, JEAN PAUL--ALFRED AND I WERE JUST LEAVING...
THE CAVE IS YOURS.
AND EVERYTHING... IN IT.
WHAT--?
AH... NOTHING, BRUCE... IT'S JUST... ALL SO NEW TO ME... SOMEWHAT OVERWHELMING.
BUT OTHER THAN THAT, EVERYTHING'S GOING WELL SO FAR? THE NEWS IS REPORTING A GENERAL DECREASE IN CRIME, SO IT MUST BE WORKING.
YES--NO PROBLEMS AT ALL SO FAR.
JUST KEEP IT LIKE THAT--BY STAYING AWAY FROM BANE... IF HE'S STILL IN GOTHAM.
YOU THINK BANE MAY BE GONE?
IT'S UNLIKELY, JEAN PAUL, BUT POSSIBLE--I'M LEAVING RIGHT NOW TO FIND OUT.
YOU AND ROBIN JUST KEEP GOTHAM UNDER CONTROL.
11

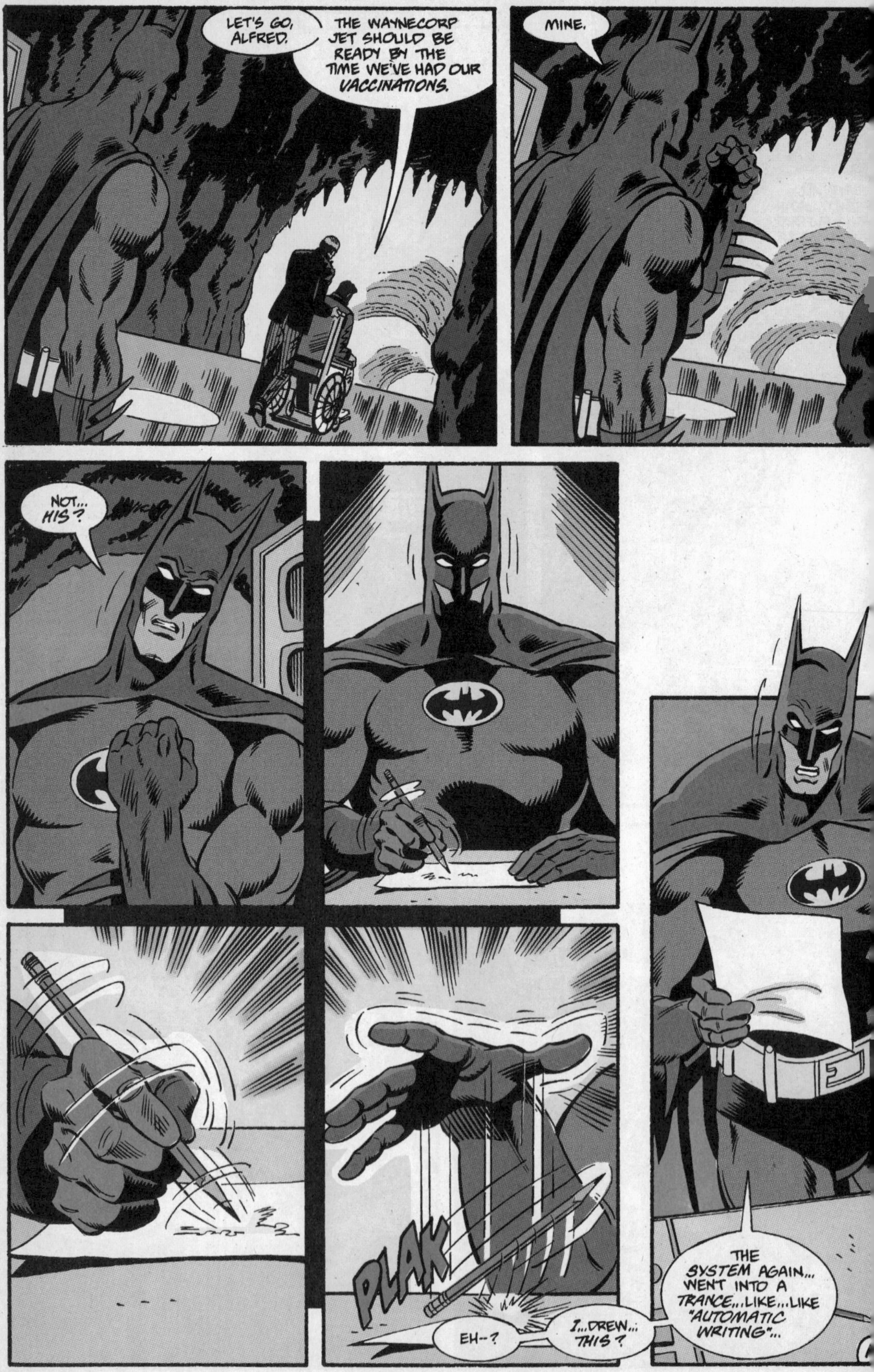

LET'S GO, ALFRED.
THE WAYNECORP JET SHOULD BE READY BY THE TIME WE'VE HAD OUR VACCINATIONS.
MINE.
NOT... HIS?
PLAK
EH--?
I...DREW... THIS?
THE SYSTEM AGAIN... WENT INTO A TRANCE...LIKE...LIKE "AUTOMATIC WRITING"...

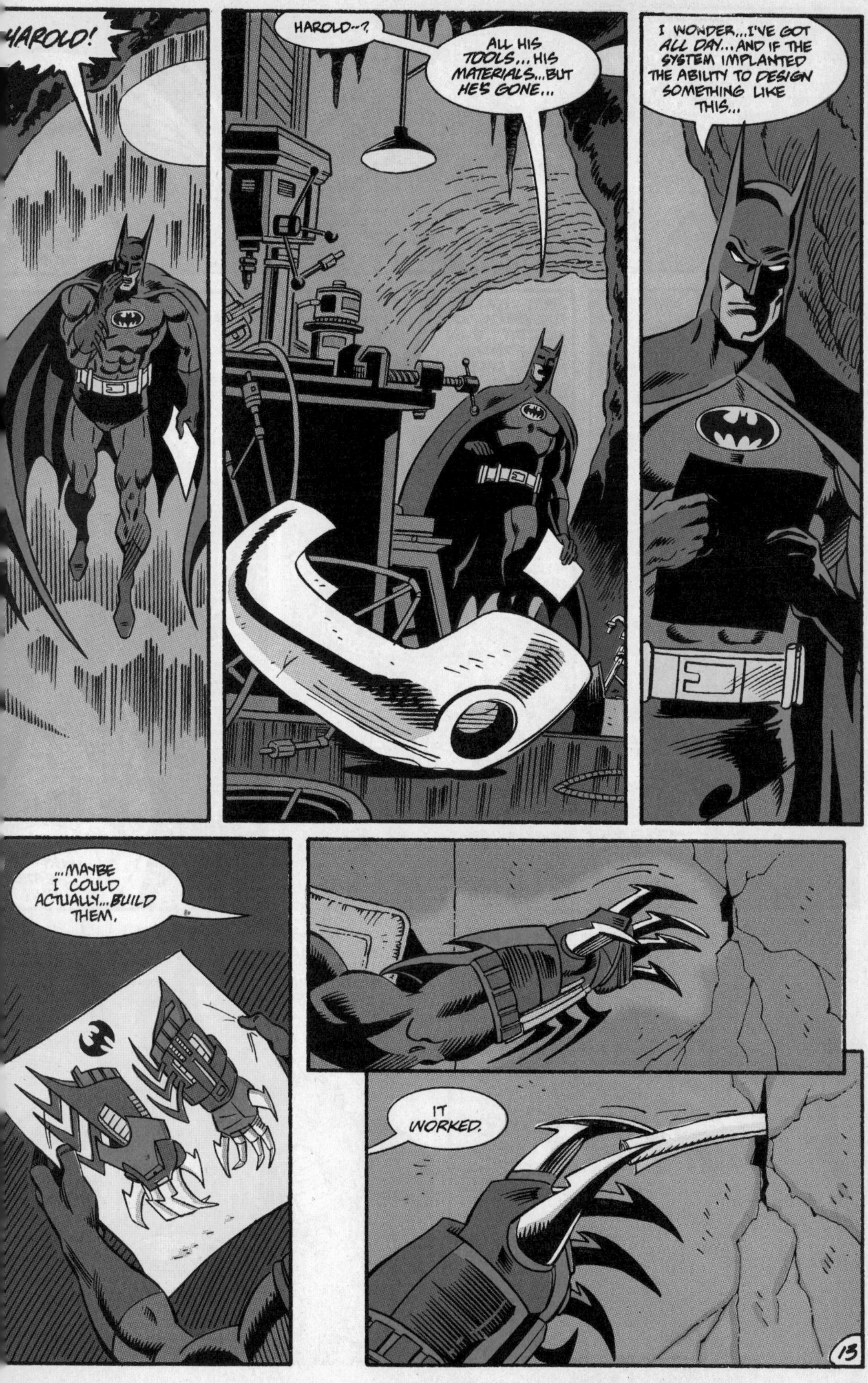
HAROLD!
HAROLD--?
ALL HIS TOOLS... HIS MATERIALS...BUT HE'S GONE...
I WONDER...I'VE GOT ALL DAY...AND IF THE SYSTEM IMPLANTED THE ABILITY TO DESIGN SOMETHING LIKE THIS...
...MAYBE I COULD ACTUALLY...BUILD THEM.
IT WORKED.
13

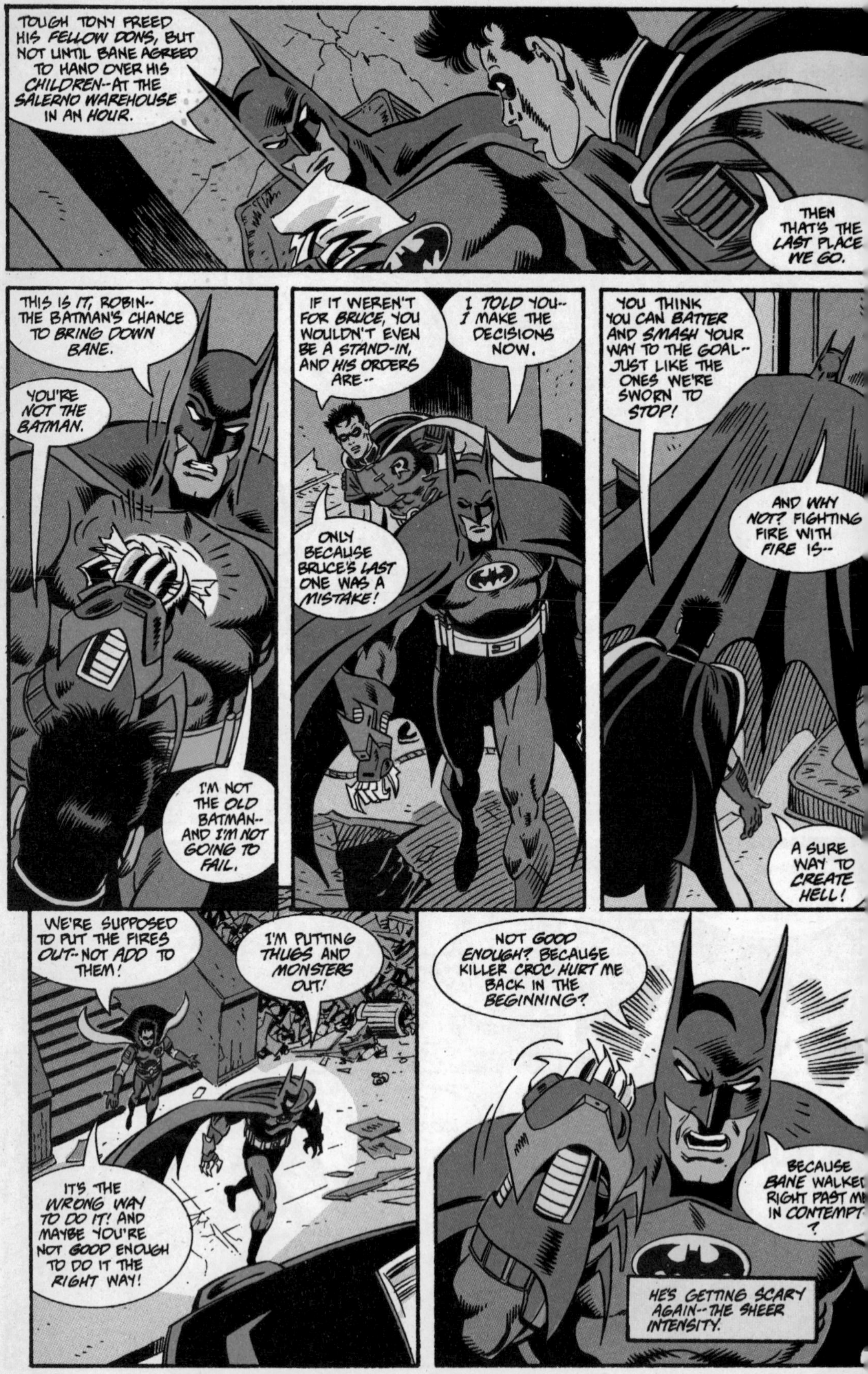

TOUGH TONY FREED HIS FELLOW DONS, BUT NOT UNTIL BANE AGREED TO HAND OVER HIS CHILDREN--AT THE SALERNO WAREHOUSE IN AN HOUR.
THEN THAT'S THE LAST PLACE WE GO.
THIS IS IT, ROBIN-- THE BATMAN'S CHANCE TO BRING DOWN BANE.
YOU'RE NOT THE BATMAN.
I'M NOT THE OLD BATMAN-- AND I'M NOT GOING TO FAIL.
IF IT WEREN'T FOR BRUCE, YOU WOULDN'T EVEN BE A STAND-IN, AND HIS ORDERS ARE--
I TOLD YOU-- I MAKE THE DECISIONS NOW.
ONLY BECAUSE BRUCE'S LAST ONE WAS A MISTAKE!
YOU THINK YOU CAN BATTER AND SMASH YOUR WAY TO THE GOAL-- JUST LIKE THE ONES WE'RE SWORN TO STOP!
AND WHY NOT? FIGHTING FIRE WITH FIRE IS--
A SURE WAY TO CREATE HELL!
WE'RE SUPPOSED TO PUT THE FIRES OUT--NOT ADD TO THEM!
I'M PUTTING THUGS AND MONSTERS OUT!
IT'S THE WRONG WAY TO DO IT! AND MAYBE YOU'RE NOT GOOD ENOUGH TO DO IT THE RIGHT WAY!
NOT GOOD ENOUGH? BECAUSE KILLER CROC HURT ME BACK IN THE BEGINNING?
BECAUSE BANE WALKED RIGHT PAST ME IN CONTEMPT?
HE'S GETTING SCARY AGAIN--THE SHEER INTENSITY.

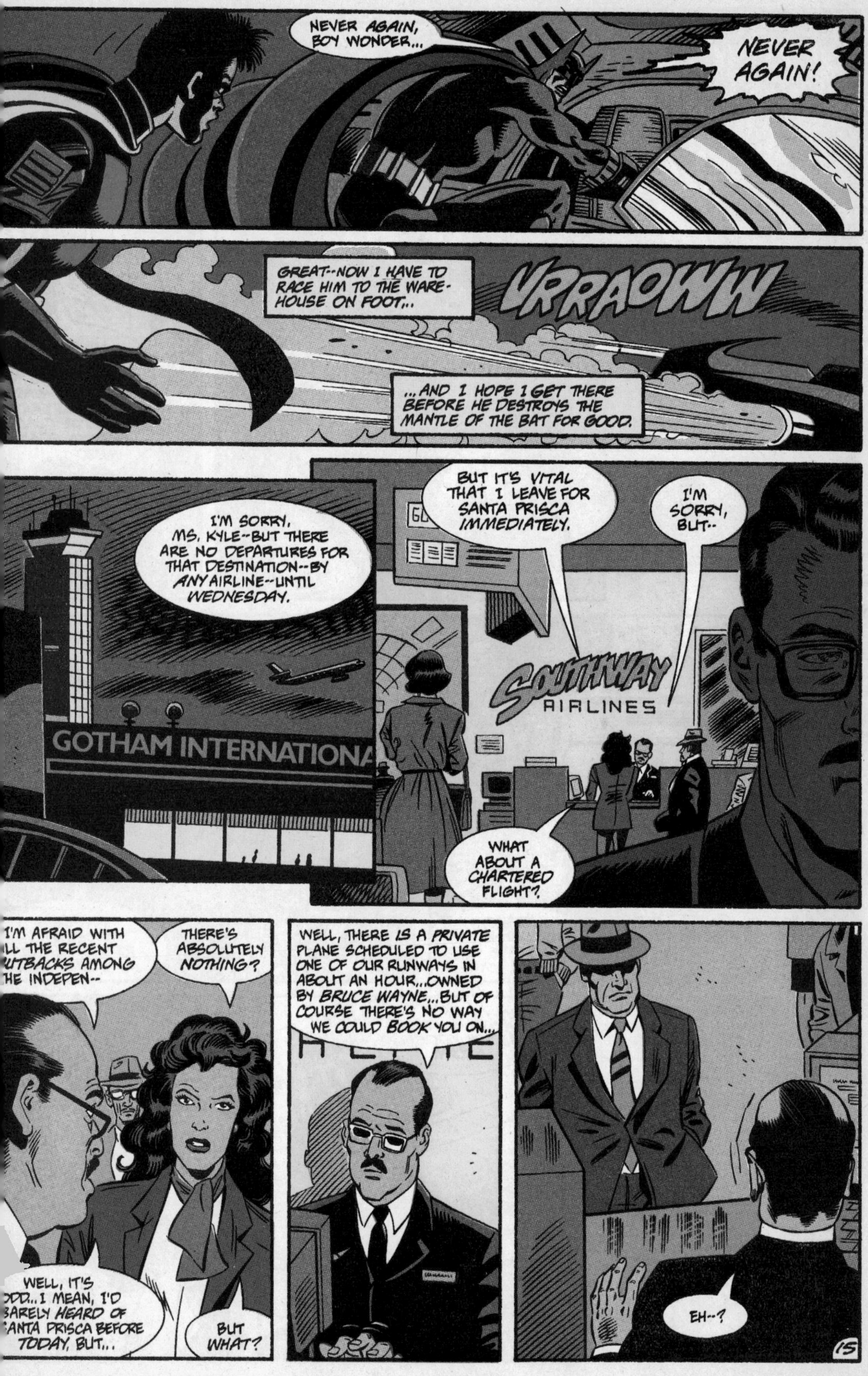
NEVER AGAIN, BOY WONDER...
NEVER AGAIN!
GREAT--NOW I HAVE TO RACE HIM TO THE WARE-HOUSE ON FOOT...
URRAOWW
...AND I HOPE I GET THERE BEFORE HE DESTROYS THE MANTLE OF THE BAT FOR GOOD.
GOTHAM INTERNATIONA
I'M SORRY, MS. KYLE--BUT THERE ARE NO DEPARTURES FOR THAT DESTINATION--BY ANY AIRLINE--UNTIL WEDNESDAY.
BUT IT'S VITAL THAT I LEAVE FOR SANTA PRISCA IMMEDIATELY.
I'M SORRY, BUT--
SOUTHWAY AIRLINES
WHAT ABOUT A CHARTERED FLIGHT?
I'M AFRAID WITH LL THE RECENT UTBACKS AMONG HE INDEPEN--
THERE'S ABSOLUTELY NOTHING?
WELL, IT'S ODD... I MEAN, I'D BARELY HEARD OF SANTA PRISCA BEFORE TODAY, BUT...
BUT WHAT?
WELL, THERE IS A PRIVATE PLANE SCHEDULED TO USE ONE OF OUR RUNWAYS IN ABOUT AN HOUR...OWNED BY BRUCE WAYNE... BUT OF COURSE THERE'S NO WAY WE COULD BOOK YOU ON...
EH--?
15

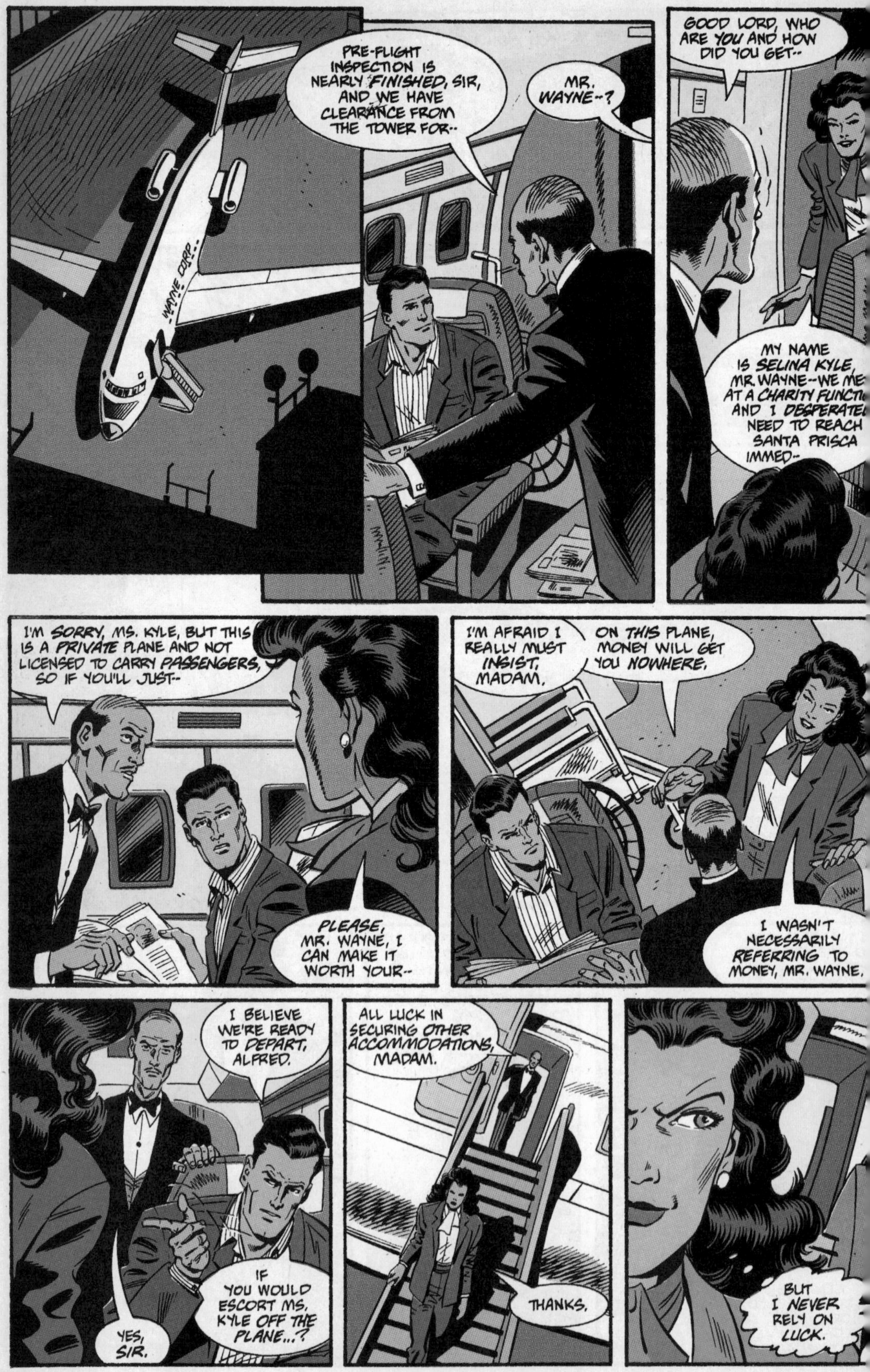
WAYNE CORP.
PRE-FLIGHT INSPECTION IS NEARLY FINISHED, SIR, AND WE HAVE CLEARANCE FROM THE TOWER FOR--
MR. WAYNE--?
GOOD LORD, WHO ARE YOU AND HOW DID YOU GET--
MY NAME IS SELINA KYLE, MR. WAYNE--WE ME AT A CHARITY FUNCTI AND I DESPERATE NEED TO REACH SANTA PRISCA IMMED--
I'M SORRY, MS. KYLE, BUT THIS IS A PRIVATE PLANE AND NOT LICENSED TO CARRY PASSENGERS, SO IF YOU'LL JUST-
PLEASE, MR. WAYNE, I CAN MAKE IT WORTH YOUR--
I'M AFRAID I REALLY MUST INSIST, MADAM.
ON THIS PLANE, MONEY WILL GET YOU NOWHERE.
I WASN'T NECESSARILY REFERRING TO MONEY, MR. WAYNE.
I BELIEVE WE'RE READY TO DEPART, ALFRED.
IF YOU WOULD ESCORT MS. KYLE OFF THE PLANE...?
YES, SIR.
ALL LUCK IN SECURING OTHER ACCOMMODATIONS, MADAM.
THANKS.
BUT I NEVER RELY ON LUCK.

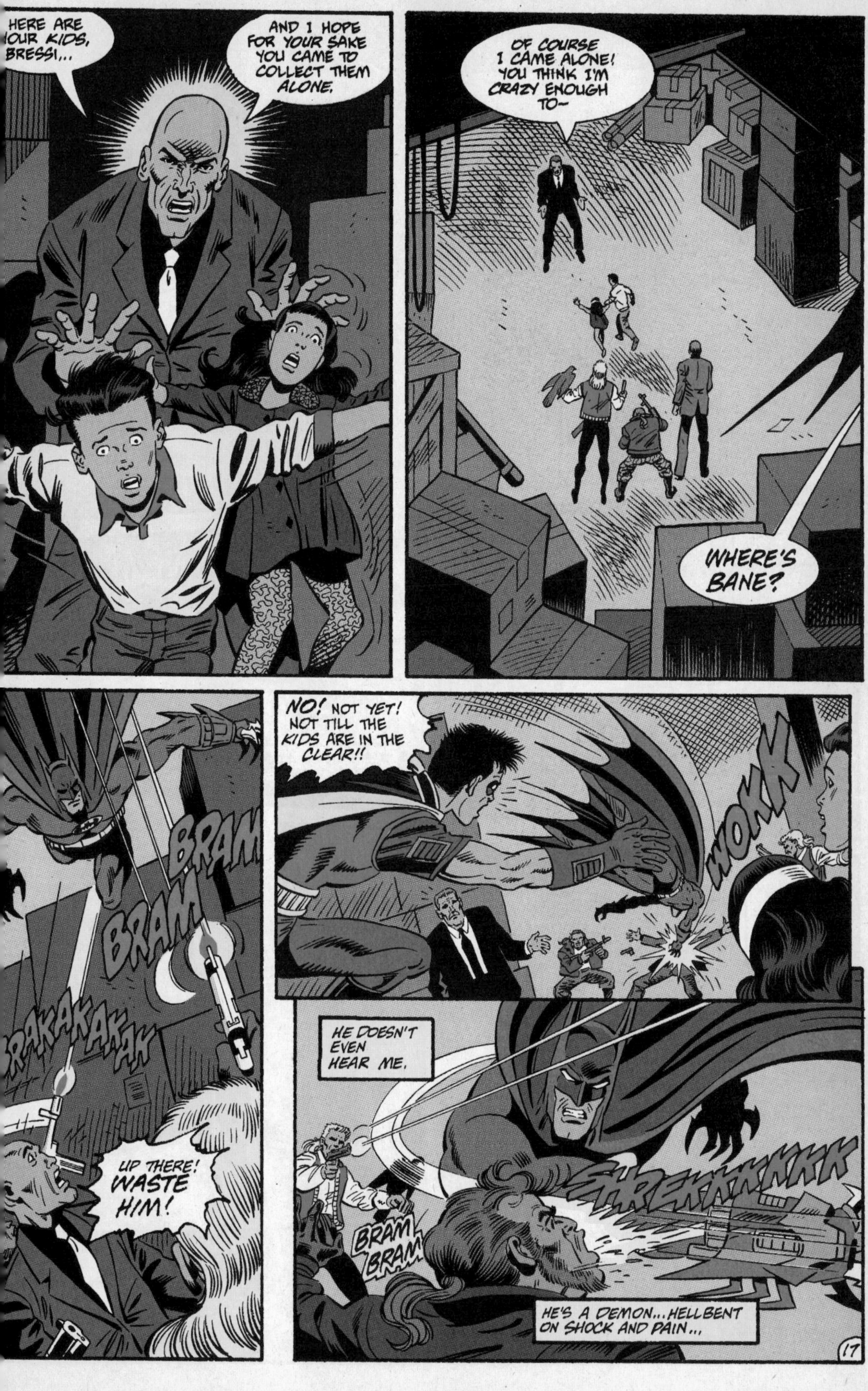
HERE ARE YOUR KIDS, BRESSI...
AND I HOPE FOR YOUR SAKE YOU CAME TO COLLECT THEM ALONE.
OF COURSE I CAME ALONE! YOU THINK I'M CRAZY ENOUGH TO~
WHERE'S BANE?
BRAM
BRAM
BRAKAKAKAKAK
UP THERE! WASTE HIM!
NO! NOT YET! NOT TILL THE KIDS ARE IN THE CLEAR!!
WOKK
HE DOESN'T EVEN HEAR ME.
SHREKKKKKKK
BRAM BRAM
HE'S A DEMON... HELLBENT ON SHOCK AND PAIN...
17

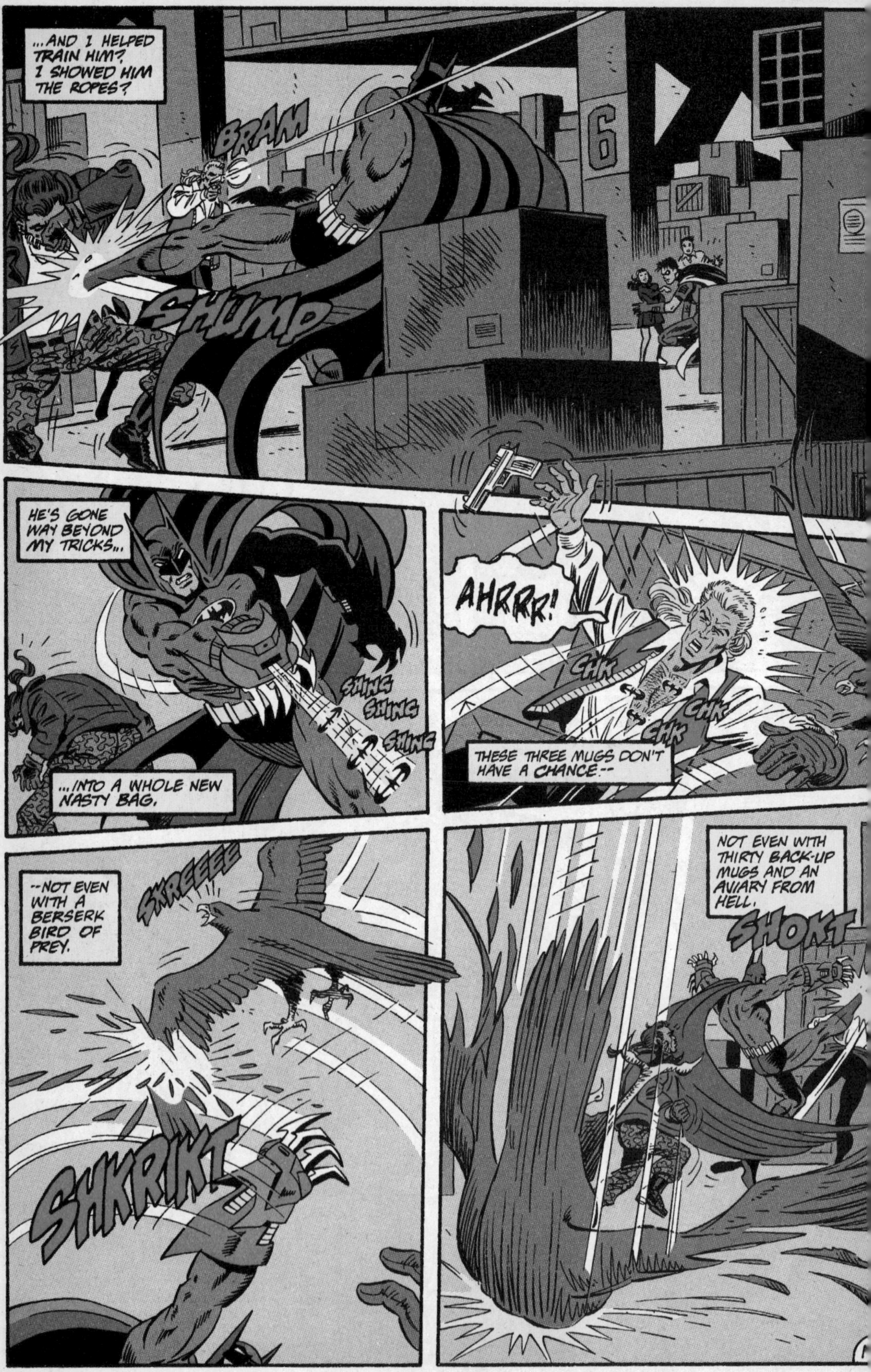
...AND I HELPED TRAIN HIM? I SHOWED HIM THE ROPES?
BRAM
SHUMP
HE'S GONE WAY BEYOND MY TRICKS...
SHING
SHING
SHING
...INTO A WHOLE NEW NASTY BAG.
AHRRR!
CHK
CHK
CHK
THESE THREE MUGS DON'T HAVE A CHANCE.--
--NOT EVEN WITH A BERSERK BIRD OF PREY.
SKREEEE
SHKRIKT
NOT EVEN WITH THIRTY BACK-UP MUGS AND AN AVIARY FROM HELL.
SHOKT

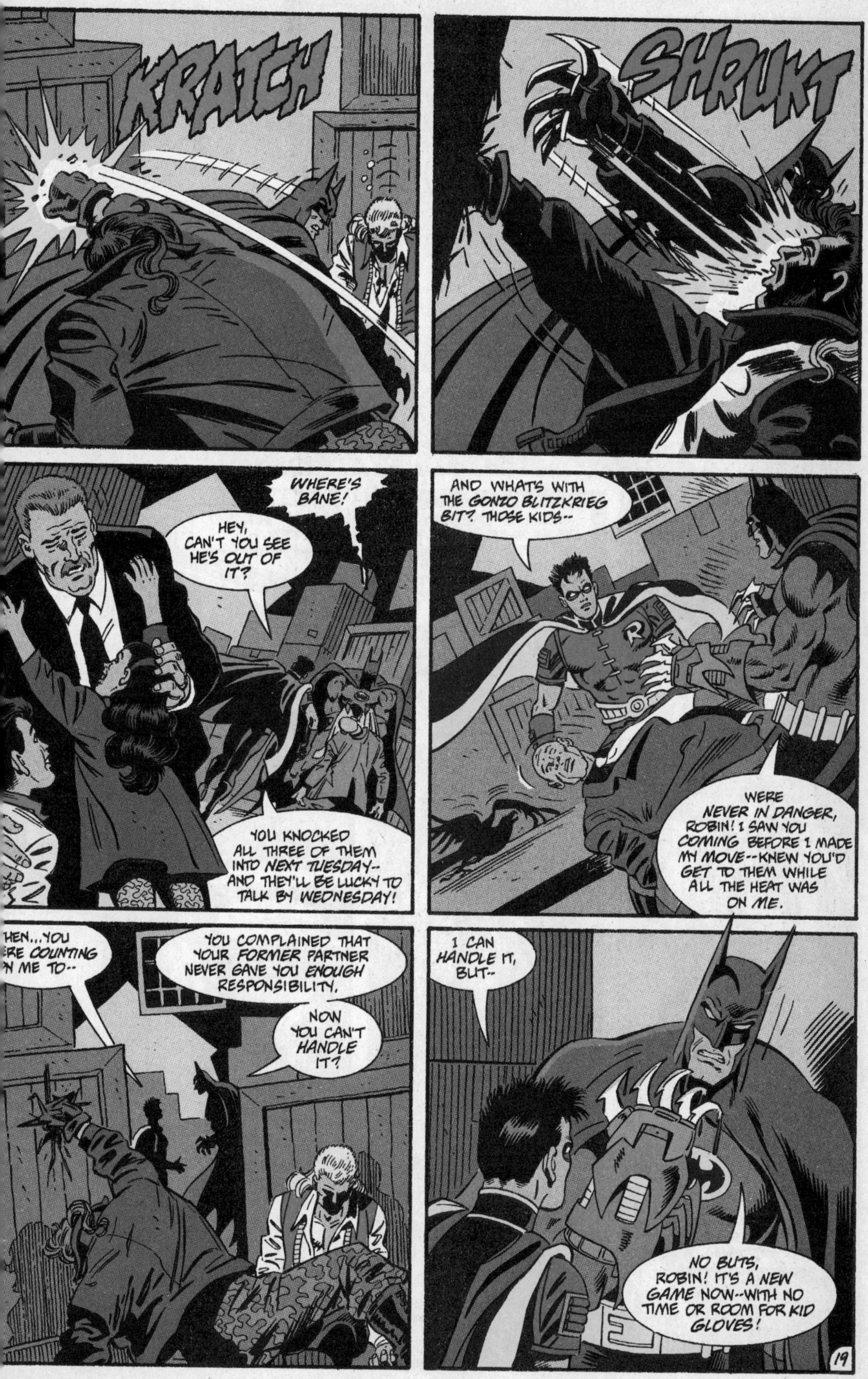
KRATCH
SHRUKT
WHERE'S BANE!
HEY, CAN'T YOU SEE HE'S OUT OF IT?
YOU KNOCKED ALL THREE OF THEM INTO NEXT TUESDAY-- AND THEY'LL BE LUCKY TO TALK BY WEDNESDAY!
AND WHAT'S WITH THE GONZO BLITZKRIEG BIT? THOSE KIDS--
WERE NEVER IN DANGER, ROBIN! I SAW YOU COMING BEFORE I MADE MY MOVE--KNEW YOU'D GET TO THEM WHILE ALL THE HEAT WAS ON ME.
HEN...YOU ERE COUNTING N ME TO--
YOU COMPLAINED THAT YOUR FORMER PARTNER NEVER GAVE YOU ENOUGH RESPONSIBILITY.
NOW YOU CAN'T HANDLE IT?
I CAN HANDLE IT, BUT--
NO BUTS, ROBIN! IT'S A NEW GAME NOW--WITH NO TIME OR ROOM FOR KID GLOVES!
19

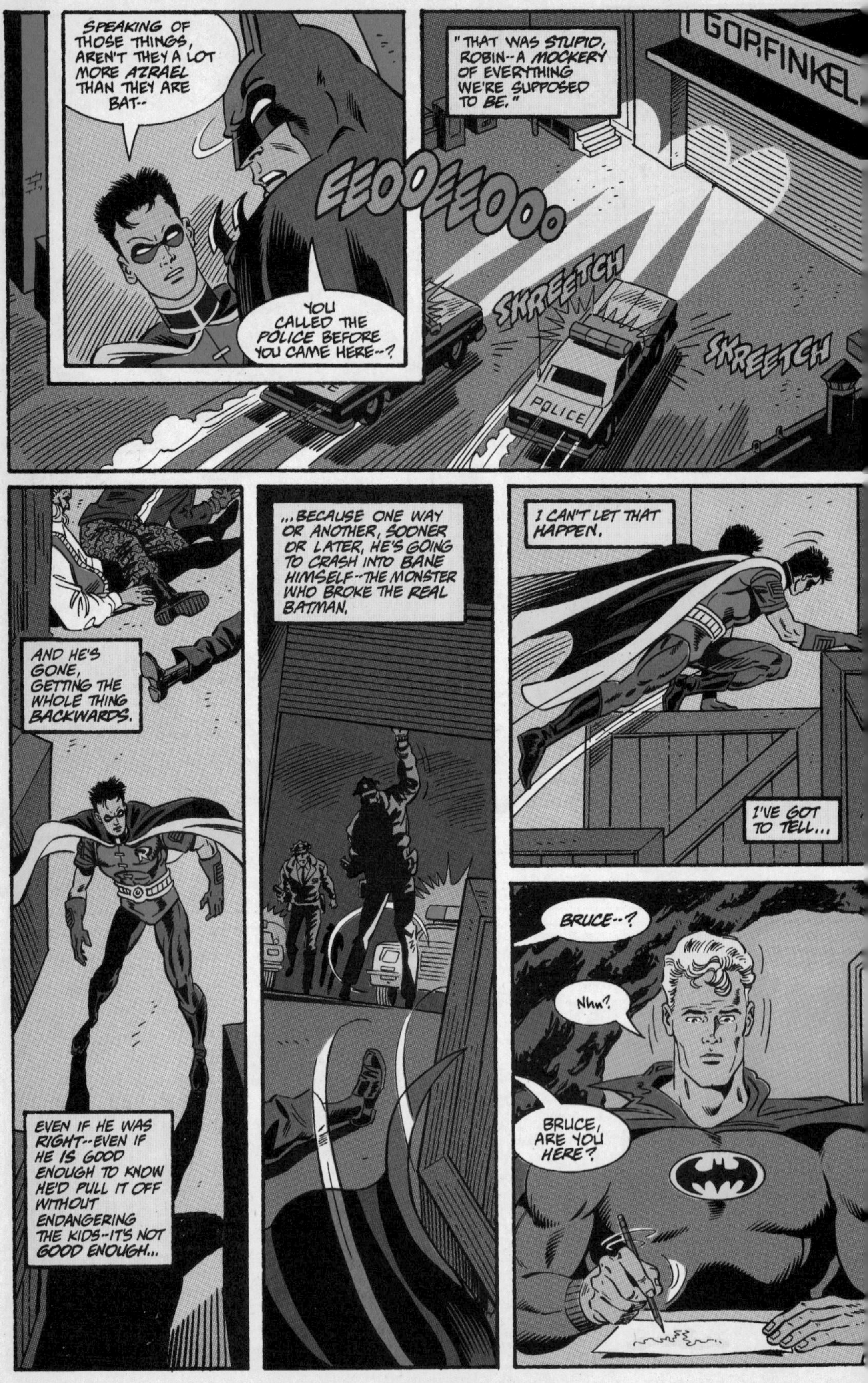
SPEAKING OF THOSE THINGS, AREN'T THEY A LOT MORE AZRAEL THAN THEY ARE BAT--
YOU CALLED THE POLICE BEFORE YOU CAME HERE--?
"THAT WAS STUPID, ROBIN--A MOCKERY OF EVERYTHING WE'RE SUPPOSED TO BE."
GORFINKEL
EEOOEEOOo
SKREETCH
SKREETCH
POLICE
AND HE'S GONE, GETTING THE WHOLE THING BACKWARDS.
EVEN IF HE WAS RIGHT--EVEN IF HE IS GOOD ENOUGH TO KNOW HE'D PULL IT OFF WITHOUT ENDANGERING THE KIDS--IT'S NOT GOOD ENOUGH...
...BECAUSE ONE WAY OR ANOTHER, SOONER OR LATER, HE'S GOING TO CRASH INTO BANE HIMSELF--THE MONSTER WHO BROKE THE REAL BATMAN.
I CAN'T LET THAT HAPPEN.
I'VE GOT TO TELL...
BRUCE--?
Nhn?
BRUCE, ARE YOU HERE?

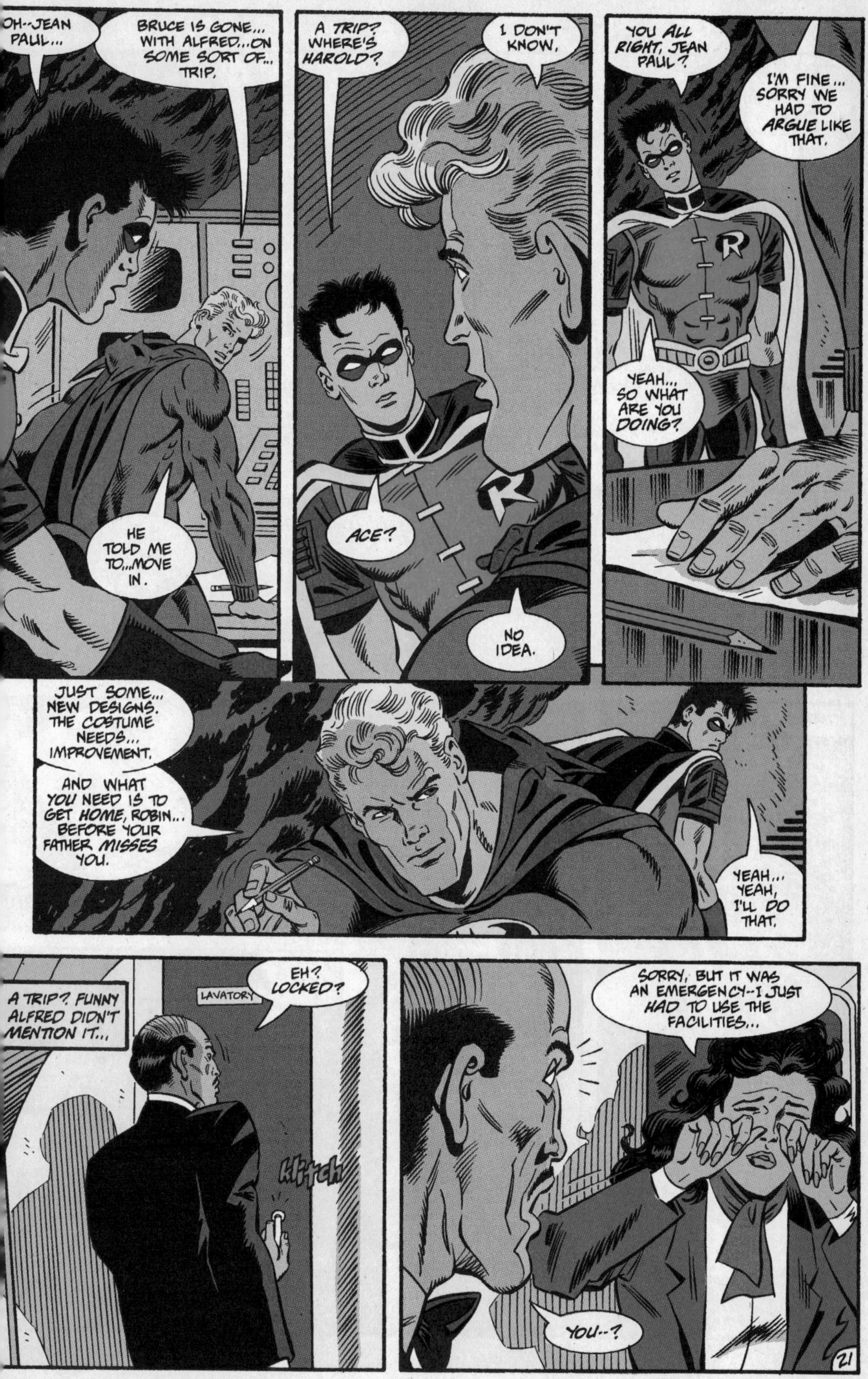
OH--JEAN PAUL...
BRUCE IS GONE... WITH ALFRED...ON SOME SORT OF... TRIP.
HE TOLD ME TO...MOVE IN.
A TRIP? WHERE'S HAROLD?
I DON'T KNOW.
ACE?
NO IDEA.
YOU ALL RIGHT, JEAN PAUL?
I'M FINE... SORRY WE HAD TO ARGUE LIKE THAT.
YEAH... SO WHAT ARE YOU DOING?
JUST SOME... NEW DESIGNS. THE COSTUME NEEDS... IMPROVEMENT.
AND WHAT YOU NEED IS TO GET HOME, ROBIN... BEFORE YOUR FATHER MISSES YOU.
YEAH... YEAH, I'LL DO THAT.
A TRIP? FUNNY ALFRED DIDN'T MENTION IT...
LAVATORY
EH? LOCKED?
klitch
SORRY, BUT IT WAS AN EMERGENCY--I JUST HAD TO USE THE FACILITIES...
YOU--?
21

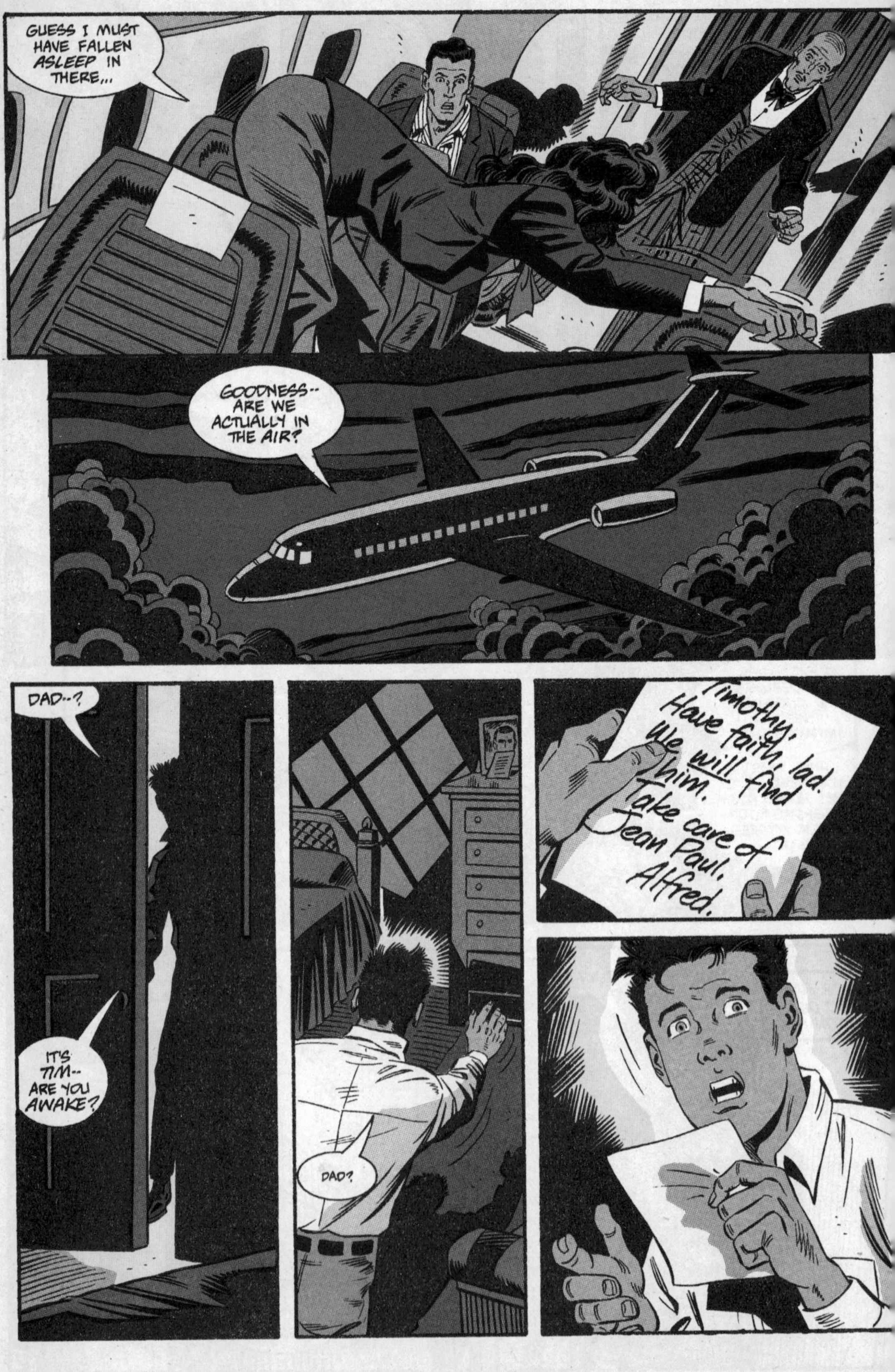
GUESS I MUST HAVE FALLEN ASLEEP IN THERE...
GOODNESS-- ARE WE ACTUALLY IN THE AIR?
DAD--?
IT'S TIM-- ARE YOU AWAKE?
DAD?
Timothy, Have faith, lad. We will find him. Take care of Jean Paul, Alfred.

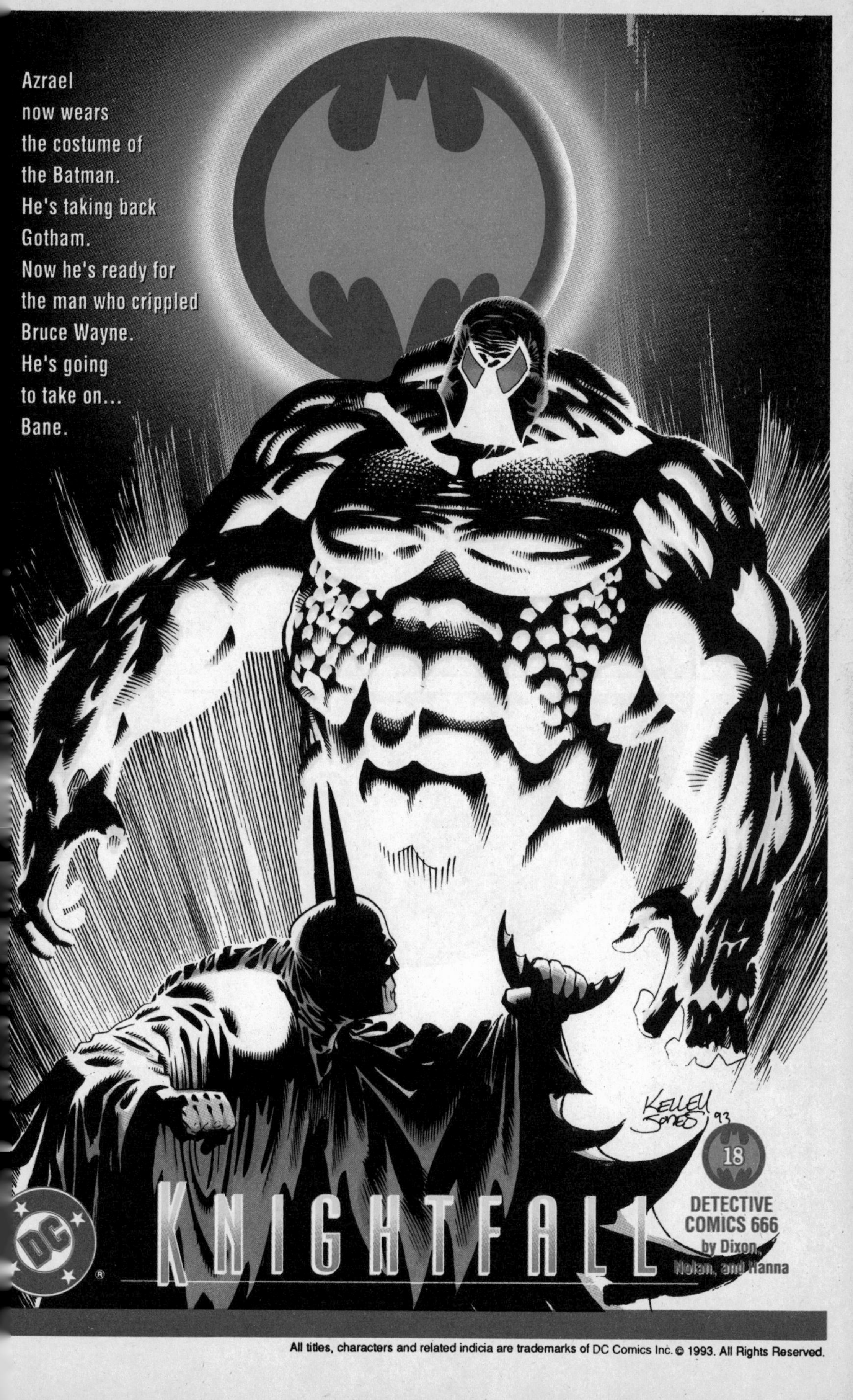
Azrael
now wears
the costume of
the Batman.
He's taking back
Gotham.
Now he's ready for
the man who crippled
Bruce Wayne.
He's going
to take on...
Bane.
KELLEY JONES '93
18
KNIGHTFALL
DETECTIVE COMICS 666
by Dixon, Nolan, and Hanna

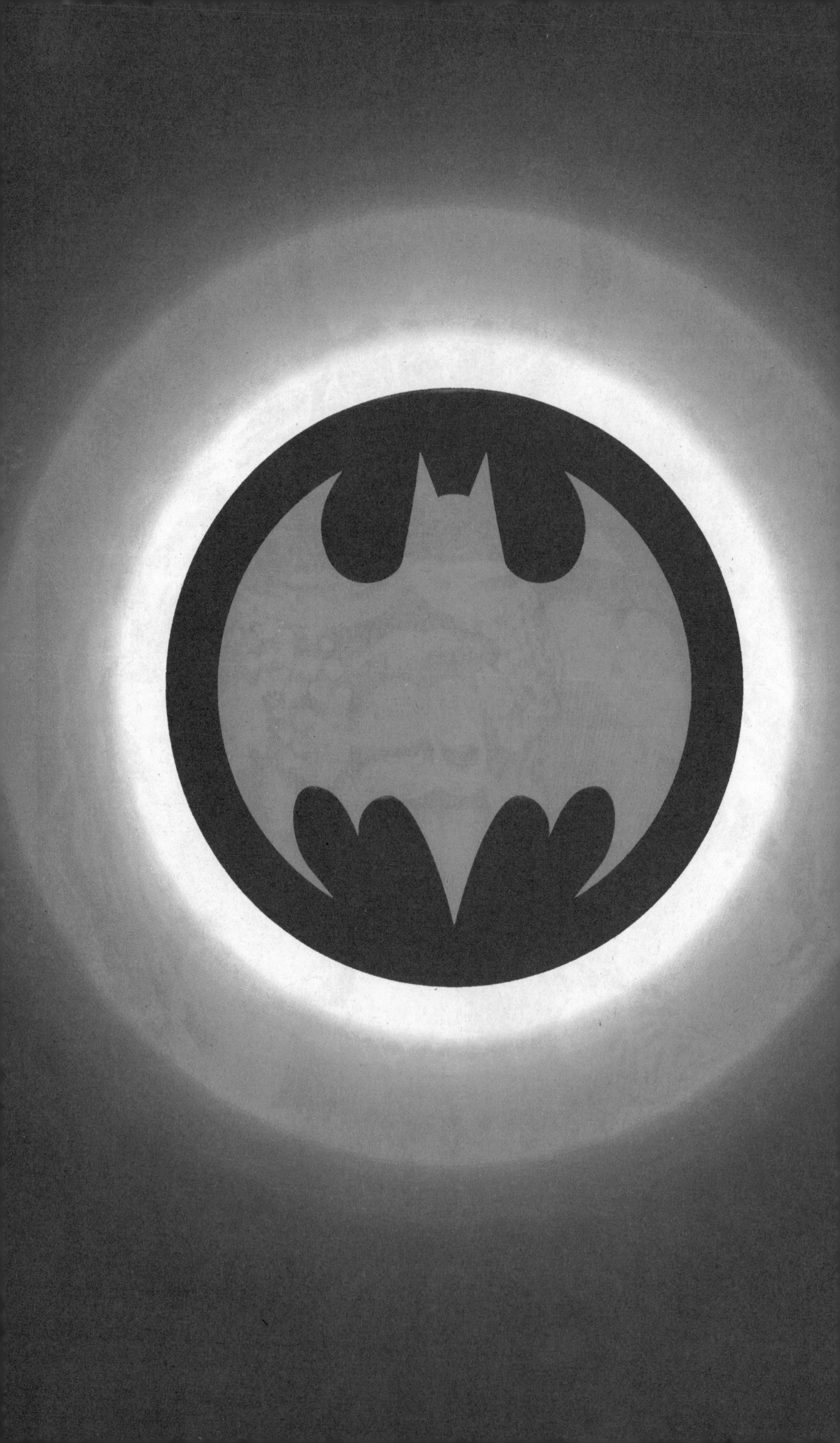

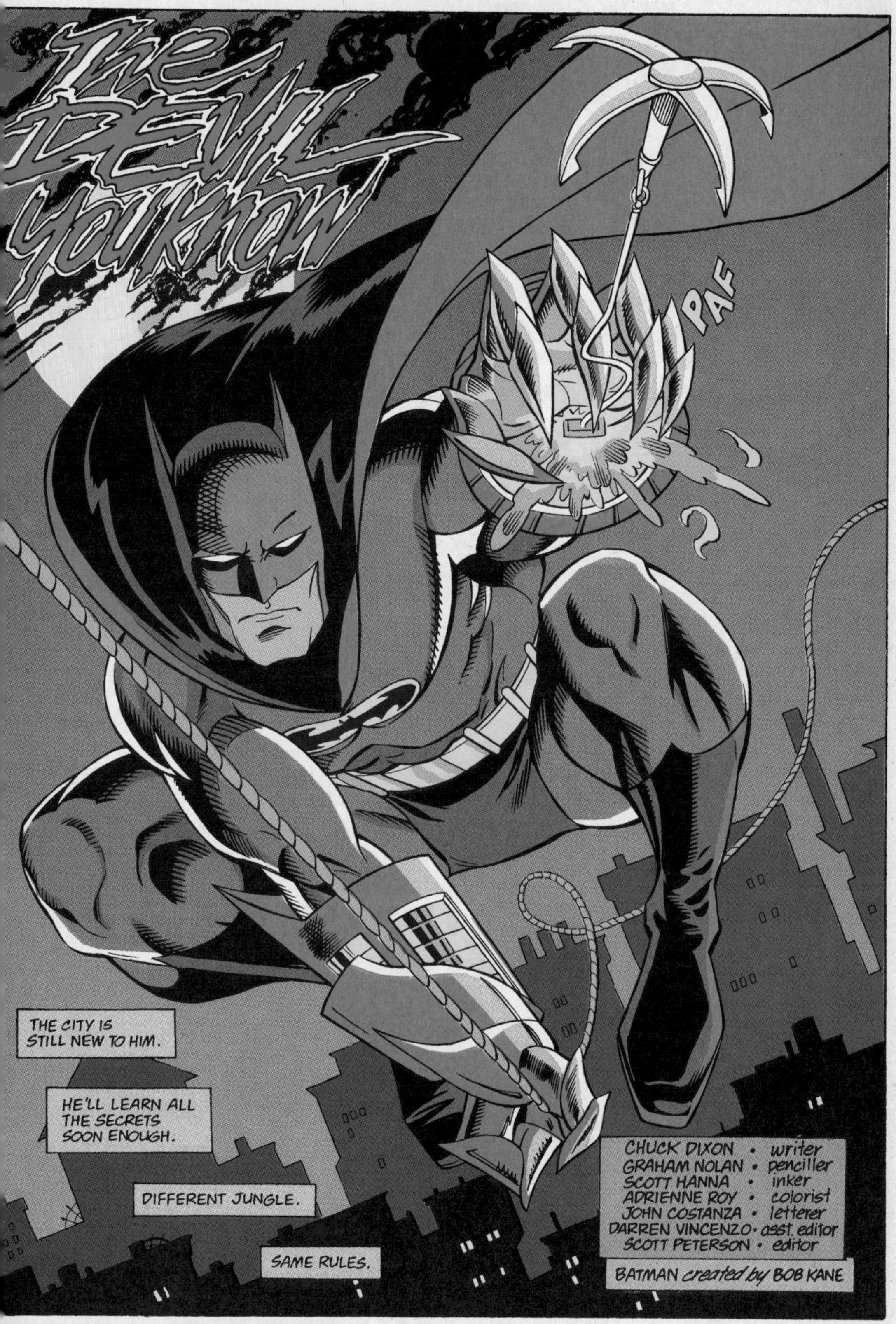

The Devil You Know
PAF
THE CITY IS STILL NEW TO HIM.
HE'LL LEARN ALL THE SECRETS SOON ENOUGH.
DIFFERENT JUNGLE.
SAME RULES.
CHUCK DIXON • writer
GRAHAM NOLAN • penciller
SCOTT HANNA • inker
ADRIENNE ROY • colorist
JOHN COSTANZA • letterer
DARREN VINCENZO • asst. editor
SCOTT PETERSON • editor
BATMAN created by BOB KANE

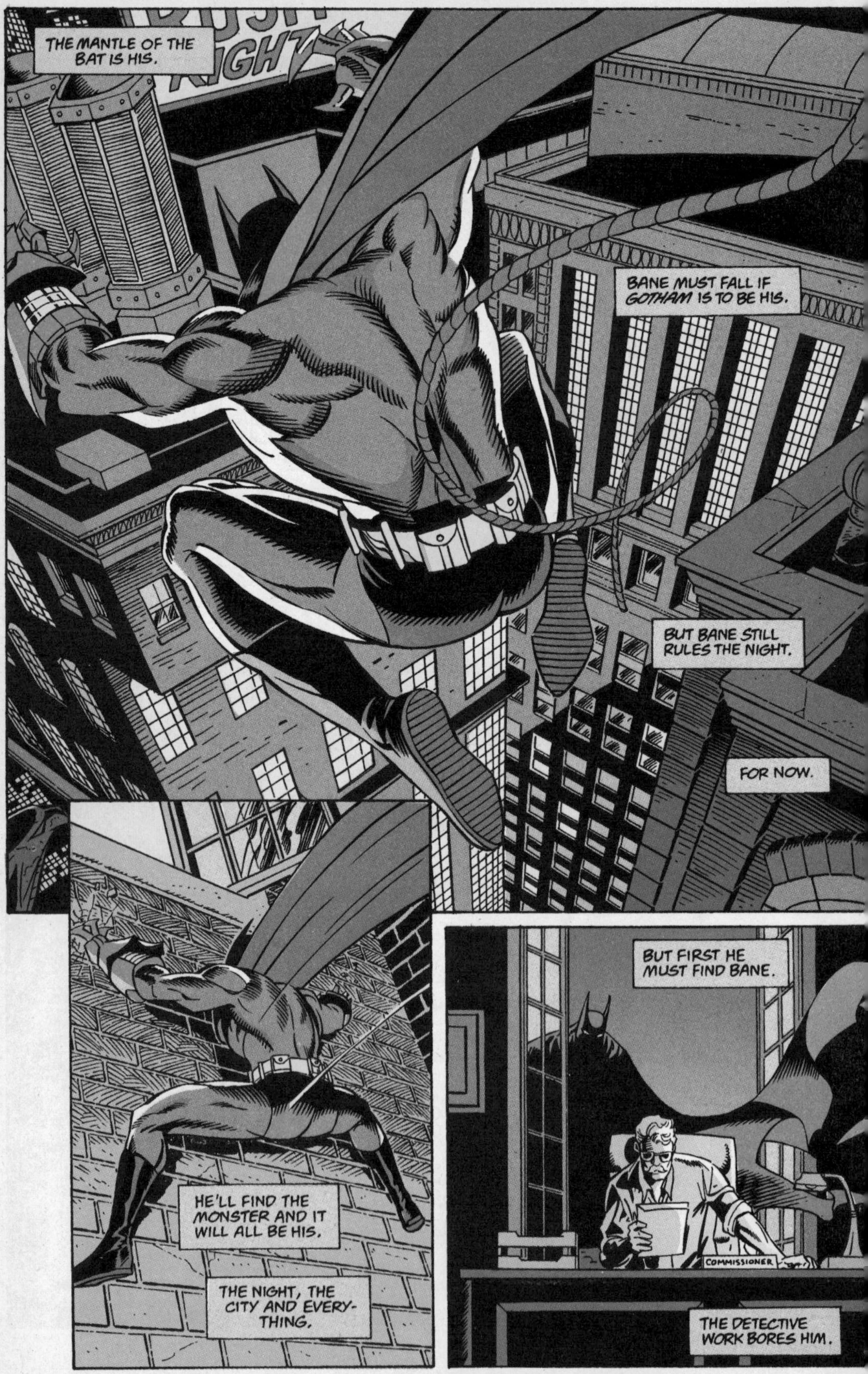
THE MANTLE OF THE BAT IS HIS.
BANE MUST FALL IF GOTHAM IS TO BE HIS.
BUT BANE STILL RULES THE NIGHT.
FOR NOW.
HE'LL FIND THE MONSTER AND IT WILL ALL BE HIS.
THE NIGHT, THE CITY AND EVERY-THING.
BUT FIRST HE MUST FIND BANE.
COMMISSIONER
THE DETECTIVE WORK BORES HIM.

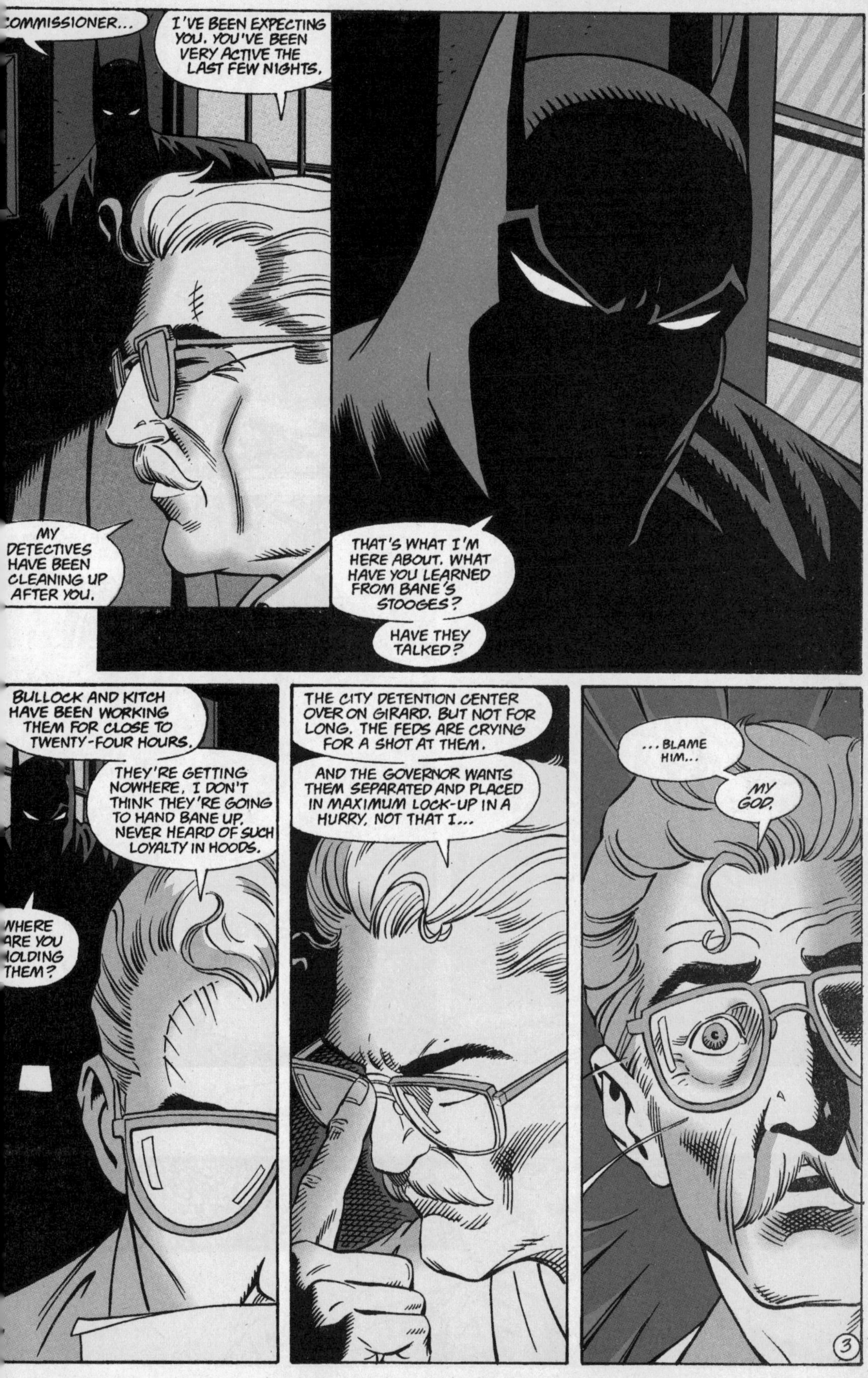
COMMISSIONER...
I'VE BEEN EXPECTING YOU. YOU'VE BEEN VERY ACTIVE THE LAST FEW NIGHTS.
MY DETECTIVES HAVE BEEN CLEANING UP AFTER YOU.
THAT'S WHAT I'M HERE ABOUT. WHAT HAVE YOU LEARNED FROM BANE'S STOOGES?
HAVE THEY TALKED?
BULLOCK AND KITCH HAVE BEEN WORKING THEM FOR CLOSE TO TWENTY-FOUR HOURS.
THEY'RE GETTING NOWHERE. I DON'T THINK THEY'RE GOING TO HAND BANE UP. NEVER HEARD OF SUCH LOYALTY IN HOODS.
WHERE ARE YOU HOLDING THEM?
THE CITY DETENTION CENTER OVER ON GIRARD. BUT NOT FOR LONG. THE FEDS ARE CRYING FOR A SHOT AT THEM.
AND THE GOVERNOR WANTS THEM SEPARATED AND PLACED IN MAXIMUM LOCK-UP IN A HURRY. NOT THAT I...
...BLAME HIM...
MY GOD.
3

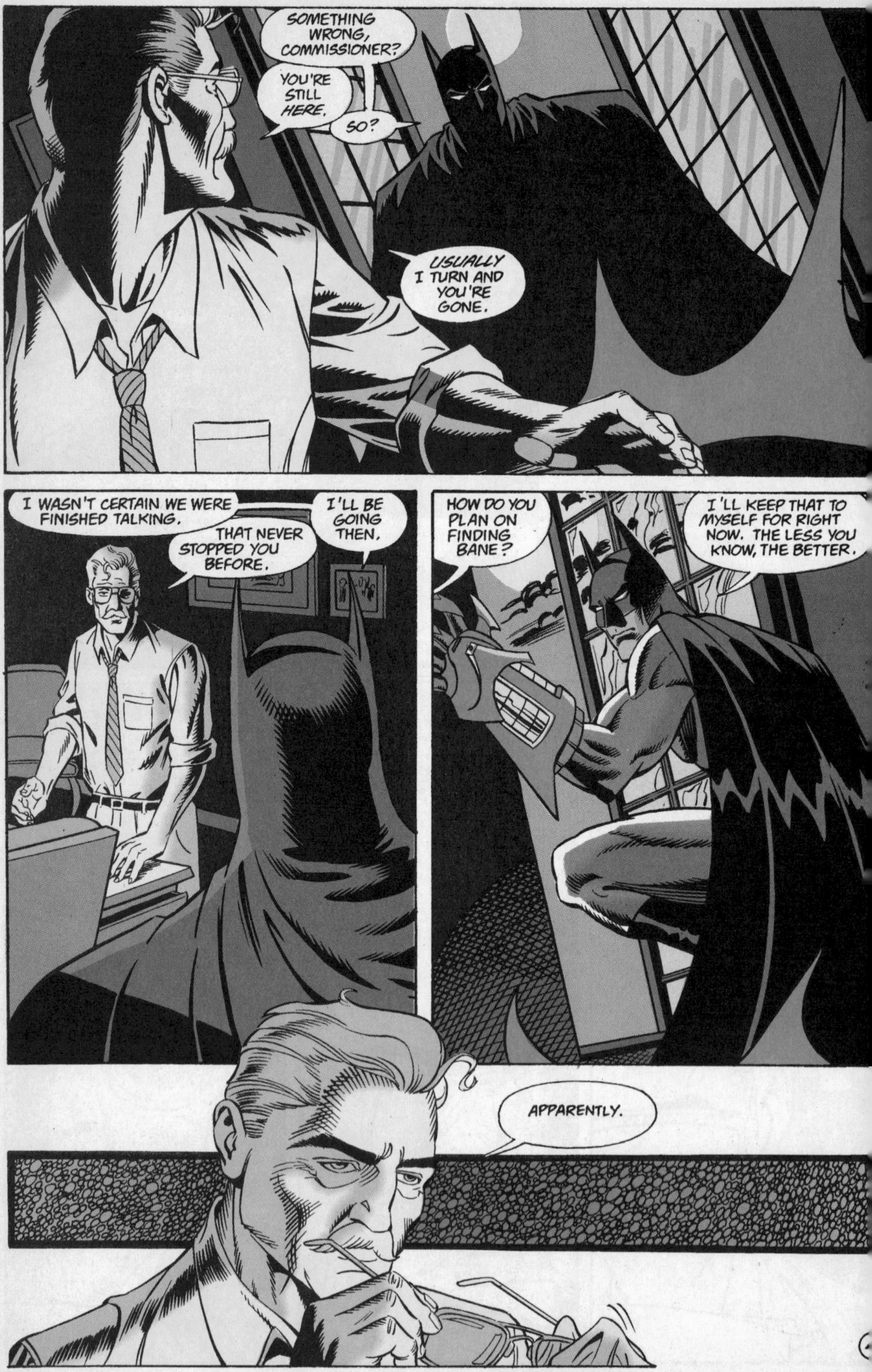
SOMETHING WRONG, COMMISSIONER?
YOU'RE STILL HERE.
SO?
USUALLY I TURN AND YOU'RE GONE.
I WASN'T CERTAIN WE WERE FINISHED TALKING.
THAT NEVER STOPPED YOU BEFORE.
I'LL BE GOING THEN.
HOW DO YOU PLAN ON FINDING BANE?
I'LL KEEP THAT TO MYSELF FOR RIGHT NOW. THE LESS YOU KNOW, THE BETTER.
APPARENTLY.

YOU GUYS ARE NEVER GONNA SEE THE LIGHT OF DAY, YOU KNOW THAT?

ARE YOU TRYING TO FRIGHTEN ME, SERGEANT?

WITH *WHAT*, SERGEANT? IMPRISONMENT?

I HAVE SERVED HARD TIME IN *PENA DURO*, THE HELLHOLE OF THE UNIVERSE. YOUR PRISONS ARE SOFT, EASY.

SURE. THEY'RE *COUNTRY* CLUBS.

BUT YOU'LL SERVE *ALONE*, ZOMBIE. THE FEDS ARE COMING TOMORROW AND SPLITTING YOU AND YOUR TWO BUNKIES UP. YOU'LL BE COUNTIN' THE YEARS IN THREE SEPARATE PENS.

HARD TIME IS *HARDER* WITHOUT FRIENDS.

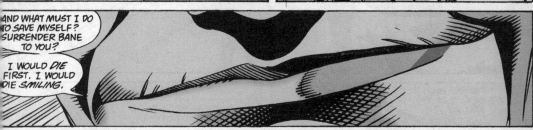

AND WHAT MUST I DO TO SAVE MYSELF? SURRENDER BANE TO YOU?

I WOULD *DIE* FIRST. I WOULD DIE *SMILING*.

GET THIS GOON OUTTA HERE BEFORE I PUT A SLUG IN HIM, LIEUTENANT.

LET'S GO, ZOMBIE. WE'RE FINISHED WITH YOU.

IMAGINE MY RELIEF.

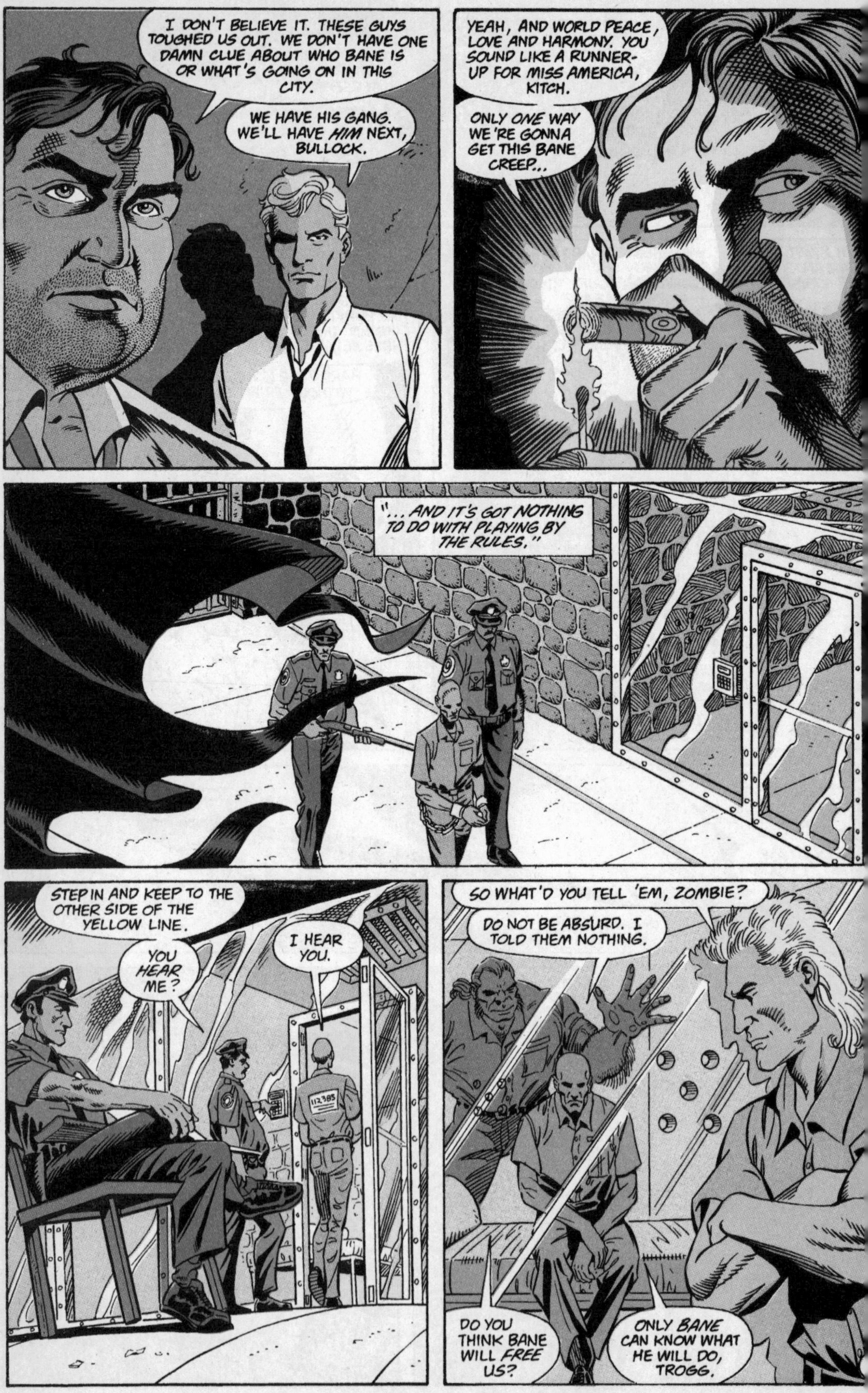
I DON'T BELIEVE IT. THESE GUYS TOUGHED US OUT. WE DON'T HAVE ONE DAMN CLUE ABOUT WHO BANE IS OR WHAT'S GOING ON IN THIS CITY.
WE HAVE HIS GANG. WE'LL HAVE *HIM* NEXT, BULLOCK.
YEAH, AND WORLD PEACE, LOVE AND HARMONY. YOU SOUND LIKE A RUNNER-UP FOR MISS AMERICA, KITCH.
ONLY *ONE* WAY WE'RE GONNA GET THIS BANE CREEP...
"... AND IT'S GOT *NOTHING* TO DO WITH PLAYING BY THE RULES."
STEP IN AND KEEP TO THE OTHER SIDE OF THE YELLOW LINE.
YOU *HEAR* ME?
I HEAR YOU.
112385
SO WHAT'D YOU TELL 'EM, ZOMBIE?
DO NOT BE ABSURD. I TOLD THEM NOTHING.
DO YOU THINK BANE WILL *FREE* US?
ONLY *BANE* CAN KNOW WHAT HE WILL DO, TROGG.

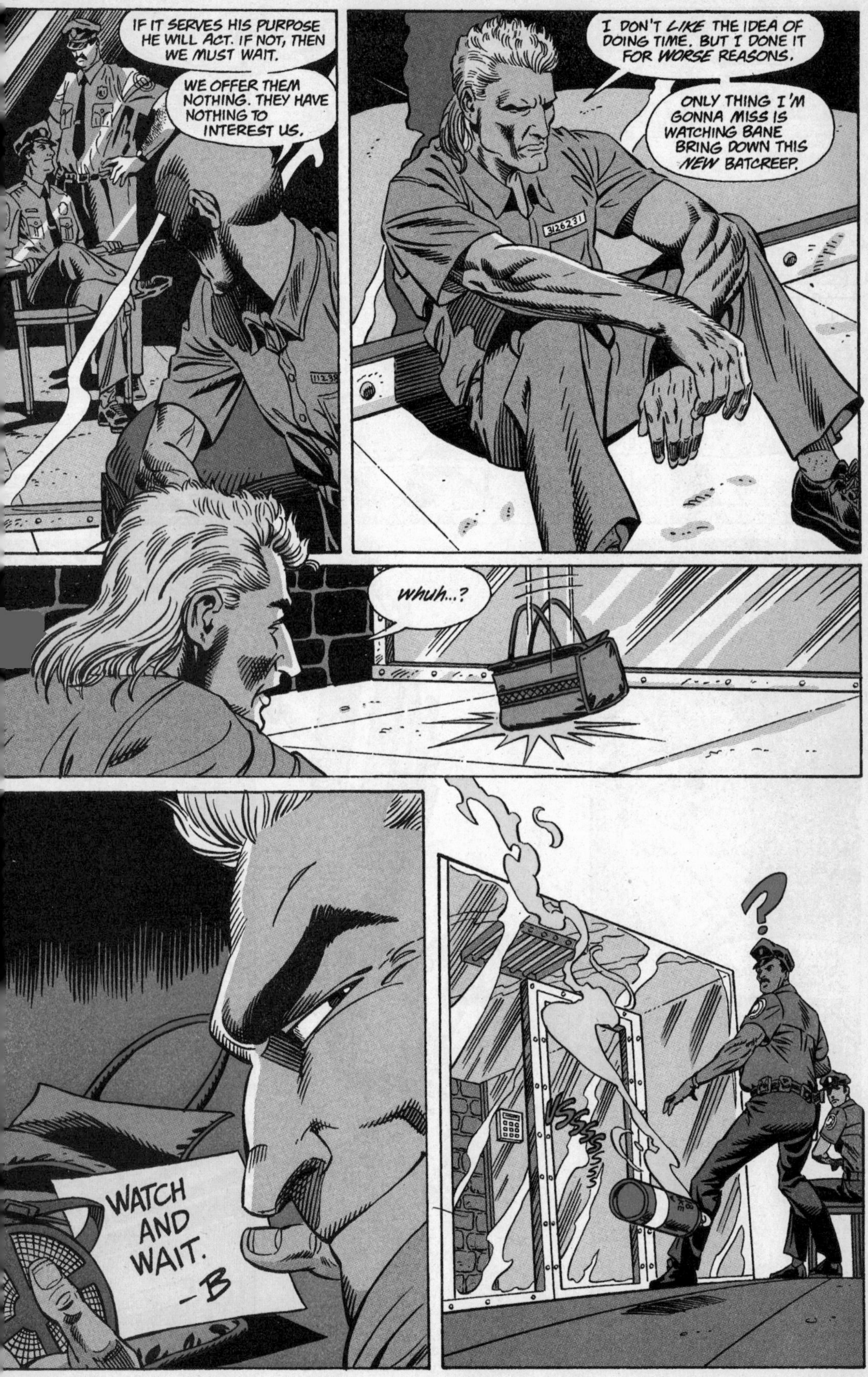
IF IT SERVES HIS PURPOSE HE WILL ACT. IF NOT, THEN WE MUST WAIT.
WE OFFER THEM NOTHING. THEY HAVE NOTHING TO INTEREST US.
I DON'T LIKE THE IDEA OF DOING TIME. BUT I DONE IT FOR WORSE REASONS.
ONLY THING I'M GONNA MISS IS WATCHING BANE BRING DOWN THIS NEW BATCREEP.
whuh...?
WATCH AND WAIT. -B
?
SSSSSS

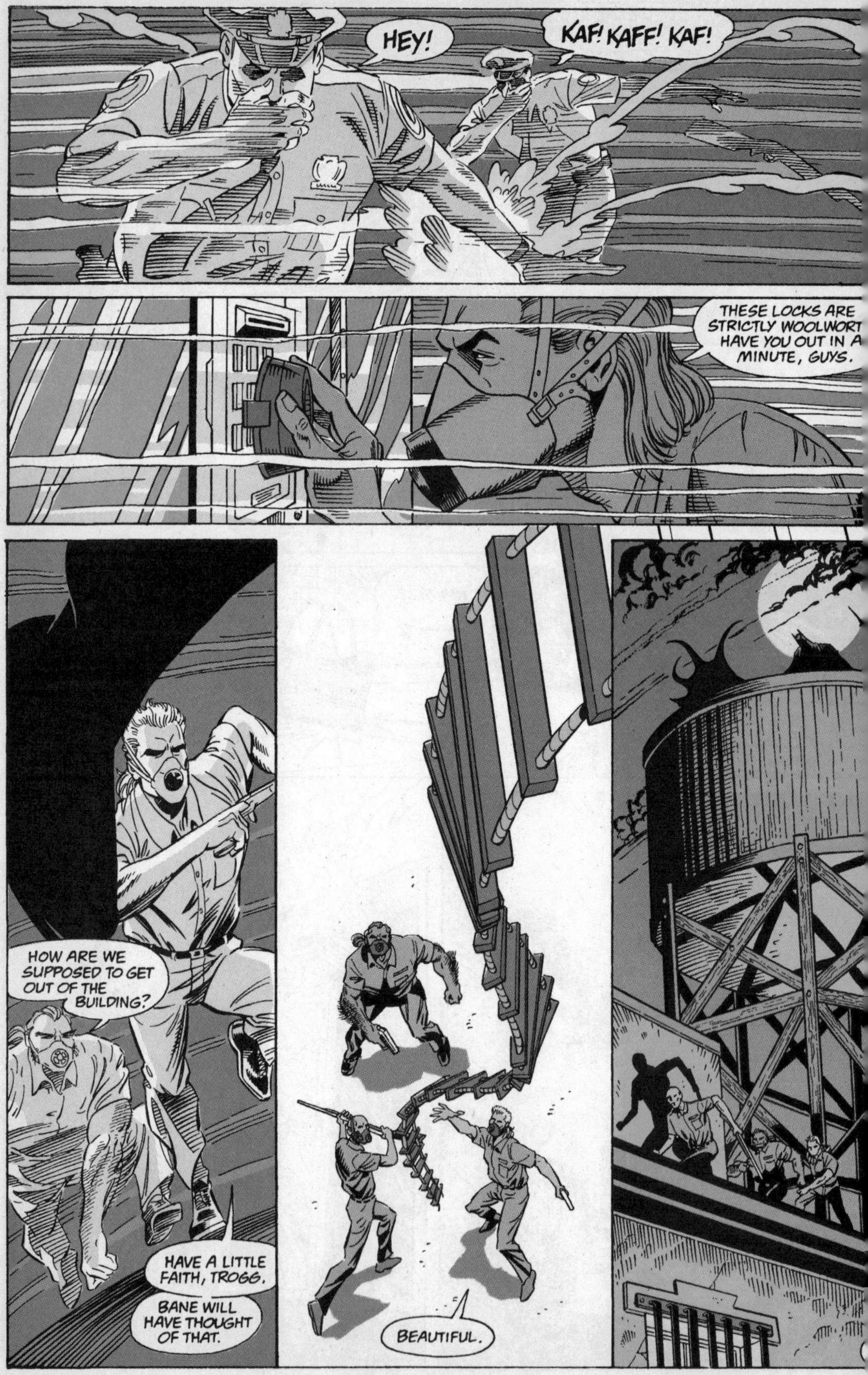
HEY!
KAF! KAFF! KAF!
THESE LOCKS ARE STRICTLY WOOLWORT HAVE YOU OUT IN A MINUTE, GUYS.
HOW ARE WE SUPPOSED TO GET OUT OF THE BUILDING?
HAVE A LITTLE FAITH, TROGG.
BANE WILL HAVE THOUGHT OF THAT.
BEAUTIFUL.

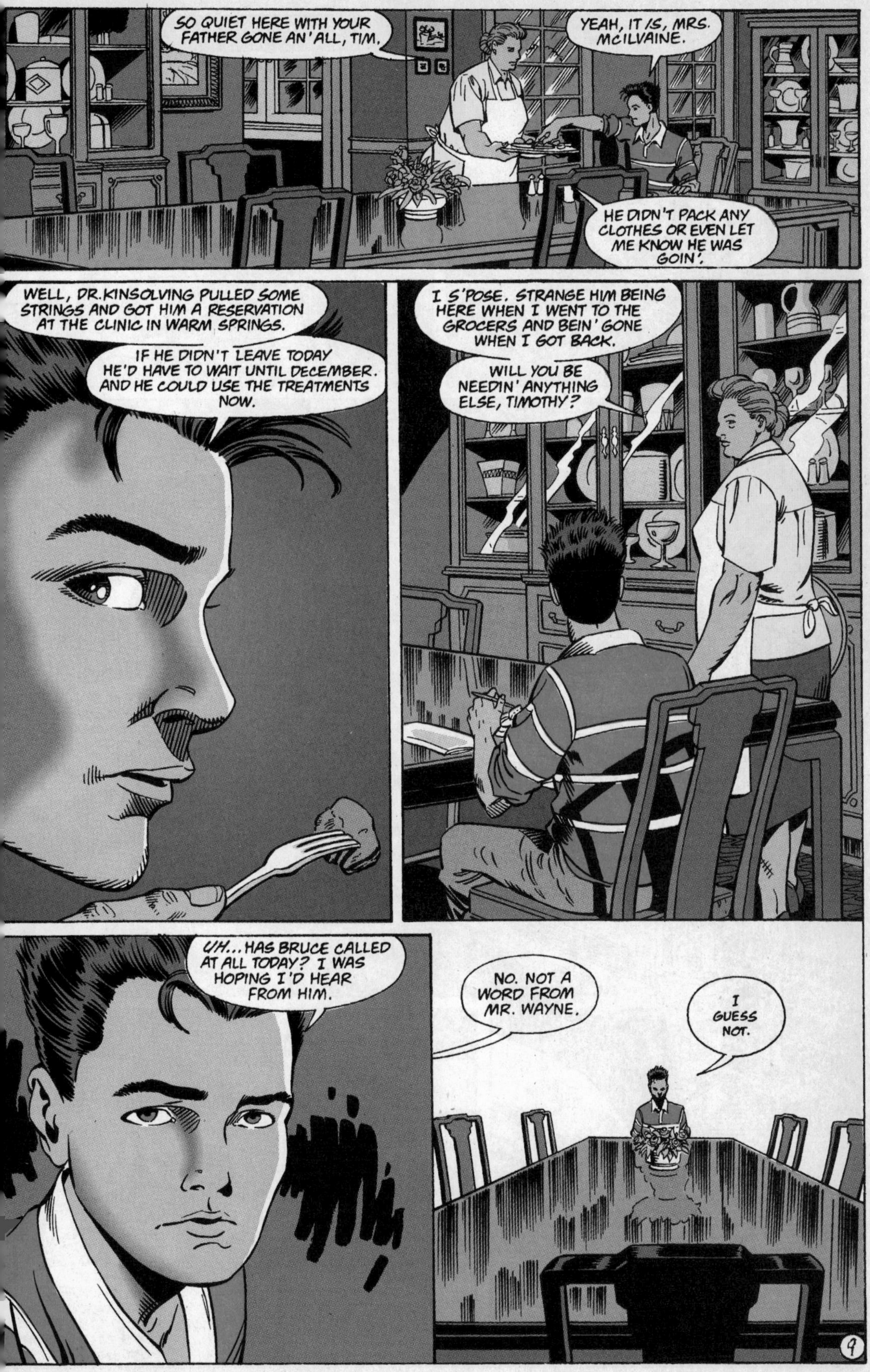
SO QUIET HERE WITH YOUR FATHER GONE AN'ALL, TIM.
YEAH, IT IS, MRS. McILVAINE.
HE DIDN'T PACK ANY CLOTHES OR EVEN LET ME KNOW HE WAS GOIN'.
WELL, DR.KINSOLVING PULLED SOME STRINGS AND GOT HIM A RESERVATION AT THE CLINIC IN WARM SPRINGS.
IF HE DIDN'T LEAVE TODAY HE'D HAVE TO WAIT UNTIL DECEMBER. AND HE COULD USE THE TREATMENTS NOW.
I S'POSE. STRANGE HIM BEING HERE WHEN I WENT TO THE GROCERS AND BEIN' GONE WHEN I GOT BACK.
WILL YOU BE NEEDIN' ANYTHING ELSE, TIMOTHY?
UH... HAS BRUCE CALLED AT ALL TODAY? I WAS HOPING I'D HEAR FROM HIM.
NO. NOT A WORD FROM MR. WAYNE.
I GUESS NOT.
9

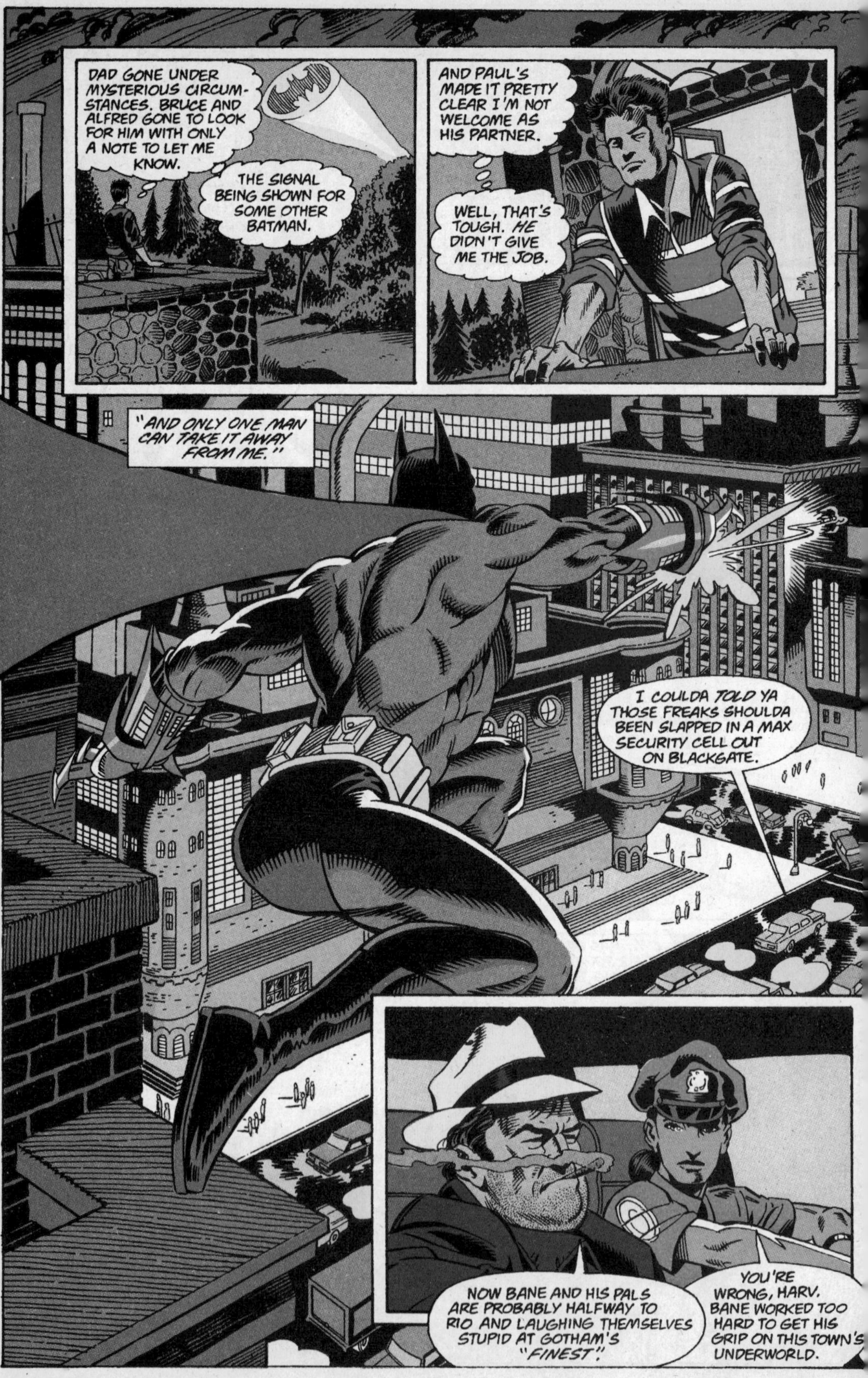
DAD GONE UNDER MYSTERIOUS CIRCUMSTANCES. BRUCE AND ALFRED GONE TO LOOK FOR HIM WITH ONLY A NOTE TO LET ME KNOW.
THE SIGNAL BEING SHOWN FOR SOME OTHER BATMAN.
AND PAUL'S MADE IT PRETTY CLEAR I'M NOT WELCOME AS HIS PARTNER.
WELL, THAT'S TOUGH. *HE* DIDN'T GIVE ME THE JOB.
"AND ONLY ONE MAN CAN TAKE IT AWAY FROM ME."
I COULDA *TOLD* YA THOSE FREAKS SHOULDA BEEN SLAPPED IN A MAX SECURITY CELL OUT ON BLACKGATE.
NOW BANE AND HIS PALS ARE PROBABLY HALFWAY TO RIO AND LAUGHING THEMSELVES STUPID AT GOTHAM'S "*FINEST*"!
YOU'RE WRONG, HARV. BANE WORKED TOO HARD TO GET HIS GRIP ON THIS TOWN'S UNDERWORLD.

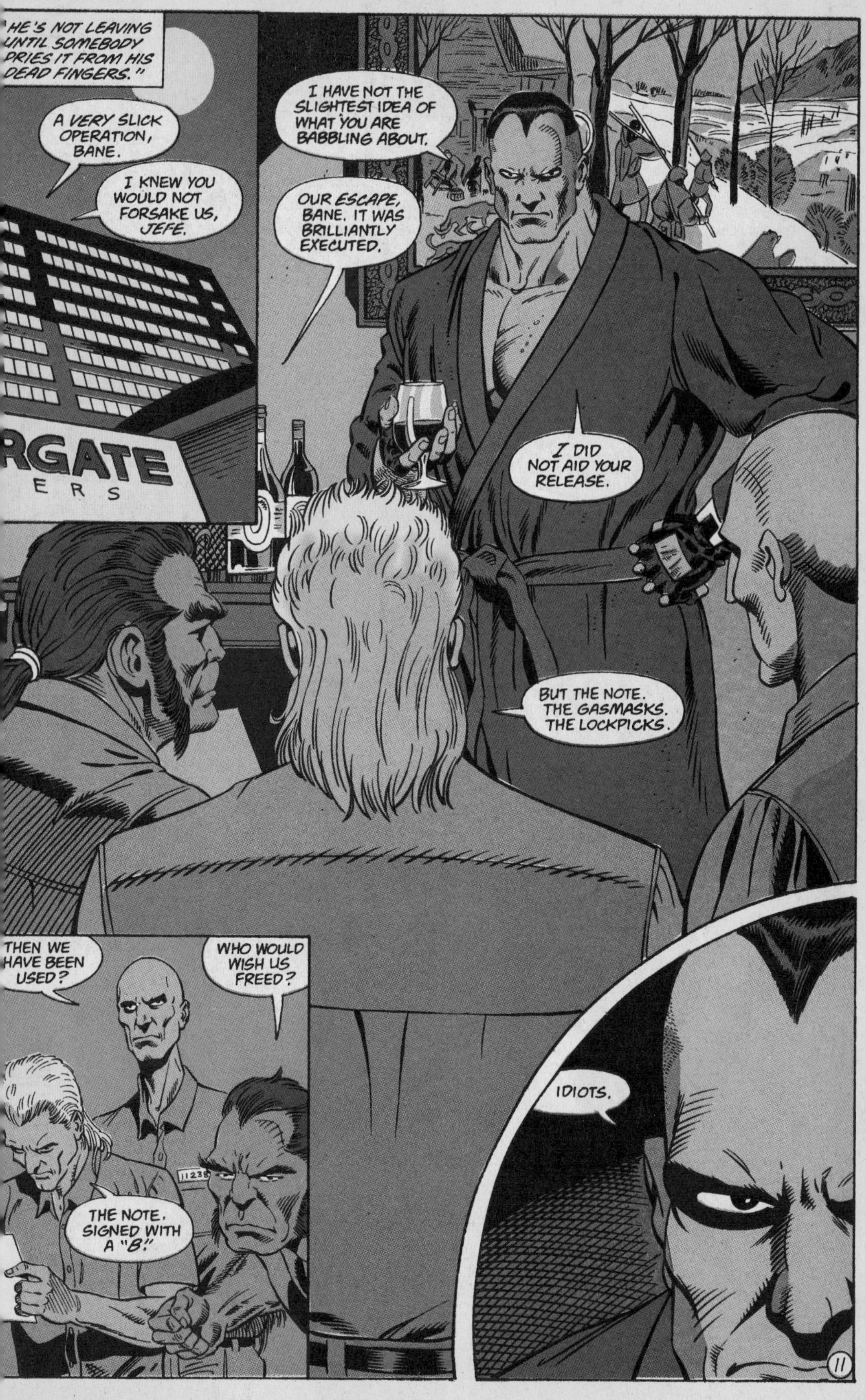
"HE'S NOT LEAVING UNTIL SOMEBODY PRIES IT FROM HIS DEAD FINGERS."
A VERY SLICK OPERATION, BANE.
I KNEW YOU WOULD NOT FORSAKE US, JEFE.
RGATE
ERS
I HAVE NOT THE SLIGHTEST IDEA OF WHAT YOU ARE BABBLING ABOUT.
OUR ESCAPE, BANE. IT WAS BRILLIANTLY EXECUTED.
I DID NOT AID YOUR RELEASE.
BUT THE NOTE. THE GASMASKS. THE LOCKPICKS.
THEN WE HAVE BEEN USED?
WHO WOULD WISH US FREED?
11238
THE NOTE. SIGNED WITH A "B."
IDIOTS.
11

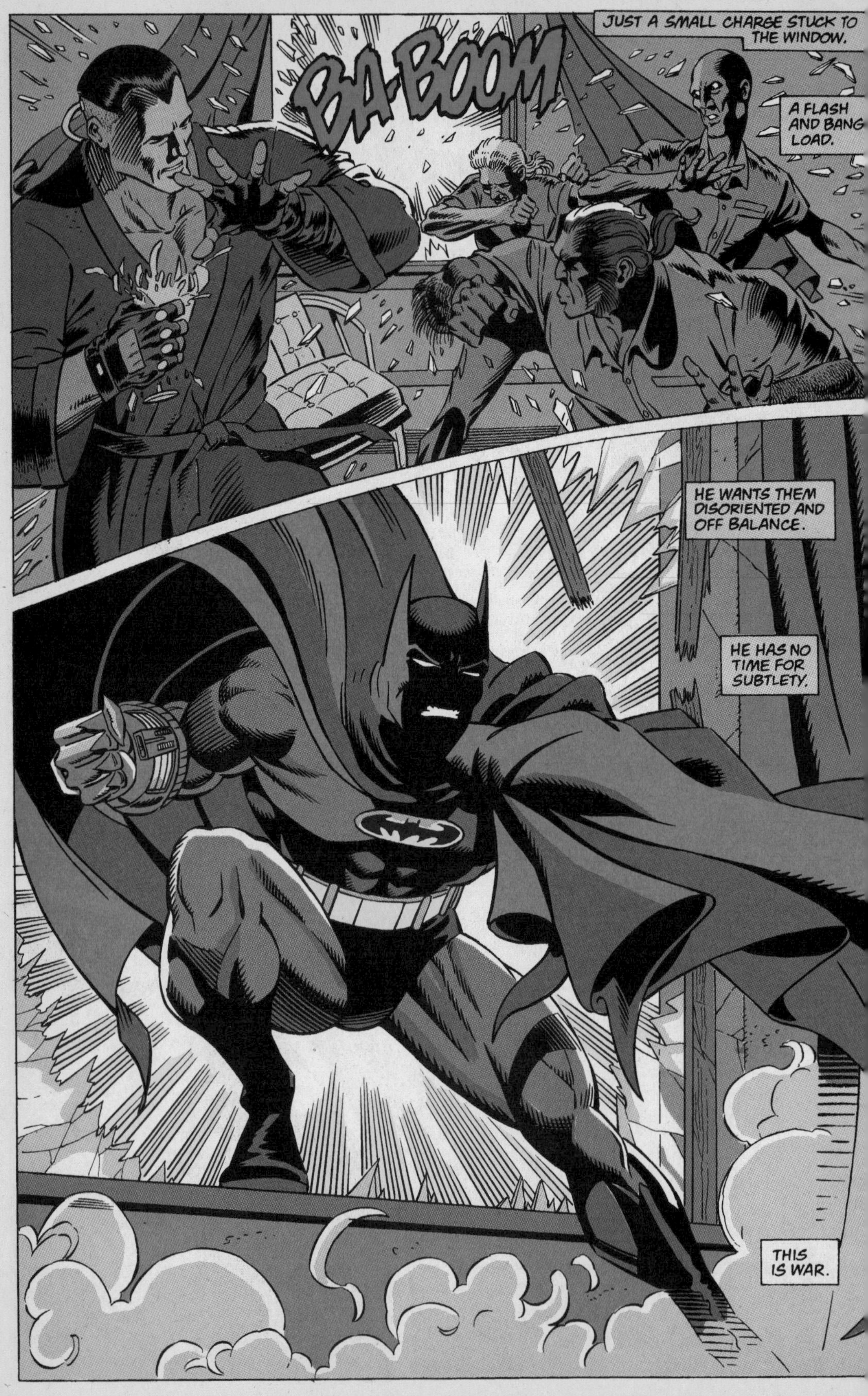

JUST A SMALL CHARGE STUCK TO THE WINDOW.
BA-BOOM
A FLASH AND BANG LOAD.
HE WANTS THEM DISORIENTED AND OFF BALANCE.
HE HAS NO TIME FOR SUBTLETY.
THIS IS WAR.

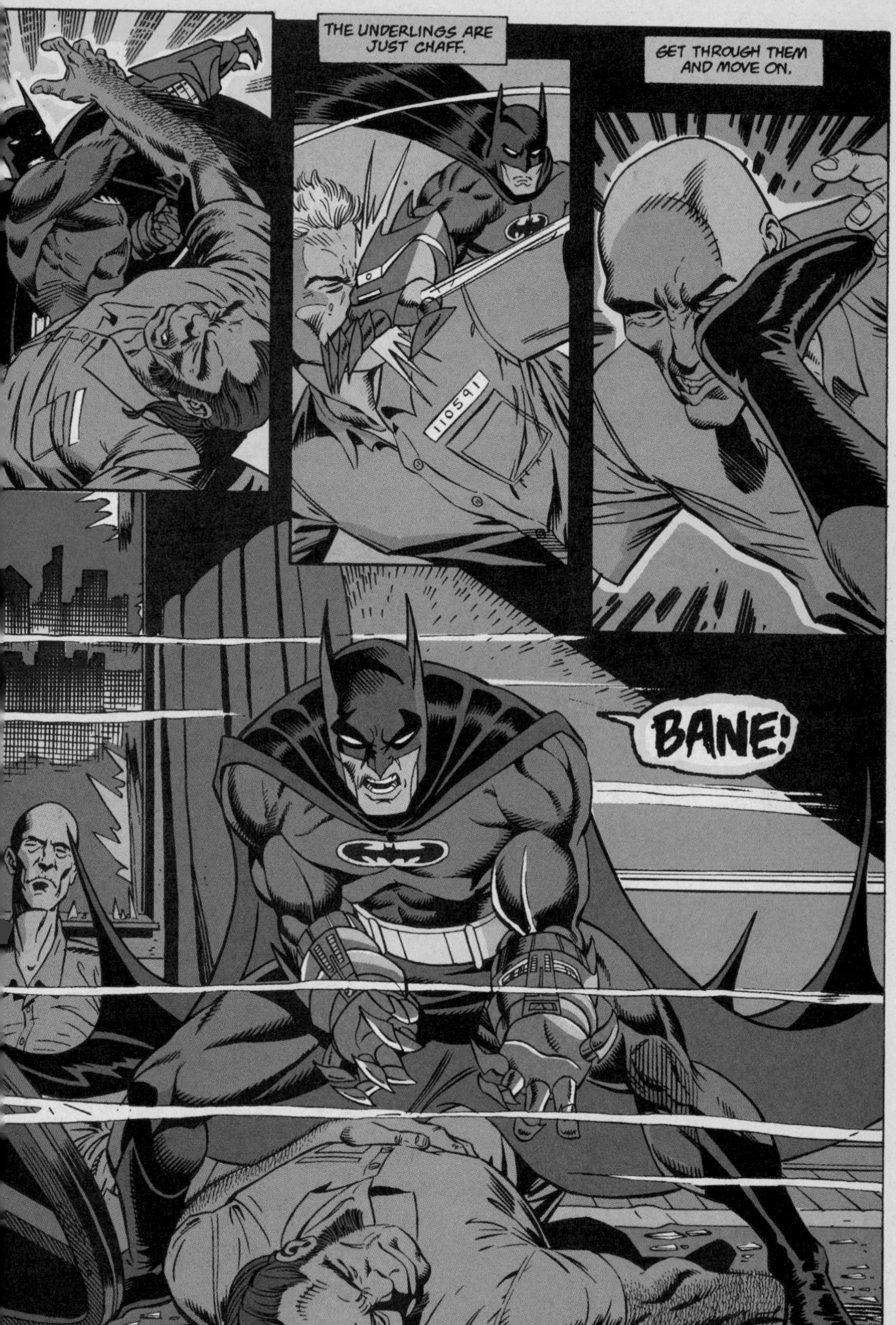
THE UNDERLINGS ARE JUST CHAFF.
GET THROUGH THEM AND MOVE ON.
BANE!
13

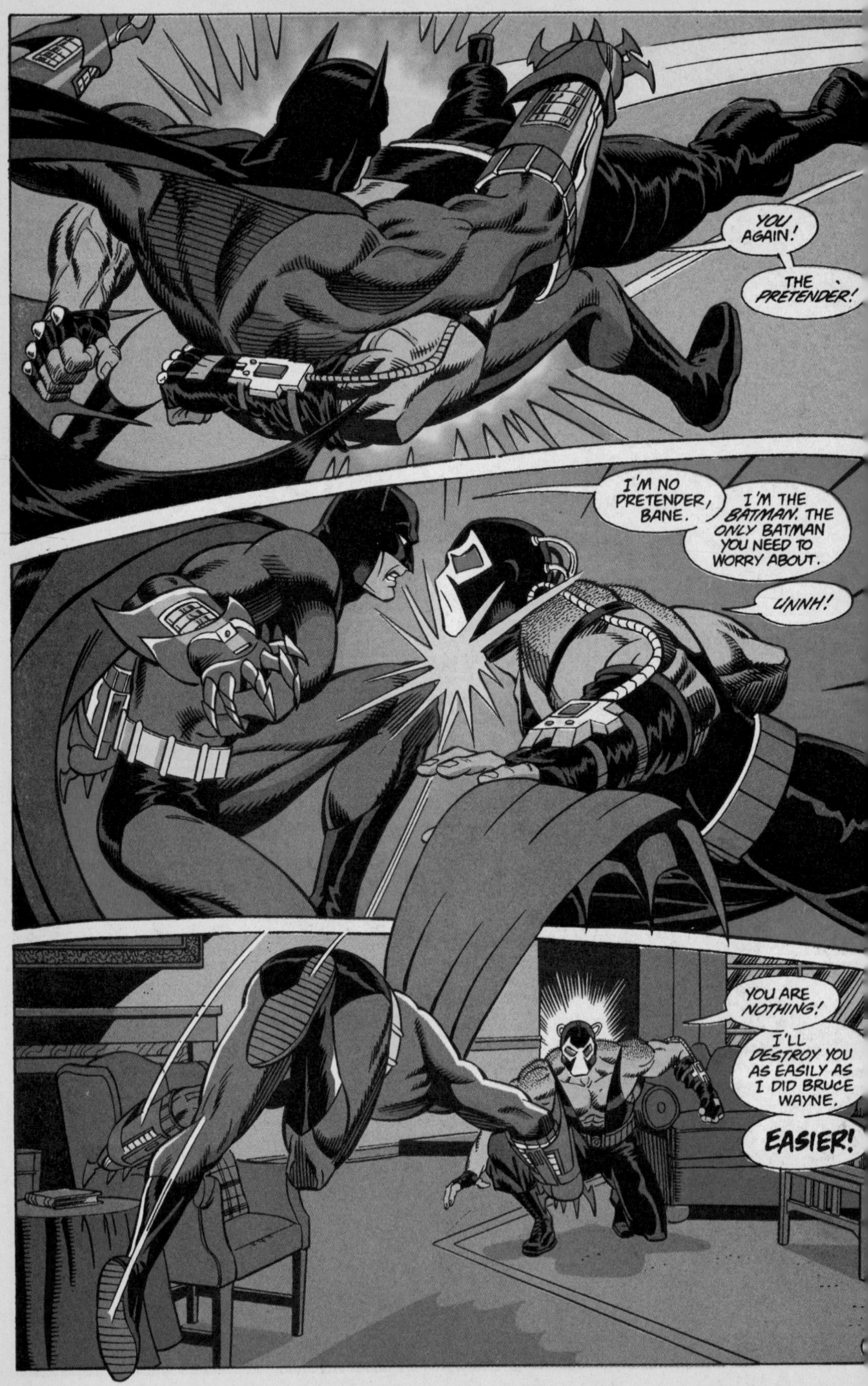

YOU AGAIN!
THE PRETENDER!
I'M NO PRETENDER, BANE.
I'M THE BATMAN. THE ONLY BATMAN YOU NEED TO WORRY ABOUT.
UNNH!
YOU ARE NOTHING!
I'LL DESTROY YOU AS EASILY AS I DID BRUCE WAYNE.
EASIER!

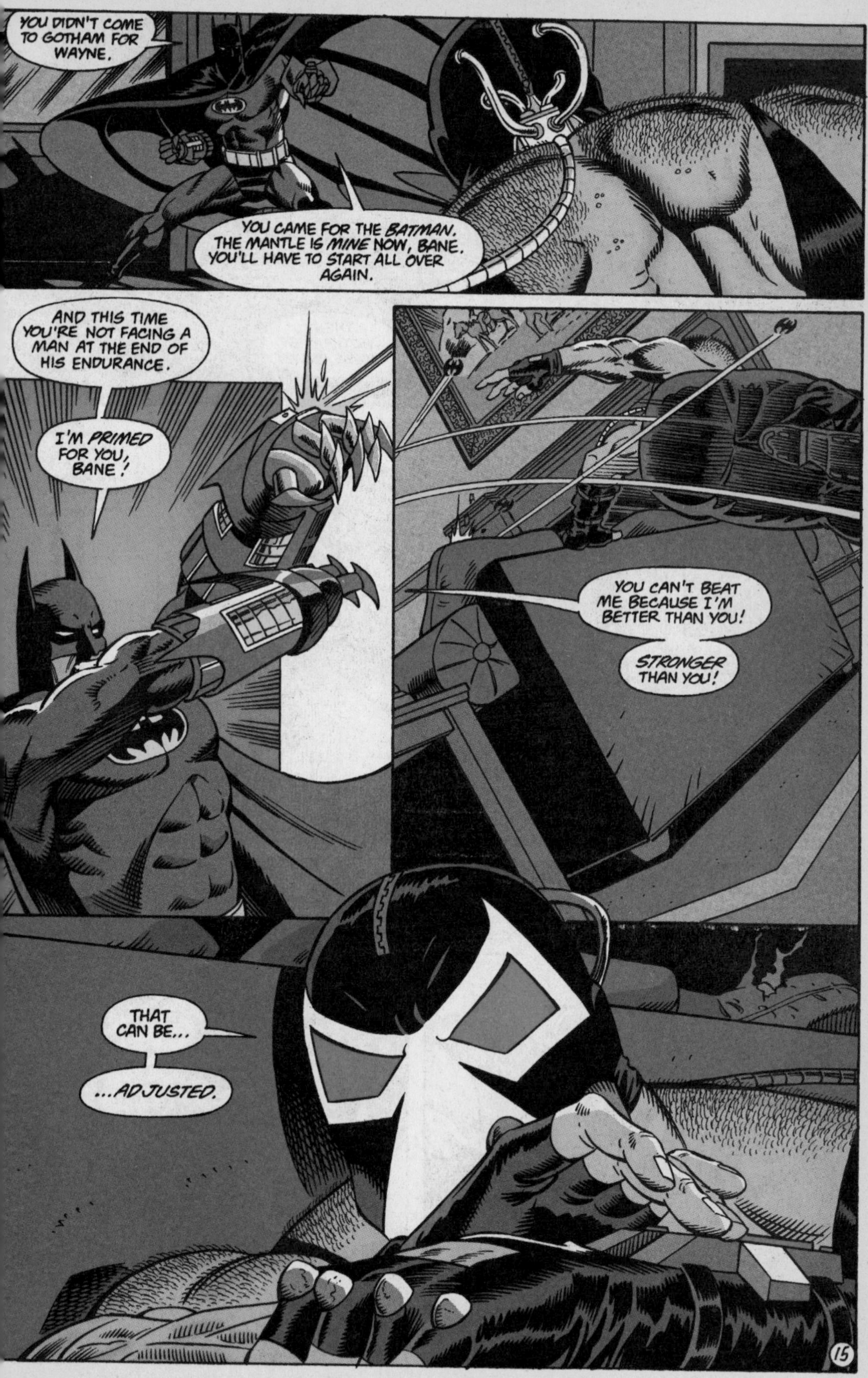
YOU DIDN'T COME TO GOTHAM FOR WAYNE.
YOU CAME FOR THE BATMAN. THE MANTLE IS MINE NOW, BANE. YOU'LL HAVE TO START ALL OVER AGAIN.
AND THIS TIME YOU'RE NOT FACING A MAN AT THE END OF HIS ENDURANCE.
I'M PRIMED FOR YOU, BANE!
YOU CAN'T BEAT ME BECAUSE I'M BETTER THAN YOU!
STRONGER THAN YOU!
THAT CAN BE...
...ADJUSTED.
15

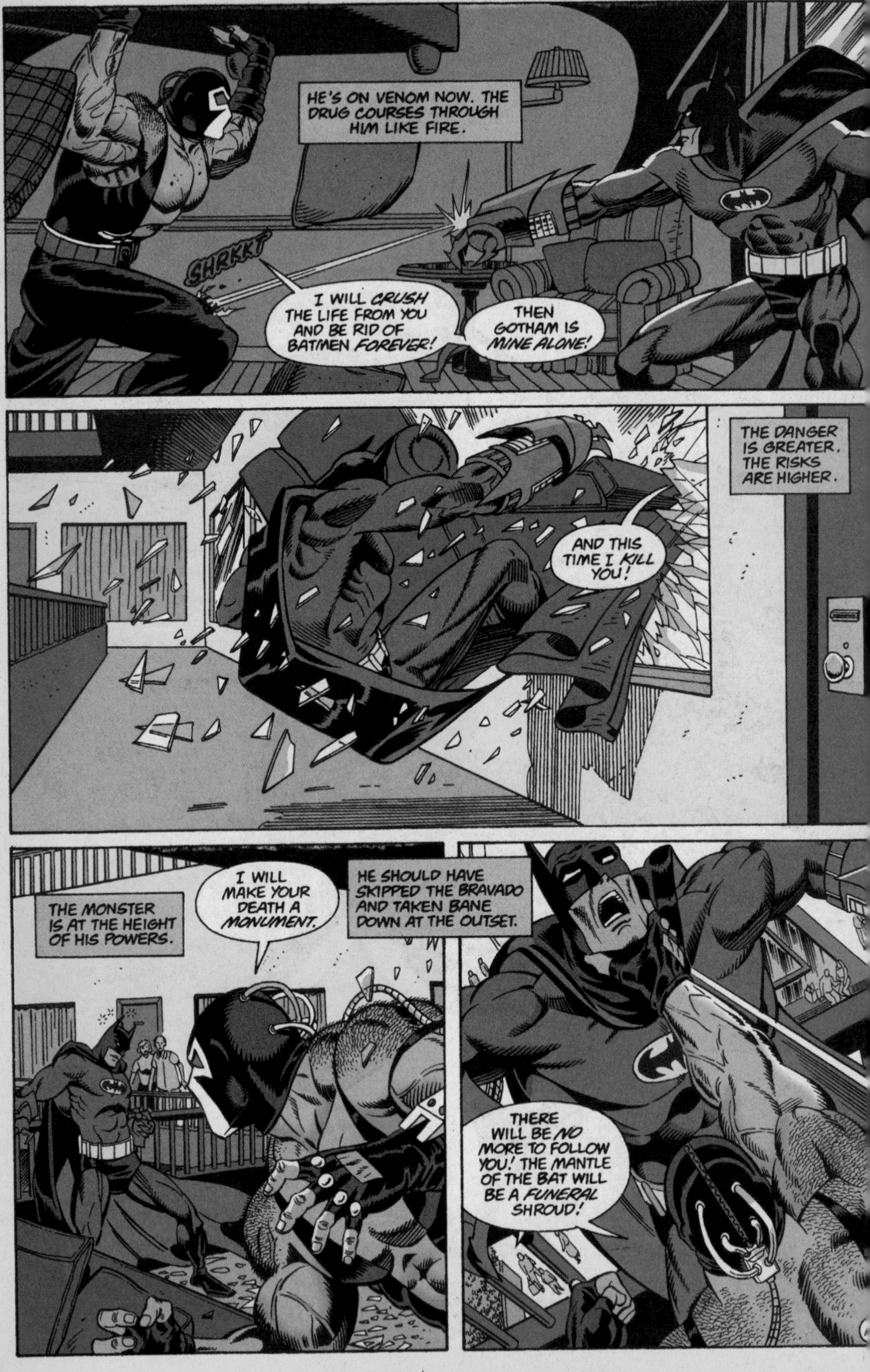
HE'S ON VENOM NOW. THE DRUG COURSES THROUGH HIM LIKE FIRE.
SHRKKT
I WILL CRUSH THE LIFE FROM YOU AND BE RID OF BATMEN FOREVER!
THEN GOTHAM IS MINE ALONE!
THE DANGER IS GREATER. THE RISKS ARE HIGHER.
AND THIS TIME I KILL YOU!
THE MONSTER IS AT THE HEIGHT OF HIS POWERS.
I WILL MAKE YOUR DEATH A MONUMENT.
HE SHOULD HAVE SKIPPED THE BRAVADO AND TAKEN BANE DOWN AT THE OUTSET.
THERE WILL BE NO MORE TO FOLLOW YOU! THE MANTLE OF THE BAT WILL BE A FUNERAL SHROUD!

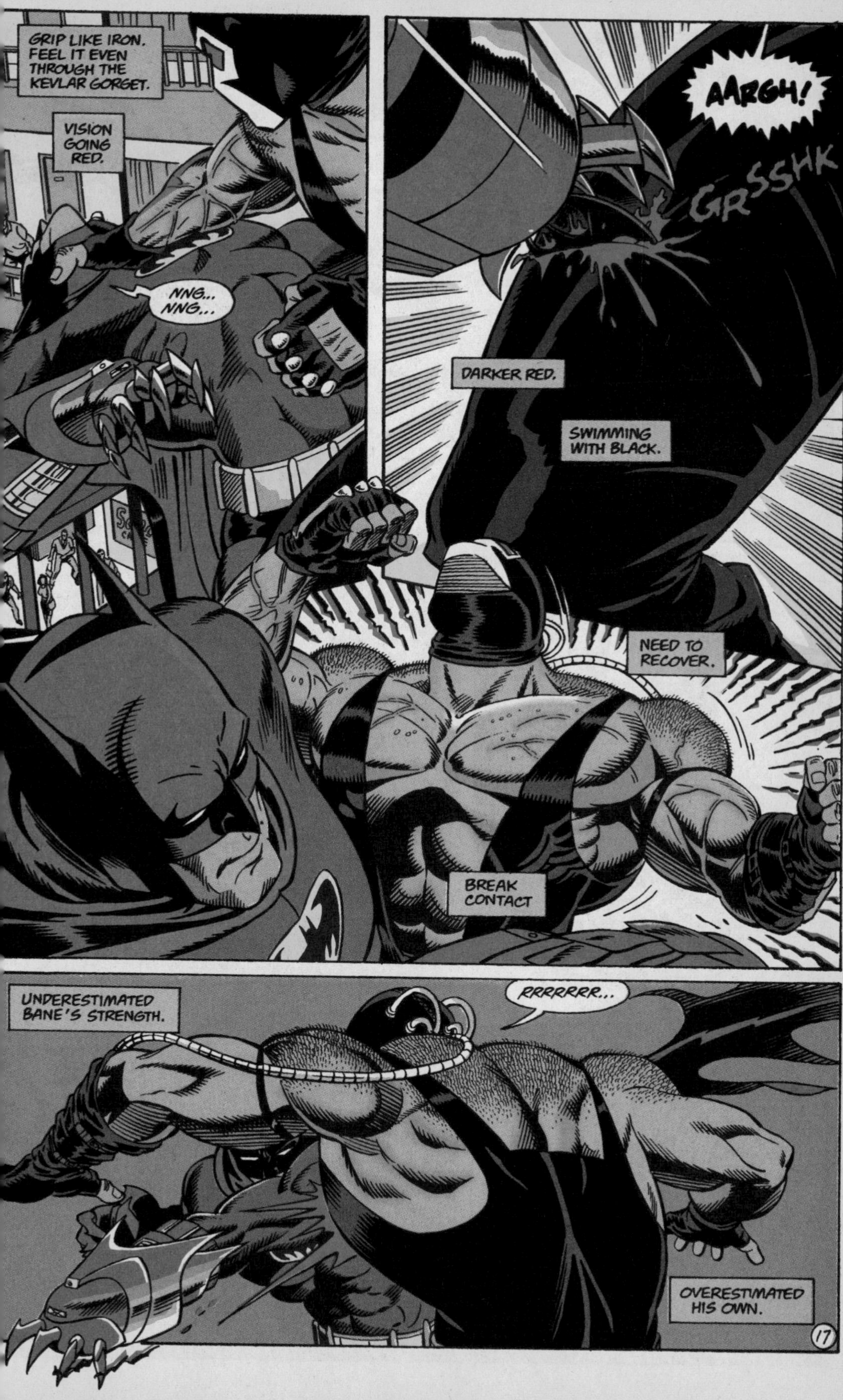
GRIP LIKE IRON. FEEL IT EVEN THROUGH THE KEVLAR GORGET.
VISION GOING RED.
NNG... NNG...
AARGH!
GRSSHK
DARKER RED.
SWIMMING WITH BLACK.
NEED TO RECOVER.
BREAK CONTACT
UNDERESTIMATED BANE'S STRENGTH.
RRRRRRR...
OVERESTIMATED HIS OWN.
17

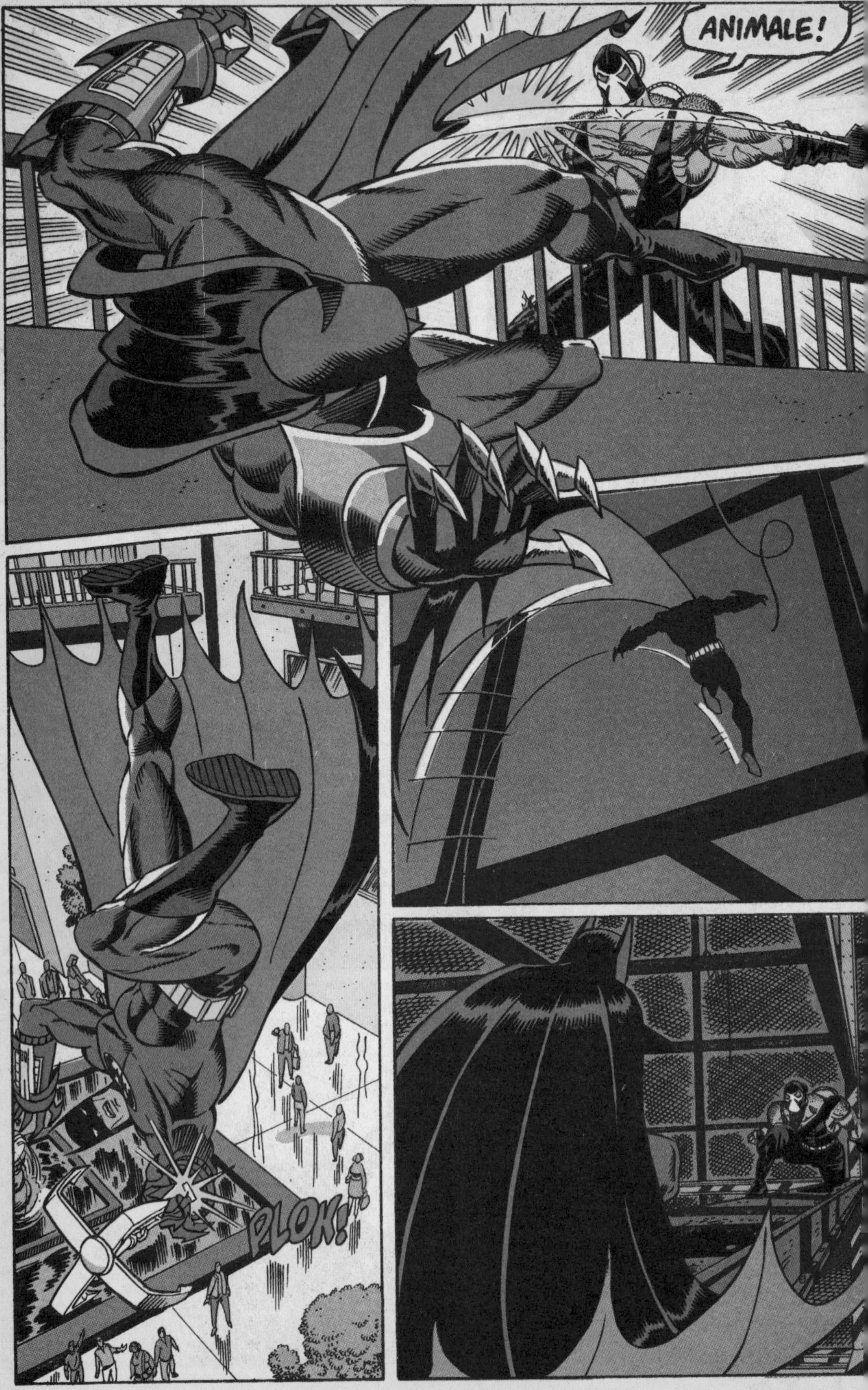
ANIMALE!
PLOK!

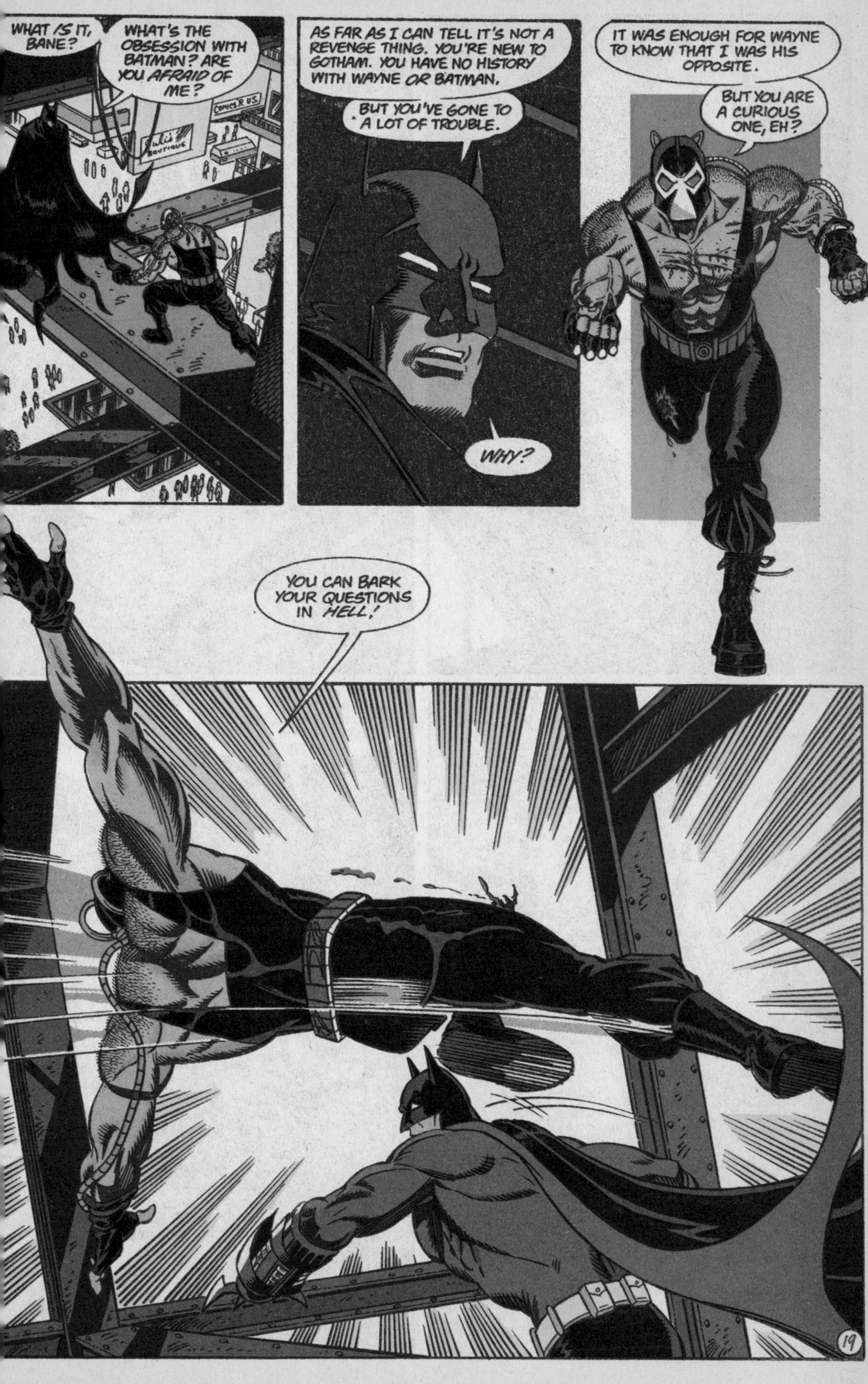
WHAT IS IT, BANE?
WHAT'S THE OBSESSION WITH BATMAN? ARE YOU AFRAID OF ME?
COMICS R US
AS FAR AS I CAN TELL IT'S NOT A REVENGE THING. YOU'RE NEW TO GOTHAM. YOU HAVE NO HISTORY WITH WAYNE OR BATMAN.
BUT YOU'VE GONE TO A LOT OF TROUBLE.
WHY?
IT WAS ENOUGH FOR WAYNE TO KNOW THAT I WAS HIS OPPOSITE.
BUT YOU ARE A CURIOUS ONE, EH?
YOU CAN BARK YOUR QUESTIONS IN HELL!
19

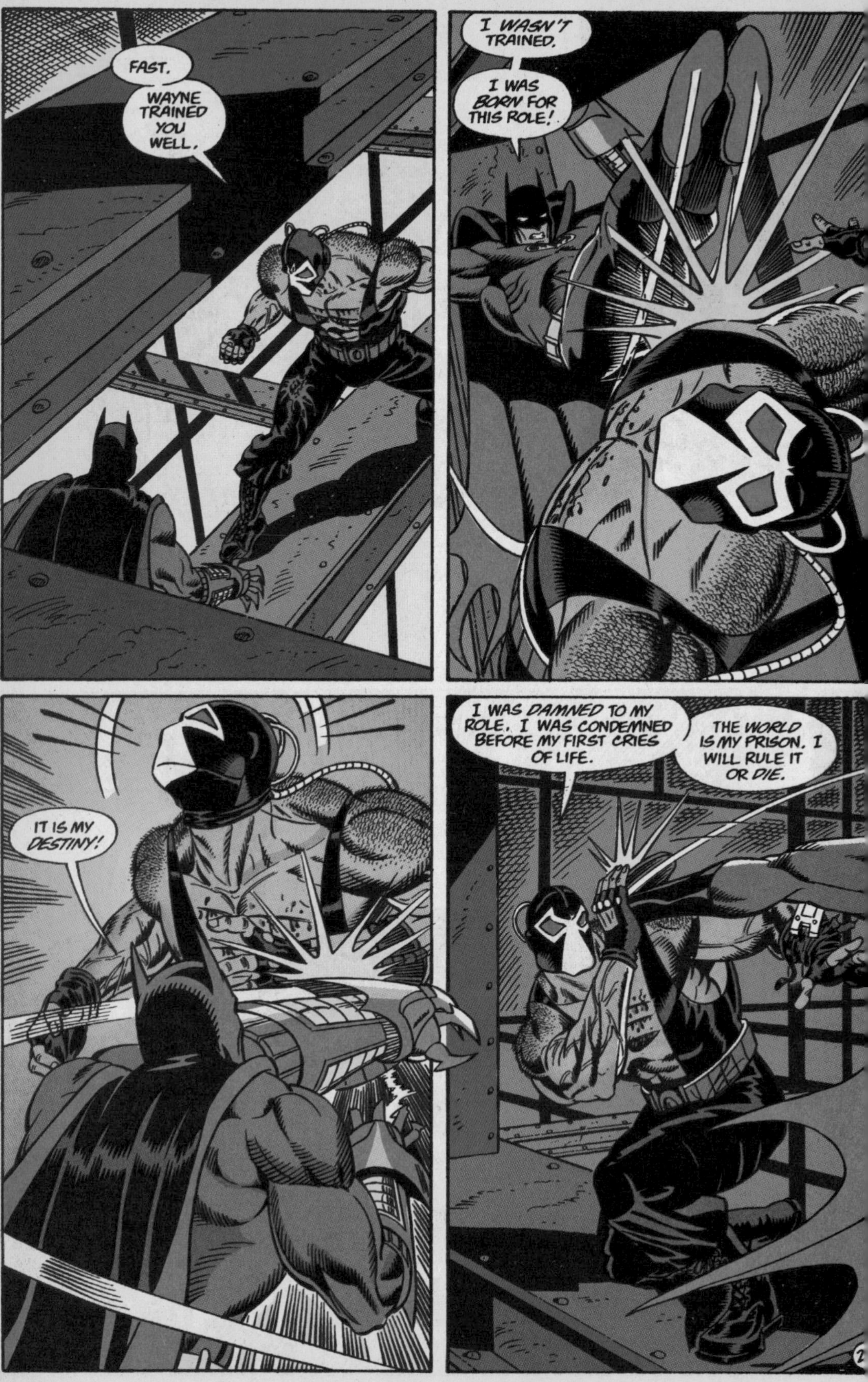
FAST.
WAYNE TRAINED YOU WELL.
I WASN'T TRAINED.
I WAS BORN FOR THIS ROLE!
IT IS MY DESTINY!
I WAS DAMNED TO MY ROLE. I WAS CONDEMNED BEFORE MY FIRST CRIES OF LIFE.
THE WORLD IS MY PRISON. I WILL RULE IT OR DIE.

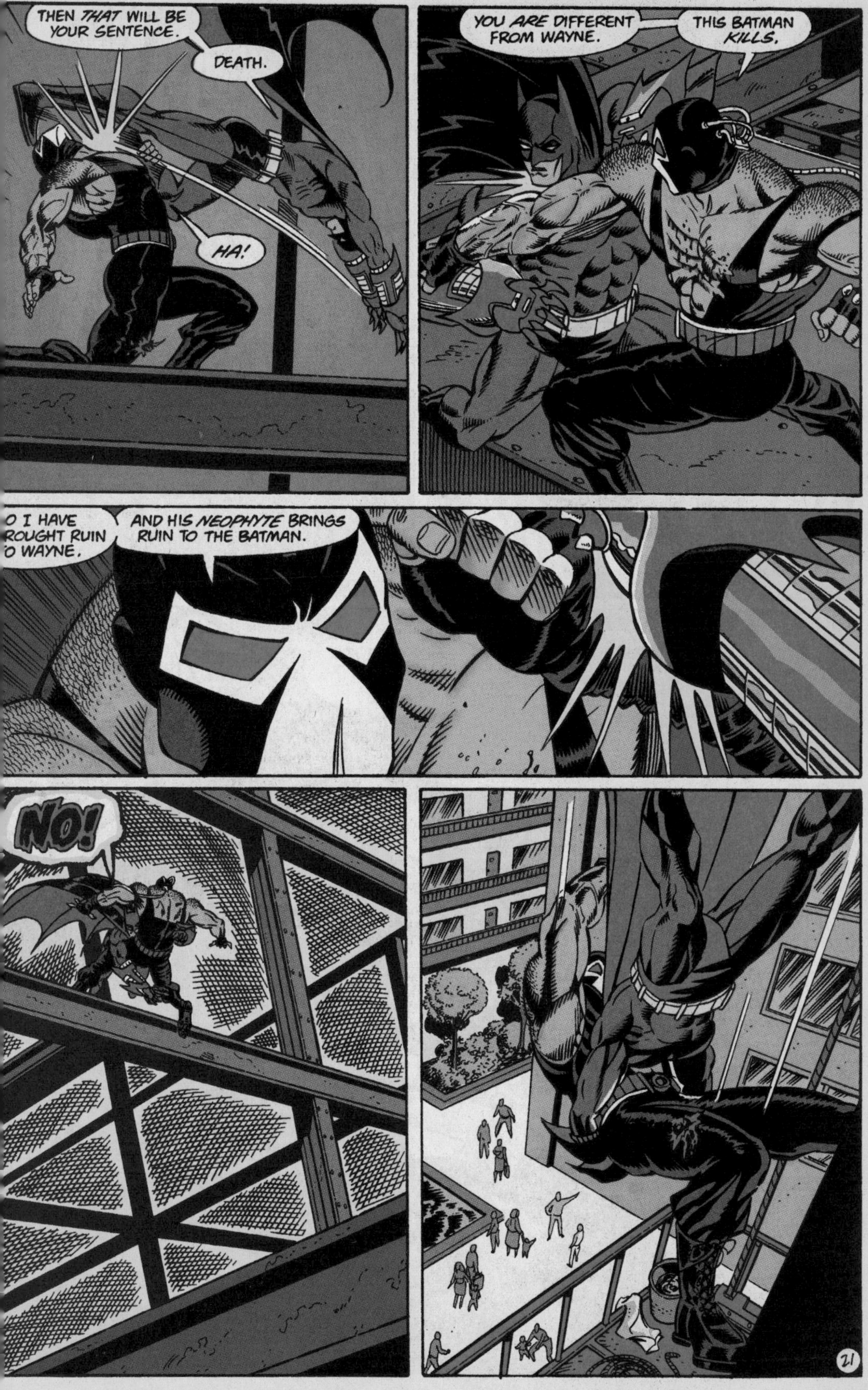
THEN THAT WILL BE YOUR SENTENCE.
DEATH.
HA!
YOU ARE DIFFERENT FROM WAYNE.
THIS BATMAN KILLS.
O I HAVE ROUGHT RUIN O WAYNE.
AND HIS NEOPHYTE BRINGS RUIN TO THE BATMAN.
NO!
21

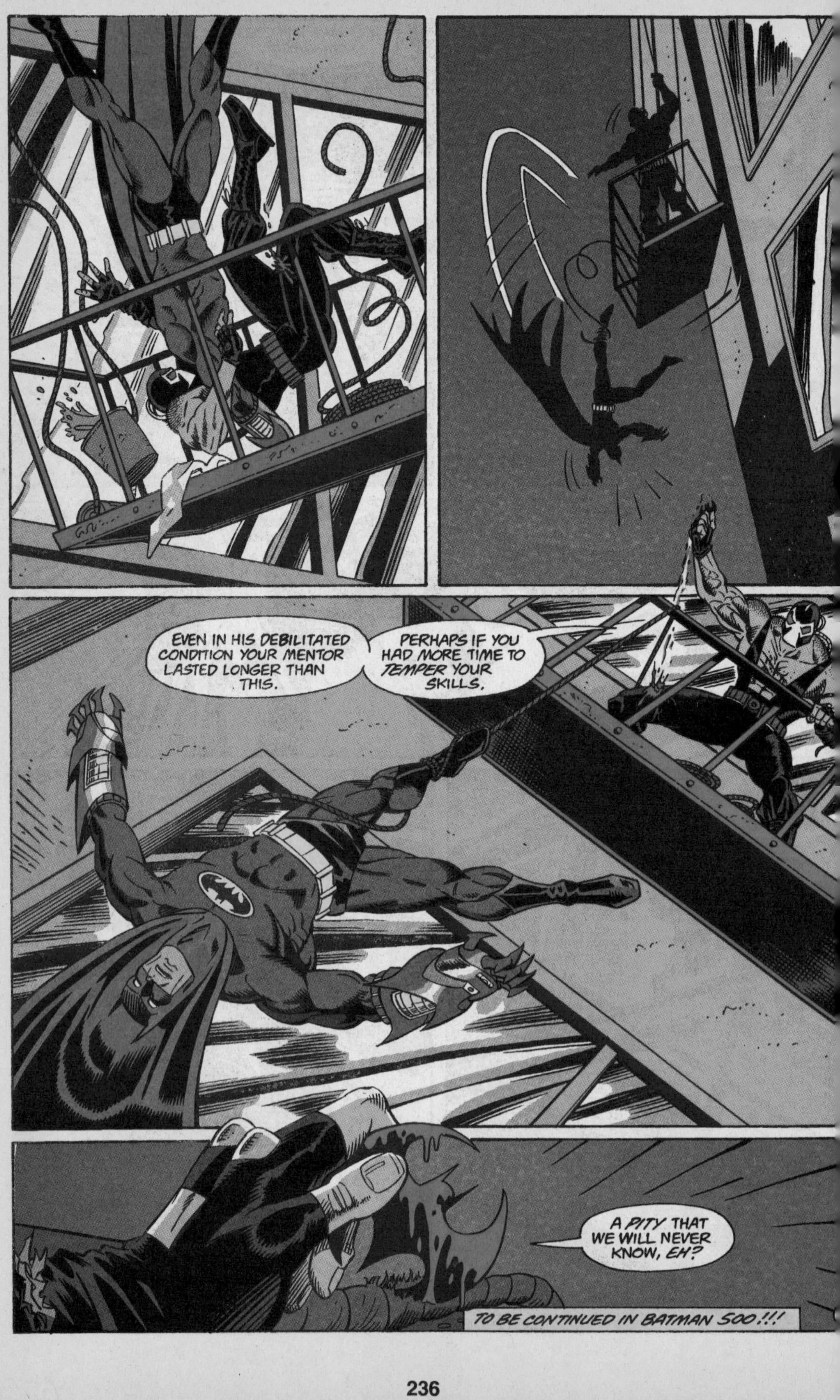
EVEN IN HIS DEBILITATED CONDITION YOUR MENTOR LASTED LONGER THAN THIS.
PERHAPS IF YOU HAD MORE TIME TO TEMPER YOUR SKILLS.
A PITY THAT WE WILL NEVER KNOW, EH?
TO BE CONTINUED IN BATMAN 500!!!

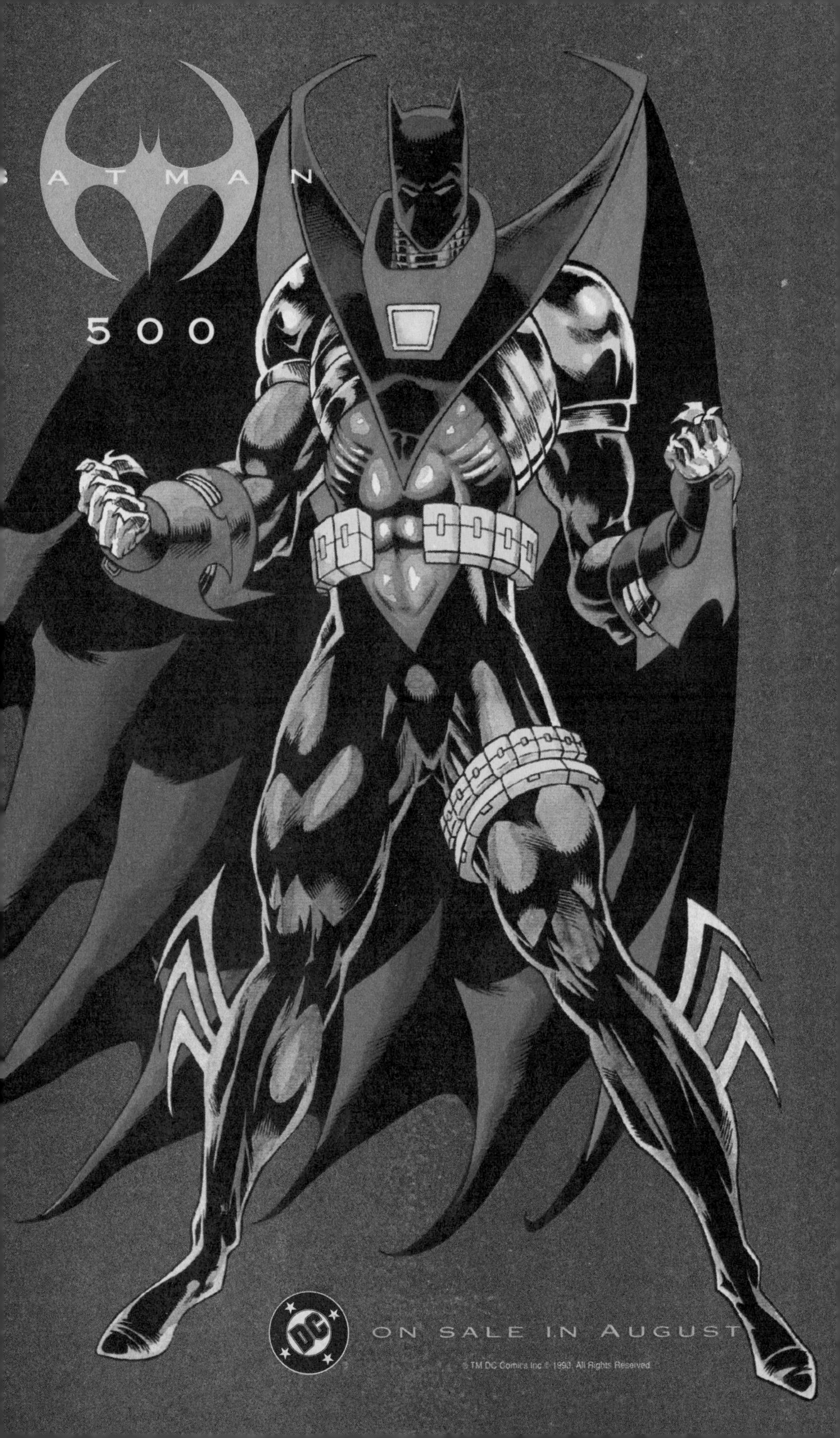

ATMAN
500
ON SALE IN AUGUST
® TM DC Comics Inc © 1993. All Rights Reserved

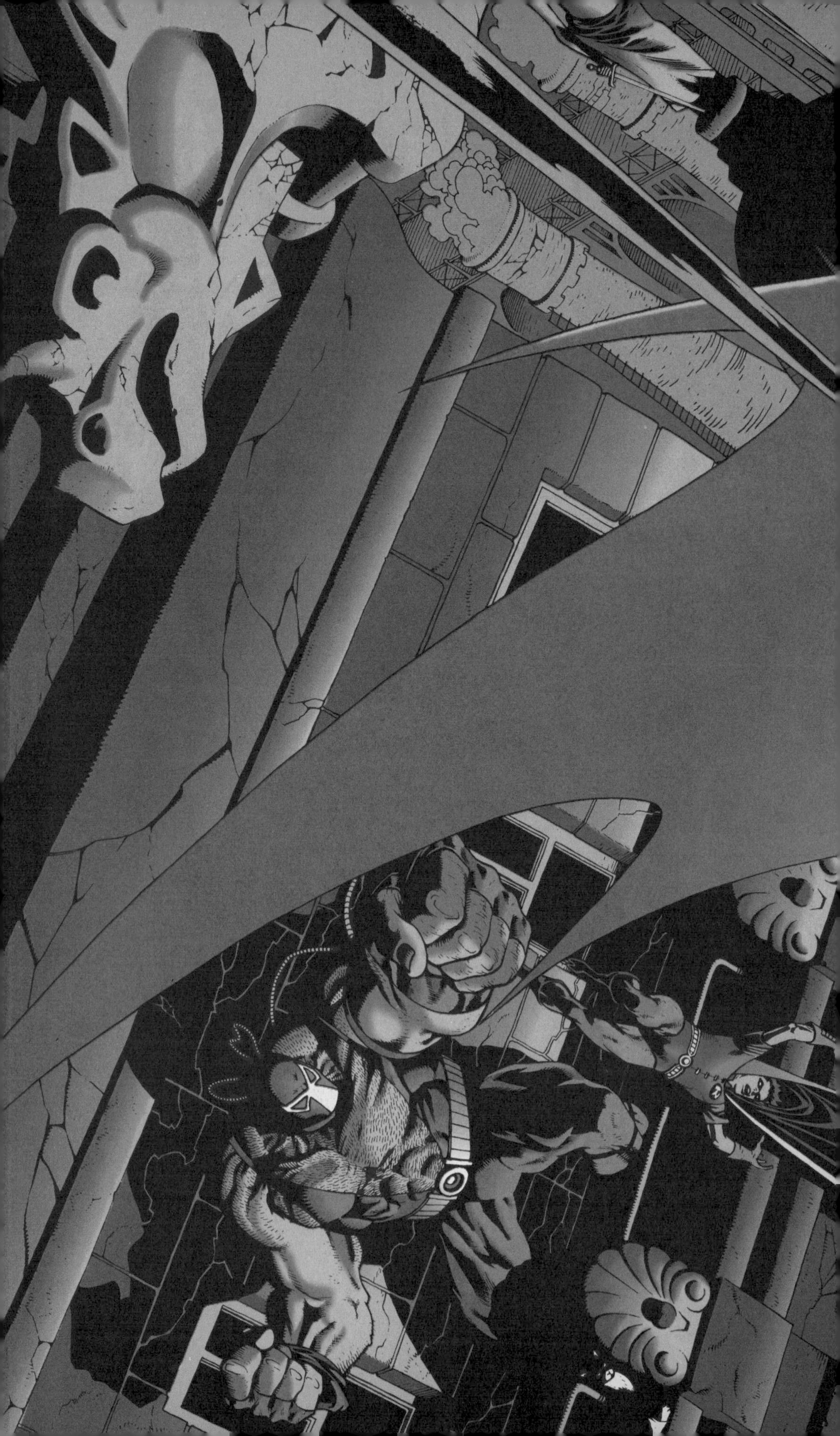

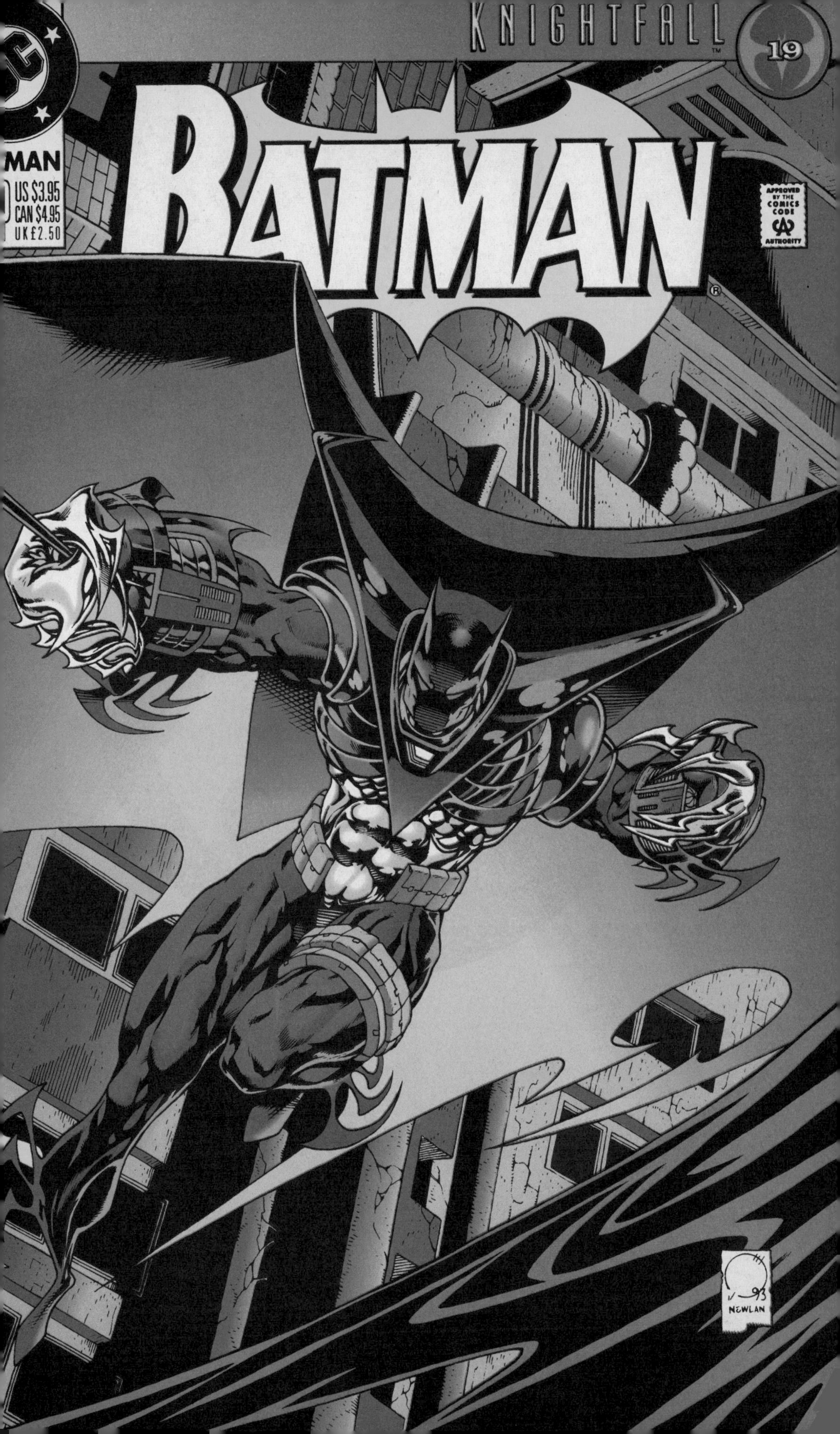
KNIGHTFALL
19
BATMAN
MAN
US $3.95
CAN $4.95
UK £2.50
APPROVED BY THE COMICS CODE AUTHORITY
NEWLAN

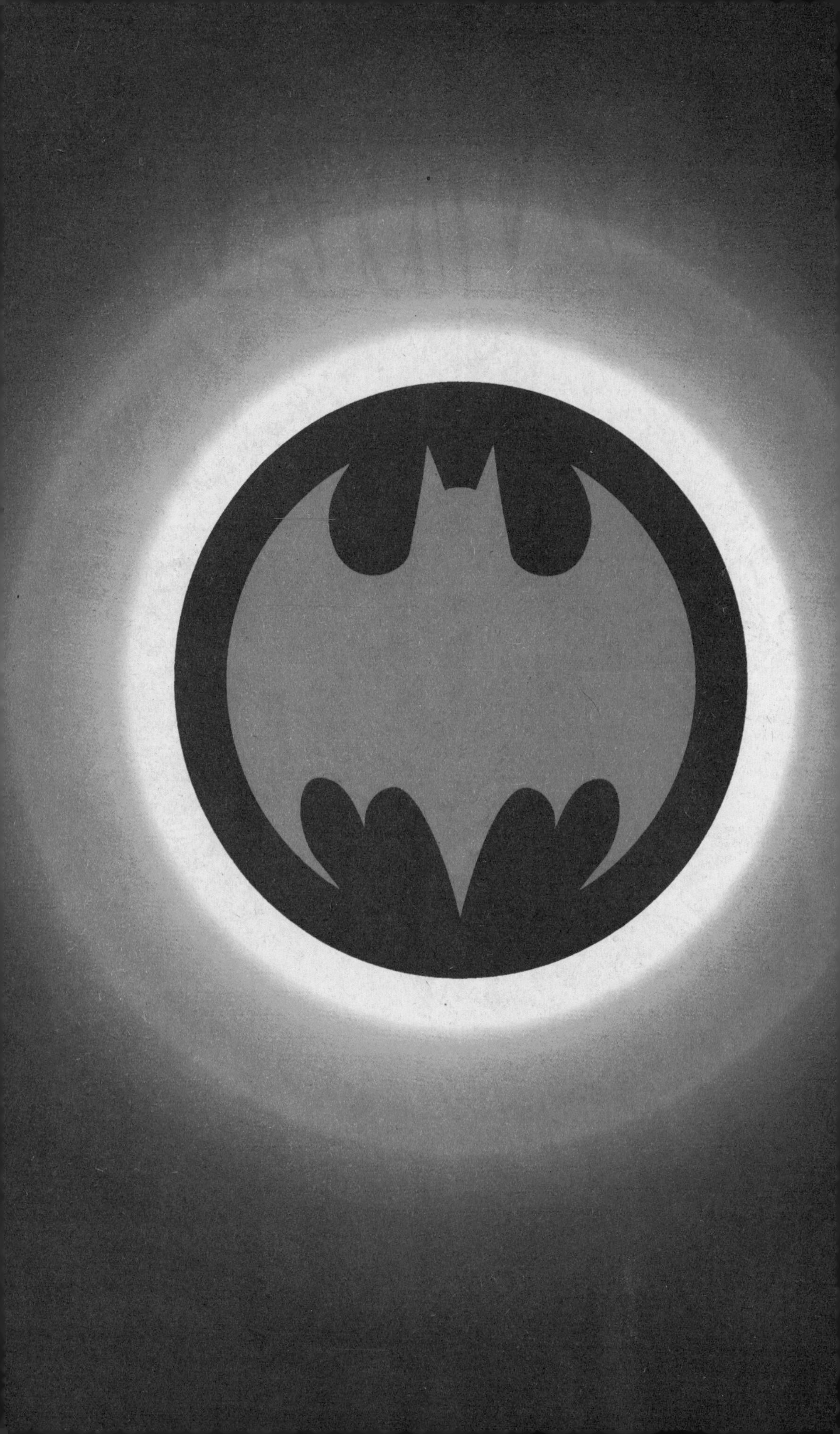

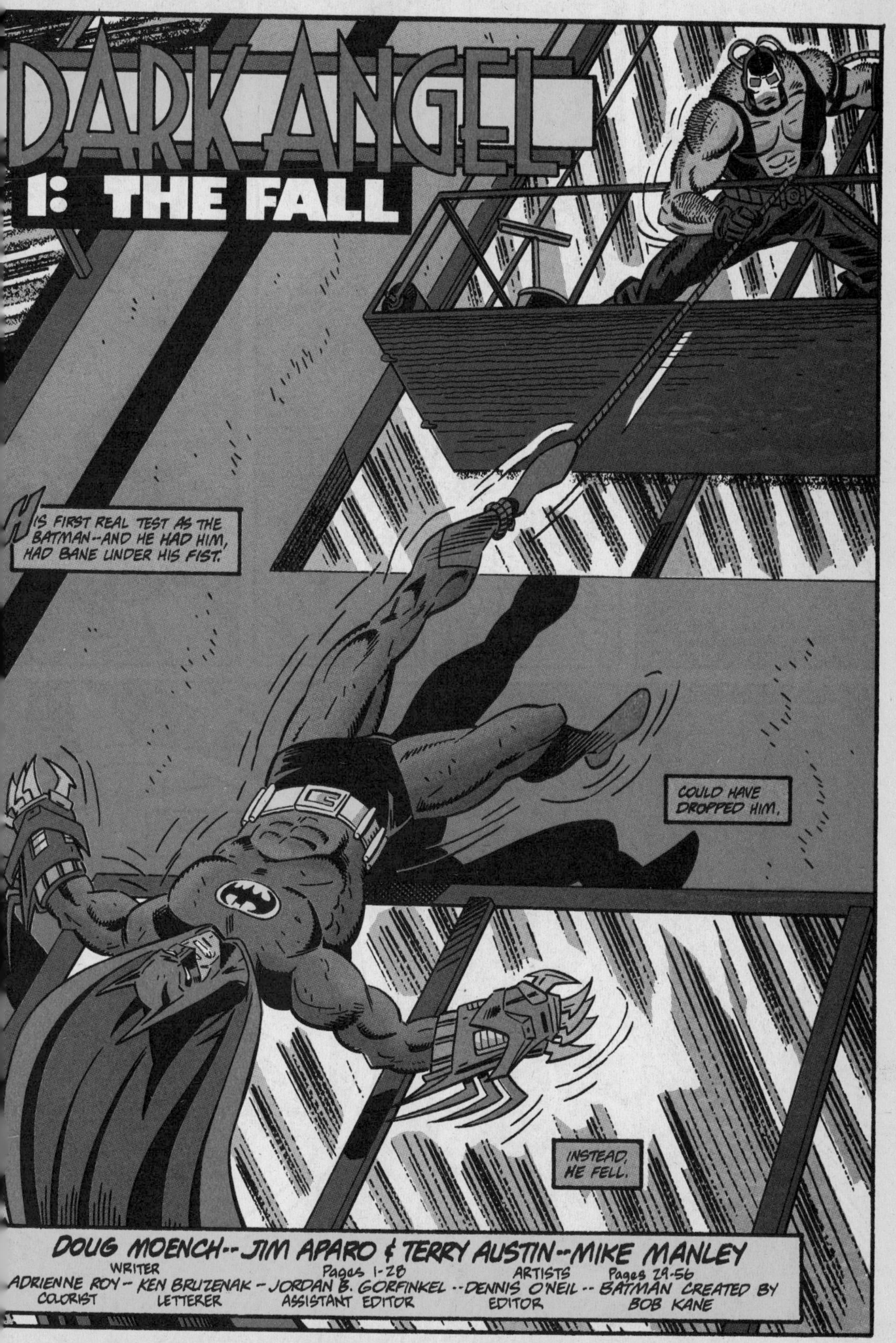
DARK ANGEL
1: THE FALL
HIS FIRST REAL TEST AS THE BATMAN--AND HE HAD HIM, HAD BANE UNDER HIS FIST.
COULD HAVE DROPPED HIM.
INSTEAD, HE FELL.
DOUG MOENCH--JIM APARO & TERRY AUSTIN--MIKE MANLEY
WRITER Pages 1-28 ARTISTS Pages 29-56
ADRIENNE ROY-KEN BRUZENAK-JORDAN B. GORFINKEL--DENNIS O'NEIL--BATMAN CREATED BY
COLORIST LETTERER ASSISTANT EDITOR EDITOR BOB KANE

AND NOW BANE IS USING A SHURIKEN-- ONE OF HIS OWN NEW WEAPONS--TO MAKE THE FALL PERMANENT.

WRNCH

RNCH

TO HELL WITH BUYING TIME.

HE TRIES TO SMASH AND GRAB IT, SHOOTING MORE OF THE BLADES.

SHING

SHING

SHING

DRIVING BANE BACK.

PRESERVING THE ROPE.

CHICH

CHU

SHING

THE RESPITE WON'T LAST LONG. HE MUST PULL HIMSELF UP SWIFTLY--BUT SMOOTHLY, WITH NO LURCHES.

THE ROPE IS ALREADY FRAYED.

CAN'T RISK MAKING IT--

SPLAP

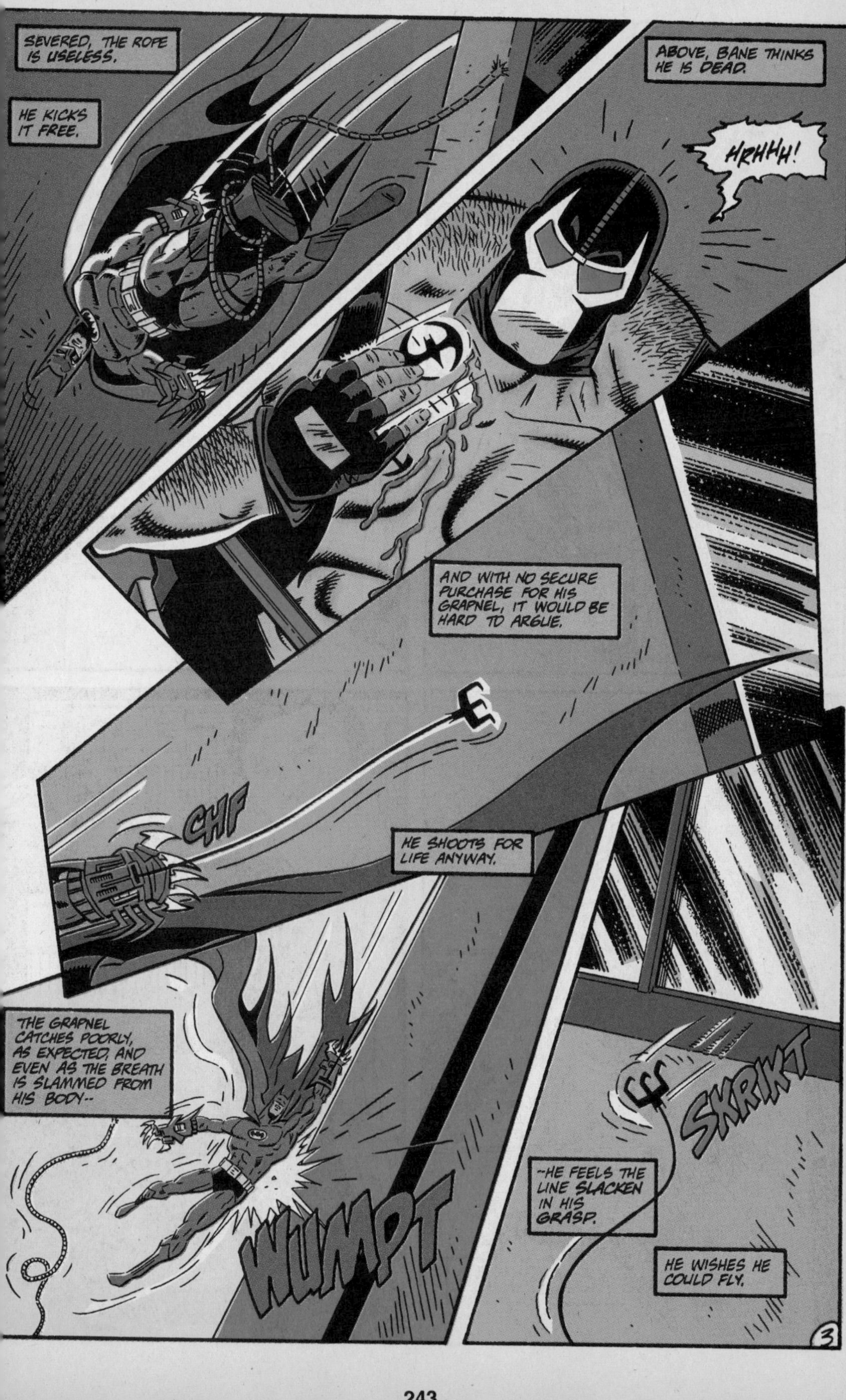
SEVERED, THE ROPE IS USELESS.
HE KICKS IT FREE.
ABOVE, BANE THINKS HE IS DEAD.
HRHHH!
AND WITH NO SECURE PURCHASE FOR HIS GRAPNEL, IT WOULD BE HARD TO ARGUE.
CHF
HE SHOOTS FOR LIFE ANYWAY.
THE GRAPNEL CATCHES POORLY, AS EXPECTED, AND EVEN AS THE BREATH IS SLAMMED FROM HIS BODY--
WUMPT
SKRIKT
--HE FEELS THE LINE SLACKEN IN HIS GRASP.
HE WISHES HE COULD FLY.
3

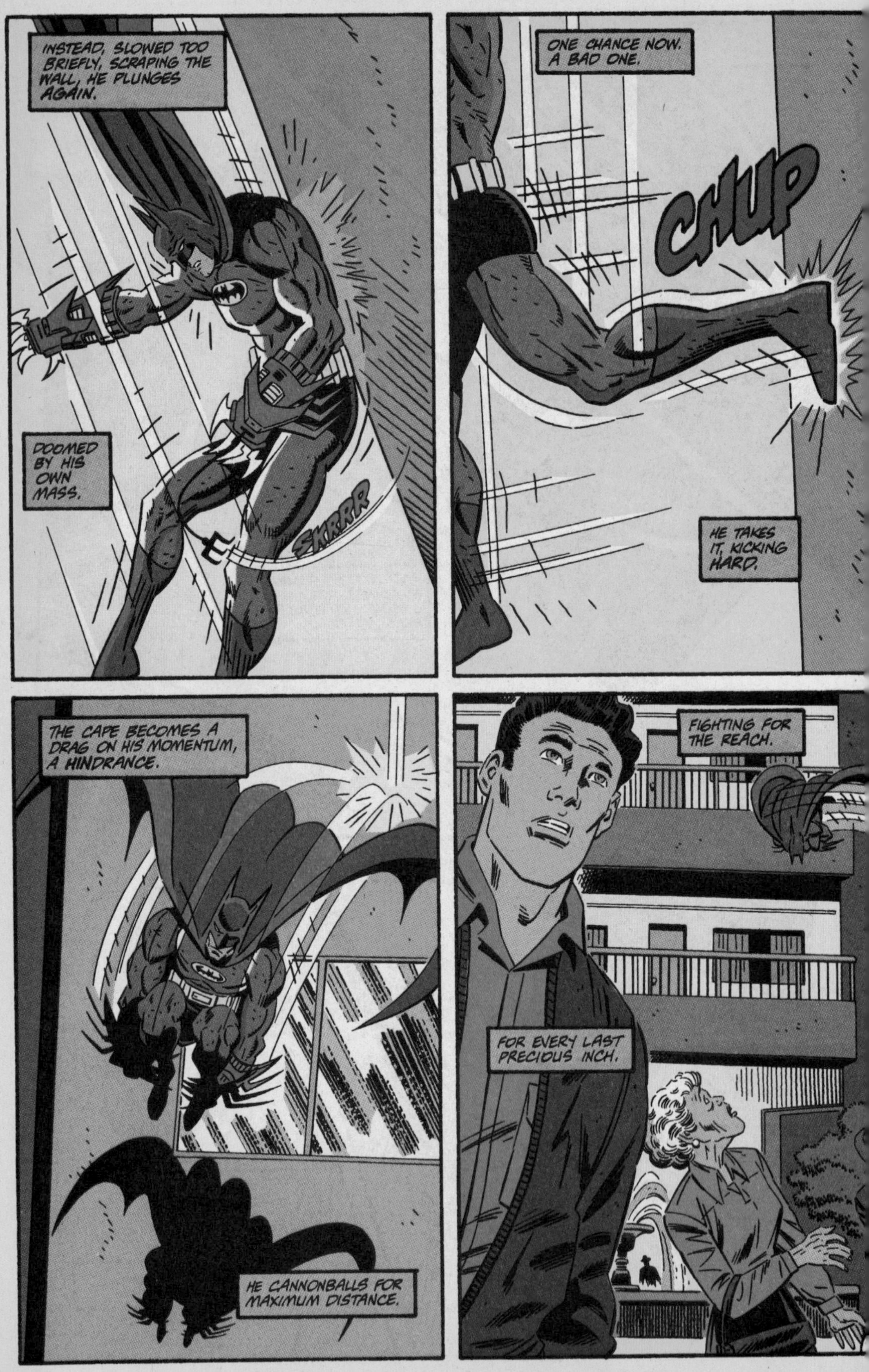
INSTEAD, SLOWED TOO BRIEFLY, SCRAPING THE WALL, HE PLUNGES AGAIN.
DOOMED BY HIS OWN MASS.
SKRRR
ONE CHANCE NOW. A BAD ONE.
CHUP
HE TAKES IT, KICKING HARD.
THE CAPE BECOMES A DRAG ON HIS MOMENTUM, A HINDRANCE.
HE CANNONBALLS FOR MAXIMUM DISTANCE.
FIGHTING FOR THE REACH.
FOR EVERY LAST PRECIOUS INCH.

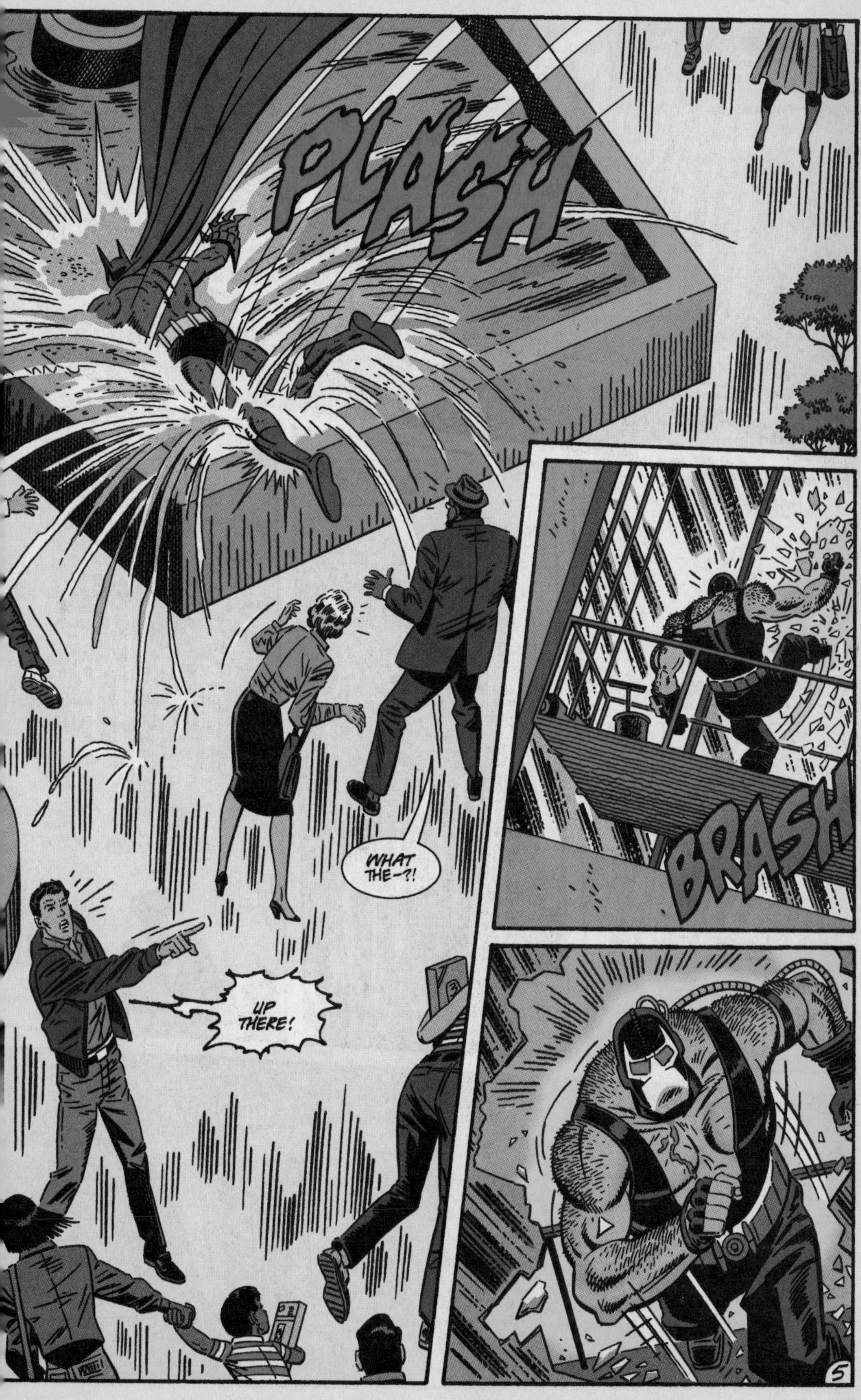
PLASH
WHAT THE-?!
UP THERE!
BRASH
5

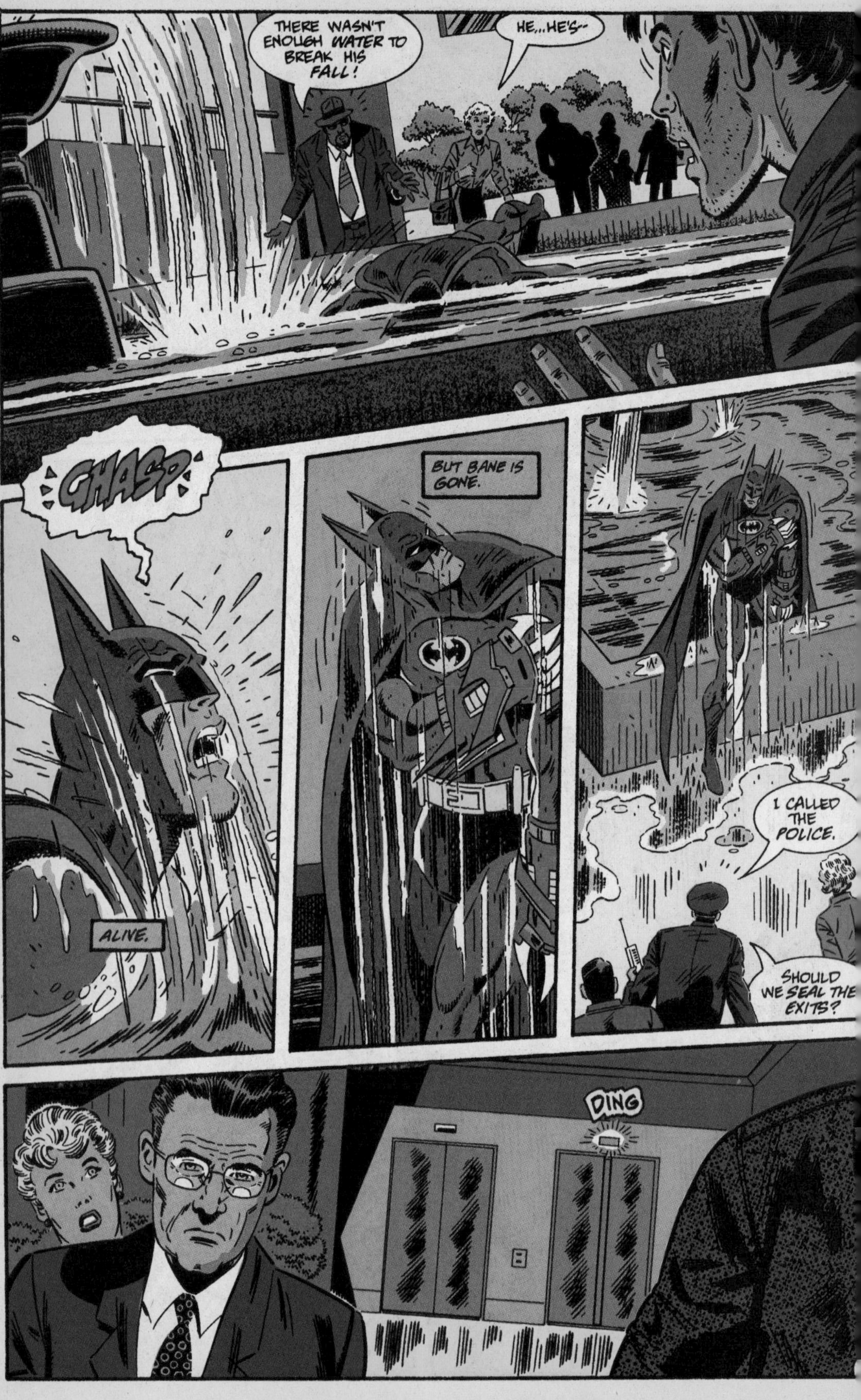
THERE WASN'T ENOUGH WATER TO BREAK HIS FALL!
HE... HE'S--
GHASP
ALIVE.
BUT BANE IS GONE.
I CALLED THE POLICE.
SHOULD WE SEAL THE EXITS?
DING

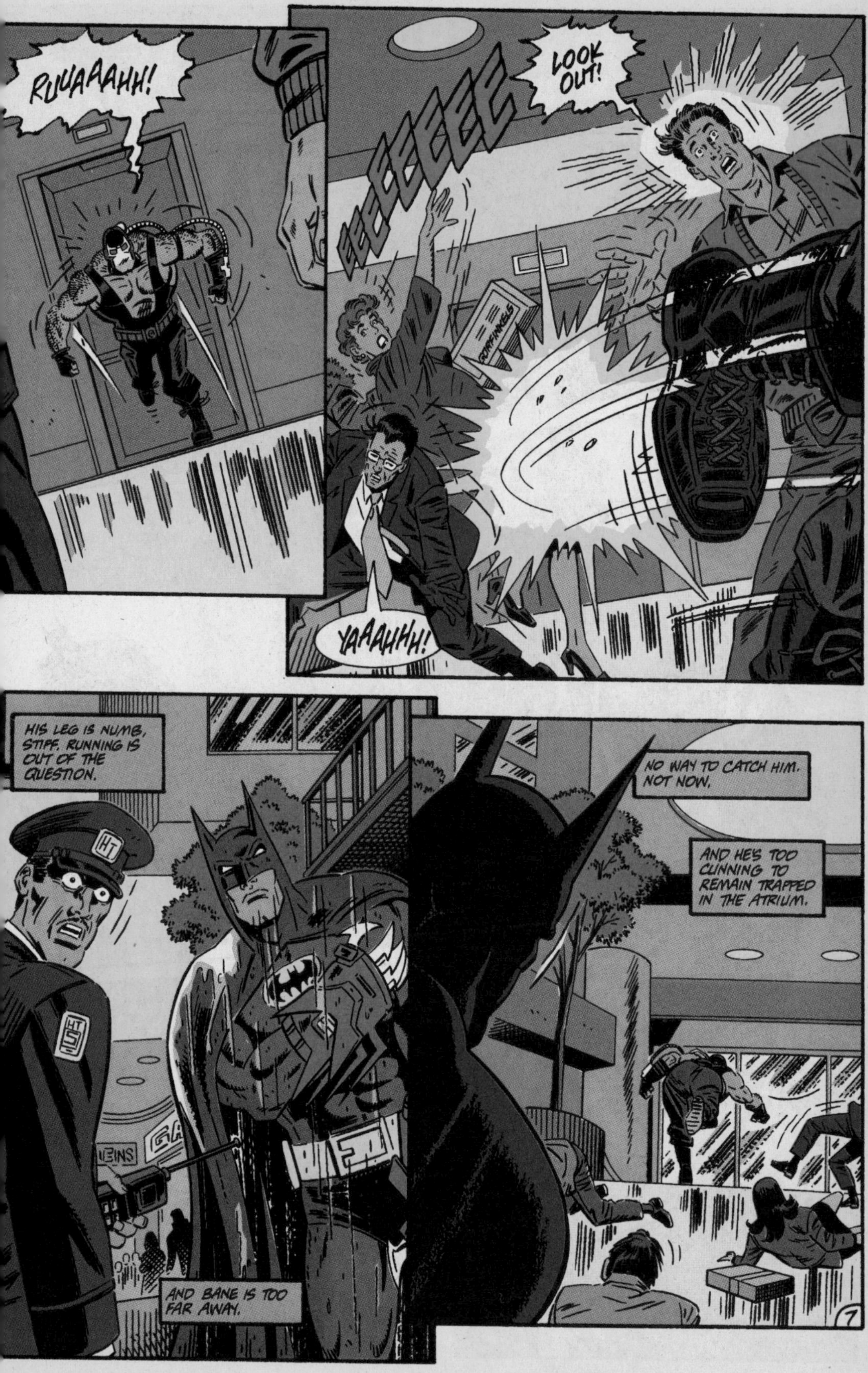
RUUAAAHH!
EEEEEEEEE
LOOK OUT!
GOTTFINKELS
YAAAHHH!
HIS LEG IS NUMB, STIFF. RUNNING IS OUT OF THE QUESTION.
AND BANE IS TOO FAR AWAY.
NO WAY TO CATCH HIM. NOT NOW.
AND HE'S TOO CUNNING TO REMAIN TRAPPED IN THE ATRIUM.
7

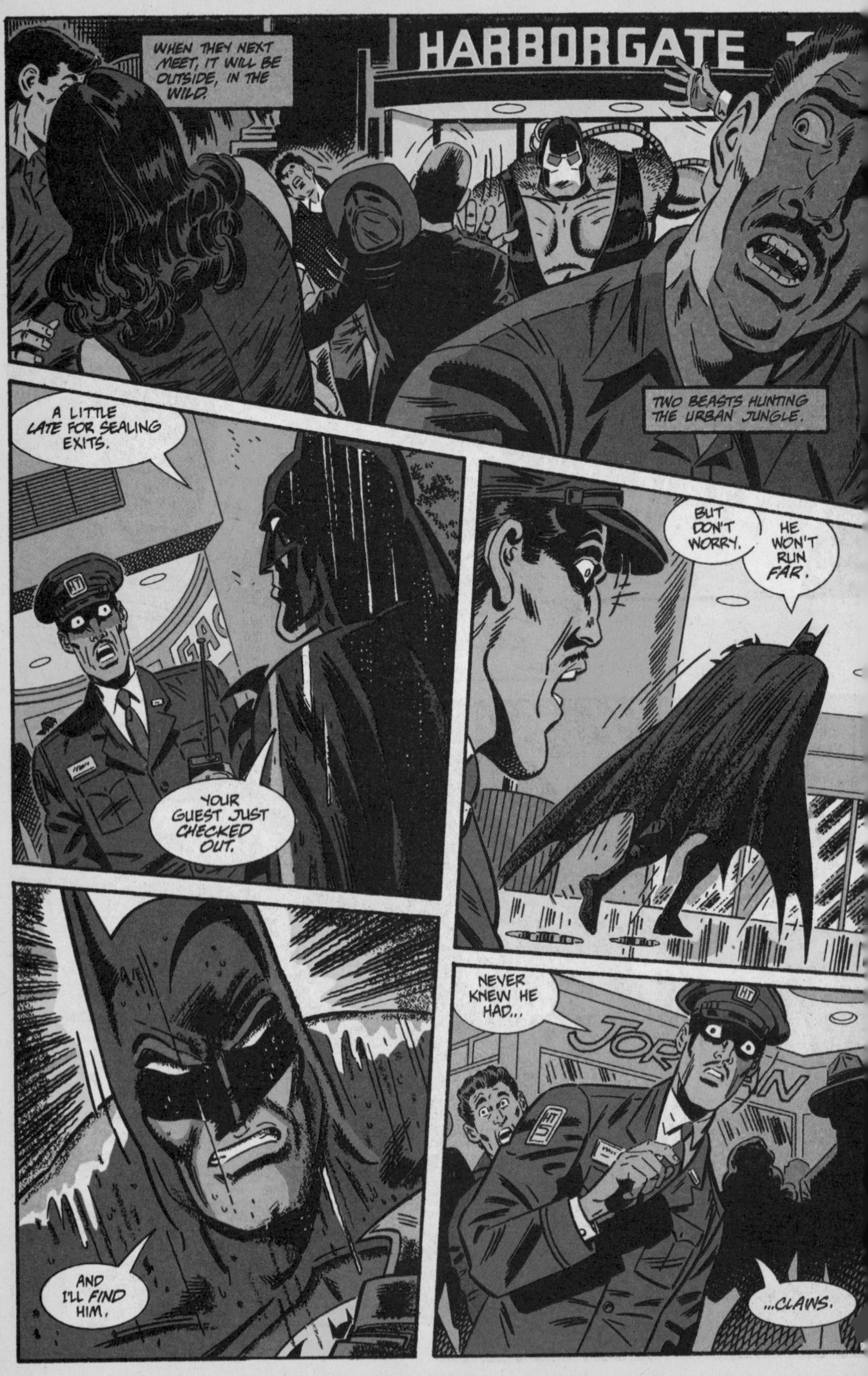
HARBORGATE
WHEN THEY NEXT MEET, IT WILL BE OUTSIDE, IN THE WILD.
TWO BEASTS HUNTING THE URBAN JUNGLE.
A LITTLE LATE FOR SEALING EXITS.
YOUR GUEST JUST CHECKED OUT.
BUT DON'T WORRY.
HE WON'T RUN FAR.
AND I'LL FIND HIM.
NEVER KNEW HE HAD...
...CLAWS.

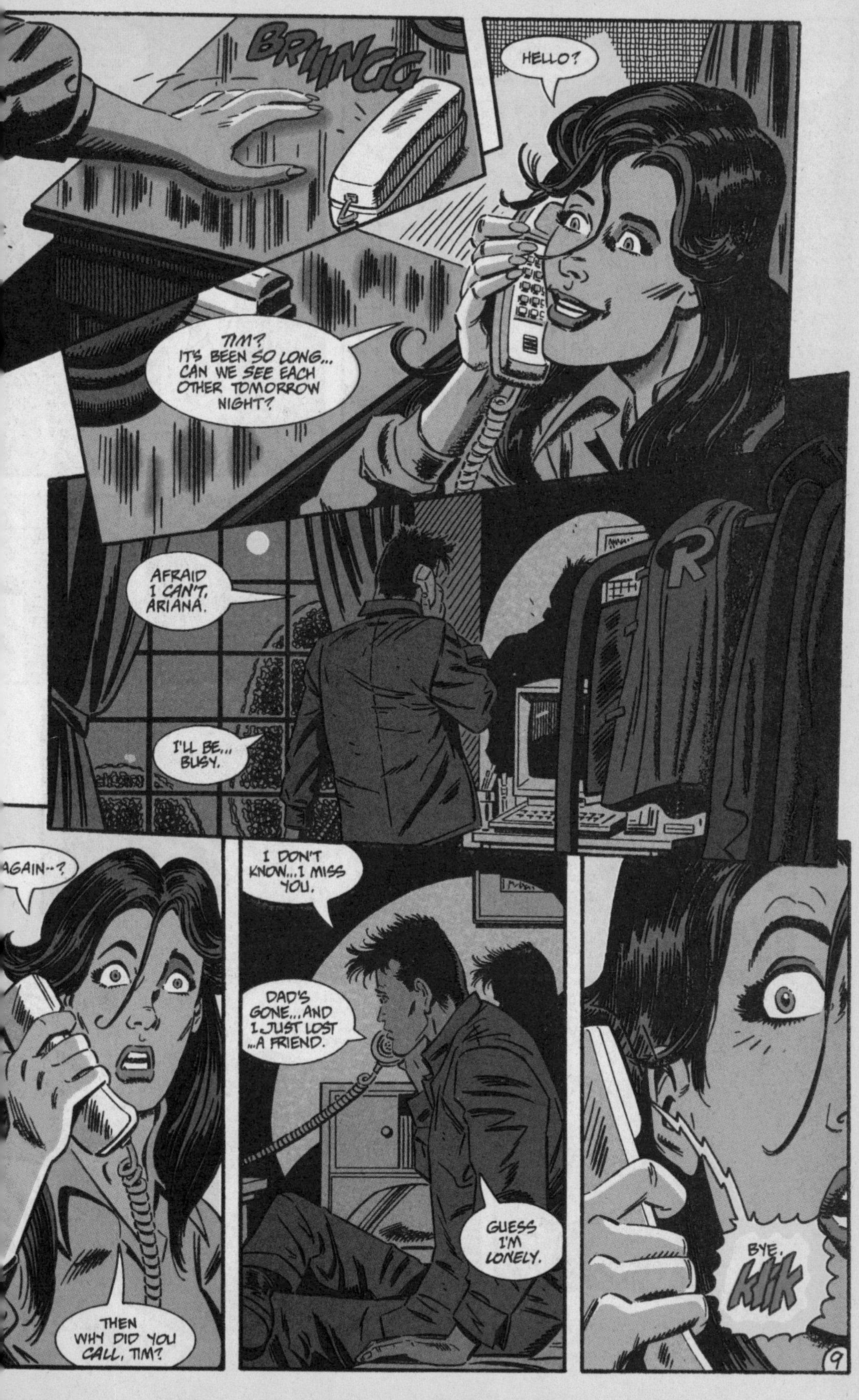
BRIIINGG
HELLO?
TIM? IT'S BEEN SO LONG... CAN WE SEE EACH OTHER TOMORROW NIGHT?
AFRAID I CAN'T, ARIANA.
I'LL BE... BUSY.
AGAIN--?
THEN WHY DID YOU CALL, TIM?
I DON'T KNOW...I MISS YOU.
DAD'S GONE...AND I JUST LOST ...A FRIEND.
GUESS I'M LONELY.
BYE.
klik
9

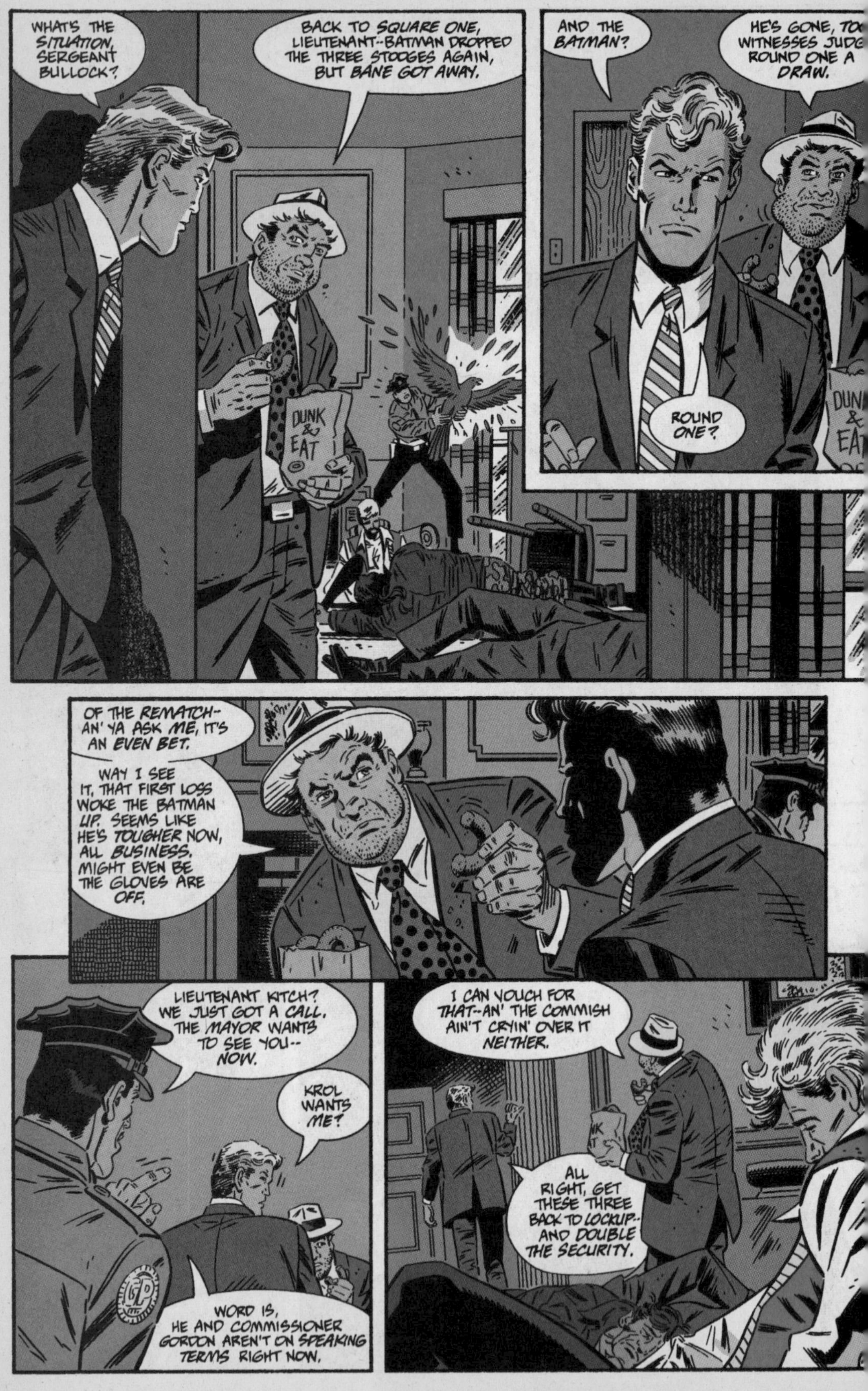
WHAT'S THE SITUATION, SERGEANT BULLOCK?
BACK TO SQUARE ONE, LIEUTENANT--BATMAN DROPPED THE THREE STOOGES AGAIN, BUT BANE GOT AWAY.
DUNK & EAT
AND THE BATMAN?
HE'S GONE, TO
WITNESSES JUDG
ROUND ONE A DRAW.
ROUND ONE?
OF THE REMATCH-- AN' YA ASK ME, IT'S AN EVEN BET.
WAY I SEE IT, THAT FIRST LOSS WOKE THE BATMAN UP. SEEMS LIKE HE'S TOUGHER NOW, ALL BUSINESS. MIGHT EVEN BE THE GLOVES ARE OFF.
LIEUTENANT KITCH? WE JUST GOT A CALL. THE MAYOR WANTS TO SEE YOU-- NOW.
KROL WANTS ME?
WORD IS, HE AND COMMISSIONER GORDON AREN'T ON SPEAKING TERMS RIGHT NOW.
I CAN VOUCH FOR THAT--AN' THE COMMISH AIN'T CRYIN' OVER IT NEITHER.
ALL RIGHT, GET THESE THREE BACK TO LOCKUP.. AND DOUBLE THE SECURITY.

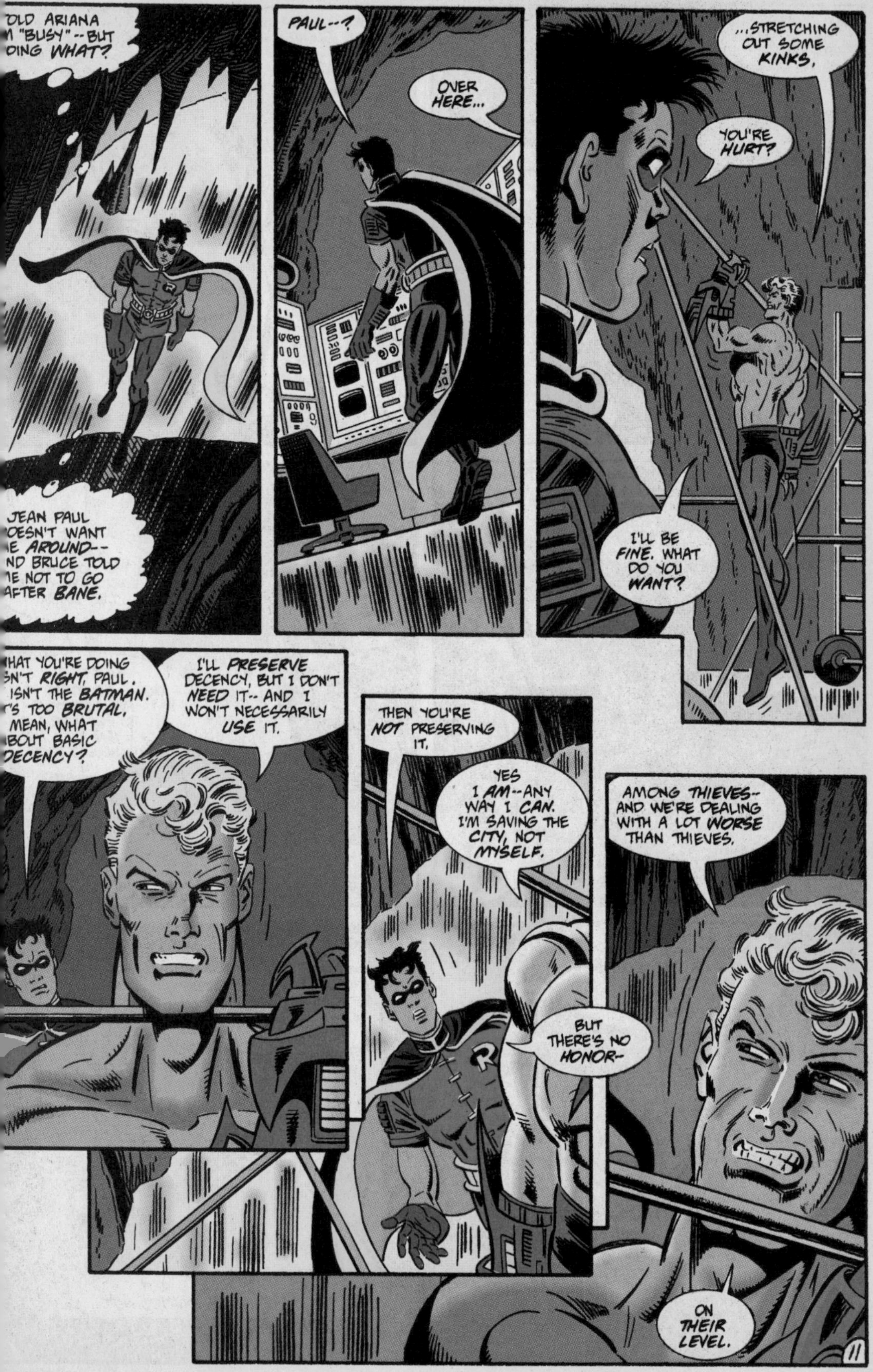

OLD ARIANA
M "BUSY"--BUT
OING WHAT?
JEAN PAUL
OESN'T WANT
E AROUND--
ND BRUCE TOLD
E NOT TO GO
AFTER BANE.
PAUL--?
OVER HERE...
...STRETCHING OUT SOME KINKS.
YOU'RE HURT?
I'LL BE FINE. WHAT DO YOU WANT?
HAT YOU'RE DOING
N'T RIGHT, PAUL.
ISN'T THE BATMAN.
'S TOO BRUTAL.
MEAN, WHAT
BOUT BASIC
ECENCY?
I'LL PRESERVE DECENCY, BUT I DON'T NEED IT-- AND I WON'T NECESSARILY USE IT.
THEN YOU'RE NOT PRESERVING IT.
YES I AM--ANY WAY I CAN. I'M SAVING THE CITY, NOT MYSELF.
BUT THERE'S NO HONOR-
AMONG THIEVES-- AND WE'RE DEALING WITH A LOT WORSE THAN THIEVES.
ON THEIR LEVEL.
11

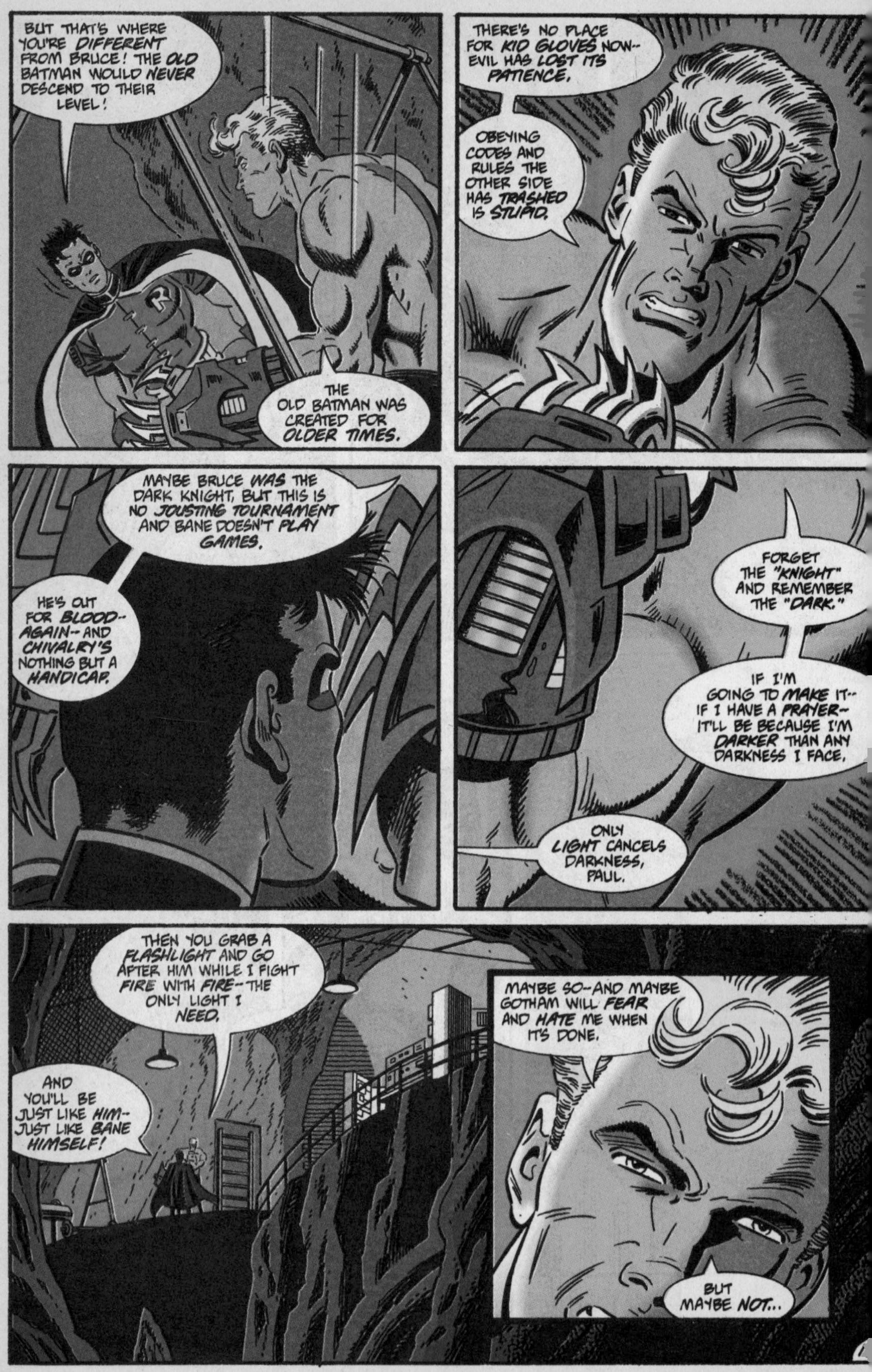
BUT THAT'S WHERE YOU'RE DIFFERENT FROM BRUCE! THE OLD BATMAN WOULD NEVER DESCEND TO THEIR LEVEL!
THE OLD BATMAN WAS CREATED FOR OLDER TIMES.
THERE'S NO PLACE FOR KID GLOVES NOW-- EVIL HAS LOST ITS PATIENCE.
OBEYING CODES AND RULES THE OTHER SIDE HAS TRASHED IS STUPID.
MAYBE BRUCE WAS THE DARK KNIGHT, BUT THIS IS NO JOUSTING TOURNAMENT AND BANE DOESN'T PLAY GAMES.
HE'S OUT FOR BLOOD-- AGAIN-- AND CHIVALRY'S NOTHING BUT A HANDICAP.
FORGET THE "KNIGHT" AND REMEMBER THE "DARK."
IF I'M GOING TO MAKE IT-- IF I HAVE A PRAYER-- IT'LL BE BECAUSE I'M DARKER THAN ANY DARKNESS I FACE.
ONLY LIGHT CANCELS DARKNESS, PAUL.
THEN YOU GRAB A FLASHLIGHT AND GO AFTER HIM WHILE I FIGHT FIRE WITH FIRE-- THE ONLY LIGHT I NEED.
AND YOU'LL BE JUST LIKE HIM-- JUST LIKE BANE HIMSELF!
MAYBE SO--AND MAYBE GOTHAM WILL FEAR AND HATE ME WHEN IT'S DONE.
BUT MAYBE NOT...

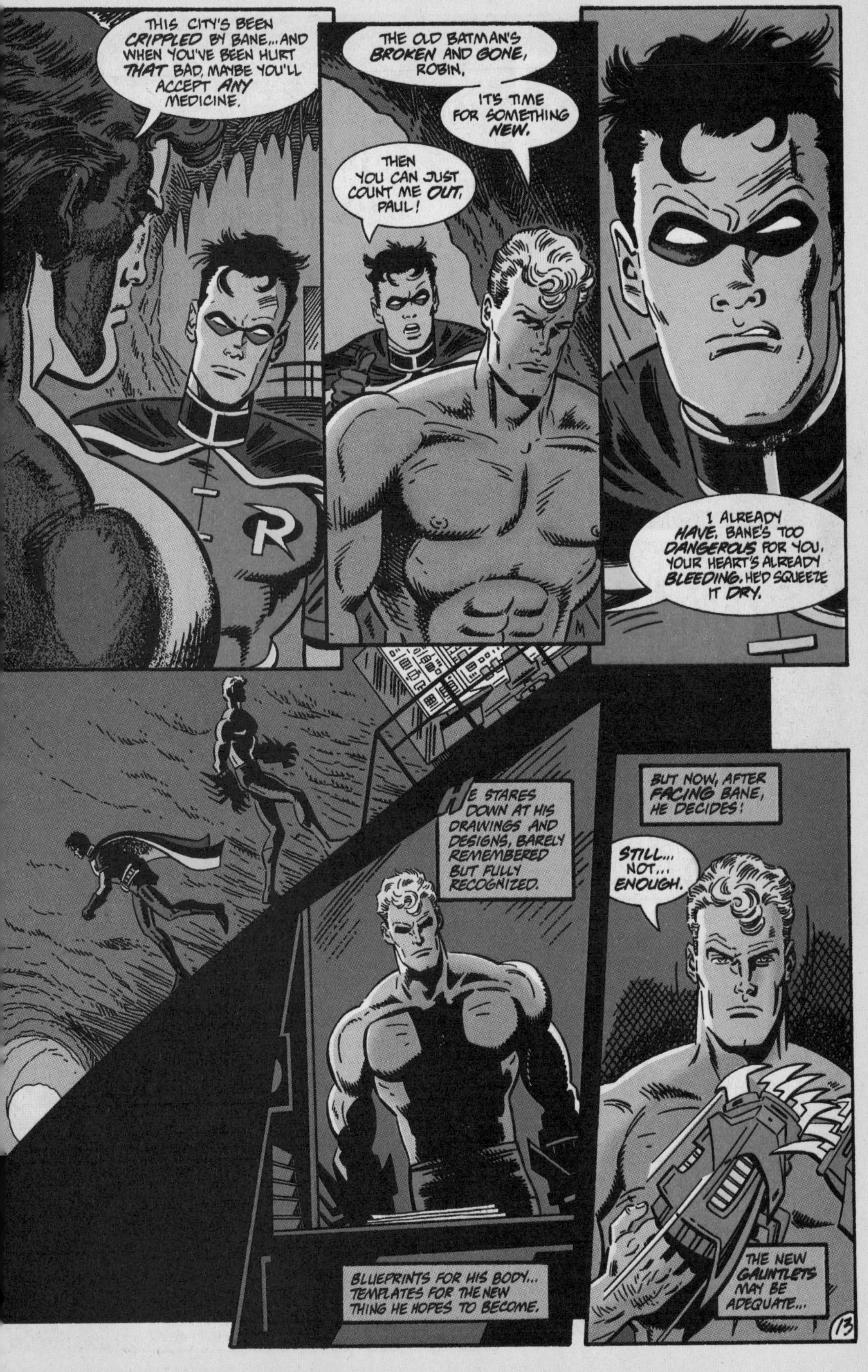
THIS CITY'S BEEN CRIPPLED BY BANE... AND WHEN YOU'VE BEEN HURT THAT BAD, MAYBE YOU'LL ACCEPT ANY MEDICINE.
THE OLD BATMAN'S BROKEN AND GONE, ROBIN.
IT'S TIME FOR SOMETHING NEW.
THEN YOU CAN JUST COUNT ME OUT, PAUL!
I ALREADY HAVE. BANE'S TOO DANGEROUS FOR YOU. YOUR HEART'S ALREADY BLEEDING. HE'D SQUEEZE IT DRY.
HE STARES DOWN AT HIS DRAWINGS AND DESIGNS, BARELY REMEMBERED BUT FULLY RECOGNIZED.
BLUEPRINTS FOR HIS BODY... TEMPLATES FOR THE NEW THING HE HOPES TO BECOME.
BUT NOW, AFTER FACING BANE, HE DECIDES:
STILL... NOT... ENOUGH.
THE NEW GAUNTLETS MAY BE ADEQUATE...
13

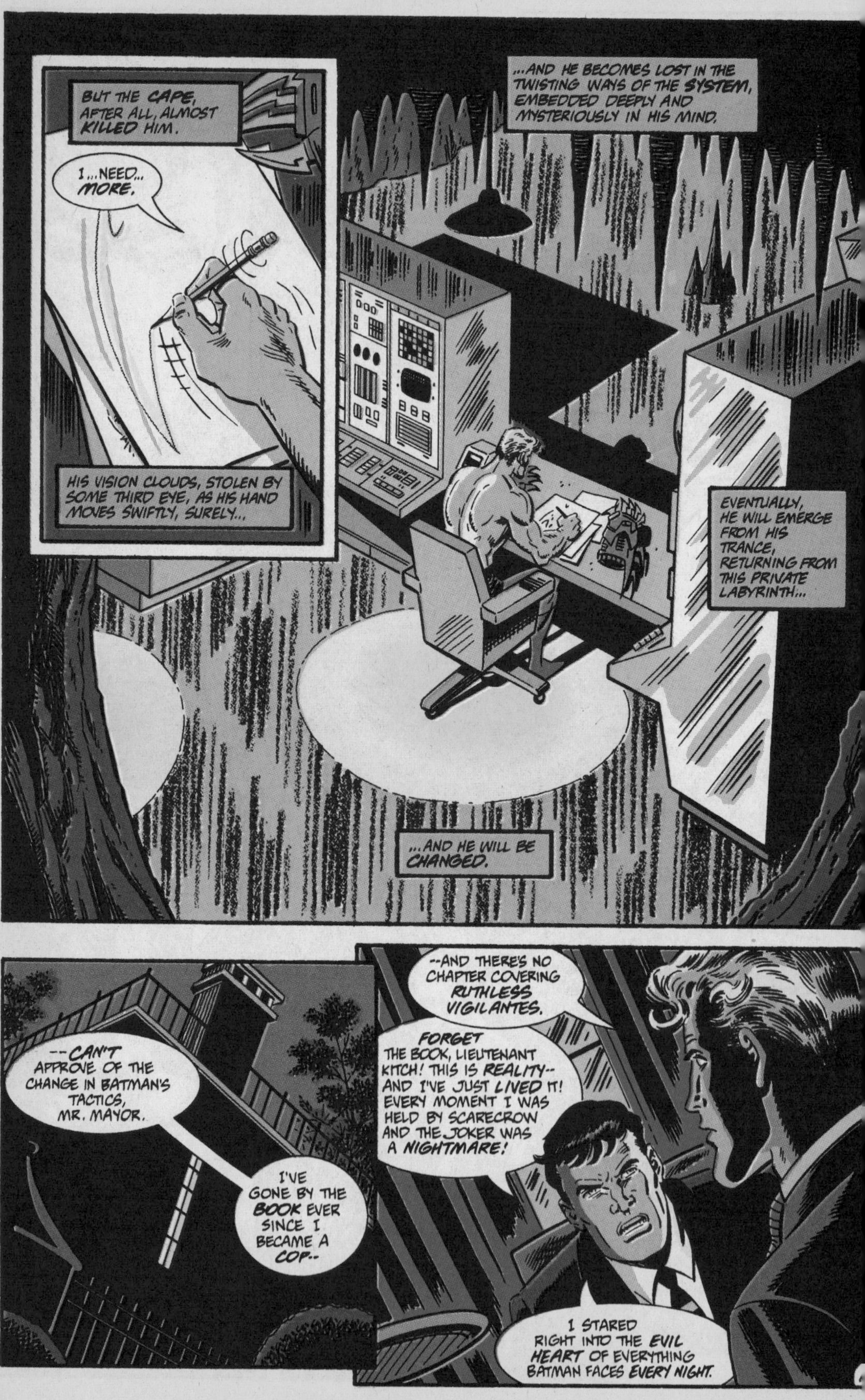
BUT THE CAPE, AFTER ALL, ALMOST KILLED HIM.
I...NEED... MORE.
HIS VISION CLOUDS, STOLEN BY SOME THIRD EYE, AS HIS HAND MOVES SWIFTLY, SURELY...
...AND HE BECOMES LOST IN THE TWISTING WAYS OF THE SYSTEM, EMBEDDED DEEPLY AND MYSTERIOUSLY IN HIS MIND.
EVENTUALLY, HE WILL EMERGE FROM HIS TRANCE, RETURNING FROM THIS PRIVATE LABYRINTH...
...AND HE WILL BE CHANGED.
--CAN'T APPROVE OF THE CHANGE IN BATMAN'S TACTICS, MR. MAYOR.
I'VE GONE BY THE BOOK EVER SINCE I BECAME A COP--
--AND THERE'S NO CHAPTER COVERING RUTHLESS VIGILANTES.
FORGET THE BOOK, LIEUTENANT KITCH! THIS IS REALITY-- AND I'VE JUST LIVED IT! EVERY MOMENT I WAS HELD BY SCARECROW AND THE JOKER WAS A NIGHTMARE!
I STARED RIGHT INTO THE EVIL HEART OF EVERYTHING BATMAN FACES EVERY NIGHT.

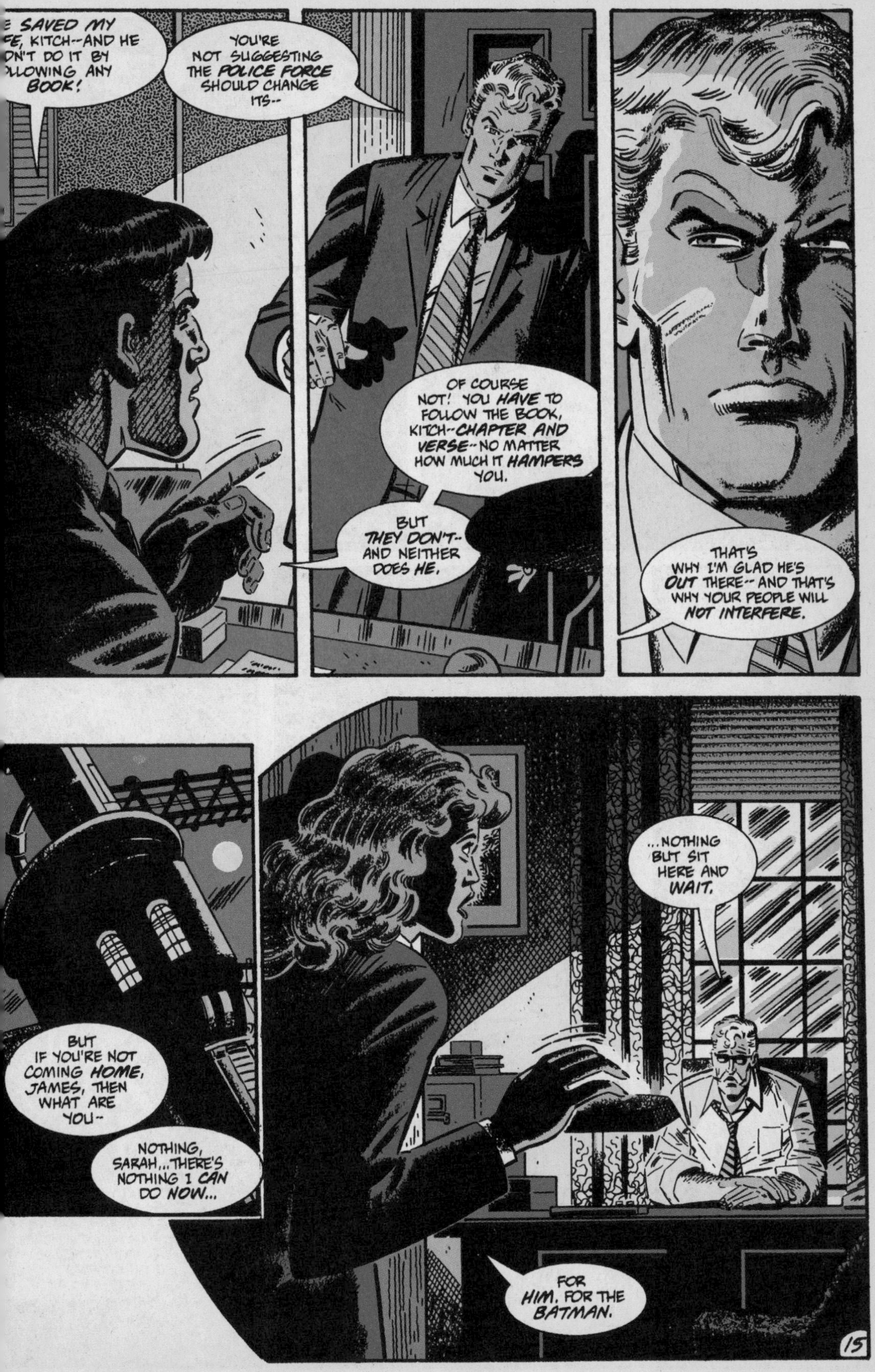

E SAVED MY FE, KITCH--AND HE DN'T DO IT BY LLOWING ANY BOOK!
YOU'RE NOT SUGGESTING THE POLICE FORCE SHOULD CHANGE ITS--
OF COURSE NOT! YOU HAVE TO FOLLOW THE BOOK, KITCH--CHAPTER AND VERSE--NO MATTER HOW MUCH IT HAMPERS YOU.
BUT THEY DON'T--AND NEITHER DOES HE.
THAT'S WHY I'M GLAD HE'S OUT THERE--AND THAT'S WHY YOUR PEOPLE WILL NOT INTERFERE.
BUT IF YOU'RE NOT COMING HOME, JAMES, THEN WHAT ARE YOU--
NOTHING, SARAH... THERE'S NOTHING I CAN DO NOW...
...NOTHING BUT SIT HERE AND WAIT.
FOR HIM. FOR THE BATMAN.
15

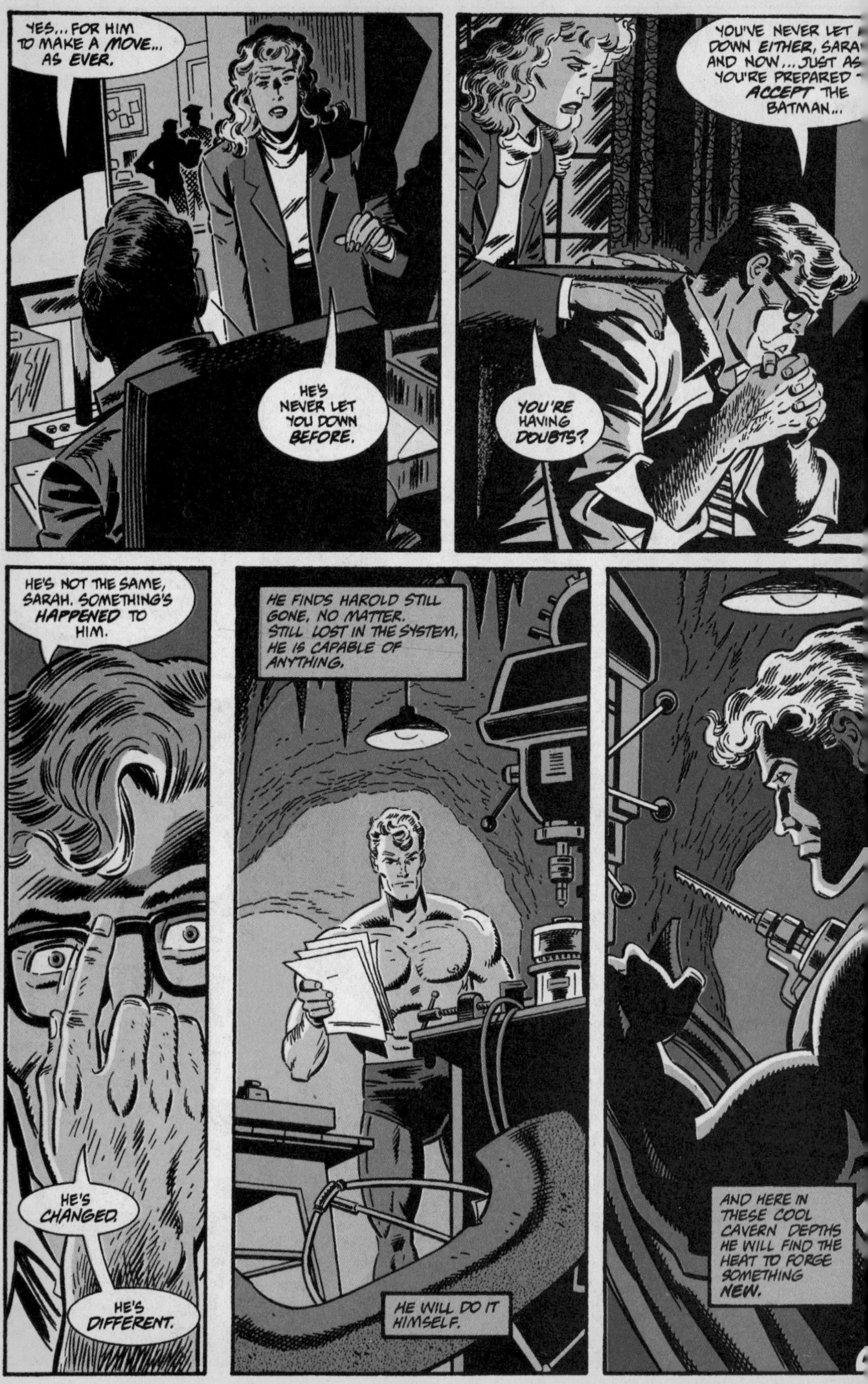
YES... FOR HIM TO MAKE A MOVE... AS EVER.
HE'S NEVER LET YOU DOWN BEFORE.
YOU'VE NEVER LET DOWN EITHER, SARA AND NOW... JUST AS YOU'RE PREPARED ACCEPT THE BATMAN...
YOU'RE HAVING DOUBTS?
HE'S NOT THE SAME, SARAH. SOMETHING'S HAPPENED TO HIM.
HE'S CHANGED.
HE'S DIFFERENT.
HE FINDS HAROLD STILL GONE, NO MATTER. STILL LOST IN THE SYSTEM, HE IS CAPABLE OF ANYTHING.
HE WILL DO IT HIMSELF.
AND HERE IN THESE COOL CAVERN DEPTHS HE WILL FIND THE HEAT TO FORGE SOMETHING NEW.

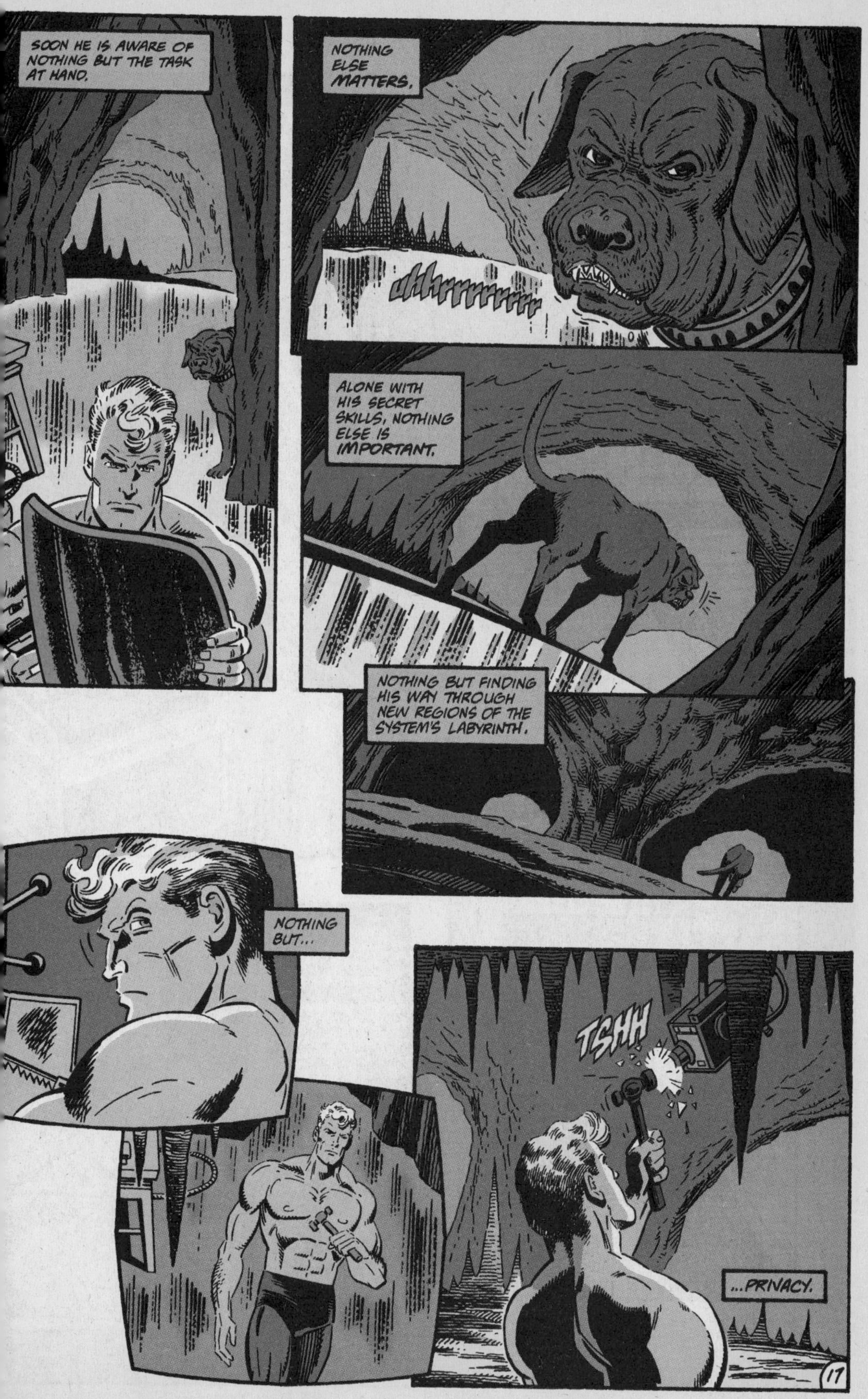
SOON HE IS AWARE OF NOTHING BUT THE TASK AT HAND.
NOTHING ELSE MATTERS.
uhhrrrrrrrrr
ALONE WITH HIS SECRET SKILLS, NOTHING ELSE IS IMPORTANT.
NOTHING BUT FINDING HIS WAY THROUGH NEW REGIONS OF THE SYSTEM'S LABYRINTH.
NOTHING BUT...
TSHH
...PRIVACY.
17

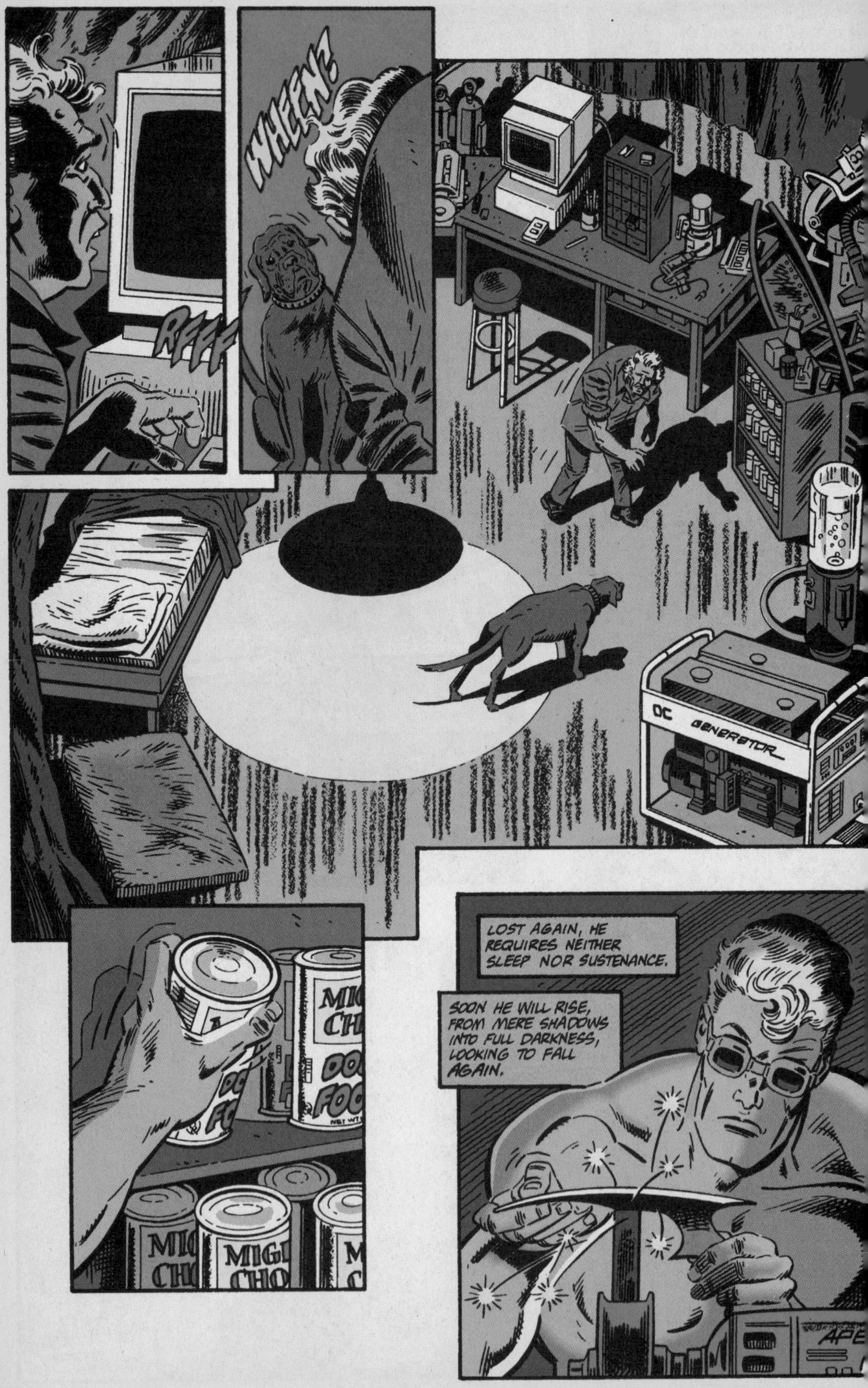
RFFF
WHEEEN!
DC GENERATOR
LOST AGAIN, HE REQUIRES NEITHER SLEEP NOR SUSTENANCE.
SOON HE WILL RISE, FROM MERE SHADOWS INTO FULL DARKNESS, LOOKING TO FALL AGAIN.

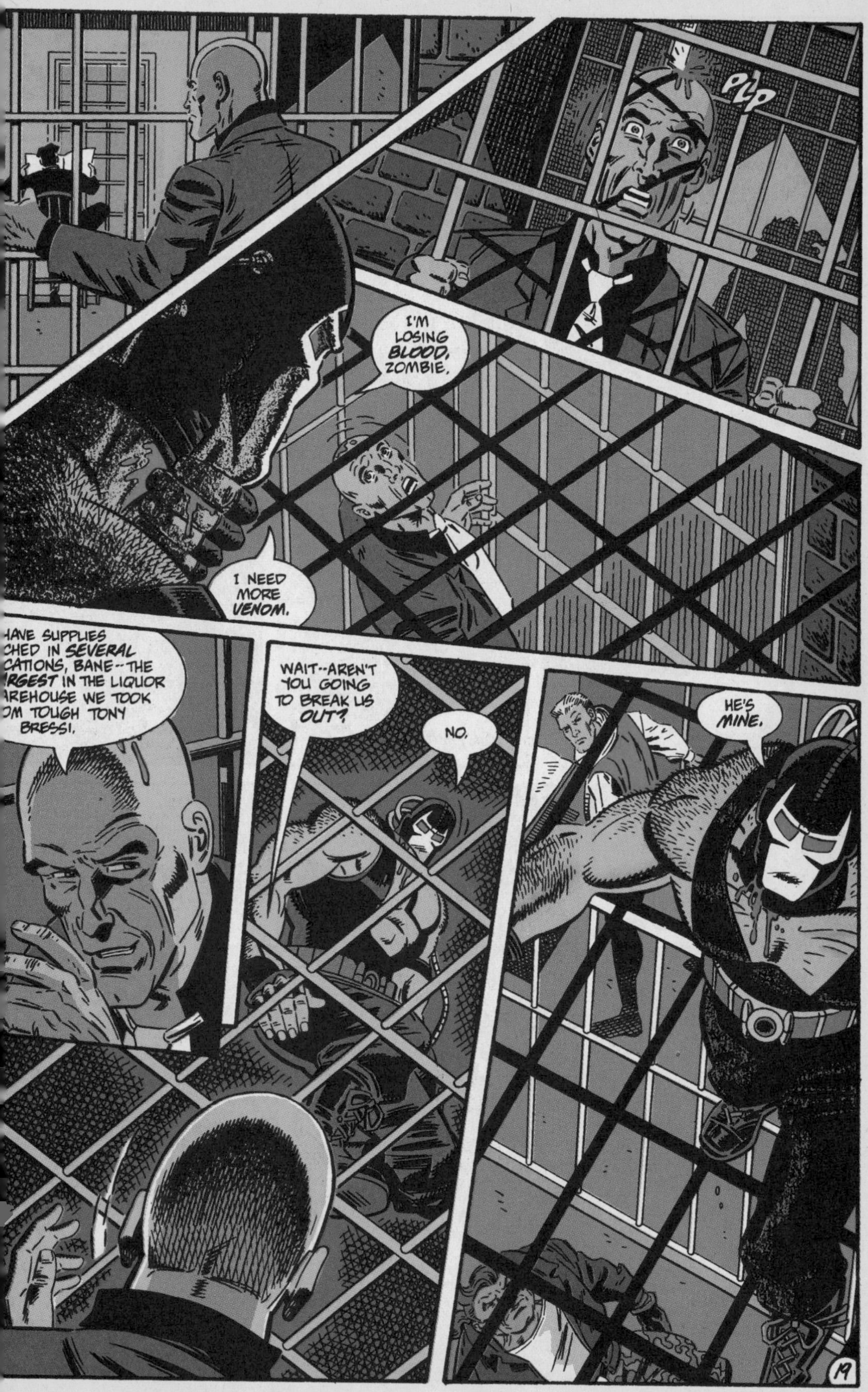
PLIP
I'M LOSING BLOOD, ZOMBIE.
I NEED MORE VENOM.
HAVE SUPPLIES
CHED IN SEVERAL
CATIONS, BANE-- THE
RGEST IN THE LIQUOR
AREHOUSE WE TOOK
OM TOUGH TONY
BRESSI.
WAIT--AREN'T YOU GOING TO BREAK US OUT?
NO.
HE'S MINE.
19

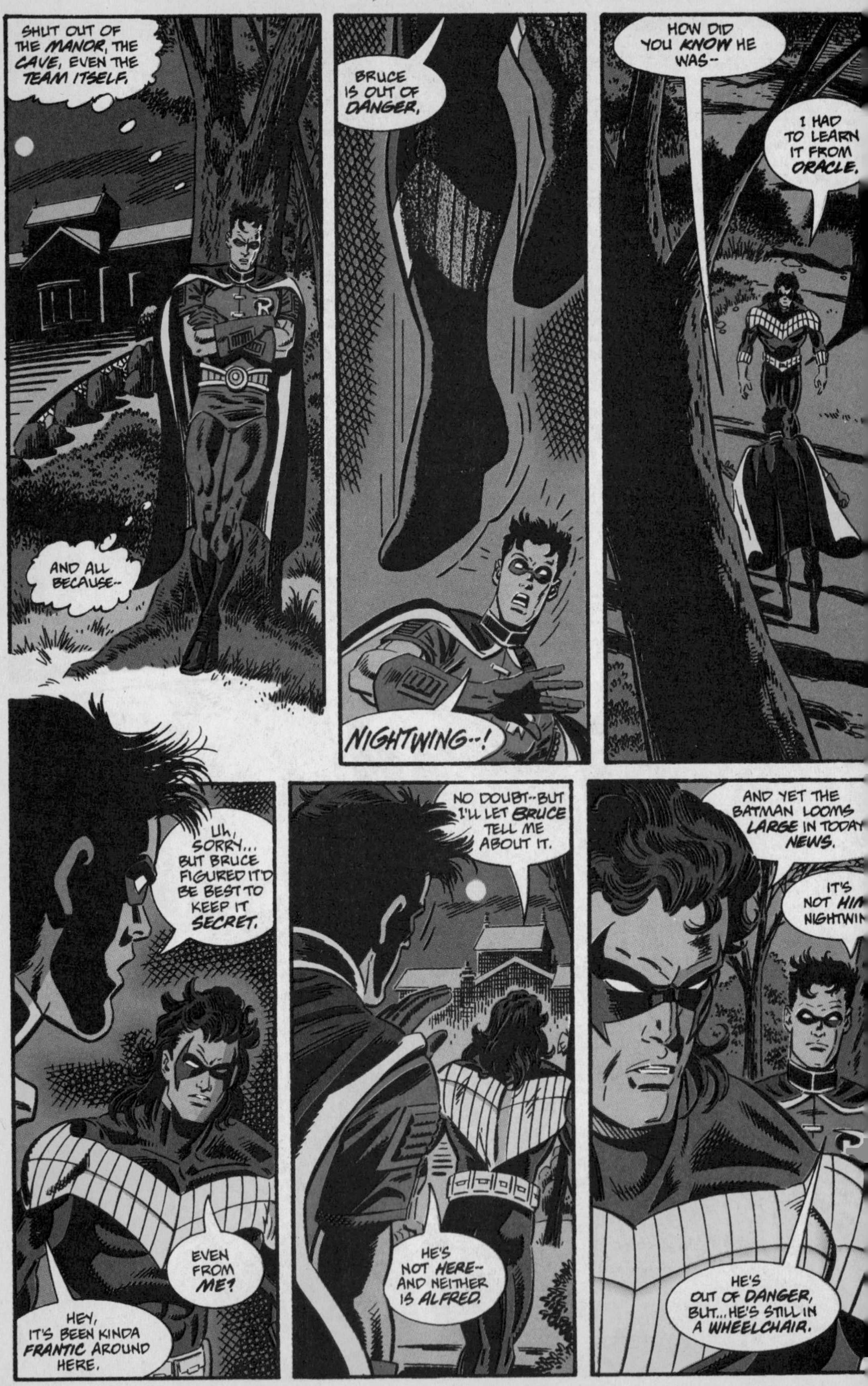
SHUT OUT OF THE MANOR, THE CAVE, EVEN THE TEAM ITSELF.
AND ALL BECAUSE--
BRUCE IS OUT OF DANGER.
NIGHTWING--!
HOW DID YOU KNOW HE WAS--
I HAD TO LEARN IT FROM ORACLE.
UH, SORRY... BUT BRUCE FIGURED IT'D BE BEST TO KEEP IT SECRET.
EVEN FROM ME?
HEY, IT'S BEEN KINDA FRANTIC AROUND HERE.
NO DOUBT--BUT I'LL LET BRUCE TELL ME ABOUT IT.
HE'S NOT HERE-- AND NEITHER IS ALFRED.
AND YET THE BATMAN LOOMS LARGE IN TODAY
NEWS.
HE'S OUT OF DANGER, BUT... HE'S STILL IN A WHEELCHAIR.

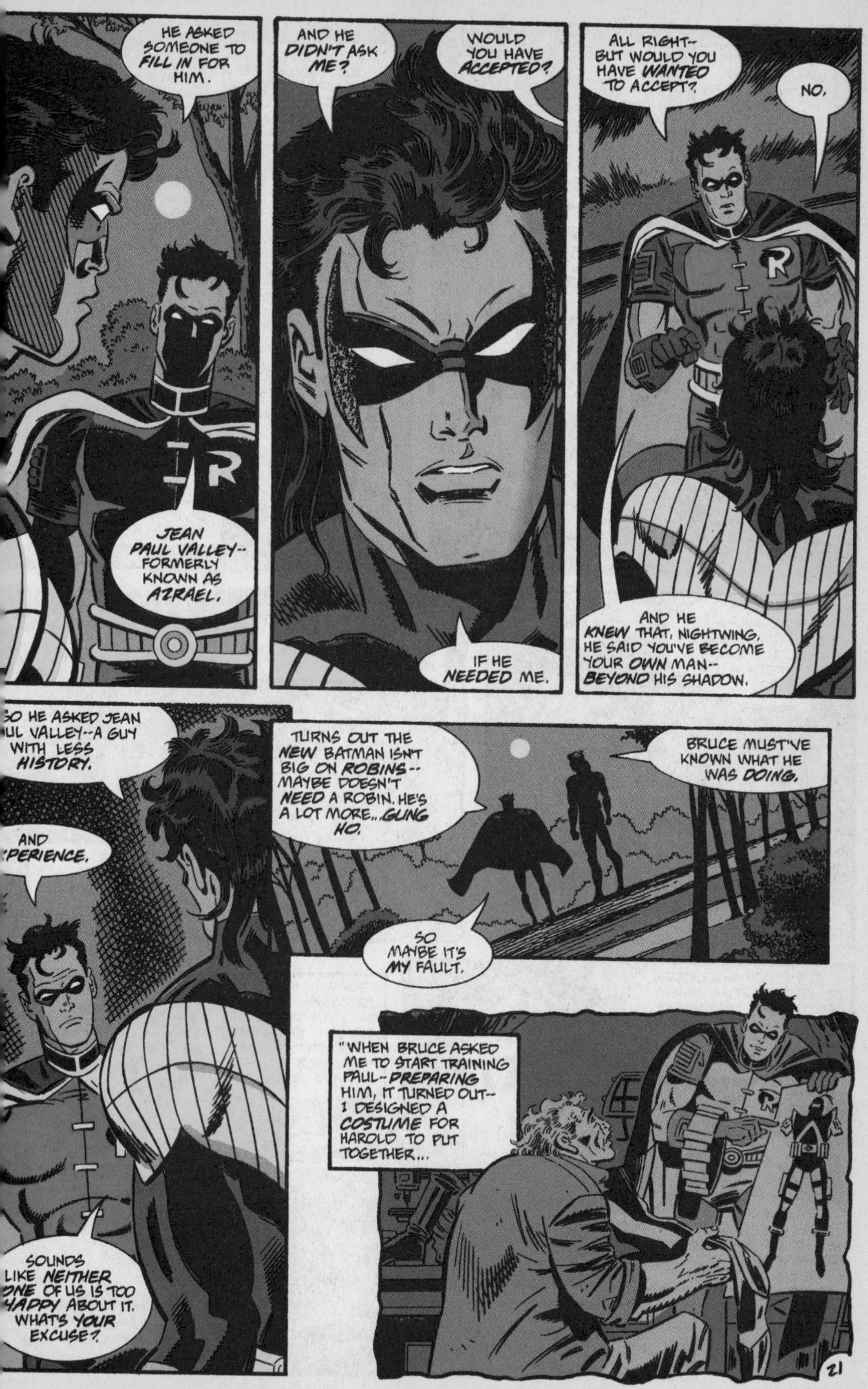

HE ASKED SOMEONE TO FILL IN FOR HIM.
JEAN PAUL VALLEY-- FORMERLY KNOWN AS AZRAEL.
AND HE DIDN'T ASK ME?
WOULD YOU HAVE ACCEPTED?
IF HE NEEDED ME.
ALL RIGHT-- BUT WOULD YOU HAVE WANTED TO ACCEPT?
NO.
AND HE KNEW THAT, NIGHTWING. HE SAID YOU'VE BECOME YOUR OWN MAN-- BEYOND HIS SHADOW.
SO HE ASKED JEAN PAUL VALLEY--A GUY WITH LESS HISTORY.
AND EXPERIENCE.
SOUNDS LIKE NEITHER ONE OF US IS TOO HAPPY ABOUT IT. WHAT'S YOUR EXCUSE?
TURNS OUT THE NEW BATMAN ISN'T BIG ON ROBINS -- MAYBE DOESN'T NEED A ROBIN. HE'S A LOT MORE... GUNG HO.
BRUCE MUST'VE KNOWN WHAT HE WAS DOING.
SO MAYBE IT'S MY FAULT.
"WHEN BRUCE ASKED ME TO START TRAINING PAUL-- PREPARING HIM, IT TURNED OUT-- I DESIGNED A COSTUME FOR HAROLD TO PUT TOGETHER...
21

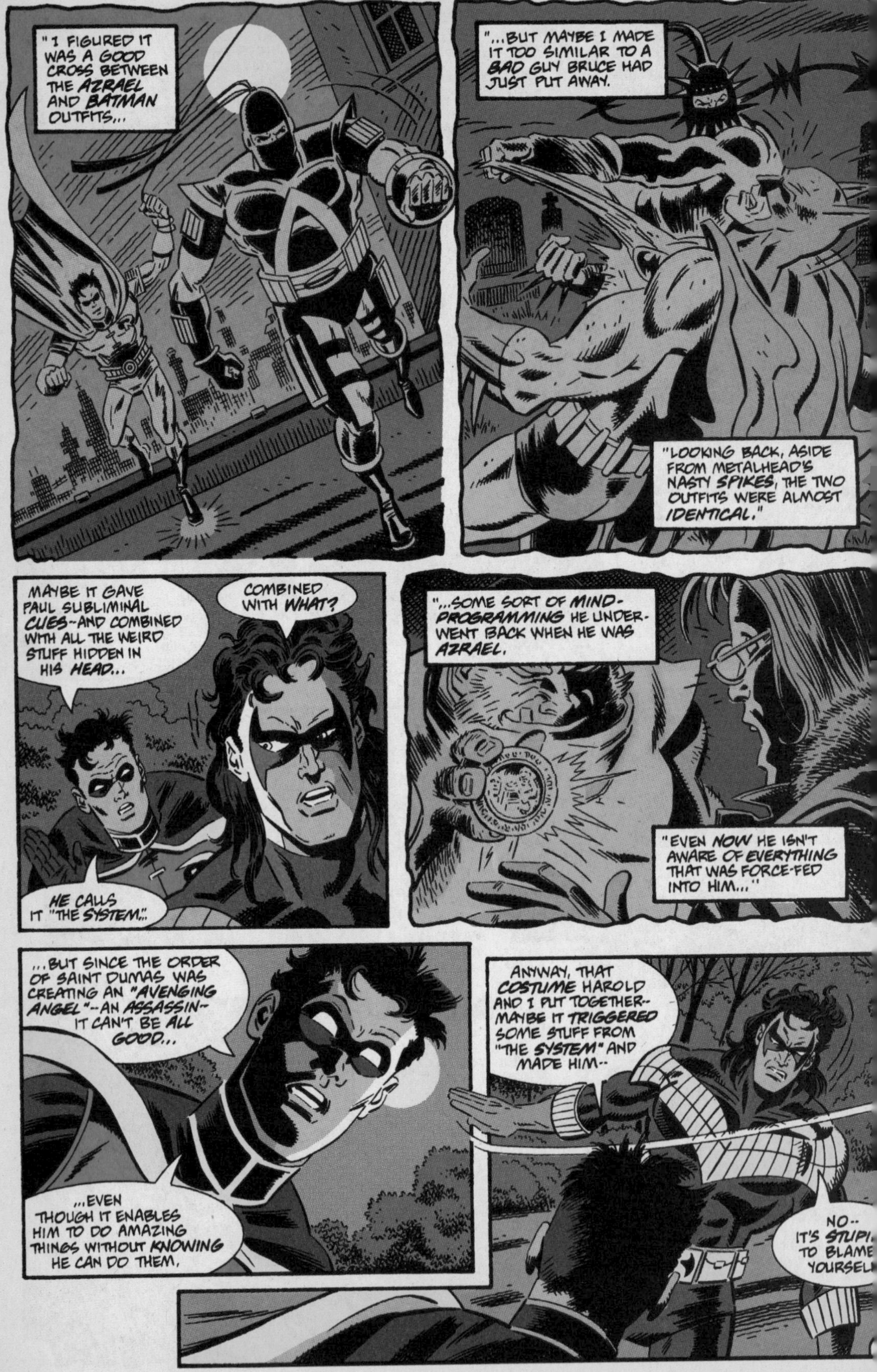
"I FIGURED IT WAS A GOOD CROSS BETWEEN THE AZRAEL AND BATMAN OUTFITS...
"...BUT MAYBE I MADE IT TOO SIMILAR TO A BAD GUY BRUCE HAD JUST PUT AWAY.
"LOOKING BACK, ASIDE FROM METALHEAD'S NASTY SPIKES, THE TWO OUTFITS WERE ALMOST IDENTICAL."
MAYBE IT GAVE PAUL SUBLIMINAL CUES--AND COMBINED WITH ALL THE WEIRD STUFF HIDDEN IN HIS HEAD...
COMBINED WITH WHAT?
HE CALLS IT "THE SYSTEM."
"...SOME SORT OF MIND-PROGRAMMING HE UNDERWENT BACK WHEN HE WAS AZRAEL.
"EVEN NOW HE ISN'T AWARE OF EVERYTHING THAT WAS FORCE-FED INTO HIM..."
...BUT SINCE THE ORDER OF SAINT DUMAS WAS CREATING AN "AVENGING ANGEL"--AN ASSASSIN--IT CAN'T BE ALL GOOD...
...EVEN THOUGH IT ENABLES HIM TO DO AMAZING THINGS WITHOUT KNOWING HE CAN DO THEM.
ANYWAY, THAT COSTUME HAROLD AND I PUT TOGETHER--MAYBE IT TRIGGERED SOME STUFF FROM "THE SYSTEM" AND MADE HIM--
NO-- IT'S STUPI. TO BLAME YOURSEL

EITHER THIS JEAN PAUL VALLEY IS GOOD ENOUGH OR HE ISN'T.

BRUCE THINKS HE IS,

THEN THAT'S IT--

--AND THERE'S NOTHING HERE FOR EITHER OF US TO DO,

MAYBE NOT...

... BUT I'M GAME FOR ONE LAST TRY,

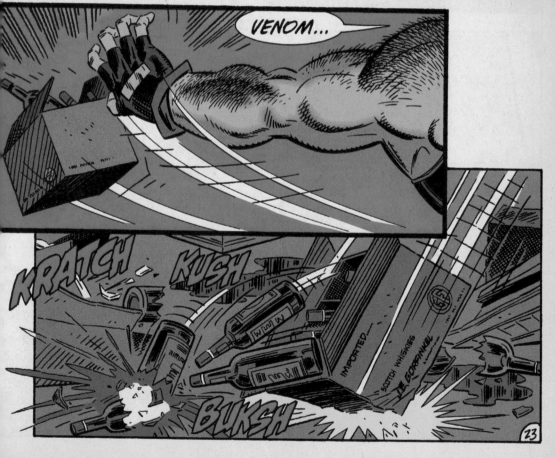

VENOM...

KRATCH KUSH

BUKSH

IMPORTED

SCOTCH WHISKIES

23

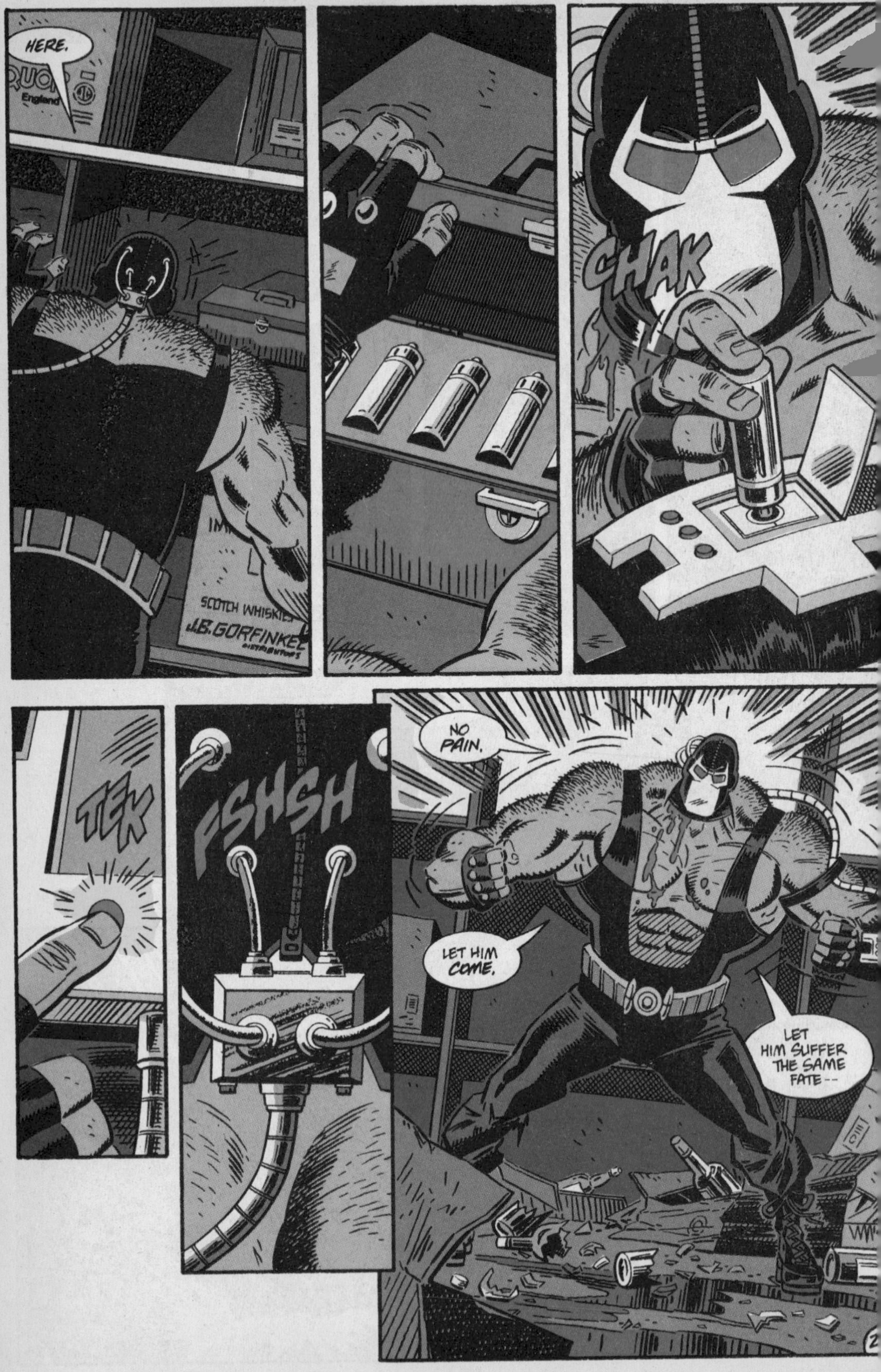
HERE.
CHAK
TEK
FSHSH
NO PAIN.
LET HIM COME.
LET HIM SUFFER THE SAME FATE --

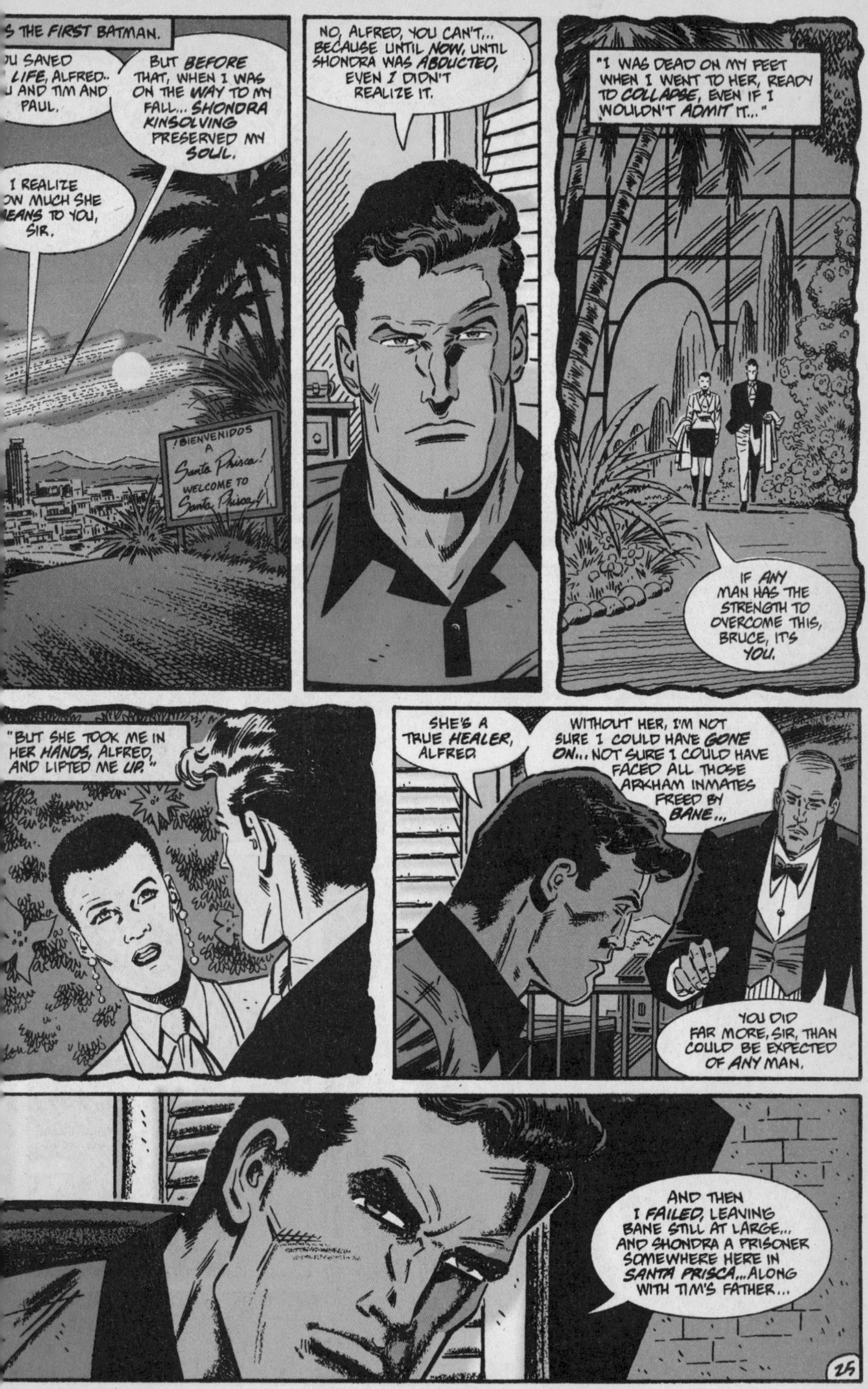
...S THE FIRST BATMAN.
...U SAVED ... LIFE, ALFRED.. ...U AND TIM AND PAUL.
BUT BEFORE THAT, WHEN I WAS ON THE WAY TO MY FALL... SHONDRA KINSOLVING PRESERVED MY SOUL.
I REALIZE ...W MUCH SHE ...EANS TO YOU, SIR.
¡BIENVENIDOS A Santa Prisca! WELCOME TO Santa Prisca!
NO, ALFRED, YOU CAN'T... BECAUSE UNTIL NOW, UNTIL SHONDRA WAS ABDUCTED, EVEN I DIDN'T REALIZE IT.
"I WAS DEAD ON MY FEET WHEN I WENT TO HER, READY TO COLLAPSE, EVEN IF I WOULDN'T ADMIT IT..."
IF ANY MAN HAS THE STRENGTH TO OVERCOME THIS, BRUCE, IT'S YOU.
"BUT SHE TOOK ME IN HER HANDS, ALFRED, AND LIFTED ME UP."
SHE'S A TRUE HEALER, ALFRED.
WITHOUT HER, I'M NOT SURE I COULD HAVE GONE ON... NOT SURE I COULD HAVE FACED ALL THOSE ARKHAM INMATES FREED BY BANE...
YOU DID FAR MORE, SIR, THAN COULD BE EXPECTED OF ANY MAN.
AND THEN I FAILED, LEAVING BANE STILL AT LARGE... AND SHONDRA A PRISONER SOMEWHERE HERE IN SANTA PRISCA...ALONG WITH TIM'S FATHER...
25

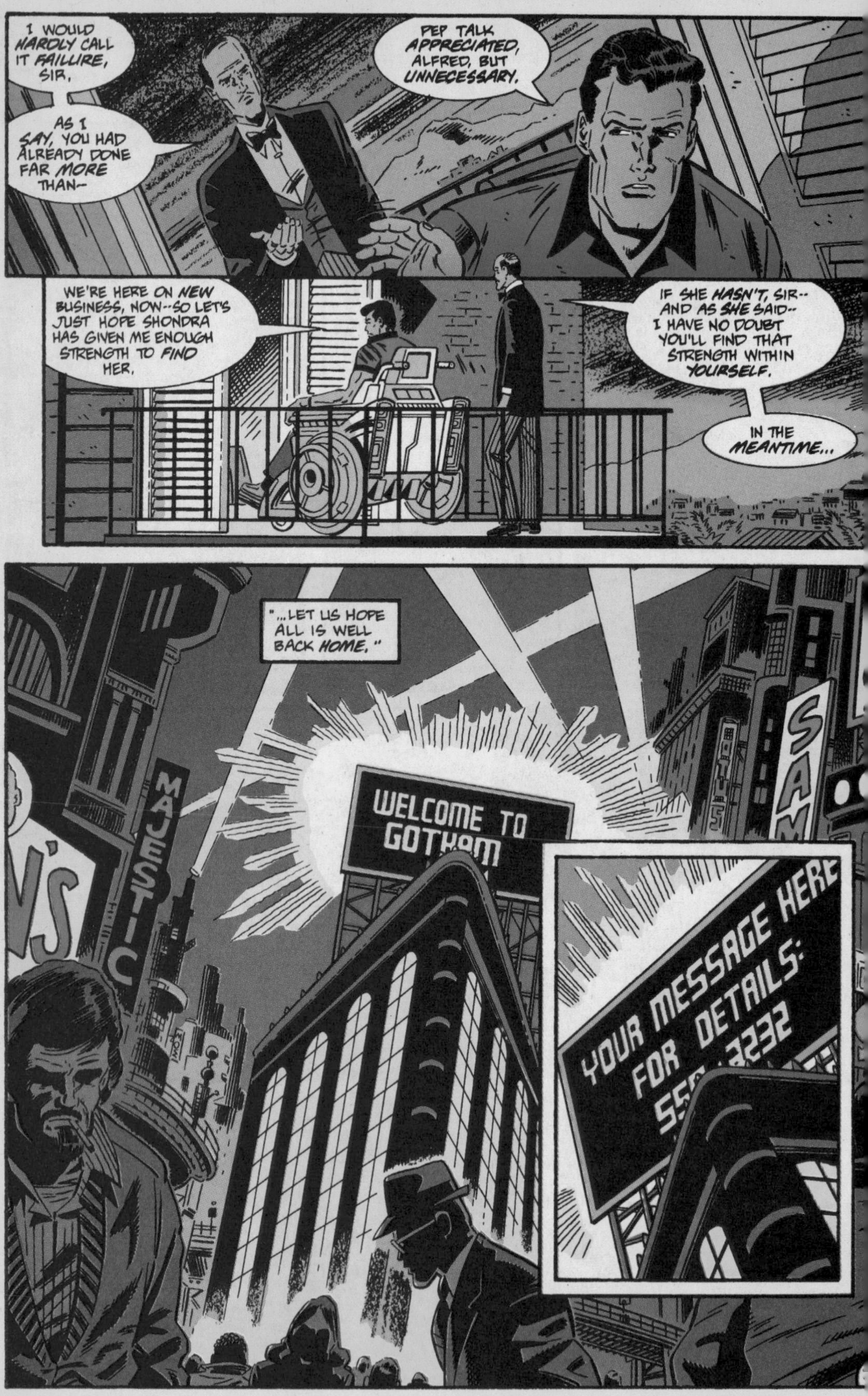

I WOULD HARDLY CALL IT FAILURE, SIR.
AS I SAY, YOU HAD ALREADY DONE FAR MORE THAN--
PEP TALK APPRECIATED, ALFRED, BUT UNNECESSARY.
WE'RE HERE ON NEW BUSINESS, NOW--SO LET'S JUST HOPE SHONDRA HAS GIVEN ME ENOUGH STRENGTH TO FIND HER.
IF SHE HASN'T, SIR-- AND AS SHE SAID-- I HAVE NO DOUBT YOU'LL FIND THAT STRENGTH WITHIN YOURSELF.
IN THE MEANTIME...
"...LET US HOPE ALL IS WELL BACK HOME."
MAJESTIC
WELCOME TO GOTHAM
YOUR MESSAGE HERE
FOR DETAILS:

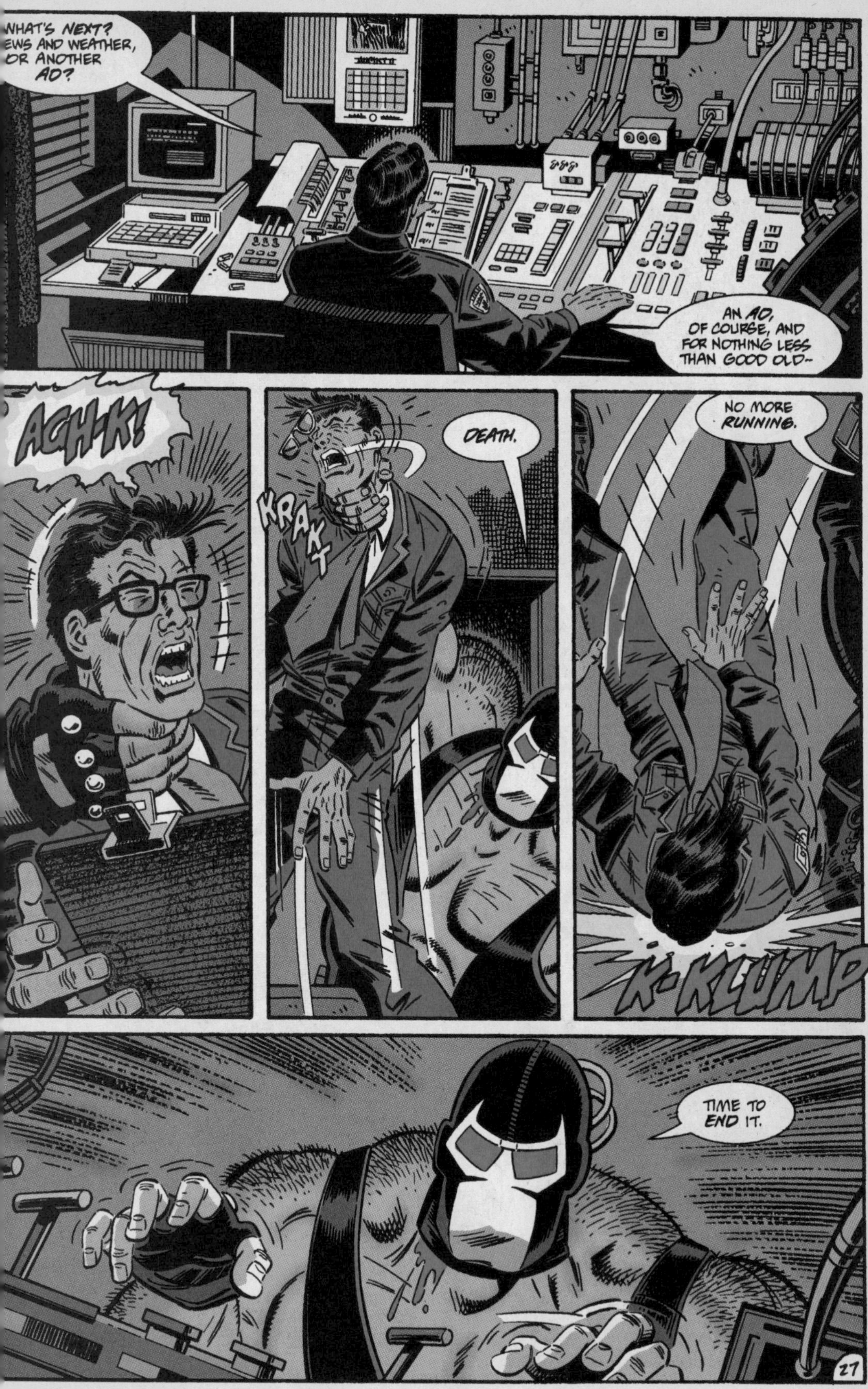
WHAT'S NEXT? NEWS AND WEATHER, OR ANOTHER AD?
AN AD, OF COURSE, AND FOR NOTHING LESS THAN GOOD OLD--
AGH-K!
KRAKT
DEATH.
NO MORE RUNNING.
K-KLUMP
TIME TO END IT.
27

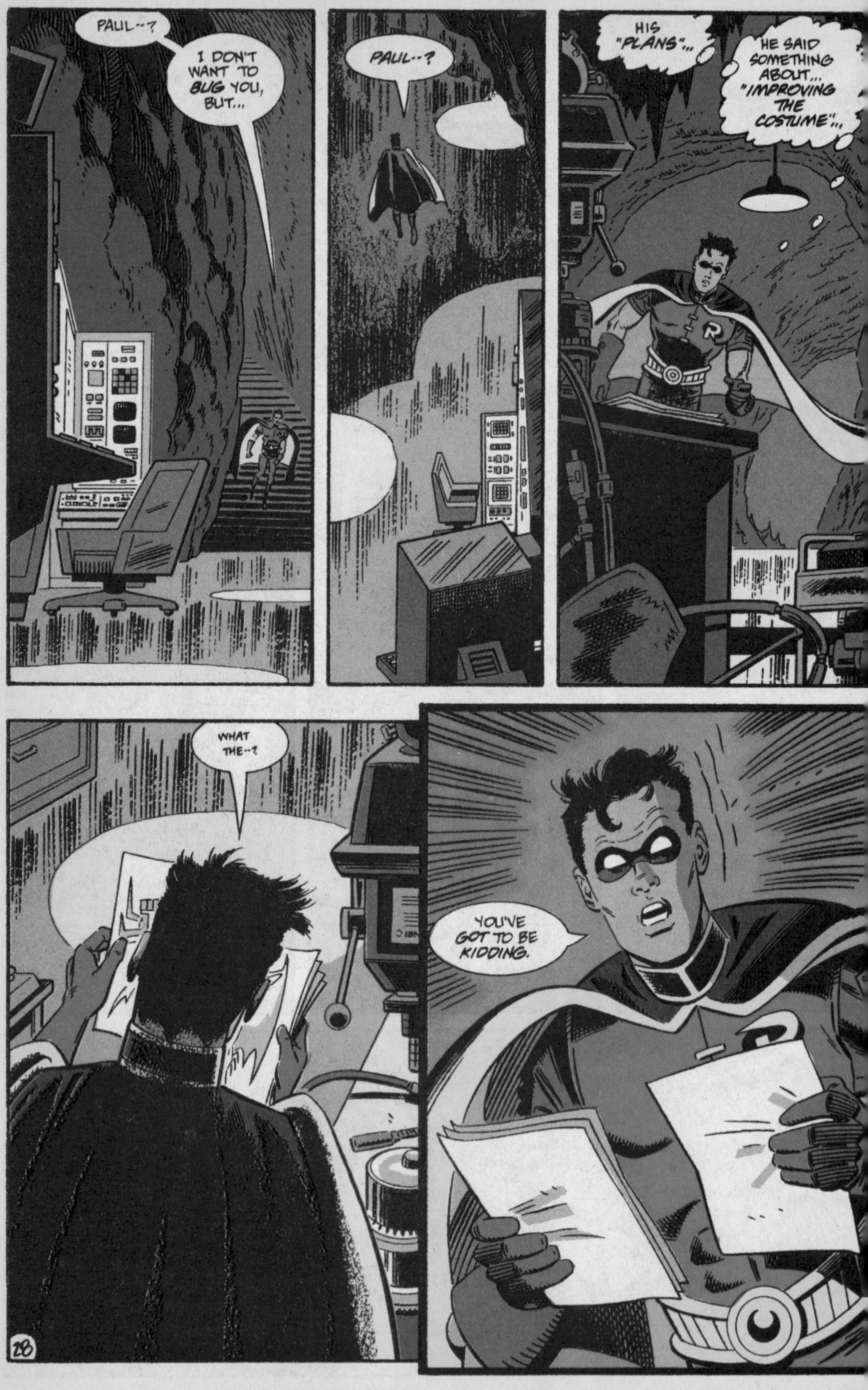
PAUL--?
I DON'T WANT TO BUG YOU, BUT...
PAUL--?
HIS "PLANS"...
HE SAID SOMETHING ABOUT... "IMPROVING THE COSTUME"...
WHAT THE--?
YOU'VE GOT TO BE KIDDING.
28

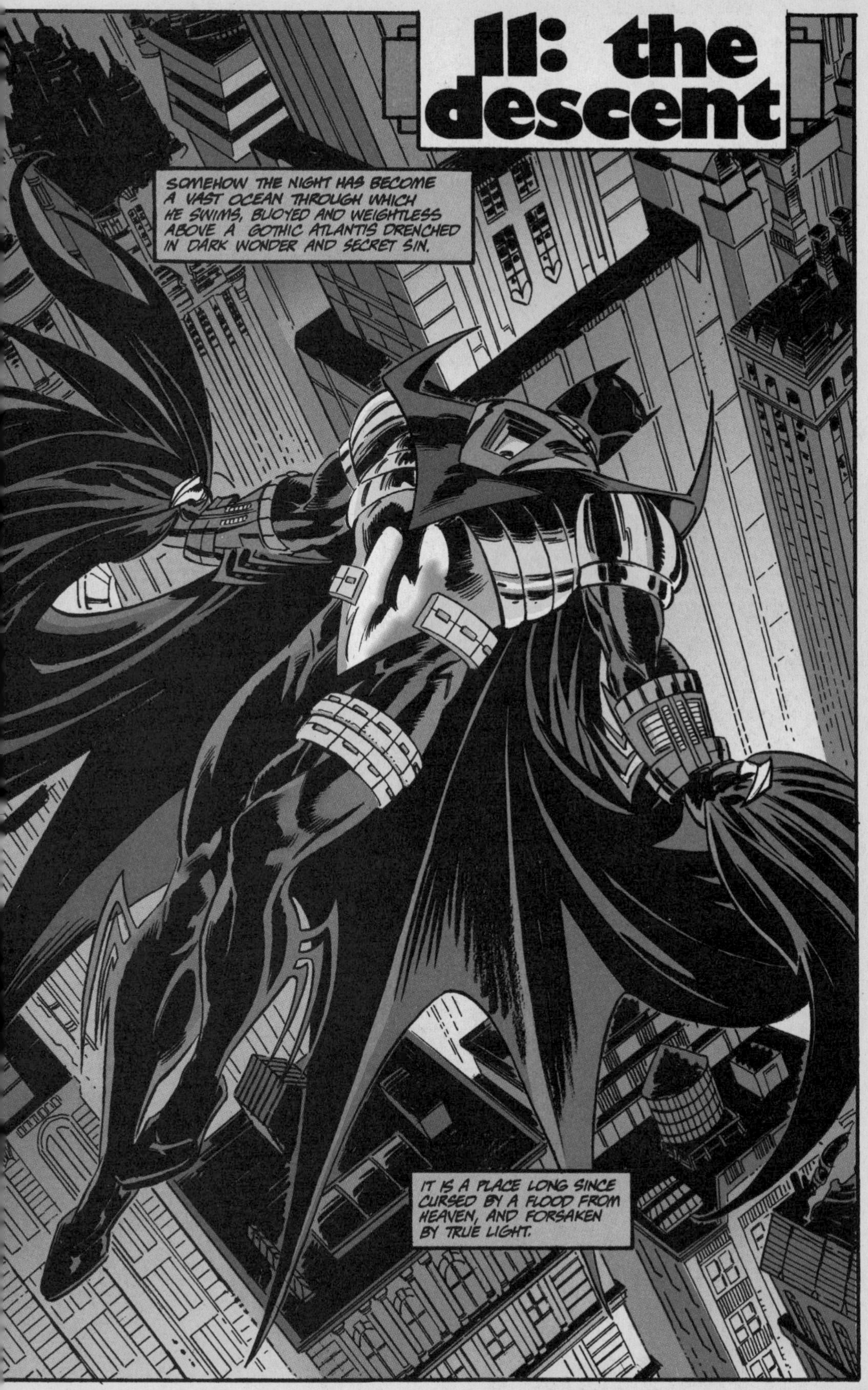
II: the descent
SOMEHOW THE NIGHT HAS BECOME A VAST OCEAN THROUGH WHICH HE SWIMS, BUOYED AND WEIGHTLESS ABOVE A GOTHIC ATLANTIS DRENCHED IN DARK WONDER AND SECRET SIN.
IT IS A PLACE LONG SINCE CURSED BY A FLOOD FROM HEAVEN, AND FORSAKEN BY TRUE LIGHT.

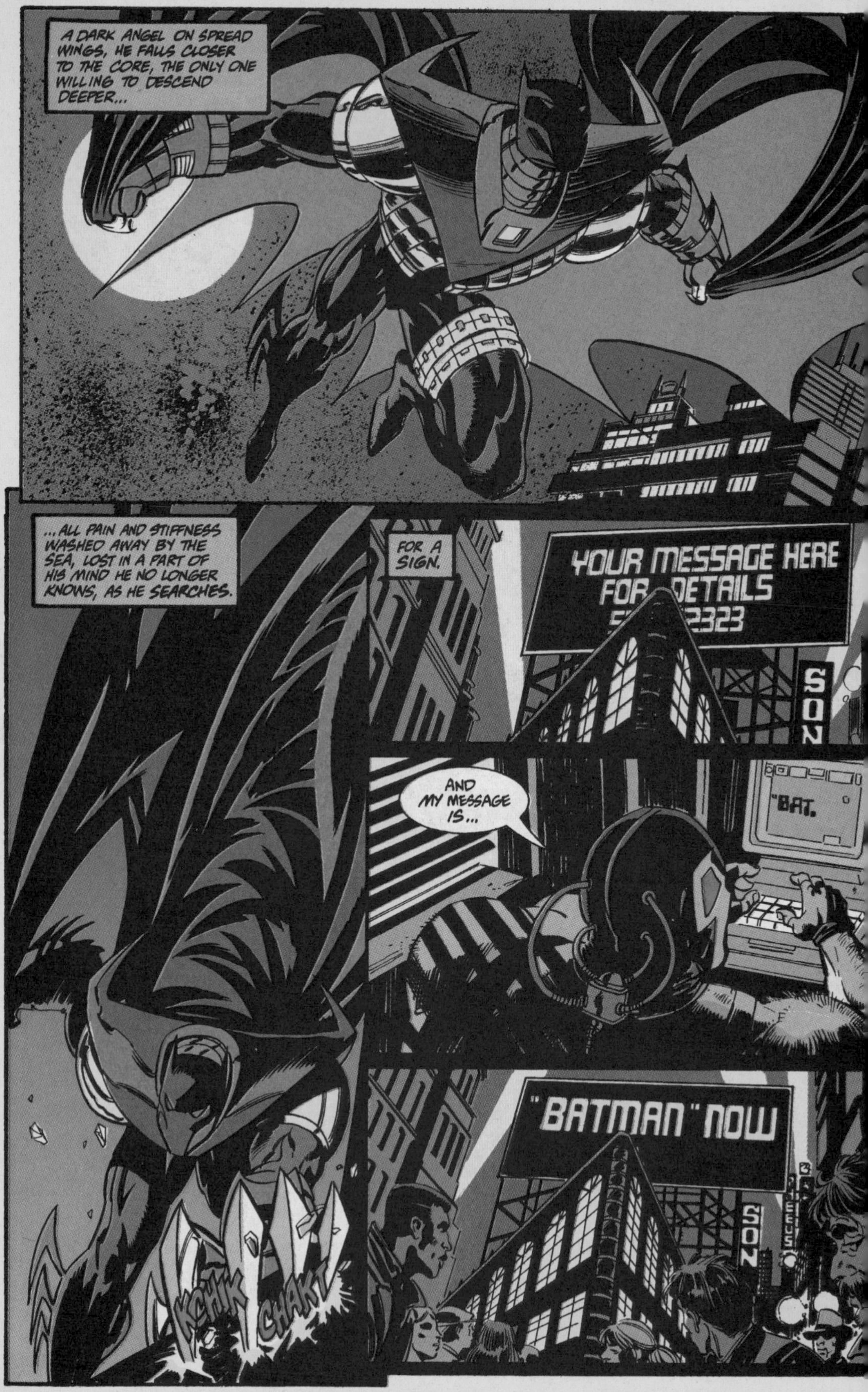
A DARK ANGEL ON SPREAD WINGS, HE FALLS CLOSER TO THE CORE, THE ONLY ONE WILLING TO DESCEND DEEPER...
...ALL PAIN AND STIFFNESS WASHED AWAY BY THE SEA, LOST IN A PART OF HIS MIND HE NO LONGER KNOWS, AS HE SEARCHES.
FOR A SIGN.
YOUR MESSAGE HERE
FOR DETAILS
AND MY MESSAGE IS...
"BAT.
"BATMAN" NOW
KCHIK
CHAKT

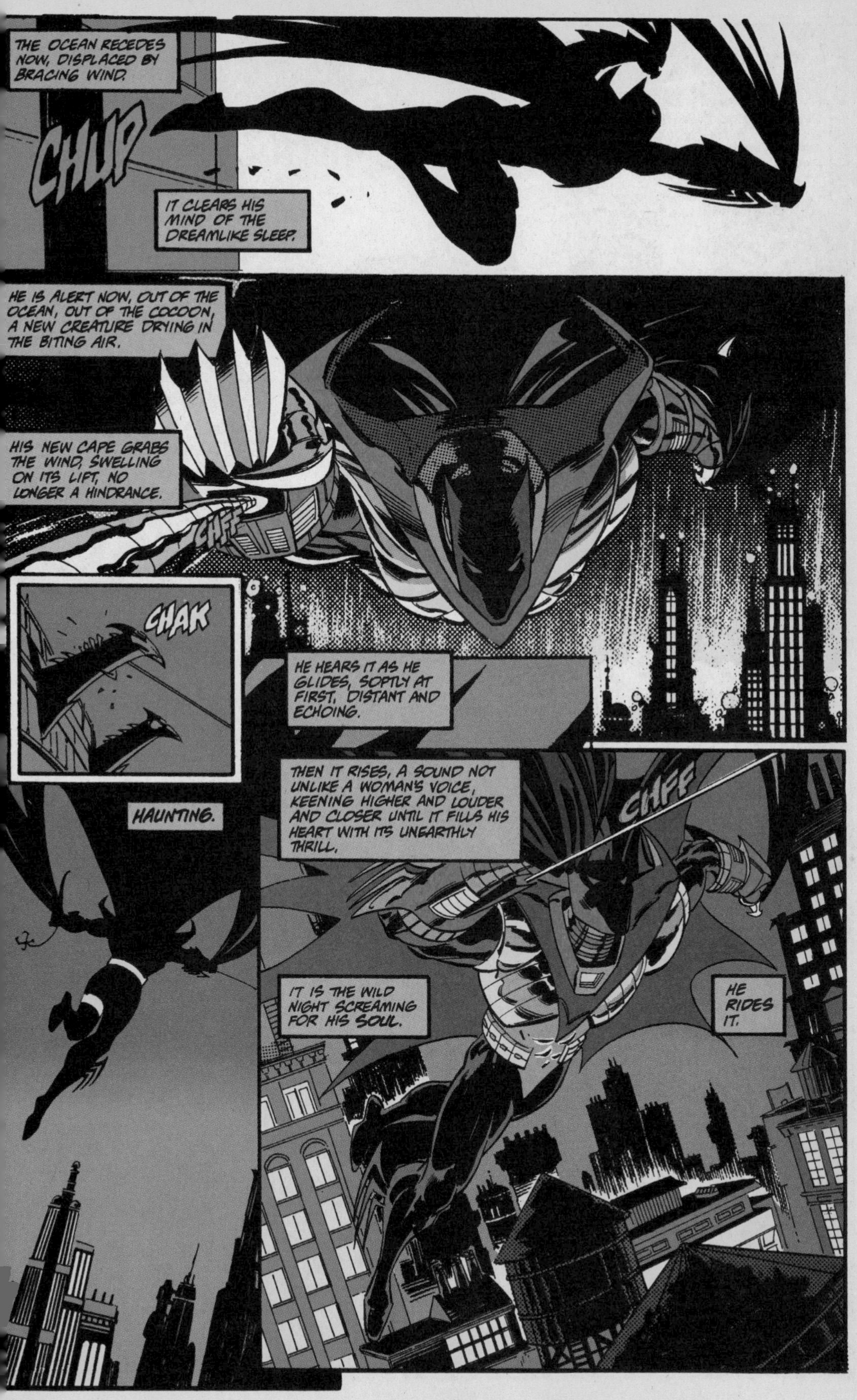
THE OCEAN RECEDES NOW, DISPLACED BY BRACING WIND.
CHUP
IT CLEARS HIS MIND OF THE DREAMLIKE SLEEP.
HE IS ALERT NOW, OUT OF THE OCEAN, OUT OF THE COCOON, A NEW CREATURE DRYING IN THE BITING AIR.
HIS NEW CAPE GRABS THE WIND, SWELLING ON ITS LIFT, NO LONGER A HINDRANCE.
CHFF
CHAK
HE HEARS IT AS HE GLIDES, SOFTLY AT FIRST, DISTANT AND ECHOING.
HAUNTING.
THEN IT RISES, A SOUND NOT UNLIKE A WOMAN'S VOICE, KEENING HIGHER AND LOUDER AND CLOSER UNTIL IT FILLS HIS HEART WITH ITS UNEARTHLY THRILL,
CHFF
IT IS THE WILD NIGHT SCREAMING FOR HIS SOUL.
HE RIDES IT.

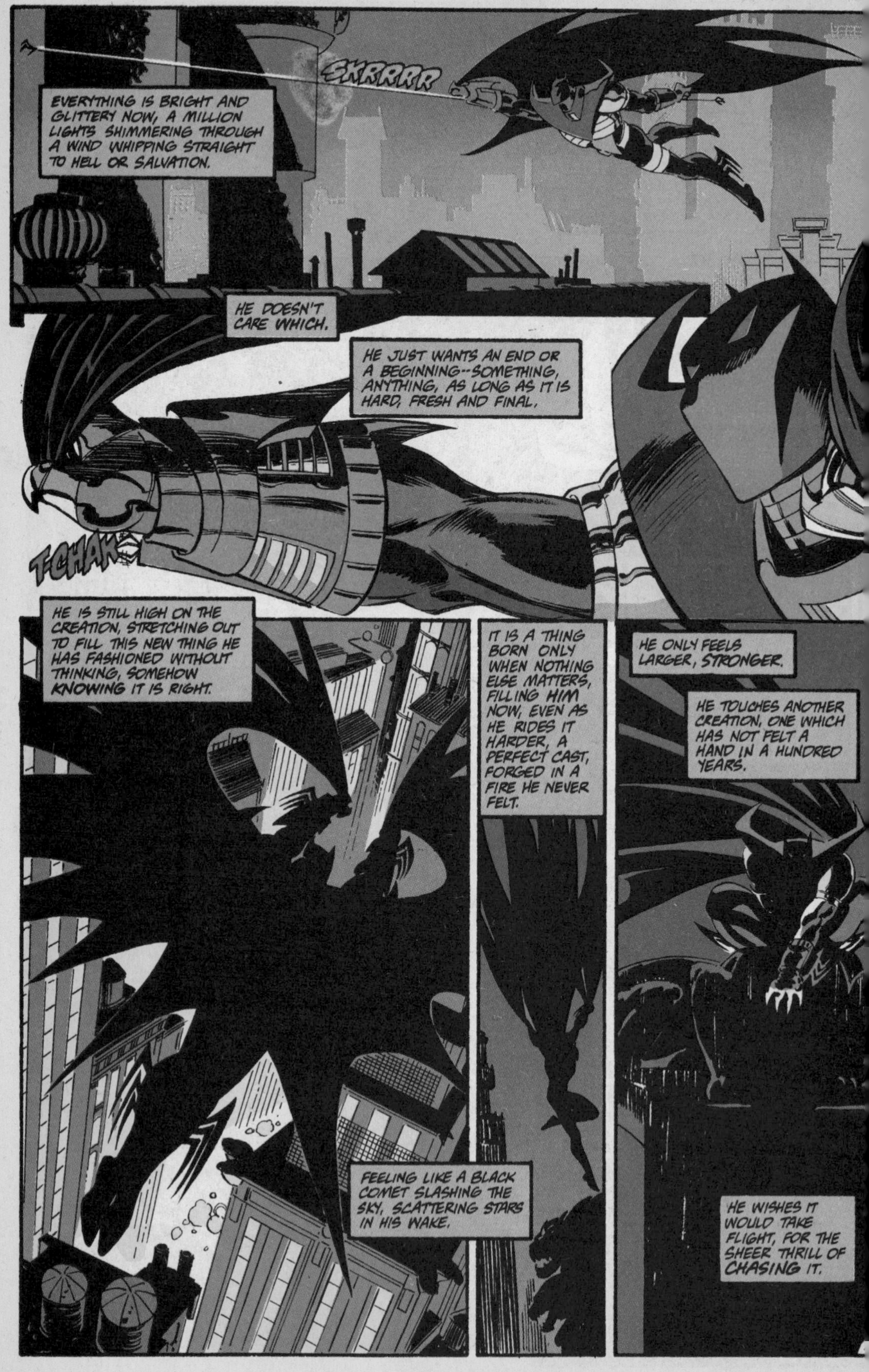
EVERYTHING IS BRIGHT AND GLITTERY NOW, A MILLION LIGHTS SHIMMERING THROUGH A WIND WHIPPING STRAIGHT TO HELL OR SALVATION.
SKRRRRR
HE DOESN'T CARE WHICH.
HE JUST WANTS AN END OR A BEGINNING--SOMETHING, ANYTHING, AS LONG AS IT IS HARD, FRESH AND FINAL.
T-CHAK
HE IS STILL HIGH ON THE CREATION, STRETCHING OUT TO FILL THIS NEW THING HE HAS FASHIONED WITHOUT THINKING, SOMEHOW KNOWING IT IS RIGHT.
FEELING LIKE A BLACK COMET SLASHING THE SKY, SCATTERING STARS IN HIS WAKE.
IT IS A THING BORN ONLY WHEN NOTHING ELSE MATTERS, FILLING HIM NOW, EVEN AS HE RIDES IT HARDER, A PERFECT CAST, FORGED IN A FIRE HE NEVER FELT.
HE ONLY FEELS LARGER, STRONGER.
HE TOUCHES ANOTHER CREATION, ONE WHICH HAS NOT FELT A HAND IN A HUNDRED YEARS.
HE WISHES IT WOULD TAKE FLIGHT, FOR THE SHEER THRILL OF CHASING IT.

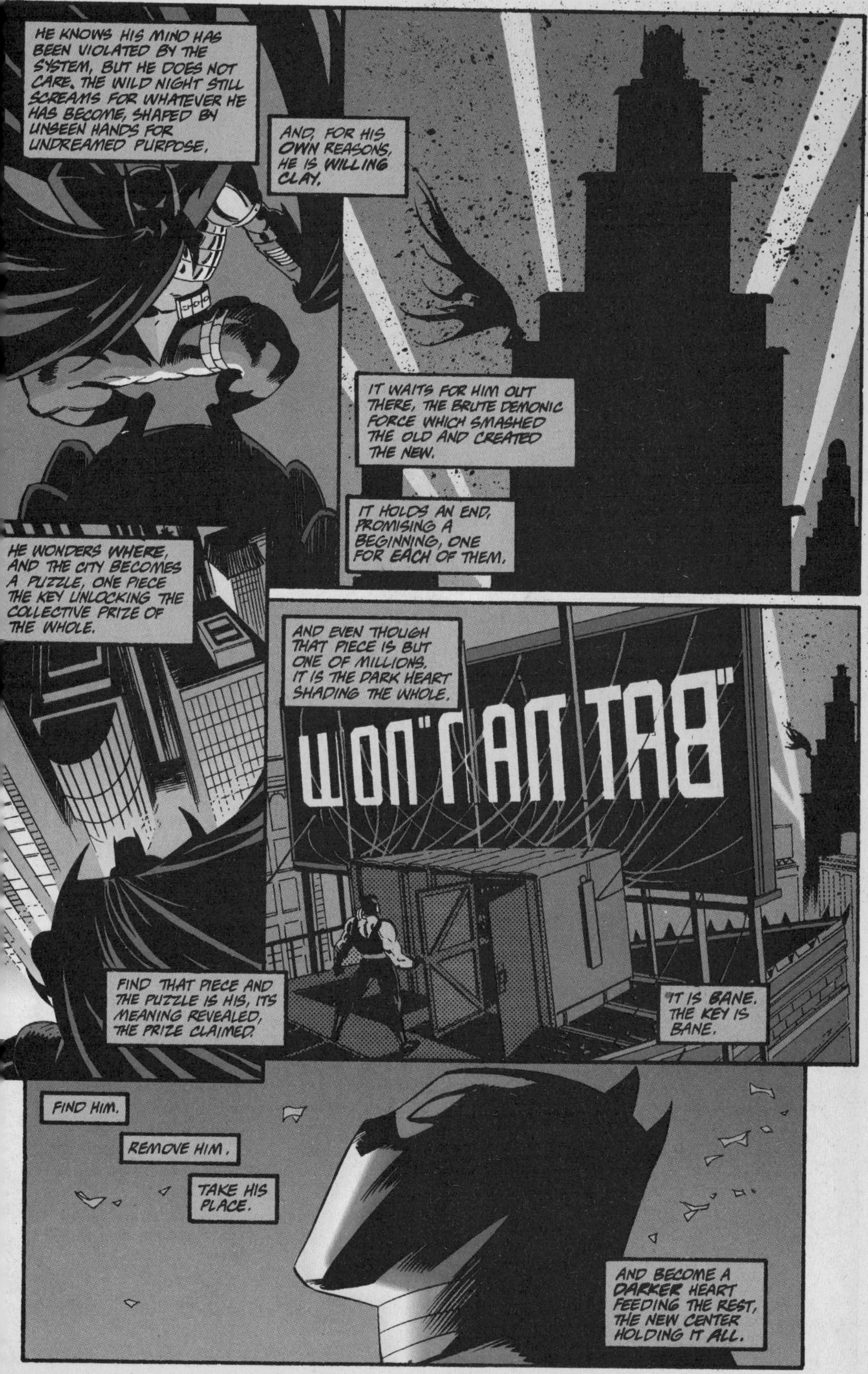
HE KNOWS HIS MIND HAS BEEN VIOLATED BY THE SYSTEM, BUT HE DOES NOT CARE. THE WILD NIGHT STILL SCREAMS FOR WHATEVER HE HAS BECOME, SHAPED BY UNSEEN HANDS FOR UNDREAMED PURPOSE.
AND, FOR HIS OWN REASONS, HE IS WILLING CLAY.
IT WAITS FOR HIM OUT THERE, THE BRUTE DEMONIC FORCE WHICH SMASHED THE OLD AND CREATED THE NEW.
IT HOLDS AN END, PROMISING A BEGINNING, ONE FOR EACH OF THEM.
HE WONDERS WHERE, AND THE CITY BECOMES A PUZZLE, ONE PIECE THE KEY UNLOCKING THE COLLECTIVE PRIZE OF THE WHOLE.
AND EVEN THOUGH THAT PIECE IS BUT ONE OF MILLIONS, IT IS THE DARK HEART SHADING THE WHOLE.
FIND THAT PIECE AND THE PUZZLE IS HIS, ITS MEANING REVEALED, THE PRIZE CLAIMED.
IT IS BANE. THE KEY IS BANE.
FIND HIM.
REMOVE HIM.
TAKE HIS PLACE.
AND BECOME A DARKER HEART FEEDING THE REST, THE NEW CENTER HOLDING IT ALL.

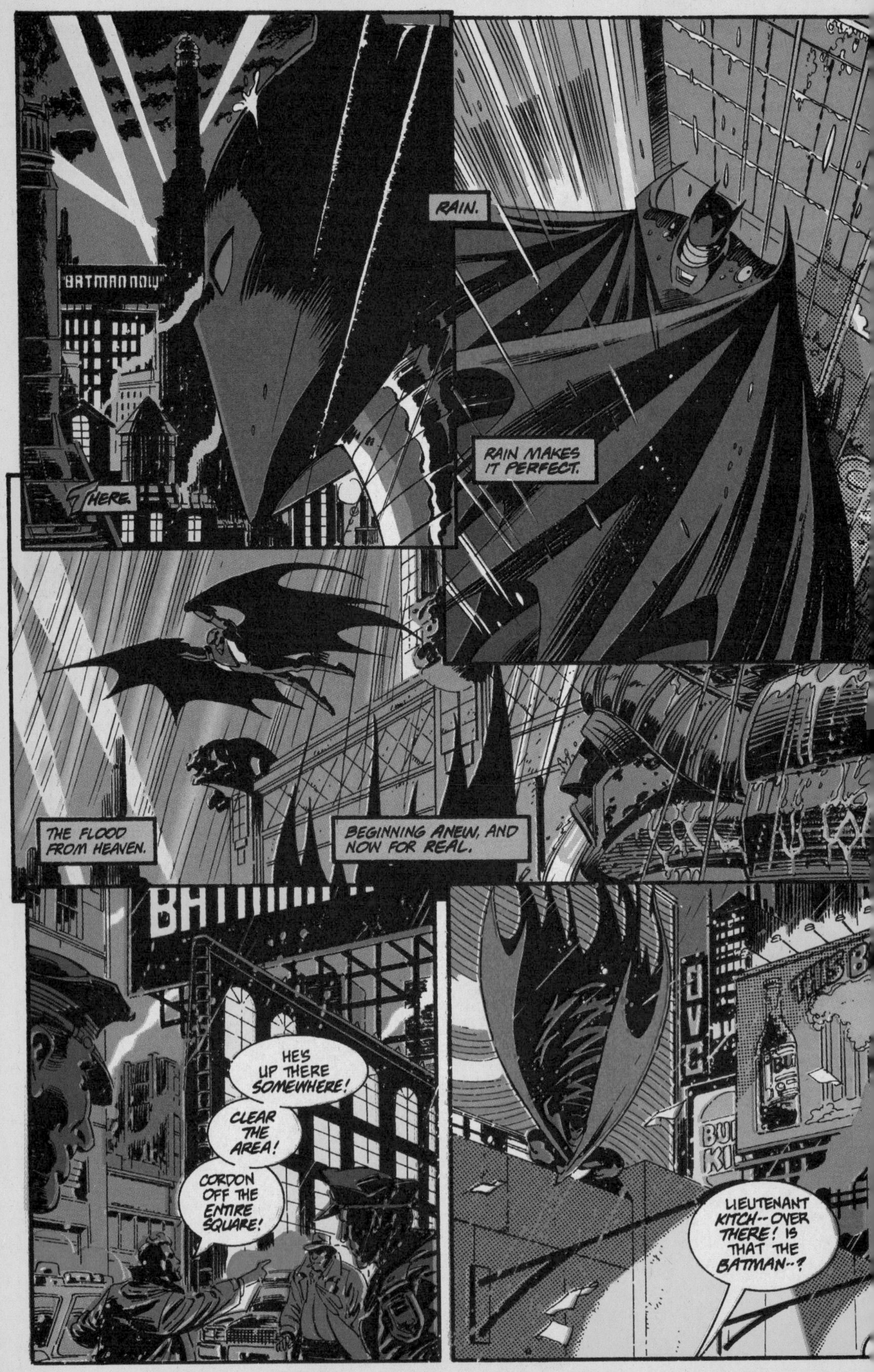
BATMAN NOW
THERE.
RAIN.
RAIN MAKES IT PERFECT.
THE FLOOD FROM HEAVEN.
BEGINNING ANEW, AND NOW FOR REAL.
HE'S UP THERE SOMEWHERE!
CLEAR THE AREA!
CORDON OFF THE ENTIRE SQUARE!
LIEUTENANT KITCH--OVER THERE! IS THAT THE BATMAN--?

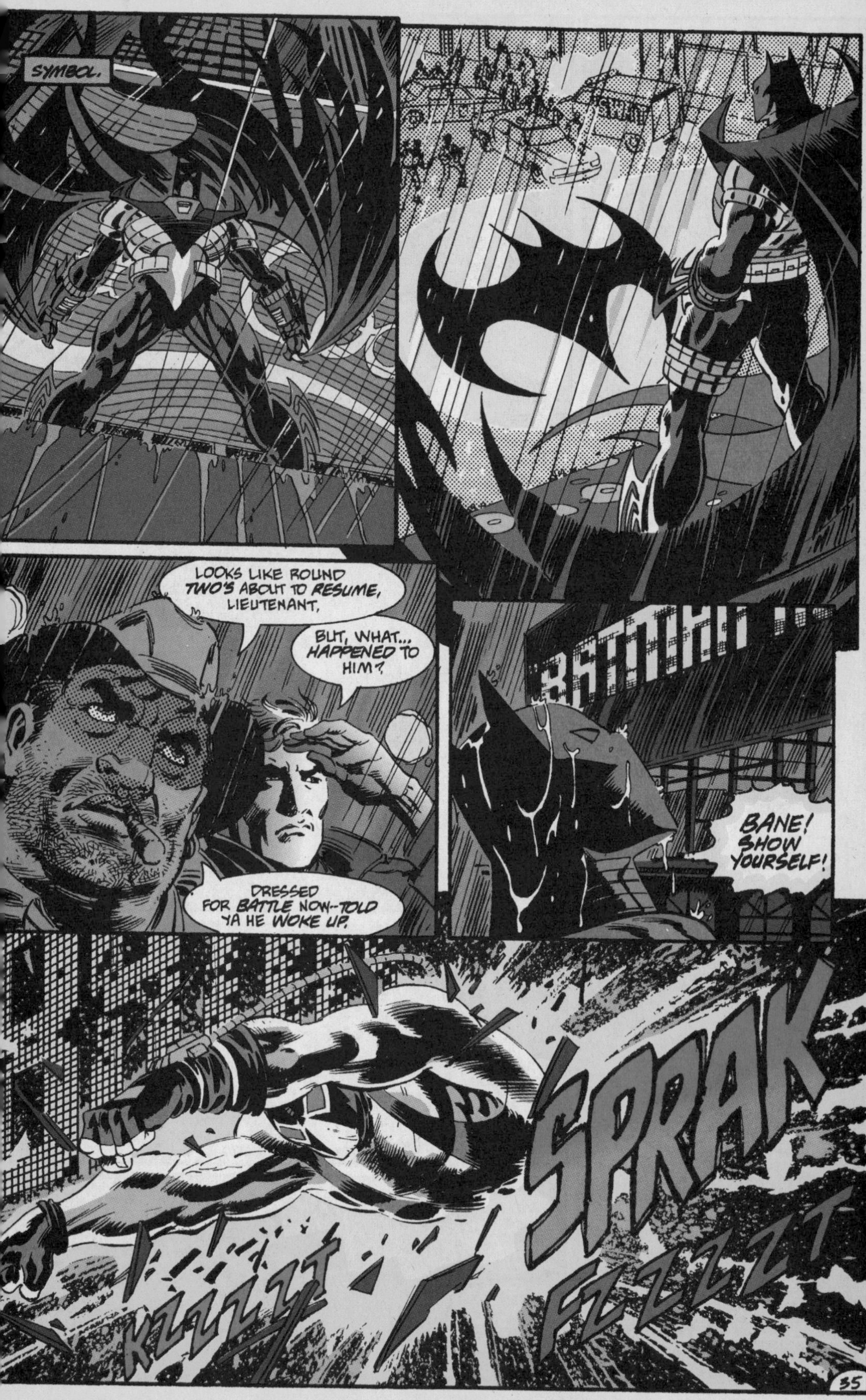
SYMBOL.
LOOKS LIKE ROUND TWO'S ABOUT TO RESUME, LIEUTENANT,
BUT, WHAT... HAPPENED TO HIM?
DRESSED FOR BATTLE NOW--TOLD YA HE WOKE UP.
BANE! SHOW YOURSELF!
SPRAK
KZZZZT
FZZZZZT
35

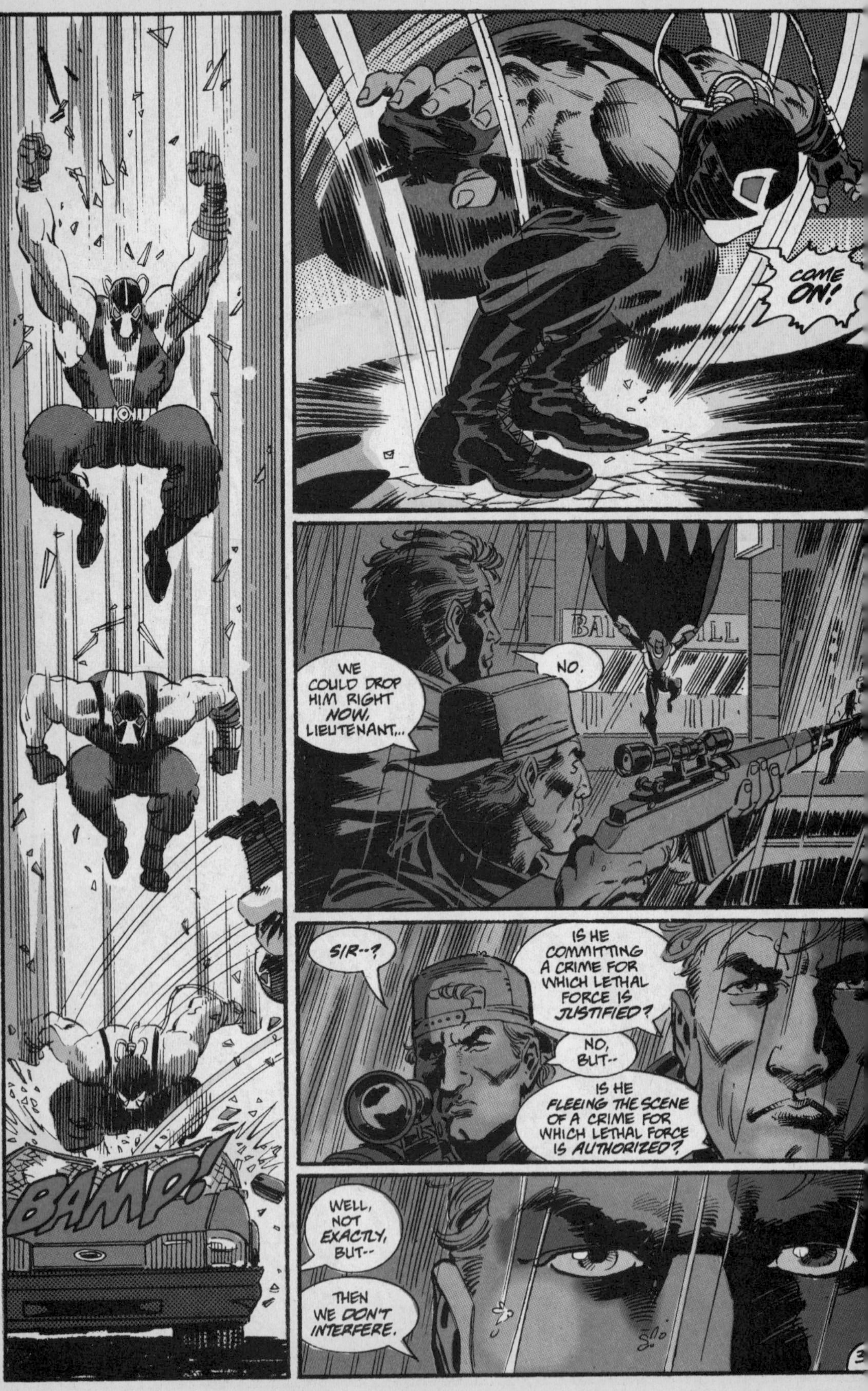
COME ON!
BAMP!
WE COULD DROP HIM RIGHT NOW, LIEUTENANT...
NO.
SIR--?
IS HE COMMITTING A CRIME FOR WHICH LETHAL FORCE IS JUSTIFIED?
NO, BUT--
IS HE FLEEING THE SCENE OF A CRIME FOR WHICH LETHAL FORCE IS AUTHORIZED?
WELL, NOT EXACTLY, BUT--
THEN WE DON'T INTERFERE.

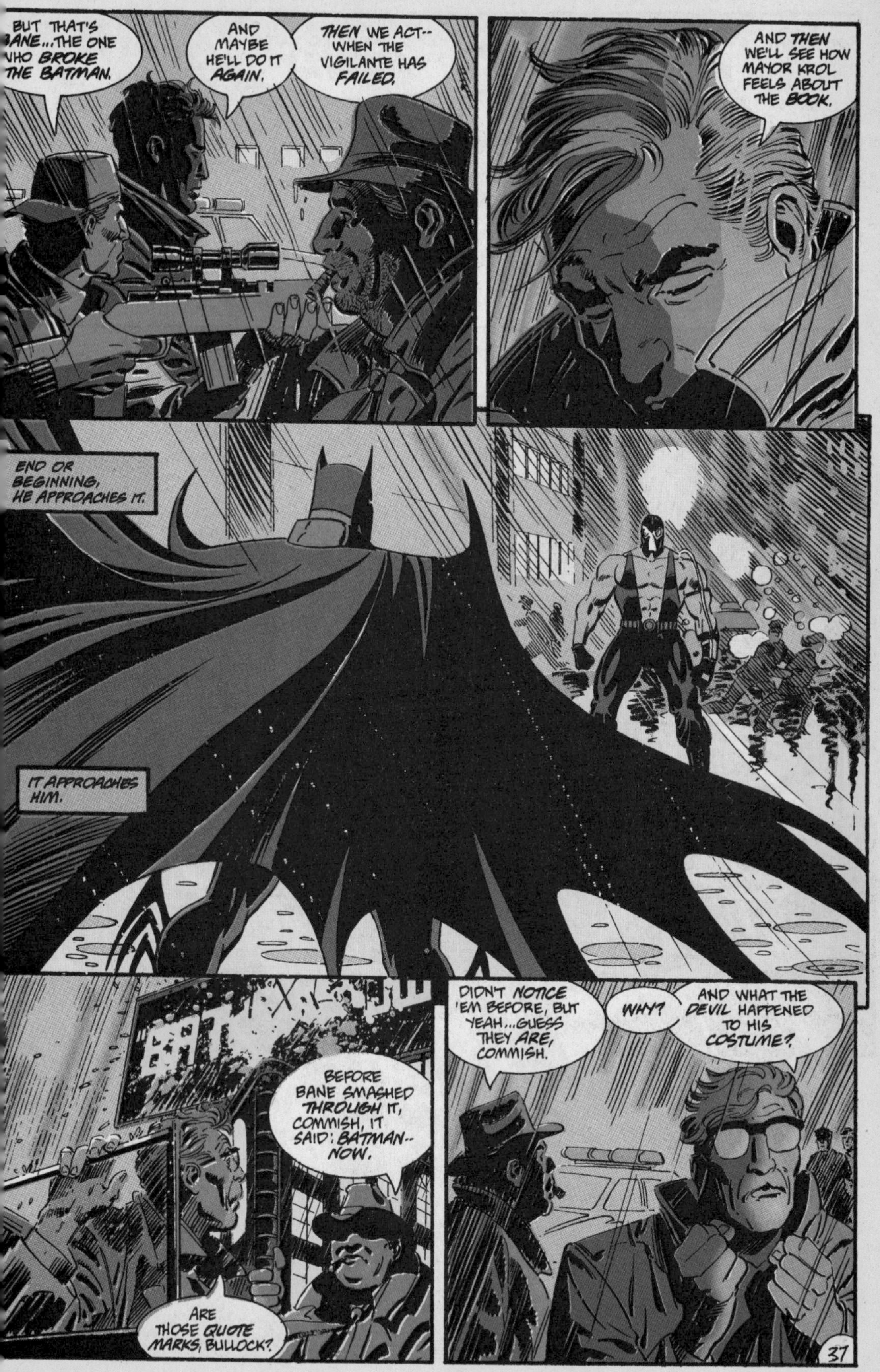

BUT THAT'S BANE...THE ONE WHO BROKE THE BATMAN.
AND MAYBE HE'LL DO IT AGAIN.
THEN WE ACT-- WHEN THE VIGILANTE HAS FAILED.
AND THEN WE'LL SEE HOW MAYOR KROL FEELS ABOUT THE BOOK.
END OR BEGINNING, HE APPROACHES IT.
IT APPROACHES HIM.
BEFORE BANE SMASHED THROUGH IT, COMMISH, IT SAID: BATMAN-- NOW.
ARE THOSE QUOTE MARKS, BULLOCK?
WHY?
DIDN'T NOTICE 'EM BEFORE, BUT YEAH...GUESS THEY ARE, COMMISH.
AND WHAT THE DEVIL HAPPENED TO HIS COSTUME?
37

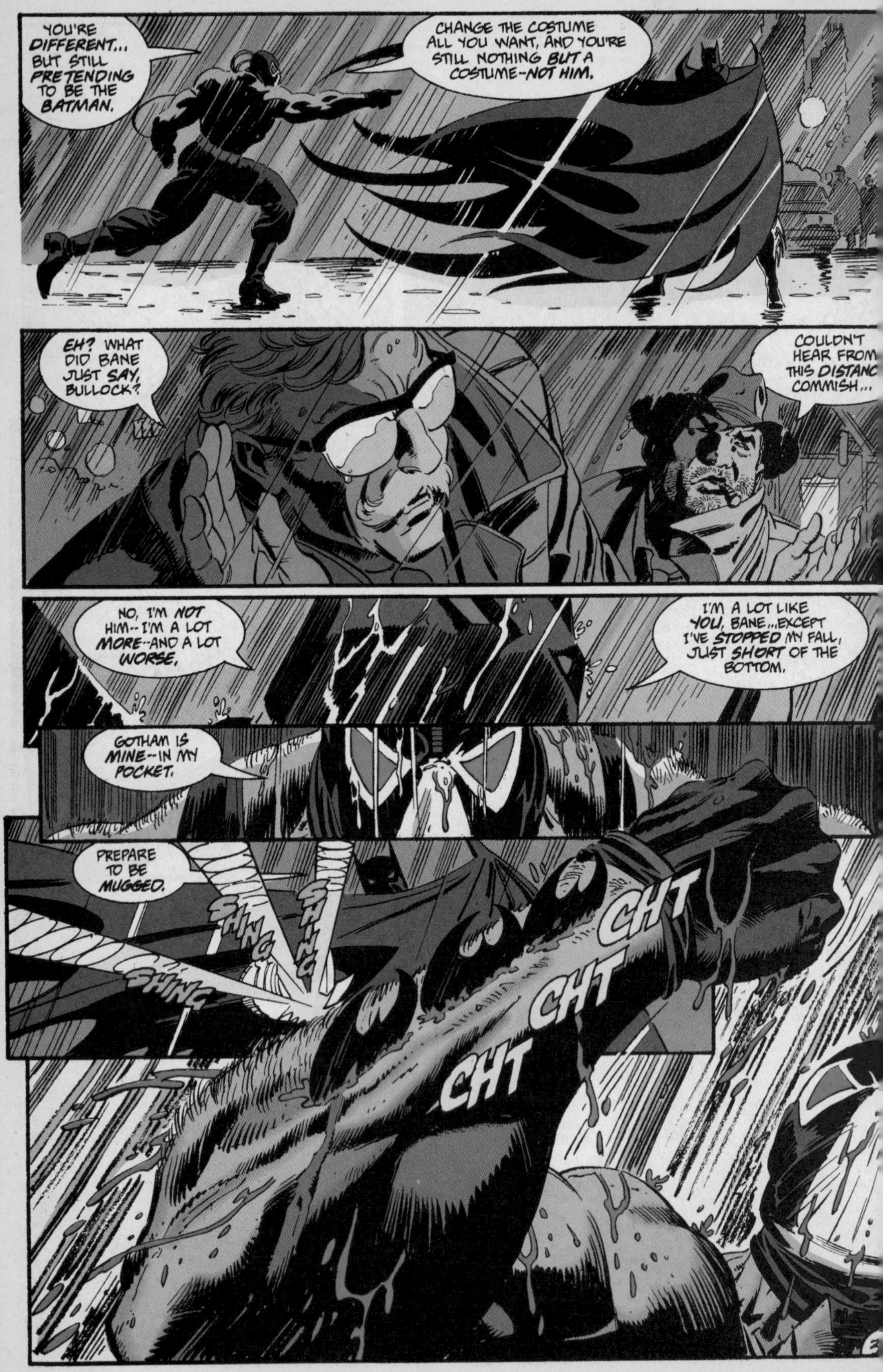
YOU'RE DIFFERENT... BUT STILL PRETENDING TO BE THE BATMAN.
CHANGE THE COSTUME ALL YOU WANT, AND YOU'RE STILL NOTHING BUT A COSTUME--NOT HIM.
EH? WHAT DID BANE JUST SAY, BULLOCK?
COULDN'T HEAR FROM THIS DISTANC COMMISH...
NO, I'M NOT HIM--I'M A LOT MORE--AND A LOT WORSE.
I'M A LOT LIKE YOU, BANE...EXCEPT I'VE STOPPED MY FALL, JUST SHORT OF THE BOTTOM.
GOTHAM IS MINE--IN MY POCKET.
PREPARE TO BE MUGGED.
SHING
SHING
SHING
CHT
CHT
CHT
CHT

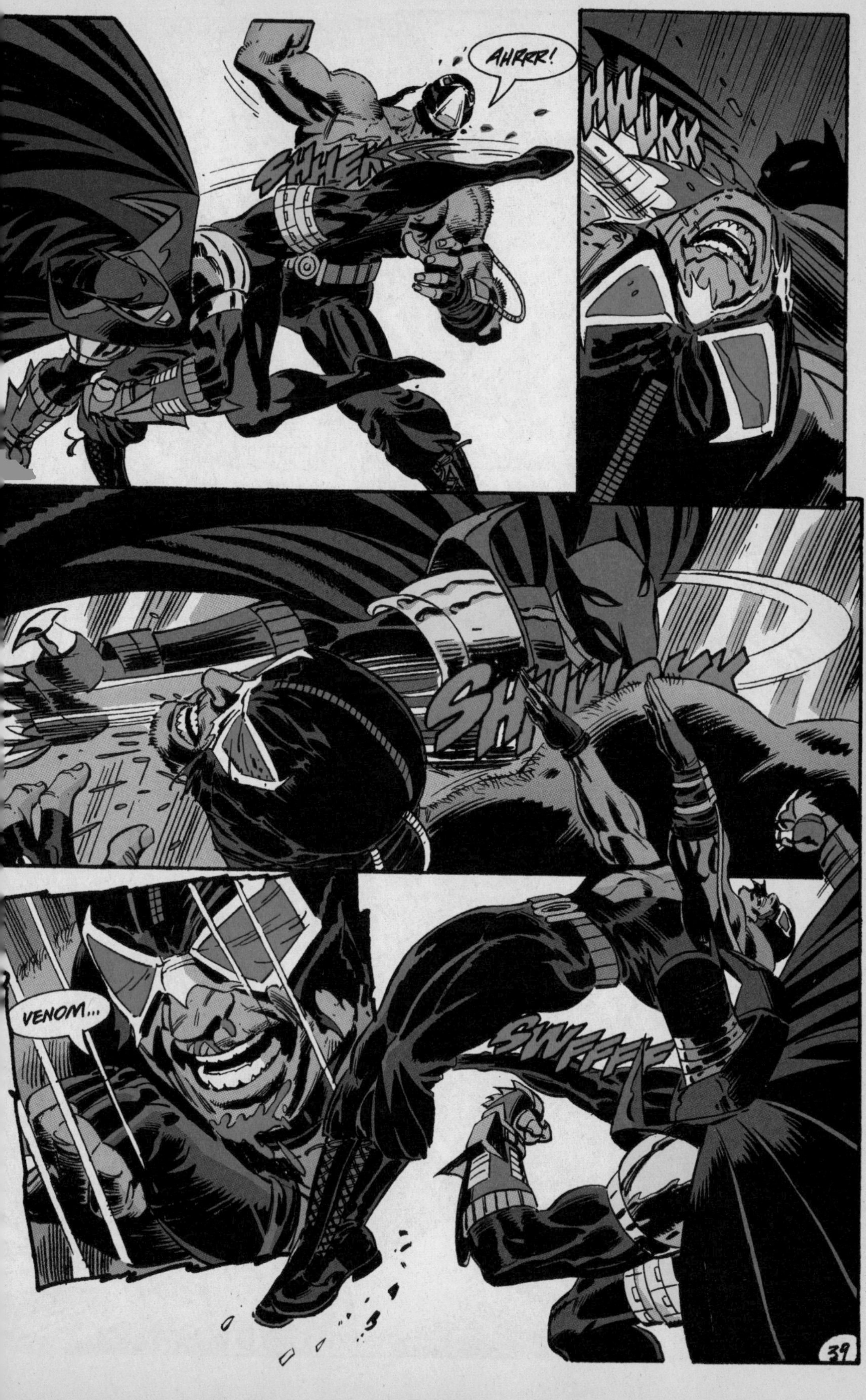
AHRRR!
SHHEK
HWUKK
SHWUN
VENOM...
SWFFFT
39

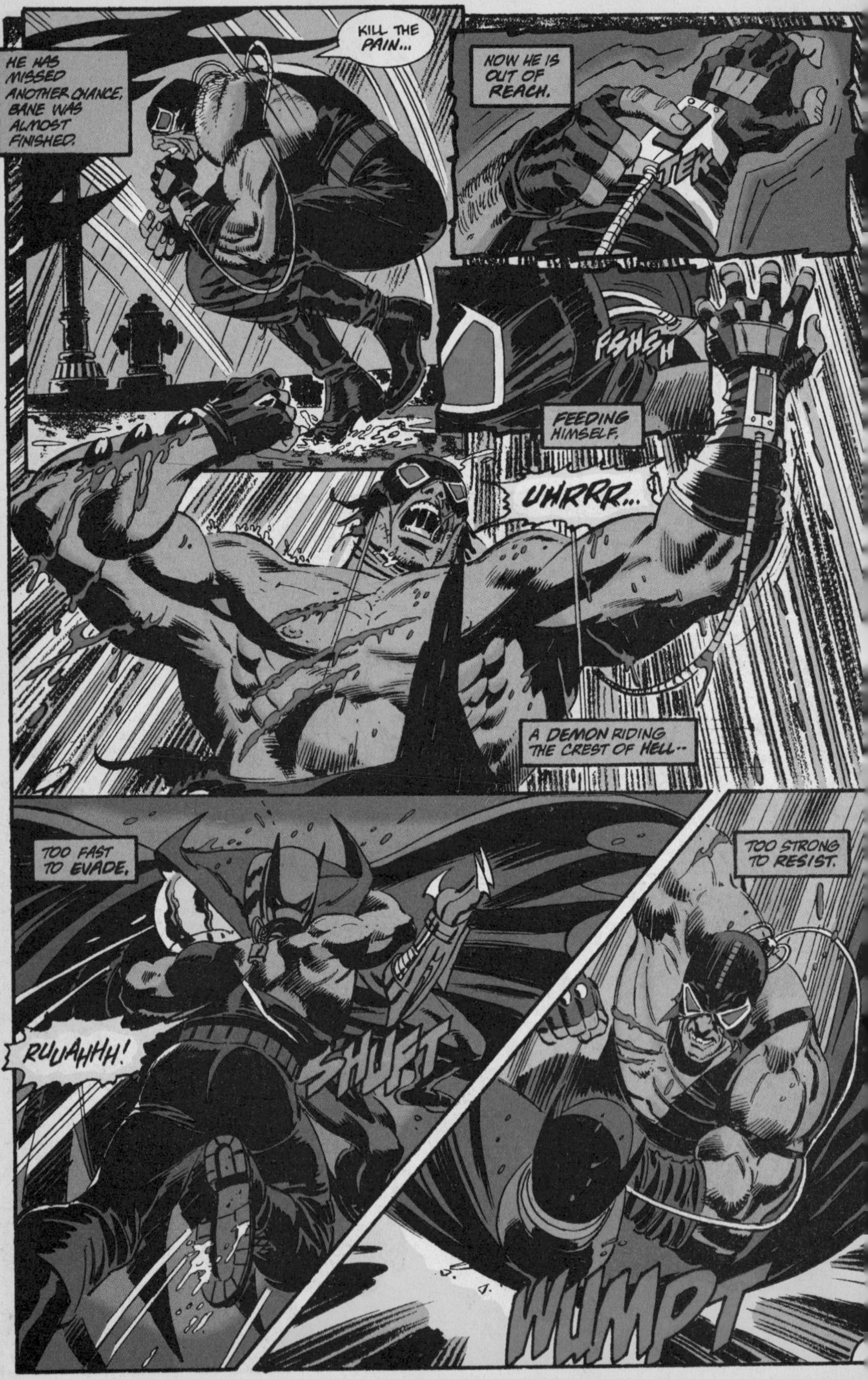

KILL THE PAIN...
HE HAS MISSED ANOTHER CHANCE. BANE WAS ALMOST FINISHED.
NOW HE IS OUT OF REACH.
FSHSH
FEEDING HIMSELF.
UHRRR...
A DEMON RIDING THE CREST OF HELL--
TOO FAST TO EVADE.
TOO STRONG TO RESIST.
RUUAHHH!
SHUFT
WUMPT

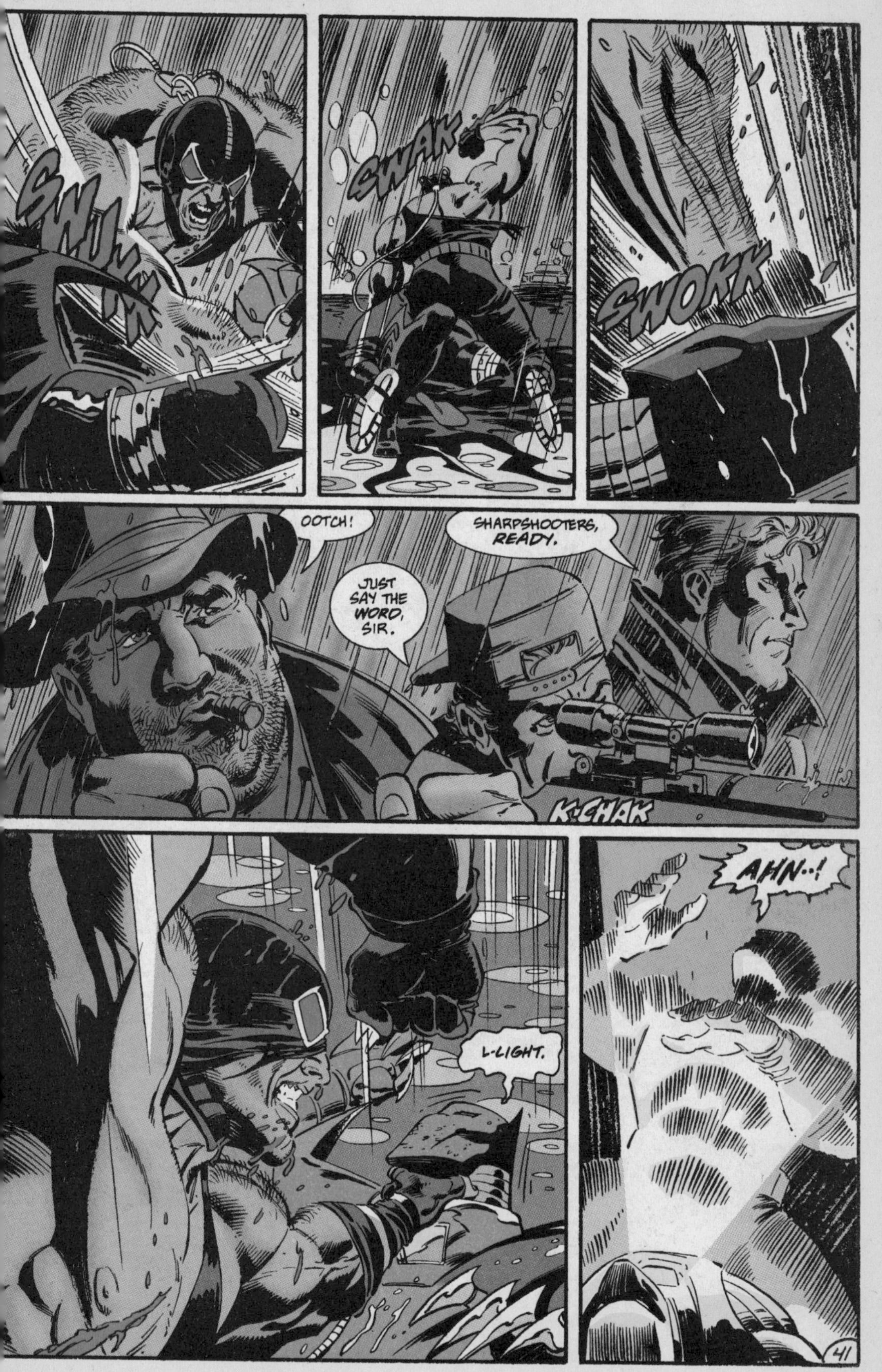
SWUNK
SWAK
SWOKK
OOTCH!
SHARPSHOOTERS, READY.
JUST SAY THE WORD, SIR.
K-CHAK
L-LIGHT.
AHN..!
41

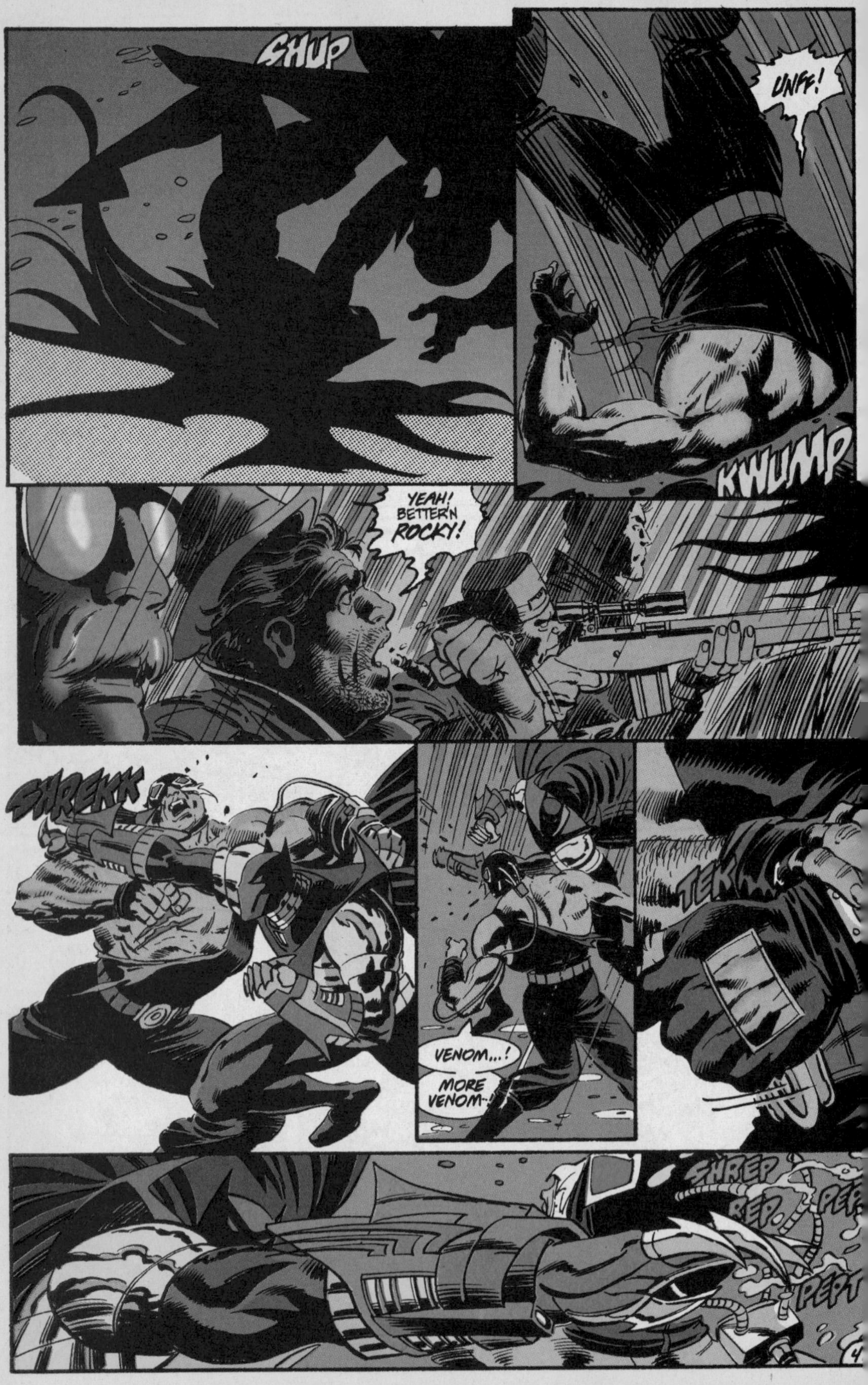
SHUP
UNFF!
KWUMP
YEAH! BETTER'N ROCKY!
SHREKK
VENOM...!
MORE VENOM--!
SHREP
REP
PEP
PEPT
4

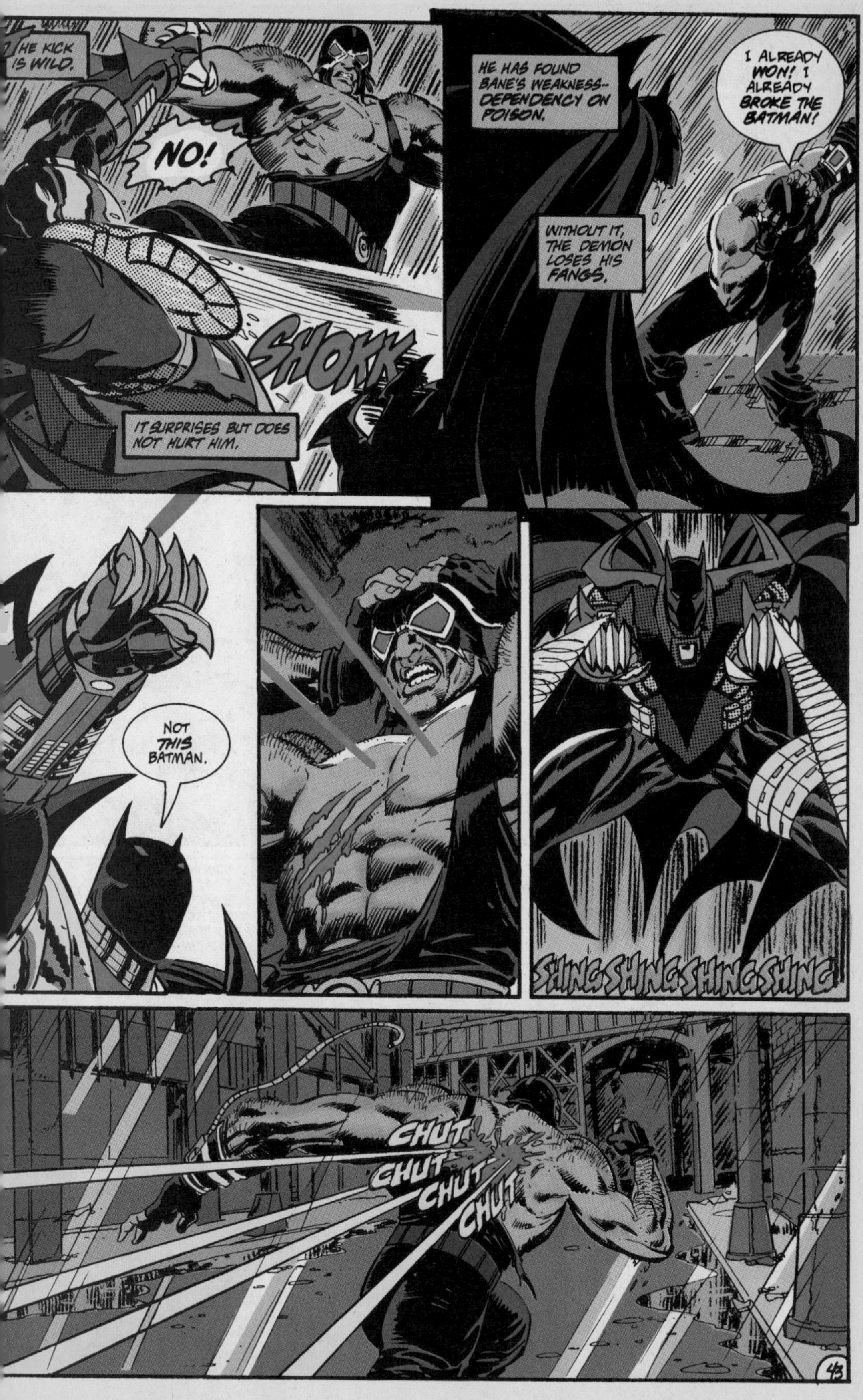

THE KICK IS WILD.
NO!
SHOKK
IT SURPRISES BUT DOES NOT HURT HIM.
HE HAS FOUND BANE'S WEAKNESS-- DEPENDENCY ON POISON.
WITHOUT IT, THE DEMON LOSES HIS FANGS.
I ALREADY WON! I ALREADY BROKE THE BATMAN!
NOT THIS BATMAN.
SHING SHING SHING SHING
CHUT CHUT CHUT CHUT
43

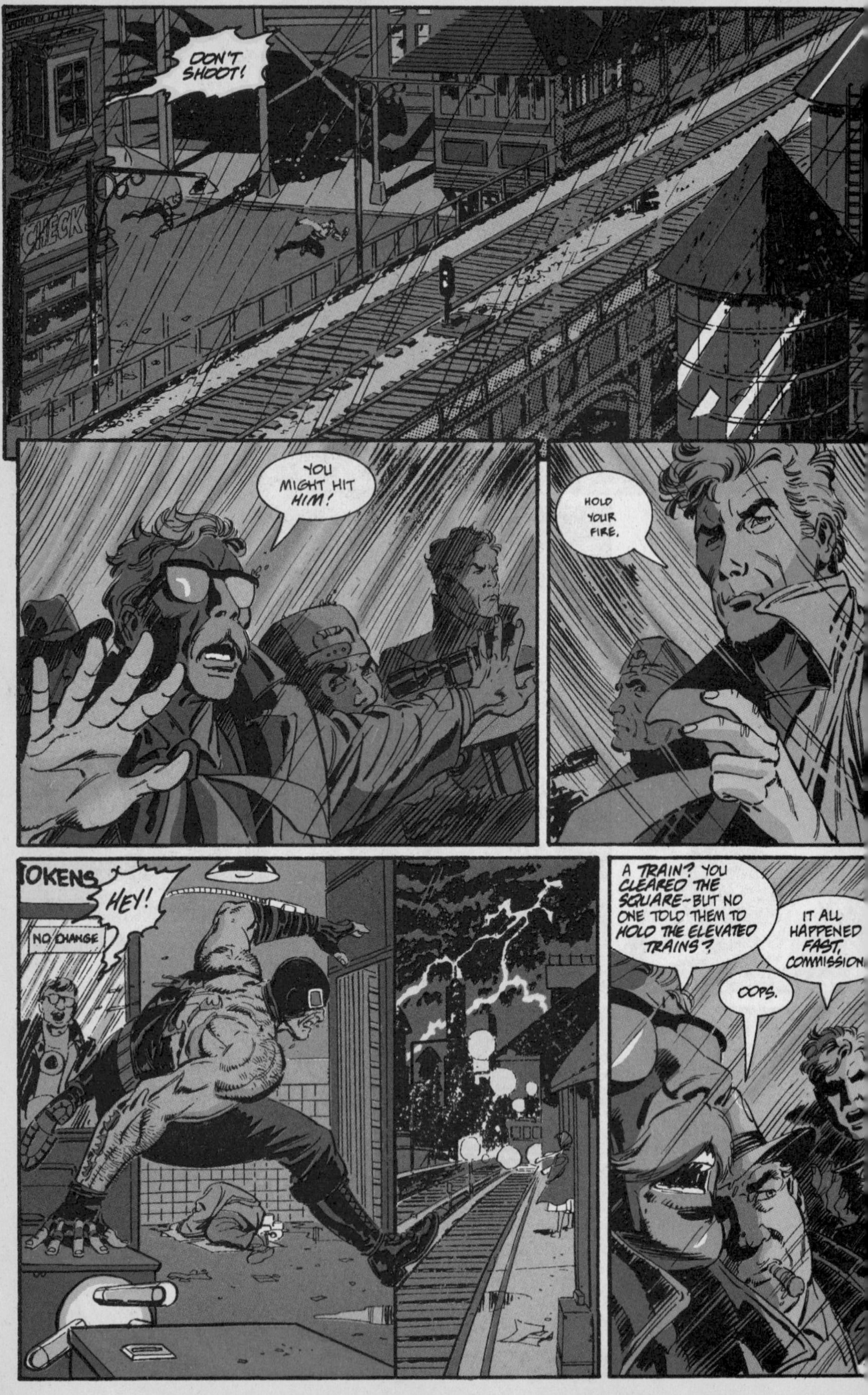
DON'T SHOOT!
CHECK
YOU MIGHT HIT HIM!
HOLD YOUR FIRE.
TOKENS
NO CHANGE
HEY!
A TRAIN? YOU CLEARED THE SQUARE-- BUT NO ONE TOLD THEM TO HOLD THE ELEVATED TRAINS?
IT ALL HAPPENED FAST, COMMISSION
OOPS.

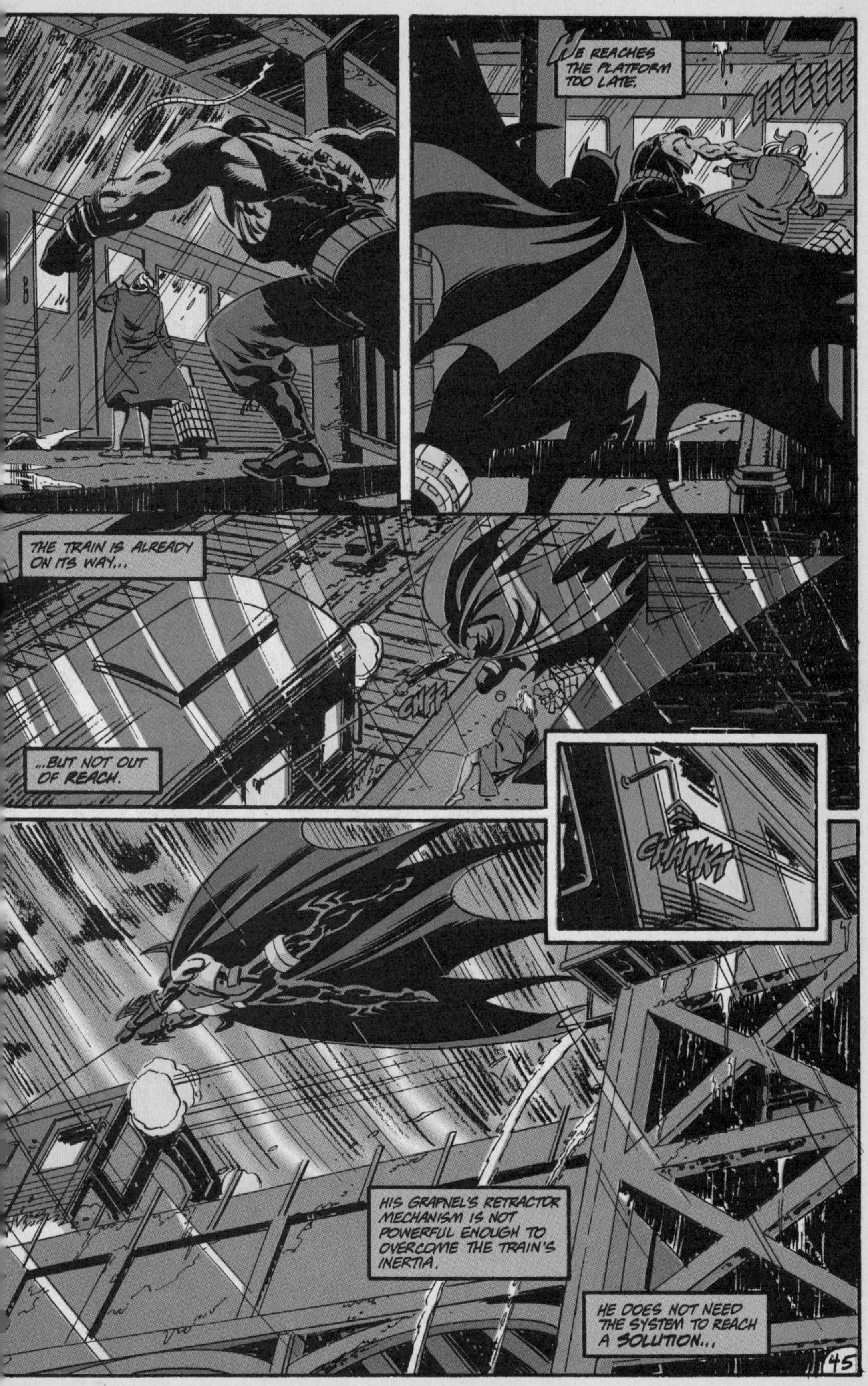
HE REACHES THE PLATFORM TOO LATE.
EEEEEEE
THE TRAIN IS ALREADY ON ITS WAY...
CHFF
...BUT NOT OUT OF REACH.
CHANK
HIS GRAPNEL'S RETRACTOR MECHANISM IS NOT POWERFUL ENOUGH TO OVERCOME THE TRAIN'S INERTIA.
HE DOES NOT NEED THE SYSTEM TO REACH A SOLUTION...
45

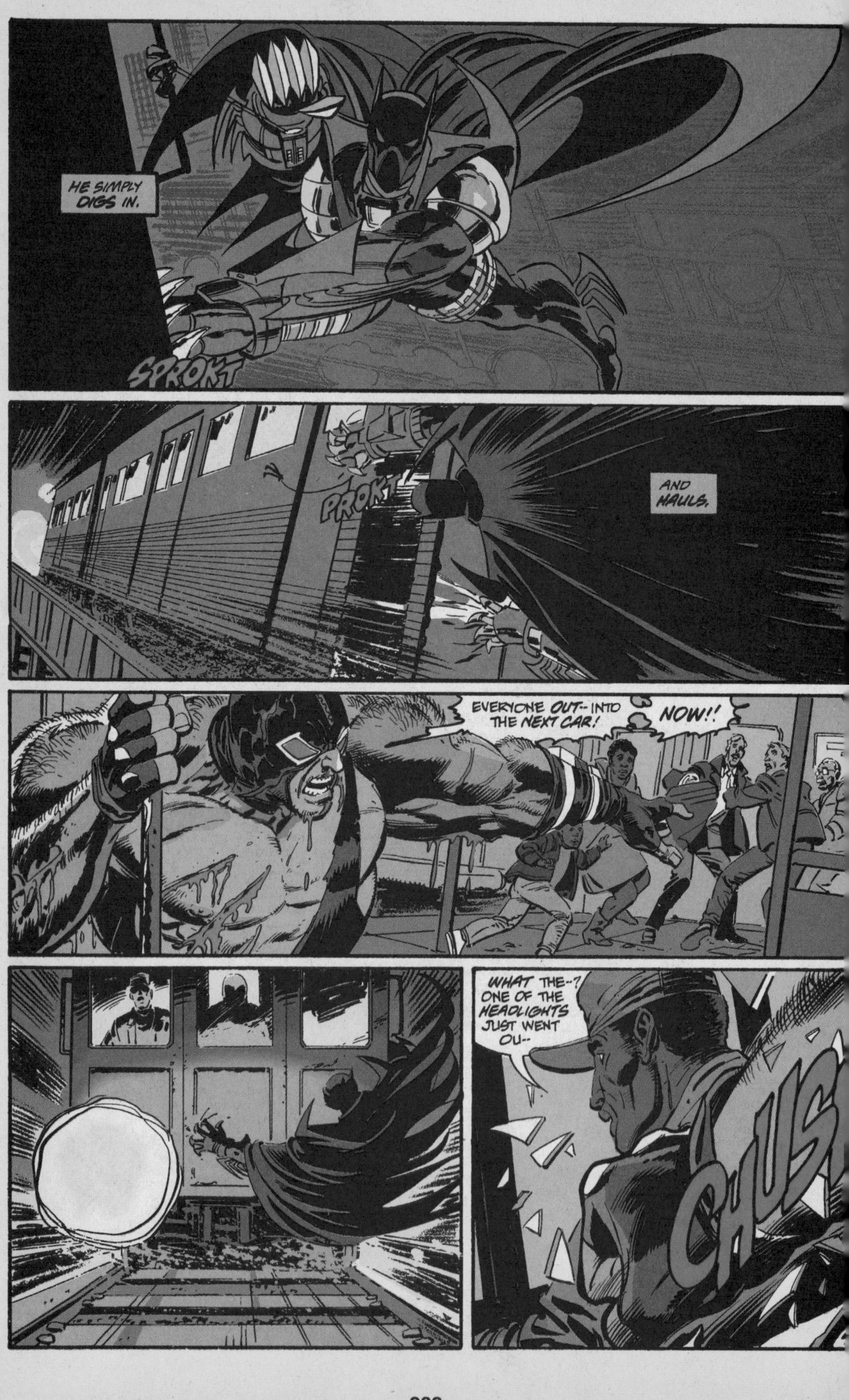
HE SIMPLY DIGS IN.
SPROKT
PROKT
AND HAULS.
EVERYONE OUT-- INTO THE NEXT CAR!
NOW!!
WHAT THE--? ONE OF THE HEADLIGHTS JUST WENT OU--

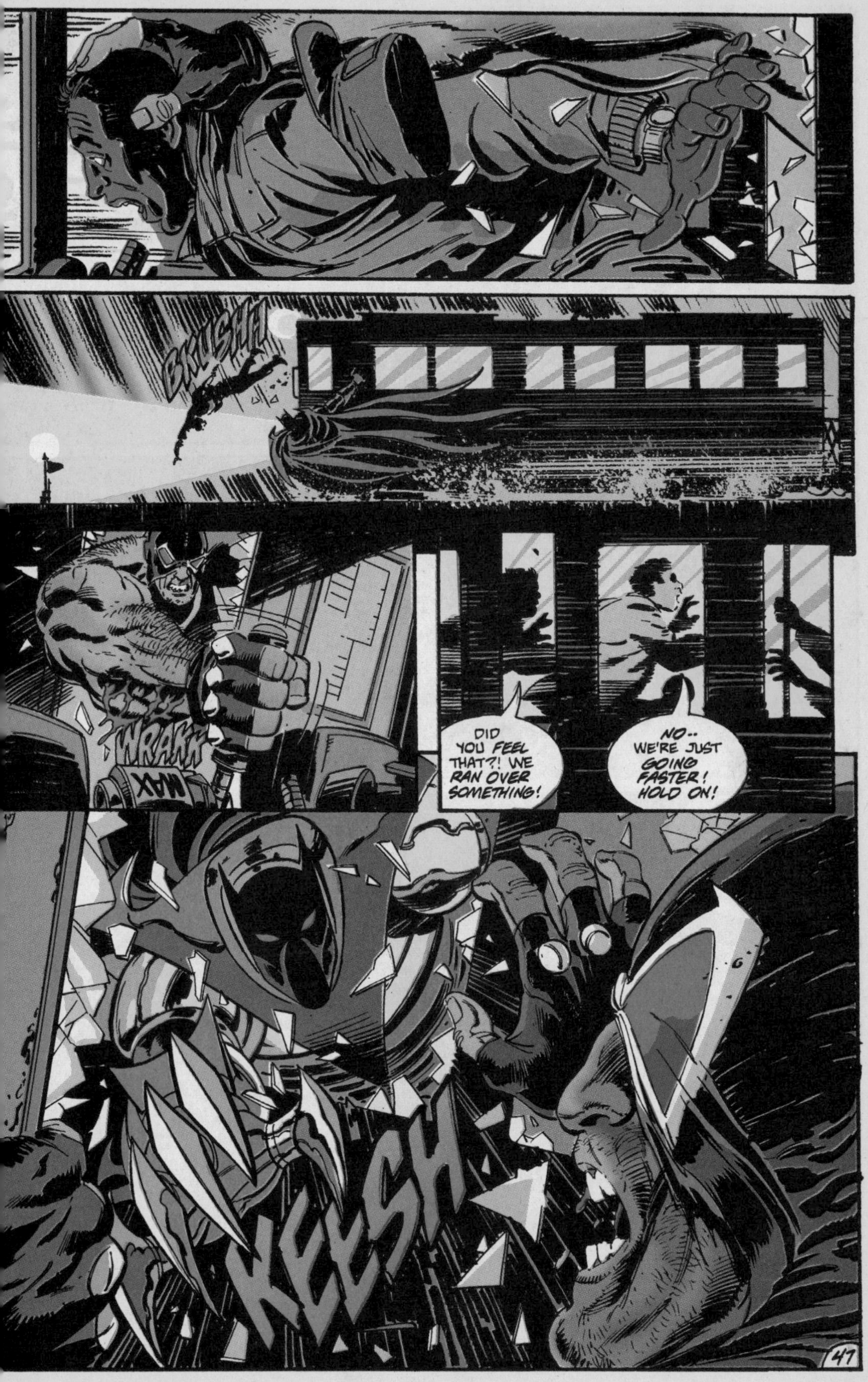
BKRSHH
WRAKK
DID YOU FEEL THAT?! WE RAN OVER SOMETHING!
NO.. WE'RE JUST GOING FASTER! HOLD ON!
KEESH
47

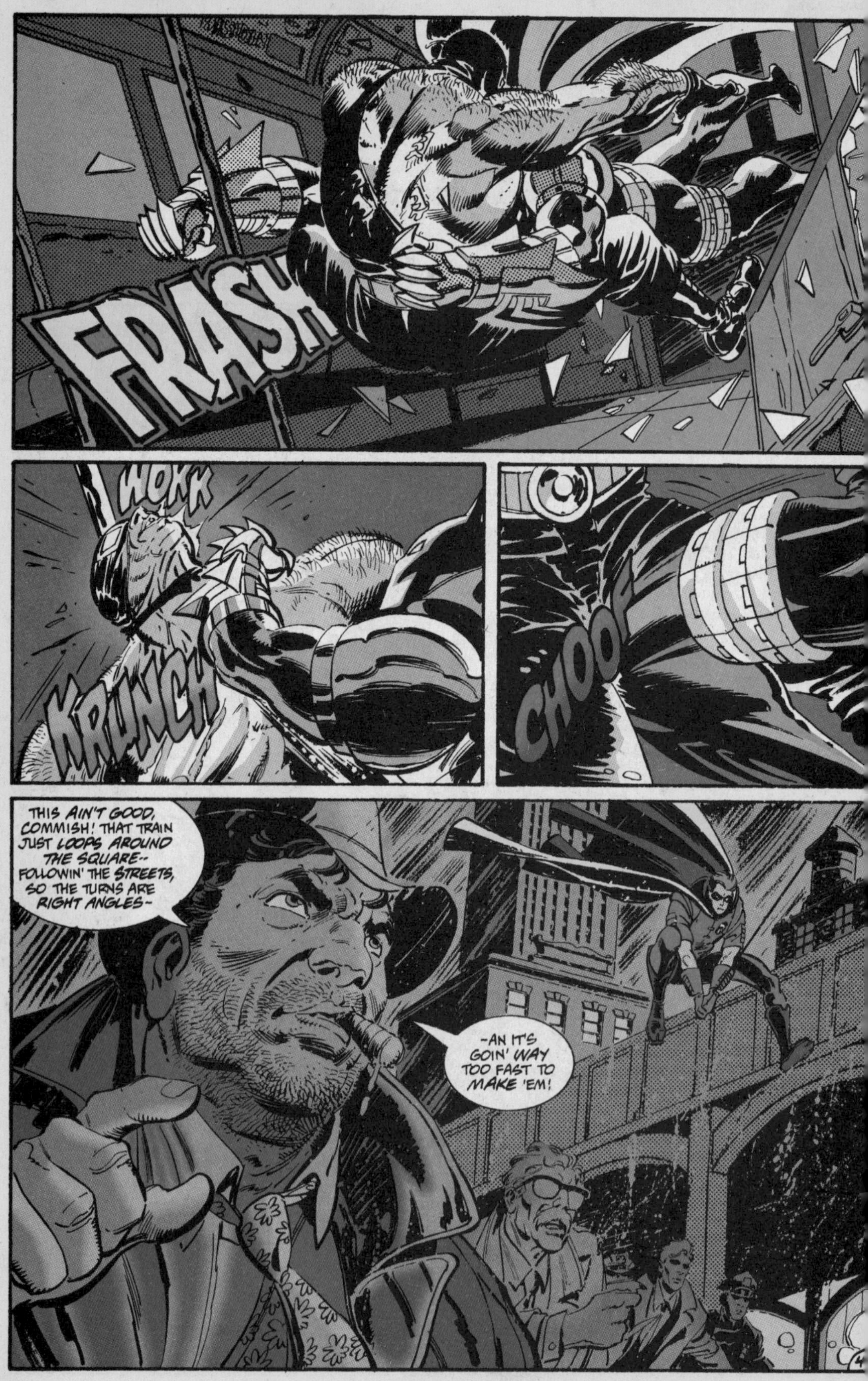
FRASH
WOKK
KRUNCH
CHOOF
THIS AIN'T GOOD, COMMISH! THAT TRAIN JUST LOOPS AROUND THE SQUARE-- FOLLOWIN' THE STREETS, SO THE TURNS ARE RIGHT ANGLES-
-AN IT'S GOIN' WAY TOO FAST TO MAKE 'EM!

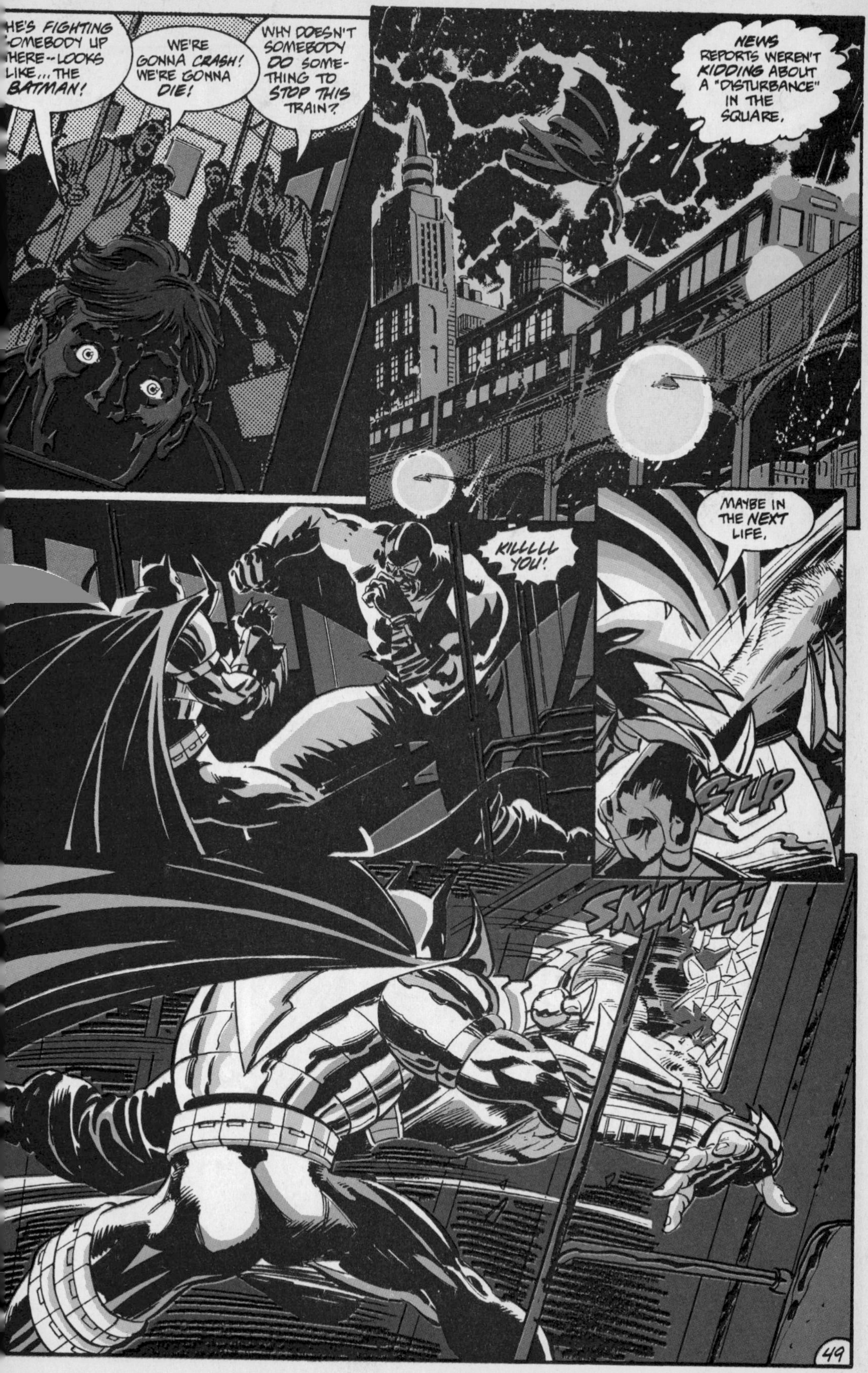
HE'S FIGHTING SOMEBODY UP THERE--LOOKS LIKE... THE BATMAN!
WE'RE GONNA CRASH! WE'RE GONNA DIE!
WHY DOESN'T SOMEBODY DO SOMETHING TO STOP THIS TRAIN?
NEWS REPORTS WEREN'T KIDDING ABOUT A "DISTURBANCE" IN THE SQUARE.
KILLLLL YOU!
MAYBE IN THE NEXT LIFE.
STUP
SKUNCH
49

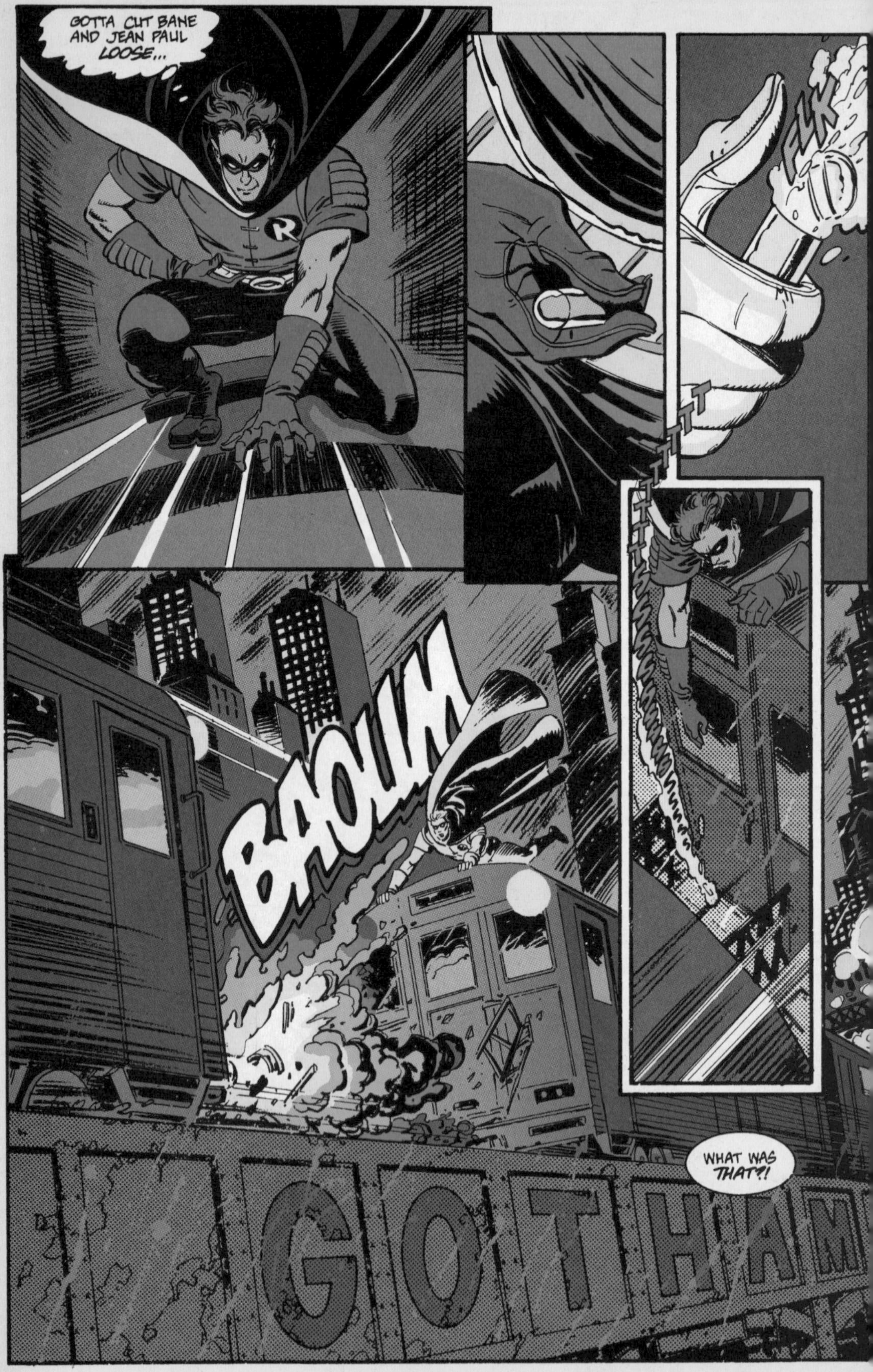
GOTTA CUT BANE AND JEAN PAUL LOOSE...
FLK
BAOUM
WHAT WAS THAT?!
GOTHAM

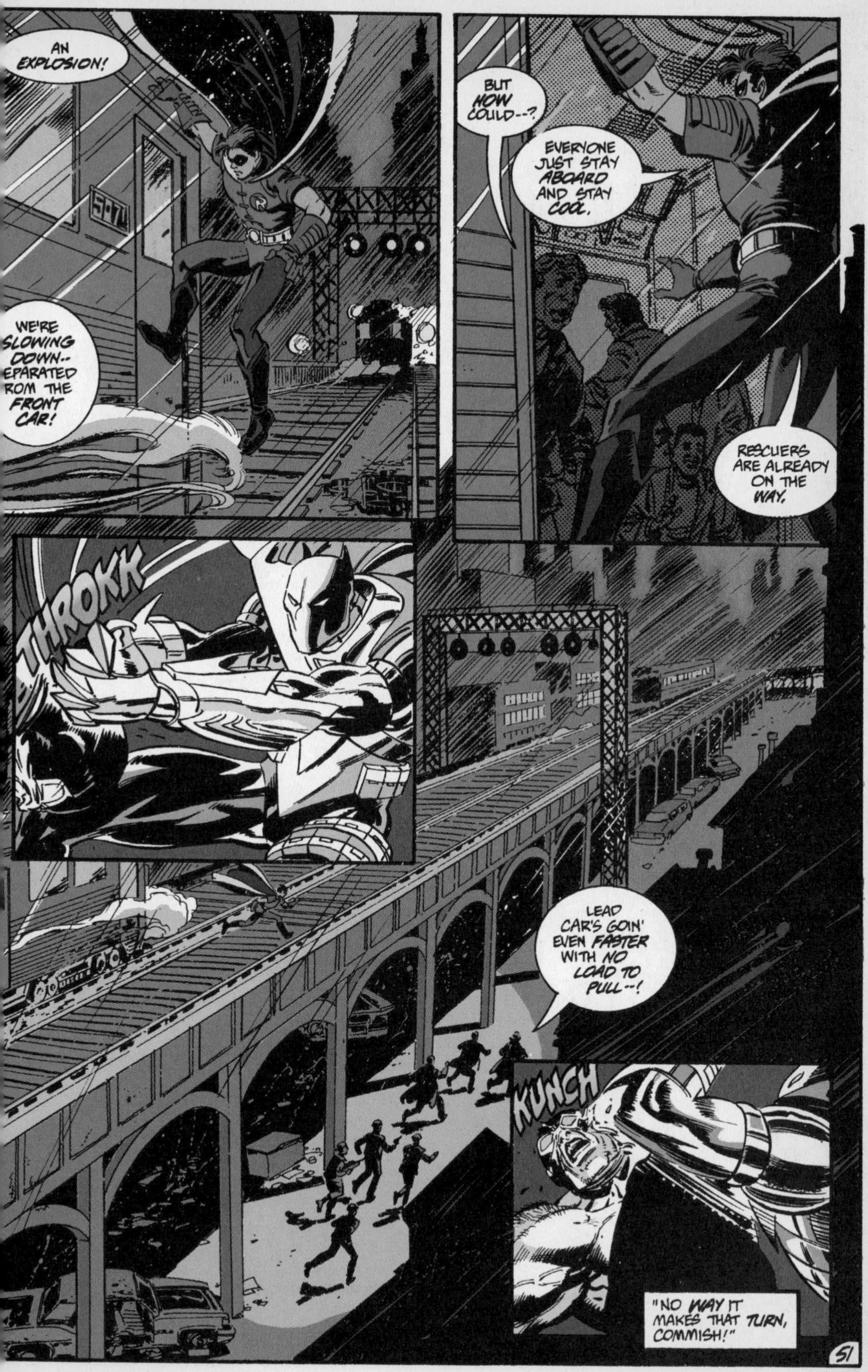
AN EXPLOSION!
WE'RE SLOWING DOWN-- EPARATED ROM THE FRONT CAR!
BUT HOW COULD--?
EVERYONE JUST STAY ABOARD AND STAY COOL.
RESCUERS ARE ALREADY ON THE WAY.
THROKK
LEAD CAR'S GOIN' EVEN FASTER WITH NO LOAD TO PULL--!
KUNCH
"NO WAY IT MAKES THAT TURN, COMMISH!"
51

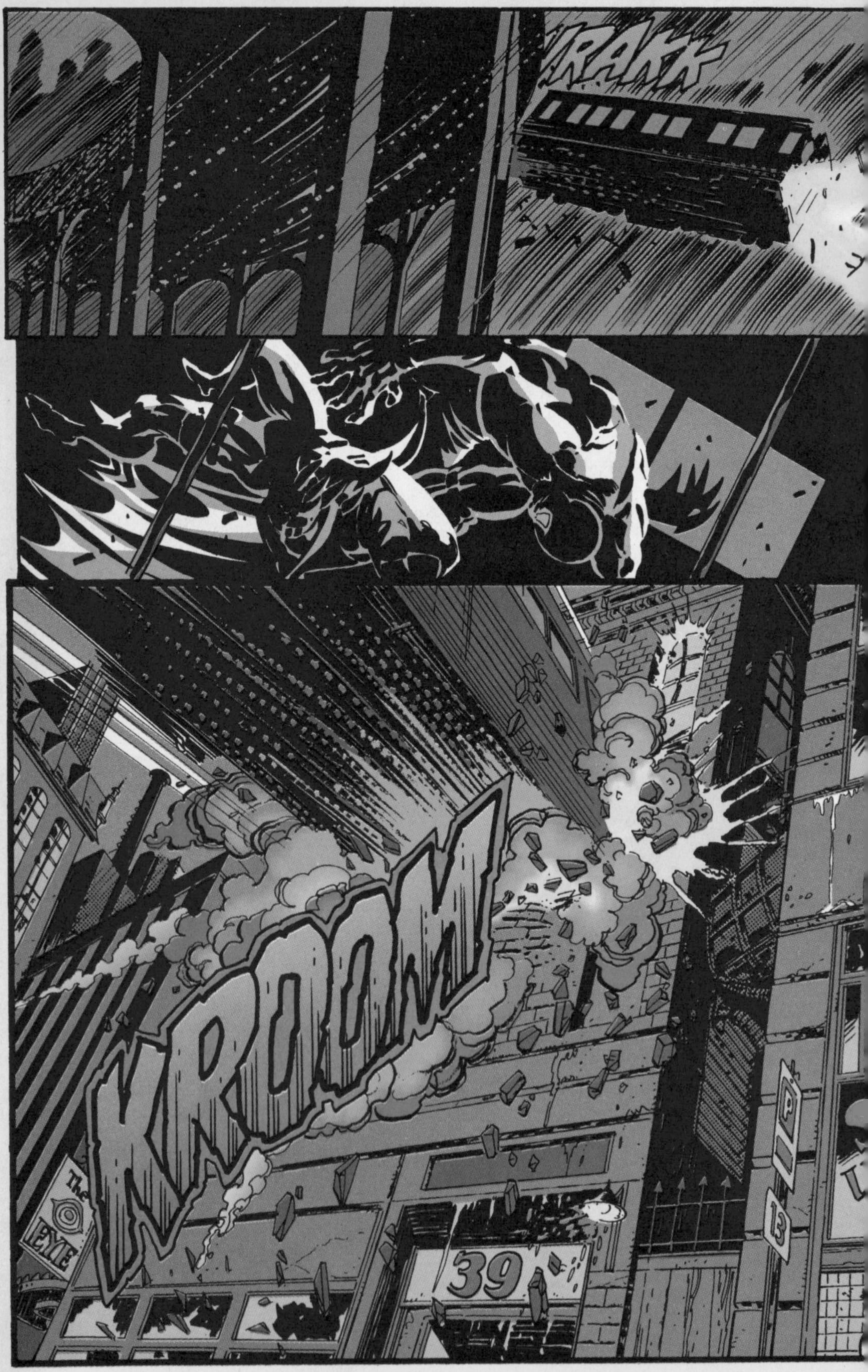

KRAKK
KROOM
The EYE
39
P
13

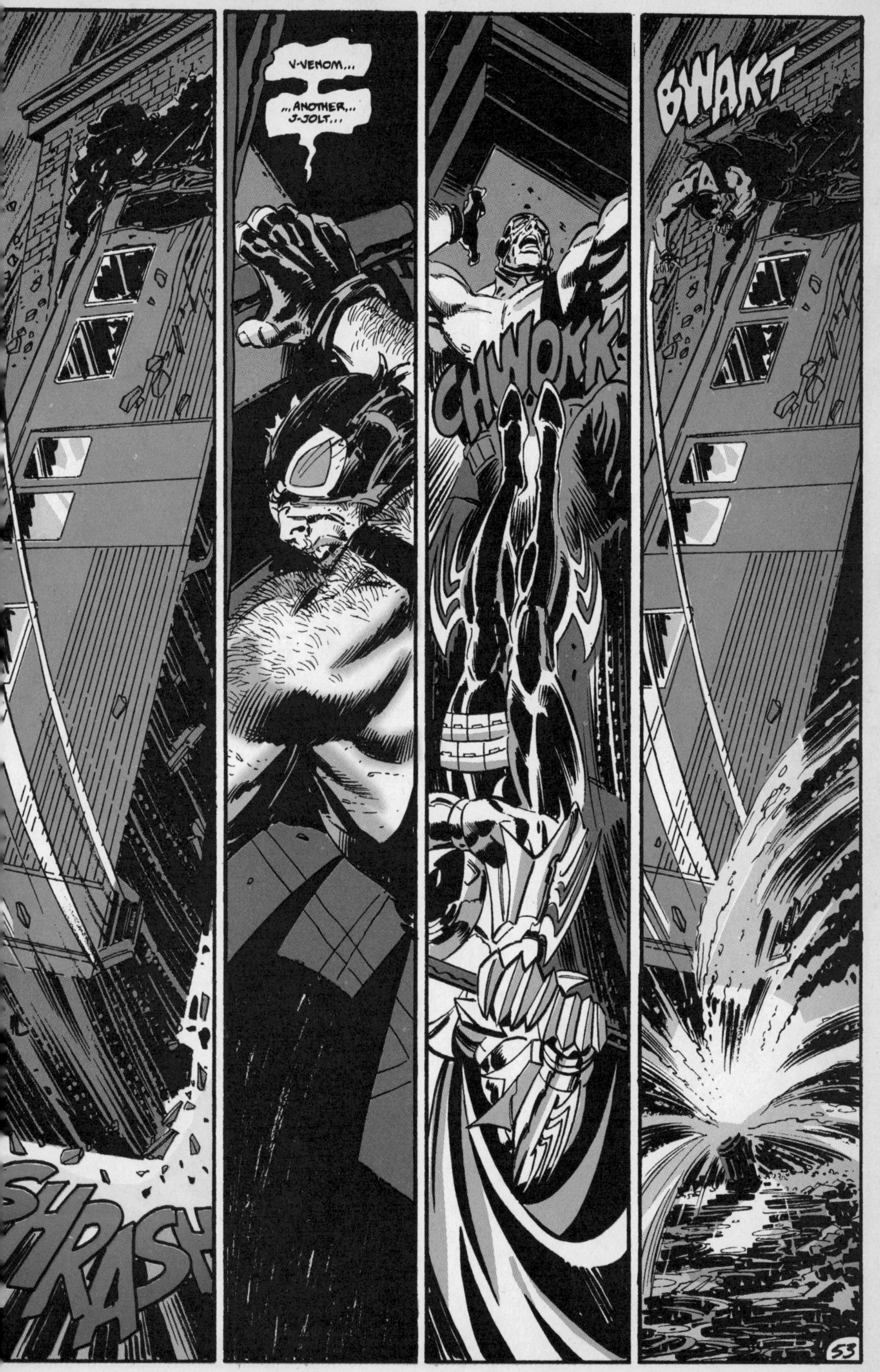
V-VENOM...
...ANOTHER...
J-JOLT...
CHWOKK
BWAKT
SHRASH
53

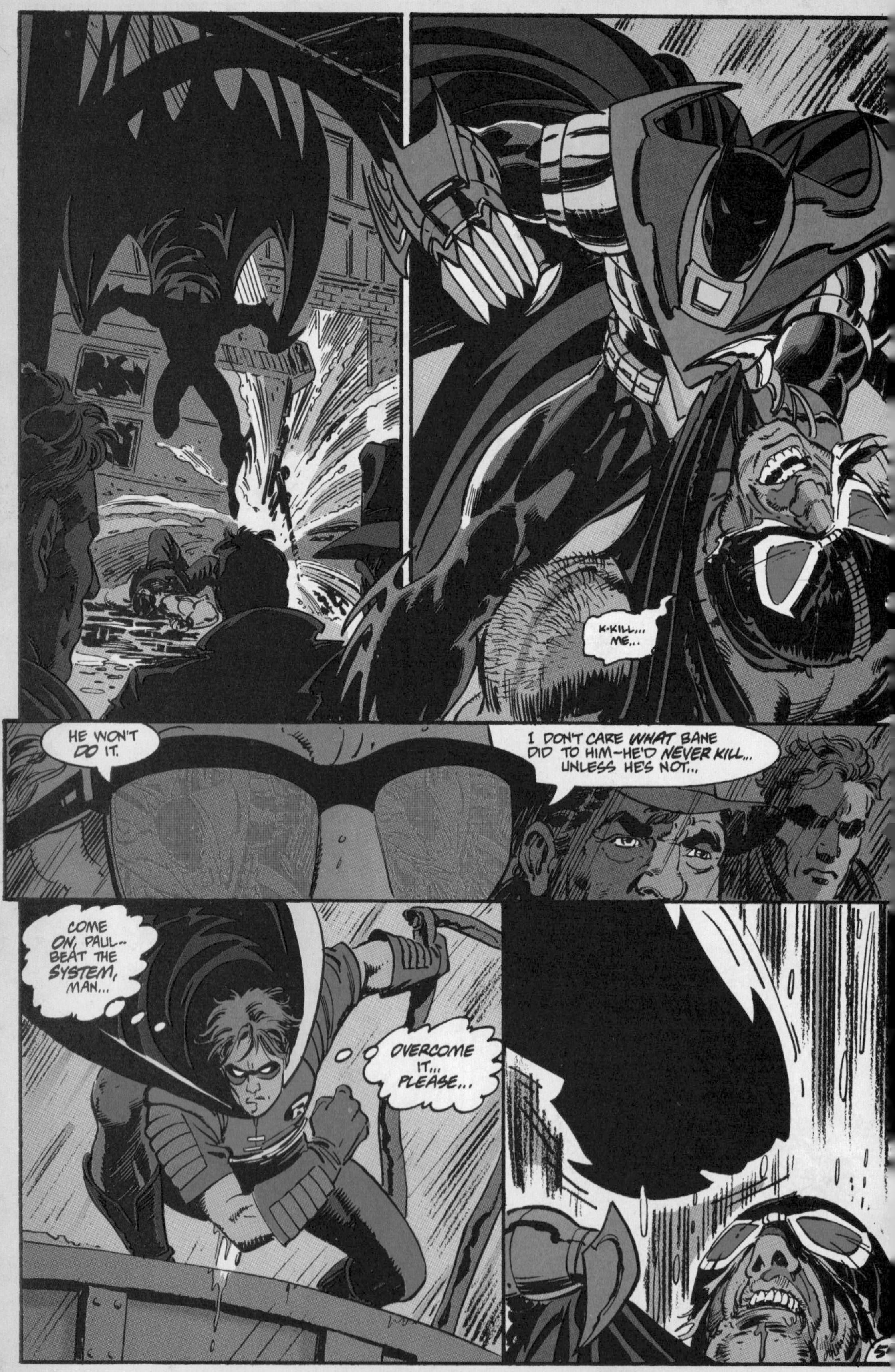
K-KILL... ME...
HE WON'T DO IT.
I DON'T CARE WHAT BANE DID TO HIM--HE'D NEVER KILL... UNLESS HE'S NOT...
COME ON, PAUL-- BEAT THE SYSTEM, MAN...
OVERCOME IT... PLEASE...

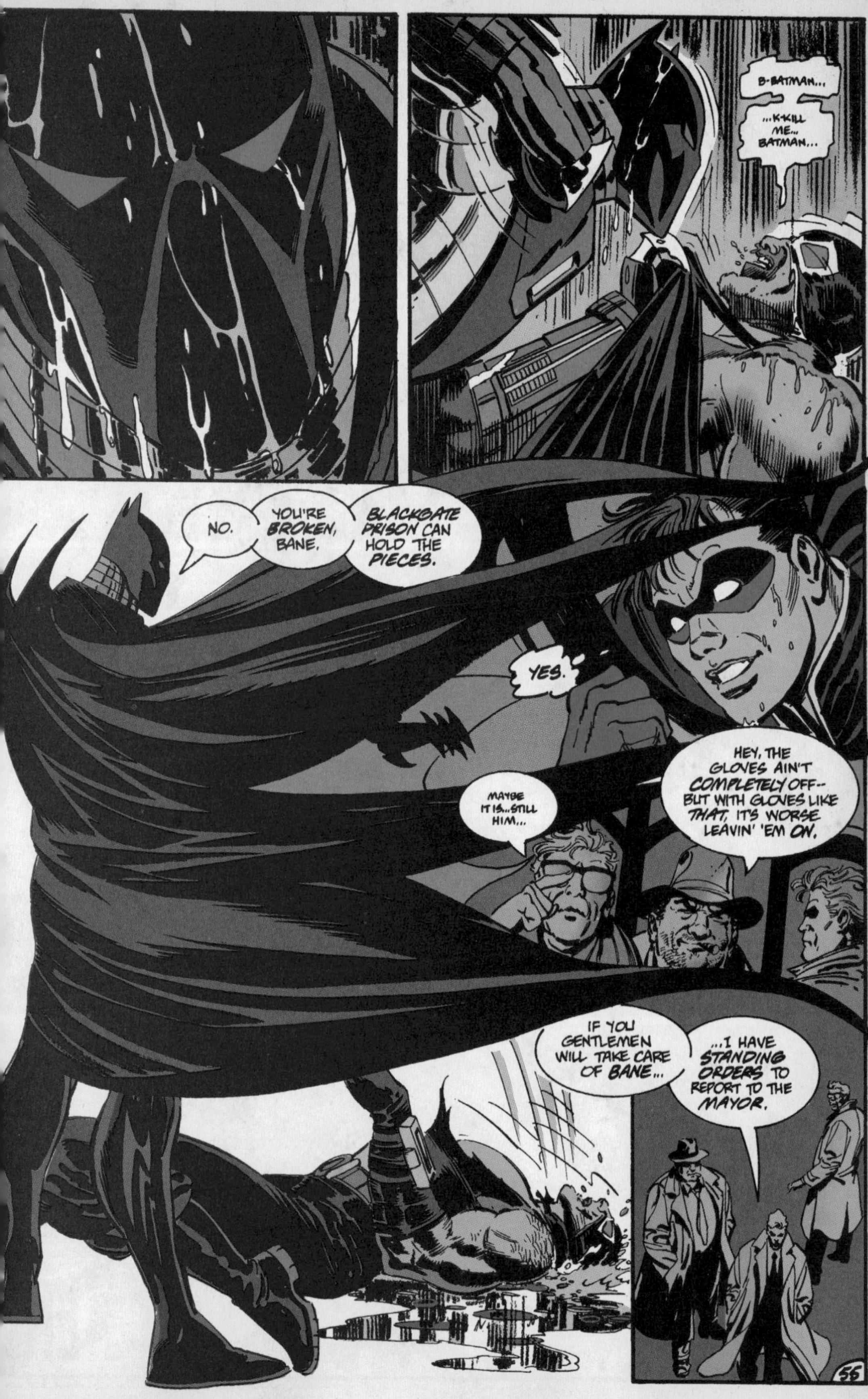
B-BATMAN...
...K-KILL ME... BATMAN...
NO.
YOU'RE BROKEN, BANE.
BLACKGATE PRISON CAN HOLD THE PIECES.
YES.
MAYBE IT IS...STILL HIM...
HEY, THE GLOVES AIN'T COMPLETELY OFF-- BUT WITH GLOVES LIKE THAT, IT'S WORSE LEAVIN' 'EM ON.
IF YOU GENTLEMEN WILL TAKE CARE OF BANE...
...I HAVE STANDING ORDERS TO REPORT TO THE MAYOR.
56

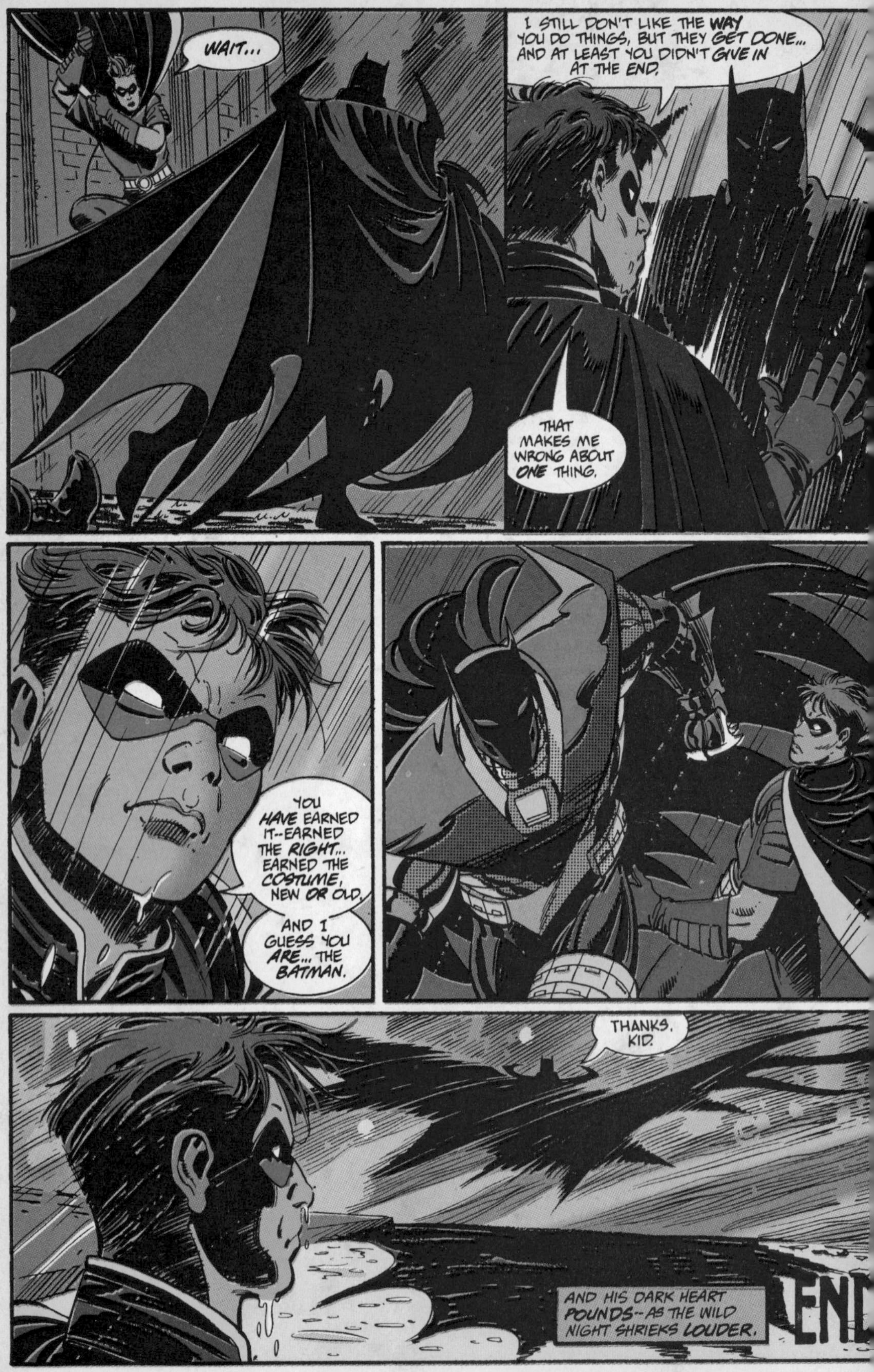
WAIT...
I STILL DON'T LIKE THE WAY YOU DO THINGS, BUT THEY GET DONE... AND AT LEAST YOU DIDN'T GIVE IN AT THE END.
THAT MAKES ME WRONG ABOUT ONE THING.
YOU HAVE EARNED IT--EARNED THE RIGHT... EARNED THE COSTUME, NEW OR OLD.
AND I GUESS YOU ARE... THE BATMAN.
THANKS, KID.
AND HIS DARK HEART POUNDS-- AS THE WILD NIGHT SHRIEKS LOUDER.
END